# THE
# ENCYCLOPEDIA
## OF
# MODERN
# WARPLANES

# THE
# ENCYCLOPEDIA
## OF
# MODERN
# WARPLANES

### THE DEVELOPMENT AND SPECIFICATIONS
### OF ALL ACTIVE MILITARY AIRCRAFT

**General Editor: Bill Gunston**

MetroBooks

# MetroBooks

This edition published by MetroBooks, an imprint
of Friedman/Fairfax Publishers, by arrangement with
Amber Books Ltd

2000 MetroBooks

M 10 9 8 7 6 5 4 3 2 1

ISBN: 1-58663-207-8

First published in Great Britain in 1985 as the partwork
*Warplane* by Orbis Publishing Ltd

Editorial and design by Amber Books Ltd
Bradley's Close, 74–77 White Lion Street,
London N1 9PF

Printed in Hong Kong by Dai Nippon Printing Co. (H.K.) Ltd.

# Introduction

This book describes some 300 types of modern warplane. Clearly, their diversity is astonishing, but what exactly is a "warplane" ?

Obviously, the term covers all the types of aircraft that engage in direct operations against an enemy, such as air-combat fighters and ground-attack aircraft. But also featured in the following pages are large airlift transports, ocean-patrol and anti-submarine aircraft, various trainers, several distinct species of reconnaissance and air-control aircraft, and a multitude of helicopters.

This introduction serves to give an overview of this profusion of contrasting warplanes. To make it more manageable and easy to follow it is broken down into different classes, though of course many types are so versatile they can perform several quite different tasks. For example, the McDonnell Douglas F-4 Phantom was originally designed as a radar-equipped interceptor to fly from the decks of aircraft carriers, whereas today it flies from land runways in the ground attack, all-weather fighter, reconnaissance and electronic warfare support roles.

## Reconnaissance

Reconnaissance was the first task to be performed by warplanes. Three-quarters of a century ago there were no air forces, and the army generals and naval admirals regarded flying machines as distasteful things that no gentleman would even notice. Virtually to a man, they dismissed the idea that they could serve any useful purpose – though a few were slightly apprehensive about airships – and the notion that warfare could take place in the skies was ridiculed.

Reluctantly, by the time World War 1 broke out in 1914 they had to admit that an observer in an aeroplane had a better view than one on the ground, and so the first warplanes were bought for the reconnaissance role. In the course of that bloody conflict the note pad began to be backed up by cameras. Soon the cameras were specially designed, becoming

large and ponderous things able to take clear photographs on glass negatives from heights of 15,000 feet or more. A few of the latest cameras had roll film fed by clockwork, and some even had means of heating the lens to stop it from becoming covered by frost.

In World War 2 the cameras got larger still, some being almost as big as a man. There were few specially designed reconnaissance aircraft. Most were versions of fighters or bombers, with everything possible done to increase the height at which they could fly, to avoid interception. In contrast, some tactical reconnaissance aircraft flew at tree-top height, roaring at full throttle past their targets with a camera clicking away pointing out to the left side. Often these aircraft were unarmed, with extra fuel replacing the guns.

By the 1950s better anti-aircraft guns and guided missiles made it suicidal to fly at much below 50,000 feet, and a few designers produced special aircraft able to fly considerably higher still. The outstanding example of the high-flying reconnaissance aircraft was the Lockheed U-2, first flown in 1955. This was essentially a very large metal glider fitted with a powerful turbojet, and it could fly up to 4,000 miles carrying special cameras at a height of around 75,000 feet. A number made illegal "overflights" across the Soviet Union until, on 1 May 1960, one was shot down by a missile.

Lockheed went on to develop the U-2R and TR-1, which

*Left: The MiG-29 has been the most successful and impressive Russian fighter of recent years. Widely exported, the highly agile and well-armed 'Fulcrum' also forms the backbone of Frontal Aviation fighter forces. This aircraft is an advanced 'Fulcrum-C', with an enlarged spine housing additional fuel and avionics, perhaps including an active jammer. The key to the MiG-29's success lies in its carefree handling characteristics, especially at low speed and high angles of attack.*

*The European Fighter Aircraft is typical of the current generation of canard-Delta configured advanced fighters, like the French Rafale and the Swedish Gripen. The aircraft is optimised for the air defence role, but has a significant all-weather ground attack capability.*

# Introduction

*Right: The General Dynamics F-16 Fighting Falcon's agility and power make it one of the world's most effective close-in dogfighters, although its superb air-to-ground capabilities mean that it is most often assigned to tactical fighter duties, and not to air defence. These two aircraft wear the markings of the Royal Danish Air Force.*

were even bigger and are still flying, but on what might be termed peacekeeping surveillance. Their cameras are now accompanied by high-tech 'synthetic-aperture' radars which can look obliquely down over large areas of country and spot almost any kind of surface activity. Moreover, today's surveillance sensors often have real-time unjammable data links, so that pictures formed by various optical and opto-electronic methods can be built up back at a friendly headquarters "in real time".

Lockheed followed the U-2 with an equally dramatic aircraft, the SR-71 "Blackbird". This was designed to fly not only higher but also faster than any other warplanes, at speeds of up to Mach 3.2. The Soviet Union built the MiG-25R to fly missions similar to the SR-71, but rather more simply and at lower cost. Both aircraft can be equipped with extremely impressive sensors including special cameras and radars. Even today aircraft flying at over Mach 3 at some 80,000 feet pose problems to most air-defence systems.

In complete contrast, many battlefield reconnaissance missions are flown by small UAVs (unmanned air vehicles) resembling large models. Some have propellers and some jets, but they are relatively cheap and surprisingly difficult to shoot down. Other classes of reconnaissance aircraft are discussed later under the headings of Electronic Warfare and Air Control.

# Fighters

*Below: A McDonnell Douglas F-15A Eagle fires an AIM-7 Sparrow semi-active radar homing missile. The F-15 is arguably the finest air defence fighter in service today. It enjoys excellent performance characteristics and is commendably agile, but the secret of its success lies mainly in its powerful, versatile pulse Doppler radar and well designed weapons system.*

At the start of World War 1 some reconnaissance aircraft defended themselves with a pistol, rifle or even a machine gun. By 1915 a few aircraft were being specially built to shoot down enemy aircraft. Some had a pusher propeller at the back so that a machine gun could be fired from the front, but they tended to be slow. A breakthrough was the development of mechanisms to enable a machine gun to be fixed on the nose to fire straight ahead, the bullets being timed so that they always passed safely between the blades of the propeller without hitting them.

From 1916 until about 1935 most fighters were biplanes capable of about 150 mph, armed with two machine guns. Then designers learned how to make streamlined monoplanes without bracing struts or wires, with the landing gear retracting into the wings or fuselage. Engine power doubled, from 500 hp to 1,000, and then doubled again. Speeds rose to over 300 mph, and instead of two small machine guns some fighters had eight, while others even fitted four 20-mm cannon which could penetrate any aircraft armour with devastating effect.

By 1945 the latest fighters had jet engines and could fly at 600 mph, while their service ceiling – the greatest practical height they could reach under full control – rose from 30.000 to over 45,000 feet. Aerodynamicists then found that sweeping the wings back in an arrowhead shape allowed fighters to go still faster, while fitting a turbojet with an afterburner – a jetpipe in which additional fuel could be burned – could greatly increase the engine's thrust and make possible speeds

faster than sound. By 1955 fighters were in service in the Soviet Union and USA which could exceed Mach 1 (the local speed of sound) in level flight, and by 1960 Mach 2 fighters were not uncommon.

These highly supersonic fighters had very powerful engines, with a sea-level thrust of 15,000 lb or more, and wings and tail surfaces that were extremely thin and almost sharp along the edges. Such thin wings had to be made extremely strong to stand up to the colossal forces of air combat at high speed, but in fact it is impossible for traditional close-range air combat to take place at speeds much higher than 400 mph, because at supersonic speed the minimum radius of a turn is several miles. Indeed, 40 years ago it was widely considered that close combat was becoming impossible, because fighters were so fast. Thus, the F-4 Phantom was designed without a gun, because it was never expected to need one. The agile MiG-21 began life with two guns, but soon threw these out in favour of two missiles.

The development of guided air-to-air missiles was expected to revolutionize fighter design. Studies were made of how fighters fitted with powerful radars could detect and identify hostile aircraft BVR (beyond visual range), and shoot them down with long-range missiles. The AIM-54 Phoenix missiles carried by the US Navy F-14 Tomcat have ranges exceeding 100 miles ! In 1960 the US Navy even asked Douglas to build a fighter called the F6D Missileer whose speed was judged of little importance. The F6D was intended to carry giant Eagle missiles and shoot down its enemies from nearly 100 miles away while it cruised quite slowly over the fleet it was protecting.

Gradually, after experience in the Vietnam War, it was recognised that such ideas were unsound. For one thing, it is very difficult to be certain of the identity of other aircraft at such distances, and the reliability of missiles was often so unpredictable that they could home on to the wrong aircraft. Col. Robin Olds, flying Phantoms as CO of the 8th Tactical Fighter Wing in Vietnam, proclaimed "A fighter without a gun is like a bird without a wing". The theoreticians did a hurried rethink, and (for example) the Phantom was hastily produced in the F-4E version with a gun under the nose, and with powerful slats along the leading edge of the wing to improve its turning ability in combat. Equally hastily, the Mikoyan design bureau in Moscow produced new versions of MiG-21 with an inbuilt gun, as well as missiles.

In World War 2 the development of airborne radar led to the production of large twin-engined fighters, usually with a crew of at least two, able to shoot down hostile aircraft at night or in bad weather. Today virtually all fighters have this capability, but 40 years ago there were many who thought fighters should be quite different, and as small and agile as possible. This was partly because of the Korean war (1950-53), when American fighters found that the simple Soviet MiG-15 could in general fly at least as fast, climb faster and more steeply to higher altitudes, and then out-turn them at great heights. Pilots began to say such things as "I want a fighter that will

do better than the MiG-15 even if it means throwing out half the heavy equipment, even including the ejection seat. Let's throw out the complicated gunsight; I'll take aim with a piece of chewing gum stuck on the windscreen".

The result was such fighters as the MiG-21, the Lockheed F-104, the British Lightning and the French Mirage. They were all in the Mach-2 class, had short range and extremely limited armament. They were exciting to fly, but it was gradually realised that they were not terribly useful except for point defence. They were the opposite of the big interceptors with powerful radar and long-range missiles. Indeed, some companies even tried to build so-called light fighters which were even smaller, but these were not adopted by major air forces.

What made neat classifications more difficult is that back in the 1930s the US Navy began making their fighters carry bombs of up to 500-lb total weight. By World War 2 most fighters could also attack ground targets with bombs and rockets, and in the Korean War most of the ground-attack missions were flown by aircraft designated as fighters. Even in the supersonic era it became common for fighters to be equipped to fly ground-attack missions.

This began to confuse the mass media. To the popular newspapers and TV an F-111, Su-24, AJ37 Viggen, Jaguar or Tornado GR.1 are obviously fighters, because they look like fighters. This is discussed under the heading Attack aircraft.

In the days of the Cold War the Soviet Union had to design new aircraft to meet the threat posed by the Americans, and vice versa. In 1967 a ripple of fear went through the Pentagon because of the highly supersonic aircraft that NATO called 'Foxbat'. This, the MiG-25, appeared to be a true successor to the MiG-15 in that it was able to fly faster and higher than anything in the West. In fact, the MiG-25 was optimised for reconnaissance, and as an interceptor it was limited to "stand-off" engagements. At its maximum speed it had to travel virtually in a straight line, unable to manoeuvre.

The USAF decided that a new fighter was required to counter the threat. Having tried to get an all-can-do fighter and attack aircraft in the shape of the F-111, which turned out to be a fine attack aircraft but useless as a fighter, the USAF decided to go for an uncompromised air-combat aircraft. The resulting FX competition was won by McDonnell Douglas with the F-15, first flown in July 1972. To achieve the best possible air-combat performance it had a huge (608 square foot) wing, sharply tapered on the leading edge but without any slats, leading-edge flaps or 'droops', and with only simple and quite small trailing-edge flaps. The tail comprised twin vertical fins and large sweptback tailplanes. These were 'slab' surfaces able to act as elevators but not designed to assist the ailerons in rolling the aircraft.

A few years later General Dynamics won a contract for an LWF, Lightweight Fighter with the F-16, later named Fighting Falcon. This was designed around a single engine of the type used in the F-15. For several years it was scorned by many in the US Air Force; there was much talk of "Why buy a Volkswagen when you can have a Cadillac?" Gradually two things happened. The F-16 became not merely accepted but accepted as being in many respects a superior aircraft. The second thing that happened was the development of a special two-seat version of the F-15 – the F-15E – specifically tailored to ground attack, completely reversing the policy pursued earlier.

Of course, another thing that happened is that the F-15 triggered off development of the MiG-29 and Su-27 in the Soviet Union, and these in turn are so good that the USAF has had to go back to square one and launch development of a totally new fighter. This time the winner was Lockheed, with the F-22A. This will be even bigger than the F-15, with two engines in the 35,000-lb class with vectored nozzles, a wing

*Above: The Lockheed YF-22 was the winner of the competition to find the USAF's next superfighter, the so-called Advanced Tactical Fighter. It combines incredible levels of performance with the latest in Stealth technology.*

*Below: The Dassault Rafale is France's latest fighter. Here the two-seat Rafale B leads a naval Rafale M and a single seat Rafale C.*

# Introduction

of 840 square feet and missiles carried internally. Like all the latest warplanes, it will be a 'stealth' design, as described later. Many people question whether it is really needed at all.

No other country can afford aircraft in this class, but it is worth taking note of how many countries wish to build their own warplanes. Before World War 2 virtually every country with an air force tried to build the simple aircraft of those times, but by 1950 the picture had changed. The new technologies of jet propulsion and transonic aerodynamics meant that almost every air force bought aircraft from the USA, Great Britain or the Soviet Union. Gradually France's Dassault company began to compete, while Sweden tried to remain independent with Saab, but they were the exceptions. Today, however, new fighter and attack aircraft are being developed in 20 countries! Almost all are relatively small aircraft, with loaded weights in the fighter role around 10 tons. Again, most are either tailless deltas or canards, with a powered foreplane instead of a tailplane. (Grumman tested an aircraft with an FSW, forward-swept wing, and achieved all that was expected of this supposed superior shape, but nobody has yet started an FSW fashion in warplane design.) Many of the new crop of light fighters will fall by the wayside, but France's Rafale, the Eurofighter being developed by Britain, Germany, Italy and Spain, and Sweden's Gripen are likely to reach front-line squadrons.

## Attack aircraft

This class of warplane hardly existed in most air forces until quite recently. It was a job done mainly by fighters, such as the Fw 190 and Typhoon in World War 2 and by a host of jet fighters since. Even today, the most important attack aircraft

in the USAF are the F-16 and a special version of the F-15.

Going back to World War 1 we find a few aircraft specially fitted out with extra guns, light bombs and defensive armour. Between the wars attention was paid to this mission mainly by the Soviet Union, which never stopped developing special Shturmovik armoured attack aircraft. In World War 2 one such machine, the Ilyushin Il-2, was made in greater numbers (36,163) than any other warplane in history. In 1954, however, it was decided that the ordinary MiG-17 and MiG-19 fighters could handle the attack role just as well, and the Il-40, a jet successor to the Il-2, was scrapped.

But the Vietnam war repeatedly drove home the lesson that there was a need for something with more armour, longer endurance and greater firepower than ordinary fighters, and after prolonged discussion of light turboprops – resulting in the Grumman OV-1 Mohawk and Rockwell OV-10 Bronco – development went ahead on the Fairchild Republic A-10A. This was built around a gun able to kill the latest battle tanks, and longspan unswept wings able to carry a large assortment of ordnance. Every part of the A-10A is designed to keep flying after being hit by battlefield anti-aircraft fire.

The A-10A generated a lot of argument from people who found the concept hard to understand. In the Soviet Union the Sukhoi bureau encountered even more scornful resistance, but kept pushing for a similar aircraft and eventually obtained an order for the Su-25. In Afghanistan these repeatedly proved their immense value, one aircraft being hit by 62 shells and three SAMs yet appearing immaculate at the 1989 Paris airshow! Even today such aircraft are still little understood; for example, there is nothing like them in the RAF.

Most air forces do, however, have fast jets which were specially designed for the ground-attack mission. Almost certainly, the best have been subsonic, examples being the Grumman A-6 Intruder and, recently withdrawn from service, the BAe Buccaneer. They are superior because, compared with supersonic aircraft, they carry more, fly further, and can make their attack with at least equal precision and probably at lower altitude. As for speed, none of the supersonic types can actually attack at supersonic speed, and with its internal bombload of 4,000 lb the Buccaneer was faster than (for example) a Jaguar, Phantom, F-111, Mirage, F-15E, Tornado or Su-24 with the same load!

Today the traditional ground-attack role merges into many others. An important attack role is to destroy enemy ships, and this is discussed under the next heading (Bombers). In land battles a significant role can be played by armed and armoured helicopters, while to survive in future wars attack aircraft (even more than others) will have to be 'stealth' designs, as discussed later.

# Bombers

This, with 'fighter', is one of the roles understood by the media. Until fairly recently there was no problem, because almost all air forces had some. Today the picture has changed. The traditional large bomber has become ever-rarer, until now such aircraft are found only in the air forces of the USA, Russia, China, Ukraine and France, the last-named having a tiny handful of Mirage IVPs. In the RAF the Jaguar and the Tornado GR.1 are used primarily as bombers, but to call them by that name would make their pilots incensed! So the once mighty RAF, which 50 years ago had over 5,000 bombers, today has none.

In contrast, the previously insignificant Ukraine has a number of bombers including 19 of the Tu-160, the heaviest and most powerful warplane in all history. These great aircraft were made at Kazan, in what is now Russia, but Russia itself has only 12 of them in combat-ready service. Nobody thought, when the monster bombers were flown to the 184th Regiment, that their base at Priluki, Ukraine, would soon be in a foreign country, which would lay claim to the aircraft !

At first glance the Tu-160 looks like an enlarged Rockwell B-1B Lancer, but in fact they are totally different aircraft. The engines of the Tu-160 are getting on for twice as powerful as those of the B-1B, yet the fuselage is more slender and the radar cross-section (the degree of stealth) is better. Both aircraft are armed primarily with stand-off missiles dispersed from rotary launchers, but they can also carry free-fall nuclear or conventional bombs.

Five years ago the USAF had over 500 bombers, but today it has funding for an active-duty bomber force of just 69 aircraft, made up of 38 B-1Bs, 24 B-52Hs and a mere seven examples of the marvellous but costly Northrop Grumman B-2 Spirit. It is hoped that eventually 20 B-2s will enter service (indeed almost all these have already been built), and many studies show that, despite awesome costs ($44,400,000,000 for 20 aircraft), B-2s can do so much more than the older bombers that they are good value for money. They are discussed briefly under the Stealth heading.

Russia retains significant forces of Tupolev Tu-95 bombers, which uniquely combine sweptback wings and tail with propulsion by amazing 15,000-hp turboprops which have hardly changed in 40 years. Today's versions carry long-range missiles, the number carried by each aircraft having been reduced from 16 to six to comply with the Strategic Arms treaties. In the same way, the Tu-22M swing-wing bombers have had their flight-refuelling probes removed. Strangely, nobody has said anything about the USAF having to seal off the flight-refuelling sockets of its own bombers.

*Left: The Northrop B-2 is the world's most advanced bomber. Effectively invisible to radar, the aircraft can find and attack even mobile targets. The small number now being delivered to the 509th Bomb Wing will give the USAF perhaps its most formidable strike asset.*

# Stealth

Though not a mission, this subject will eventually affect the design of almost every warplane. As long ago as 1937 a British radar pioneer said "I would expect aircraft designers now to take into account the need to minimise the way future bombers act as a mirror to radio waves". Amazingly, this advice was almost ignored for about 40 years, before being suddenly thought of in the USA as if it was something new. The subject is called LO (low observables) but is popularly called stealth.

In general terms, a large bomber such as a B-52 can be seen on enemy radar screens from perhaps 200 miles away if it is side-on, or 100 miles from head-on. But if this aircraft was replaced by a modern LO bomber, of which the B-2 is the only known example, it could probable get within two or three miles of its target without being detected. Indeed, carrying stand-off stealthy missiles it would not need to go near its target at all, and the enemy would never know what had hit them.

Stealth design is partly a matter of getting the shape right, partly a matter of selecting the right materials and partly a matter of surface coatings. The entire airframe has to be designed with amazing care. The first LO aircraft in service, the Lockheed F-117, used a method called faceting, in which the external skin is made up of hundreds of flat mirrorlike surfaces which all reflect hostile radar waves in directions other than back to the place they came from. Later Stealth aircraft have absolutely smooth outer skins, but with strange shapes, such as a leading edge that curves from above to a sharp lower edge, and with all edges (air inlets, landing-gear doors and bomb doors) with precisely made zigzags, which like every other part, have to be kept in perfect condition, without

*Below: The Lockheed F-117A was the world's first operational Stealth aircraft, designed to avoid detection by enemy air defences by reducing radar signature to a point where the aircraft appears to be little bigger than a bird on enemy radar screens.*

*Above: The Lockheed P-3C is a highly effective and widely exported long range maritime patrol aircraft, packed with advanced sensors and able to carry the latest anti-submarine and anti-ship weapons. This aircraft, like most USN Orions, carries very low-visibility markings.*

the slightest damage or dirt, at all times. Such considerations must eventually influence the design of helicopters, maritime patrol and all other true combat aircraft.

# Maritime patrol

In peacetime these are among the warplanes which work hard flying 'for real' missions, because they are often called to assist stricken ships in storms, search for survivors or smugglers and carry out many other tasks. Some are quite small coastal aircraft, such as the Pilatus Britten-Norman Defender, with radar, binoculars, cameras and perhaps simple weapons to control vessels suspected of carrying arms or drugs. A bigger version of this class is the An-72P, which carries all-weather sensors and heavy armament including cannon, rockets and bombs.

For use in all-out warfare aircraft need to have capability against surface warships and, especially, submarines. Modern submarines can travel deeply submerged at high speed whilst sending out little noise through the ocean. This means that the airborne sensors — radar, infra-red heat detectors, MAD (magnetic-anomaly detectors to measure disturbance of the Earth's magnetic field) and sonobuoys which float in the sea and send back by radio any likely noise spectrum – have to be much better than ever before, and complemented by a massive amount of receiver and computer power in the aircraft.

Russia's most important ocean-patrol aircraft are all versions of the Tu-95 and Tu-142, so they all have unrivalled range and endurance (as well as a flight-refuelling probe) and suites of sensors which have been repeatedly upgraded. Russia and Japan use small numbers of jet and turboprop flying boats. but most Western air forces and navies use the Lockheed P-3 Orion, based on the Lockheed Electra turboprop airliner of 1955.

Compared with this the RAF's turbofan-engined BAe Nimrod might seem far more up to date, but in fact in 1995 the RAF was even thinking of replacing these fine aircraft by the much smaller and slower P-3! To some degree this is because avionics are more important than airframes in this role, and partly because Britain no longer has an aircraft industry with the funds required to keep British forces properly equipped. This in turn is largely because of an active "buy American" policy on the part of successive Governments, on the grounds of economy. This in turn means that British forces could never again envisage taking part in any conflict which the US Government did not approve of. An alternative to the P-3 would be to build a maritime patrol version of a modern jetliner, such as the A310. This would outperform the P-3 in every respect, besides having far more potential for future development. Boeing is pushing its 767 for the same role.

*Right: Reconnaissance is a vital, but often neglected role for today's air arms. The Lockheed U-2R is a dedicated high altitude reconnaissance aircraft. A variety of reconnaissance sensors can be mounted in the extended nose, and in the Q-bay behind the cockpit. The US Air Force is the only user of the type.*

# Transports

At the end of World War 2 military transports were typified by the Dakota (military DC-3), with tailwheel landing gear and a

rather cramped cabin which (on the ground) sloped steeply. Everything had to be loaded through a door in the side and pushed uphill inside. Anything dropped by parachute had to be manhandled out through the side door or else carried underneath the aircraft. All this severely limited what could be carried to such things as troops, oil drums and perhaps a motorcycle. With great difficulty a Jeep could be carried.

In 1954 Lockheed flew the first C-130 Hercules, and this changed everything. For a start it had a big unobstructed hold, 10 feet wide and up to 9 feet high, which on the ground was level. At the back was a ramp door up which one could drive trucks or even light armoured vehicles. In flight four turboprop engines gave sparkling performance (as good in climb and speed as a Spitfire), and the cabin was pressurized for high-altitude cruise. Depressurized, the rear ramp door could be opened to para-drop anything from inside, or heavy loads could be extracted and dropped free while the C-130 flew over a drop zone at about 15 feet altitude. Should it have to land, big low-pressure tyres supported the weight on soft airstrips.

Lockheed have delivered well over 2,000 Hercules to customers all over the world, and in 1995 were aggressively still marketing updated versions of this 43-year-old design. Meanwhile, an obvious replacement, the all-new An-70 from Ukraine, was written-off in February 1995 after a mid-air collision. The only other likely C-130 replacement is the FLA (Future Large Airlifter), being developed by a consortium of European nations including Britain, but this is still not a completely firm programme.

Russia still has many of the 1,247 An-12BP airlifters in service, but the design bureaux are eagerly fighting to replace them with a new design (the An-70 now being a foreign aircraft). Russia also has small numbers of huge An-22 and An-124 transports, which are most valuable aircraft. The only other transports in this larger class are the USAF's Lockheed C-5 Galaxy, McDonnell Douglas KC-10 Extender and McDonnell Douglas C-17 Globemaster III, but for reasons of cost there are strong moves to make the USAF start accepting military versions of established civil aircraft.

The KC-10 is a tanker/transport, with enormous fuel capacity which can be transferred through a Flying Boom at the tail to receive aircraft equipped with a suitable socket receptacle. The USAF and France use the KC-135 tanker, which like the KC-10 is based on a civil airliner. The impoverished RAF goes further, and its tankers are actually modified civil airliners (TriStars and VC10s) bought secondhand. These all employ the more versatile probe/drogue method, also used by Russia and the US Navy. A few fighters can carry "buddy packs" on weapon pylons, with which they can refuel their friends.

# Electronic warfare

Today EW aircraft can be grouped into several distinct species. One group, whose mission is ECM (electronic

countermeasures), look like fast jet attack aircraft, and can if necessary actually precede or accompany such aircraft as they penetrate hostile airspace. The job of such EW platforms is to clear the way by confusing or jamming the enemy's radar-based defence systems. This involves listening to the hostile emissions, sorting them into a scale of priorities and then re-broadcasting (with timed delay) or simply jamming those posing the greatest threat. The Grumman EA-6B needs a crew of four to do this, and carries its jammers in underwing pods, each with its own windmill-driven electric generator. The same contractor's EF-111 A Raven does much the same job with a crew of two and internal jammers.

Some EW aircraft carry nothing but sensors to gather Elint (electronic intelligence). This is the role of several species of Boeing EC-135, which at one time almost filled the skies around (but never across) the borders of the Soviet Union and China, listening, recording, comparing, analysing and, sometimes, deliberately provoking responses by appearing to pose an air-defence threat.

The same job on a smaller scale is done by USAF Wild Weasel aircraft, which today comprise F-4G Phantoms and F-16C fighters armed with HARM anti-radar missiles. A special version of the Tornado called ECR (Electronic Combat and Reconnaissance) flies the same missions. Of course, with money ever tighter, an obvious objective is to equip the same aircraft to fly ECR one day and all-weather attack a few hours later. In former Warsaw Pact air forces many of the battlefield EW systems are carried aloft by special helicopters, most of them versions of the Mi-8.

# Helicopters

Today helicopters are increasingly flying almost the entire spectrum of warplane missions, even including air combat, bombing and electronic-warfare. They add a few of their own. Their ability to hover motionless and land in confined spaces opens up a host of tasks right up to the front line, while a duty no other aircraft can perform (except for special magnetic-ring conversions in World War 2) is MCM, mine countermeasures. For example, the mighty MH-53E is designed to tow a heavy sled across the ocean, sending out various disturbances designed to explode every mine over which it passes. Modern sea mines can be triggered in several totally different ways, and the MCM sweep has to try to activate every kind of exploder.

Of course, helicopters in this class are also important as transports, some being specially equipped with sensors and weapons for clandestine or even direct assaults on the enemy. Another special transport class is medevac (medical evacuation), calling for something better than the M*A*S*H external stretcher! Some big helicopters are fully equipped flying surgical hospitals, and all Medevac machines have comprehensive equipment to help casualties survive until a hospital is reached.

A visually different category is the battlefield armed helicopter, with a slim two-seat (or, in the case of the outstanding Ka-50, single-seat) fuselage, every possible form of armour and protection of the dynamic parts against ground fire, and the best possible combination of night and all-weather sensors, aiming systems and weapons. The weapons almost always include a powerful gun and a battery of self-homing missiles. The latest such helicopters naturally put their sighting systems on top of the main rotor, so that the helicopter does not have to expose itself to the enemy but – like a soldier in a World War 1 trench using a periscope – can hide behind any available cover.

Another extremely important role is ASW (anti-submarine warfare). Special ASW helicopters can carry essentially all the sensors and weapons needed to find and kill modern submarines. Of course, unlike large land-based aeroplanes, they cannot range independently over the open ocean but must stay within less than an hour's flight of their parent surface ship,

which can be a destroyer or frigate. Many helicopters are equipped for probe/drogue air refuelling.

## Air control

Development of large high-power radars and computers made it possible to create long endurance high-flying aircraft which can in effect manage a cheese-shaped block of airspace with a radius exceeding 200 miles. The obvious example to cite is the Boeing E-3 Sentry, called the AWACS (Airborne Warning and Control System), which carries its main antenna on a rotating pivot high above the rear fuselage. Using special secure communications, this can keep track (literally) of hundreds of aircraft in a war zone and direct friendly fighters on to targets that should be shot down. Of course, the crew have to be alert, and communicate all the required information, or there may be friendly-fire 'blue-on-blue' shoot-downs of friendly aircraft.

The Soviet counterpart was the Tu-126, which was scorned by Western (Pentagon) experts who derided its capability, especially over water. In fact its Liana radar was in many respects superior to the Westinghouse radar fitted to the E-3. When the time came to replace these aircraft the job fell on the Ilyushin 76, but General Designer Novozhilov was reluctant to commit his bureau to the timescale, so the job was passed to the G.M.Beriev bureau. Today the Beriev A-50 has been in service four years, using the Il-76 as the basic carrier. Grumman produces the E-2C Hawkeye of the US Navy, but Yakovlev has no funds to build the very similar Yak-44E. Boeing, however, is building an AWACS version of the 767 airliner, the first customer being Japan.

## Trainers

The only comment to make here is that today there are 72 active programmes for military trainers! Of these, 21 have piston engines, 15 are turboprops and 136 are jets. Many trainers have important secondary capabilities as liaison, AOP, medevac or light strike aircraft, and some of the advanced jet trainers (like the BAe Hawk) are formidable ground attack aircraft in their own right.

**Bill Gunston**

*Above: The Grumman EA-6B Prowler is arguably the world's most effective and capable tactical electronic warfare aircraft. It serves with the US Navy and the US Marine Corps, and has reportedly been evaluated by the RAF, the Luftwaffe and the US Air Force.*

*Below: The McDonnell Douglas Helicopters AH-64 Apache is a devastatingly effective attack helicopter, heavily armed, agile, well-armoured, and fitted with advanced targeting sensors.*

# Aeritalia (Lockheed) F-104S ASA Starfighter

*Aeritalia (Lockheed) F-104S ASA Starfighter (demonstrator).*

### Role
Fighter
Close support
Counter-insurgency
Tactical strike
Strategic bomber
Tactical reconnaissance
Strategic reconnaissance
Maritime patrol
Anti-ship strike
Anti-submarine warfare
Search and rescue
Assault transport
Transport
Liaison
Trainer
Inflight-refuelling tanker
Specialized

### Performance
All-weather capability
Rough field capability
STOL capability
VTOL capability
Airspeed 0-250 mph
Airspeed 250 mph-Mach 1
Airspeed Mach 1 plus
Ceiling 0-20,000 ft
Ceiling 20,000-40,000 ft
Ceiling 40,000 ft plus
Range 0-1,000 miles
Range 1,000-3,000 miles
Range 3,000 miles plus

### Weapons
Air-to-air missiles
Air-to-surface missiles
Cruise missiles
Cannon
Trainable guns
Naval weapons
Nuclear-capable
Rockets
'Smart' weapon kit
Weapon load 0-4,000 lb
Weapon load 4,000-15,000 lb
Weapon load 15,000 lb plus

### Avionics
Electronic Counter Measures
Electronic Support Measures
Search radar
Fire control radar
Look-down/shoot-down
Terrain-following radar
Forward-looking infra-red
Laser
Television

The Aeritalia (Lockheed) F-104S Starfighter was an Italian advanced derivative of the Lockheed F-104G. Following the F-104S's initial flight on 30 December 1968 and service debut with the Aeronautica Militare Italiana in June 1969, production continued until March 1979.

With the AMI in the early 1980s facing at minimum a decade before a replacement such as the Eurofighter EFA was likely to become available for service, plans were drawn up for a mid-life updated version of the F-104S to be known as the **Aeritalia F-104S ASA** (Aggiornamento Sistemi d'Arma, or updated weapons system). Approval for a prototype conversion was given in 1983, and this aircraft was delivered to the AMI's flight test centre on 12 December 1981.

Intended to give Italian Starfighters enhanced capability in the interception and interdiction/strike roles, the improvement package was confined to aircraft equipment and there was no intention to update the airframe and/or powerplant, although later there was discussion about the retrofit on an inflight-refuelling system. The most vital part of the update was the installation of the FIAR R21G/M1 Setter radar, which gives a look-down/shoot-down capability against low-flying targets.

To provide an effective weapon against such low-flying targets, the Italian company Selenia developed for the F-104S ASA a more advanced version of its Asplde AAM. Known as the Aspide IA, this is is an all-weather, all-aspect missile, offering quick reaction time, improved manoeuvrability at medium and long ranges, and increased resistance to advanced ECM. The Aspide IA is paired with the AIM-9L Sidewinder for close-range combat, and introduction of the new and more compact missile guidance system makes it possible to reinstate, if desired, the 20-mm General Electric M61A1 Vulcan cannon removed from the F-104S.

Some 160 F-104S aircraft were updated to F-104S ASA standard, and in the mid-1990s a further limited upgrade of some of these aircraft was undertaken. Five squadrons remain in use.

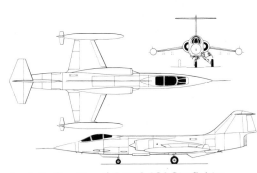

*Aeritalia (Lockheed) F-104S ASA Starfighter*

*Most of Italy's surviving F-104S multi-role fighters were upgraded for an improved interception and self-defence capablity through the Aggiornamento Sistemi d'Arma programme.*

**The F-104S ASA incorpororates new ECM, weapons delivery system, IFF, pitch control computer and radar for a genuine look-down/shoot-down capability against low-level targets.**

**Specification:** Aeritalia F-104S ASA Starfighter
**Origin:** Italy
**Type:** single-seat multi-role combat aircraft
**Powerplant:** one 8119-kg (17,900-lb) afterburning thrust Fiat (General Electric) J79-GE-19 turbojet
**Performance:** maximum speed Mach 2.2 or 1,261 kt (2337 km/h; 1,452 mph) at 36,089 ft (11000 m); maximum cruising speed 529 kt (980 km/h; 609 mph) at 36,089 ft (11000 m); service ceiling 58,070 ft (17700 m); combat radius 1250 km (777 miles) with maximum fuel; ferry range 2920 km (1,814 miles)
**Weights:** empty 6760 kg (14,903 lb); maximum take-off 14060 kg (30,997 lb)
**Dimensions:** span 6.68 m (21 ft 11 in); length 16.69 m (54 ft 9.1 in); height 4.11 m (13 ft 5.8 in); wing area 18.22 m² (196.12 sq ft)
**Armament:** provision for a maximum external load of 3400 kg (7,496 lb) on nine external hardpoints, including Aspide IA and AIM-9L Sidewinder AAMs; one 20-mm General Electric M61A1 cannon can also be installed

# Aeritalia (Lockheed) F-104S Starfighter

*Aeritalia (Lockheed) F-104S of the Turkish air force.*

The spectacular and often controversial Lockheed F-104 Starfighter proved to be of comparatively little interest to the US Air Force. The XF-104 prototype had flown on 4 March 1954, but four years of development ensued before the F-104A became operational in 1958. Two-seat F-104B aircraft followed, but although the USAF was disenchanted with the type it was too far committed to refuse the improved F-104C which served with Tactical Air Command until 1965. This could easily have been the end of the Starfighter story, but in the late 1950s Denmark, Italy, the Netherlands, Norway and West Germany (under the leadership of West Germany) together with Canada and Japan, made an extensive evaluation of about 12 aircraft, finally selecting the F-104 as the subject for an international manufacturing programme, at that time the world's largest, to provide these nations with a multi-mission attack fighter.

Following its major participation in the international programme that produced the F-104G (G = Germany), Aeritalia initiated the development of an advanced version for service specifically with the Aeronautica Militare Italiana. This had the designation **Aeritalia F-104S** (S = Sparrow), and was basically similar to (and incorporated the various improvements standard in) late production F-104Gs. It differed from the F-104G primarily by introducing a weapon system configured specifically for the air combat rather than ground attack role: thus its primary armament changed from bombs and rockets to Sidewinder and Sparrow III AAMs. The first of 205 F-104S aircraft for the AMI was flown on 30 December 1968 with deliveries following in 1969. Despite its optimization for the air-to-air role, the F-104S was generally deployed in the air-to-surface role in much the same way as the F-104G. Aeritalia also built 40 examples of the F-104S for the Turkish air force, the last of them delivered in mid-1976, of these totals approximately 165 and 36 remained in service with the respective air forces in early 1985 These 245 F-104S aircraft were the final examples of the Lockheed Starfighter to be built.

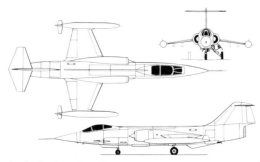

**Aeritalia (Lockheed) F-104S Starfighter**

*Forty examples of the F-104S were built for the Turkish air force, and 21 of these aircraft are still in service as interceptors.*

*The F-104S served with the 4°, 5°, 9°, 36°, 50°, 51° and 53° Stormi of the AMI, and were employed mostly for ground attack, in which it supplanted the North American F-86E Sabre.*

**Specification:** Aeritalia (Lockheed) F-104S Starfighter
**Origin:** Italy
**Type:** single-seat multi-role combat aircraft
**Powerplant:** one 8119-kg (17,900-lb) afterburning thrust General Electric J79 GE-19 turbojet
**Performance:** maximum speed Mach 2.2 or 1,257 kt (2330 km/h; 1,448 mph) at 36,089 ft (11000 m); maximum cruising speed 529 kt (980 km/h; 609 mph) at 36,089 ft (11000 m); time to 35,007 ft (10670 m) 1 minute 20 seconds; service ceiling 58,070 ft (17700 m); combat radius 1250 km (777 miles with maximum fuel; ferry range 2920 km (1,814 miles) with external and internal fuel
**Weights:** empty 6760 kg (14,903 lb); maximum take-off 14060 kg (31,000 lb)
**Dimensions:** span 6.68 m (21 ft 11 in); length 16.69 m (54 ft 9.1 in); height 4.11 m (13 ft 5.8 in); wing area 18.22 m² (196.12 sq ft)
**Armament:** provision for a maximum external load 3400 kg (7,500 lb) on nine external hardpoints for AAMs, bombs, rocket pods and fuel tanks; standard weapon load two wingtip Sidewinder plus two underwing Sparrow III AAMs, the wingtip Sidewinders being replaceable by 645-litre (142-lmp gal) auxiliary fuel tanks

**Role**
Fighter
Close support
Counter-insurgency
Tactical strike
Strategic bomber
Tactical reconnaissance
Strategic reconnaissance
Maritime patrol
Anti-ship strike
Anti-submarine warfare
Search and rescue
Assault transport
Transport
Liaison
Trainer
Inflight-refuelling tanker
Specialized

**Performance**
All-weather capability
Rough field capability
STOL capability
VTOL capability
Airspeed 0-250 mph
Airspeed 250 mph-Mach 1
Airspeed Mach 1 plus
Ceiling 0-20,000 ft
Ceiling 20,000-40,000 ft
Ceiling 40,000ft plus
Range 0-1,000 miles
Range 1,000-3,000 miles
Range 3,000 miles plus

**Weapons**
Air-to-air missiles
Air-to-surface missiles
Cruise missiles
Cannon
Trainable guns
Naval weapons
Nuclear-capable
Rockets
'Smart' weapon kit
Weapon load 0-4,000 lb
Weapon load 4,000-15,000 lb
Weapon load 15,000 lb plus

**Avionics**
Electronic Counter Measures
Electronic Support Measures
Search radar
Fire control radar
Look-down/shoot-down
Terrain-following radar
Forward-looking infra-red
Laser
Television

13

# Aeritalia G222

*Aeritalia G222L of the Libyan air force.*

**Role**
Fighter
Close support
Counter-insurgency
Tactical strike
Strategic bomber
Tactical reconnaissance
Strategic reconnaissance
Maritime patrol
Anti-ship strike
Anti-submarine warfare
Search and rescue
Assault transport
Transport
Liaison
Trainer
Inflight-refuelling tanker
Specialized

**Performance**
All-weather capability
Rough field capability
STOL capability
VTOL capability
Airspeed 0-250 mph
Airspeed 250 mph-Mach 1
Airspeed Mach 1 plus
Ceiling 0-20,000 ft
Ceiling 20,000-40,000 ft
Ceiling 40,000ft plus
Range 0-1,000 miles
Range 1,000-3,000 miles
Range 3,000 miles plus

**Weapons**
Air-to-air missiles
Air-to-surface missiles
Cruise missiles
Cannon
Trainable guns
Naval weapons
Nuclear-capable
Rockets
'Smart' weapon kit
Weapon load 0-4,000 lb
Weapon load 4,000-15,000 lb
Weapon load 15,000 lb plus

**Avionics**
Electronic Counter Measures
Electronic Support Measures
Search radar
Fire control radar
Look-down/shoot-down
Terrain-following radar
Forward-looking infra-red
Laser
Television

The **Fiat G222** was initiated in an effort to meet NATO's Basic Military Requirement Four of 1962, which sought to develop a practical V/STOL transport for service with NATO air forces. Although a number of advanced proposals came from several manufacturers, none seemed sufficiently practical to gain even a prototype contract. However, the Aeronautica Militare Italiana believed that Fiat's proposal could provide a useful transport if finalized as a more conventional design in terms of powerplant and aerodynamics. In 1969 the AMI signed a contract for two **G222TCM** prototypes and one static test airframe. The manufacture of these machines was delayed by two successive redesigns, and it was not until 18 July 1970 that the first prototype (MM582) was flown, the second following on 22 July 1971. These began evaluation with the AMI on 21 December 1971, highly successful tests resulting in a contract for 44 (later 46) production G222s, first flown on 23 December 1975.

From the outset other major Italian manufacturers were involved in the programme, with Aermacchi responsible for the outer wings, CIRSEA for the landing gear, Piaggio for the wing centre-section, SIAI-Marchetti for the tail unit, and Aeritalia (as Fiat had become before its 1990 merger with Selenia to become Alenia) for the fuselage, final assembly and testing. The G222 continued in production up to the early 1990s and was built in several versions. These include the G222 standard military transport with the armed forces of Argentina (3), Dubai (1), Italy (30), Nigeria (5), Somalia (2) and Venezuela (8); the **G222RM** (Radio Misure) for radio/radar calibration used by Italy (4); the **G222SAA** (Sistema Aeronautico Antincendio) fire-fighter with equipment to disburse water of fire-retardant chemicals used by Italy (10); the **G222T** with Rolls-Royce Tyne engines, of which Libya took 20 with the local designation G222L; and the **G222VS** (Versione Speziale) electronic intelligence model used by Italy (2).

The manufacturer also studied other stillborn versions of the G222 included an AEW type, an inflight-refuelling tanker, a launcher for drones, an Earth resources reconnaissance platform and an ASW/ASV mission version.

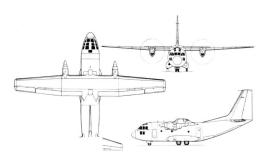

**Aeritalia G222**

*This was a trials aircraft for the G222RM radar and radio calibration type, used for the testing of airfield installations. Aeritalia also developed an Elint version as the G222Vs for the Italian air force.*

*G222 of the 98° Gruppo, 46a Aerobrigata Trasporto Medio. The G222 suffered a protracted development, but since entering Italian and export service the type has more than proved its tactical worth.*

## Specification: Aeritalia G222

**Origin:** Italy

**Type:** general-purpose transport

**Powerplant:** two Fiat (General Electric) T64-GE-P4D turboprops each flat-rated at 2535 kW (3,400 shp)

**Performance:** maximum speed 292 kt (540 km/h; 336 mph) at 15,010 ft (4575 m); long-range cruising speed 237 kt (439 km/h; 273 mph) at 19,685 ft (6000 m); initial rate of climb 1,706 ft (520 m) per minute; service ceiling 25,000 ft (7620 m); range 1370 km (851 miles) with maximum payload; ferry range 4633 km (2,879 miles) with maximum fuel 4633 km (2,879 miles)

**Weights:** empty 14590 kg (32,165 lb); maximum take-off 28000 kg (61,729 lb)

**Dimensions:** span 28.70 m (94 ft 1.9 in); 1ength 22.70 m (74 ft 5.7 in); height 9.80 m (32 ft 1.8 in); wing area 82.00 m² (882.67 sq ft)

**Armament:** none

# Aeritalia/Aermacchi/EMBRAER AMX

*Aeritalia/Aermacchi/**EMBRAER AMX** of the Brazilian air force.*

Looking a decade ahead to the anticipated rundown from 1987 of its Fiat G91R/Ys and licence-built Lockheed F-104Gs, the Aeronautica Militare Italiana began to formulate its specification for a small tactical fighter-bomber. Other elements of the requirement included the reconnaissance, support for ground and naval forces, and complementing the Panavia Tornado. At about the same time the Força Aérea Brasileira identified its A-X requirement for a somewhat similar aircraft to supplement and then supplant its EMBRAER AT-26 Xavantes, and this led to discussions between the Brazilian company EMBRAER and the Italy's Aermacchi about collaboration on an adaptation of the Aermacchi M.B.340 design to meet the combined need. Finalization of the AMI's requirement brought a co-operative agreement between Aermacchi and Aeritalia, and following selection of the Rolls-Royce Spey turbofan as powerplant for the aircraft, by then identified as the Aeritalia/Aermacchi AMX, in July 1980 EMBRAER became a member of the design and production team for what then became known as the **Aeritalia/Aermacchi/EMBRAER AMX** and later as the **AMX International AMX**.

A compact shoulder-wing monoplane with swept wings and tail surfaces, the AMX accommodates the pilot on a Martin-Baker Mk 10L zero-zero ejector seat. Shared manufacture sees major assemblies coming from Aeritalia (central fuselage section, vertical tail surfaces and elevators), Aermacchi (forward and rear fuselage sections) and EMBRAER (wings, tailplane and engine inlets). The Rolls-Royce Spey Mk 807 is licence-built in Italy by Alfa Romeo, Fiat and Piaggio. The first of seven prototypes flew in May 1984, and the type entered service with Italy and, as the **A-1, Brazil** during April and October 1989 respectively. The first **AMX-T** combat-capable two-seat operational trainer flew in March 1990, and current orders amount to 110 and 26 single- and two-seat aircraft for Italy, plus 65 and 14 respectively for the Brazilian air force.

**Specification:** AMX International AMX
**Origin:** Italy and Brazil
**Type:** single-seat multi-role combat aircraft
**Powerplant:** one 11,030-lb (5003-kg) dry thrust Fiat/Piaggio/Alfa-Romeo (Rolls-Royce) Spey Mk 807 turbofan
**Performance:** maximum speed 565 kt (1047 km/h; 651 mph) at sea level; initial rate of climb 10,250 ft (3124 m) per minute; service ceiling 13000 m (42,650 ft); combat radius 345 miles (556 km) on a lo-lo-lo mission or 553 miles (889 km) on a hi-lo-hi mission; ferry range with maximum external and internal fuel 2,073 miles (3336 km)
**Weights:** empty 6700 kg (14,771 lb); maximum take-off 13000 kg (28,660 lb)
**Dimensions:** span 8.874 m (29 ft 1.5 in) excluding wingtip missile rails; 1ength 13.23 m (43 ft 5 in); height 4.55 m (14 ft 11.25 in); wing area 21.00 m² (226.04 sq ft)
**Armament:** one 20-mm M61A1 Vulcan cannon or (Brazilian version) two 30 mm DEFA Cannon plus provision for up to 3800 kg (8,377 lb) of stores carried on five external hardpoints (one twin unit under the fuselage and four under the wings) together with two wingtip rails for Sidewinder or similar AAMs

**AMX International AMX**

*The AMX is the answer to the Italian air force's need for a successor to the Aeritalia G91 and also the F-104G version of the Starfighter. This AMX prototype was unfortunately lost on its fifth flight.*

*The second AMX prototype displays Sidewinder air-to-air missiles at its wingtips, while five pylons under the fuselage and wings can carry a wide assortment of other stores.*

| Role |
|---|
| Fighter |
| Close support |
| Counter-insurgency |
| Tactical strike |
| Strategic bomber |
| Tactical reconnaissance |
| Strategic reconnaissance |
| Maritime patrol |
| Anti-ship strike |
| Anti-submarine warfare |
| Search and rescue |
| Assault transport |
| Transport |
| Liaison |
| Trainer |
| Inflight-refuelling tanker |
| Specialized |

| Performance |
|---|
| All-weather capability |
| Rough field capability |
| STOL capability |
| VTOL capability |
| Airspeed 0-250 mph |
| Airspeed 250 mph-Mach 1 |
| Airspeed Mach 1 plus |
| Ceiling 0-20,000 ft |
| Ceiling 20,000-40,000 ft |
| Ceiling 40,000ft plus |
| Range 0-1,000 miles |
| Range 1,000-3,000 miles |
| Range 3,000 miles plus |

| Weapons |
|---|
| Air-to-air missiles |
| Air-to-surface missiles |
| Cruise missiles |
| Cannon |
| Trainable guns |
| Naval weapons |
| Nuclear-capable |
| Rockets |
| 'Smart' weapon kit |
| Weapon load 0-4,000 lb |
| Weapon load 4,000-15,000 lb |
| Weapon load 15,000 lb plus |

| Avionics |
|---|
| Electronic Counter Measures |
| Electronic Support Measures |
| Search radar |
| Fire control radar |
| Look-down/shoot-down radar |
| Terrain-following radar |
| Forward-looking infra-red |
| Laser |
| Television |

# Aermacchi M.B.326K/Atlas Impala

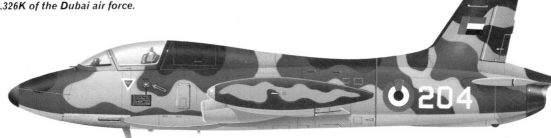

*Aermacchi M.B.326K of the Dubai air force.*

**Role**
Fighter
Close support
Counter-insurgency
Tactical strike
Strategic bomber
Tactical reconnaissance
Strategic reconnaissance
Maritime patrol
Anti-ship strike
Anti-submarine warfare
Search and rescue
Assault transport
Transport
Liaison
Inflight-refuelling tanker
Trainer
Specialized

**Performance**
All-weather capability
Rough field capability
STOL capability
VTOL capability
Airspeed 0-250 mph
Airspeed 250 mph-Mach 1
Airspeed Mach 1 plus
Ceiling 0-20,000 ft
Ceiling 20,000-40,000 ft
Ceiling 40,000ft plus
Range 0-1,000 miles
Range 1,000-3,000 miles
Range 3,000 miles plus

**Weapons**
Air-to-air missiles
Air-to-surface missiles
Cruise missiles
Cannon
Trainable guns
Naval weapons
Nuclear-capable
Rockets
'Smart' weapon kit
Weapon load 0-4,000 lb
Weapon load 4,000-15,000 lb
Weapon load 15,000 lb plus

**Avionics**
Electronic Counter Measures
Electronic Support Measures
Search radar
Fire control radar
Look-down/shoot-down
Terrain-following radar
Forward-looking infra-red
Laser
Television

Early use of the two-seat M.B.326 had shown that the aircraft was an excellent and stable weapons platform, which resulted in the light attack variants of that sturdy and popular machine. It seems surprising, therefore, that it was not until 22 August 1970 that the prototype of the **Aermacchi M.B.326K** single-seat close support aircraft was flown with the Viper 20 Mk 540 of the late-production M.B 326 family.

From the outset it had been intended to provide more power for production aircraft, and the second prototype thus introduced the 1814-kg (4,000-lb) thrust Viper 632-43. This made it possible to add more potent armament, in the form of two cannon installed in the lower part of the forward fuselage The increased fuselage volume gained by elimination of the second seat provided space for the cannon armament's ammunition drums, tankage for additional fuel and for the avionics which had formerly been squeezed into the nose. In most other respects the airframe was similar to that of the M.B.326GB but some additional localized structural reinforcement was intro-duced to cater for the increased stress of low-level manoeuvres, and for this latter reason hydraulically servo-powered ailerons were also provided for improved lateral control.

Although the test and development programme proceeded without major hitches, there was a gap of almost two years before the first order was finalized for three M.B.326Ks to provide Dubai with a counter-insurgency flight. Later deliveries included six more for Dubai, with others for the air forces of Ghana (six), Tunisia (eight) and Zaire (eight). In 1974 Aermacchi delivered to South Africa seven M.B.326Ks in component form, followed by 15 more sets in the following year for assembly by Atlas Aircraft Corporation. After that Atlas continued to build the type under licence as the **Impala Mk 2** with the same Viper 20 Mk 540 turbojet as used in the two-seater. Production continued into the mid-1980s and amounted to 73 aircraft. Early in 1995 the South African air force had some 79 of the aircraft in service for the light attack, close support and weapons training roles.

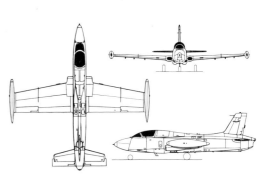

**Aermacchi M.B.326K**

*The Aermacchi M.B.326K can carry a great variety of attack stores on its six underwing pylons. Air-to-air capability comes in the form of two Matra Magic missiles.*

*The single-seat arrangement of the M.B.326K is plain to see in this photograph, as is the port 30-mm DEFA 533 cannon, not fitted to the two-seat variant.*

**Specification:** Aermacchi M.B.326K
**Origin:** Italy
**Type:** single-seat close support, tactical reconnaissance or limited air interception aircraft
**Powerplant:** one 1814-kg (4,000-lb) dry thrust Piaggio (Rolls-Royce) Viper 632-43 turbojet
**Performance:** maximum speed, clean 480 kt (890 km/h; 553 mph) at 5,000 ft (1525 m) or with armament 370 kt (685 km/h; 426 mph) at 30,020 ft (9150 m); initial rate of climb, clean 6,500 ft (1980 ft) per minute or with armament 3,750 ft (1143 m) per minute; combat radius 268 km (167 miles) on a lo-lo-lo mission with maximum armament; ferry range 2130 km (1,324 miles) with two drop tanks
**Weights:** empty 3123 kg (6,885 lb); norma take-off 4625 kg (10,240 lb); maximum take-off 5895 kg (13,000 lb)
**Dimensions:** span 10.85 m (35 ft 7.2 in) over tiptanks; length 10.67 m (35 ft 0 in); height 3.72 m (12 ft 2.5 in); wing area 19.35 m² (208.29 sq ft)
**Armament:** two 30-mm DEFA 553 cannon, each with 125 rounds, plus provision for up to 4,000 lb (1814 kg) of stores on six underwing hardpoints, generally detailed as for the M.G.326GB plus two Matra 550 Magic AAMs, launchers for a wide assortment of air-to-surface rockets, or (on inner port station) a four-camera reconnaissance pod

# Aermacchi M.B.326

*Aermacchi M.B.326GB of the Zaïre air force.*

Design of the **Aermacchi M.B.326** two-seat basic trainer was started by Dr.-Ing. Ermanno Bazzocchi in 1954, and the first of two prototypes flew on 10 December 1957. This aircraft had a 794-kg (1,750-lb) dry thrust Bristol Siddeley (now Rolls-Royce) Viper 8 turbojet, but the second prototype and 15 pre-production aircraft standardized on the 1134-kg (2,500-lb) thrust Viper 11. The Aeronautica Militare Italiana then received the first of 85 examples of this jet trainer, designated just M.B.326 in its initial form, during February 1962, in addition to the 15 pre-production aircraft. Intended for all stages of flying training, the aircraft has a simple and robust airframe with viceless handling characteristics.

In production for 20 years, the M.B.326 was designed with straight flying surfaces and a pressurized cockpit section equipped with a tandem pair of vertically unstaggered ejector seats, and was built in many variants. From an early stage it was clear that the type had potential for use in a light attack role. Such capability was offered by Aermacchi on the M.B.326A with six underwing hardpoints for a variety of external stores. but the AMI at that time had no requirement for such an aircraft. However, orders for similar aircraft were received from Ghana (nine **M.B.326F**s)

and Tunisia (eight **M.B.326B**s). The **M.B.326H** with full armament capability was assembled or licence-built in Australia by the Commonwealth Aircraft Corporation for the Royal Australian Air Force (87) and Navy (10). Last of the early versions. all powered by the Viper 11, were 40 **M.B.326M** unarmed trainers built in Italy for the South African air force, plus about 125 known as the **Impala Mk 1** assembled or licence-built in the Transvaal by the Atlas Aircraft Corporation.

The more powerful Viper 20 engine was introduced in early 1967. Combined with a strengthened airframe in the M.B.326G prototype, the improved type had double the weapon load of the earlier versions. It was built as the **M.B.326GB** for the Argentine navy (eight) and the air forces of Zaire (17) and Zambia (23): EMBRAER in Brazil licence-built 182 similar **M.B.326GC** aircraft for the air forces of Brazil (167 **AT-26 Xavante**), Paraguay (nine) and Togo (six). Aermacchi also supplied the AMI with six **M.B.326E** aircraft with basically the M.B 326GB airframe but the Viper 11 engine, and converted six earlier M.B.326s to the same configuration The final two-seat version was the **M.B.326L** advanced trainer based on the single-seat M.B.326K: two and four were supplied to the Dubai and Tunisian air forces respectively.

## Specification: Aermacchi M.B.326GB
**Origin:** Italy
**Type:** two-seat basic/advanced trainer and light attack aircraft
**Powerplant:** one 1547-kg (3,410-lb) dry thrust Piaggio (Rolls-Royce) Viper 20 Mk 54-0 turbojet
**Performance:** maximum speed, clean 468 kt (867 km/h; 539 mph); initial rate of climb with armament 3,100 ft (945 m) per minute; service ceiling with armament 39,040 ft (11900 m); combat radius 648 km (403 miles); maximum range, clean 1850 km (1,150 miles)
**Weights:** empty 2685 kg (5,919 lb); maximum take-off 5215 kg (11,497 lb)
**Dimensions:** span 10.85 m (35 ft 7.2 in) over tiptanks; length 10.67 m (35 ft 0 in); height 3.72 m (12 ft 2.5 in); wing area 19.35 m² (208.29 sq ft)
**Armament:** provision for up to 1814 kg (4,000 lb) of stores carried on six underwing hardpoints suitable for gun pods, rocket-launcher pods and/or bombs, or camera pod(s)

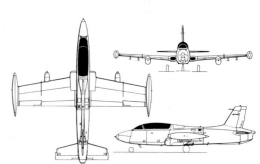

**Aermacchi M.B.326E**

*The M.B.326 was found ideal for training and light attack duties by several countries, especially some wealthier third-world nations. Ghana has operated nine examples of the M.B.326F.*

*The Aermacchi M.B.326 has proved excellent in the training role, where its sprightly performance and tandem seating prepared students for faster and more potent jets.*

**Role**
Fighter
Close support
Counter-insurgency
Tactical strike
Strategic bomber
Tactical reconnaissance
Strategic reconnaissance
Maritime patrol
Anti-ship strike
Anti-submarine warfare
Search and rescue
Assault transport
Transport
Liaison
Trainer
Inflight-refuelling tanker
Specialized

**Performance**
All-weather capability
Rough field capability
STOL capability
VTOL capability
Airspeed 0-250 mph
Airspeed 250 mph-Mach 1
Airspeed Mach 1 plus
Ceiling 0-20,000 ft
Ceiling 20,000-40,000 ft
Ceiling 40,000ft plus
Range 0-1,000 miles
Range 1,000-3,000 miles
Range 3,000 miles plus

**Weapons**
Air-to-air missiles
Air-to-surface missiles
Cruise missiles
Cannon
Trainable guns
Naval weapons
Nuclear-capable
Rockets
'Smart' weapon kit
Weapon load 0-4,000 lb
Weapon load 4,000-15,000 lb
Weapon load 15,000 lb plus

**Avionics**
Electronic Counter Measures
Electronic Support Measures
Search radar
Fire control radar
Look-down/shoot-down
Terrain-following radar
Forward-looking infra-red
Laser
Television

# Aermacchi M.B.339

*Aermacchi M.B.339A of the Argentine navy.*

## Role
Fighter
Close support
Counter-insurgency
Tactical strike
Strategic bomber
Tactical reconnaissance
Strategic reconnaissance
Maritime patrol
Anti-ship strike
Anti-submarine warfare
Search and rescue
Assault transport
Transport
Liaison
Trainer
Inflight-refuelling tanker
Specialized

## Performance
All-weather capability
Rough field capability
STOL capability
VTOL capability
Airspeed 0-250 mph
Airspeed 250 mph-Mach 1
Airspeed Mach 1 plus
Ceiling 0-20,000 ft
Ceiling 20,000-40,000 ft
Ceiling 40,000ft plus
Range 0-1,000 miles
Range 1,000-3,000 miles
Range 3,000 miles plus

## Weapons
Air-to-air missiles
Air-to-surface missiles
Cruise missiles
Cannon
Trainable guns
Naval weapons
Nuclear-capable
Rockets
'Smart' weapon kit
Weapon load 0-4,000 lb
Weapon load 4,000-15,000 lb
Weapon load 15,000 lb plus

## Avionics
Electronic Counter Measures
Electronic Support Measures
Search radar
Fire control radar
Look-down/shoot-down
Terrain-following radar
Forward-looking infra-red
Laser
Television

Realizing that it would within the foreseeable future require a second-generation jet trainer to supersede its current M.B.326 and Aeritalia (Fiat) G91T, the Aeronautica Militare Italiana awarded a wide-ranging study contract to Aermacchi. No fewer than nine design studies were investigated under the designations M.B.338 and M.B.339 to the extent of seven and two variants respectively. Selection of one of the purpose-designed M.B.338 proposals would probably have provided a greater increase in performance and capability, but would equally have proved more costly to develop. With no vast sums available, the AMI thus opted for closer examination of the two M.B.339 proposals, the M.B.339L with a SNECMA Larzac turbofan and the M.B.339V retaining the Rolls-Royce Viper turbojet of the M.B.326 series.

It was the latter, based closely on the airframe and powerplant of the M.B.326K, that was finally selected for full-scale development. The principal revision was effected in the forward fuselage to provide a new cockpit with a raised rear seat to that the instructor could see over the head of his pupil for take-off and landing, an extended canopy for improved all-round view, and more advanced avionics. Revision of the aerodynamics and an enlarged vertical tail surface also gave improved performance and better handling. The first (MM588) of an eventual three M.B.339X prototypes, one of them for static test, was flown on 12 August 1976. The first of 101 production M.B.339A trainers for the AMI was flown on 20 July 1978 and began service trials on 8 August 1979. In 1982 the AMI's aerobatic team received 15 **M.B.339PAN** aircraft with a smoke-generating system and no wingtip tanks. Other operators of the M.B.339A include the Argentine navy (10), Dubai (5), Ghana (2), Malaysia (12), Nigeria (12) and Peru (16). It is thus clear that the M.B.339's performance limitations, imposed by a turbojet powerplant and stright flying surfaces, combined with the availability of more advanced turbofan-powered trainers such as the BAe Hawk and Dassault/Dornier Alpha Jet, to reduce sales potential relative to the M.B.326.

*Aermacchi M.B.339A*

## Specification: Aermacchi M.B.339A
**Origin:** Italy
**Type:** basic/advanced trainer and close-support aircraft
**Powerplant:** one 1814-kg ( 4,000-lb) dry thrust Piaggio (Rolls-Royce) Viper 632-43 turbojet
**Performance:** limiting Mach number 0.85 or 499 kt (925 km/h, 575 mph); maximum speed 485 kt (900km/h; 559 mph) at sea level; initial rate of climb 6,594 ft (2010 m) per minute; service ceiling 48,000 ft (14630 m); combat radius 593 km (368 miles) on a hi-lo-hi mission with maximum warload, or 371 km (231 miles) on a lo-lo-lo mission with maximum warload; ferry range 2110 km (1,311 miles) with external fuel
**Weights:** empty 3125 kg (6,889 1b); normal take-off 4400 kg (9,700 lb); maximum take-off 5895 kg (13,000 lb)
**Dimensions:** span 10.858 m (35 ft 7.5 in) over tiptanks; 1ength 10.97 m (36 ft 0 in): height 3.99 m (13 ft 1.1 in): wing area 19 30 m² (207.75 sq ft)
**Armament:** provision for up to 1814 kg) (4,000 lb) of stores carried on six underwing hardpoints; the two inboard points can each carry a 30-mm cannon or 7 62-mm (0.3-in) multi-barrel Minigun in a Macchi pod, and the two centre points are 'wet' for the carriage of drop tanks; a wide variety of weapon loads includes bombs, napalm, AS.11/AS.12 or Magic missiles, rocket launchers, and a single four-camera reconnaissance pod

*In addition to its role as an advanced trainer, the M.B.339A is employed by the Italian air force for weapons training. Some 1814 kg (4,000 lb) of stores can be carried on the underwing hardpoints.*

*Dubai has received five M.B.339s, which it uses for advanced training and light strike purposes. The Matra Magic can be carried for a limited air-to-air capability.*

# Aermacchi M.B.339K

*Aermacchi M.B.339K (company demonstrator).*

The successful reception of the M.B.339A trainer encouraged Aermacchi to adopt for this aircraft a treatment similar to that which had seen the evolution of the single-seat M.B.326K out of the two-seat M.B.326. The company thus developed a single-seat **Aermacchi M.B.339K** which was originally named Veltro 2 in remembrance of the Macchi M.C.205V Veltro (greyhound), the best Italian fighter/fighter-bomber of World War II.

The development process saw the adoption of a new forward fuselage with a single-seat, the increased fuselage volume being gainfully employed for avionics, more fuel, and the internal installation of two DEFA cannon. In other respects the M.B.339K differed little from its two-seat counterpart, but for customers who might require more sophistication a wide range of optional avionics was available, including an ECM jammer pod, plus head-up and/or TV display. The prototype (I-BITE), built as a private venture, had the standard licence-built Viper Mk 632-43 turbojet as its powerplant. This machine was flown for

the first time on 30 May 1980.

No orders were received for the type, possibly because potential customer felt that the M.B.339K offered insufficient improvement in capability and performance over the M.B.326K. Conformation of this supposition may be found in plans for an uprated version announced in the mid-1980s with the uprated 2018-kg (4,450-lb) thrust Viper Mk 680-43 turbojet, and a nav/attack system incorporating inertial navigation, stores management system, weapon-aiming computer and HUD. Still no orders were placed, and the M.B.339K was cancelled in the early 1990s.

Features of the type, most notably the powerplant and nav/attack system, were incorporated in the improved **M.B.339C** combat-capable mission trainer ordered by New Zealand, which received six such aircraft from 1991. The M.B.339C is notable for the diversity of the modern weapons that can be carried on its six hardpoints and delivered with very considerable accuracy as a result of the type's advanced combination of sensors and computing capability.

## Specification: Aermacchi M.B.339C
**Origin:** Italy
**Type:** fighter and ground attack lead-in trainer with full operational capability
**Powerplant:** one 2018-kg (4,450-lb) thrust Piaggio (Rolls-Royce) Viper Mk 680-43 turbojet
**Performance:** maximum speed 441 kt (815 km/h) 508 mph) at 30,000 ft (9145 m); initial rate of climb 7,085 ft (2160 m) per minute; time to 30,000 ft (9145 m) 6 minutes 42 seconds; service ceiling 46,700 ft (14240 m); ferry range 2038 km (1,266 miles) with two underwing drop tanks
**Weights:** empty 3310 kg (7,297 lb); normal take-off 4884 kg (10,767 lb); maximum take-off 6350 kg (14,000 lb)
**Dimensions:** span 11.22 m (36 ft 9.7 in) over tiptanks; length 11.24 m (36 ft 10.5 in); height 3.994 m (13 ft 1.25 in); wing area 19.30 m² (207.75 sq ft)
**Armament:** provision for up to 1814 kg (4,000 lb) of stores carried on six underwing hardpoints; typical weapons are two cannon or machine-gun pods, two Sidewinder AAMs, two AGM-65 Maverick ASMs, or up to six bombs and/or rocket-launcher pods

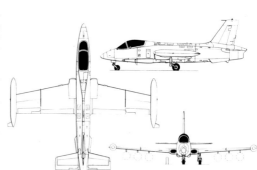

**Aermacchi M.B.339K**

*The M.B.339K could carry a wide variety of stores on its six underwing pylons, including air-to-air missiles. Jamming pods could be carried for self-protection.*

*The port for the starboard 30-mm **DEFA** cannon is clearly visible in this banked view of the M.B.339K prototype. As well as light attack, the aircraft could be used as a weapons trainer.*

| Role |
|---|
| Fighter |
| Close support |
| Counter-insurgency |
| Tactical strike |
| Strategic bomber |
| Tactical reconnaissance |
| Strategic reconnaissance |
| Maritime patrol |
| Anti-ship strike |
| Anti-submarine warfare |
| Search and rescue |
| Assault transport |
| Transport |
| Liaison |
| Trainer |
| Inflight-refuelling tanker |
| Specialized |

| Performance |
|---|
| All-weather capability |
| Rough field capability |
| STOL capability |
| VTOL capability |
| Airspeed 0-250 mph |
| Airspeed 250 mph-Mach 1 |
| Airspeed Mach 1 plus |
| Ceiling 0-20,000 ft |
| Ceiling 20,000-40,000 ft |
| Ceiling 40,000ft plus |
| Range 0-1,000 miles |
| Range 1,000-3,000 miles |
| Range 3,000 miles plus |

| Weapons |
|---|
| Air-to-air missiles |
| Air-to-surface missiles |
| Cruise missiles |
| Cannon |
| Trainable guns |
| Naval weapons |
| Nuclear-capable |
| Rockets |
| 'Smart' weapon kit |
| Weapon load 0-4,000 lb |
| Weapon load 4,000-15,000 lb |
| Weapon load 15,000 lb plus |

| Avionics |
|---|
| Electronic Counter Measures |
| Electronic Support Measures |
| Search radar |
| Fire control radar |
| Look-down/shoot-down |
| Terrain-following radar |
| Forward-looking infra-red |
| Laser |
| Television |

# Aero L-29 Delfin

*Aero L-29 Delfin 'Maya' of the Soviet air force.*

## Role

Fighter
Close support
Counter-insurgency
Tactical strike
Strategic bomber
Tactical reconnaissance
Strategic reconnaissance
Maritime patrol
Anti-ship strike
Anti-submarine warfare
Search and rescue
Assault transport
Transport
Liaison
Trainer
Inflight-refuelling tanker
Specialized

## Performance

All-weather capability
Rough field capability
STOL capability
VTOL capability
Airspeed 0-250 mph
Airspeed 250 mph-Mach 1
Airspeed Mach 1 plus
Ceiling 0-20,000 ft
Ceiling 20,000-40,000 ft
Ceiling 40,000ft plus
Range 0-1,000 miles
Range 1,000-3,000 miles
Range 3,000 miles plus

## Weapons

Air-to-air missiles
Air-to-surface missiles
Cruise missiles
Cannon
Trainable guns
Naval weapons
Nuclear-capable
Rockets
'Smart' weapon kit
Weapon load 0-4,000 lb
Weapon load 4,000-15,000 lb
Weapon load 15,000 lb plus

## Avionics

Electronic Counter Measures
Electronic Support Measures
Search radar
Fire control radar
Look-down/shoot-down
Terrain-following radar
Forward-looking infra-red
Laser
Television

Designed by Z. Rublic and K. Tomás to supersede the piston-engined trainers then in service with the Czech air force, the XL-29 prototype was flown for the first time on 5 April 1959 as a mid-wing monoplane with an unstaggered cockpit locating the instructor at the same height as his pupil. Following the flight of a second prototype in mid-1960, a small pre-production batch built for service evaluation was flown in competition with the PZL-Mielec TS-11 Iskra and Yakovlev Yak-30 during 1961. The XL-29's excellent all-round performance resulted in the type's selection as the standard trainer for all Warsaw Pact air forces with the exception of Poland, which opted for the TS-11. The first prototype had been powered by a Bristol Siddeley Viper turbojet, but the second adopted the Czech-designed Motorlet M 701 turbojet that was selected for production aircraft.

A straightforward design, the **Aero L-29 Delfln** (dolphin) does not readily stall or spin, and can also operate from grass, sand or waterlogged strips. Pupil and instructor are seated in tandem on synchronized ejector seats and there is underwing provision for

the carriage of light armament for training purposes. The first L-29s entered service in 1963, and by the time that production ended in 1974 some 3,600 aircraft of this type had been built. On the face of it, the large scale of this manufacturing programme may seem surprising until it is remembered that the type was also procured for the Soviet air force, in whose service the L-29 gained the NATO reporting name **'Maya'**: the Soviets took more than 2,000 of the production total. In addition to deliveries for the air forces of Bulgaria, Czechoslovakia, East Germany, Hungary, Romania and the USSR, L-29s were exported to several other countries including Egypt, Guinea, Indonesia, Iraq, Nigeria, Syria and Uganda, and many of these aircraft remain in service, although maintenance has now become a problem and successors have been bought or considered where finances permit.

There have been just two variants of the type, the first being the single-seat **L-29A Delfin Akrobat** built in only small numbers for aerobatic displays, and the second the L-29R dedicated attack version which appeared only in prototype form.

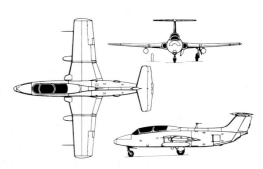

**Aero L-29 'Maya'**

*The L-29 Delfin was selected as the basic jet trainer of the USSR, and as such gained the NATO reporting name 'Maya'. Over 2,000 were delivered to the Soviet air force.*

*Some 3,600 Delfins were built, the majority of which went to the Warsaw Pact. The Czech air force was a major user, but in all countries the L-29 has been largely supplanted by the L-39.*

**Specification:** Aero L-29 Delfin 'Maya'
**Origin:** Czechoslovakia
**Type:** basic and advanced trainer
**Powerplant:** one 890-kg (1,962-lb) dry thrust Motorlet M 701c500turbojet
**Performance:** maximum speed 353 kt (655 km/h; 407 mph) at 16,404 ft (5000 m) or 332 kt (615 km/h; 382 mph) at sea level; initial rate of climb 2,756 ft (840 m) per minute; service ceiling 36,092 ft (11000 m); range 640 km (398 miles) on internal fuel or 895 km (556 miles) with external tanks
**Weights:** empty 2280 kg (5,027 1b); normal take-off 3280 kg (7,231 lb); maximum take-off 3540 kg (7,804 lb)
**Dimensions:** span 10.29 m (33 ft 9.1 in); length 10.81 m (35 ft 5.6 in); height 3.13 m (10 ft 3.2 in); wing area 19.80 m² (213.13 sq ft)
**Armament:** provision for a gunsight and gun camera, and two 100-kg (220-lb) bombs, or eight air-to-surface rockets, or two 7.62-mm (0.3-in) machine-gun pods

# Aero L-39Albatros

*Aero L-39ZA Albatros of the Czech air force.*

The evolution of a successor to the L-29 Delfin began about three years after that aircraft had entered production. The new type was developed in close co-operation with the USSR, which expected to adopt it as successor to the L-29 as its standard jet trainer. A key to much enhanced performance was adoption of the Ivchyenko AI-25 turbofan engine of practically double the power output of the Motorlet turbojet in the L-29, and the achievement of full compatibility of this engine with an airframe of similar overall dimensions to the L-29 brought delays in design finalization. The second of the first three prototypes (the first and third being used for structural test) was initially flown on 4 November 1968, and was joined later by four other flying prototypes. It was not until late 1972 that a production go-ahead confirmed the **Aero L-39 Albatros** as a successor to the L-29 in the air forces of the USSR, Czechoslovakia and East Germany. Full trials were conducted during 1973 and the L-39 entered service with the Czech air force early in 1974.

A cantilever low-wing monoplane, the L-39 carries instructor and pupil on rocket-assisted ejector seats. During the design process, emphasis was placed on modular construction to simplify repair and to allow assemblies to be dismantled easily for major overhauls; there is an ample provision of access panels to facilitate servicing, and adoption of an APU makes the aircraft independent of ground facilities.

Some 2,800 L-39s were built in the main production effort up to 1992: variants include the **L-39C** basic and advanced trainer; the **L-39V** target tug; the **L-39Z0** weapons trainer with reinforced wings and four underwing weapon stations; and the **L-39ZA** dedicated ground attack and reconnaissance version of the L-39Z0 with reinforced landing gear and an underfuselage gun pod. The L-39 series serves with the air forces of Afghanistan, Algeria, Bulgaria, Cuba, Czechoslovakia, East Germany, Ethiopia, Iraq, Libya, Nigeria, Romania, Syria, the USSR and Vietnam. Production has now switched to the **L-59** development with a strengthened airframe, upgraded avionics, and the 2200-kg (4,850-lb) dry thrust ZMDB Progress DV-2 turbofan: Egypt is buying 48 of this variant with further sales to Thailand and the Philippines possible. A 'westernized' **L-159** is also under development with Bendix/King avionics and the 4,000-lb (1814-kg) dry thrust Garrett TFE731-4 turbofan.

**Specification:** Aero L-39ZA Albatros
**Origin:** Czechoslovakia
**Type:** light attack and weapons training aircraft
**Powerplant:** one 1720-kg (3,792-lb) dry thrust Ivchyenko AI-25TL turbofan
**Performance:** maximum speed 340 kt (630 km/h; 391 mph) at 16,404 ft (5000 m) or 329 kt (610 km/h; 379mph) at sea level; initial rate of climb 2,657 ft (810 m) per minute; service ceiling 24,606 ft (7500 m); range (L-39C) 1100 km (683 miles) with internal fuel
**Weights:** empty 3565 kg (7,859 lb); normal take-off 4635 kg (10,218 lb); maximum take-off 5600 kg (12,346 lb)
**Dimensions:** span 9.46 m (31 ft 0.4 in) over tiptanks; length 12.13 m (39 ft 9.6 in); height 4.77 m (15 ft 7.8 in); wing area 18.80 m² (202.36 sq ft)
**Armament:** one 23-mm GSh-23L two-barrel cannon with 150 rounds, and provision for up to 1100 kg (2,425 lb) of weapons on four underwing hardpoints, including bombs of up to 500 kg (1,102 lb), rocket and gun pods, or two drop tanks

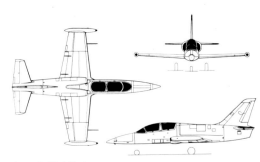

*Aero L-39 Albatros*

*In a way similar to the BAe Hawk, the L-39 can be fitted with a cannon pod and air-to-air missiles for a limited point-defence capability. The missiles are IR-homing AA-2 'Atolls'.*

*The primary role of the Albatros is advanced training, and the type was adopted as such by several countries of the previous Warsaw Pact, including the USSR.*

**Role**
Fighter
Close support
Counter-insurgency
Tactical strike
Strategic bomber
Tactical reconnaissance
Strategic reconnaissance
Maritime patrol
Anti-ship strike
Anti-submarine warfare
Search and rescue
Assault transport
Transport
Liaison
Trainer
Inflight-refuelling tanker
Specialized

**Performance**
All-weather capability
Rough field capability
STOL capability
VTOL capability
Airspeed 0-250 mph
Airspeed 250 mph-Mach 1
Airspeed Mach 1 plus
Ceiling 0-20,000 ft
Ceiling 20,000-40,000 ft
Ceiling 40,000ft plus
Range 0-1,000 miles
Range 1,000-3,000 miles
Range 3,000 miles plus

**Weapons**
Air-to-air missiles
Air-to-surface missiles
Cruise missiles
Cannon
Trainable guns
Naval weapons
Nuclear-capable
Rockets
'Smart' weapon kit
Weapon load 0-4,000 lb
Weapon load 4,000-15,000 lb
Weapon load 15,000 lb plus

**Avionics**
Electronic Counter Measures
Electronic Support Measures
Search radar
Fire control radar
Look-down/shoot-down
Terrain-following radar
Forward-looking infra-red
Laser
Television

# Aérospatiale AS.350 Ecureuil/AStar and AS.355 Ecureuil 2/Twinstar

*Aérospatiale AS.350B of the Singapore air force.*

### Role
Fighter
Close support
Counter-insurgency
Tactical strike
Strategic bomber
Tactical reconnaissance
Strategic reconnaissance
Maritime patrol
Anti-ship strike
Anti-submarine warfare
Search and rescue
Assault transport
Transport
Liaison
Trainer
Inflight-refuelling tanker
Specialized

### Performance
All-weather capability
Rough field capability
STOL capability
VTOL capability
Airspeed 0-250 mph
Airspeed 250 mph-Mach 1
Airspeed Mach 1 plus
Ceiling 0-20,000 ft
Ceiling 20,000-40,000 ft
Ceiling 40,000 ft plus
Range 0-1,000 miles
Range 1,000-3,000 miles
Range 3,000 miles plus

### Weapons
Air-to-air missiles
Air-to-surface missiles
Cruise missiles
Cannon
Trainable guns
Naval weapons
Nuclear-capable
Rockets
'Smart' weapon kit
Weapon load 0-4,000 lb
Weapon load 4,000-15,000 lb
Weapon load 15,000 lb plus

### Avionics
Electronic Counter Measures
Electronic Support Measures
Search radar
Fire control radar
Look-down/shoot-down
Terrain-following radar
Forward-looking infra-red
Laser
Television

The first prototype (F-VWKH) of the Aérospatiale **AS.350 Ecureuil** was flown initially on 27 June 1974 after the type had been designed as successor to the Alouette. Special efforts had been made to ensure that the AS.350 would have good fuel economy and low maintenance costs. The second prototype (F-WVKI), flown on 14 February 1975, had a powerplant of one Turbomeca Arriel turboshaft, and is marketed throughout the rest of the world as the AS.350B Ecureuil (squirrel). Development of the AS.355E twin-turbine version began in mid-1978: this differed from its predecessors by having two Allison 250-C20 turboshafts, and the first of two prototypes (F-WZLA) made its maiden flight on 28 September 1979. The AS.355E became the Ecureuil 2 or, in North America, the TwinStar. The AS.355F development introduced a rotor blade of a new aerofoil section and greater chord for increased payload, and the AS.350B introduced the 478-kW (641-shp) Arriel 1B.

Military interest was only modest, with a few air arms adopting the Ecureuil for utility roles. This began to change with the debut of two dedicated military variants as the **AS.350L** (later **AS.550 Fennec**) with one 478-kW (641-shp) Arriel 1B turboshaft and the **AS.355M** (later **AS.555 Fennec**) with two 420-shp (313-kW) Allison 250-C20F turboshafts and outrigger pylons for light armament. The first of 52 **AS.335F** helicopters for the Armée de l'Air was delivered in 1984 and from the eighth machine onward they have two 330-kW (443-shp) Turbomeca TM 319 Arrius turboshafts and the designation **AS.555AN.** Several AS.550 and AS.555 variants have since been developed in land-based and maritime versions with uprated powerplants, different avionics and provision for a number of different armament fits based on varying numbers of missiles, torpedoes, guns and/or rockets. Customers include Australia (24 AS.350Bs), Bophuthatswana (AS.355), Brazil (24 AS.555), Central African Republic (AS.350), Denmark (12 AS.550s), Djibouti (AS.355), France (152+ AS.550 and AS.555), Singapore (AS.350) and Tunisia (AS.350 and AS.355).

*Aérospatiale AS.355M Ecureuil*

*Singapore operates the AS.350 Ecureuil on light utility duties. The AS.355 (now AS.555) was offered by Aérospatiale (now Eurocopter France) with stub pylons for anti-tank and other missiles.*

*An important operator of the Ecureuil is the Brazilian navy, which uses its helicopters on light duties from ship to shore. Ecureuils operate from the aircraft carrier **Minas Gerais**.*

**Specification:** Aérospatiale AS.555N Fennec
**Origin:** France
**Type:** six-seat naval utility helicopter
**Powerplant:** two 340-kW (456-shp) Turbomeca TM 319 1M Arrius turboshafts
**Performance:** maximum cruising speed 121 kt (225 km/h; 140 mph); initial rate of climb 408 m (1,340 ft) per minute; hovering ceiling in ground effect 2600 m (8,530 ft); range 722 km (448 miles) with maximum fuel and no reserves
**Weights:** empty 1382 kg (3,046 lb); maximum take-off 2540 kg (5,600 lb) with an internal load or 2600 kg (5,732 lb) with a slung load
**Dimensions:** main rotor diameter 10.69 m (35 ft 0.9 in); length of fuselage 10.93 m (35 ft 10.5 in); height 3.34 m (10 ft 11.5 in); main rotor disc area 89.75 m² (966.12 sq ft)
**Armament:** provision for weapon loads such as two torpedoes, or one 20-mm cannon plus two rocket-launcher pods

# Aérospatiale AS.332 Super Puma

*Aérospatiale AS.332 Super Puma (AS.532SC Cougar) of the Chilean air force.*

In 1974 Aérospatiale began a programme to improve the capability of the SA.330 Puma. Experience had shown the need for better payload, performance and survivability. First, a Puma was fitted with two Turbomeca Makila turboshafts and an uprated transmission: the resulting AS.331 was flown on 5 September 1977. In the meantime construction of the new **Aérospatiale SA.332 Super Puma**, with the same powerplant, was in progress. Major changes included a lengthened nose, high energy absorption landing gear and a small ventral fin. Not so apparent, but vital to improved survivability, were the new composite advanced-aerofoil rotor blades, damage-resistant transmission operable for one hour without lubricant, duplicated electric and hydraulic systems, self-sealing fuel tanks, and optional crew armour.

The prototype (F-WZJA) was flown on 13 September 1978 and deliveries began in late 1981. By mid-1985 about 195 had entered civil and military service in five versions. The first two were the military **AS.332B** (now

**AS.532UC** Cougar) for a crew of two and 21 troops, and its AS.332C civil equivalent with two crew and 17/19 passengers. These two initial versions have increased-capacity equivalents, with the cabin lengthened by 0.76 m (2 ft 5.9 in), in the forms of the military **AS.332M** (now **AS.532UL** Cougar). The fifth version is the navalized **AS.332F** (now **AS.532MC** Cougar) Frégate (frigate) model suitable for ASV, ASW and SAR roles. The military variants are available in **AS.532AC/AL** short/long-fuselage armed form and the naval variant in the **AS.532SC** short-fuselage armed form. Military sales have been made to countries including Abu Dhabi (8), Argentina (6), Brazil (16), Cameroun (1), Chile (6), China (6), Ecuador (8), Finland (3) France (29), Gabon (1), Germany (3), Indonesia (33+ licence-built **IPTN NAS-332**), Japan (3) Jordan (8), Kuwait (6), Mexico (2), Nepal (2), Nigeria (2), Oman (2), Panama (1), Saudi Arabia (12), Singapore (22), Spain (12), Sweden (10), Switzerland (15), Togo (1), Venezuela (8) and Zaïre (1).

## Specification: Aérospatiale AS.532AL Cougar
**Origin:** France
**Type:** transport helicopter
**Powerplant:** two 1400-kW (1,877-shp)Turbomeca Makila turboshafts
**Performance:** maximum cruising speed 141 kt (262 km/h; 163 mph) at sea level; initial rate of climb 420 m (1,378 ft per minute; hovering ceiling in ground effect 2800 m (9,185 ft); service ceiling 4100m (13,450 ft); range 842 km (523 miles) with standard fuel or 1245 km (773 miles) with maximum internal and external fuel
**Weights:** empty 4460 kg (9,832 lb); maximum take-off 9000 kg (19,841 lb) with an internal load or 9350 kg (20,615 lb) with a slung load
**Dimensions:** main rotor diameter 15.60 m (51 ft 2.2 in); length, rotors turning 18.70 m (61 ft 4.2 in); height 4.92 m (16 ft 1.7 in); main rotor disc area 191.13 m² (2,057.43 sq ft)
**Armament:** optional cannon, machine-guns or rocket-launcher pods

*Aérospatiale AS.332L Super Puma*

*For the anti-ship role, the Super Puma (Cougar) can carry two Aérospatiale AM.39 Exocet missiles, although no operator yet uses this configuration.*

*The primary role of the Super Puma (Cougar) is assault transport. Improvements over the original Puma include an uprated powerplant and far greater crash survivability.*

Role
Fighter
Close support
Counter-insurgency
Tactical strike
Strategic bomber
Tactical reconnaissance
Strategic reconnaissance
Maritime patrol
Anti-ship strike
Anti-submarine warfare
Search and rescue
Assault transport
Transport
Liaison
Trainer
Inflight-refuelling tanker
Specialized

Performance
All-weather capability
Rough field capability
STOL capability
VTOL capability
Airspeed 0-250 mph
Airspeed 250 mph-Mach 1
Airspeed Mach 1 plus
Ceiling 0-20,000 ft
Ceiling 20,000-40,000 ft
Ceiling 40,000ft plus
Range 0-1,000 miles
Range 1,000-3,000 miles
Range 3,000 miles plus

Weapons
Air-to-air missiles
Air-to-surface missiles
Cruise missiles
Cannon
Trainable guns
Naval weapons
Nuclear-capable
Rockets
'Smart' weapon kit
Weapon load 0-4,000 lb
Weapon load 4,000-15,000 lb
Weapon load 15,000 lb plus

Avionics
Electronic Counter Measures
Electronic Support Measures
Search radar
Fire control radar
Look-down/shoot-down radar
Terrain-following radar
Forward-looking infra-red
Laser
Television

23

# Aérospatiale/Westland SA.330 Puma

*Aérospatiale SA.330 Puma of the Abu Dhabi air force.*

In the mid-1960s the Aviation Légère de l'Armèe de Terre (ALAT) drew up the specification of a medium-size helicopter required for operation by day or night in all weathers and all climates. To meet this requirement, Sud-Aviation designed the **Sud SA.330** with four-blade main rotor, a powerplant of two Turbomeca Turmo turboshafts, semi-retractable tricycle landing gear, a cabin large enough for a crew of two and 16/20 troops, or six stretchers and six seated casualties, or an equivalent weight of cargo, and large doors for fast loading and unloading. The type could also, by installation of optional armament, serve in an assault fire-support role. The first of two prototypes (F-ZWWN/O) was flown on 15 April 1965, and the last of six pre-production SA.330s (F-ZWWP/T and XW241 ) on 30 July 1968. By that date the SA.330, now named **Puma**, had become the second helicopter in the Anglo/French helicopter co-production agreement of 1967 (the first being the Gazelle). This followed selection of the SA.330 as a tactical transport for the RAF, to

be built in the UK by Westland Helicopters.

The first production SA.330B was rolled out on 12 September 1968, and the first of an initial 88 for ALAT was delivered in March 1969. When production ended in 1984 a total of 692 had been built. Variants included the SA.330B with Turmo IIICJ engines, followed by the **SA.330C** export equivalent. The first of the 48 Westland-assembled **SA.330E** helicopters was flown on 25 November 1970, with RAF designation **Puma HC.Mk 1**. The SA.330F was a 15/17-passenger and cargo civil version with Turmo IVA engines, and was followed by the similar SA.330G with uprated Turmo IVCs, and the military **SA.330H** which was a version of the SA.330C with Turmo IVCs. The last two production models were the civil SA.330J and the military **SA.330L** models that introduced de-iced inlets for the Turmo IVC engines and composite rotor blades. ICA at Brasov in Romania completed more than 100 under the designation **IAR-330**, and Nurtanio (later IPTN) in Indonesia assembled 11 from knock-down kits.

**Specification:** Aérospatiale SA.330L Puma
**Origin:** France
**Type:** medium transport helicopter
**Powerplant:** two 1175-kW (1,575-shp) Turbomeca Turmo IVC turboshafts
**Performance:** maximum permissible speed 142 kt (263 km/h; 163 mph); maximum cruising speed 139 kt (258 km/h; 160 mph); initial rate of climb 366 m (1,201 ft) per minute; hovering ceiling in ground effect 2300m (7,546 ft); service ceiling 4800 m (15,748 ft); maximum range without reserves 550 km (342 miles)
**Weights:** empty 3615 kg (7,970 lb); maximum take-off 7400 kg (16,314 lb) with an internal load or 7500 kg (16,535 lb) with a slung load
**Dimensions:** main rotor diameter 15.00 m (49 ft 2.6 in): length, rotors turning 18.15 m (59 ft 6.6 in); height 5.14 m (16 ft 10.4 in); main rotor disc area 176.72 m² (1,902.21 sq ft)
**Armament:** generally none, but can include 7.62-mm (0.3-in) forward-firing machine guns, 20-mm side-firing cannon, missiles and rocket-launcher pods

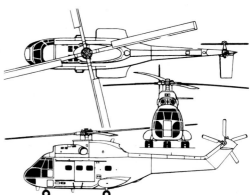

*Aérospatiale SA.330 Puma*

*Spain is a major operator of the Puma, operating the type on many duties including the VIP, liaison, and assault transport roles. Search and rescue missions are also undertaken by the SA.330.*

*The Royal Air Force has two squadrons of Pumas (a helicopter of No.230 Squadron being illustrated here) for battlefield support duties. These are based at Odiham but deploy regularly to Germany.*

# Aérospatiale SA.341 Gazelle

*Aérospatiale Gazelle HT.Mk 2 of No.705 Squadron, Royal Navy, at Culdrose.*

Aérospatiale's X.300 programme was originated to meet a requirement of the Aviation Légère de l'Armée de Terre (ALAT) for a light observation helicopter. Soon designated **Aérospatiale SA.340**, the new type had a kinship with the SA.318C Alouette II as it used the earlier machine's Turbomeca Astazou II powerplant and transmission system, but introduced a new enclosed fuselage seating two pilots side-by-side, a rigid main rotor of the type developed by Bölkow in Germany, and the patented 'fenestron' tail rotor. Early interest in the UK for this helicopter to equip its three armed forces brought about the Anglo-French helicopter development and manufacturing programme, finalized on 22 February 1967, under which Gazelles were produced jointly with Westland Helicopters of Yeovil, Somerset.

The first SA.340 prototype (with the Alouette III's conventional tail rotor) was flown initially on 7 April 1967. The second flew on 12 April 1968 with the fenestron, followed by four **SA.341 Gazelle** pre-production helicopters The first production SA.341, flown on 6 August 1971, introduced the uprated Astazou IIIA engine, a lengthened cabin and enlarged tail surfaces. Initial versions included the **SA.341B** for the British army (**Gazelle AH.Mk 1**) with the Astazou IIIN engine, the similar **SA.341C** for the Royal Navy (**Gazelle HT.Mk 2**), the **SA.341D** trainer for the RAF (**Gazelle HT.Mk 3**), the **SA.341E** communications type for the RAF (**Gazelle HCC.Mk 4**), and with the Astazou IIIC engine the original **SA.341F** for the ALAT. A military version known as the **SA.341H** was built under licence by SOKO in Yugoslavia, and these can operate in the anti-tank role with an armament of four Soviet AT-3 'Sagger' missiles.

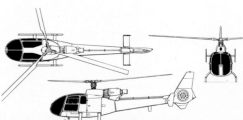

**Aérospatiale SA.341D Gazelle (Gazelle HT.Mk 2)**

**Gazelle HT.Mk 2s were used by No.705 Squadron from RNAS Culdrose for basic helicopter training. Most Fleet Air Arm pilots trained on the type, including pilots destined for the BAe Sea Harrier.**

**The Royal Air Force's basic helicopter training is handled by the Gazelle HT.Mk 3s of No.2 Flying Training School at RAF Shawbury. Other RAF Gazelles are flown in the communications role.**

**Specification:** Aérospatiale SA.341 Gazelle
**Origin:** France
**Type:** five-seat utility helicopter
**Powerplant:** one 440-kW (590-shp) Turbomeca Astazou IIIA turboshaft
**Performance:** maximum cruising speed 142 kt (264 km/h; 164 mph) at sea level; initial rate of climb 540 m (1,772 ft) per minute; hovering ceiling in ground effect 9,300 ft (2835 m); service ceiling 16,400 ft (5000 m); range 360 km (224 miles) with pilot and payload of 500 kg (1,102 lb) or 670 km (416 miles) with maximum fuel
**Weights:** empty 917 kg (2,0221b): maximum take-off 1800 kg (3,968lb)
**Dimensions:** main rotor diameter 10.50 m (34 ft 5.4 in); length, rotors turning 11.97 m (39 ft 3.3 in); height 3.18 m (10 ft 5.2 in); main rotor disc area 86.59 m² (932.08 sq ft)
**Armament:** (SA.341H) usually four (sometimes two) AT-3 'Sagger' anti-tank missiles and two SA-7 'Grail' anti-helicopter missiles

Fighter
Close support
Counter-insurgency
Tactical strike
Strategic bomber
Strategic reconnaissance
Tactical reconnaissance
Maritime patrol
Anti-ship strike
Anti-submarine warfare
Search and rescue
Assault transport
Transport
Liaison
Trainer
Inflight-refuelling tanker
Specialized

**Performance**
All-weather capability
Rough field capability
STOL capability
VTOL capability
Airspeed 0-250 mph
Airspeed 250 mph-Mach 1
Airspeed Mach 1 plus
Ceiling 0-20,000 ft
Ceiling 20,000-40,000 ft
Ceiling 40,000ft plus
Range 0-1,000 miles
Range 1,000-3,000 miles
Range 3,000 miles plus

**Weapons**
Air-to-air missiles
Air-to-surface missiles
Cruise missiles
Cannon
Trainable guns
Naval weapons
Nuclear-capable
Rockets
'Smart' weapon kit
Weapon load 0-4,000 lb
Weapon load 4,000-15,000 lb
Weapon load 15,000 lb plus

**Avionics**
Electronic Counter Measures
Electronic Support Measures
Search radar
Fire control radar
Look-down/shoot-down radar
Terrain-following radar
Forward-looking infra-red
Laser
Television

# Aérospatiale SA.342 Gazelle

*Aérospatiale SA.342 Gazelle of the Moroccan air force.*

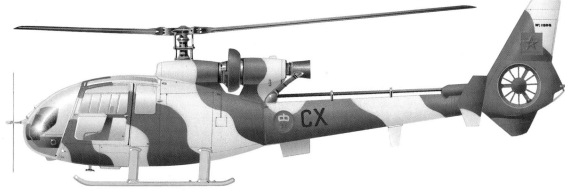

## Role

Fighter
Close support
Counter-insurgency
Tactical strike
Strategic bomber
Tactical reconnaissance
Strategic reconnaissance
Maritime patrol
Anti-ship strike
Anti-submarine warfare
Search and rescue
Assault transport
Transport
Liaison
Trainer
Inflight-refuelling tanker
Specialized

## Performance

All-weather capability
Rough field capability
STOL capability
VTOL capability
Airspeed 0-250 mph
Airspeed 250 mph-Mach 1
Airspeed Mach 1 plus
Ceiling 0-20,000 ft
Ceiling 20,000-40,000 ft
Ceiling 40,000ft plus
Range 0-1,000 miles
Range 1,000-3,000 miles
Range 3,000 miles plus

## Weapons

Air-to-air missiles
Air-to-surface missiles
Cruise missiles
Cannon
Trainable guns
Naval weapons
Nuclear-capable
Rockets
'Smart' weapon kit
Weapon load 0-4,000 lb
Weapon load 4,000-15,000 lb
Weapon load 15,000 lb plus

## Avionics

Electronic Counter Measures
Electronic Support Measures
Search radar
Fire control radar
Look-down/shoot-down
Terrain-following radar
Forward-looking infra-red
Laser
Television

Early utilization of the SA.341 Gazelle confirmed that this new helicopter was a worthy successor to the Alouette II, with satisfactory reliability as a result of adoption of the powerplant and transmission of the Alouette and the rigid main rotor which Bölkow had developed for the BO 105 five-seat helicopter. Aérospatiale realized very quickly, however, that a version with uprated powerplant would offer greater scope for military use, and the changed designation **Aérospatiale SA.342** emphasized the difference. For hot and dry conditions the SA.342K introduced the 649-kW (870-shp) Turbomeca Astazou XIVH with momentum-separation shrouds over the engine inlets. First flown on 11 May 1973, the type secured initial sales to Kuwait for a total 20 aircraft for use in attack and AOP roles.

Continuing development resulted in civil and military versions designated SA.342J and **SA.342L** respectively, these having the Astazou XIV turboshaft engine, an improved fenestron, and certification for take-off at higher weights. The military SA.342L was able to carry a wide range of weapons, and from this version has been developed for ALAT the more capable **SA.342M** especially for the anti-tank role or **SA.342M/Canon** for the escort role with an armament of one 20-mm M621 fixed cannon. The SA.342M has the Astazou XIVM with automatic start-up, and an instrument panel specified by ALAT. Workload in the demanding anti-tank role has been reduced by provision of an autopilot, a self-contained navigation system plus Doppler radar, and a SFIM APX 397 gyro-stabilized sight for guiding the four Euromissile HOT anti-tank missiles. ALAT procurement of the SA.342M amounted to more than 150 helicopters delivered from 9 June 1980. The SA.342L has been built under licence by SOKO in Yugoslavia and the Arab British Helicopter Company at Helwan in Egypt.

### Specification: Aérospatiale SA.342M Gazelle

**Origin:** France
**Type:** anti-tank helicopter
**Powerplant:** one 640-kW (858-shp) Turbomeca Astazou XIVM turboshaft
**Performance:** maximum permissible speed 168 kt (310 km/h; 193 mph); cruising speed 142 kt (264 km/h; 164 mph); initial rate of climb 510 m (1,673 ft) per minute; hovering ceiling in ground effect 3650 m (12,000 ft); service ceiling 4300 m (14,100ft); range 755 km (469 miles) with maximum fuel and no reserves
**Weights:** empty 975 kg (2,150 lb); maximum take-off 1900 kg (4,189 lb)
**Dimensions:** main rotor diameter 10.50 m (34 ft 5.4 in); length, rotors turning 11.97 m (39 ft 3.3 in); height 3.18 m (10 ft 5.2 in); main rotor disc area 86.59 m² (932.08 sq ft)
**Armament:** can include one or two 7.62-mm (0.3-in) machine-guns, or one 20-mm GIAT M621 cannon, plus four or six HOT anti-tank missiles, or two rocket-launcher pods, or two AS.12 wire-guided missiles

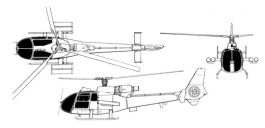

*Aérospatiale SA.342 Gazelle*

**The SA.342 has an uprated engine for better performance under 'hot and high' conditions. Four Euromissile HOT anti-tank missiles are carried in launcher tubes on stub pylons.**

**Comparatively large numbers of SA.342 helicopters have been delivered to the ALAT. These are used mostly for anti-armour operations, but also perform other battlefield roles.**

# Aérospatiale SA.365 Dauphin 2

*Aérospatiale SA.365M Dauphin 2, licence-built as the Harbin Z-9 Haitun, of the Chinese air force.*

In the early 1970s Aérospatiale began the full-scale development of a helicopter to supersede the Alouette III. The resulting Aérospatiale SA.360 Dauphin initial version had a four-blade main rotor, a 13-blade fenestron ducted-fan anti-torque rotor, tailwheel landing gear, and standard accommodation for a pilot and nine passengers. The first prototype (F-WSQL) flew on 2 June 1972 with a powerplant of one 731-kW (980-shp) Turbomeca Astazou XVI turboshaft, but after 180 flights this machine was re-engined by the 783-kW (1,050-shp) Astazou XVIIIA that was adopted for production aircraft. The roomy cabin gave scope for optional layouts seating pilot, co-pilot and 12 passengers, a two-crew ambulance with four litters and medical attendant, a mixed-traffic version with six passengers and 2.50 m³ (88.29 cu ft) of cargo, and executive interior for four to six passengers. A military SA.361H for assault transport and anti-tank operations was developed as a private venture with the 1044-kW (1,400-shp) Astazou XXB, but it was soon clear that for both civil and military use the future lay with the **SA.365C Dauphin 2** twin-turbine version.

The SA.365C prototype (F-WVKE) flew on 24 January 1975 with a powerplant of two 485-kW (650-shp) Turbomeca Arriel turboshafts, but production aircraft have the 492-kW (660-shp) Arriel 1A. Variants include the **SA.365N** similar to the SA.365C except for retractable tricycle landing gear, 529-kW (710-shp) Arriel 1C engines and a high proportion of composite materials in its structure. The **SA.365F**, ordered first by Saudi Arabia (24), is intended primarily for the anti-ship role as 20 examples of the missile-armed **AS.565SA Panther** and four examples of the **AS.565MA** unarmed SAR type with Omera ORB 32 search radar; the anti-ship helicopters carry Thomson-CSF Agrion 15 radar, a Crouzet MAD bird and an armament of two or four AS.15TT missiles. Ireland has five SA.365Fs for the SAR and fishery surveillance roles. The most important military variant was developed as the **SA.365M** with a powerplant of two 584-kW (783-shp) Arriel 1M1 turboshafts and crash-resistant fuel tanks but entered service as the **AS.565UA** high-speed assault transport for 8/10 troops. Armament on the outriggers for anti-armour or fire support on the **SA.565AA/CA** armed variants can include SNEB 68-mm (2.68-in) rockets, HOT anti-tank missiles, and GIAT 20-mm cannon pods. The only current operator of the land-based Panther is Brazil.

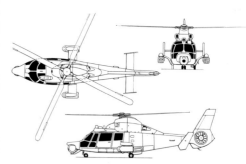

*Aérospatiale SA.365M Dauphin 2 (AS 565 Panther)*

*Hong Kong's small air arm operates three SA.365Cs on light duties around the territory. These include SAR, medevac, firefighting, liaison and VIP transport.*

*The SA.365F is available in AS.565SA anti-ship and AS.565MA SAR versions. In the former, Agrion 15 radar is carried under the nose with four AS.15TT missiles providing the punch.*

**Specification:** Aérospatiale AS 565A Panther
**Origin:** France
**Type:** two-crew multi-role military helicopter
**Powerplant:** two 584-kW (783-shp) Turbomeca Arriel 1M1 turboshafts
**Performance:** maximum cruising speed 150 kt (278 km/h; 173 mph) at sea level; initial rate of climb 420 m (1,378 ft) per minute; hovering ceiling in ground effect 2600 m (8,531 ft); range 875 km (544 miles) with standard fuel
**Weights:** empty 2193 kg (4,835 lb); maximum take-off 4250 lb (9,369 lb)
**Dimensions:** main rotor diameter 11.94 m (39 ft 2 in); length, rotor turning 13.68 m (44 ft 10.625 in); height 3.99 m (13 ft 1 in); main rotor disc area 111.97 m² (1,205.26 sq ft)
**Armament:** HOT anti-tank missiles, Mistral air-to-air missiles, cannon or machine-guns pods, or rocket-launcher pods

## Role
Fighter
Close support
Counter-insurgency
Tactical strike
Strategic bomber
Tactical reconnaissance
Strategic reconnaissance
Maritime patrol
Anti-ship strike
Anti-submarine warfare
Search and rescue
Assault transport
Transport
Liaison
Trainer
Inflight-refuelling tanker
Specialized

## Performance
All-weather capability
Rough field capability
STOL capability
VTOL capability
Airspeed 0-250 mph
Airspeed 250 mph-Mach 1
Airspeed Mach 1 plus
Ceiling 0-20,000 ft
Ceiling 20,000-40,000 ft
Ceiling 40,000ft plus
Range 0-1,000 miles
Range 1,000-3,000 miles
Range 3,000 miles plus

## Weapons
Air-to-air missiles
Air-to-surface missiles
Cruise missiles
Cannon
Trainable guns
Naval weapons
Nuclear-capable
Rockets
'Smart' weapon kit
Weapon load 0-4,000 lb
Weapon load 4,000-15,000 lb
Weapon load 15,000 lb plus

## Avionics
Electronic Counter Measures
Electronic Support Measures
Search radar
Fire control radar
Look-down/shoot-down
Terrain-following radar
Forward-looking infra-red
Laser
Television

# Aérospatiale SA.366 Dauphin 2/HH-65A Dolphin

*Aérospatiale HH-65A of the United States Coast Guard*

## Role

Fighter
Close support
Counter-insurgency
Tactical strike
Strategic bomber
Tactical reconnaissance
Strategic reconnaissance
Maritime patrol
Anti-ship strike
Anti-submarine warfare
Search and rescue
Assault transport
Transport
Liaison
Trainer
Inflight-refuelling tanker
Specialized

## Performance

All-weather capability
Rough field capability
STOL capability
VTOL capability
Airspeed 0-250 mph
Airspeed 250 mph-Mach 1
Airspeed Mach 1 plus
Ceiling 0-20,000 ft
Ceiling 20,000-40,000 ft
Ceiling 40,000ft plus
Range 0-1,000 miles
Range 1,000-3,000 miles
Range 3,000 miles plus

## Weapons

Air-to-air missiles
Air-to-surface missiles
Cruise missiles
Cannon
Trainable guns
Naval weapons
Nuclear-capable
Rockets
'Smart' weapon kit
Weapon load 0-4,000 lb
Weapon load 4,000-15,000 lb
Weapon load 15,000 lb plus

## Avionics

Electronic Counter Measures
Electronic Support Measures
Search radar
Fire control radar
Look-down/shoot-down
Terrain-following radar
Forward-looking infra-red
Laser
Television

In the late 1970s the US Coast Guard drew up details of its requirement for an SRR (ShortRange Recovery) helicopter for operation from shore bases, as well as from its cutters and icebreakers. As the requirement fell within the performance envelope and capabilities of its SA.365N Dauphin 2, Aérospatiale formulated to this requirement a submission which it designated as the **Aérospatiale SA.366G Dauphin 2**, and at the Paris Air Show of 1979 the company was able to announce that it had been the successful competitor. Later that year Aérospatiale received an initial order for 23 out of a total requirement for 90 helicopters, and the type was subsequently allocated the US Coast Guard designation **HH-65A Dolphin**.

Although the airframe of the HH-65A is basically similar to that of the SA.365N, the powerplant (two Lycoming LTS101-750A-1 turboshafts) and operational equipment are of US manufacture, and in terms of unit cost represent some 60 per cent of the total. The cabin is equipped for a crew of three, comprising pilot, co-pilot and crewman/hoist operator, and the specialized equipment includes inflatable flotation bags that would, in the event of an emergency ditching,

enable the occupants to evacuate in sea state 5 and keep the aircraft afloat for salvage. The primary avionics include an advanced FLIR (Forward-Looking Infra-Red) sensor to ease the task of SAR by night in bad weather and/or high sea states. Accurate navigation is critical, but no less important is automatic communication to the helicopter's base, via a data link system, of the various parameters of its flight path so that in emergency its position can at once be pinpointed.

The first SA.366G was flown on 23 July 1980, and this helicopter was later transferred to the Aérospatiale Helicopter Corporation in Texas for installation of the specified US equipment and avionics. During subsequent flight tests there were problems with the fenestron, and a larger fin and an 11-blade fan of increased diameter both constructed of carbonfibre were introduced, the resulting helicopter receiving the revised designation **SA.366G-1**. Initial deliveries to the USCG began in early 1984, and in-service helicopters have been somewhat upgraded in equipment to help in the interdiction of drug smugglers.

**Aérospatiale SA.366G-1 (HH-65A Dolphin)**

**Specification:** Aérospatiale HH-65A Dolphin
**Origin:** France
**Type:** search and rescue helicopter
**Powerplant:** two 461-kW (618-shp) LycomingLTS101-750A-1 turboshafts
**Performance:** maximum cruising speed 139 kt (257 km/h; 160 mph); hovering ceiling in ground effect 7,500ft (2290 m); range 400 km (249 miles) with maximum passenger load or 760 km (472 miles) with maximum fuel; endurance 4 hours with maximum fuel
**Weights:** empty 2718 kg (5,992 lb); maximum take-off 4050 kg (8,929 lb)
**Dimensions:** main rotor diameter 11.93 m (39 ft 1.7 in);1cngth, rotors turning 13.46 m ( 44 ft 1.9 in); height 3.51 m (11 ft 6.2 in); main rotor disc area 111.78 m² (1,203.25 sq ft)
**Armament:** none

*Deliveries of the HH-65A to the USCG began in 1984 and amounted to 90 helicopters replacing the Sikorsky HH-3 and HH-52 in the SAR role.*

*The HH-65A Dolphin is packed with complex communications, navigation and search equipment. An important addition to the basic fit was the Forward-Looking Infra-Red search system for adverse-weather SAR capability.*

# Aérospatiale SA.316B/SA.319B Alouette III

*Aérospatiale Alouette III of the South African Air Force.*

The reliability and sales success of its Alouette II prompted Sud-Aviation to initiate development of an advanced version: the incorporation of both a more powerful turboshaft engine and improved aerodynamics was considered essential for greater payload capability and enhanced performance and, at the same time, the opportunity was taken to introduce new equipment. Initially designated as the SE.3160, the prototype Alouette III introduced a larger and more enclosed cabin than that of its predecessor, able to carry a pilot and sixequipped troops. In the casevac role two litters and two seated casualties or medical attendants could be accommodated behind the pilot, or alternatively the six seats could easily be removed for the carriage of cargo: there was also provision for an external sling for loads of up to 750 kg (1,653 lb).

A prototype was flown for the first time on 28 February 1959 and early production examples followed in 1961. The initial production SA.316A helicopter, built for home and export markets, became the subject of a licence agreement with Hindustan Aeronautics Ltd in India, where the type is still

built as the **HAL Chetak**. Subsequent development produced the main production model, the **SA.316B** which was first flown on 27 June 1968. This introduced the Turbomeca Artouste IIIB turboshaft with uprated main and tail rotor transmissions, and was able to carry more payload. Last of the Artouste-powered Alouette IIIs was the **SA.316C**, built in only small numbers with the Artouste IIID engine. The SA.316B was also the subject of licence agreements with the Swiss Federal Aircraft Factory, and ICA-Brasov in Romania where the type continued in production into the later 1980s. The capability of the SA.316B soon led to two-seat military versions deployed in a variety of roles with a range of weapon options that made them suitable for light attack and ASW. As with the Alouette II, a version was introduced with the Turbomeca Astazou turboshaft, this being the **SA.319B Alouette III Astazou** with a 649-kW (870-shp) Astazou XIV derated to 447 kW (600 shp). Both the SA.316B and SA.319B were included in the production total of 1,453 helicopters, and a considerable number of these were for military service.

**Specification:** Aérospatiale SA.316B Alouette III (standard version)
**Origin:** France
**Type:** general-purpose helicopter
**Powerplant:** one 649-kW (870-shp) Turbomeca Artouste IIIB turboshaft
**Performance:** maximum cruising speed 100 kt (185 km/h; 115 mph) at sea level; initial rate of climb 260 m (853 ft) per minute; service ceiling 3200 m (10,499 ft); range 540 km (336 miles) with maximum fuel at optimum altitude
**Weights:** empty 1143 kg (2520 kg); maximum take-off 2200 kg (4,850 lb)
**Dimensions:** main rotor diameter 11.02 m (36 ft 1.9 in); length, rotors turning 12.84 m (42 ft 2.5 in); height 3.00 m (9 ft 10.1 in); main rotor disc area 95.38 m² (1,026.7 sq ft)
**Armament:** one 7.62-mm (0.3-in) AA52 machine-gun with 1,000 rounds and tripod-mounted in the cabin to fire to starboard (four crew), or one 20-mm MG151/20 or GIAT M621 cannon, or four AS.11 or two AS.12 air-to-surface missiles; (two crew), or two Mk 44 torpedoes, or one Mk 44 torpedo and MAD gear in the ASW role, or two AS.12 air-to-surface missiles in the ASV role

**Aérospatiale SA.316B Alouette III**

*The Swiss Federal Aircraft Factory licence-built the Alouette III for the Swiss army, which operates the helicopters throughout the nation's mountainous areas for roles that include rescue.*

*The French Armée de l'Air operated the Alouette III in large numbers for a variety of tasks. In the anti-armour role the type was flown with AS.11 missiles controlled via a sight above the cockpit.*

**Role**
Fighter
Close support
Counter-insurgency
Tactical strike
Strategic bomber
Tactical reconnaissance
Strategic reconnaissance
Maritime patrol
Anti-ship strike
Anti-submarine warfare
Search and rescue
Assault transport
Transport
Liaison
Trainer
Inflight-refuelling tanker
Specialized

**Performance**
All-weather capability
Rough field capability
STOL capability
VTOL capability
Airspeed 0-250 mph
Airspeed 250 mph-Mach 1
Airspeed Mach 1 plus
Ceiling 0-20,000 ft
Ceiling 20,000-40,000 ft
Ceiling 40,000ft plus
Range 0-1,000 miles
Range 1,000-3,000 miles
Range 3,000 miles plus

**Weapons**
Air-to-air missiles
Air-to-surface missiles
Cruise missiles
Cannon
Trainable guns
Naval weapons
Nuclear-capable
Rockets
'Smart' weapon kit
Weapon load 0-4,000 lb
Weapon load 4,000-15,000 lb
Weapon load 15,000 lb plus

**Avionics**
Electronic Counter Measures
Electronic Support Measures
Search radar
Fire control radar
Look-down/shoot-down
Terrain-following radar
Forward-looking infra-red
Laser
Television

# Aérospatiale SA.321 Super Frelon

*Aérospatiale SA.321 Super Frelon of the Libyan air force.*

## Role

Fighter
Close support
Counter-insurgency
Tactical strike
Strategic bomber
Tactical reconnaissance
Strategic reconnaissance
Maritime patrol
Anti-ship strike
Anti-submarine warfare
Search and rescue
Assault transport
Transport
Liaison
Trainer
Inflight-refuelling tanker
Specialized

## Performance

All-weather capability
Rough field capability
STOL capability
VTOL capability
Airspeed 0-250 mph
Airspeed 250 mph-Mach 1
Airspeed Mach 1 plus
Ceiling 0-20,000 ft
Ceiling 20,000-40,000 ft
Ceiling 40,000 ft plus
Range 0-1,000 miles
Range 1,000-3,000 miles
Range 3,000 miles plus

## Weapons

Air-to-air missiles
Air-to-surface missiles
Cruise missiles
Cannon
Trainable guns
Naval weapons
Nuclear-capable
Rockets
'Smart' weapon kit
Weapon load 0-4,000 lb
Weapon load 4,000-15,000 lb
Weapon load 15,000 lb plus

## Avionics

Electronic Counter Measures
Electronic Support Measures
Search radar
Fire control radar
Look-down/shoot-down
Terrain-following radar
Forward-looking infra-red
Laser
Television

To meet requirements of the French armed services for a medium transport helicopter, on 10 June 1959 Sud-Aviation flew its SA.3200 Frelon (hornet) prototype. Powered by three Turbomeca Turmo IIIB turboshaft engines, the SA.3200 had large external fuel tanks that left the interior clear for a maximum 28 troops, and a swing-tail fuselage to simplify loading cargo. However, development was terminated in favour of a larger and more capable helicopter designed in conjunction with Sikorsky in the USA, and with Fiat in Italy producing the main gearbox and transmission. What was to become Europe's largest production helicopter clearly shows Sikorsky influence in its rotor system (designed by Sikorsky) and watertight hull suitable for amphibious operation. Two military prototypes of the new type were built as the SA.3210.01 troop transport (F-ZWWE) flown on 7 December 1962, and the SA.3210.02 maritime version (F-ZWWF) for the Aéronavale on 28 May 1963.

The designation changed to **SA.321 Super Frelon** for the four pre-production aircraft, and the initial production version was

the maritime **SA.321G** ASW aircraft for the Aéronavale, which received 24. Iraq and Libya took 16 and six similar helicopters. The SA.321G was identifiable by the small stabilizing float (incorporating search radar) attached to the support structure of each main unit of the tricycle landing gear. This model was followed by the 34/37-passenger SA.321F airliner and the SA.321J intended for use as a 27-passenger transport, or cargo carrier with a 4000-kg (8,818-lb) internal or 5000-kg (11,023-lb) external load, or other utility purposes such as firefighting. This was superseded by the higher-weight **SA.321Ja**, of which China took 16 for civil and military use before reverse-engineering the type as the **Changhe Z-8**. Non-amphibious military export versions included 14 **SA.321K** transports for Israel that were later revised with 1,895-shp (1413-kW) General Electric T58-GE-16 turboshafts, and the similar **SA.321L** and **SA.321M** of which 16 and eight were supplied to South Africa and Libya respectively. When production ended in 1983, a total of 99 Super Frelons had been built.

## Specification: Aérospatiale SA.321G Super Frelon

**Origin:** France
**Type:** ASW helicopter
**Powerplant:** three 1,171-kW (1,570-shp) Turbomeca Turmo IIIC6 turboshafts
**Performance:** cruising speed 134 kt (248 km/h; 154 mph) at sea level; initial rate of climb 300 m (984 ft) per minute; hovering ceiling in ground effect 1950 m (6,398 ft); service ceiling 3100 m (10,170 ft); endurance 4 hours in the ASW role
**Weights:** empty 6863 kg (15,130 lb); maximum take-off 13000 kg (228,660 lb)
**Dimensions:** main rotor diameter 18.90 m (62 ft 0 in); length, rotors turning 23.03 m (75 ft 6.7 in); height 6.76 m (22 ft 2.1 in); main rotor disc area 280.55 m² (3,019.94 sq ft)
**Armament:** four homing torpedoes in the ASW role or two Exocet missiles in the ASV role

*Aérospatiale SA.321G Super Frelon*

*During the mid-1980s the Super Frelons of the Aéronavale were revised in overall grey scheme. A more important improvement was the addition of a large search radar in the nose.*

*Principal role for the Aéronavale's Super Frelons is shielding the submarine force as they leave harbour. Other roles are also undertaken.*

# Agusta A 129 Mangusta

*Agusta A 129 Mangusta of the Italian army.*

To meet a requirement of the Aviazione Leggera dell'Esercito for a dedicated light anti-tank helicopter, Agusta began work in 1978 on a development of its A 109A. It was soon realized this would not be good enough, and a completely new design was initiated under the designation **Agusta A 129 Mangusta** (mongoose). Adopting the form that has become almost standard for anti-armour helicopters, this type has a narrow fuselage incorporating separate tandem cockpits for the co-pilot/gunner and pilot (in a raised rear cockpit) on energy-absorbing armoured seats. The fuselage carries mid-mounted stub wings, each with two underwing pylons that allow the carriage of a 1000-kg (2,205-lb) weapon load. Other design features include robust impact-absorbing fixed tailwheel landing gear; a powerplant of two Rolls-Royce Gem turboshaft engines partially built, in the case of production helicopters, by Piaggio; a crashworthy fuselage structure with ballistic tolerance against 12.7-mm (0.5-in) armour-piercing ammunition; and a transmission, four-blade main and three-blade tail rotor all with similar ballistic tolerance. The first 'official'

flight of the A 129 prototype (MM 590/E 1901) was made on 15 September 1983.

An initial production batch of 66 (later 60) was approved by the Italian government, six of them being allocated for training and the remainder split between two operational squadrons, and the Italian army hopes to procure an additional 30 helicopters, plus reserves, to equip a third squadron. The A 129 with full day and night operational capability is regarded by the Italian army as a very useful helicopter. This results from the adoption of an integrated multiplex system (IMS), managed by two computers, which controls and/or monitors aircraft performance, autopilot, caution/warning systems, communications, engine condition, flight director, fly-by-wire system, navigation, electronic warfare systems, rocket fire control, and the status of electrical, fuel and hydraulic systems. An A 129 Mk 2 Tonal was developed in partnership with Westland for British and other markets but has not been built, but Agusta is developing a revised version with an uprated powerplant and a trainable nose-mounted 20-mm cannon for the effective suppression of battlefield anti-aircraft fire.

## Specification: Agusta A 129 Mangusta
**Origin:** Italy
**Type:** light anti-tank and multi-role military helicopter
**Powerplant:** two 608-kW (815-shp) Piaggio (Rolls-Royce) Gem 2 Mk 1004D turboshafts each with an emergency rating of 772 kW (1,035 shp)
**Performance:** maximum speed 179 kt (315 km/h; 196 mph) at 6,560 ft (2000 m); initial rate of climb 2,150 ft (65 m) per minute; hovering ceiling in ground effect 12,305 ft (3750 m); endurance 3 hours
**Weights:** empty 2520 kg (5,575 lb; maximum take-off 4100 kg (9,038 lb)
**Dimensions:** main rotor diameter 11.90 m (39 ft 0.5 in); length, rotors turning 14.29 m (46 ft 10.6 in); height 3.315 m (10 ft 10.5 in); main rotor disc area 111.22 m² (1,197.20 sq ft)
**Armament:** provision for 1200 kg (2,646 lb) of stores carried on four hardpoints, and generally comprising eight TOW anti-tank missiles and two machine-gun or rocket-launcher pods

*Agusta A 129 Mangusta*

*The A 129 exhibits the classic layout for gunship helicopters, with the pilot sitting in the raised rear seat and the weapons system officer in the forward station, closer to the action.*

*Primary weapon for the A 129 in the anti-armour role is the TOW, carried on the stub pylons. The sight in mounted in the nose, but the helicopter had provision for a mast-mounted sight.*

**Role**

Fighter
Close support
Counter-insurgency
Tactical strike
Strategic bomber
Tactical reconnaissance
Strategic reconnaissance
Maritime patrol
Anti-ship strike
Anti-submarine warfare
Search and rescue
Assault transport
Transport
Liaison
Trainer
Inflight-refuelling tanker
Specialized

**Performance**

All-weather capability
Rough field capability
STOL capability
VTOL capability
Airspeed 0-250 mph
Airspeed 250 mph-Mach 1
Airspeed Mach 1 plus
Ceiling 0-20,000 ft
Ceiling 20,000-40,000 ft
Ceiling 40,000ft plus
Range 0-1,000 miles
Range 1,000-3,000 miles
Range 3,000 miles plus

**Weapons**

Air-to-air missiles
Air-to-surface missiles
Cruise missiles
Cannon
Trainable guns
Naval weapons
Nuclear-capable
Rockets
'Smart' weapon kit
Weapon load 0-4,000 lb
Weapon load 4,000-15,000 lb
Weapon load 15,000 lb plus

**Avionics**

Electronic Counter Measures
Electronic Support Measures
Search radar
Fire control radar
Look-down/shoot-down
Terrain-following radar
Forward-looking infra-red
Laser
Television

# Agusta-Bell AB 205

*Agusta-Bell AB 205 of the Greek Aeroporta Statou.*

**Role**
Fighter
Close support
Counter-insurgency
Tactical strike
Strategic bomber
Tactical reconnaissance
Strategic reconnaissance
Maritime patrol
Anti-ship strike
Anti-submarine warfare
Search and rescue
Assault transport
Transport
Liaison
Trainer
Inflight-refuelling tanker
Specialized

**Performance**
All-weather capability
Rough field capability
STOL capability
VTOL capability
Airspeed 0-250 mph
Airspeed 250 mph-Mach 1
Airspeed Mach 1 plus
Ceiling 0-20,000 ft
Ceiling 20,000-40,000 ft
Ceiling 40,000ft plus
Range 0-1,000 miles
Range 1,000-3,000 miles
Range 3,000 miles plus

**Weapons**
Air-to-air missiles
Air-to-surface missiles
Cruise missiles
Cannon
Trainable guns
Naval weapons
Nuclear-capable
Rockets
'Smart' weapon kit
Weapon load 0-4,000 lb
Weapon load 4,000-15,000 lb
Weapon load 15,000 lb plus

**Avionics**
Electronic Counter Measures
Electronic Support Measures
Search radar
Fire control radar
Look-down/shoot-down
Terrain-following radar
Forward-looking infra-red
Laser
Television

Basically similar to the earlier Bell Model 204, the Bell Helicopter Model 205 introduced a number of improvements. The most significant was a lengthened fuselage providing an enlarged cabin seating 11/14 troops or, when used in a medevac role, six litters, a seated casualty and a medical attendant. Several nations have built the Model 204/205 under licence, but the major licensee is Agusta which as early as 10 May 1961 flew its first AB 204.

The **Agusta-Bell AB 205**, which continued in production into the late 1980s, corresponds to the UH-1D/UH-1H 'Huey' versions built by Bell in the USA. It is suitably equipped for one pilot operation by day (VFR or IFR) and night; in its AB 205 military version it has proved a useful multi-role utility helicopter and has been built in considerable numbers for the Italian armed forces and for export. When stripped of all internal fittings the cabin has a clear volume of 6.2 m³ (220 cu ft), making it easily adaptable as a cargo carrier or as a SAR helicopter. Agusta also expanded the AB 205's overall capabilities by providing kits for the installation of auxiliary fuel tanks, a rescue hoist or a rotor brake; for the engine there is filter/separation protection and winterization; and emergency flotation gear, regular flotation gear and skis for operation from snow. There are also a number of weapon systems involving machine guns, missiles and singly or multiply launched rockets, plus armour protection and a gyro-stabilized sight.

From 1969 Agusta also built the **AB 205A-1** as a slightly modified version of the Bell civil Model 205A-1, and this proved a useful utility helicopter. It has only minor modifications by comparison with the Bell 205A-1, and uses a similarly powered sub-type of the T53 turboshaft engine which powers the military AB 205.

*Agusta-Bell AB 205*

## Specification: Agusta-Bell AB 205
**Origin:** USA and Italy
**Type:** multi-role military helicopter
**Powerplant:** one 1,400-shp (1044-kW) Avco Lycoming T53-L-1 3B turboshaft flat-rated at 1,100 shp (820 kW)
**Performance:** maximum speed 120 kt (222 km/h; 138 mph); cruising speed 110 kt (204 km/h; 127 mph); initial rate of climb 1,680 ft (512 m) per minute; service ceiling 15,010 ft (4,575 m); maximum range 580 km (360 miles) with standard fuel and no reserves
**Weights:** empty 2177 kg (4,800 lb); maximum take-off 4309 kg (9,500 lb)
**Dimensions:** main rotor diameter 14.71 m (48 ft 3.2 in); length, rotors turning 17.39 m (57 ft 0.7 in); height 4.48 m (14 ft 8.4 in); main rotor disc area 169.95 m² (1,829.36 sq ft)
**Armament:** can include, singly or in combination, 7.62-mm (0.3-in) and 12.7-mm (0.5-in) machine guns, 7.62-mm (0.3-in) Minigun, 70-mm (2.75-in) rockets, AS.12 air-to-surface missiles, and TOW anti-tank missiles

*This AB 205 serves with the Greek air force's 359 Mira, and is used primarily for search and rescue. The yellow band facilitates visibility and the helicopter mounts a hoist above the door.*

*The AB 205 performs general transport duties in the Italian army, involving mainly liaison and battlefield assault. This helicopter serves with the 13° Graco at Verona-Boscomantico.*

# Agusta-Bell AB 212ASW/ASV

*Agusta-Bell AB 212ASW/ASV of the Turkish navy.*

Under licence from Bell Helicopters, Agusta began production of the **Agusta-Bell AB 212** utility transport helicopter which is essentially the same as the Bell Model 212 Twin Two-Twelve (UH-1N). This differs from the earlier Model 205 by introduction of a twin-turbine powerplant, a revised and uprated transmission and generally improved dynamics, structure and systems.

The capability and reliability of this twin-turbine helicopter soon induced Agusta to develop a specialized version primarily for ASW but suitable also for deployment in ASV, SAR, utility and Vertrep roles. Work began on this project in late 1971, the resulting **AB 212ASW/ASV** prototype being evaluated by the Aviazione per la Marina Militare Italiana during 1973. Externally it can be identified by its dorsal radome, but otherwise the structure differs little from that of the basic AB 212: changes include localized strengthening, the addition of deck-mooring attachments, and features to improve resistance to salt-water corrosion. The most important changes are internal, and include a crew of three or four for combat missions;

two pilots four litters and a medical attendant for casevac; and two pilots and seven passengers for light transport.

Key to the AB 212ASW/ASV's mission capability is its onboard equipment. For ASW the automatic flight-control system combines inputs from the automatic stabilization system, radar altimeter, Doppler navigation system and other sensors to give hands-off flight from the cruise state to sonar hover under all weather conditions. The automatic navigation system pinpoints the helicopter's position on the radar tactical display together with target information from the AQS-18 low-frequency variable-depth sonar. For the ASV mission a high-performance long-range search radar, such as the SMA (Ferranti) Seaspray is introduced for helicopter-launched anti-ship missiles, and optional avionics such as the TG-2 Teseo data link system can provide the helicopter with capability for the mid-course guidance of the OTO Melara Otomat 2 anti-ship missile used by the Italian navy. More than 100 AB 212ASW/ASV helicopters are in service world-wide.

*Agusta-Bell AB 212ASW/ASV*

**The Peruvian navy is one of the many users that have found the AB 212ASW/ASV a capable and versatile naval helicopter. It is able to perform anti-submarine and anti-ship roles.**

**The AB 212ASW/ASV is widely used by the Italian navy for anti-submarine and anti-ship duties. This helicopter carries an MM/APS-705 search radar above the cabin and is seen dunking a sonar.**

## Specification: Agusta-Bell AB 212ASW/ASV
**Origin:** USA and Italy
**Type:** ASW and multi-role naval helicopter
**Powerplant:** one 1398-kW (1,875-shp) Pratt & Whitney Canada PT6T-6 Turbo Twin Pac coupled-turboshaft engine
**Performance:** maximum speed 106 kt (196 mph; 122 mph); cruising speed 100 kt (185 mph; 115 mph) with weapons; initial rate of climb 1,300 ft (396 m) per minute; hovering ceiling in ground effect 10,500 ft (3200 m); maximum range 667 km (414 miles) with auxiliary fuel; endurance 3 hours on a search and rescue mission
**Weights:** empty 3420 kg (7,540 lb); maximum take-off 5070 kg (11,175 lb)
**Dimensions:** main rotor diameter 14.63 m (48 ft 0 in); length, rotors turning 17.40 m (57 ft 1 in): height 4.53 m (14 ft 10.25 in); main rotor disc area 168.11 m² (1,809.586 sq ft)
**Armament:** two Mk 44/46 or Moto Fides A 244/S homing torpedoes in the ASW role, or two Marte Mk 2 or Sea Skua air-to-surface missiles in the ASV role

**Role**
Fighter
Close support
Counter-insurgency
Tactical strike
Strategic bomber
Tactical reconnaissance
Strategic reconnaissance
Maritime patrol
Anti-ship strike
Anti-submarine warfare
Search and rescue
Assault transport
Transport
Liaison
Trainer
Inflight-refuelling tanker
Specialized

**Performance**
All-weather capability
Rough field capability
STOL capability
VTOL capability
Airspeed 0-250 mph
Airspeed 250 mph-Mach 1
Airspeed Mach 1 plus
Ceiling 0-20,000 ft
Ceiling 20,000-40,000 ft
Ceiling 40,000ft plus
Range 0-1,000 miles
Range 1,000-3,000 miles
Range 3,000 miles plus

**Weapons**
Air-to-air missiles
Air-to-surface missiles
Cruise missiles
Cannon
Trainable guns
Naval weapons
Nuclear-capable
Rockets
'Smart' weapon kit
Weapon load 0-4,000 lb
Weapon load 4,000-15,000 lb
Weapon load 15,000 lb plus

**Avionics**
Electronic Counter Measures
Electronic Support Measures
Search radar
Fire control radar
Look-down/shoot-down
Terrain-following radar
Forward-looking infra-red
Laser
Television

# Agusta-Bell AB 412 and Griffon

*Agusta-Bell AB 412 Griffon of the Lesotho air force.*

Licensed production by Agusta of the Bell Model 412 began during 1981 under the designation **Agusta-Bell AB 412**. This helicopter represents an extension of the Bell Model 205/212 range, the Model 212 having introduced a twin-turbine powerplant and the subsequent Model 412 adding a four-blade rotor for more efficient performance and smoother flight. Agusta offers a number of layouts of the AB 412 for different civil applications, and has also developed a dedicated multi-purpose military version known as the **Griffon**. Intended for the attack of ships, tanks and other hard targets when suitably armed, the Griffon can carry up to 15 troops and be adapted quickly for such roles as casevac (six stretchers/two attendants) logistic transport patrol SAR and tactical support.

To achieve the military Griffon, modification of the basic AB 412 added crash-resistant seats (armour-plated for the crew), high-absorption landing gear, self-sealing fuel tanks, and armament attachment points.

The helicopter's survivability can be further enhanced by the installation of ECM, decoy and jamming, missile detection, and radar/laser warning systems. External weapon options for the Griffon include two 12.7-mm (0.5-in) machine-gun pods, two 25-mm Oerlikon cannon, two launchers each with 19 81-mm (3.2-in) SNORA rockets, four or eight TOW anti-tank missiles, four air-to-air or air-defence suppression missiles, and for the ASV role four BAe Sea Skua or similar missiles.

Agusta's Griffon prototype first flew during August 1982 and the first production helicopter was delivered in January 1983. Initial orders were received from the Italian army and Carabinieri, Spain, Uganda and Zimbabwe. The Turkish navy planned to acquire an ASV version armed with Sea Skua missiles, but this plan fell in abeyance. It is still early days for predicting sales of this comparatively new helicopter, but the Griffon seems likely to be in production for some time.

*Agusta-Bell AB 412 Griffon*

## Specification: Agusta-Bell AB 412 Griffon
**Origin:** USA and Italy
**Type:** multi-role military helicopter
**Powerplant:** one 1342-kW (1,800-shp) Pratt & Whitney Canada PT6T-6 Turbo Twin Pac coupled-turboshaft engine
**Performance:** maximum speed 125 kt (232 km/h; 144 mph) at 4,920 ft (1500 m); initial rate of climb 1,440 ft (438 m) per minute: service ceiling 16,995 ft (5180 m); hovering ceiling in ground effect 4,100 ft (1250 m); maximum range 500 km (311 miles) with standard fuel and no reserves
**Weights:** empty 2841 kg (6,263 lb); maximum take-off 5261 kg (11,600 lb)
**Dimensions:** main rotor diameter 14.02 m (46 ft 0 in); length, rotors turning 17.07 m (56 ft 0 in); height 4.32 m (14 ft 2.5 in); main rotor disc area 154.39 m² (1,661.90 sq ft)
**Armament:** combinations of weapons detailed in the text, according to role

*The AB 412 can perform many battlefield roles, including fire support, anti-armour and, as here, combat assaults and extractions.*

*The capabilities of the AB 412 have meant encouraging sales so far. The major customer is the Italian army, although Spain originally ordered 24. Most of the helicopters undertake several roles.*

# Agusta-Sikorsky AS-61

*Agusta-Sikorsky AS-61-TS of the 93° Gruppo, 31° Stormo, Italian air force.*

Sikorsky's production of its extensively built S-61 series has ended, but the basic type continues in production with the two of the company's licensees, namely Agusta in Italy and Westland in the UK; Mitsubishi, the Japanese licensee, completed its last S-61 series helicopter in 1990. Agusta began licensed construction of the civil S-61 and military SH-3D in 1967, delivering its first **Agusta-Sikorsky ASH-3D** anti-submarine helicopter to the Italian navy in 1969. Although generally similar to the Sikorsky S-61, the Agusta production model differs in its local strengthening of the airframe, revised horizontal tail, uprated powerplant.

Agusta then built the military **ASH-3H**, which is basically equivalent to the US Navy's SH-3H and can be equipped for roles that include ASV, ASW, anti-surface missile defence, SAR, tactical transport, and Vertrep. The primary use of the ASH-3D and ASH-3H has been in the ASV and ASW roles, for which the two variants have advanced avionics: for the ASW roles they carry two or four Mk 44/46 or Moto Fides A 244/S homing torpedoes, or four depth charges, while for the ASV role their armament can include

four short-range Aérospatiale AS.12 missiles or two long-range OTO Melara Marte Mk 2, AM.39 Exocet or McDonnell Douglas Harpoon missiles. ASH-3D and ASH-3H helicopters have been supplied to Argentina, Brazil, Iran and Peru, but the Italian navy is the major operator. An unarmed version for VIP transport, variously designated as the **ASH-3D/TS** (Trasporto Speciale), **AS-61A4**, and **AS-61VIP**, was built for Iran, Iraq, Italy and Saudi Arabia.

With an end to Sikorsky construction of the S-61N civil helicopter, Agusta obtained the production rights and modified the design to provide reduced capacity and increased range. Designated as the AS-61N1 Silver, the civil prototype flew initially on 25 July 1984; this and initial aircraft retain the General Electric CT58 powerplant of the Sikorsky S-61N, but Agusta has plans for any resumption of production to offer two 1312-kW (1,760-shp) General Electric CT7 turboshafts. Agusta also builds the very different Sikorsky S-61R transport under the designation **HH-3F** for use in SAR and utility roles. The Aeronautica Militare Italiana received 20; others were built for export.

**Agusta-Sikorsky ASH-3H**

*The ASH-3H carries state-of-the-art submarine detection gear, communications and weapons, similar to those of the US Navy's SH-3H. This pair is operated by Brazil's naval air arm.*

*Agusta builds the HH-3F, similar to its US counterpart. This is primarily used by the Italian navy for SAR. This example displays its amphibious capability.*

**Specification:** Agusta-Sikorsky ASH-3H (ASW role)
**Origin:** USA and Italy
**Type:** all-weather anti-submarine helicopter
**Powerplant:** two 1118-kW (1,500-shp) General Electric T58-GE-100 turboshafts
**Performance:** cruising speed 120 kt (222 km/h; 138 mph); initial rate of climb 2,200 ft (670 m) per minute; hovering ceiling in ground effect 8,200 ft (2500 m); service ceiling 12,205 ft (3720 m); range 1165 km (724 miles) with standard fuel
**Weights:** empty 5895 kg (12,995 lb); maximum take-off 9525 kg (21,000 lb)
**Dimensions:** main rotor diameter 18.90 m (62 ft 0 in): length, rotors turning 21.91 m (71 ft 10.7 in); height 4.93 m (16 ft 2 in): main rotor disc area 280.47 m² (3.019.1 sq ft)
**Armament:** as detailed in text for ASW and ASV roles

**Role**
Fighter
Close support
Counter-insurgency
Tactical strike
Strategic bomber
Tactical reconnaissance
Strategic reconnaissance
Maritime patrol
Anti-ship strike
Anti-submarine warfare
Search and rescue
Assault transport
Transport
Liaison
Trainer
Inflight-refuelling tanker
Specialized

**Performance**
All-weather capability
Rough field capability
STOL capability
VTOL capability
Airspeed 0-250 mph
Airspeed 250 mph-Mach 1
Airspeed Mach 1 plus
Ceiling 0-20,000 ft
Ceiling 20,000-40,000 ft
Ceiling 40,000ft plus
Range 0-1,000 miles
Range 1,000-3,000 miles
Range 3,000 miles plus

**Weapons**
Air-to-air missiles
Air-to-surface missiles
Cruise missiles
Cannon
Trainable guns
Naval weapons
Nuclear-capable
Rockets
'Smart' weapon kit
Weapon load 0-4,000 lb
Weapon load 4,000-15,000 lb
Weapon load 15,000 lb plus

**Avionics**
Electronic Counter Measures
Electronic Support Measures
Search radar
Fire control radar
Look-down/shoot-down
Terrain-following radar
Forward-looking infra-red
Laser
Television

# AIDC AT-3 Tzu-chung

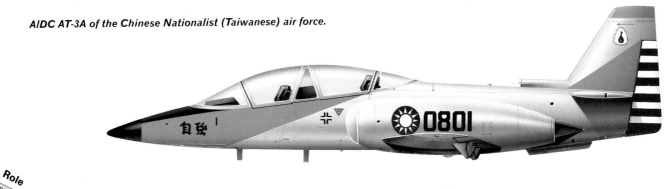

*AIDC AT-3A of the Chinese Nationalist (Taiwanese) air force.*

## Role

Fighter
Close support
Counter-insurgency
Tactical strike
Strategic bomber
Tactical reconnaissance
Strategic reconnaissance
Maritime patrol
Anti-ship strike
Anti-submarine warfare
Search and rescue
Assault transport
Transport
Liaison
Trainer
Inflight-refuelling tanker
Specialized

## Performance

All-weather capability
Rough field capability
STOL capability
VTOL capability
Airspeed 0-250 mph
Airspeed 250 mph-Mach 1
Airspeed Mach 1 plus
Ceiling 0-20,000 ft
Ceiling 20,000-40,000 ft
Ceiling 40,000ft plus
Range 0-1,000 miles
Range 1,000-3,000 miles
Range 3,000 miles plus

## Weapons

Air-to-air missiles
Air-to-surface missiles
Cruise missiles
Cannon
Trainable guns
Naval weapons
Nuclear-capable
Rockets
'Smart' weapon kit
Weapon load 0-4,000 lb
Weapon load 4,000-15,000 lb
Weapon load 15,000 lb plus

## Avionics

Electronic Counter Measures
Electronic Support Measures
Search radar
Fire control radar
Look-down/shoot-down
Terrain-following radar
Forward-looking infra-red
Laser
Television

In July 1975 the Aero Industry Development Center was awarded a contract to design and develop for the Chinese Nationalist air force a twin-turbofan military trainer. Its design, as the **AIDC AT-3**, was finalized in collaboration with the Chungshan Institute of Science and Technology and the US manufacturer Northrop. The result is a low-wing monoplane with retractable tricycle landing gear and tandem accommodation for a crew of two in an air-conditioned and pressurized cockpit on zero-zero ejector seats beneath a long transparency with individual side-opening canopy sections: unusually, the two members of the crew are separated by an internal windscreen. The two Garrett TFE731 turbofans are mounted in nacelles, one on each side of the fuselage; standard fuel is contained in two fuselage bladder tanks, but can be augmented by a 568-litre (150-US gal) drop tank on each inboard underwing pylon. Advanced avionics are provided for communication and navigation, and seven external stores stations allow the carriage of a maximum external weapon

load of 2720 kg (5,998 lb).

Following evaluation of the design proposal, the CNAF ordered two prototypes whose construction began in January 1978; these flew respectively on 16 September 1980 and 30 October 1981. Following evaluation the CNAF awarded AIDC a contract for 60 aircraft under the designation **AT-3A Tzu-chung**, and the first of these made its maiden flight on 6 February 1984.

In service with the CNAF, the AT-3A was flown mainly in the advanced training role for which it is optimized. The aircraft has first-class manoeuvrability as a result of its small size and high power, and can also undertake the weapons training, Sidewinder-equipped air combat and light attack roles. These capabilities have been exploited in the **AT-3B** conversion, of which some 45 or more are being effected in the 1990s with more capable electronics including radar and a HUD. A variant that proceeded no further than the design stage was the A-3 Lui-meng single-seat attack derivative of the AT-3.

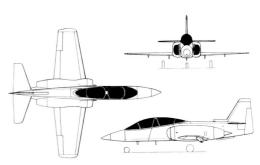

*AIDC AT-3A Tzu-chung*

**The AT-3A was developed indigenously around a pair of Garrett TFE731 turbofans. These engines give sufficient power for light combat duties to be undertaken.**

## Specification: AIDC AT-3A Tzu-chung

**Origin:** Taiwan
**Type:** advanced flying and weapons trainer
**Powerplant:** two 1588-kg (3,500-lb) dry thrust Garrett TFE731-2-2L turbofans
**Performance:** maximum speed 488 kt (904 km/h; 562 mph) at 36,089 ft (11000 m); initial rate of climb 10,105 ft (3080 m) per minute; service ceiling 48,065 ft (14650 m); range 1,417 miles (2280 km) on internal fuel; endurance 3 hours 12 minutes on internal fuel
**Weights:** empty 3855 kg (8,500lb); maximum take-off 7940 kg (17,505 lb)
**Dimensions:** span 10.46 m (34 ft 3.75 in); length 12.90 m (42 ft 4 in) including probe; height 4.36 m (14 ft 3.75 in); wing area 21.93 m² (236.05 sq ft)
**Armament:** provision for two 12.7 mm (0.5 in) machine-guns in a ventral pack and for up to 2720 kg (5,998 lb) of disposable stores carried on seven external hardpoints; typical weapons are two AIM-9 Sidewinder AAMs on wingtip rails, ASMs, cannon and machine-gun pods, rocket-launchers pods, and free-fall bombs of the unitary and cluster types

*This view of the XAT-3 prototype shows the simple yet effective lines of this trainer. Avionics are of a high standard, and the aircraft has good weapons capability, including air-to-air.*

# AIDC Ching-Kuo IDF (Indigenous Fighter)

Developed as the **Indigenous Defence Fighter** but now named **Ching-Kuo**, this lightweight air-defence fighter was developed in Taiwan to reduce the country's susceptibility to politically motivated import problems. The basic design was finalized in 1985 with considerable bought-in support from General Dynamics (airframe), Menasco (landing gear), Garrett (engine), Westinghouse (radar), Bendix/King (avionics) and Lear Astronics (digital fly-by-wire control system using a sidestick controller). Appearing late in 1988 and flying on 28 May 1989 in the form of the first of one two-seat and three single-seat prototypes, the A-1 is of the relaxed-stability type based on a blended wing/fuselage design with large LERXes, a modestly swept mid-set wing, a tail unit with all-moving horizontal surfaces, and a broad centre and rear fuselage accommodating the powerplant of two side-by-side afterburning turbofans.

All in all, therefore, the design resembles that of the General Dynamics (now Lockheed) F-16 Fighting Falcon with the exception of its engine inlets, which have a strong similarity to those of the McDonnell Douglas F/A-18 Hornet. These inlets are elliptical in shape and feed engines that exhaust via fully variable nozzles. The first of a pre-production batch of 10 aircraft was delivered in March 1992, and the first of a planned initial series of 120 production aircraft was due for delivery in January 1994 as replacements for the Chinese Nationalist air force's Lockheed F-104 Starfighters and Northrop F-5E Tiger IIs.

The Ching-Kuo's main sensor is the Green Dragon 53, a local adaptation of the General Electric APG-67(V) radar with features of the Westinghouse APG-66 to create a capable air/sea-search radar with a range of 150 km (93 miles) and lookdown/shoot-down capability. It is anticipated that more advanced avionics will be retrofitted as these become available. In 1992 it was revealed that the USA is to sell the F-16 Fighting Falcon to Taiwan, and this has led to the restriction of the production programme to a mere 130 aircraft including a number of the two-seat version, which is a combat-capable operational conversion and proficiency trainer. The type entered service in 1994.

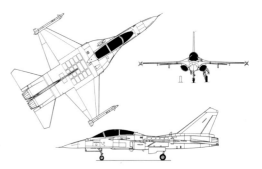

*AIDC Ching-Kuo IDF*

**Above:** *Three two-seat Ching-Kuo trainers in formation, the prototype two-seater flying closest to the camera ship. The single- and two-seat aircraft share a common designation.*

**Below:** *A production-standard Ching-Kuo single-seater of the 8th Fighter Squadron, the first operational IDF unit and one of three constituent squadrons of the 3rd Fighter Group.*

## Specification: AIDC Ching-Kuo
**Origin:** Taiwan
**Type:** lightweight air-defence fighter with anti-ship capability
**Powerplant:** two 4291-kg (9,460-lb) afterburning thrust ITEC (Garrett/AIDC) TFE1042-70 turbofans
**Performance:** maximum speed more than Mach 1.2 or 688 kt (1275 km/h; 792 mph) at 36,000 ft (10975 m); maximum rate of climb at sea level 50,000 ft (15240 m) per minute; service ceiling 55,000 ft (16760 m)
**Weights:** normal take-off 9072 kg (20,000 lb
**Dimensions:** (estimated) span 9.00 m (29 ft 6 in) over missile rails; length 14.48 m (47 ft 6 in) including probe
**Armament:** one 20-mm General Electric M61A1 Vulcan rotary six-barrel cannon, and provision for an unrevealed weight of disposable stores carried on six external hardpoints (two under the fuselage, two under the wings and two at the wingtips) for four Tien Chien 1 short-range AAMs, or two Tien Chien 2 medium-range AAMs, or four Tien Chien 1 and two Tien Chien 2 AAMs, or three Hsiung Feng II anti-shiPmissiles and two Tien Chien 1 AAMs, or AGMs, or various combinations of cannon pods, rocket-launcher pods and bombs

# Airtech CN-235

*Military transport version of the Airtech CN-235.*

### Role

Fighter
Close support
Counter-insurgency
Tactical strike
Strategic bomber
Tactical reconnaissance
Strategic reconnaissance
Maritime patrol
Anti-ship strike
Anti-submarine warfare
Search and rescue
Assault transport
Transport
Liaison
Trainer
Inflight-refuelling tanker
Specialized

### Performance

All-weather capability
Rough field capability
STOL capability
VTOL capability
Airspeed 0-250 mph
Airspeed 250 mph-Mach 1
Airspeed Mach 1 plus
Ceiling 0-20,000 ft
Ceiling 20,000-40,000 ft
Ceiling 40,000ft plus
Range 0-1,000 miles
Range 1,000-3,000 miles
Range 3,000 miles plus

### Weapons

Air-to-air missiles
Air-to-surface missiles
Cruise missiles
Cannon
Trainable guns
Naval weapons
Nuclear-capable
Rockets
'Smart' weapon kit
Weapon load 0-4,000 lb
Weapon load 4,000-15,000 lb
Weapon load 15,000 lb plus

### Avionics

Electronic Counter Measures
Electronic Support Measures
Search radar
Fire control radar
Look-down/shoot-down
Terrain-following radar
Forward-looking infra-red
Laser
Television

Construcciones Aeronauticas SA (CASA) of Spain and PT Industri Pesawat Terbang Nurtanio (now IPTN) of Indonesia formed a joint company named Aircraft Technology Industries (Airtech) to develop a twin-turbo-prop 40/44-passenger transport aircraft. CASA's selection of Nurtanio as partner for this venture, with each company sharing the financial, design and production loads, hinged upon the fact that Nurtanio was already building the CASA C-212 under licence. Such an arrangement offered benefits to both companies, plus the prospect of initial contracts from the Indonesian armed forces.

Designated **Airtech CN-235**, this new transport is smaller than the Lockheed C-130 and Transall C.160, but is generally similar to the latter. It has the same high-wing cantilever monoplane layout to ensure an unrestricted cabin, unswept rear fuselage incorporating a cargo ramp/door, and retractable tricycle landing gear of the levered-suspension type with each tandem-wheel main unit retracting into an external fuselage fairing. The powerplant comprises two General

Electric CT7 turboprops in nacelles on the wing leading edge. The pressurized accommodation can be used to seat 40/44 passengers, or in a mixed passenger/freight layout 18 passengers and two LD3 containers, or in all-freight layout four LD3 containers. The military **CN-235M** has seating for 48 troops or 46 paratroops, and in an aeromedical role the type can carry 24 litters and a four-man medical team. Airtech also delivers the **CN-235MPA** maritime patrol version with a longer nose (carrying FLIR and ECM sensors), 360° search radar and armament such as anti-ship missiles or lightweight torpedoes on a maximum of six underwing hardpoints, and also offers EW and aerial survey/photography variants.

Each of the partners built a prototype, the Spanish-built aircraft (ECT 100) being flown initially on 11 November 1983, and the Indonesian prototype (PK-XNC) following on 30 December. By the mid-1990s, orders for the military version stood at well over 150 aircraft, and included sizeable sales to France (8), Indonesia (42), Morocco (7), South Korea (12), Spain (20) and Turkey (52).

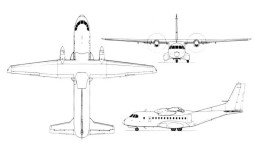

*Airtech CN-235*

*This view of the Indonesian CN-235 prototype shows the advanced wing employed on the type. Indonesia is taking more than 40 examples, divided between the air force and the navy.*

*Airtech has envisaged many military roles for the CN-235, including one version dedicated to electronic intelligence and ECM. Primary role will be assault transport, as this impression shows.*

## Specification: Airtech CN-235M Series 100

**Origin:** Indonesia and Spain
**Type:** multi-role transport
**Powerplant:** two General Electric CT7-9C turboprops each flat-rated at 1305 kW (1,750 shp)
**Performance:** maximum speed 240 kt (445 km/h; 276 mph) at sea level; maximum cruising speed 248 kt (460 km/h; 286 mph) at 15,000 ft (4570 m); initial rate of climb 1,900 ft (579 m) per minute; service ceiling 26,600 ft (8110 m); range 4355 km (2,706 miles) with a 3600-kg (7,936-lb) payload or 1500 km (932 miles) with maximum payload
**Weights:** empty 8800 kg (19,400 lb); maximum take-off 16500 kg (36,376 lb)
**Dimensions:** span 25.81 m (84 ft 8 1 in); length 21.35m (70 ft 0.6 in); height 8.18 m (26 ft 10 in); wing area 59.10 m² (636.17 sq ft)
**Armament:** see text

# Antonov An-2 'Colt'

*Float-equipped An-2 'Colt' of the Polish air force.*

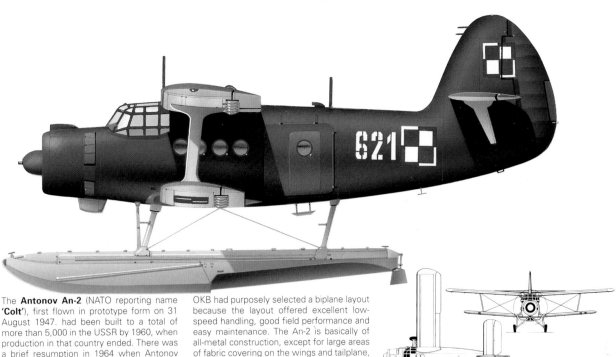

The **Antonov An-2** (NATO reporting name **'Colt'**), first flown in prototype form on 31 August 1947. had been built to a total of more than 5,000 in the USSR by 1960, when production in that country ended. There was a brief resumption in 1964 when Antonov built a number of An-2M agricultural aircraft, but since 1960 the main source of production has been WSK-PZL Mielec in Poland, which had built an estimated total of more than 10,000 aircraft by 1985 with production continuing at a low rate into the mid-1990s. Since 1957 this remarkable biplane has also been built under licence as the **Shijiazhuang Y-5** in communist China, where production is estimated to be well in excess of 1,500. If this assumed grand total of 17,000 aircraft or more is correct, then the An-2 has the distinction of being one of the most extensively manufactured aircraft of the period since the end of World War II.

When photographs of the An-2 were first seen in the West, in late 1947, the aircraft was regarded as outdated and without significant sales potential. But the Antonov OKB had purposely selected a biplane layout because the layout offered excellent low-speed handling, good field performance and easy maintenance. The An-2 is basically of all-metal construction, except for large areas of fabric covering on the wings and tailplane, and the wing design incorporates such features as full-span slats and differential ailerons on the upper wing, together with electrically actuated slotted flaps on both upper and lower wings. Perhaps the significance of the design lies in the fact that the An-3, the An-2's successor in the agricultural role, is basically similar but with a turbopropInstead of a piston engine.

Antonov-built An-2s not only went to the Soviet armed forces, but also to Aeroflot and other civil organizations, and were also widely exported. Some 80 per cent of Polish production has been supplied to the USSR, and most of the balance exported. Those built in China serve with the air arm of the People's Liberation Army, with the state airline CAAC, and also find extensive and highly gainful employment in the agricultural role.

**Antonov An-2 'Colt'**

*The Antonov An-2 has been used throughout the Communist world for all manner of light transport duties. Training of parachutists is an important task, demonstrated here by this Hungarian machine.*

*The majority of An-2s built since 1960 have come from the WSK-PZL Mielec factories in Poland, supplying these to the Soviet Union and for export. The Polish air force itself operates many An-2s.*

**Specification:** WSK-PZL Mielec An-2 'Colt'
**Origin:** USSR (now CIS)
**Type:** 14-seat transport and general utility aircraft
**Powerplant::** one 746-kW (1,000-hp) PZL Kalisz (Shvetsov) ASz-62IR radial piston engine
**Performance:** maximum speed 139 kt (258 km/h; 160 mph) at 5,740 ft (1750 m); initial rate of climb 670 ft (210 m) per minute; service ceiling 14,435 ft (4400 m); range 900 km (559 miles) with a 500-kg (1,102-lb) payload
**Weights:** empty 3450 kg (7,606 lb); maximum take-off 5500 kg (12,125lb)
**Dimensions:** span, upper18.18 m (59 ft 7.7 in) and lower 14.24 m (46 ft 8.6 in); length 12.74 m (41 ft 9.6 in); height 4.00 m (13 ft 1.5 in):wing area, total71.6 m² (770.72 sq ft)
**Armament:** none

**Role**
Fighter
Close support
Counter-insurgency
Tactical strike
Strategic bomber
Tactical reconnaissance
Strategic reconnaissance
Maritime patrol
Anti-ship strike
Anti-submarine warfare
Search and rescue
Assault transport
Transport
Liaison
Trainer
Inflight-refuelling tanker
Specialized

**Performance**
All-weather capability
Rough field capability
STOL capability
VTOL capability
Airspeed 0-250 mph
Airspeed 250 mph-Mach 1
Airspeed Mach 1 plus
Ceiling 0-20,000 ft
Ceiling 20,000-40,000 ft
Ceiling 40,000ft plus
Range 0-1,000 miles
Range 1,000-3,000 miles
Range 3,000 miles plus

**Weapons**
Air-to-air missiles
Air-to-surface missiles
Cruise missiles
Cannon
Trainable guns
Naval weapons
Nuclear-capable
Rockets
'Smart' weapon kit
Weapon load 0-4,000 lb
Weapon load 4,000-15,000 lb
Weapon load 15,000 lb plus

**Avionics**
Electronic Counter Measures
Electronic Support Measures
Search radar
Fire control radar
Look-down/shoot-down
Terrain-following radar
Forward-looking infra-red
Laser
Television

# Antonov An-12 'Cub-A'

*Antonov An-12 'Cub-A' of the Indonesian air force.*

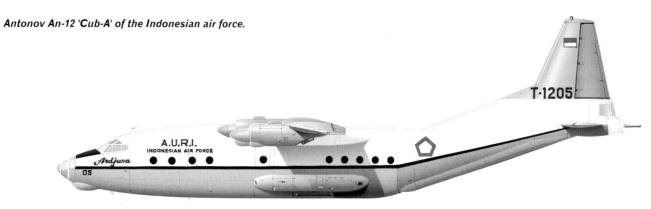

## Role

Fighter
Close support
Counter-insurgency
Tactical strike
Strategic bomber
Tactical reconnaissance
Strategic reconnaissance
Maritime patrol
Anti-ship strike
Anti-submarine warfare
Search and rescue
Assault transport
Transport
Liaison
Trainer
Inflight-refuelling tanker
Specialized

## Performance

All-weather capability
Rough field capability
STOL capability
VTOL capability
Airspeed 0-250 mph
Airspeed 250 mph-Mach 1
Airspeed Mach 1 plus
Ceiling 0-20,000 ft
Ceiling 20,000-40,000 ft
Ceiling 40,000ft plus
Range 0-1,000 miles
Range 1,000-3,000 miles
Range 3,000 miles plus

## Weapons

Air-to-air missiles
Air-to-surface missiles
Cruise missiles
Cannon
Trainable guns
Naval weapons
Nuclear-capable
Rockets
'Smart' weapon kit
Weapon load 0-4,000 lb
Weapon load 4,000-15,000 lb
Weapon load 15,000 lb plus

## Avionics

Electronic Counter Measures
Electronic Support Measures
Search radar
Fire control radar
Look-down/shoot-down
Terrain-following radar
Forward-looking infra-red
Laser
Television

Sometimes described as the Soviet equivalent version of the Lockheed C-130 Hercules, the **Antonov An-12** civil and military cargo transport has not, however, been produced on such a large scale and in so many variants. Having said that, though, it must be realized that more than 900 An-12s were built before production ended in the USSR in 1973, and the type still serves with the V-TA (Military Transport Aviation) of the Soviet (now CIS) air force, and with the air arms of Algeria, China, Ethiopia, India, Iraq, Madagascar, Poland, Syria and Yugoslavia. Civil versions are used by Aeroflot, as well as by Air Guinee, Balkan Air, CAAC in the People's Republic of China and the Polish airline LOT.

Flown in prototype form in 1958, the An-12 was built in parallel with the An-10 Ukraina and had the same basic airframe, but the rear fuselage was modified to incorporate two large longitudinal doors that hinge upwards into the cabin to allow direct loading of cargo from trucks. Behind the two doors is a full-width door that also hinges upwards into the cabin to improve headroom and access during

loading/unloading operations, but it is not possible to load or unload vehicles without the use of a separate ramp.

In the mid-1990s there are still large numbers of the **'Cub-A'** transport still in service with the CIS air force, although the majority of the aircraft have been replaced and augmented by Ilyushin Il-76s. The An-12s of the state airline Aeroflot are also available to military commanders for transport duties. The 'Cub-A' in V-TA service is designated **An-12BP** and in the 1980s saw much use in Afghanistan, where its rear-loading doors made it useful for paradropping supplies to outlying garrisons. Troops can also be dropped from the 'Cub-A', which can carry up to 100 men in full combat gear. Several of the Aeroflot aircraft appeared alongside their V-TA counterparts on the airlift from the USSR to Afghanistan, and these notionally civil aircraft had the tail gun turret of the military model. A later addition to the aircraft were attachments for the flares used to decoy heat-seeking missiles away from the aircraft, a feature made necessary by the Afghan freedom fighters' acquisition of shoulder-launched SAMs.

### Specification: Antonov An-12BP 'Cub-A'
**Origin:** USSR (now Ukraine)
**Type:** military transport
**Powerplant:** four 2983-ekW (4,000-eshp) IvchyenkoAl-20K turboprops
**Performance:** maximum speed 419kt (777 km/h; 483 mph); cruising speed 361 kt (670 km/h; 416 mph); initial rate of climb 1,970 ft (600 m) per minute; service ceiling 33,465 ft (10200 m); range 3600 km (2,237 miles) with maximum payload or 5700 km (3,542 miles) with maximum fuel
**Weights:** empty 28000 kg (61,729lb); maximum take-off 61000 kg (134,482 lb)
**Dimensions:** span 38.00 m (124 ft 8.1 in); length 33.10 m (108 ft 7.1 in); height 10.53 m (34 ft 6.6 in); wing area 121.70 m² (1,310. 0 sq ft)
**Armament:** two 23-mm NR-23 cannon in the tail turret

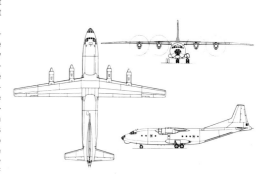

*Antonov An-12 'Cub-A '*

*Most An-12s are used for cargo transport and for assault duties. However, this Polish machine was been fitted out for VIP work. Many civil aircraft have a secondary military application.*

*Partially replaced by the Il-76, the An-12 has been operated by the Indian air force for many years as its prime heavy transport. These have to undertake regular flights through the Himalayas.*

# Antonov An-12 'Cub-B/C/D'

*Soviet air force Antonov An-12 'Cub-C', flying in Egyptian air force colours.*

The good range and ceiling of the An-12, and above all its capacious fuselage, made the type an obvious choice for conversion for various electronic roles. The first to appear was the **'Cub-B'** which has been seen over international waters. especially the Baltic Sea, sporting four additional blister fairings under the forward and centre fuselage and many small blade aerials. The role is electronic intelligence, and the 'Cub- B' has appeared over NATO exercises and snooping around Western coastlines. Ten aircraft are believed to have been to have been modified, and these serve with the AV-MF (naval air arm). It seems they are involved primarily with RINT (radiation intelligence), producing electronic 'fingerprints' of NATO ships and radar installations to gain information about radar wavelengths and strengths.

Another important role for the An-12 is ECM, and there are two variants which operate with both the air fore and the naval air arm. The **'Cub-C'** has a solid ogival tailcone in place of the otherwise standard tail turret, while the **'Cub-D'** has two large blister fairings running side by side longitudinally between the nose and main landing gear; this model retains the conventional tail turret. The

'Cub-D' is a highly complex jamming platform carrying several tons of specialized equipment, much of it palletized for ease of change. At least five wavebands can be jammed, and judging by the number of extra aerials, foreign language specialists may be carried to transmit confusing messages on enemy frequencies. Physical ECM means are also carried in the form of chaff and flares. Several Soviet-flown aircraft were seen during the 1970s in Egyptian air force markings for service in the Mediterranean theatre.

In a similar way to the Hercules ABCCC, the An-12 has been adapted to the airborne control and command post. This variant was used to good effect in Afghanistan, where the terrain made radio contact with the ground base and other air elements difficult. The command equipment was probably palletized like that of the Hercules, and the aircraft used are likely to be standard transport 'Cub-As'.

One An-12 (SSSR-11916) was seen under test with a long ogival tail fairing and a long, slim nose radome similar to that of the Beriev M-12 'Mail' amphibian. The intended role was anti- submarine warfare, but it is probable that no other conversions were made.

**Antonov An-12 'Cub-B'**

*The 'Cub-B ' is the electronic intelligence version of the An-12, distinguished by the three radomes under the fuselage. This example sports deceptive civil registrations.*

*This An-12 was spotted over the Baltic Sea in Aeroflot colours and civil registration, with large radomes in the nose and tail, presumably housing anti-submarine gear.*

## Specification: Antonov An-12 'Cub-B/C/D'
**Origin:** USSR (now Ukraine)
**Type:** electronic intelligence platform ('Cub-B') or ECM platform ('Cub-C/D')
**Powerplant:** four 2983-ekW (4,000-eshp) Ivchenko AI-20K turboprops
**Performance:** maximum speed 419 kt (777 km/h; 483 mph); cruising speed 361 kt (670 km/h; 416 mph); initial rate of climb 1,970 ft (600 m) per minute; service ceiling 33,465 ft (10200 m); range 3600 km (2,237 miles) with maximum payload or 5700 km (3,542 miles) with maximum fuel
**Weights:** empty 28000 kg (61,729 lb); maximum take-off 61000 kg (134,482 lb)
**Dimensions:** span 38.00 m (124 ft 8.1 in); length 33.10 m (108 ft 7.1 in); height 10.53 m (34 ft 6.6 in);wing area 121.70 m² (1,310.0 sq ft)
**Armament:** two 23-mm NR-23 cannon in tail turret ('Cub-B/D') or none ('Cub-C')

**Role**
Fighter
Close support
Counter-insurgency
Tactical strike
Strategic bomber
Tactical reconnaissance
Strategic reconnaissance
Maritime patrol
Anti-ship strike
Anti-submarine warfare
Search and rescue
Assault transport
Transport
Liaison
Trainer
Inflight-refuelling tanker
Specialized

**Performance**
All-weather capability
Rough field capability
STOL capability
VTOL capability
Airspeed 0-250 mph
Airspeed 250 mph-Mach 1
Airspeed Mach 1 plus
Ceiling 0-20,000 ft
Ceiling 20,000-40,000 ft
Ceiling 40,000ft plus
Range 0-1,000 miles
Range 1,000-3,000 miles
Range 3,000 miles plus

**Weapons**
Air-to-air missiles
Air-to-surface missiles
Cruise missiles
Cannon
Trainable guns
Naval weapons
Nuclear-capable
Rockets
'Smart' weapon kit
Weapon load 0-4,000 lb
Weapon load 4,000-15,000 lb
Weapon load 15,000 lb plus

**Avionics**
Electronic Counter Measures
Electronic Support Measures
Search radar
Fire control radar
Look-down/shoot-down
Terrain-following radar
Forward-looking infra-red
Laser
Television

# Antonov An-14 Pchelka 'Clod'

*Antonov An-14 Pchelka 'Clod' of the East German air force.*

### Role
Fighter
Close support
Counter-insurgency
Tactical strike
Strategic bomber
Tactical reconnaissance
Strategic reconnaissance
Maritime patrol
Anti-ship strike
Anti-submarine warfare
Search and rescue
Assault transport
Transport
Liaison
Trainer
Inflight-refuelling tanker
Specialized

### Performance
All-weather capability
Rough field capability
STOL capability
VTOL capability
Airspeed 0-250 mph
Airspeed 250 mph-Mach 1
Airspeed Mach 1 plus
Ceiling 0-20,000 ft
Ceiling 20,000-40,000 ft
Ceiling 40,000ft plus
Range 0-1,000 miles
Range 1,000-3,000 miles
Range 3,000 miles plus

### Weapons
Air-to-air missiles
Air-to-surface missiles
Cruise missiles
Cannon
Trainable guns
Naval weapons
Nuclear-capable
Rockets
'Smart' weapon kit
Weapon load 0-4,000 lb
Weapon load 4,000-15,000 lb
Weapon load 15,000 lb plus

### Avionics
Electronic Counter Measures
Electronic Support Measures
Search radar
Fire control radar
Look-down/shoot-down
Terrain-following radar
Forward-looking infra-red
Laser
Television

The primary need that shaped the design of the **Antonov An-14 Pchelka** (little bee) was the requirement for a twin-engined light general-purpose aircraft that would be easy to maintain and could be flown safely by pilots of only moderate experience. Its braced high-wing configuration ensures maximum cabin space for passengers or cargo, as does the fixed tricycle landing gear. Power is provided by two wing-mounted radial engines, and access to the cabin for passengers or cargo is via clamshell doors in the upswept rear fuselage The flight deck is occupied by the pilot and one passenger, and the cabin can seat a maximum of seven more passengers. In a casevac role the cabin can accommodate six stretchers and a medical attendant, the stretchers being in tiers of three on each side.

The first of two prototypes was flown on 15 March 1958, then powered by 149-kW (200-hp) Ivchyenko AI-14R radial engines, and production of the An-14 (NATO reporting

name **'Clod'**) for Aeroflot and the Soviet armed forces began at Arsenyev in 1965. When production ended some 10 years later, it was estimated that about 300 had been built. Most of these saw either civil or military service in the USSR (now CIS), but some were also supplied to Bulgaria, the German Democratic Republic and Guinea. Small numbers remain in service with the CIS and Guinea.

A larger (15-passenger) version with turboprop engines was flown in prototype form during September 1969 under the designation **Antonov An-14M** that was later changed to **An-28**, but there was little progress towards production of this aircraft. However, in 1978 PZL Mielec in Poland was given responsibility for manufacture of the An-28 (which has been given the NATO reporting name **'Cash'**) and production of an initial batch of aircraft began at Mielec in early 1984, three of them going to the Polish air force in the SAR role.

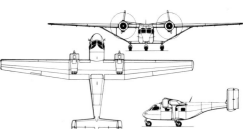

*Antonov An-14 Pchelka 'Clod'*

*The Antonov An-14 saw widespread service with the Soviet airline Aeroflot, as well as with the air force. It is being replaced in both services by the An-28 turboprop-powered derivative.*

*The Antonov An-14 provided the Soviet (now CIS) air force with a light transport and 'run-about' for many years, but the type is being replaced with more modern types.*

**Specification:** Antonov An-14 'Clod'
**Origin:** USSR (now Ukraine)
**Type:** light utility transport
**Powerplant:** two 224-kW (300-hp) Ivchyenko AI-14RF radial piston engines
**Performance:** maximum speed 120 kt (222 km/h; 138 mph) at 3,280 ft (1000 m); cruising speed 97 kt (180 km/h;112 mph) at 6,560 ft (2000 m); initial rate of climb 1,005 ft (306 m) per minute; service ceiling 17,060 ft (5200 m); range 650 km (404 miles) with maximum payload and 800 km (497 miles) with maximum fuel
**Weights:** empty 2000 kg (4,409 lb); maximum take-off 3600 kg (7,937 lb)
**Dimensions:** span 21.99 m (72 ft 1.7 in); length 11.44 m (37 ft 6.4 in); height 4.63 m (15 ft 2.3 in); wing area 39.72 m² (427.56 sq ft)
**Armament:** none

# Antonov An-22 'Cock'

*Antonov An-22 'Cock' of the Soviet air force's V-TA.*

On 27 February 1965 Antonov flew the prototype of its **Antonov An-22 Antei** (Antheus) long-range heavy-lift transport, and the appearance of the type at the Paris Air Show a few months late created considerable surprise among Western nations. Subsequently gaining the NATO reporting name **'Cock'**, the An-22 is in overall configuration basically a scaled-up version of the An-12 'Cub', but differs principally in having a tail unit incorporating twin endplate vertical surfaces which extend above and below the tailplane.

With a high aspect ratio wing and a maximum take-off weight of 246 tons, the An-22 possesses an understandably high wing loading. In fact, at 724.6 kg/m2 (148.8 lb/sq ft) this is the highest of any military transport in service: for comparison, the dimensionally larger Lockheed C-5 Galaxy wing loading is 661.6 kg/m2 (135.5 lb/sq ft). Under these conditions one might expect sluggish field performance, but four powerful turboprop engines, each driving a pair of four-blade contra-rotating propellers, provide a massive slipstream which is 'blown' over the double-slotted flaps that represent 60 per cent of the wing trailing edges. The combination has

proved good enough for a maximum-weight take-off run of only 1300 m (4,265 ft), and for the establishment of 27 FAI records for speed with payload and payload to height. The retractable tricycle landing gear is designed for off-runway operation, the nosewheel unit having twin wheels, and each main unit possessing three levered-suspension levered-suspension units in tandem; the tyre pressures are adjustable in flight or on the ground for optimum airfield performance. Pressurization is provided for the crew of five or six, and for the 28/29 passengers seated in a forward cabin section, but the 33.0-m (10.83-ft) long main cargo hold is unpressurized. Crew/passenger access is via a door in each landing gear fairing, cargo being loaded and unloaded by means of a ramp in the upswept aft fuselage.

As with most aircraft of Soviet (now CIS) manufacture, production is a matter for conjecture, but it is believed that Aeroflot and the Soviet air force's V-TA had each received about 50 when production ended in 1974. The An-22 was being supplemented and partially replaced by the Antonov An-124 Ruslan 'Condor' from 1987.

## Specification: Antonov An-22 Antei 'Cock'

**Origin:** USSR (now Ukraine)
**Type:** long-range heavy transport
**Powerplant:** four 11186-kW (15,000-shp) Kuznetsov NK-12MA turboprops
**Performance:** maximum speed 399 kt (740 km/h; 460 mph); cruising speed 324 kt (600 km/h; 373 mph); range 5000 km (3,107 miles) with maximum payload of 80000 kg (176,370 lb) or 10950 km (6,804 miles) with maximum fuel
**Weights:** empty 114000 kg( 251,327 lb); maximum take-off 250000 kg (551,156 lb)
**Dimensions:** span 64.40 m (211 ft 3.4 in); length 57.90 m (189 ft 11.5 in); height 12.53 m (41 ft 1.3 in); wing area 345 .00 m² (3,713 .67 sq f t)
**Armament:** none

**Antonov An-22 Antei 'Cock'**

*The An-22 features three radars in the nose to aid navigation and to avoid bad weather. The An-22 has excellent range performance which, like the Galaxy, enables it to deploy around the world.*

*The enormous rear loading ramp of the An-22 can be opened in flight to allow paradropping of material. The aircraft has low-pressure tyres to enable it to operate from rough ground .*

# Antonov An-24 'Coke'

*Antonov An-24 'Coke ' of the Czechoslovakian air force.*

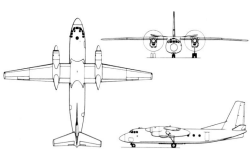

*Antonov An-24 'Coke'*

**Role**

Fighter
Close support
Counter-insurgency
Tactical strike
Strategic bomber
Tactical reconnaissance
Strategic reconnaissance
Maritime patrol
Anti-ship strike
Anti-submarine warfare
Search and rescue
Assault transport
Transport
Liaison
Trainer
Inflight-refuelling tanker
Specialized

**Performance**

All-weather capability
Rough field capability
STOL capability
VTOL capability
Airspeed 0-250 mph
Airspeed 250 mph-Mach 1
Airspeed Mach 1 plus
Ceiling 0-20,000 ft
Ceiling 20,000-40,000 ft
Ceiling 40,000ft plus
Range 0-1,000 miles
Range 1,000-3,000 miles
Range 3,000 miles plus

**Weapons**

Air-to-air missiles
Air-to-surface missiles
Cruise missiles
Cannon
Trainable guns
Naval weapons
Nuclear-capable
Rockets
'Smart' weapon kit
Weapon load 0-4,000 lb
Weapon load 4,000-15,000 lb
Weapon load 15,000 lb plus

**Avionics**

Electronic Counter Measures
Electronic Support Measures
Search radar
Fire control radar
Look-down/shoot-down
Terrain-following radar
Forward-looking infra-red
Laser
Television

The **Antonov An-24**, which was first flown in December 1959 with a powerplant of two turboprops, was designed to replace the piston-engined transports used by Aeroflot on its internal feederline routes. Though in the class of the Fokker F.27, the new design was heavier and fitted with more powerful engines, and as a consequence was less economic in service as it used more fuel for the same task. Aeroflot began passenger services with the initial An-24s (NATO reporting name **'Coke'**) in October 1962, flying the Kiev-Kherson route.

With construction of the An-24, Antonov for the first time made extensive use of bonding and welding. Major production versions were the **An-24V** with 28/40 seats, and the **An-24V Series II** of 1967 with accommodation for uPto 50 passengers. An unusual development in the **An-24RV** of 1967 replaced the TG-16 gas-turbine auxiliary power unit, mounted in the starboard engine nacelle, by a Tumanskii RU-19-300 turbojet which not only served the functions of an APU but could be used on the ground or in the air to improve performance, especially under 'hot-and-high' conditions. Other versions included a specialized freighter,

the **An-24T**, with the passenger door at the rear of the cabin deleted and a new freight door incorporated in the undersurface of the rear fuselage; addition of the Tumanskii auxiliary turbojet resulted in the **An-24RT**. In 1971 an **An-22P** firefighting version was evaluated: this carried equipment and a firefighting team that could be paradropped to tackle forest fires.

Although production of the An-24 ended in the USSR during 1978, after more than 1,100 had been built, the type is still manufactured in China as the **Xian Y-7** passenger transport with a higher-rated powerplant, wider fuselage and wing of increased span, and as the **Xian Y-8** tactical transport with a rear ramp/door. Of the Soviet construction total, almost 75 per cent were exported, serving with at least 15 airlines. They were also used in small numbers by the air forces of Bangladesh, Bulgaria, Congo, Cuba, Czechoslovakia. Egypt, East Germany, Hungary, Iraq, Laos, North Korea, Mongolia, Romania, Somalia, South Yemen, Sudan, Vietnam and, of course, the USSR (now CIS). Most of these nations continue to use the An-24.

**Specification:** Antonov An-24RV 'Coke'
**Origin:** USSR (now Ukraine)
**Type:** short-range transport
**Powerplant:** two 2103-ekW (2,820-ehp) Ivchyenko AI-24T turboprops, plus one 900-kg (1,984-lb) dry thrust Tumanskii RU-19-300 auxiliary turbojet
**Performance:** maximum cruising speed 270 kt (500 km/h; 311 mph) at 20,015 ft (6100 m); normal cruising speed 243 kt (450 km/h; 280 mph); initial rate of climb 675 ft (205 m) per minute; service ceiling 29,530 ft( 9000 m); range 550 km (342 miles) with maximum payload
**Weights:** empty 14060 kg (30,997 lb); maximum take-off 21800 kg(48,061 lb)
**Dimensions:** span 29.20 m (95 ft 9.6 in); length 23.53 m (77 ft 2.4 in); height 8.32 m (27 ft 3.6 in); wing area 74 98 m² (807.10 sq ft)
**Armament:** none

*This Somalian air force An-24V wears Italian air force registrations. The An-24 has provided many third-world countries with a cheap workhorse.*

*The An-24 did not have appeal for foreign users in the same way as the later An-26, yet 17 countries operated the type, including the Congo, which uses this aircraft for general transport duties.*

# Antonov An-26 'Curl'

*Antonov An-26 'Curl' of the Mali air force.*

When first seen by Westerners, the **Antonov An-26** was at first thought to be merely a variant of the An-24T with a revised cargo door; only later was it learned that while it was indeed derived from the An-24, the An-26 incorporated a number of important new design features. As the type was intended as a dedicated cargo transport, is rear fuselage was completely redesigned to incorporate a full-width door/ramp in the undersurface, and this aircraft also had the distinction of being the first Soviet transport to introduce a pressurized cargo hold. Then an unusual feature, the rear door/ramp was revised so that in addition to its use as a ramp it could be positioned just below the rear fuselage to leave a clear aperture: on the ground this made it easier to load at truck-bed height, and in the air made possible the air-dropping of freight items.

For its specialized cargo role the An-26 (NATO reporting name **'Curl-A'**) was equipped to simplify the movement and positioning of loads: these features included an electrically powered winch of 2000-kg

(4,409-lb) capacity moving on a track the length of the cabin, and an electrically/manually actuated conveyor built flush with the cabin floor; this latter proves particularly valuable for the paradropping of freight. Tip-up seats are provided along each cabin wall to seat 38/40 paratroops or to allow the aircraft's use as a troop transport, and the machine can also be adapted quickly for use as an air ambulance carrying 24 litters and a medical attendant.

An improved **An-26B** was introduced in 1981 with a revised handling system that facilitates the loading/unloading by a two-man of three standard freight pallets with a combined weight of 5500 kg (12,125 lb). In addition to service with the Soviet (now CIS) armed forces, which also operate small numbers of the **'Curl-B'** Sigint version, the An-26 is believed to have been used by the air arms of Angola, Bangladesh, Benin, China (locally built **Xian Y-7H-500**), Cuba, Czechoslovakia, East Germany, Ethiopia, Hungary, Iraq, Madagascar, Mozambique, Peru, Poland, Romania, Somalia, Tanzania and Yugoslavia.

## Specification: Antonov An-26 'Curl-A'

**Origin:** USSR (now Ukraine)
**Type:** short-range transport
**Powerplant:** two 2103-ekW (2,820-ehp) Ivchyenko AI-24VT turboprops, plus one 800-kg (1,764-lb) dry thrust Tumanskii RU-19A-300 turbojet
**Performance:** cruising speed 237 kt (440 km/h; 273 mph); initial rate of climb 1,575 ft (480 m ) per minute; service ceiling 24,605 ft (7500 m); range 1100 km (684 miles) with maximum payload and no reserves, or 2550 km (1,275 miles) maximum fuel and no reserves
**Weights:** empty 15020 kg (33,113 lb); maximum take-off 24000 kg (52,911 lb)
**Dimensions:** span 29.20 m (95 ft 9.6 in); length 23.80 m (78 ft I in); height 8.58 m(28 ft 1.8 in); wing area 74.98 m² (807.10 sq ft)
**Armament:** none

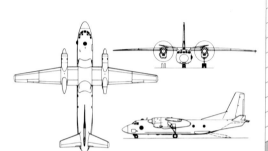

**Antonov An-26 'Curl'**

*The air force of the former Yugoslavia used the An-26 for light transport duties and liaison. The An-24 took over from the An-24 as the major transport type throughout the Communist world.*

*In common with other WarPac countries, East Germany relied on the An-26 for most of its transport duties. The rear cargo door can be swung under the rear fuselage for paradropping.*

Role
Fighter
Close support
Counter-insurgency
Tactical strike
Strategic bomber
Tactical reconnaissance
Strategic reconnaissance
Maritime patrol
Anti-ship strike
Anti-submarine warfare
Search and rescue
Assault transport
Transport
Liaison
Trainer
Inflight-refuelling tanker
Specialized

Performance
All-weather capability
Rough field capability
STOL capability
VTOL capability
Airspeed 0-250 mph
Airspeed 250 mph-Mach 1
Airspeed Mach 1 plus
Ceiling 0-20,000 ft
Ceiling 20,000-40,000 ft
Ceiling 40,000ft plus
Range 0-1,000 miles
Range 1,000-3,000 miles
Range 3,000 miles plus

Weapons
Air-to-air missiles
Air-to-surface missiles
Cruise missiles
Cannon
Trainable guns
Naval weapons
Nuclear-capable
Rockets
'Smart' weapon kit
Weapon load 0-4,000 lb
Weapon load 4,000-15,000 lb
Weapon load 15,000 lb plus

Avionics
Electronic Counter Measures
Electronic Support Measures
Search radar
Fire control radar
Look-down/shoot-down
Terrain-following radar
Forward-looking infra-red
Laser
Television

# Antonov An-30 'Clank'

*Antonov An-30 'Clank' of the Romanian air force.*

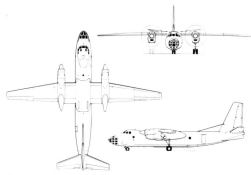

## Role

Fighter
Close support
Counter-insurgency
Tactical strike
Strategic bomber
Tactical reconnaissance
Strategic reconnaissance
Maritime patrol
Anti-ship strike
Anti-submarine warfare
Search and rescue
Assault transport
Transport
Liaison
Trainer
Inflight-refuelling tanker
Specialized

## Performance

All-weather capability
Rough field capability
STOL capability
VTOL capability
Airspeed 0-250 mph
Airspeed 250 mph-Mach 1
Airspeed Mach 1 plus
Ceiling 0-20,000 ft
Ceiling 20,000-40,000 ft
Ceiling 40,000ft plus
Range 0-1,000 miles
Range 1,000-3,000 miles
Range 3,000 miles plus

## Weapons

Air-to-air missiles
Air-to-surface missiles
Cruise missiles
Cannon
Trainable guns
Naval weapons
Nuclear-capable
Rockets
'Smart' weapon kit
Weapon load 0-4,000 lb
Weapon load 4,000-15,000 lb
Weapon load 15,000 lb plus

## Avionics

Electronic Counter Measures
Electronic Support Measures
Search radar
Fire control radar
Look-down/shoot-down
Terrain-following radar
Forward-looking infra-red
Laser
Television

In the same way that the An-26 is a cargo version of the An-24, the **Antonov An-30** is a dedicated aerial survey/mapping version of the An-24/An-26 family. It is, in fact, one of only very few types for this specialized role to have been produced anywhere in the world.

While based on the basic airframe and powerplant of the An-24/An-26, the An-30 is easily identified by the much modified forward fuselage that incorporates a raised flight deck to provide access to the completely new glazed nose which gives the navigator a wide field of view. The main cabin retains the standard door and forward freight door, but differs by having fewer windows because part of the interior is converted for use as a darkroom and for film storage. There are five glazed apertures (two of them oblique) for survey cameras, each of them protected by a remotely operated door, and in addition to a flight crew of five there are two specialized photographers/surveyors to control the onboard equipment. Cameras vary according to the type of mission, and these can be replaced by alternative kinds of survey equipment, such as various magnetometers, to obtain data on land resources. Sophisticated navigation equipment is used, and the aircraft's flight path over the area to be photographed and/or surveyed is controlled accurately in terms of altitude, direction and speed by an onboard computer. The An-30 retains the cargo hoist and handling system of its predecessors, which means that it needs only the installation of closure plates over the camera apertures to make it suitable for use as a transport.

First flown in prototype form during 1974, the An-30 (NATO reporting name **'Clank'**) has been built in modest numbers. The major user is Aeroflot, which in 1984 had 14 in service, and Balkan Bulgarian Airlines has one. Military operators include the air arms of Bulgaria and Romania.

**Antonov An-30 'Clank'**

## Specification: Antonov An-30 'Clank'
**Origin:** USSR (now Ukraine)
**Type:** photographic/survey aircraft
**Powerplant:** two 2103-ekW (2,820-ehp) Ivchyenko AI-24VT turboprops, plus one 800-kg (1,764-lb) dry thrust Tumanskii RU-19A-300 turbojet
**Performance:** maximum speed 291 kt (540 km/h; 335 mph); cruising speed 232 kt (430 km/h; 267 mph); service ceiling without auxiliary turbojet 23,950 ft (7300 m); range 2630 km (1,634 miles) with maximum fuel and no reserves
**Weights:** empty 15590 kg (34,370 lb); maximum take-off 23000 kg (50,706 lb)
**Dimensions:** span 29.20 m (95 ft 9.6 in); length 24.26 m (79 ft 7.1 in); height 8.32 m (27 ft 3.6 in); wing area 74.98 m² (807.10 sq ft)
**Armament:** none

*Based on the An-26, the An-30 is readily identifiable by its raised cockpit and extensively glazed nose. Aeroflot operates several aircraft, which can have quasi-military applications.*

*The Romanian air force operates the An-30 for cartographic and earth resources programmes. The aircraft still retains some transport capabilities with its specialized role equipment removed.*

# Antonov An-32 'Cline'

*Antonov An-32 'Cline' under evaluation by Aeroflot.*

In May 1977 the first details were released of a new short-range transport which is now recognized as the best derivative of the Antonov An-24/26 family. In this aircraft, designated **Antonov An-32** (NATO reporting name **'Cline'**), the Antonov design bureau set out to eliminate the 'hot-and-high' performance shortcomings of the earlier members of the family: this objective has been attained without major alterations to the basic airframe.

The changes that were introduced to enhance performance included new high-lift devices and Ivchyenko AI-20D turboprops which give almost 84 per cent more power than the AI-24VT engines which they replace. Aerodynamic changes to the wings provide automatic leading-edge slats and triple-slotted trailing-edge flaps, while the tail unit gains a full-span leading-edge slat for the tailplane and a much larger ventral fin. Apart from structural strengthening the fuselage is little changed from that of the An-26, and retains the rear door/ramp which can, alternatively, be swung down to a position below the rear fuselage.

The An-32 has a flight crew of three, and its cabin can carry alternative payloads of 12 freight pallets, or 50 passengers, or 42 paratroops, or 24 litters plus three medical attendants within its payload limit of 6700 kg (14,770 lb).

Introduction of the new powerplant has made it possible to dispense with the auxiliary turbojet of the An-24RT/An-26, although a conventional APU is provided for self-start capability at airfields below 14,765 ft (4500 m). The new engines are mounted much higher, serving the triple purposes of reducing the likelihood of debris ingestion when operating from unpaved airstrips, of limiting cabin noise from the increased-diameter propellers, and of providing adequate ground clearance for the increased-diameter propellers. What appear to be unusually deep engine nacelles result from the fact that they still have to house the retracted main landing gear units.

The An-32 prototype had been around for almost three years without gaining an order when, in late 1980, India began to show interest in the type to replace its ageing fleet of Douglas C-47 and Fairchild C-119 transports in air force service. Indian air force An-32s, of which 113 are in service, have the name **Sutlej**: the first three were delivered in July 1984. Other confirmed operators include the air forces of Afghanistan, CIS and Peru, although several other countries may also operate the type.

**Specification:** Antonov An-32 'Cline'
**Origin:** USSR (now Ukraine)
**Type:** short/medium-range transport
**Powerplant:** two 3812-ekW (5,112-ehp) Ivchyenko AI-20D turboprops
**Performance:** cruising speed 286 kt (530 km/h; 329 mph) at 26,245 ft (8000 m); service ceiling 29,530 ft (9000 m); range 1200 km (746 miles) with maximum payload or 2520 km (1,565 miles) with maximum fuel
**Weights:** empty 17308 kg (38,158 lb); maximum take-off 27000 kg (59,525 lb)
**Dimensions:** span 29.20 m (95 ft 9.6 in); length 23.78 m (78 ft 0.25 in); height 8.75 m (28 ft 8.5 in); wing area 74.98 m² (807.10 sq ft)
**Armament:** none

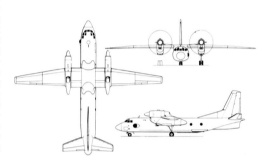

**Antonov An-32 'Cline'**

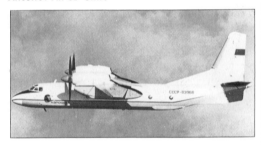

*This An-32 was tested by Aeroflot as a potential transport for the hot regions of the Soviet Union. The Soviet (later CIS) air force subsequently ordered the type.*

*The massive engine installation is readily apparent in this pre-production machine on a sales tour of South America. Only a few countries have bought the type.*

## Role
Fighter
Close support
Counter-insurgency
Tactical strike
Strategic bomber
Tactical reconnaissance
Strategic reconnaissance
Maritime patrol
Anti-ship strike
Anti-submarine warfare
Search and rescue
Assault transport
Transport
Liaison
Trainer
Inflight-refuelling tanker
Specialized

## Performance
All-weather capability
Rough field capability
STOL capability
VTOL capability
Airspeed 0-250 mph
Airspeed 250 mph-Mach 1
Airspeed Mach 1 plus
Ceiling 0-20,000 ft
Ceiling 20,000-40,000 ft
Ceiling 40,000ft plus
Range 0-1,000 miles
Range 1,000-3,000 miles
Range 3,000 miles plus

## Weapons
Air-to-air missiles
Air-to-surface missiles
Cruise missiles
Cannon
Trainable guns
Naval weapons
Nuclear-capable
Rockets
'Smart' weapon kit
Weapon load 0-4,000 lb
Weapon load 4,000-15,000 lb
Weapon load 15,000 lb plus

## Avionics
Electronic Counter Measures
Electronic Support Measures
Search radar
Fire control radar
Look-down/shoot-down
Terrain-following radar
Forward-looking infra-red
Laser
Television

# Antonov An-72 and An-74 'Coaler'

*Antonov An-72 'Coaler' of the Soviet air force.*

### Role
Fighter
Close support
Counter-insurgency
Tactical strike
Strategic bomber
Tactical reconnaissance
Strategic reconnaissance
Maritime patrol
Anti-ship strike
Anti-submarine warfare
Search and rescue
Assault transport
Transport
Liaison
Trainer
Inflight-refuelling tanker
Specialized

### Performance
All-weather capability
Rough field capability
STOL capability
VTOL capability
Airspeed 0-250 mph
Airspeed 250 mph-Mach 1
Airspeed Mach 1 plus
Ceiling 0-20,000 ft
Ceiling 20,000-40,000 ft
Ceiling 40,000ft plus
Range 0-1,000 miles
Range 1,000-3,000 miles
Range 3,000 miles plus

### Weapons
Air-to-air missiles
Air-to-surface missiles
Cruise missiles
Cannon
Trainable guns
Naval weapons
Nuclear-capable
Rockets
'Smart' weapon kit
Weapon load 0-4,000 lb
Weapon load 4,000-15,000 lb
Weapon load 15,000 lb plus

### Avionics
Electronic Counter Measures
Electronic Support Measures
Search radar
Fire control radar
Look-down/shoot-down
Terrain-following radar
Forward-looking infra-red
Laser
Television

The **Antonov An-72 STOL** STOL light transport, allocated the NATO reporting name **'Coaler'**, was designed to supersede the Antonov An-26. To achieve good STOL capability, the An-72 has a Lotarev turbofan engine mounted above and well forward on each wing, with the efflux ejected over the wing's upper surface. Thus when the inboard double-slotted and outboard triple-slotted trailing-edge flaps are deployed, the engine exhaust deflected over the inboard flaps is 'attached' to them by the so-called 'Coanda effect', creating considerably increased lift.

The An-72 is of a configuration now typical for transport aircraft, with the wing high on the fuselage to maximize internal capacity. High-lift features include full-span leading-edge flaps outboard of the engines, with five-section upper-surface spoilers forward of the trailing- edge multi-slotted flaps. These last extend over some 70 per cent of the wing trailing edge, conventional ailerons accounting for the remainder. To cater for the high-temperature engine efflux, adjacent wing skins, spoilers is upswept at the rear to incorporate a loading ramp-door, mounts a T-tail with the tailplane well clear of the engine efflux, and has retractable tricycle landing gear with a twin-wheel nose unit and main units each with two legs in tandem carrying single wheels. This multi-wheel gear

combines with low-pressure tyres to permit operation from unprepared airfields, or surfaces covered by ice or snow. The An-72 is usually operated by a crew of three (pilot, co-pilot and light engineer) on a spacious flight deck. The main cabin is intended primarily for a normal cargo payload of 10000 kg (22,046 lb), but can carry 32 passengers on sidewall folding seats, or 24 litters plus one medical attendant in the air ambulance role.

The An-72 was first seen in the West at the Paris Air Show of 1979, and limited numbers entered Soviet air force service as the **An-72A 'Coaler-C'** with extended-span wings and a longer fuselage, and as the **An-72AT 'Coaler-C'** freighter.

In February 1984 a new **An-74 'Coaler-C'** transport was announced for service in Arctic/Antarctic regions, and the first example was seen in the West during July 1986. Although based on the airframe of the 'Coaler-A', the An-74 had a five-man flight crew, much improved de-icing, provision for ski landing gear, much enlarged fuel capacity, and upgraded avionics including a navigation system based on an inertial navigation system. The only external distinguishing features are the larger radome and the addition of two blister windows at the rear of the flight deck and forward of the cabin on the port side.

## Specification: Antonov An-72A 'Coaler-C'
**Origin:** USSR (now Ukraine)
**Type:** STOL transport
**Powerplant:** two 6500-kg (14,330-lb) dry thrust Zaporozhye/Lotarev D-36 turbofans
**Performance:** maximum speed 380 kt (705 km/h, 438 mph) at 32,810 ft (10000 m); cruising speed 324 kt (600 km/h; 373 mph) at 32,810 ft (10000 m); service ceiling 38,715 ft (11800 m); range 800 km (497 miles) with maximum payload or 4800 km (2,980 miles) with maximum fuel
**Weights:** empty 19050 kg (41,997 lb); maximum take-off 34500 kg (76,059 lb)
**Dimensions:** span 31.89 m (104 ft 7.5 in); length 28.07 m (92 ft 1.1 in); height 8.65 m (28 ft 4.5in); wing area 98.62 m² (1,062.0 sq ft)
**Armament:** none

*Antonov An-74 'Coaler'*

**The An-74 is a version of the An-72 for transport operations in the Antarctic, with improved avionics, greater fuel capacity and provision for skis landing gear.**

**The An-72 and An-74 are dedicated STOL transports, and their basic design was clearly influenced by the Boeing YC-14 experimental transport aircraft first flown on 9 August 1976.**

# Antonov An-124 Ruslan 'Condor'

*Antonov An-124 Ruslan 'Condor' of Aeroflot.*

In summer 1977 it was reported that the Antonov design bureau had started work on a huge transport probably larger than the Lockheed C-5 Galaxy. The new type was needed primarily as replacement for the same bureau's An-22 Antei 'Cock' but carrying a maximum payload of 150000 kg (330,688 lb), but was also required as a heavy transport with a hold large enough to accommodate an entire SS-20 'Saber' inter-mediate-range ballistic missile system. Initially the provisional designation An-40 was reported, subsequently 'confirmed' as An-400 and receiving the NATO reporting name **'Condor'**. The first aircraft flew in December 1982, and in May 1985 came information that the type was in fact the **Antonov An-124 Ruslan**.

As the An-124 has the same role as the C-5, it is hardly surprising that its configuration is similar with a exception of a low-set tailplane in place of the C-5's T-tail configuration. The An-124's zero-fuel weight is much heavier, so payloads are much greater. Cabin width and height are bigger than those of the C-5, and the supercritical-section wings (with gigantic one-piece skins) hold 220 tonnes of fuel, an all-time record. The high-bypass-ratio (5.7:1) turbofan engines incorporate thrust reversers.

The fuselage has a visor-type nose door/folding ramp, and the upswept rear fuselage carries a four-section door/ramp. With both open, there is a through cargo hold 36.0 m (118.1 ft) long, 6.4 m (21 ft) wide and 4.4 m (14.4 ft) high. Two travelling gantries, each with a capacity of 10000 kg (22,046 lb), extend the length of the hold, front to rear, each mounting two 5000-kg (11,023-lb) hoists that travel the cabin width. Above the lightly pressurized cargo hold is the fully pressurized flight deck for a crew of six, with accommodation to its rear for a relief crew, and behind the wing is a cabin for 88 passengers. Each main landing gear comprises five pairs of wheels in tandem, the front two pairs being steerable, and there are two independently steerable twin-wheel nose gear units.

The An-124 is designed for operation from any 1200-m (3,800-ft) strip of rough field or packed snow and has a kneeling capability, front or rear, to speed loading and unloading. Flight control is via a quadruplex fly-by-wire system, permitting relaxed static stability, and the An-124's avionics include triplex inertial navigation systems.

Intended for use by both Aeroflot and the Soviet (now CIS) air force's V-TA, the An-124 entered service in January 1986.

## Specification: Antonov An-124 Ruslan 'Condor'
**Origin:** USSR (now Ukraine)
**Type:** heavy-lift strategic transport
**Powerplant:** four 23401-kg (51,590-lb) dry thrust Zhaporozhye/Lotarev D-18T turbofans
**Performance:** maximum cruising speed 467 kt (865 km/h; 537 mph) at 39,370 ft (12000 m); normal cruising speed 432 kt (800 km/h; 497 mph); range 4500 km (2,795 miles) with maximum payload or 16500 km (10,250 miles) with maximum fuel
**Weights:** empty 175000 kg (385,802 lb); maximum take-off 405000 kg (832,872 lb)
**Dimensions:** span 73.30 m (240 ft 5.8 in); length 69.10 m (226 ft 8.5 in); height 20.78 m (68 ft 2.25 in); wing area 628.0 m² (6,760.0 sq ft)
**Armament:** none

**Antonov An-124 Ruslan 'Condor'**

*The nose of the An-124 swivels upwards, like that of the C-5, to reveal a folding ramp across which loads can be moved easily. Two pads support the ramp when extended and distribute weight.*

*The An-124 is unusual in having twin nosewheel units. The wing is festooned with lift-enhancing devices including full-span leading-edge slats and large flaps.*

**Role**
Fighter
Close support
Counter-insurgency
Tactical strike
Strategic bomber
Tactical reconnaissance
Strategic reconnaissance
Maritime patrol
Anti-ship strike
Anti-submarine warfare
Search and rescue
Assault transport
Transport
Liaison
Trainer
Inflight-refuelling tanker
Specialized

**Performance**
All-weather capability
Rough field capability
STOL capability
VTOL capability
Airspeed 0-250 mph
Airspeed 250 mph-Mach 1
Airspeed Mach 1 plus
Ceiling 0-20,000 ft
Ceiling 20,000-40,000 ft
Ceiling 40,000ft plus
Range 0-1,000 miles
Range 1,000-3,000 miles
Range 3,000 miles plus

**Weapons**
Air-to-air missiles
Air-to-surface missiles
Cruise missiles
Cannon
Trainable guns
Naval weapons
Nuclear-capable
Rockets
'Smart' weapon kit
Weapon load 0-4,000 lb
Weapon load 4,000-15,000 lb
Weapon load 15,000 lb plus

**Avionics**
Electronic Counter Measures
Electronic Support Measures
Search radar
Fire control radar
Look-down/shoot-down
Terrain-following radar
Forward-looking infra-red
Laser
Television

49

# Atlas Cheetah

*The Atlas Cheetah prototype conversion.*

## Role

Fighter
Close support
Counter-insurgency
Tactical strike
Strategic bomber
Tactical reconnaissance
Strategic reconnaissance
Maritime patrol
Anti-ship strike
Anti-submarine warfare
Search and rescue
Assault transport
Transport
Liaison
Trainer
Inflight-refuelling tanker
Specialized

## Performance

All-weather capability
Rough field capability
STOL capability
VTOL capability
Airspeed 0-250 mph
Airspeed 250 mph-Mach 1
Airspeed Mach 1 plus
Ceiling 0-20,000 ft
Ceiling 20,000-40,000 ft
Ceiling 40,000ft plus
Range 0-1,000 miles
Range 1,000-3,000 miles
Range 3,000 miles plus

## Weapons

Air-to-air missiles
Air-to-surface missiles
Cruise missiles
Cannon
Trainable guns
Naval weapons
Nuclear-capable
Rockets
'Smart' weapon kit
Weapon load 0-4,000 lb
Weapon load 4,000-15,000 lb
Weapon load 15,000 lb plus

## Avionics

Electronic Counter Measures
Electronic Support Measures
Search radar
Fire control radar
Look-down/shoot-down
Terrain-following radar
Forward-looking infra-red
Laser
Television

Faced with continuing action against hostile forces on the nation's borders, the South African Air Force attached high priority to a mid-life update of the survivors of the 74 Mirage IIIs procured from Dassault during the period 1963-70. The urgency of such a programme was accentuated by the fact that after November 1977 South Africa was prevented by a United Nations embargo from importing more advanced aircraft. The realization of this update programme became known on 16 July 1986, when South Africa's President P. W. Botha unveiled a two-seat Mirage IIID2Z which had been extensively modified by Atlas as the prototype of the **Atlas Cheetah**.

According to sources in the SAAF, the programme initiated by Atlas results in some 50 per cent of the airframe being reconstructed in a process that also involves the replacement of many components. At the same time the opportunity was taken to upgrade the flight systems. The aerodynamic changes include the adoption of inlet-mounted canard foreplanes, small sidestrakes on the nose, curved lower forward fuselage side strakes and 'dog-tooth' wing leading edges. The powerplant of the Cheetah has also been the subject of conjecture, some sources claiming that the aircraft retains the original SNECMA Atar 9C/D turbojet that originally equipped the Mirage IIIs supplied by France, but others

opining that the original engine has been replaced by an uprated type. The only realistic possibility for an uprated powerplant is the Atar 9K-50 as supplied by France with the SAAF's Dassault Mirage F1 warplanes, and for which South Africa has a manufacturing licence. The Cheetah certainly possesses better performance than the Mirage III, but it is arguable that this derives from aerodynamic rather than propulsion enhancements despite the revised fighter's presumably higher structure weight. Operational enhancements are new navigation and weapon-delivery systems, as well as chaff and flare dispensers. The Cheetah carries indigenously developed weapons including the Armscor V3B/C Kukri IR-homing dogfight AAM.

The future of the Cheetah programme has been questioned since the ending of apartheid and the induction of a multi-racial government in 1994, but current Cheetah variants include the **Cheetah DZ** conversions from Mirage IIIBZ, DZ and D2Z standard with the two-seaters possessing more advanced systems to serve as pathfinders for the single-seaters; the **Cheetah EZ** conversions from Mirage IIIEZ, RZ and R2Z standards; and the **Cheetah R2** revealed in April 1992 with the Advanced Combat Wing characterized by fixed and drooped leading edges for reduced supersonic drag, increased turn rate, and greater fuel capacity.

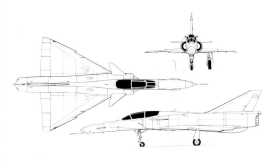

*Atlas Cheetah*

**Specification:** Atlas Cheetah (estimated)
**Origin:** South Africa
**Type:** one/two-seat combat and training aircraft
**Powerplant:** one7200-kg (15,873-lb) afterburning thrust SNECMA Atar 9K-50 turbojet
**Performance:** maximum speed, clean Mach 2.2 or 1,261 kt (2337 km/h 1,452 mph) above 39,370 ft (12000 m); service ceiling 55,775 ft (17000 m)
**Weights:** not revealed
**Dimensions:** span 8.22 m (26 ft 11.6 in); length 15.40 m (50 ft 6.3 in); height 4.25 m (13 ft 11.3 in); wing area 35.0 m² (376.75 sq ft)
**Armament:** can include Armscor V3 AAM, bombs, cluster bombs and other weapons of South African origin

*The Cheetah is essentially a Kfir-style conversion of the original Mirage III incorporating modernized avionics, possibly a new multi-mode radar and various aerodynamic improvements.*

*All weaponry intended for the Kfir is of South African origin, and includes the formidable new Armscor V3 Kukri AAM, which can be used in conjunction with a helmet-mounted sight.*

# Bell Model 204 (UH-1 Iroquois)

*Bell Model 204 of the Austrian air force.*

In the early 1950s the US Army notified its requirement for a helicopter with a primary casevac mission, but suitable also for use in the utility and instrument training roles. In 1955 the design submitted by Bell was announced as the winner, three prototypes of the **Bell Model 204** being ordered under the designation XH-40. The first of these (55-4459) was flown initially on 22 October 1956, its 615-kW (825-hp) Lycoming XT53-L-1 turboshaft, derated to 522 kW (700 shp), making this the first turbine-powered aircraft to be acquired by the US Army. The XH-40s were followed by six YH-40 service trials helicopters with minor changes including a 30.5-cm (1-ft) fuselage 'stretch'.

When the Model 204 was ordered into production, the service designation **HU-1A** was allocated, the letter prefix prompting the 'Huey' nickname that survived the helicopter's 1962 redesignation as the **UH-1A** and became far better known than the official name **Iroquois**. The initial version was the HU-1A with the T53-L-1 engine and accommodation for a crew of two plus six passengers or two litters. It was followed by the **HU-1B** with revised main rotor blades and an enlarged cabin seating two crew plus seven passengers or three litters: early- and late-

production helicopters had the 716-kW (960-shp) T53-L-5 and 820-kW (1,100-shp) T53-L-11 engines respectively. In 1962 the HU-1A and **HU-1B** were redesignated as the UH-1A and UH-1B and in 1965 the UH-1B was superseded in production by the **UH-1C**. This had a 'door-hinge' main rotor with wide-chord blades for significant improvement in performance and manoeuvrability. Other military versions include the US Marine Corps' **UH-1E** with a rescue hoist, rotor brake and special avionics; the USAF's **UH-1F** and similar **TH-1F** trainer with the 962-kW (1,290-shp) General Electric T58-GE-3 and increased-diameter rotor; the US Navy's search and rescue **HH-1K** similar to the UH-1E except for the 1044-kW (1,400-shp) T53-L-13, plus the **TH-1L** trainer and **UH-1L** utility versions of the UH-1E with the T53-L-13 engine; and the US Army's **UH-1M** with night sensor equipment (three acquired for evaluation).

In addition to production for the US armed forces Bell also built the **Model 204B** for military export, and this version was extensively licence-built for both civil and military use by Agusta in Italy (**Agusta-Bell AB 204**) and by Fuji in Japan, where the **Fuji-Bell 204B-2** was developed with increased engine power and a tractor tail rotor.

## Specification: Bell UH-1E Iroquois
**Origin:** USA
**Type:** assault support helicopter
**Powerplant:** one 820-kW (1,100-shp) Lycoming T53-L-1 turboshaft
**Performance:** maximum speed 120 kt (222 km/h; 138 mph); initial rate of climb 2,350 ft (716 m) per minute; service ceiling 16,700 ft (5090 m); range 341 km (212 miles) with maximum fuel
**Weights:** empty 2155 kg (4,750 lb); maximum take-off 3856 kg (8,500 lb)
**Dimensions:** main rotor diameter 13.41 m (44 ft 0 in); length of fuselage 12.98 m (42 ft 7 in); height 4.44 m (14 ft 7 in); main rotor disc area 141.26 m² (1,520.5 sq ft)
**Armament:** some UH-1A/Bs were operated in Vietnam with up to four side-mounted 7.62-mm (0.3-in) machine-guns, or two packs each containing 24 rockets

*Bell Model 204 (UH-1B)*

**The Bell 204 was licence-built by Agusta and Fuji. The former built this example for the Austrian air force, which uses it for many co-operation duties and mountain rescue.**

**HT-18 at Whiting Field operated this UH-1E as part of the US Navy's helicopter training force. The 'Huey' was a good trainer for pilots moving forward to large helicopters.**

### Role
Fighter
Close support
Counter-insurgency
Tactical strike
Strategic bomber
Tactical reconnaissance
Strategic reconnaissance
Maritime patrol
Anti-ship strike
Anti-submarine warfare
Search and rescue
Assault transport
Transport
Liaison
Trainer
Inflight-refuelling tanker
Specialized

### Performance
All-weather capability
Rough field capability
STOL capability
VTOL capability
Airspeed 0-250 mph
Airspeed 250 mph-Mach 1
Airspeed Mach 1 plus
Ceiling 0-20,000 ft
Ceiling 20,000-40,000 ft
Ceiling 40,000ft plus
Range 0-1,000 miles
Range 1,000-3,000 miles
Range 3,000 miles plus

### Weapons
Air-to-air missiles
Air-to-surface missiles
Cruise missiles
Cannon
Trainable guns
Naval weapons
Nuclear-capable
Rockets
'Smart' weapon kit
Weapon load 0-4,000 lb
Weapon load 4,000-15,000 lb
Weapon load 15,000 lb plus

### Avionics
Electronic Counter Measures
Electronic Support Measures
Search radar
Fire control radar
Look-down/shoot-down
Terrain-following radar
Forward-looking infra-red
Laser
Television

51

# Bell Model 205 (UH-1D/H Iroquois)

*Bell Model 205 of the Moroccan air force.*

## Role

Fighter
Close support
Counter-insurgency
Tactical strike
Strategic bomber
Tactical reconnaissance
Strategic reconnaissance
Maritime patrol
Anti-ship strike
Anti-submarine warfare
Search and rescue
Assault transport
Transport
Liaison
Trainer
Inflight-refuelling tanker
Specialized

## Performance

All-weather capability
Rough field capability
STOL capability
VTOL capability
Airspeed 0-250 mph
Airspeed 250 mph-Mach 1
Airspeed Mach 1 plus
Ceiling 0-20,000 ft
Ceiling 20,000-40,000 ft
Ceiling 40,000ft plus
Range 0-1,000 miles
Range 1,000-3,000 miles
Range 3,000 miles plus

## Weapons

Air-to-air missiles
Air-to-surface missiles
Cruise missiles
Cannon
Trainable guns
Naval weapons
Nuclear-capable
Rockets
'Smart' weapon kit
Weapon load 0-4,000 lb
Weapon load 4,000-15,000 lb
Weapon load 15,000 lb plus

## Avionics

Electronic Counter Measures
Electronic Support Measures
Search radar
Fire control radar
Look-down/shoot-down
Terrain-following radar
Forward-looking infra-red
Laser
Television

With production of the Model 204 for the US armed services totalling some 2,500 examples, it is not surprising that an improved **Bell Model 205**, proposed in 1960, was of interest to the US Army: a contract followed in July 1960 for seven YUH-1D service test helicopters. These retained the Lycoming T53-L-11 turboshaft, but differed from the Model 204 by having a larger-diameter main rotor; a lengthened fuselage for a pilot and increased payload (12/14 troops, or six litters and one medical attendant, or 1814 kg/4,000 lb of freight), increased fuel capacity, and provision for auxiliary fuel.

The first YUH-1D was flown on 16 August 1961 and the type was ordered into production for the US Army with the designation **UH-1D**. A total of 2,008 was built for the US Army, followed by the generally similar **UH-1H**, which differed by introducing the 1044-kW (1,400-shp) T53-L-13 turboshaft: final production of the UH-1H (55 for the Turkish army) ended in 1987. Variants included three **EH-1H** ECM conversions from UH-1H standard, with many more planned before the intended mission was assumed by the Sikorsky EH-60A (later EH-60C) Black Hawk,

plus some 220 **UH-1V** medevac conversions from UH-1H standard carried out by the US Army Electronics Command. Other military versions of the Model 205, generally similar to the UH-1H, have included 10 **CUH-1H** operational trainers for the Canadian Armed Forces (which designated them **CH-118**) and 30 **HH-1H** rescue helicopters for the USAF. Production of the UH-1H for the US Army totalled 3,573, and it was planned to retain some 2,700 of these in service into the 21st century. Under a product improvement programme these have gained new avionics and equipment, and new composite main rotor blades are to be introduced as well as Doppler navigation and an improved cockpit.

In addition to military exports by Bell, a multi-role utility helicopter for both civil and military use was extensively built in Italy as the Agusta-Bell AB 205 (see separate entry). Dornier in Germany completed 352 helicopters equivalent to the UH-1D, which serve with the Luftwaffe and Heeresfliegertruppen. In Taiwan AIDC built 118 helicopters similar to the UH-1H for the Chinese Nationalist army. In Japan Fuji continues to build the Model 205 as the **Fuji-Bell HU-1H**.

## Specification: Bell UH-1H Iroquois
**Origin:** USA
**Type:** general-purpose helicopter
**Powerplant:** one 1044-kW (1,400-shp) Lycoming T53-L-13 turboshaft
**Performance:** maximum speed 110 kt (204 km/h; 127 mph); initial rate of climb 1,600 ft (488 m) per minute; service ceiling 12,600 ft (3840 m); range 318 miles (512 km) with maximum fuel
**Weights:** empty 2363 kg (5,210 lb); maximum take-off 4309 kg (9,500 lb)
**Dimensions:** main rotor diameter 14.63 m ( 48 ft 0 in); length, rotors turning 17.62 m (57 ft 9.7 in); height 4.41 m (14 ft 5.5 in); main rotor disc area 168.11 m² (1,809.56 sq ft)
**Armament:** none

**Bell Model 205 (UH-1D/H Iroquois)**

*Fuji builds the Model 205 as the HU-1H for local military use. This helicopter is typical of Japanese 'Hueys', which are used for general duties and for search and rescue.*

*The US Army plans to retain numbers of the UH-1H into the next century, despite the wide adoption of the Sikorsky UH-60 Black Hawk. Many of the helicopters now serve with the National Guard.*

# Bell Model 206/206L TexasRanger, TH-57 SeaRanger and AB 206

*Bell Model 206 of the Pakistani army.*

The US Navy showed little interest in the US Army's OH-58 Kiowa light observation helicopter, but with a requirement identified in 1967 for a turbine-powered light training helicopter decided, if possible, to procure an 'off-the-shelf' type already in production. On 31 January 1968, therefore, the US Navy ordered from Bell 40 examples of what was basically a standard civil Model 206A JetRanger II: these differed only in having US Navy avionics and having the optional dual controls installed as standard. Designated **TH-57A SeaRanger**, the 40 helicopters were delivered during 1968 to Training Squadron HT-8 at NAS Whiting Field, Milton, Florida, and these machines remained in service until well into the 1980s. Expanding requirements then led to the delivery of 51 new-production **TH-57B** primary trainers, the last of them handed over in late 1984: these later helicopters are based on the later Model 206B JetRanger III, and introduced a number of detail improvements suggested by experience with the TH-57A. In January 1982 the US Navy

ordered the **TH-57C**, a new-production advanced instrument trainer.In 1980 Bell began development of a military Bell Model 206L TexasRanger which did not proceed past the demonstration helicopter phase. Powered by a single 373-kW (500-shp) Allison 250-C28B turboshaft, the TexasRanger incorporated the lengthened fuselage of the Model 206L LongRanger to seat a pilot and up to six passengers, but for anti-armour/armed reconnaissance missions carried the pilot and weapons operator on side-by-side armoured seats. Weapons included air-to-air or TOW missiles, or two pods containing Folding-Fin Air Rockets or 7.62-mm (0.3-in) machine-guns.

Agusta in Italy has built versions of Bell's Models 206A JetRanger, 206B JetRanger II and 206B JetRanger III under equivalent AB 206 designations. The most recent version of the **Agusta-Bell AB 206 B JetRanger III** has the quieter Allison 250-C20J engine, increased fuel capacity and other improvements. Italian production for civil andmilitary customers, now exceeds 1,000 helicopters.

## Specification: Bell TH-57C SeaRanger
**Origin:** USA
**Type:** advanced instrument training helicopter
**Powerplant:** one 313-kW (420-shp) Allison 250-C20J turboshaft flat-rated at 236 kW (317 shp)
**Performance:** maximum cruising speed 114 kt (211 km/h; 131 mph) at sea level; initial rate of climb 1,540 ft (469 m) per minute; range 692 km (430 miles) at sea level with maximum fuel or 848 km (527 miles) at 10,000 ft (3050 m)
**Weights:** empty 840 kg (1,852 lb); maximum take-off 1520 kg (3,350 lb)
**Dimensions:** main rotor diameter 10.16 m (33 ft 4 in); length, rotors turning 11.82 m (38 ft 9.5 in); height 2.91 m (9 ft 6.5in); main rotor disc area 81.07 m² (872.67sq ft)
**Armament:** none

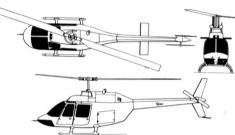

**Bell Model 206A JetRanger**

*Australia is one of the many operators of the Model 206, which has been successfully sold around the world. Several have been converted to carry guns and light missiles.*

*Differing little from the civil JetRanger, the TH-57 SeaRanger forms the bulk of the US Navy's helicopter training fleet. This TH-57A served with HT-8 at NAS Whiting Field.*

Role
Fighter
Close support
Counter-insurgency
Tactical strike
Strategic bomber
Strategic reconnaissance
Tactical reconnaissance
Maritime patrol
Anti-ship strike
Anti-submarine warfare
Search and rescue
Assault transport
Transport
Liaison
Trainer
Inflight-refuelling tanker
Specialized

Performance
All-weather capability
Rough field capability
STOL capability
VTOL capability
Airspeed 0-250 mph
Airspeed 250 mph-Mach 1
Airspeed Mach 1 plus
Ceiling 0-20,000 ft
Ceiling 20,000-40,000 ft
Ceiling 40,000ft plus
Range 0-1,000 miles
Range 1,000-3,000 miles
Range 3,000 miles plus

Weapons
Air-to-air missiles
Air-to-surface missiles
Cruise missiles
Cannon
Trainable guns
Naval weapons
Nuclear-capable
Rockets
'Smart' weapon kit
Weapon load 0-4,000 lb
Weapon load 4,000-15,000 lb
Weapon load 15,000 lb plus

Avionics
Electronic Counter Measures
Electronic Support Measures
Search radar
Fire control radar
Look-down/shoot-down
Terrain-following radar
Forward-looking infra-red
Laser
Television

# Bell Model 209 (AH-1 HueyCobra)

*Bell AH-1S HueyCobra of the Israeli air force (Heyl Ha'Avir).*

When details were issued of the US Army's AAFSS (Advanced Aerial Fire Support System) requirement to replace the failed Lockheed AH-56 Cheyenne, Bell initiated crash development of a company-funded prototype derived from the Model 204: this had the powerplant, transmission and wide-chord rotor of the UH-1C but introduced a new fuselage seating the gunner in the nose with the pilot behind and above him. The fuselage was very narrow, only 0.97 m (3 ft 2 in) at its widest point and this, coupled with a low silhouette, made the helicopter easy to conceal on the ground and a more difficult target in the air. The **Bell Model 209 HueyCobra** prototype (N209J) was flown for the first time on 7 September 1965. This began service tests in December 1965, and then gained an order for two pre-production **AH-1G** helicopters on 4 April 1966 and, such was the degree of urgency, for 110 production AH-1Gs only nine days later. Initial deliveries reached the US Army in June 1967, and within weeks the type had become operational in Vietnam. AH-1G production totalled 1,119 for the US Army, which transferred 38 to the US Marine Corps for train-ing; some US Army AH-1Gs were converted as **TH-1G** dual-control trainers. Later variants included 92 **AH-1Q** conversions from AH-1G standard to fire TOW missiles, and the **AH-1R** conversion with the 1342-kW (1,800-shp) T53-L-703 turboshaft and no TOW capability.

The designation **Modified AH-1S** applies to 245 AH-1Gs and 92 AH-1Q helicopters retrofitted with a TOW system and the powerplant of the AH-1R. These 337 machines were followed by 100 **Production AH-1S** (from 1987 **AH-1P**) helicopters with improved avionics and an uprated powerplant and transmission; 98 similar **Up-gun AH-1S** (later **AH-1E**) helicopters with a universal 20/30-mm cannon turret and other refinements, and 151 **Modernized AH-1S** (later **AH-1F**) helicopters with the AH-1P and AH-1E improvements as well as new air data, Doppler navigation and fire-control systems. Continuing programmes are ensuring the continued capabilities of the HueyCobra by the retrofit of improved sighting systems, provision for Stinger AAMs, laser warning system, and engine enhancements.

As well as the US Army, the AH-1S has also been built for several overseas air arms.

**Specification:** Bell AH-1F HueyCobra
**Origin:** USA
**Type:** anti-armour and close support/attack helicopter
**Powerplant:** one 1342-kW (1,800-shp) Lycoming T53-L-703 turboshaft
**Performance:** maximum speed 123 kt (227 km/h; 141 mph) with TOW missiles; initial rate of climb l,620 ft (494 m) per minute; service ceiling 12,200 ft (3720 m); range 507 km (305 miles) with maximum fuel and reserves
**Weights:** empty 2993 kg (6,598 lb); maximum take-off 4536 kg (10,000 lb)
**Dimensions:** main rotor diameter 13.41 m (44 ft 10 in); length, rotors turning 16.18 m (53 ft 1 in); height 4.09 m (13 ft 5 in); main rotor disc area 141.26 m² (1,520.23 sq ft)
**Armament:** one General Electric Universal Turret for one 20- or 30-mm cannon, and provision for eight TOW missiles on the outboard hardpoints and on the inboard hardpoints weapons such as Stinger AAMs and rocket-launcher pods

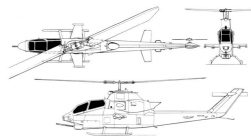

*Bell AH-1S HueyCobra*

*Early AH-1Gs are still in service with the US Army National Guard. This example serves in Utah.*

*Helicopters of modernized AH-1s standard are now being supplied in some numbers to foreign users. The Pakistani army has received 20 for anti-armour duties with TOW missiles.*

# Bell Model 209 (AH-1J/T SeaCobra)

*Bell AH-1J SeaCobra of the US Marine Corps.*

Following its evaluation of the AH-1G, the US Marine Corps decided to procure this type in a form with a twin-engined powerplant for extra reliability. In May 1968 the USMC ordered 49 **AH-1J SeaCobra** helicopters, and as an interim measure procured 38 AH-1G HueyCobras which were used for training and initial deployment until delivery of the SeaCobras during 1970-1. The AH-1J retained basically the same airframe as the AH-1G with some detail changes to cater for the higher output of the 1342-kW (1,800-shp) Pratt & Whitney Canada T400-CP-400 coupled-turboshaft powerplant. Flat-rated at 820 kW (1,100 shp) and with a take-off and emergency rating of 932 kW (1,250 shp), the T400 is a militarized version of Pratt & Whitney Canada's PT6T-3 Turbo Twin Pac using aluminium instead of magnesium alloys in its construction as is essential for a maritime or seaboard environment. Bell was also contracted by Iran to build 202 similar AH-1Js with TOW capability.

An additional 20 AH-1Js were delivered to the USMC in 1974-5, the last two of this batch later being modified as **AH-1T Improved SeaCobra** prototypes. Retaining many features of the AH-1J airframe, this model has a longer fuselage for increased fuel capacity, a lengthened tail boom, improved main and tail rotors as developed for the Bell Model 214, and an uprated transmission to handle the full rated power of the 1469-kW (1,970-shp) T400-WV-402 powerplant. The first of 57 AH-1Ts (59228) was flown on 20 May 1976 and delivered to the USMC on 15 October 1977. Of these machines, 51 were later equipped to carry TOW missiles.

In 1980 Bell was loaned an AH-1T by the USMC, and converted this machine with two General Electric T700-GE-700 turboshafts having a combined output of 2386 kW (3,200 shp). This paved the way for an upgraded AH-1T which, in its **AH-1T Improved SeaCobra** production form, has two T700-GE-401 turboshafts, a new combining gearbox and other improvements. Some 57 such helicopters were delivered, and from 1992 all 42 surviving machines were upgraded to **AH-1W SuperCobra** standard complementing new-build helicopters that were delivered from March 1986. The AH-1W had upgraded avionics and improved weapons capability. The latest version offered by Bell is the **AH-1W(4B) Viper** with a four-blade main rotor, provision for up to 1444 kg (3,184 lb) of weapons on six hardpoints, improved avionics and a digital flight-control system.

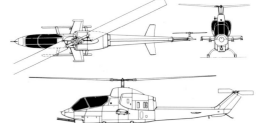

*Bell AH-1T SeaCobra*

*Sporting black markings, this AH-1J displays the far bulkier engine bay of the twin-engined version. These helicopters were later fitted with infra-red countermeasures.*

*The US Marine Corps' Cobras are used for support of ground operations, especially beach assaults. TOW missiles are used, and the Rockwell Hellfire missile has also entered service on the type.*

**Specification:** Bell AH-1W SuperCobra
**Origin:** USA
**Type:** close-support and attack helicopter
**Powerplant:** two 1212-kW (1,625-shp) General Electric T700-GE-401 turboshafts
**Performance:** maximum speed 152 kt (282 km/h; 175 mph) at sea level; initial rate of climb 800 ft (244 m) with one engine inoperative; hovering ceiling in ground effect 14,750 ft (4495 m); service ceiling 14,000+ ft (4270+ m); range 587 km (365 miles)
**Weights:** empty 4627 kg (10,200 lb); maximum take-off 6690 kg (14,750 lb)
**Dimensions:** main rotor diameter 14.63 m (48 ft 0 in); length, rotors turning 17.68 m (58 ft 0 in); height 4.32 m (14 ft 2 in); main rotor disc area 168.11 m² (1,806.56 sq ft)
**Armament:** chin turret housing a 20-mm M197 three-barrel cannon, plus four underwing attachments for 2.75 in (70-mm) rocket-launcher pods, flare dispensers, grenade launchers, parachute flares, Minigun pods. or alternative TOW or Hellfire anti-tank missile installations

## Role
Fighter
Close support
Counter-insurgency
Tactical strike
Strategic bomber
Tactical reconnaissance
Strategic reconnaissance
Maritime patrol
Anti-ship strike
Anti-submarine warfare
Search and rescue
Assault transport
Transport
Liaison
Trainer
Inflight-refuelling tanker
Specialized

## Performance
All-weather capability
Rough field capability
STOL capability
VTOL capability
Airspeed 0-250 mph
Airspeed 250 mph-Mach 1
Airspeed Mach 1 plus
Ceiling 0-20,000 ft
Ceiling 20,000-40,000 ft
Ceiling 40,000 ft plus
Range 0-1,000 miles
Range 1,000-3,000 miles
Range 3,000 miles plus

## Weapons
Air-to-air missiles
Air-to-surface missiles
Cruise missiles
Cannon
Trainable guns
Naval weapons
Nuclear-capable
Rockets
'Smart' weapon kit
Weapon load 0-4,000 lb
Weapon load 4,000-15,000 lb
Weapon load 15,000 lb plus

## Avionics
Electronic Counter Measures
Electronic Support Measures
Search radar
Fire control radar
Look-down/shoot-down
Terrain-following radar
Forward-looking infra-red
Laser
Television

# Bell Model 212 Twin Two-Twelve (UH-1N)

*Bell Model 212 as used by CAAC in China. These helicopters are used for quasi-civil duties but would be operated by the military in time of war.*

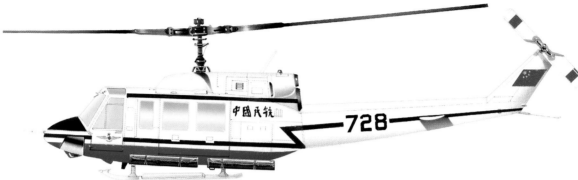

## Role
Fighter
Close support
Counter-insurgency
Tactical strike
Strategic bomber
Tactical reconnaissance
Strategic reconnaissance
Maritime patrol
Anti-ship strike
Anti-submarine warfare
Search and rescue
Assault transport
Transport
Liaison
Trainer
Inflight-refuelling tanker
Specialized

## Performance
All-weather capability
Rough field capability
STOL capability
VTOL capability
Airspeed 0-250 mph
Airspeed 250 mph-Mach 1
Airspeed Mach 1 plus
Ceiling 0-20,000 ft
Ceiling 20,000-40,000 ft
Ceiling 40,000ft plus
Range 0-1,000 miles
Range 1,000-3,000 miles
Range 3,000 miles plus

## Weapons
Air-to-air missiles
Air-to-surface missiles
Cruise missiles
Cannon
Trainable guns
Naval weapons
Nuclear-capable
Rockets
'Smart' weapon kit
Weapon load 0-4,000 lb
Weapon load 4,000-15,000 lb
Weapon load 15,000 lb plus

## Avionics
Electronic Counter Measures
Electronic Support Measures
Search radar
Fire control radar
Look-down/shoot-down
Terrain-following radar
Forward-looking infra-red
Laser
Television

Following negotiations in early 1968 between Bell Helicopters, the Canadian government, and Pratt & Whitney Canada, it was mutually agreed to initiate a jointly-funded program covering the development of a twin-turbine version of the Bell Model 205 (UH-1H) Iroquois. Selected as powerplant for this new venture was the PT6T Turbo Twin Pac: this comprised two turboshaft engines mounted side-by-side to drive, through a combining gearbox, a single output shaft. An advantage was provided by the provision in the gearbox of sensing torquemeters which, in the event of an engine failure, would signal the still-operative turbine to develop either emergency or continuous power in order that the flight could be concluded in safety.

Adaptation of the initial production PT6T-3 Turbo Twin Pac to the airframe of the Model 205 proceeded without serious problem, and the first deliveries of **Bell Model 212** helicopters to the US Air Force began during 1970 under the tri-service designation **UH-1N**. The USAF acquired a total of 79 UH-1Ns which have seen service world-wide in support of Special Operations Force counter-insurgency activities. A larger number went to the US Navy US and Marine Corps, which by 1978 had received a total of 221. Those of the US Marine Corps include two converted to **VH-1N** VIP transports plus six built as new to this configuration The Canadian Armed Forces acquired 50 Bell 212s, the first of them handed over on 3 May 1971 and the last of them just over a year later. These were initially designated **CUH-1N**, but have since been redesignated **CH-135**.

The improved safety offered by the Twin Pac powerplant made this helicopter attractive to companies providing support to offshore gas/oil operations, and while Bell soon had the commercial Twin Two-Twelve in full-scale production, it also built small numbers of military helicopters for other nations. Agusta in Italy soon acquired a licence for the Model 212, producing the AB 212 for civil and military customers, and also developed a specialized maritime version as the AB 212ASW/ASV, these being described separately.

## Specification: Bell UH-1N
**Origin:** USA
**Type:** utility and transport helicopter
**Powerplant:** one Pratt & Whitney Canada T400-CP-400 coupled turboshaft rated at rated at 962 kW (1,290 shp) for take-off
**Performance:** maximum speed 110 kt (204 km/h; 127 mph) at sea level: initial rate of climb 1,745 ft (532 m) per minute; service ceiling 17,300 ft (5275 m); maximum range 460 km (286 miles)
**Weights:** empty 2722 kg (6,000 lb); maximum take-off 4536 kg (10,000 lb)
**Dimensions:** main rotor diameter 14.69 m (48 ft 2.25 in); length, rotors turning 17.46 m (57 ft 3.25 in); height 4.53 m (14 ft 10.25 in); main rotor disc area 173.90 m² (1,871.91 sq ft)
**Armament:** none

**Bell Model 212 (UH-1N)**

*The twin-engined Huey version is used in numbers by the US Marine Corps. Eight aircraft are used as VIP transports under the designation VH-1N. This is a UH-1N of the standard variant used for general transport duties.*

*Most of the UH-1Ns supplied to the USAF are employed on covert duties with Special Operations Forces. These two sport a jungle camouflage for counter-insurgency duties in the Panama Canal Zone.*

# Bell Model 214

*Bell Model 214ST of the Venezuelan air force.*

When Bell announced on 12 October 1970 that it had completed a new prototype, there was little doubt of its derivation when it was named as the Bell Model 214 Huey Plus. A developed version of the military UH-1H Iroquois, the new helicopter had a number of detail improvements plus a measure of structural strengthening for operation at a higher gross weight. Improved performance also resulted from installation of an advanced main rotor allied to a more powerful 1417-kW (1,900-shp) Lycoming T53-L-702 turboshaft. From this Bell prototype developed the 16-seat utility **Model 214A** powered by a 2185-kW (2,930-shp) Lycoming LTC4B-8D turboshaft, and following interest from Iran the Model 214A was demonstrated there. This resulted in Bell announcing during late 1972 an order for 287 Model 214As to serve with the Iranian army under the name **Isfahan**; subsequent orders included an additional six Model 214As for the army, and for the air force 39 generally similar **Model 214C** helicopters, which differed by being equipped specifically for the SAR role.

Plans for the production of the Model

214A and a **Model 214ST Stretched Twin** to form the basis of an Iranian helicopter industry, with the Iranian government and Bell in partner-ship, came to an end with overthrow of the Shah in 1979. By then Bell had flown a prototype and the first of three pre-production Model 214STs, and decided to continue alone with development of this twin-turbine utility helicopter which could accommodate a crew of two and 16 (later 18) passengers. Initial deliveries followed in 1982, major interest and procurement coming from operators providing commuter and offshore support services. Nevertheless, the capacity and capability of the helicopter, now known as the **Model 214ST Super Transport**, has also appealed to a number of military operators.

Bell also began development of the Model 214A as a general-purpose civil helicopter designated **Model 214B BigLifter**. This was envisaged as a two-crew/14-passenger transport but which, equipped with a cargo hook of 3629-kg (8,000-lb) capacity, would also be suitable for a wide variety of civil and military uses. Only a few military sales were secured.

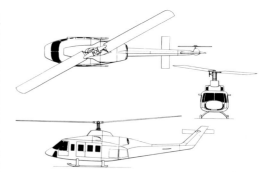

*Bell Model 214ST Super Transport*

**Specification:** Bell Model 214ST Super Transport
**Origin:** USA
**Type:** civil and military transport helicopter
**Powerplant:** two 1212-kW (1,625-shp) General Electric CT7-2 turboshafts
**Performance:** cruising speed 138 kt (256 km/h; 159 mph) at sea level or 135 kt (249 km/h; 155 mph) at 4,000 ft (1220 m); initial rate of climb 1,850 ft (564 m) per minute; hovering ceiling in ground effect 6,400 ft (1950 m); range 805 km (500 miles) with maximum fuel and no reserves
**Weights:** maximum take-off 7938 kg (17,500 lb)
**Dimensions:** main rotor diameter 15.85 m (52 ft 0 in); length, rotors turning 18.95 m (62 ft 2.05 in); height 4.84 m (15 ft 10.5 in); main rotor disc area 197.29 m² (2,123.72 sq ft)
**Armament:** none

*The Bell Model 214A is centred around a powerful Lycoming LTC4B-8D turboshaft, which gives the helicopter its characteristic large exhaust. Iran was the major customer.*

*Iran's large Model 214A force saw considerable action during the war with Iraq. Further examples were supplied to the air force as Model 214Cs for SAR duties.*

**Role**
Fighter
Close support
Counter-insurgency
Tactical strike
Strategic bomber
Tactical reconnaissance
Strategic reconnaissance
Maritime patrol
Anti-ship strike
Anti-submarine warfare
Search and rescue
Assault transport
Transport
Liaison
Trainer
Inflight-refuelling tanker
Specialized

**Performance**
All-weather capability
Rough field capability
STOL capability
VTOL capability
Airspeed 0-250 mph
Airspeed 250 mph-Mach 1
Airspeed Mach 1 plus
Ceiling 0-20,000 ft
Ceiling 20,000-40,000 ft
Ceiling 40,000ft plus
Range 0-1,000 miles
Range 1,000-3,000 miles
Range 3,000 miles plus

**Weapons**
Air-to-air missiles
Air-to-surface missiles
Cruise missiles
Cannon
Trainable guns
Naval weapons
Nuclear-capable
Rockets
'Smart' weapon kit
Weapon load 0-4,000 lb
Weapon load 4,000-15,000 lb
Weapon load 15,000 lb plus

**Avionics**
Electronic Counter Measures
Electronic Support Measures
Search radar
Fire control radar
Look-down/shoot-down
Terrain-following radar
Forward-looking infra-red
Laser
Television

# Bell Models 206 and 406 (OH-58 Kiowa)

Bell OH-58A Kiowa of the 25th Aviation Company, US Army, based in Germany.

The US Army's competition for a four-seat LOH (Light Observation Helicopter), announced in 1960, drew design proposals from no fewer than 12 US manufacturers. Bell, Hiller and Hughes each gained contracted to build five prototypes for evaluation, and the Hughes Model 369 was later selected for production as the OH-6 Cayuse. Convinced that its design had merit, however, Bell built a new five-seat prototype, and this **Bell Model 206A JetRanger** made its first flight on 10 January 1966 and soon entered commercial production in the USA and, as the **Agusta-Bell AB 206A**, in Italy.

In 1967 the US Army, worried by the slow delivery rate and rising cost of the OH-6A, reopened its LOH competition: on 8 March 1968 the Model 206A was declared winner and ordered into production as the **OH-58A Kiowa**. Deliveries to the US Army began on 23 May 1969, and over five years a total of 2,200 such helicopters was procured; the Canadian Armed Forces also acquired 74 with the designation **COH-58A** that was later changed to **CH-136**. In June 1976 the US Army awarded Bell a contract to convert one OH-58A to improved **OH-58C** standard

with a flat glass canopy, uprated engine and IR suppression system. Two more prototype conversions followed before modification of an eventual 435 OH-58As to OH-58C standard was completed between March 1978 and March 1985.

In September 1981 the **Bell Model 406** proposal won the AHIP (Army Helicopter Improvement Program) competition to provide close combat reconnaissance, support of attack helicopters and direction of artillery fire. The Model 406 thus introduced a McDonnell Douglas/Northrop mast-mounted sight with advanced optronic and thermal sights as well as a laser rangefinder and designator, specialized avionics, a control and display subsystem in a 'glass' cockpit, and an uprated powerplant driving a four-blade main rotor in place of the original two-blade unit. The US Army wanted to upgrade 578 OH-58As to this standard, but it now seems that as few as 243 may be converted to this **OH-58D Kiowa** standard. Variants on this basic theme include the **OH-58D Kiowa Warrior** with provision for a miscellany of weapons on external hardpoints, and the **Model 406 Combat Scout** export model.

## Specification: Bell OH-58D Kiowa Warrior
**Origin:** USA
**Type:** two-seat scout and attack helicopter
**Powerplant:** one 485-kW (650-shp) Allison T63-AD-700 turboshaft
**Performance:** maximum speed 128 kt (237 km/h; 147 mph) at 4,000 ft (1220 m); initial rate of climb 1,540 ft (469 m) per minute; hovering ceiling in ground effect 12,000+ ft (3660+ m); service ceiling 12,000+ ft (3660+ m); range 463 km (288 miles)
**Weights:** empty 1492 kg (3,289 lb); maximum take-off 2495 kg (5500 kg)
**Dimensions:** main rotor diameter 10.67 m (35 ft 0 in); length, rotors turning 12.85 m (42 ft 2 in); height 3.93 m (12 ft 10.625 in); main rotor disc area 89.37 m² (962.0 sq ft)
**Armament:** four Stinger AAMs, or four Hellfire ASMs, or two 2.75-in (70-mm) rocket-launcher pods, or two 12.7-mm (0.5-in) machine gun pods, or a mix of these weapons

Bell OH-58A Kiowa

Many early Kiowas have been rebuilt to OH-58D standard with a four-blade rotor and mast-mounted sight. Completely revised avionics and other enhancements are also fitted.

The OH-58A serves in large numbers with the US Army for use in the spotting role. A six-barrel machine-gun can provide suppressive fire whilst operating in hostile areas.

<table>
<tr><td>
Role<br>
Fighter<br>
Close support<br>
Counter-insurgency<br>
Tactical strike<br>
Strategic bomber<br>
Tactical reconnaissance<br>
Strategic reconnaissance<br>
Maritime patrol<br>
Anti-ship strike<br>
Anti-submarine warfare<br>
Search and rescue<br>
Assault transport<br>
Transport<br>
Liaison<br>
Trainer<br>
Inflight-refuelling tanker<br>
Specialized<br>
<br>
Performance<br>
All-weather capability<br>
Rough field capability<br>
STOL capability<br>
VTOL capability<br>
Airspeed 0-250 mph<br>
Airspeed 250 mph-Mach 1<br>
Airspeed Mach 1 plus<br>
Ceiling 0-20,000 ft<br>
Ceiling 20,000-40,000 ft<br>
Ceiling 40,000ft plus<br>
Range 0-1,000 miles<br>
Range 1,000-3,000 miles<br>
Range 3,000 miles plus<br>
<br>
Weapons<br>
Air-to-air missiles<br>
Air-to-surface missiles<br>
Cruise missiles<br>
Cannon<br>
Trainable guns<br>
Naval weapons<br>
Nuclear-capable<br>
Rockets<br>
'Smart' weapon kit<br>
Weapon load 0-4,000 lb<br>
Weapon load 4,000-15,000 lb<br>
Weapon load 15,000 lb plus<br>
<br>
Avionics<br>
Electronic Counter Measures<br>
Electronic Support Measures<br>
Search radar<br>
Fire control radar<br>
Look-down/shoot-down<br>
Terrain-following radar<br>
Forward-looking infra-red<br>
Laser<br>
Television
</td></tr>
</table>

# Bell/Boeing
# V-22 Osprey

*The second prototype V-22 briefly wore US Marines/Navy/Air Force/Army titles and grey/green camouflage, before reverting to white and high visibility orange for the test programme. A later prototype remained in camouflage.*

Under development as a V/STOL assault transport for the US Marine Corps in response to the advanced JVX (Joint Services Vertical Lift Aircraft - Experimental) requirement of 1982 to supersede the Boeing Vertol CH-46 and Sikorsky CH-53 helicopters, the **Bell/Boeing V-22 Osprey** is a fascinating tilt-rotor hybrid rotary/fixed-wing transport offering an excellent combination of payload/range and VTOL capability in the manner validated by the Bell Model 301 (XV-15) research type that flew in May 1977. The Osprey is in some ways a typical tactical airlifter in its rectangular-section fuselage, upswept tail unit, high-set wing, and retractable tricycle landing gear with its twin-wheel main units retracting into lateral lower-fuselage fairings.

The chief difference between the typical tactical airlifter and the Osprey, however, lies in the latter's propulsion/vertical lift system of a single large proprotor and its engine located at each wing tip. The proprotors, complete with their engines and associated nacelles, can be turned between the vertical position in which they deliver direct lift and the horizontal position

in which they deliver direct thrust, under command of the triplex digital fly-by-wire control system.

Six prototypes were ordered in May 1986, and the first of these flew in March 1989 before achieving its first full translation from helicopter to aeroplane mode in September 1989. It was planned that the type should enter service in the early 1990s, but the programme has been delayed by a measure of service antipathy as well as technical problems. The Osprey is fitted with two external hooks able to carry 4536 kg (10,000 lb) individually or 6804 kg (15,000 lb) collectively, and also has a hold fitted with a 907-kg (2,000-lb) capacity winch and removable roller rails for the handling of freight items. The hold can carry 24 men or 9072 kg (20,000 lb) of freight, and is accessed by a ventral ramp/door arrangement under the upswept tail unit.

Procurement of 552 Ospreys was planned for the period between December 1991 and April 1992, but this programme has been set back by a considerable period and the Osprey will probably only enter service in the first part of the next century.

### Specification: Bell/Boeing V-22A Osprey
**Origin:** USA
**Type:** multi-role assault and logistic V/STOL tilt-rotor transport
**Powerplant:** two 4586-kW (6,150-shp) Allison T406-AD-400 turboshafts
**Performance:** maximum cruising speed 314 kt (582 km/h; 361 mph) in aeroplane mode at optimum altitude; maximum cruising speed 100 kt (185 km/h; 115 mph) in helicopter mode at sea level; service ceiling 26,000 ft (7925 m); range 2224 km (1,382 miles) after VTO with a 5443-kg (12,000-lb) payload or 3336 km (2,075 miles) after STO with a 9072-kg (20,000-lb) payload; ferry range 3892 km (2,418 miles)
**Weights:** empty 14463 kg (31,886 lb); normal take-off 21545 kg (47,500 lb) for VTO and 24947 kg (55,000 lb) for STO; maximum take-off 27442 kg (60,500 lb) for STO
**Dimensions:** proprotor diameter, each 11.58 m (38 ft 0 in); width overall 25.78 m (84 ft 6.8 in) with proprotors turning; length, fuselage 17.47 m (57 ft 4 in) excluding probe; height 5.238 m (17 ft 4 in); proprotor disc area, total 210.72 m² (2,268.23 sq ft) ; wing area 35.59 m2 (382.0 sq ft)
**Armament:** none

**Bell/Boeing V-22A Osprey**

*The V-22 combines the payload/range capability of the fixed-wing transport aircraft with the versatility and freedom from runways of the helicopter.*

*The V-22 in hovering flight, with its engine/rotor pods in the vertical position. The V-22 prototypes have proved the practicality and advantages of the concept, but full-scale production has yet to be funded.*

## Role
Fighter
Close support
Counter-insurgency
Tactical strike
Strategic bomber
Tactical reconnaissance
Strategic reconnaissance
Maritime patrol
Anti-ship strike
Anti-submarine warfare
Search and rescue
Assault transport
Transport
Liaison
Trainer
Inflight-refuelling tanker
Specialized

## Performance
All-weather capability
Rough field capability
STOL capability
VTOL capability
Airspeed 0-250 mph
Airspeed 250 mph-Mach 1
Airspeed Mach 1 plus
Ceiling 0-20,000 ft
Ceiling 20,000-40,000 ft
Ceiling 40,000ft plus
Range 0-1,000 miles
Range 1,000-3,000 miles
Range 3,000 miles plus

## Weapons
Air-to-air missiles
Air-to-surface missiles
Cruise missiles
Cannon
Trainable guns
Naval weapons
Nuclear-capable
Rockets
'Smart' weapon kit
Weapon load 0-4,000 lb
Weapon load 4,000-15,000 lb
Weapon load 15,000 lb plus

## Avionics
Electronic Counter Measures
Electronic Support Measures
Search radar
Fire control radar
Look-down/shoot-down
Terrain-following radar
Forward-looking infra-red
Laser
Television

# Boeing B-52H Stratofortress

*Boeing B-52H Stratofortress of the US Air Force.*

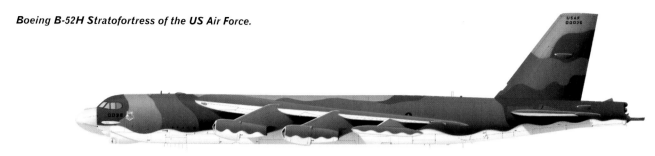

## Role
Fighter
Close support
Counter-insurgency
Tactical strike
Strategic bomber
Tactical reconnaissance
Strategic reconnaissance
Maritime patrol
Anti-ship strike
Anti-submarine warfare
Search and rescue
Assault transport
Transport
Liaison
Trainer
Inflight-refuelling tanker
Specialized

## Performance
All-weather capability
Rough field capability
STOL capability
VTOL capability
Airspeed 0-250 mph
Airspeed 250 mph-Mach 1
Airspeed Mach 1 plus
Ceiling 0-20,000 ft
Ceiling 20,000-40,000 ft
Ceiling 40,000ft plus
Range 0-1,000 miles
Range 1,000-3,000 miles
Range 3,000 miles plus

## Weapons
Air-to-air missiles
Air-to-surface missiles
Cruise missiles
Cannon
Trainable guns
Naval weapons
Nuclear-capable
Rockets
'Smart' weapon kit
Weapon load 0-4,000 lb
Weapon load 4,000-15,000 lb
Weapon load 15,000 lb plus

## Avionics
Electronic Counter Measures
Electronic Support Measures
Search radar
Fire control radar
Look-down/shoot-down
Terrain-following radar
Forward-looking infra-red
Laser
Television

The final production member of the B-52 family of strategic heavy bombers, the **Boeing B-52H Stratofortress** shared the same derivation as the B-52G, but because it was intended for a new task it was not merely a slightly improved variant but differed in some important ways. Instead of being required for the bomber role of its predecessors, the B-52H was intended to serve as a carrier for the Douglas GAM-87A Skybolt air-launched ballistic missile then under development. The most significant of the changes for this mission was to ensure that the B-52H would be able to penetrate enemy airspace at low level, demanding structural modification to ensure the airframe would be able to withstand the effects of low-level turbulence. The changes were barely visible externally, but two other external modifications did permit simple identification. One of the early-build B-52Gs (57-6471) had flown in July 1960 as a test-bed for the Pratt & Whitney TF33-P-1 turbofan, and more powerful versions of the same engine were installed in revised cowlings to enhance the performance of the B-52H, giving a range increase of almost one-third by comparison with the B-52G. The second noticeable external change was replacement of the four 12.7-mm (0.5-in) machine-guns in the tail turret of the B-52G by a 20-mm Vulcan six-barrel cannon. Internal changes included revised ECM equipment and provision of terrain-avoidance radar.

A total of 102 B-52H Stratofortresses was built, the first (60-006) being flown on 6 March 1961 and the last being completed in June 1962: six months the Skybolt programme was cancelled. Since then this aircraft has followed an upgrade path similar to that of the B-52G in its armament (being equipped up to the early 1990s to carry 20 AGM-69 SRAM stand-off defence-suppression missiles) and in its offensive and defensive electronics, which include the ASQ-151 Electro-optical Viewing System, Phase VI ECM and Offensive Avionics System. Toward the end of the 1980s most of the surviving aircraft were modified to carry up to 20 AGM-86 ALCMs (six on each of the underwing pylons and eight on a Common Strategic Rotary Launcher in the weapon bay). From the early 1990s the aircraft were revised for the carriage of conventional weapons for support of US ground and maritime operations.

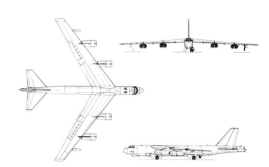

**Boeing B-52H Stratofortress**

*The primary differences between the B-52H and other marks are the turbofan engines with distinctive cowlings and the six-barrel rotary cannon in the tail turret.*

*In the early 1990s the USAF operated the B-52H in the cruise missile launch platform role with 12 ALCMs on the wing pylons and a further eight on an internal rotary launcher.*

**Specification:** Boeing B-52H Stratofortress
**Origin:** USA
**Type:** long-range strategic cruise missile carrier and bomber
**Powerplant:** eight 7711-kg (17,000-lb) dry thrust Pratt & Whitney TF33-P-3 turbofans
**Performance:** maximum speed 516 kt (956 km/h; 594 mph) at optimum altitude; cruising speed 442 kt (819 km/h; 509 mph) at optimum altitude; maximum penetration speed 365 kt (676 km/h; 420 mph) at low level; service ceiling 55,000 ft (16765 m); range 16093 km (10,000 miles) with maximum internal fuel
**Weight:** maximum take-off more than 221353 kg (488,000lb)
**Dimensions:** span 56.39 m (185 ft 0 in); length 49.04 m (160 ft 10.8 in); height 12.40 m (40 ft 8 in); wing area 371.60 m² (4,000.0sq ft)
**Armament:** provision for up to approximately 22680 kg (50,000 lb) of disposable stores

# Boeing EC-135

*Boeing EC-135H of the 6th ACCS, 1st Tactical Fighter Wing, USAF.*

In the early days of KC-135A production, the USAF's Strategic Air Command identified the requirement for an airborne command post (ABCP). The idea was for an aircraft equipped for this vital role to be airborne at all times so that, in the event of a devastating strike against SAC's fixed-location ground control centres, it would still be possible to maintain command of its strategic retaliatory force from a command post that was on the move and high above the ground. Therefore the 17 TF33-engined KC-135B tankers delivered to the command also had comprehensive communications systems, were equipped to receive fuel in flight, and had work areas and living quarters laid out within the large cabin area. By 1964 the fact that these aircraft were dedicated ABCPs was recognized by their receipt of the revised designation **Boeing EC-135C**, and in the mid-1990s 13 of the aircraft remained in service.

Over the years the number of EC-135 variants has grown, the EC-135C being joined first by six **EC-135A** conversions from J57-engined KC-135A tankers to provide communications relay aircraft able to double in the ABCP role; five of these aircraft are still operating as relay aircraft. Other variants are still

in use, although the numbers quoted have been altered by subsequent conversions. The **EC-135G** (four KC-135A conversions) serve as airborne control centres for ballistic missile launch but can double for communications relay. Five advanced airborne command posts for European operations were one VC-135A and four KC-135A conversions, and had the designation **EC-135H** until withdrawal in 1992. Other command post variants include the **EC-135J** (four EC-135C conversions for use as National Emergency Airborne Command Posts but later transferred to the Pacific Air Forces), the **EC-135K** (two KC-135A fighter-deployment shepherds), and the **EC-135P** (four conversions from NKC-135A, KC-135A and EC-135H standards as Tactical Air Command airborne command posts). There are also five **EC-135L** SAC communications relay aircraft with a reverse refuelling capability for extended-endurance missions. Another known variant is the **EC-135N**, of which eight were produced for satellite tracking and other space-related activities. At least four **EC-135B ARIA** (Advanced Range Instrumentation Aircraft), each with a steerable antenna in a bulbous nose radome, were derived as conversions from C-135B standard.

**Specification:** Boeing EC-135A
**Origin:** USA
**Type:** communications relay aircraft
**Powerplant:** four 6237-kg (13,750-lb) dry thrust Pratt & Whitney J57-59W turbojets
**Performance:** maximum speed 508 kt (941 km/h; 585 mph) at 30,000 ft (9145 m); average cruising speed 460 kt (853 km/h; 430 mph) between 30,500 and 40,000 ft (9300 and 12190 m); initial rate of climb 2,000 ft (609 m) per minute; service ceiling 50,000 ft (15240 m)
**Weights:** empty 46633kg (98,466 lb); maximum take-off 134717 kg (297, 000 lb)
**Dimensions:** span 39.88 m (130 ft 10 in); length 41.53 m (136 ft 3 in); height 12.70 m (41 ft 8 in); wing area 226.03 m² (2,433.0 sq ft)
**Armament:** none

*Boeing EC-135C*

**This collection of EC-135B and EC-135N ARIA aircraft was brought together for Apollo space missions. The large antenna in the bulbous nose is for tracking missiles and spacecraft.**

**The EC-135J is a rebuild of the EC-135C for airborne command post duties. These are typical of the ABNCP EC-135s and are active with the 9th ACCS, 15th ABW.**

**Role**
Fighter
Close support
Counter-insurgency
Tactical strike
Strategic bomber
Strategic reconnaissance
Tactical reconnaissance
Strategic reconnaissance
Maritime patrol
Anti-ship strike
Anti-submarine warfare
Search and rescue
Assault transport
Transport
Liaison
Trainer
Inflight-refuelling tanker
Specialized

**Performance**
All-weather capability
Rough field capability
STOL capability
VTOL capability
Airspeed 0-250 mph
Airspeed 250 mph-Mach 1
Airspeed Mach 1 plus
Ceiling 0-20,000 ft
Ceiling 20,000-40,000 ft
Ceiling 40,000ft plus
Range 0-1,000 miles
Range 1,000-3,000 miles
Range 3,000 miles plus

**Weapons**
Air-to-air missiles
Air-to-surface missiles
Cruise missiles
Cannon
Trainable guns
Naval weapons
Nuclear-capable
Rockets
'Smart' weapon kit
Weapon load 0-4,000 lb
Weapon load 4,000-15,000 lb
Weapon load 15,000 lb plus

**Avionics**
Electronic Counter Measures
Electronic Support Measures
Search radar
Fire control radar
Look-down/shoot-down
Terrain-following radar
Forward-looking infra-red
Laser
Television

# Boeing KC-135E and KC-135R Stratotanker

*Boeing KC-135E Stratotanker of the 108th ARS, 126th ARW, Illinois Air National Guard.*

### Role
Fighter
Close support
Counter-insurgency
Tactical strike
Strategic bomber
Tactical reconnaissance
Strategic reconnaissance
Maritime patrol
Anti-ship strike
Anti-submarine warfare
Search and rescue
Assault transport
Transport
Liaison
Trainer
Inflight-refuelling tanker
Specialized

### Performance
All-weather capability
Rough field capability
STOL capability
VTOL capability
Airspeed 0-250 mph
Airspeed 250 mph-Mach 1
Airspeed Mach 1, plus
Ceiling 0-20,000 ft
Ceiling 20,000-40,000 ft
Ceiling 40,000ft plus
Range 0-1,000 miles
Range 1,000-3,000 miles
Range 3,000 miles plus

### Weapons
Air-to-air missiles
Air-to-surface missiles
Cruise missiles
Cannon
Trainable guns
Naval weapons
Nuclear-capable
Rockets
'Smart' weapon kit
Weapon load 0-4,000 lb
Weapon load 4,000-15,000 lb
Weapon load 15,000 lb plus

### Avionics
Electronic Counter Measures
Electronic Support Measures
Search radar
Fire control radar
Look-down/shoot-down
Terrain-following radar
Forward-looking infra-red
Laser
Television

Modern performance requirements for fighter/interceptor aircraft are an antithesis to range, yet the policy of major air forces (rapid reaction when needed in a far distant policing role) demands unprecedented range. It is a constantly growing demand which makes the requirement for inflight-refuelling tankers increase by leaps and bounds, and thus it is important for an air arm to get the maximum utilization from its existing fleet.

When production of Boeing KC-135 tankers for the US Air Force ended, a total of 724 had been built of which about 650 remained in service during the mid-1980s. It was then decided to ensure that these aircraft should be kept operational into the next century, the major requirement being replacement of the underwing skin. This task, started as early as 1975, had progressed steadily and by mid-1985 more than 500 aircraft had benefited from this modification designed to extend service life by some 27,000 hours. This primary improvement was followed by a programme to re-engine Air National Guard and Air Force Reserve KC-135s with the JT3D turbofan that is the civil equivalent of the TF33. These powerplants were removed and refurbished from ex-commercial Boeing 707s acquired by the USAF, and at the same time the KC-135s also gained also the larger tail units, engine pylons and cowlings from the Model 707s. Simultaneously new brakes and anti-skid units are installed and, upon completion of the work, the 130 or so aircraft are redesignated **KC-135E**.

Far more comprehensive is the programme to update the main tanker fleet with the 9979-kg (22,000-lb) dry thrust CFM International F108-CF-100 turbofan equivalent to the civil CFM56-2B-1. The first of these **KC-135R** upgrades was delivered to the Strategic Air Command's 384th Air Refueling Wing at McConnell AFB, near Wichita in Kansas, in July 1984, the 200th conversion was delivered in April 1990, and by the middle of the decade more than 250 of the USAF's 500 or so KC-135As had been improved, albeit in a somewhat lethargic programme. The upgrade also involves the installation of an APU to give self-start capability; a flight deck with a more advanced autopilot, avionics, controls and displays; strengthened main landing gear incorporating anti-skid units; revised hydraulic and pneumatic systems; and an enlarged tailplane. Its improved capabilities enable the improved type to operate with much improved safety from shorter runways (civil airports if necessary) and to transfer more fuel at a longer radius: thus two KC-135Rs can undertake the work of three KC-135As. In addition to KC-135R conversions for the USAF, Boeing received a contract to modify the 11 remaining French C-135F tankers to this same standard with the designation **C-135FR**.

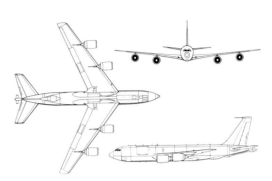

**Boeing KC-135R Stratotanker**

*An early KC-135R shows the large high-bypass-ratio CFM F108 turbofans which have replaced the thirsty J57 turbojets. Fuel receiving capability has also been added.*

*The whole first-line KC-135 fleet will eventually be re-engined, giving a planned service life into the 21st century. This example is from the 384th ARW at McConnell AFB.*

## Specification: Boeing KC-135R Stratotanker
**Origin:** USA
**Type:** inflight-refuelling tanker/cargo/transport aircraft
**Powerplant:** four 9979-kg (22,000 lb) dry thrust CFM International F108-CF-100 turbofans
**Performance:** average cruising speed 460 kt (853 km/h; 530 mph) between 30,500 and 40,000 ft (9300 and 12190 m); radius 4627 km (2,875 miles) to offload 150 per more fuel than the KC-135A
**Weight:** maximum take-off 146284 kg (322,500 lb); maximum fuel load 92210 kg (203,288 lb)
**Dimensions:** span 39.88 m (130 ft 10 in); length 41.53 m (136 ft 3 in); height 12.70 m (41 ft 8 in); wing area 226.03 m² (2,433.0 sq ft)
**Armament:** none

# Boeing RC-135

*Boeing RC-135V of the 55th Strategic Reconnaissance Wing, USAF.*

The capability of the Boeing Model 707 in its C-135 tanker/transport versions suggested its suitability for deployment in a reconnaissance role. Initial procurement covered four new-build aircraft. Given the company designation Model 739-700, these were delivered for the use by the 1,370th Photo Mapping Wing of the Military Aircraft Command of the USAF with the designation **RC-135A**. Similar to the Boeing C-135A and with J57-59W turbojets, they had cameras behind three ports in the underfuselage, aft of the nosewheel, and special equipment was carried for electronic surveillance. These four RC-135As were subsequently converted to serve as transports, and again in 1980 to tanker configuration as **KC-135D** aircraft. In the mid-1960s the RC-135As were followed by 10 new-build RC-135B electronic reconnaissance aircraft (Boeing Model 739445B) with an airframe similar to that of the KC-135B but with TF33-P-9 turbofan engines. The aircraft were used for a variety of purposes, and there was no standardization in the electronics installed by various military establishments. Later the RC-135Bs were rebuilt, losing their inflight-refuelling booms but gaining side-looking airborne radar (SLAR) undernose radomes and a ventral camera bay to gain the revised designation **RC-135C**. Four conversions from KC-135A (one) and C-135A (three) produced the **RC-135D** with modified SLAR and thimble-nose radome, and one **RC-135E** (formerly C-135B) except for the wide glassfibre radome around the forward fuselage. By conversion of C/VC-135B transports at least six **RC-135M** electronic reconnaissance aircraft appeared with thimble nose, teardrop fairings each side of the fuselage forward of the tailplane, and a twin-lobe ventral aerial; these were associated with the 'Rivet Card' and 'Rivet Quick' programmes. Other rebuilds for the reconnaissance role include the **RC-135S** (three aircraft and one **TC-135S** trainer) with large external dipole aerials and a variety of blisters and pods; one **RC-135T** for classified electronic surveillance in support of SAC; two **RC-135U** aircraft with SLAR, a chin radome and a variety of aerials; eight **RC-135V** rebuilds (from RC-135Cs and an RC-135U) with a thimble nose, SLAR and a farm of underfuselage blade aerials; six **RC-135W** operational and one **TC-135W** trainer conversions from RC-135M standard to an improved RC-135V standard; and one **RC-135X** conversion to an improved RC-125S standard.

## Specification: Boeing RC-135C
**Origin:** USA
**Type:** electronic reconnaissance aircraft
**Powerplant:** four 8165-kg (18,000-lb) dry thrust Pratt & Whitney TF33-P-9 turbofans
**Performance:** maximum speed 535 kt (991 km/h; 616 mph) at 25,000 ft (7620 m); cruising speed 486 kt (901 km/h; 560 mph) at 35,000 ft (10670 m); service ceiling 40,600 ft (12375 m); operational radius 4305 km (2,675 miles); ferry range 9100 km (5,655 miles)
**Weights:** empty 46403 kg (102,300 lb); maximum take-off 124965 kg (275,500 lb)
**Dimensions:** span 39.88 m (130 ft 10 in); length 39 20 m (128 ft 7.3 in); height (tall fin) 12.70 m (41 ft 8 in); wing area 226.03m² (2,433.0 sq ft)
**Armament:** none

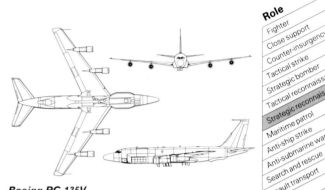

**Boeing RC-135V**

*Two RC-135U aircraft are on the strength of the 55th SRW. These do not have the 'thimble' nose, but possess extra aerials located on the wingtips, cheeks and tail area.*

*Six RC-135Ws serve on general Elint duties around the world. These aircraft have been modified from the RC-135M, introducing SLAR cheek antenae and extra blade aerials.*

**Role**
Fighter
Close support
Counter-insurgency
Tactical strike
Strategic bomber
Tactical reconnaissance
Strategic reconnaissance
Maritime patrol
Anti-ship strike
Anti-submarine warfare
Search and rescue
Assault transport
Transport
Liaison
Trainer
Inflight-refuelling tanker
Specialized

**Performance**
All-weather capability
Rough field capability
STOL capability
VTOL capability
Airspeed 0-250 mph
Airspeed 250 mph-Mach 1
Airspeed Mach 1 plus
Ceiling 0-20,000 ft
Ceiling 20,000-40,000 ft
Ceiling 40,000ft plus
Range 0-1,000 miles
Range 1,000-3,000 miles
Range 3,000 miles plus

**Weapons**
Air-to-air missiles
Air-to-surface missiles
Cruise missiles
Cannon
Trainable guns
Naval weapons
Nuclear-capable
Rockets
'Smart' weapon kit
Weapon load 0-4,000 lb
Weapon load 4,000-15,000 lb
Weapon load 15,000 lb plus

**Avionics**
Electronic Counter Measures
Electronic Support Measures
Search radar
Fire control radar
Look-down/shoot-down
Terrain-following radar
Forward-looking infra-red
Laser
Television

# Boeing Model 707 (C-137)

*Boeing VC-137C used as a presidential transport.*

Being's Model 367-80 private-venture prototype proved an important aircraft for the USAF, for from it has come the family of C-135, EC-135, KC-135 and RC-135 separately described tankers, transports and special-purpose aircraft. It was equally important to the Boeing Airplane Company (as it then was), which had gambled on gaining USAF interest and contracts for a tanker version equipped with the Boeing-developed refuelling boom; income from this source would then enable the company to develop a new range of civil transports This gamble paid off when the company gained USAF contracts plus approval to proceed with design and production of a civil version. This **Boeing Model 707** won orders from October 1955.

The original civil version was the Model 707-120 and differed somewhat from the USAF tanker/transports, The biggest change was in the fuselage which was increased in width by 0.41 m (1 ft 4 in) to a maximum of 3.76 m (12 ft 4 in), and lengthened to 42.32 m (138 ft 10 in) to carry up to 181 passengers in a high-density layout; at the same time it gained closely-spaced cabin windows.

There were also, of course, many detail changes to suit these aircraft for civil rather than military use, and when the USAF decided to acquire the civil version, as a transport for VIP personnel (primarily the president of the USA) or high-priority cargo, the combination of changes was considered sufficient for the new designation **Boeing C-137** to be allocated.

USAF procurement was very limited, amounting to three Model 707-153s allocated the designation **VC-137A**. When delivered in 1959 these had four 6123-kg (13,500-lb) dry thrust Pratt & Whitney JT3C-6 turbojets; when subsequently re-engined with 8165-kg (18,000-lb) dry thrust TF33-P-5 turbofans they were redesignated **VC-137B**. Only one other variant served with the USAF: this was the **VC-137C** Presidential transport, the two examples of which, apart from interior furnishings, are similar to the Model 707-320B Intercontinental; two further non-presidential **C-137C** aircraft were later added. To supplement its VC-137s, the USAF converted several C-135 airframes to **VC-135** VIP standard, and these are used for staff transport mainly within the United States. In 1981 the USAF bought eight ex-airline Model 707-320s with the designation **C-18A**, and of these four and two have been modified to **C-18B ARIA** (Advanced Range Instrumentation Aircraft) and **EC-18C** cruise missile mission control aircraft respectively.

Several other air arms operate modest numbers of Model 707 transports in special VIP/transport tanker roles, and during the later 1980s and 1990s there has emerged a small but significant market for tanker/cargo versions operated by Saudi Arabia with the designation **KE-3A** and other nations with the portmanteau designation **KC-707**.

## Specification: Boeing VC-137C

**Origin:** USA
**Type:** VIP transport
**Powerplant:** four 8165-kg (18,000-lb) dry thrust Pratt & Whitney JT3D-3 turbofans
**Performance:** maximum speed 544 kt (1009 km/h; 627mph); maximum cruising speed 521 kt (966 km/h; 600 mph) at 25,000 ft (7620 m); range 12247 km (7,610 miles) with maximum fuel, allowances but no reserves
**Weights:** maximum take-off 148325 kg (327,000 lb)
**Dimensions:** span 44.42 m (145 ft 9 in); length 46.61 m (152 ft 11 in); height 12.93 m (42 ft 5 in); wing area 279.63 m² (3,010.0 sq ft)
**Armament:** none

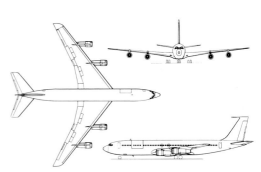

**Boeing VC-137C**

*As well as the VC-137, several C-135 airframes were adapted for staff transport, including this VC-135B. Some have been returned to cargo configuration.*

*'Air Force One ' is the call-sign of the presidential transport. Three VC-137A/B and two VC-137C aircraft were reserved for this role at Andrews AFB in Maryland, near Washington DC, but have now been replaced by Boeing E-4s.*

# Boeing Vertol Model 107 (CH-46 Sea Knight)

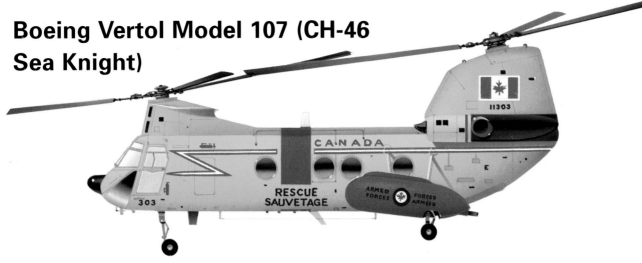

The Piasecki Helicopter Corporation, formed in 1955, had a change of management in March 1956 and was renamed the Vertol Aircraft Corporation. Almost at once the company began design and development of a twin-rotor transport helicopter, ostensibly for civil use, but engineered for military employment if sales could be won. This Vertol Model 107 had a powerplant of two light yet powerful turboshafts mounted above the fuselage to give maximum cabin volume; a large loading ramp in the upswept rear fuselage, strong enough for direct onloading of wheeled vehicles; and a sealed compartmented fuselage for emergency water operations.

The Model 107 prototype was first flown on 22 April 1958 and soon gained a US Army order for 10 similar YHC-1A helicopters, the first of these flying on 27 August 1959; the order was later reduced to three helicopters when the army became interested in a larger helicopter being developed by Vertol. At the end of March 1960 Vertol became a division of the Boeing Airplane Company with the name Boeing Vertol Company: by then the US Marine Corps was looking closely at one of the YHC-1As then flying with General Electric T58 turboshafts, and in February 1961 the **Boeing Vertol Model 107M** development of this helicopter won a USMC design competition and was ordered into production for service from June 1964 with

the designation **CH-46A Sea Knight**. The type was used mainly in the assault transport role with 17 troops or 15 litters, and the logistics transport role with a payload of 1814 kg (4,000 lb). Production totalled 160 CH-46As with 932-kW (1,250-shp) T58-GE8/8B turboshafts. Later production for the USMC included the **CH-46D** (266 built plus about 12 conversions) with uprated T68-GE-10 engines for an internal payload of 3175 kg (7,000 lb) including 25 troops, and the **CH-46F** (174 built) with improved avionics and equipment. US Navy procurement of the Sea Knight included the **UH-46A** (14 built) and **UH-46D** (10 plus at least five conversions), respectively similar to the CH-46A and CH-46D, and used in the Vertrep role. More than 250 USMC Sea Knights have been updated to **CH-46E** standard with 1394-kW (1,870-shp) T58-GE-16 turboshafts and other improvements including, in the **CH-46E 'Bullfrog'** conversion, almost doubled fuel capacity. Other naval versions include small numbers of **HH-46A** and **HH-46D** helicopters for SAR, a few RH-46 helicopters for the minesweeping role, and five **VH-46F** VIP helicopters.

In addition to civil production of the Model 107, Boeing Vertol supplied the type to other air forces, and in 1965 Kawasaki in Japan acquired world-wide sales rights for the improved Model 107-II.

**Specification:** Boeing Vertol CH-4D Sea Knight
**Origin:** USA
**Type:** twin-rotor military transport helicopter
**Powerplant:** two 1004-kW (1,400-shp) General Electric T58-GE-10 turboshafts
**Performance:** maximum cruising speed 140 kt (259 km/h; 161 mph); economical cruising speed 134 kt (248 km/h;154mph); initial rate of climb 1,660 ft (506 m) per minute; service ceiling 14,000 ft (4265 m); range 380 km (236 miles) at maximum weight with 10 per cent fuel reserve
**Weights:** empty 5827kg (13,067 lb); maximum take-off 10433 kg (23,000 lb)
**Dimensions:** rotor diameter, each 15.54 m (51 ft 0 in); length, rotors turning 25.40 m (83 ft 4 in); height 5.09 m (16 ft 8.5 in); rotor disc area, total 379.56 m² (4,085.65 sq ft)
**Armament:** none

*Boeing Vertol Model 107 (CH-113 Labrador/Voyageur) of the Canadian Armed Forces.*

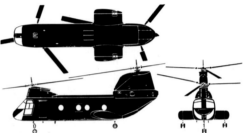

*Boeing Vertol CH-46 Sea Knight*

*The CH-46 is a true warhorse, having seen action in Vietnam, Lebanon and Grenada. USMC helicopters operate from assault carriers.*

*These CH-46s are lined up on deck on an assault carrier sailing off Grenada. The type acquitted itself well in this campaign.*

**Role**
Fighter
Close support
Counter-insurgency
Tactical strike
Strategic bomber
Strategic reconnaissance
Tactical reconnaissance
Strategic reconnaissance
Maritime patrol
Anti-ship strike
Anti-submarine warfare
Search and rescue
Assault transport
Transport
Liaison
Trainer
Inflight-refuelling tanker
Specialized

**Performance**
All-weather capability
Rough field capability
STOL capability
VTOL capability
Airspeed 0-250 mph
Airspeed 250 mph-Mach 1
Airspeed Mach 1 plus
Ceiling 0-20,000 ft
Ceiling 20,000-40,000 ft
Ceiling 40,000ft plus
Range 0-1,000 miles
Range 1,000-3,000 miles
Range 3,000 miles plus

**Weapons**
Air-to-air missiles
Air-to-surface missiles
Cruise missiles
Cannon
Trainable guns
Naval weapons
Nuclear-capable
Rockets
'Smart' weapon kit
Weapon load 0-4,000 lb
Weapon load 4,000-15,000 lb
Weapon load 15,000 lb plus

**Avionics**
Electronic Counter Measures
Electronic Support Measures
Search radar
Fire control radar
Look-down/shoot-down
Terrain-following radar
Forward-looking infra-red
Laser
Television

# Boeing Vertol Model 114 (CH-47 Chinook)

*Boeing Vertol CH-47 Chinook of the Royal Australian Air Force.*

## Role
Fighter
Close support
Counter-insurgency
Tactical strike
Strategic bomber
Tactical reconnaissance
Strategic reconnaissance
Maritime patrol
Anti-ship strike
Anti-submarine warfare
Search and rescue
Assault transport
Transport
Liaison
Inflight-refuelling tanker
Trainer
Specialized

## Performance
All-weather capability
Rough field capability
STOL capability
VTOL capability
Airspeed 0-250 mph
Airspeed 250 mph-Mach 1
Airspeed Mach 1 plus
Ceiling 0-20,000 ft
Ceiling 20,000-40,000 ft
Ceiling 40,000ft plus
Range 0-1,000 miles
Range 1,000-3,000 miles
Range 3,000 miles plus

## Weapons
Air-to-air missiles
Air-to-surface missiles
Cruise missiles
Cannon
Trainable guns
Naval weapons
Nuclear-capable
Rockets
'Smart' weapon kit
Weapon load 0-4,000 lb
Weapon load 4,000-15,000 lb
Weapon load 15,000 lb plus

## Avionics
Electronic Counter Measures
Electronic Support Measures
Search radar
Fire control radar
Look-down/shoot-down
Terrain-following radar
Forward-looking infra-red
Laser
Television

Further development by Vertol of the Model 107 resulted in a considerably larger all-weather helicopter. Evaluation of the **Vertol Model 114** design submission and those from four other manufacturers resulted in Vertol's contract for five YCH-1B (from 1962 YCH-47A) pre-production helicopters. By comparison with the CH-46D, the production **Boeing Vertol CH-47A Chinook** had a fuselage lengthened by 1.88 m (6 ft 2 in), rotors of increased diameter, two 1641-kW (2,200-shp) Lycoming T55-L-5 or later 1976-kW (2,650-shp) T55-L-7 engines, and fixed quadricycle landing gear, but retained the CH-46's type of fuselage for operation from water. The CH-47A could carry 44 troops or a 7257-kg (16,000-lb) external load compared to the CH-46's 25 troops or 4536 kg (10,000 lb).

Production of the CH-47A for the US Army totalled 349. Subsequent versions have included the **CH-47B** (108 built) with modified rotor blades, detail improvements and 2125-kW (2,850-shp) T55-L-7C turboshafts. The final production version for the US Army was the **CH-47C** (270 built) with 2796-kW (3,750-shp) T55-L-11A turboshafts, increased internal fuel and strengthened transmission; under a 1978 contract Boeing

Vertol upgraded the dynamic systems of surviving CH-47As and CH-47Bs to CH-47C standard. Since then one of each variant served for prototype conversion to the latest and much enhanced **CH-47D** standard to which the US Army plans the upgrade of 472 older helicopters for operation into the next century. After airframe refurbishment, the helicopters gain higher-rated T55 turboshafts, an advanced and uprated transmission, composite rotor blades, an improved flight deck, and more advanced systems and equipment. The first 'production' conversions were redelivered to the US Army in May 1982, and the CH-47D programme continues in the mid-1990s. Another US Army variant is the **MH-47E** for clandestine operations with an inflight-refuelling probe, armament, armour, and advanced avionics and electronics.

In addition to Model 234 civil versions of the Chinook, Boeing Vertol has supplied the military **Model 414 International Chinook** to several other air arms, and in 1968 Meridionali in Italy acquired production and marketing rights for the CH-47C and has since built considerable numbers for Italian army aviation and other armed forces.

*Boeing Vertol CH-47C Chinook*

**Specification:** Boeing Vertol CH-47D Chinook
**Origin:** USA
**Type:** medium transport helicopter
**Powerplant:** two Lycoming T55-L-712 turboshafts each with a standard rating of 2796 kW (3,750 shp) and emergency rating of 3356 kW (4,500shp)
**Performance:** maximum speed 157 kt (291 km/h; 181 mph); cruising speed 138 kt (256 km/h; 159 mph) at maximum take-off weight; initial rate of climb 1,330 ft (405 m) per minute; service ceiling 22,100 ft (6735 m); ferry range 2020 km ( 1,255 miles); radius 185 km (115 miles) with an 8164-kg (18,000-lb) payload
**Weights:** empty 10475 kg (23,093 lb); maximum take-off 22680 kg (50,000 lb) Dimensions: rotor diameter, each 18.29 m (60 ft 0 in); length, rotors turning 30.18 m (99 ft 0 in); height 5.68 m (18 ft 7.8 in); rotor disc area, total 525.34 m² (5,654.88 sq ft)
**Armament:** none

*The Chinook is the main heavy helicopter for the US Army's airborne divisions. These are used to airlift artillery and other heavy equipment following infantry landings.*

*The RAF belatedly adopted the Chinook HC.Mk 1 for army support, principally in Germany. Nos 7 and 18 Sqns are the users, as well as No.1310 Flt in the Falklands.*

# British Aerospace (HS) 146

*BAe 146 C.Mk 1 as evaluated for The Queen's Flight, RAF.*

In August 1973 Hawker Siddeley announced that with British government backing it intended to initiate the design and development of a new short-range civil transport with it identified as the HS 146. This was to be powered by four turbofans, and a stated aim was to the production of an aircraft with operational noise levels considerably below announced future legislation on noise emission. The new project had hardly got under way before imminent nationalization of the British aircraft manu-facturing industry led to the shelving of the scheme in the hope that more money would then become available. It was not until 10 July 1978 that the board of what had by then become British Aerospace gave approval for a resumption of the programme. This involved not only British Aerospace but also, as risk-sharing partners, Avco Corporation in the USA and Saab Scania in Sweden. Avco supplies the ALF 502R turbofan (the letter suffix signifying a reduced rating, which ensures the already quiet basic engine has an even lower nose signature) and, through its Avco Aerostructures division, manufactures the wing boxes. Saab is responsible for the tailplane and all moving control surfaces, while in the UK Short Brothers was subcontracted to fabricate the ALF 502 engine pods.

Three versions are in production, the prototype of the **BAe 146-100** making the type's maiden flight on 3 September 1981. CAA certification was gained on 20 May 1983, and on the following day Dan-Air became the first airline to take delivery of the BAe 146. This initial version is intended for operation from short semi-prepared airstrips with capacity for 71/93 passengers. The later **BAe 146-200**, with 3162-kg (6970-lb) dry thrust ALF 502R-5 engines and a fuselage lengthened by 2.39 m (7 ft 10 in) to seat 82/109 passengers, is intended for operation from paved runways. The **BAe 146-300**, with its fuselage lengthened by 2.41 m (7 ft 11 in) over that of the BAe 146-200 for 103/128-seat accommodation, first flew in May 1987.

Only a few aircraft have achieved government and military sales. The British Ministry of Defence has bought three examples of the **BAe 146 Statesman** executive version for service with The Queen's Flight under the designation **BAe 146 CC.Mk 2** after evaluating a single machine as the BAe 146 CC.Mk 1. In August 1990 the BAe 146 was redesignated as the **Regional Jet** series.

## Specification: BAe 146-100

**Origin:** UK
**Type:** short-range transport
**Powerplant:** four 3039-kg (6,700-lb) dry thrust Lycoming ALF 502R-3 turbofans
**Performance:** maximum cruising speed 426 kt (789 km/h; 490 mph) at 23,000 ft (7010 m); economical cruising speed 382 kt (708 km/h; 440 mph) at 30,000 ft (9145 m); range 797 km (495 miles) with maximum payload with allowances and reserves, and 2961 km (1,840 miles) with maximum fuel with allowances and reserves
**Weights:** empty 21319 kg (47,000 lb); maximum take-off 34473 kg (76,000 lb)
**Dimensions:** span 26.34 m (86 ft 5 in); length 26.16 m (85 ft 10 in); height 8.61 m (28 ft 3 in); wing area 77.29 m2 (832.0 sq ft)
**Armament:** none

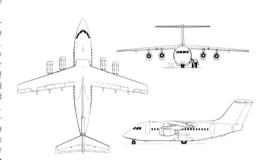

**BAe 146-100**

*The BAe 146's short-field performance, quiet operation, excellent fuel economy and four-jet safety make it a good choice for VIP transport.*

*This BAe 146 C.Mk 1 was evaluated by No.242 OCU. It has since passed to a civil operator, while the RAF now has three BAe 146 CC.Mk 2 aircraft for use by The Queen's Flight at RAF Benson.*

**Role**
Fighter
Close support
Counter-insurgency
Tactical strike
Strategic bomber
Tactical reconnaissance
Strategic reconnaissance
Maritime patrol
Anti-ship strike
Anti-submarine warfare
Search and rescue
Assault transport
Transport
Liaison
Trainer
Inflight-refuelling tanker
Specialized

**Performance**
All-weather capability
Rough field capability
STOL capability
VTOL capability
Airspeed 0-250 mph
Airspeed 250 mph-Mach 1
Airspeed Mach 1 plus
Ceiling 0-20,000 ft
Ceiling 20,000-40,000 ft
Ceiling 40,000ft plus
Range 0-1,000 miles
Range 1,000-3,000 miles
Range 3,000 miles plus

**Weapons**
Air-to-air missiles
Air-to-surface missiles
Cruise missiles
Cannon
Trainable guns
Naval weapons
Nuclear-capable
Rockets
'Smart' weapon kit
Weapon load 0-4,000 lb
Weapon load 4,000-15,000 lb
Weapon load 15,000 lb plus

**Avionics**
Electronic Counter Measures
Electronic Support Measures
Search radar
Fire control radar
Look-down/shoot-down
Terrain-following radar
Forward-looking infra-red
Laser
Television

# British Aerospace (Avro/HS) 748 and Andover

*British Aerospace 748 of the Ecuadorian air force.*

## Role

Fighter
Close support
Counter-insurgency
Tactical strike
Strategic bomber
Tactical reconnaissance
Strategic reconnaissance
Maritime patrol
Anti-ship strike
Anti-submarine warfare
Search and rescue
Assault transport
Transport
Liaison
Trainer
Inflight-refuelling tanker
Specialized

## Performance

All-weather capability
Rough field capability
STOL capability
VTOL capability
Airspeed 0-250 mph
Airspeed 250 mph-Mach 1
Airspeed Mach 1 plus
Ceiling 0-20,000 ft
Ceiling 20,000-40,000 ft
Ceiling 40,000ft plus
Range 0-1,000 miles
Range 1,000-3,000 miles
Range 3,000 miles plus

## Weapons

Air-to-air missiles
Air-to-surface missiles
Cruise missiles
Cannon
Trainable guns
Naval weapons
Nuclear-capable
Rockets
'Smart' weapon kit
Weapon load 0-4,000 lb
Weapon load 4,000-15,000 lb
Weapon load 15,000 lb plus

## Avionics

Electronic Counter Measures
Electronic Support Measures
Search radar
Fire control radar
Look-down/shoot-down
Terrain-following radar
Forward-looking infra-red
Laser
Television

The Avro 748 was the last aircraft to be identified as a product of the once famous Avro (A. V. Roe) company, and represented an attempt to get a foot in the post-war civil market after the design and production of some superb military aircraft which had spanned two world wars. When a decision to proceed with the 748 twin-turboprop transport was taken, in January 1959, Avro was a member of the Hawker Siddeley Group, and in due course the aircraft was redesignated **HS 748**. Later, in 1977, the Hawker Siddeley identity was lost with the formation of British Aerospace, and it is this latter company which built this aircraft up to the mid-1980s with the designation **BAe 748**.

The Avro 748 prototype (G-APZV) was flown for the first time on 24 June 1960, but even before this event the Indian air force had shown interest in a slightly heavier **Avro 748M** and began negotiations for licensed construction of the type: 72 were eventually assembled for the Indian Air Force by Hindustan Aeronautics Ltd on the basis of British-built components.

The Royal Air Force is numbered among the armed services which have procured the HS 748 series. The RAF needed a tactical transport version, and this was evolved as the HS 780 with the fuselage lengthened to

23.75 m (77 ft 11 in) and revised with an upswept tail unit allowing the incorporation of a rear ramp/door providing straight-in access to a hold with a strengthened floor. The RAF took 31 of this **Andover C.Mk 1**, which served between July 1966 and 1975, when defence cuts forced the retirement of the aircraft. Ten were sold to the Royal New Zealand Air Force, but seven were later returned to service as four **Andover E.Mk 3** and three **Andover E.Mk 3A** radar calibration aircraft.

Two versions of the HS 748 offered for government and/or military use were the **HS 748 Series 2 Military Transport** (in Series 2A and 2B variants, the latter with uprated engines and a 1.22-m/4-ft increase in span) and the HS 748 Coastguarder. The latter failed to secure orders, but the Military Transport was considerably more successful with small but collectively useful orders. The type has the stronger floor and rear freight door optional for civil transports, and can be operated at higher weights with a payload of 58 troops, or 48 paratroops and dispatchers, or 24 litters and nine attendants, or 5885 kg (12,975 lb) of freight. The RAF took six of the type with the designation **Andover C.Mk 2** for four general-purpose transports and **Andover CC.Mk 2** for two VIP aircraft for The Queen's Flight.

## Specification: BAe 748 Series 2B Military Transport

**Origin:** UK
**Type:** short/medium-range utility transport aircraft
**Powerplant:** two 1700-ekW (2,280-ehp) Rolls-Royce Dart RDa.7 Mk 536-2 turboprops
**Performance:** cruising speed 243 kt (451 km/h; 280 mph); initial rate of climb 1,420 ft (433 m) per minute. Service ceiling 25,000 ft (7620 m); range 1456 km (905 miles) with maximum payload
**Weights:** empty 11671 kg (25,730 lb); maximum take-off 23133 kg (51,000 lb)
**Dimensions:** span 31.23 m (102 ft 5.5 in); length 20.42 m (67 ft 0 in); height 7.57 m (24 ft 10 in); wing area 77.00 m² (828.87 sq ft)
**Armament:** none

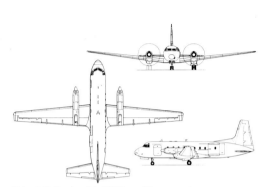

*BAe 748 Series 2A Military Transport*

*British Aerospace modified the 748 airframe to maritime patrol configuration with moderately advanced electronics and provision for armament. Named Coastguarder, this variant found no customer.*

*Several air forces adopted the Military Transport for general light transport operations. This aircraft flies with the Ecuadorian air force.*

# British Aerospace (EECo/BAC) Canberra (bomber versions)

*BAe (EECo/BAC) Canberra B.Mk 62 of the Argentine air force, as seen on Falklands duty.*

The **English Electric Canberra** was first flown as the A.1 prototype on 13 May 1949. It had been planned as a high-altitude bomber with a crew of two and a radar bomb sight, but the sight never materialized and the Canberra B.Mk 2 entered service with the RAF No.101 Squadron in May 1951 as a traditional level bomber with a visual bomb sight in a glazed nose and the crew increased to three. New features included ejector seats and a pressurized cabin with an enormous glazed bulge over the pilot's cockpit. The navigator sat at the rear alongside the bomb-aimer, who moved forward to the nose on bombing runs.

The basic design reflected that of the earlier Gloster Meteor, with the engines mounted outboard of the fuselage in nacelles centred on the extremely broad wing. This large wing, very lightly loaded, gave the Canberra outstanding manoeuvrability at low levels and great altitude performance. The flight controls were manual, the tailplane was used for trimming, and the wing had split flaps. The whole aircraft was extremely traditional and simple, which made it cheap and acceptable to many air forces which could not have operated more advanced aircraft.

The fuel was housed in the upper half of the circular-section fuselage above the bomb bay, and in tip tanks which were removable on the ground. The front and rear bomb bays each had twin hydraulically opened doors of traditional type, although the aircraft sat very low on the ground in order that the main landing gears could be retracted into the short inboard wing sections, The twin-wheel nose gear used a Liquid Spring strut, but in most marks was not steerable. Almost the only novel feature was the row of 40 air-brake fingers which could be extended above and below the wings.

The original Canberra B.Mk 2 was followed by the **Canberra B.Mk 6** with more powerful Avon engines with triple-breech cartridge starters, extra integral wing tanks and improved avionics, and by the **Canberra B(I).Mk 8** night interdictor with the navigator in the nose and the pilot (the only other occupant) in a fighter type cockpit offset to the left, and with four 20-mm cannon in the rear weapon bay and stores pylons under the outer wings. Hundreds of new and refurbished examples of all three basic offensive versions were sold all over the world, and remain in limited service.

## Specification: Canberra B.Mk 6
**Origin:** UK
**Type:** bomber and visual attack aircraft
**Powerplant:** two 3402-kg (7,500-lb) dry thrust Rolls-Royce Avon Mk 109 turbojets
**Performance:** maximum speed 525 kt (973 km/h; 605 mph) up to 15,000 ft (4570 m) thereafter falling to 470 kt (871 km/h; 541 mph) at 40,000ft (12190 m); service ceiling 48,000 ft (14630 m); combat radius 1778 km (1,105 miles)
**Weights:** empty 10099 kg (22,265 lb); maximum take-off 24040 kg (53,000 lb)
**Dimensions:** span 19.51 m (64 ft 0 in) excluding tip tanks; length 19.96 m (65 ft 6 in); height 4.75 m (15 ft 7 in); wing area 89.18 m² (960.0 sq ft)
**Armament:** normal bomb load six 454-kg (1 ,000-lb) bombs internally, plus two more such bombs, or AS.30 air-to-surface missiles, rocket-launcher pods or other stores on two underwing pylons

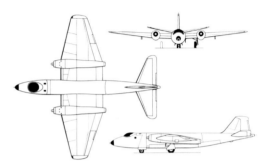

*BAe (EECo/BAC) Canberra B.Mk 6*

*The Peruvian air force uses the Canberra in many marks, including this Canberra B(I).Mk 68. The interdictor versions feature an offset, fighter-type canopy, with the navigator/bombardier in the nose.*

*South Africa used its Canberra B(I).Mk 12 in operations against Angolan forces. As can be seen, the aircraft is very short of markings.*

# British Aerospace (EECo/BAC) Canberra (reconnaissance versions)

*BAe (EECo/BAC) Canberra PR.Mk 9 of No.1 Photographic Reconnaissance Unit, RAF.*

## Role

Fighter
Close support
Counter-insurgency
Tactical strike
Strategic bomber
Tactical reconnaissance
Strategic reconnaissance
Maritime patrol
Anti-ship strike
Anti-submarine warfare
Search and rescue
Assault transport
Transport
Liaison
Trainer
Inflight-refuelling tanker
Specialized

## Performance

All-weather capability
Rough field capability
STOL capability
VTOL capability
Airspeed 0-250 mph
Airspeed 250 mph-Mach 1
Airspeed Mach 1 plus
Ceiling 0-20,000 ft
Ceiling 20,000-40,000 ft
Ceiling 40,000ft plus
Range 0-1,000 miles
Range 1,000-3,000 miles
Range 3,000 miles plus

## Weapons

Air-to-air missiles
Air-to-surface missiles
Cruise missiles
Cannon
Trainable guns
Naval weapons
Nuclear-capable
Rockets
'Smart' weapon kit
Weapon load 0-4,000 lb
Weapon load 4,000-15,000 lb
Weapon load 15,000 lb plus

## Avionics

Electronic Counter Measures
Electronic Support Measures
Search radar
Fire control radar
Look-down/shoot-down
Terrain-following radar
Forward-looking infra-red
Laser
Television

The outstanding altitude capability and overall cost-effectiveness of the Canberra B.Mk 2 made a photo-reconnaissance conversion a natural early development, and the prototype **English Electric Canberra PR.Mk 3** flew as early as 19 March 1950. It differed from the B.Mk 2 in having its fuselage 'stretched' by 0.356 m (1 ft 2 in) to increase the internal fuel from 6260 litres (1,377 Imp gal) to 8715 litres (1,917 Imp gal), and carried seven optical cameras instead of bombs. One section of the bay was equipped for carriage of photoflash stores and markers. This mark was followed in 1953 by the **Canberra PR.Mk 7**, which was vas a similar conversion of the B.Mk 6 with integral wing tanks and uprated engines.

In typical British style production of the Canberra PR.Mk 3 totalled 35, and of the PR.Mk 7 no fewer than 74, while the number built of the definitive PR version amounted to only 23. Napier developed a controllable rocket engine to boost the altitude performance of this **Canberra PR.Mk 9** variant, but the booster was the cancelled. The Canberra PR.Mk 9 was thus left with uprated Avon Mk 206 engines and a modified wing with extended span and a centre section, inboard of the nacelles, of extended chord. Although nothing remotely comparable with the American RB-57 versions, these changes did give a significant increase in altitude. The engineering was entrusted to Shorts, which also built the production aircraft. The pilot was seated on the left under a fixed fighter-type canopy and the navigator (the only other occupant) entered via a hinged metal nose to sit on the nose centreline under a frangible escape hatch. Other features include increased internal fuel, powered ailerons and a totally different avionics and electronic warfare fit.

The latter was upgraded during the Canberra PR.Mk 9's long service with Nos 58 and later 39 Squadrons The original Canberra PR.Mk 9 force was disbanded in 1983, but five of the aircraft were ferried to Shorts for a further conversion which is the most extensive and costly of any applied to UK-built Canberras. The details are classified, but these five aircraft were eventually used for advanced Elint and reconnaissance duties, using sensors and other equipment not previously carried by British aircraft. Three Canberra PR.Mk 9s were sold to Chile, where one later crashed while serving with Grupo 2.

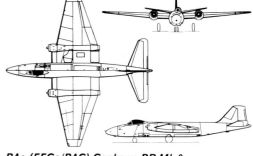

*BAe (EECo/BAC) Canberra PR.Mk 9*

*The Canberra PR.Mk 7 was based on the B.Mk 6 airframe, but featured a lengthened forward fuselage. All RAF aircraft served with No. 100 Sqn.*

*No. 1 PRU's Canberra PR.Mk 9s underwent much updating after their introduction into service. This type has been tipped to carry the CASTOR battlefield surveillance radar.*

**Specification:** Canberra PR.Mk 9 (pre-rebuild)
**Origin:** UK
**Type:** photo-reconnaissance aircraft
**Powerplant:** two 4763-kg (10,500-lb) dry thrust Rolls-Royce Avon Mk 206 turbojets
**Performance:** maximum speed about 564 kt (1050 km/h; 650 mph) at medium altitude; service ceiling classified but about 60,000 ft (18290 m); range classified but in excess of 5875 km (3,650 miles)
**Weights:** empty not published but about 11790 kg (26,000 lb): maximum take-off not published but similar to the Canberra B(I).Mk 8's 25514 kg (56,250 lb)
**Dimensions:** span 20.68 m (67 ft 10 in); length 20.32 m (66 ft 8 in); height 4.78 m (15 ft 8 in); wing area 97.08m2 (1,045.0 sq ft)
**Armament:** none

# British Aerospace (HS) Harrier T.Mk 4

*British Aerospace Harrier T.Mk 4 of No.4 Squadron, RAF.*

At an early stage of the Harrier programme it was realized that the special techniques needed to fly this STOVL type called for a dual-control trainer version, and the prototype of such a variant first flew in April 1969 just as the Harrier GR.Mk 1 was entering service. After much refinement of the trainer's concept, 21 **Harrier T.Mk 2** two-seaters were built for the RAF. The main difference between the two variants lay in the fuselage, which in the trainer was lengthened at nose and tail to accommodate and balance the tandem stepped cockpits, each with a Martin-Baker Mk 9A or Mk 9D seat and enclosed by a single canopy hinged to the right. The tailcone with its vital reaction control jets was extended aft, the tailplane was structurally different and the vertical tail was taller.

The **Harrier T.Mk 4** and **Harrier T.Mk 4A**, respectively retrofitted with the Pegasus Mk 103 engine and built with it from the start, serve with No. 233 Operational Conversion Unit and with the operational squadrons. In an emergency, the rear seats and tail ballast would be removed so that the aircraft could be flown operationally by the instructors, allowing the trainers to take their place in the dispersed Harrier operating force. The aircraft carry a similar range of external loads, including the guns under the fuselage and a wide assortment of guided and unguided ordnance carried on four hardpoints under the wings, and are equipped with the LRMTS (laser rangefinder and marked-target seeker) but not with the ARI.18223 radar warning receiver.

For the Fleet Air Arm BAe delivered four **Harrier T.Mk 4N** aircraft differing only in having no LRMTS, and then two **Harrier T.Mk 8** conversions with the cockpit of the Sea Harrier. The US Marine Corps received eight TAV-8A aircraft without LRMTS, RWR or gun pods, but with large dorsal blades for tactical radio, and three similar VAE-1 (TAV-8S or Mk 54/58) aircraft were delivered to the Spanish navy. All these aircraft retained operational capability, though weapons were not normally fitted.

The Indian Navy's No. 300 Squadron operates a slightly different variant, the **Harrier T.Mk 60**. This looks similar to the T.Mk 4N but has the complete avionics systems of the Sea Harrier apart from the Blue Fox radar.

The next-generation TAV-8B Harrier II, trainer version of the McDonnell Douglas/BAe AV-8B, is described separately, together with its BAe Harrier T.Mk 10 British counterpart.

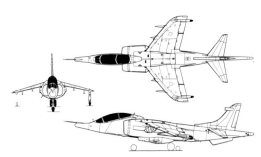

*British Aerospace Harrier T.Mk 4*

*The Royal Navy's No.899 Sqn, based at RNAS Yeovilton, uses the two-seat Harrier T. Mk 4N for initial STOVL training for its potential Sea Harrier pilots.*

*The 'T-bird' Harrier is used for conversion, continuation training and for demonstration purposes. It retains full combat capability.*

**Specification:** BAe Harrier T.Mk4/4A
**Origin:** UK
**Type:** STOVL dual-control trainer with combat capability
**Powerplant:** one 9752-kg (21,500-lb) dry thrust Rolls-Rove Pegasus Mk 103 vectored-thrust turbofan
**Performance:** maximum speed (dive limit) Mach 1.3 or (clean at low altitude) 625 kt (1159 km/h; 720 mph); initial rate of climb about 28,000 ft (8534 m) per minute; service ceiling 50,000 ft (15240 m); range not published
**Weights:** empty 6849 kg (15,100 lb): maximum take-off 11884 kg (26,200 lb)
**Dimensions:** span 7.70 m( 25 ft 3in) or 9.04 m (29 ft 8 in) with bolt-on ferry tips; length 17.50 m (57 ft 5 in) or, non-RAF aircraft, 17.00 m (55 ft 9.5 in); height 4.17 m (13 ft 8 in); wing area 18.68 m² (201.1 sq ft)
**Armament:** two 30 mm Aden cannon each with 120/150 rounds, plus provision for up to 2268 kg (5,000 lb) of diverse stores carried on five stations

## Role
Fighter
Close support
Counter-insurgency
Tactical strike
Strategic bomber
Tactical reconnaissance
Strategic reconnaissance
Maritime patrol
Anti-ship strike
Anti-submarine warfare
Search and rescue
Assault transport
Transport
Liaison
Trainer
Inflight-refuelling tanker
Specialized

## Performance
All-weather capability
Rough field capability
STOL capability
VTOL capability
Airspeed 0-250 mph
Airspeed 250 mph-Mach 1
Airspeed Mach 1 plus
Ceiling 0-20,000 ft
Ceiling 20,000-40,000 ft
Ceiling 40,000ft plus
Range 0-1,000 miles
Range 1,000-3,000 miles
Range 3,000 miles plus

## Weapons
Air-to-air missiles
Air-to-surface missiles
Cruise missiles
Cannon
Trainable guns
Naval weapons
Nuclear-capable
Rockets
'Smart' weapon kit
Weapon load 0-4,000 lb
Weapon load 4,000-15,000 lb
Weapon load 15,000 lb plus

## Avionics
Electronic Counter Measures
Electronic Support Measures
Search radar
Fire control radar
Look-down/shoot-down
Terrain-following radar
Forward-looking infra-red
Laser
Television

# British Aerospace (HS) Hawk

*British Aerospace Hawk T.Mk 53 of the Indonesian air force.*

## Role
Fighter
Close support
Counter-insurgency
Tactical strike
Strategic bomber
Tactical reconnaissance
Strategic reconnaissance
Maritime patrol
Anti-ship strike
Anti-submarine warfare
Search and rescue
Assault transport
Transport
Liaison
Trainer
Inflight-refuelling tanker
Specialized

## Performance
All-weather capability
Rough field capability
STOL capability
VTOL capability
Airspeed 0-250 mph
Airspeed 250 mph-Mach 1
Airspeed Mach 1 plus
Ceiling 0-20,000 ft
Ceiling 20,000-40,000 ft
Ceiling 40,000 ft plus
Range 0-1,000 miles
Range 1,000-3,000 miles
Range 3,000 miles plus

## Weapons
Air-to-air missiles
Air-to-surface missiles
Cruise missiles
Cannon
Trainable guns
Naval weapons
Nuclear-capable
Rockets
'Smart' weapon kit
Weapon load 0-4,000 lb
Weapon load 4,000-15,000 lb
Weapon load 15,000 lb plus

## Avionics
Electronic Counter Measures
Electronic Support Measures
Search radar
Fire control radar
Look-down/shoot-down
Terrain-following radar
Forward-looking infra-red
Laser
Television

Originally flown as the HS.1182 prototype on 21 August 1974, the **BAe Hawk** was from the start a truly outstanding design which gradually became recognized not only as an excellent trainer but as a world-beating all-round tactical combat aircraft which can fly medium-range attack and air-combat missions for a small fraction of the cost of more powerful types offering little more than the same capability.

Keys to the success of the Hawk in a keenly competitive field are its exceptional structure life, its unrivalled low maintenance requirements (the lowest per flight hour of any jet aircraft in the world), its unequalled low accident rate (discounting aircraft deliberately destroyed in Zimbabwe), its uniformly high technology and unrivalled fuel economy for the heavy weapon loads that can be carried.

Apart from the US Navy with its somewhat different McDonnell Douglas T-45 Goshawk variant, customers for the baseline trainer include the RAF (**Hawk T.Mk 1**), Finland (**Hawk Mk 51**), Kenya (**Hawk Mk 52**) and Indonesia (**Hawk Mk 53**). The Hawk Mk 60 series has a more powerful engine

and a number of other features to improve its capabilities, and customers include Zimbabwe (**Hawk Mk 60**), Dubai (**Hawk Mk 61**), Abu Dhabi (**Hawk Mk 63**), Kuwait (**Hawk Mk 64**), Saudi Arabia (**Hawk Mk 65**), Switzerland (**Hawk Mk 66**) and South Korea (**Hawk Mk 67**).

In 1985 construction began of the **Hawk Mk 200** to meet a wide demand for a single-seat version dedicated to the tactical attack mission. Identical to the Hawk Mk 60 aft of the new cockpit, this is one of the world's most versatile aircraft with equipment for day, night and all-weather airspace denial (a mission also flown by the RAF's 72 **Hawk T.Mk 1A** conversions), close support, interdiction, reconnaissance and anti-ship strike. The first Hawk Mk 200 flew in May 1986 with the 2651-kg (5,845-lb) dry thrust Adour Mk 871 turbofan, and the type has now been ordered by Oman (**Hawk Mk 203**), Saudi Arabia (radar-equipped **Hawk Mk 205**) and Malaysia (**Hawk Mk 208**). The **Hawk Mk 100** is a two-seater with much of the Hawk Mk 200's capabilities, and this has been ordered by Abu Dhabi (**Hawk Mk 102**), Oman (**Hawk Mk 103**) and Malaysia (**Hawk Mk 108**).

## Specification: BAe Hawk Mk 60
**Origin:** UK
**Type:** trainer and multi-role tactical attack/defence aircraft
**Powerplant:** one 2586-kg (5,700-lb) dry thrust Rolls Royce/Turbomeca Adour Mk 861 turbofan
**Performance:** maximum speed (dive limit) Mach 1.2 or (clean) 560 kt (1038 km/h; 645 mph) at sea level; initial rate of climb 11,800 ft (3597 m) per minute; service ceiling 50,000 ft (15240 m); combat radius 998 km (620 miles) with a 2268-kg (5,000-lb) warload
**Weights:** empty 3636 kg (8,015 lb); maximum take-off 8568 kg (18,890 lb)
**Dimensions:** 9.39 m (30 ft 9.7 in); length 11.17 m (36 ft 7.8 in) excluding probe; height 3.99 m (13 ft 1 in); wing area 16.69m² (179.65 sq ft)
**Armament:** provision for one cannon of up to 30-mm calibre in a self-contained centreline pod and up to 3000 kg (6.614 lb) of diverse weapons carried on four underwing hardpoints

*British Aerospace Hawk T.Mk 1A*

*The Empire Test Pilots School at Boscombe Down uses four Hawks for the training of evaluation pilots. The type's high performance makes it excellent at this role.*

*Zimbabwe is one of the foreign users of the Hawk, although one was written off and three badly damaged during a sabotage attack at the Thornhill air base.*

# BAe (Hawker/HS) Hunter

*BAe (Hawker) Hunter F.Mk74 of the Singapore air force.*

The UK's lack of any competitive fighter in the early years of the jet era promised to be rectified by the first flight of Hawker's P.1067 prototype on 20 July 1951. This beautiful thoroughbred combined swept flying surfaces, excellent handling, a powerful axial-flow engine, and an armament of four 30-mm cannon installed with their magazines in a removable and there quickly replaceable pack. After prolonged development which added a rear-fuselage airbrake and bulged external boxes to collect ammunition links, the aircraft entered service as the **Hawker Hunter F.Mk 1** in July 1954. The **Hunter F.Mk 4** introduced leading-edge tanks and provision for external stores, and in June 1956 the **Hunter F.Mk 6** introduced the much more powerful Avon Mk 200 series engine. First of the 'large-bore' variants, the Hunter F.Mk 6 showed that this elegant machine could become potent.

Later Hunter F.Mk 6s had dogtoothed leading edges (introduced retrospectively), an a 'flying tail' in which the tailplane became the primary surface instead of just the trimming control. In 1959 the last basic model, the **Hunter FGA.Mk 9**, entered service with stronger landing gear, a braking parachute and a larger external load which can include four drop tanks. Two aircraft were modified as P.1109s with nose radar and Firestreak missiles (the extended nose made them the fastest service Hunters), but the rest had only a ranging gunsight. In the **Hunter FR.Mk 10** even this was removed to make way for a fan of three nose cameras.

Large export orders and licensed production in the Low Countries brought production to 1,927 including a number of two-seat trainer variants. Many of these venerable aircraft are still flying, the majority being rebuilds by BAe which have included many conversions from 'small-bore' Hunter F.Mk 4s up to the later FGA standard. Some 'advanced' countries improved the Hunter's weapon fit: the Swiss aircraft, for example, have provision for the AGM-65 Maverick TV-guided air-to-surface missile. In most of these countries the Hunter has been or is being relegated to second-line tasks, but the type is still in first-line service with some countries in South America and the Middle and Far Easts.

**Specification:** Hawker Hunter FGA.Mk 9
**Origin:** UK
**Type:** ground-attack fighter
**Powerplant:** one 4604-kg (10,150-lb) dry thrust Rolls-Royce Avon Mk 207 turbojet
**Performance:** maximum speed 610 kt (1130 km/h; 702 mph) at sea level or 538 kt (998 km/h; 622 mph) at high altitude; initial rate of climb 17.200 ft (5243 m) per minute; service ceiling 52,000 ft (15850 m); tactical radius 713 km (443 miles) on a hi-lo-hi mission with two tanks and typical attack ordnance
**Weights:** empty 6532 kg (14,400 lb); maximum take-off 11158 kg (24,600 lb)
**Dimensions:** span 10.25 m (33 ft 8 in); length 13.93 m (45 ft 10.4 in); height 4.02 m (13 ft 2 in); wing area 32.42 m² (349.0 sq ft)
**Armament:** four 30-mm Aden cannon each with 100 (maximum 135) rounds, plus provision for up to 2722 kg (6,000 lb) of external fuel and/or ordnance including all normal tactical stores up to 454-kg (1,000-lb) size

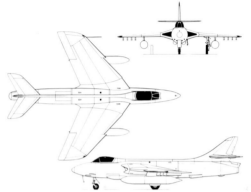

**BAe (Hawker) Hunter FGA.Mk 9**

*India still has a number of Hunters, which performed sterling work during two wars with Pakistan. The aircraft now serves mainly in the weapons training role.*

*Switzerland is still a major operator of the Hunter, employing around 80 Hunter F.Mk 58s with several Fliegerstaffeln. Swiss Hunters are Sidewinder and Maverick-capable.*

# British Aerospace (HS) Nimrod MR.Mk 2

*British Aerospace Nimrod MR.Mk 2P of No. 42 Sqn, RAF, based at St Mawgan.*

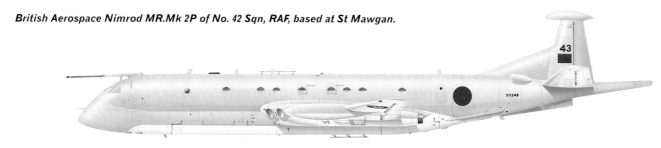

## Role

Fighter
Close support
Counter-insurgency
Tactical strike
Strategic bomber
Tactical reconnaissance
Strategic reconnaissance
Maritime patrol
Anti-ship strike
Anti-submarine warfare
Search and rescue
Assault transport
Transport
Liaison
Trainer
Inflight-refuelling tanker
Specialized

## Performance

All-weather capability
Rough field capability
STOL capability
VTOL capability
Airspeed 0-250 mph
Airspeed 250 mph-Mach 1
Airspeed Mach 1 plus
Ceiling 0-20,000 ft
Ceiling 20,000-40,000 ft
Ceiling 40,000 ft plus
Range 0-1,000 miles
Range 1,000-3,000 miles
Range 3,000 miles plus

## Weapons

Air-to-air missiles
Air-to-surface missiles
Cruise missiles
Cannon
Trainable guns
Naval weapons
Nuclear-capable
Rockets
'Smart' weapon kit
Weapon load 0-4,000 lb
Weapon load 4,000-15,000 lb
Weapon load 15,000 lb plus

## Avionics

Electronic Counter Measures
Electronic Support Measures
Search radar
Fire control radar
Look-down/shoot-down
Terrain-following radar
Forward-looking infra-red
Laser
Television

Hawker Siddeley Manchester began design of the **Hawker Siddeley Nimrod** in 1964, using the Comet 4C airliner as the basis of a new aircraft to replace the Avro Shackleton in the maritime patrol and ASW role with the RAF. The airliner's circular-section pressurized fuselage, in a form shortened by 1.98 m (6 ft 6 in), was retained but supplemented by a very large unpressurized lower lobe to accommodate search radar in the nose and a capacious weapons bay and various systems bays farther aft. Normal crew comprises two pilots and an engineer on the flight deck, route and tactical navigators, two acoustic systems operators, a radar operator and ESM/MAD (electronic support measures/magnetic-anomaly detection) operator, and two observer/loaders who look from bulged side windows or load and fire active and passive sonobuoys, marine markers and other stores from tubes in the rear fuselage. Original features included turbofan engines with reversers on the outer engines, auxiliary tanks projecting ahead of the wings with a searchlight in the right tank, a French ESM system with its antennae in a pod above the fin, and a MAD sensor in a long boom aft of the tail.

**Specification:** BAe Nimrod MR.2
**Origin:** UK
**Type:** maritime patrol and ASW aircraft
**Powerplant:** four 5507-kg (12,140-lb) dry thrust Rolls-Royce Spey Mk 250 turbofans
**Performance:** maximum speed 500 kt (925 km/h; 575 mph); patrol speed 200 kt (370 km/h; 230 mph) on two engines; service ceiling 42,000 ft (12800 m); ferry range 9262 km (5,755 miles) on internal fuel without inflight-refuelling
**Weights:** empty 39010 kg (86,000 lb); maximum take-off 87090 kg (192,000 lb)
**Dimensions:** span 35.00 m (114 ft 10 in) excluding ESM pods; length 39.34 m (129 ft l in); height 9.08 m (29 ft 9.5 in); wing area 197.04 m² (2,121.0 sq ft)
**Armament:** provision for up to 6123 kg (13,500 lb) of dropped stores carried in internal bay, including nine torpedoes, and underwing pylons can be fitted for Harpoon anti-ship missiles or pairs of Sidewinder self-defence AAMs

From 1969 the RAF received 46 **Nimrod MR.Mk 1** aircraft, deployed at Kinloss, St Mawgan and, initially, Malta. Despite intensive use in every kind of weather only one aircraft has been lost, as the result of a multiple birdstrike on take-off. The Nimrod consistently won every patrol/ ASW competition it entered, even in its Nimrod MR.Mk 1 form, and since 1979 the remaining RAF force of 31 aircraft (others having been diverted to the Nimrod R.Mk 1 and abortive Nimrod AEW.Mk 3 programmes) has been totally transformed in capability by revision to **Nimrod MR.Mk 2** standard. This provides a new tactical system, computer, radar and acoustic processing installations, upgraded communications, inertial navigation, new displays and controls and an airborne crew-training system. During the Falklands war of 1982 an inflight-refuelling probe was hastily added, and other updates include an extra environmental-control system and, some years later than planned, Loral ARI.18240/1 ESM pods were added at the wingtips. Another hurried update during the South Atlantic war resurrected the capability to carry previously neglected underwing stores.

*British Aerospace Nimrod MR.Mk 2*

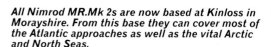

**All Nimrod MR.Mk 2s are now based at Kinloss in Morayshire. From this base they can cover most of the Atlantic approaches as well as the vital Arctic and North Seas.**

**This Nimrod MR.Mk 2P is in the most up-to-date guise, complete with refuelling boom, wingtip pods, underfuselage aerials and blade aerials on the tailplane.**

# British Aerospace (HS) Nimrod R.Mk 1

*British Aerospace Nimrod R.Mk 1 of No.51 Sqn, RAF Wyton.*

The RAF has been involved with electronic intelligence (Elint) for many years. and after World War II Nos 51 and 192 Squadrons were notable with their specially configured Avro Lincolns, Boeing Washingtons, BAe (EECo) Canberras and de Havilland Comets. By the 1960s the Comets were getting too long in the tooth and the Canberras too costly, so when the Nimrod programme went ahead in June 1965 it was recognized that the same basic aircraft could be an ideal basis for a new Elint type. In addition to the 46 Nimrod MR.Mk 1 maritime patrol aircraft, therefore, orders were placed for three further aircraft (XW664-666), which were completed to **BAe Nimrod R.Mk 1** standard. They were delivered in July 1971 to the RAF's No.51 Squadron, normally based at Wyton. After extensive fitting out, they were formally commissioned on 10 May 1974.

Originally finished in natural metal with upper surfaces painted white, the Nimrod R.Mk Is were later repainted in the less conspicuous khaki colour called hemp. They have also been progressively upgraded, receiving Loral ARI.18240/1 wingtip passive receiver pods in a fashion similar to the Nimrod MR.Mk 2. One aircraft was fitted with an inflight-refuelling probe for duty in the Falklands war. The main visible sensors are three very large spiral-helix receiver domes, one facing ahead on the front of each wing tank and one facing aft on the tailcone (replacing the MAD boom of the maritime reconnaissance Nimrod). All details are classified, but it is obvious that the main receivers must cover the widest possible band of frequencies and also have a D/F (direction finding) and ranging function to record both the character and location of all detectable hostile emissions. Most modern Elint platforms do much more than this and carry on board a library of known emitters, with which each signal is compared. Thus a detailed map can be built up of the type and location of all potentially enemy ground radio stations, navigation aids and, particularly, defence systems such as surveillance radar, SAM guidance radars and fighter direction stations (to say nothing of emissions from the fighters themselves). The Nimrod R.Mk 1s spent most of these early lives on patrol near Warsaw Pact frontiers, especially over international waters in the Baltic.

## Specification: BAe Nimrod R.Mk 1
**Origin:** UK
**Type:** electronic intelligence platform
**Powerplant:** four 5507-kg (12,140-lb) dry thrust Rolls-Royce Spey Mk 250 or 251 turbofans
**Performance:** not published, but generally closely similar to that of the Nimrod MR.Mk 2; possibly mission endurance is extended by fitting auxiliary tanks in the former weapons bay
**Weights:** not disclosed, but very close to those of the Nimrod MR.Mk 2 although empty weight may be slightly less
**Dimensions:** span 35.08 m (115 ft 1 in); length 36.50 m (119 ft 9 in); height 9.08 m (29 ft 9.5 in); wing area 197.04 m² (2,121.0 sq ft)
**Armament:** none

**British Aerospace Nimrod R.Mk 1**

*Three Nimrod airframes were delivered to No.51 Sqn for electronic intelligence. These have been gradually updated over the years at their Wyton base.*

*One Nimrod R.Mk 1 has received an inflight-refuelling probe, presumably for operations during the Falklands war. These secretive aircraft are sometimes seen over the Baltic.*

### Role
Fighter
Close support
Counter-insurgency
Tactical strike
Strategic bomber
Tactical reconnaissance
Strategic reconnaissance
Maritime patrol
Anti-ship strike
Anti-submarine warfare
Search and rescue
Assault transport
Transport
Liaison
Trainer
Inflight-refuelling tanker
Specialized

### Performance
All-weather capability
Rough field capability
STOL capability
VTOL capability
Airspeed 0-250 mph
Airspeed 250 mph-Mach 1
Airspeed Mach 1 plus
Ceiling 0-20,000 ft
Ceiling 20,000-40,000 ft
Ceiling 40,000ft plus
Range 0-1.000 miles
Range 1,000-3,000 miles
Range 3,000 miles plus

### Weapons
Air-to-air missiles
Air-to-surface missiles
Cruise missiles
Cannon
Trainable guns
Naval weapons
Nuclear-capable
Rockets
'Smart' weapon kit
Weapon load 0-4,000 lb
Weapon load 4,000-15,000 lb
Weapon load 15,000 lb plus

### Avionics
Electronic Counter Measures
Electronic Support Measures
Search radar
Fire control radar
Look-down/shoot-down radar
Terrain-following radar
Forward-looking infra-red
Laser
Television

# British Aerospace (BAC) One-Eleven

*British Aerospace One-Eleven of the Omani air force.*

## Role
Fighter
Close support
Counter-insurgency
Tactical strike
Strategic bomber
Tactical reconnaissance
Strategic reconnaissance
Maritime patrol
Anti-ship strike
Anti-submarine warfare
Search and rescue
Assault transport
Transport
Liaison
Trainer
Inflight-refuelling tanker
Specialized

## Performance
All-weather capability
Rough field capability
STOL capability
VTOL capability
Airspeed 0-250 mph
Airspeed 250 mph-Mach 1
Airspeed Mach 1 plus
Ceiling 0-20,000 ft
Ceiling 20,000-40,000 ft
Ceiling 40,000ft plus
Range 0-1,000 miles
Range 1,000-3,000 miles
Range 3,000 miles plus

## Weapons
Air-to-air missiles
Air-to-surface missiles
Cruise missiles
Cannon
Trainable guns
Naval weapons
Nuclear-capable
Rockets
'Smart' weapon kit
Weapon load 0-4,000 lb
Weapon load 4,000-15,000 lb
Weapon load 15,000 lb plus

## Avionics
Electronic Counter Measures
Electronic Support Measures
Search radar
Fire control radar
Look-down/shoot-down
Terrain-following radar
Forward-looking infra-red
Laser
Television

Developed as a company funded venture by the newly formed British Aircraft Corporation, the **BAC One-Eleven** was planned as a short-haul jet passenger airliner to succeed the Vickers Viscount. It was launched on the basis of an order for 10 aircraft from British United, and first flew in August 1963. The basic design was entirely conventional, with two of the newly developed Spey turbofans mounted on the rear of a circular-section fuselage with small elliptical passenger windows and seating for 65 to 89 passengers, who boarded via a stairway under the tail. Features included manual ailerons but powered tail surfaces (the horizontal tail being on top of the fin), very short landing gear units, engine bleed-air de-icing of wings and tail, thrust reversers, and a gas turbine APU in the tailcone for self-start capability.

Almost all production went to commercial operators. BAC built 56 Series 200, nine Series 300, 69 Series 400 (originally developed for the US market), nine Series 475 specially equipped for operations from short unpaved airstrips, and 87 of the stretched Series 500 seating up to 109 There are also mixed-traffic and cargo versions, and one of the few military buyers, the Sultan of Oman's air force, uses three **One-Eleven Series 475** aircraft with a quick-change interior and wide cargo doors. Two early **One-Eleven Series 217** aircraft have had a long career with No. 34 (VIP) Squadron, RAAF, at Canberra, and several other One-Elevens have been used as VIP aircraft by heads of state.

All production was transferred in the early 1980s to the IAv Bucuresti (now Romaero) in Romania, where the **Rombac 1-11 Series 495** and stretched **1-11 Series 560** were built up to the early 1990s for use within Romania and for export. These models have all the latest features including hushkits to quieten the engines, which were also licence-produced in Romania.

One of the first Romanian-assembled aircraft, still incorporating British-made parts, was a VIP machine for the Romanian president.

**Specification:** Rombac 1-11 Series 560
**Origin:** UK licensed to Romania
**Type:** passenger and cargo transport
**Powerplant:** two 5693-kg (12,550-lb) dry thrust Rolls-Royce Spey Mk 512-14DW turbofans
**Performance:** maximum cruising speed 470 kt (870 km/h; 541 mph) at 21,000 ft (6400 m); initial rate of climb 2,370 ft (722 m) per minute; service ceiling 35,000 ft (10670 m); range 2459 km (1,528 miles) with capacity payload and reserves
**Weights:** empty 25267 kg (55,704 lb); maximum take-off 47400 kg (104,500 lb)
**Dimensions:** span 28.50 m (93 ft 6 in) or, early Series 200/300/400 aircraft, 26.97 m (88 ft 6 in); length 32.61 m (107 ft 0 in) or, short-fuselage models, 28.50 m (93 ft 6 in); height 7.47 m (24 ft 6 in); wing area 95.78 m² (1,031.0 sq ft)
**Armament:** none

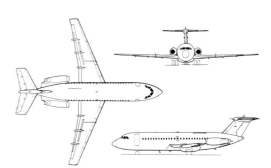

**British Aerospace One-Eleven Series 475**

*Two One-Eleven Series 479s are on the strength of the Empire Test Pilots School for training purposes. These have replaced Andovers and Viscounts for heavy type handling.*

*A handful of One-Eleven airliners have been purchased for the MoD. This example was used by the Royal Aircraft Establishment at Bedford for testing purposes.*

# British Aerospace Sea Harrier FRS.Mk 1

*British Aerospace Sea Harrier FRS.Mk 1 of No.801 Sqn, Royal Navy.*

The **BAe Sea Harrier** was born into a land whose official policy was that there must be no more Royal Navy combat aircraft unless they were helicopters. Even the 'Invincible' class of light carriers had to be called 'through-deck cruisers' to avoid the forbidden idea of a carrier. This made it impossible to begin development of a 'maritime Harrier' until May 1975, so that the Sea Harrier did not enter Fleet Air Arm service until shortly before the Argentine invasion of the Falklands in 1982. The importance of the small force of Sea Harriers in the subsequent campaign then spoke for itself.

Compared with the RAF's Harrier GR.Mk 3 the **Sea Harrier FRS.Mk 1** introduced a totally new front end (which folds to reduce length aboard ship) with a Blue Fox multimode radar, a raised cockpit giving more space for displays and avionics (and giving better all-round view), and a largely different nav/attack system tailored to maritime deployment from ships. The engine and other parts are marinized, the ventral fin incorporates a radar altimeter, the seat is a Martin-Baker Mk 10H, deck hold-down anchors are incorporated, and an air/ship communication link is added. During the Falklands war provision was added for paired Sidewinder AAMs and larger drop tanks.

Excluding three development aircraft, the RN buy comprised batches of 21, 10, 14 and nine aircraft delivered by June 1988. Losses have amounted to nine in accidents and two to enemy ground fire. The RN force comprises No.899 HQ Squadron for training and two combat units, Nos 800 and 801 Squadrons each with eight aircraft, all three of them land-based at RNAS Yeovilton with the operational squadrons deploying to the light carriers HMS *Ark Royal*, *Illustrious* and *Invincible* as required.

The Indian Navy operates the **Sea Harrier FRS.Mk 51** with gaseous instead of liquid oxygen and Magic rather than Sidewinder AAMs. The Indian buy started with six aircraft delivered between December 1983 and July 1984 for service with No.300 (White Tiger) Squadron on board the carrier *Vikrant*. The Indian Navy then ordered an additional 10 aircraft in November 1985, and these aircraft were delivered between December 1989 and September 1991. A third batch of seven aircraft was ordered in the later 1980s, and the delivery of these aircraft allowed the creation of another Sea Harrier squadron for service on the carrier *Viraat*. The Indian Navy also operates three **Harrier T.Mk 60** radarless trainers for its Sea Harrier force.

## Specification: BAe Sea Harrier FRS.Mk 1
**Origin:** UK
**Type:** shipborne multi-role combat aircraft
**Powerplant:** one 9752-kg (21,500-lb) dry thrust Rolls Royce Pegasus Mk 104 vectored-thrust turbofan
**Performance:** maximum speed (dive limit) Mach 1.25 or (level flight) 600 kt (1110 km/h; 690 mph) at sea level with full AAM load; initial rate of climb about 50,000 ft (15240 m) per minute; service ceiling 51,000 ft (15545 m); intercept radius 740 km (460 miles) on a hi-hi-hi mission with full combat reserve
**Weights:** empty 5942 kg (13,100 lb); maximum take-off 11884 kg (26,200 lb)
**Dimensions:** span 7.70 m (25 ft 3 in); length 14.50 m (47 ft 7 in); height 3.71 m (12 ft 2 in); wing area 18.68 m² (201.1 sq ft)
**Armament:** two 30-mm Aden cannon, plus provision for 3629 kg (8,000 lb) of stores carried on five pylons and including Sidewinder or Magic AAMs and two Harpoon or Sea Eagle anti-ship missiles

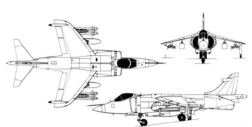

*British Aerospace Sea Harrier FRS.Mk 1*

*The only foreign customer for the Sea Harrier has been the Indian Navy, which now operates the type from two aircraft carriers, the two squadrons otherwise being shore-based at Goa-Dabolim with the operational conversion unit.*

*The Sea Harrier FRS.Mk 1 equips two operational squadrons on board carriers, and there is also a training squadron at Yeovilton.*

**Role**
Fighter
Close support
Counter-insurgency
Tactical strike
Strategic bomber
Tactical reconnaissance
Strategic reconnaissance
Maritime patrol
Anti-ship strike
Anti-submarine warfare
Search and rescue
Assault transport
Transport
Liaison
Trainer
Inflight-refuelling tanker
Specialized

**Performance**
All-weather capability
Rough field capability
STOL capability
VTOL capability
Airspeed 0-250 mph
Airspeed 250 mph-Mach 1
Airspeed Mach 1 plus
Ceiling 0-20,000 ft
Ceiling 20,000-40,000 ft
Ceiling 40,000ft plus
Range 0-1,000 miles
Range 1,000-3,000 miles
Range 3,000 miles plus

**Weapons**
Air-to-air missiles
Air-to-surface missiles
Cruise missiles
Cannon
Trainable guns
Naval weapons
Nuclear-capable
Rockets
'Smart' weapon kit
Weapon load 0-4,000 lb
Weapon load 4,000-15,000 lb
Weapon load 15,000 lb

**Avionics**
Electronic Counter Measures
Electronic Support Measures
Search radar
Fire control radar
Look-down/shoot-down
Terrain-following radar
Forward-looking infra-red
Laser
Television

# British Aerospace Sea Harrier FRS.Mk 2

*The first radar-equipped Sea Harrier FRS.Mk 2 prototype. The stretched fuselage is clearly evident.*

The **British Aerospace Sea Harrier FRS.Mk 2** is the mid-life update version of the Sea Harrier FRS.Mk 1, designed to provide the type with the ability to engage multiple beyond-visual-horizon targets (including those at a lower level than the Sea Harrier) with its primary armament of four AIM-120 AMRAAM medium-range AAMs. To this end the original Blue Fox radar is replaced by Ferranti Blue Vixen coherent pulse-Doppler track-while-scan radar to provide an all-weather look-down detection facility with track-while-scan and multiple target engagement capabilities, and other improvements are a MIL 1553B digital data-bus (making possible the full effective carriage and launch of Sea Eagle anti-ship and ALARM anti-radar missiles) and the installation of the Marconi Sky Guardian 200 RWR, the Joint Tactical Information and Distribution System for secure voice and data links, two additional underwing hardpoints, wing tip stations for two AIM-9 Sidewinder short-range AAMs, wing

improvements, a revised cockpit with HOTAS controls, provision for larger drop tanks, 25-mm Aden 25 cannon in place of the elderly 30-mm weapons, and possibly a Plessey missile-approach warning system.

British Aerospace received instructions to develop the Sea Harrier FRS.Mk 2 in January 1985, and the aerodynamic prototype made its first flight on 19 September 1988 as a Sea Harrier FRS.Mk 1 conversion with a shorter forward fuselage (including a less pointed radome) and a longer rear fuselage in a combination that produced a slight decrease in overall length. The second prototype followed in March 1989, and in December 1988 the Ministry of Defence had contracted for the conversion of 33 Sea Harrier FRS.Mk 1s to the upgraded standard, and the first of these aircraft were redelivered in April 1992. In November 1993 British Aerospace received an order for 18 new-build Sea Harrier FRS.Mk 2s to complement the conversions, giving the Fleet Air Arm total to 51 aircraft.

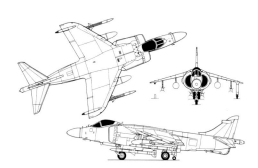

**BAe Sea Harrier FRS.Mk 2**

### Specification: BAe Sea Harrier FRS.Mk 2
**Origin:** UK
**Type:** shipborne multi-role combat aircraft
**Powerplant:** one 9752-kg (21,500-lb) dry thrust Rolls Royce Pegasus Mk 106 vectored-thrust turbofan
**Performance:** maximum speed Mach more than 1.11 or 639 kt (1185 km/h; 736 mph) at sea level with full AAM load; cruising speed 459 kt (850 km/h; 528 mph); initial rate of climb about 50,000 ft (15240 m) per minute; service ceiling 51,000 ft (15545 m); intercept radius 185 km (115 miles) on a hi-hi-hi CAP with a loiter of 90 minutes
**Weights:** (estimated) empty 5942 kg (13,100 lb); maximum take-off 11884 kg (26,200 lb)
**Dimensions:** span 7.70 m (25 ft 3 in); length 14.17 m (46 ft 6 in); height 3.71 m (12 ft 2 in); wing area 18.68 m² (201.1 sq ft)
**Armament:** two 30-mm Aden cannon, plus provision for 3629 kg (8,000 lb) of stores carried on five pylons and including four AIM-120 AMRAAM or two AMRAAM and four Sidewinder AAMs, two Harpoon or Sea Eagle anti-ship missiles and a number of other advanced weapons to complement the types carried by the Sea Harrier FRS.Mk 1

*Above: The Sea Harrier FRS.Mk 2 aerodynamic prototype was fitted with a nose-mounted test instrumentation boom.*

*Below: Sea Harrier FRS.Mk 2s (now known as FA.Mk 2s) wearing the winged fist insignia of No.899 Squadron, the training and evaluation unit for the new variant. The 'production' FRS.Mk 2 has a relocated pitot probe on the fin leading edge.*

# British Aerospace (BAC) Strikemaster

*British Aerospace Strikemaster Mk 88 of the Royal New Zealand Air Force.*

The obvious appeal of the Jet Provost as a highly developed and economical trainer prompted BAC to do what Hunting, the company that had originated the design, had lacked the funds to achieve: development of the type into a multi-role tactical aircraft able to fly both pilot training and weapon training sorties and also, should the occasion demand, go to war in the light attack and tactical reconnaissance roles. Via the **BAC.145**, sold to the Sudan as virtually an armed version of the pressurized Jet Provost T.Mk 5, BAC developed the **BAC.167 Strikemaster** by installing a more powerful version of the Viper engine and increasing the number of stores hardpoints to eight. The airframe had been strengthened several times in the course of the development of the Jet Provost and BAC.145, and in the BAC.167 it was locally reinforced yet again to make it virtually unbreakable in tactical use under even the harshest conditions.

Features include short landing gear units suitable for operation from rough airstrips, fuel housed in integral and bag tanks in the wings and in fixed tip tanks, hydraulically operated spoiler/airbrake surfaces above the wings, manual flight controls, a pressurized and airconditioned cockpit with a side-by-side pair of Martin-Baker Mk PB4 ejector seats, and comprehensive navigation and communications equipment which some customers have upgraded to include EW (electronic warfare) installations.

The first Strikemaster flew in October 1967 and the **Strikemaster Mk 80** series entered service a year later. Customers comprise Ecuador, Kenya, Kuwait, New Zealand, Oman, Saudi Arabia, Singapore, Sudan and South Yemen. The final batch of new **Strikemaster Mk 90** aircraft were delivered to the Sudan in 1984, assembly of this batch having been relocated from Warton to Hurn. Many of the Strikemasters have seen prolonged active service: for example, all 20 of the Sultan of Oman's Strikemaster Mk 82 and Mk 82A aircraft have sustained battle damage. The Strikemaster has a reputation for almost Russian toughness and longevity under the most austere of circumstances, and most still have a useful career ahead of them.

### Specification: BAe Strikemaster Mk 80
**Origin:** UK
**Type:** close-support and reconnaissance aircraft with weapons training capability
**Powerplant:** one 1547-kg (3,410-lb) dry thrust Rolls-Royce Viper Mk 535 turbojet
**Performance:** maximum speed, clean 418 kt (774 km/h; 481 mph) at 18,000 ft (5485 m); initial rate of climb 5,250 ft (1600 m) per minute; service ceiling 40,000 ft (12190 m); combat radius 397 km (247 miles) on a hi-lo-hi mission with a 1361-kg (3,000-lb) weapon load and full reserves
**Weights:** empty 2810 kg (6,195 lb); maximum take-off 5216 kg (11,500 lb)
**Dimensions:** span 11.23 m (36 ft 10 in); length 10.27 m (33 ft 8.5 in); height 3.34 m (10 ft 11.5 in); wing area 19.85 m² (213.7 sq ft)
**Armament:** two 7.62-mm (0.3-in) FN forward-firing machine-guns each with 550 rounds, plus provision for up to 1361 kg (3,000 lb) of other weapons carried on four underwing hardpoints, including gun pods, bombs, rocket-launcher pods, tanks, or a five-camera reconnaissance pod

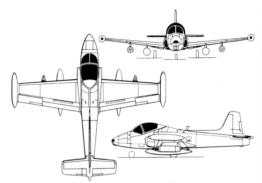

*British Aerospace Strikemaster Mk 80*

*Oman operates the Strikemaster for both weapons training and light attack duties. The type can carry small bombs and unguided rockets on its wing pylons.*

*The Saudi Arabian Strikemasters are used primarily for advanced flying training and for weapons training. The type is being supplemented and will eventually be supplanted by the Hawk.*

Role
Fighter
Close support
Counter-insurgency
Tactical strike
Strategic bomber
Tactical reconnaissance
Strategic reconnaissance
Maritime patrol
Anti-ship strike
Anti-submarine warfare
Search and rescue
Assault transport
Transport
Liaison
Trainer
Inflight-refuelling tanker
Specialized

Performance
All-weather capability
Rough field capability
STOL capability
VTOL capability
Airspeed 0-250 mph
Airspeed 250 mph-Mach 1
Airspeed Mach 1 plus
Ceiling 0-20,000 ft
Ceiling 20,000-40,000 ft
Ceiling 40,000ft plus
Range 0-1,000 miles
Range 1,000-3,000 miles
Range 3,000 miles plus

Weapons
Air-to-air missiles
Air-to-surface missiles
Cruise missiles
Cannon
Trainable guns
Naval weapons
Nuclear-capable
Rockets
'Smart' weapon kit
Weapon load 0-4,000 lb
Weapon load 4,000-15,000 lb
Weapon load 15,000 lb plus

Avionics
Electronic Counter Measures
Electronic Support Measures
Search radar
Fire control radar
Look-down/shoot-down
Terrain-following radar
Forward-looking infra-red
Laser
Television

# British Aerospace (Vickers-Armstrongs/BAC) VC10

*British Aerospace VC10 K.Mk 2 of No.101 Sqn, RAF Brize Norton.*

## Role

Fighter
Close support
Counter-insurgency
Tactical strike
Strategic bomber
Tactical reconnaissance
Strategic reconnaissance
Maritime patrol
Anti-ship strike
Anti-submarine warfare
Search and rescue
Assault transport
Transport
Liaison
Trainer
Inflight-refuelling tanker
Specialized

## Performance

All-weather capability
Rough field capability
STOL capability
VTOL capability
Airspeed 0-250 mph
Airspeed 250 mph-Mach 1
Airspeed Mach 1 plus
Ceiling 0-20,000 ft
Ceiling 20,000-40,000 ft
Ceiling 40,000ft plus
Range 0-1,000 miles
Range 1,000-3,000 miles
Range 3,000 miles plus

## Weapons

Air-to-air missiles
Air-to-surface missiles
Cruise missiles
Cannon
Trainable guns
Naval weapons
Nuclear-capable
Rockets
'Smart' weapon kit
Weapon load 0-4,000 lb
Weapon load 4,000-15,000 lb
Weapon load 15,000 lb plus

## Avionics

Electronic Counter Measures
Electronic Support Measures
Search radar
Fire control radar
Look-down/shoot-down
Terrain-following radar
Forward-looking infra-red
Laser
Television

Included in the production run of 54 **Vickers VC10** and **Super VC10** airliners were 14 aircraft for the RAF, whose **VC10 C.Mk 1** transports combined features of both civil types. Apart from having the VC10's short fuselage, almost all engineering features of the VC10 C.Mk 1 are those of the Super VC10, including uprated engines, a stronger structure, wet (integral-tank) fin, extended leading edge and increased gross weight. To meet RAF requirements the VC10 C.Mk 1 also has an APU in the tail, a strengthened floor and large cargo door for heavy freight, and a cabin laid out for 150 aft-facing seats, or mixed passenger/cargo or all cargo use, or VIP use, or casevac use with provision for up to 78 litters. One aircraft was withdrawn to flight test the Rolls-Royce RB.211 engine and was scrapped after this, but the surviving 13 aircraft have each been fitted with a inflight-refuelling probe and continue to give exemplary service with No.10 Squadron. In 1990 and 1992, Flight Refuelling was contracted to convert eight and five aircraft to **VC10 C.Mk 1(K)** partial inflight-refuelling standard with two underwing HDUs (hose-and-drogue units).

To meet an increased tanking need, No.101 Squadron in 1983-5 received nine former civil aircraft completely rebuilt by BAe Bristol. Five British Airways VC10s and four East African Airways Super VC10s became **VC10 K.Mk 2** and **VC10 K.Mk 3** tankers respectively. The two variants were generally brought to the C.Mk 1 standard but with the cabin windows plated over, cargo door sealed, five large double-skinned tanks added above the floor, and three HDUs: a Mk 17B in the rear fuselage and a Mk 32 under each wing. The VC10 K.Mk 2 carries 50802 kg (112,000 lb) of transfer fuel and the VC10 K.Mk 3 no less than 86364 kg (190,400 lb). At the front is a compartment for 17/18 passengers, and underfloor holds can carry refuelling pods or essential spares. The RAF also bought the last 14 British Airways Super VC10s, three of which were cannibalized and the rest stored for possible conversion into tankers at a later date. In March 1989 it was decided that five of these aircraft should be converted to **VC10 K.Mk 4** partial tanker configuration with three HDUs but no additional tanks.

*British Aerospace VC10 K.Mk 3*

*No.10 Sqn operates 13 VC10 C.Mk 1(K)s for global transport duties. These aircraft are often employed for transporting government officials and members of the royal family around the world.*

*The triple-point tanking capability is demonstrated by this No.101 Sqn aircraft. It is a VC10 K.Mk 2 converted from a British Airways VC10 Series 1106.*

## Specification: BAe VC 10 C.Mk 1
**Origin:** UK
**Type:** long-range transport
**Powerplant:** four 9888-kg (21,800-lb) dry thrust Rolls-Royce Conway Mk 301 turbofans
**Performance:** long-range cruising speed 369 kt (684 km/h; 425 mph) at 30,000 ft (9145 m); initial rate of climb 2,300 ft (701 m) per minute; service ceiling 42,000 ft (12800 m); range 6276 km (3,900 miles) with maximum payload
**Weights:** empty 66224 kg (146,000 lb); maximum take-off 146510 kg (323,000 lb)
**Dimensions:** span 44.55 m (146 ft 2 in); length 48.36 m (158 ft 8 in) excluding probe; height 12.04 m (39 ft 6 in); wing area 272.38 m² (2,932.0 sq ft)
**Armament:** none

# British Aerospace/McDonnell Douglas AV-8A and AV-8S Matador

*British Aerospace/McDonnell Douglas AV-8C Harrier of VMA-231, US Marine Corps, NAS Cherry Point.*

Throughout the early 1960s the US Marine Corps was urgently seeking an aircraft that could provide firepower for the support of amphibious assaults. The choice seemed to lie between an armed helicopter, or shiploads of complex prefabricated airfield hardware, or reliance on the US Navy's aircraft carriers. In 1968, however, the USMC evaluated the Hawker Siddeley Harrier and found it almost exactly the weapon of which it had dreamed. Plans were drawn up for the purchase of 114 **BAe/McDonnell Douglas AV-8A** aircraft, although this was later altered to 102 AV-8A single-seat and eight **TAV-8A** two-seat aircraft because of the latter's higher price. The aircraft were delivered from January 1971, and in 1972 were recycled through MCAS Cherry Point for adaptation to a common standard without the British inertial system, LRMTS and radar warning receiver, but with the wiring and underwing racks for Sidewinder AAMs, a manual fuel control to keep the engine running in the event of a birdstrike or other

severe disturbance, the Stencel SIII-S3 ejector seat, a non-toppling attitude and heading reference system, tactical VHF radio and, in the TAV-8A, UHF radio for command of ground forces.

The USMC pioneered the concept of VIFFing (Vectoring In Forward Flight) for improved turning capability, and accomplished a great deal with the relatively tricky and limited AV-8. From 1979 a total of 47 aircraft was reworked to AV-8C standard with airframe life extension, lift improvement devices, ALR-45 radar warning, ALE-39 chaff/flare launcher, on-board oxygen generation, secure voice link and new UHF radio.

A Spanish order was placed via the US government with final assembly by McDonnell Douglas. The purchase comprised 10 **AV-8S** (Spanish **VA-1 Matador**) and three **TAV-8S** (Spanish **VAE-1**) aircraft to improved AV-8A and TAV-8A standards respectively. These Spanish machines are the only members of the AV-8 family still in service.

**Specification:** BAe/McDonnell Douglas AV-8C
**Origin:** UK and USA
**Type:** STOVL shipborne or land-based tactical attack fighter
**Powerplant:** one 9752-kg (21,500-lb) dry thrust Rolls-Royce F402-RR-402 vectored-thrust turbofan
**Performance:** maximum speed over Mach 1, or 643 kt (1191 km/h; 740 mph) at sea level; initial rate of climb 50,000 ft (15240 m) at VTO weight; service ceiling 51,200 ft (15605 m); ferry range 3766 km (2,340 miles)
**Weights:** empty 5699 kg (12,565 lb); maximum take-off 11340 kg (25,000 lb)
**Dimensions:** span 7.70 m (25 ft 3 in); length 13.89 m (45 ft 7 in); height 3.45 m (11 ft 4 in); wing area 18.68 m² (201.1 sq ft)
**Armament:** two 30-mm Aden cannon each with 130 rounds, plus two AIM-9 Sidewinder AAMs and provision for up to 2268 kg (5,000 lb) of weapons carried on external hardpoints

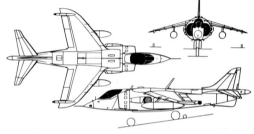

**British Aerospace/McDonnell Douglas AV-8A**

*An AV-8A of VMA-231, normally based at MCAS Cherry Point, wears an unusual winter camouflage scheme. VMA-231 was the last of the three AV-8 squadrons to form.*

*An AV-8S, locally designated VA-1 Matador, of the Spanish navy's Escuadrilla 008. The unit is based at Rota, and frequently operates from the Spanish navy's sole carrier.*

# British Aerospace/McDonnell Douglas
# T-45 Goshawk

*An operational T-45A Goshawk of Training Wing Two at Kingsville, Texas*

## Role
Fighter
Close support
Counter-insurgency
Tactical strike
Strategic bomber
Tactical reconnaissance
Strategic reconnaissance
Maritime patrol
Anti-ship strike
Anti-submarine warfare
Search and rescue
Assault transport
Transport
Liaison
Trainer
Inflight-refuelling tanker
Specialized

## Performance
All-weather capability
Rough field capability
STOL capability
VTOL capability
Airspeed 0-250 mph
Airspeed 250 mph-Mach 1
Airspeed Mach 1 plus
Ceiling 0-20.000 ft
Ceiling 20,000-40,000 ft
Ceiling 40,000ft plus
Range 0-1,000 miles
Range 1,000-3,000 miles
Range 3,000 miles plus

## Weapons
Air-to-air missiles
Air-to-surface missiles
Cruise missiles
Cannon
Trainable guns
Naval weapons
Nuclear-capable
Rockets
'Smart' weapon kit
Weapon load 0-4,000 lb
Weapon load 4,000-15,000 lb
Weapon load 15,000 lb plus

## Avionics
Electronic Counter Measures
Electronic Support Measures
Search radar
Fire control radar
Look-down/shoot-down
Terrain-following radar
Forward-looking infra-red
Laser
Television

In November 1981 the US Navy decided that in its search for a comprehensive VTXTS training system to replace the Rockwell T-2 Buckeye the clear winner was the Hawk from BAe, partnered by McDonnell Douglas and with Sperry providing academics, simulators and support. The variant selected, the **T-45 Goshawk**, differs appreciably from the Hawk T.Mk 1, notably in having full carrier capability including a strong nose-tow nose gear with twin wheels, strengthened main landing gear units of the long-stroke type, an arrester hook, and twin lateral airbrakes instead of a single ventral airbrake. Other changes include an advanced US Navy cockpit, US Navy avionics and modest use of CFRP (carbonfibre reinforced plastics) throughout the structure. The engine, like every other functioning item, has been deliberately designed not for high performance but for the lowest possible cost of procurement and operation over a service life expected to be at least 20 years and possibly 40. Fuel burn is expected to be only about 40 per cent that of the current T-2 and

McDonnell Douglas TA-4 Skyhawk, and maintenance man hours are dramatically reduced. The seat is the new NACES (Navy Aircrew Common Ejector Seat), which is basically the Martin-Baker Mk 14 zero-zero unit manufactured in the USA.

Total procurement was planned as 54 T-45B landed-based aircraft followed by 253 **T-45A** carrier-compatible aircraft, but this scheme was later revised to 300 T-45As. The first of two prototype made its first flight on 16 April 1988, but the planned in-service date of October 1989 was delayed first by USN demands for airframe and engine changes, and then by the company's December 1989 decision to transfer the whole programme from Douglas in California to McDonnell in Missouri. The first T-45A off the original Douglas production line was delivered in October 1990, the first machine from McDonnell following in December 1991. The first 96 aircraft are being completed to a reduced standard as the advanced 'glass' cockpit is being introduced only on the 97th aircraft.

**BAe/McDonnell Douglas T-45A Goshawk (prototype configuration)**

## Specification: BAe/McDonnell Douglas T-45A Goshawk
**Origin:** UK and USA
**Type:** carrier-equipped naval pilot trainer
**Powerplant:** one 2651-kg (5,845-lb) dry thrust Rolls-Royce/Turbomeca F-405-RR-401 turbofan
**Performance:** maximum speed 538 kt (997 km/h; 620 mph) at 8,000 ft (2440 m); initial climb rate 6,982 ft (2128 m) per minute; service ceiling 42,250 ft (12875 m); ferry range 1850 km (1,150b miles) with internal fuel
**Weights:** empty 4263 kg (9,399 lb); maximum take-off 5787 kg (12,758 lb) **Dimensions:** span 9.39 m (30 ft 9.75 in); length 11.97m (39 ft 3.125 in) including probe; height 4.27 m (14 ft 0 in); wing area 16.69 m² (179.6 sq ft)
**Armament:** none

*Above: The T-45A Goshawk is completely cleared for carrierborne operation, and the type regularly deploys aboard the training carrier Forrestal.*

*Below: The first prototype T-45A Goshawk was brought up to production configuration, with tall square cut fin, squared off tailplanes and wingtips, and with ventral fin, leading edge slats and aerodynamic improvements.*

# Canadair CF-5 Freedom Fighter

*Canadair CF-5A (CF-116) Freedom Fighter of No.434 (Blue Nose) Sqn, of the Canadian Armed Forces.*

In 1965 the Northrop F-5 was selected for what in 1968 became the NATO Canadian Armed Forces (Air Element). Canadair Ltd at Montreal was chosen to build the aircraft under licence in two versions which had the company design designation CL-219 but the manufacturing designations **Canadair CF-5A** and **CF-5D** for the single-seat and tandem two-seat versions respectively.

Canadair incorporated into the basic design several major improvements, the most important being uprated engines (licence-manufactured by Orenda Engines also of Montreal) and an inflight-refuelling probe. Soon after manufacture started, the Royal Netherlands air force placed an order with Canadair for 105 of the **NF-5A** variant with the wing revised for the incorporation of automatically scheduled leading-edge manoeuvring flaps, Doppler navigation system, and 1041-litre (275-US gal) drop tanks. The manufacture of these aircraft for the Netherlands air force involved the participation of Dutch companies, but this was inte-grated with CF-5 production and all assem-bly was undertaken by Canadair. In addition four CF-5Ds, with the revised designation **VF-5**, were built for Venezuela in a govern-ment-to-government transaction.

The first CF-5A flew at Cartierville on 6 May 1968, and the type entered service with the Canadian Armed Forces later in the same year with the service designation **CF-116**. The NF-5 entered Dutch service in 1969. To bring the CAF (Air Element) back up to full strength, a follow-on order was placed for 20 additional CF-5Ds, and these brought the CF-5 production total of all versions up to 240. The last aircraft were delivered in 1975, and in the mid-1990s some 80 were still in the CAF inventory, although a number of these were in store. In 1988 the CAF ordered a lift-extension upgrade of 13 CF-5A and 33 C-5D aircraft with structural revisions and improved avionics: despite this, the long-term future of the type is uncertain as Canada trims its forces. Some 15 second-hand aircraft have been sold to the Venezuelan air force.

**Specification:** Canadair CF-5A Freedom Fighter
**Origin:** USA and Canada
**Type:** fighter and light attack aircraft
**Pwerplant:** two 1950-kg (4,300-lb) afterburning thrust Orenda (General Electric) J85-CAN-15 turbojets
**Performance:** maximum speed Mach 1.4 or 849 kt (1575 km/h; 978 mph) at 36,000 ft (10970 m); initial rate of climb 32,000 ft (9750 m) per minute; service ceiling 50,850 ft (15500 m); combat radius 314 km (195 miles) at sea level with maximum fuel and two bombs with full reserves for combat and diversion
**Weights:** empty 3700 kg (8,157 lb); maximum take-off 9249 kg (20,390 lb)
**Dimensions:** span 7.87 m (25 ft 10 in ) over tiptanks); length 14.38 m (47 ft 2 in); height 4.01 m (13 ft 2 in); wing area 15.79 m² (170.0 sq ft)
**Armament:** two 20-mm M39 cannon in the upper part of the nose, plus provision for two AIM-9 Sidewinder AAMs and a wide variety of other stores, including gun pods, rocket-launcher pods and bombs, carried on underwing hardpoints

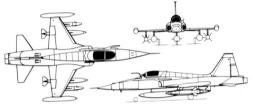

**Canadair CF-5A Freedom Fighter**

*The Koninklijke Luchtmacht operated about 70 NF-5s in five squadrons. Many received an air superiority grey colour scheme, like this NF-5B of No.316 Sqn.*

*Two Norwegian air force NF-5As are seen during a visit to RAF Gütersloh in Germany. The nearest aircraft carries on its fin the badge of the 'Flying Jokers' aerobatic display team.*

**Role**
Fighter
Close support
Counter-insurgency
Tactical strike
Strategic bomber
Tactical reconnaissance
Strategic reconnaissance
Maritime patrol
Anti-ship strike
Anti-submarine warfare
Search and rescue
Assault transport
Transport
Liaison
Trainer
Inflight-refuelling tanker
Specialized

**Performance**
All-weather capability
Rough field capability
STOL capability
VTOL capability
Airspeed 0-250 mph
Airspeed 250 mph-Mach 1
Airspeed Mach 1 plus
Ceiling 0-20,000 ft
Ceiling 20,000-40,000 ft
Ceiling 40,000ft plus
Range 0-1,000 miles
Range 1,000-3,000 miles
Range 3,000 miles plus

**Weapons**
Air-to-air missiles
Air-to-surface missiles
Cruise missiles
Cannon
Trainable guns
Naval weapons
Nuclear-capable
Rockets
'Smart' weapon kit
Weapon load 0-4,000 lb
Weapon load 4,000-15,000 lb
Weapon load 15,000 lb plus

**Avionics**
Electronic Counter Measures
Electronic Support Measures
Search radar
Fire control radar
Look-down/shoot-down radar
Terrain-following radar
Forward-looking infra-red
Laser
Television

# Canadair CL-41 Tutor

*Canadair CL-41G-5 Tebuan of the Royal Malaysian Air Force.*

### Role
Fighter
Close support
Counter-insurgency
Tactical strike
Strategic bomber
Tactical reconnaissance
Strategic reconnaissance
Maritime patrol
Anti-ship strike
Anti-submarine warfare
Search and rescue
Assault transport
Transport
Liaison
Trainer
Inflight-refuelling tanker
Specialized

### Performance
All-weather capability
Rough field capability
STOL capability
VTOL capability
Airspeed 0-250 mph
Airspeed 250 mph-Mach 1
Airspeed Mach 1 plus
Ceiling 0-20,000 ft
Ceiling 20,000-40,000 ft
Ceiling 40,000ft plus
Range 0-1,000 miles
Range 1,000-3,000 miles
Range 3,000 miles plus

### Weapons
Air-to-air missiles
Air-to-surface missiles
Cruise missiles
Cannon
Trainable guns
Naval weapons
Nuclear-capable
Rockets
'Smart' weapon kit
Weapon load 0-4,000 lb
Weapon load 4,00-15,000 lb
Weapon load 15,000 lb plus

### Avionics
Electronic Counter Measures
Electronic Support Measures
Search radar
Fire control radar
Look-down/shoot-down
Terrain-following radar
Forward-looking infra-red
Laser
Television

Standard jet trainer of the Canadian Armed Forces, the **Canadair CL-41** has the service designation **CT-114** and the name **Tutor**. It was an important aircraft for Canada, for not only was it the first aircraft ever designed by Canadair, and also financed by the company, but also launched Pratt & Whitney Canada into gas turbines with the design and manufacture of the JT-12 engine. A neat stressed-skin aircraft, the CL-4l has a low-set wing, short landing gear units, side-by-side dual controls in a pressurized cockpit, an upward-opening clamshell canopy, door-type fuselage airbrakes, and wing-root air inlets for the engine.

The prototype made its maiden flight on 13 January 1960. The day before the official evaluation of the type was due to begin, the canopy was inadvertently jettisoned in flight: Canadair managed to locate the errant item, which was back in place next day! The production aircraft introduced a number of changes, by far the biggest being a switch from the JT12 to the General Electric CJ610, made in Canada as the J85-CAN-40. Production orders totalled 190, delivered in 1963-6 for service with

the designation **CT-114**. Standard aircraft at CFB Moose Jaw are unpainted except for bright red nose, wingtips and tail. Aircraft of the official aerobatic team were originally golden, as 'The Golden Centennaires', but are today 'The Snowbirds' with a red/white/blue livery and with an all-red 'Red Knight' solo aircraft. Reliability is excellent and service life has been extended to the mid-1990s, when there are still 140 aircraft available, although some are in storage.

In 1966 the Royal Malaysian air force ordered 20 examples of a modified version designated **CL-41G-5 Tebuan** (wasp). These have the 1338-kg (2,950-lb) dry thrust J85-CAN-J4 turbojet, six underwing hardpoints for an external load of up to 1814 kg (4,000 lb), zero-zero ejector seats, long-stroke landing gear units strengthened for rough-field operation, and other detail changes. Of these six remained on strength in 1986, but were retired shortly after this time. Total CL-41 production was 212 including the prototype and the sole CL-41R with the nose and NASARR radar of the Canadair (Lockheed) CF-104 Starfighter.

**Canadair CL-41 Tutor**

### Specification: Canadair CT-114 Tutor
**Origin:** Canada
**Type:** pilot trainer
**Powerplant:** one 1338-kg (2,950-lb) thrust Orenda (General Electric) J85-CAN-40 or J85-CAN-J4 turbojet
**Performance:** maximum speed 430 kt (797 km/h; 495mph); service ceiling 43,000 ft (13100 m); range 1000 km (621 miles) with internal fuel
**Weights:** empty 2220 kg (4,895 lb); maximum take-off 3532 kg (7,787 lb)
**Dimensions:** span 11.13 m (36 ft 6 in); length 9.75 m (32 ft 0 in); height 2.76 m (9 ft 1 in); wing area 20.44 m² (220.0 sq ft)
**Armament:** none

*These are Canadair CL-41 (CT-114) Tutors operated by No.2 CFFTS at Moose Jaw in Saskatchewan. The CL-41 was the first aircraft designed by Canadair, and has seen service into the mid-1990s.*

*The CL-41 has been the mount of Canada 's aerobatic team for many years, first with 'The Golden Centennaires' and then with 'The Snowbirds', who fly from Moose Jaw.*

# CASA C-212 Aviocar

*CASA C-212 Aviocar of the Spanish air force.*

The **CASA C-212 Aviocar** was designed by CASA, Spain's largest aircraft manufacturer, under air ministry contract for replacement of Spain's current piston-engine transports. The first C-212 flew on 26 March 1971.

An all-metal machine, the C-212 is a simple and economical design, essentially a C-130 on a much reduced twin-engined scale and without pressurization. A basic requirement was the ability to operate from austere rough airstrips without ground facilities and with an available run of 400 m (1,310 ft). The cabin of the original **C-212 Series 100** has a rectangular cross-section with internal dimensions of 5.0 m (16 ft 5 in) usable length, 2.0 m (6 ft 6.5 in) width and 1.7 m (5 ft 7 in) height. A full-section rear ramp/door can be used for loading vehicles, or for truck-bed loading of cargo, and can be opened in flight for paradropping of freight items. Accommodation includes two pilots plus 19 passengers, or up to 2000 kg (4,409 lb) of cargo, or 15 paratroops and an instructor, or 12 litters and three sitting casualties plus attendants.

CASA delivered 10 development and 125 C-212 Series 100 production aircraft, and a further 29 were made in a partnership deal by PT Nurtanio in Indonesia. In 1979 the production line switched to the stretched **C-212 Series 200**, of which some 240 were delivered with more powerful engines, increased weights and a stretched fuselage giving a usable cabin length of 6.5 m (21 ft 4 in) for 23 passengers, or 24 equipped troops, or 23 paratroops, or 2770 kg (6,107 lb) of cargo.

By 1986 total sales of all versions had reached 400, of which half were military. Production by CASA and Nurtanio continued, a new version marketed from that time being the **C-212 Series 300** with greater weight and span, and many new features. Subvariants of the **C-212 Series 300M** specifically military model include the **C-212 Series 300ASW** anti-submarine model with specialized electronics and provision for armament, the **C-212 Series 300 Elint/ECM** special-missions model with a customer-specified electronics, and the **C-212 Series 300MP** maritime patrol model with specialized electronics but no armament. Sales have been made to air forces and paramilitary customers all over the world, partly because the Aviocar is the cheapest certificated aircraft in its class.

**Specification:** CASA C-212 Series 300M Aviocar
**Origin:** Spain
**Type:** STOL utility transport
**Powerplant:** two Garrett TPE331-10R-513C turboprops each flat-rated at 671 kW (900 shp)
**Performance:** maximum cruising speed 191 kt (354 km/h; 220 mph) at 10,000 ft (3050 m); initial rate of climb 1,630 ft (497 m) per minute; service ceiling 26,000 ft (7925 m); range 835 km (519 miles) with maximum payload or 2680 km (1,665 miles) with maximum fuel and a 2,628-lb (1192-kg) payload
**Weights:** empty 9,700 lb (4400 kg); maximum take-off 17,637 lb (8000 kg)
**Dimensions:** span 20.28 m (66 ft 6.5 in); length 16.15 m (52 ft 11.75 in); height 6.60 m (21 ft 7.75 in); wing area 41.0 m² (441.33 sq ft)
**Armament:** none

*CASA C-212 Aviocar*

**A CASA C-212 Aviocar of the Comando de Aviación del Ejercito de Chile, which operates six of these aircraft. The Chilean naval air arm operates a further four of the type.**

**A CASA C-212 Aviocar of the Spanish air force, which uses the type for tactical and assault transport, search and rescue, paratroop transport, and various support duties.**

**Role**
Fighter
Close support
Counter-insurgency
Tactical strike
Strategic bomber
Tactical reconnaissance
Strategic reconnaissance
Maritime patrol
Anti-ship strike
Anti-submarine warfare
Search and rescue
Assault transport
Transport
Liaison
Trainer
Inflight-refuelling tanker
Specialized

**Performance**
All-weather capability
Rough field capability
STOL capability
VTOL capability
Airspeed 0-250 mph
Airspeed 250 mph-Mach 1
Airspeed Mach 1 plus
Ceiling 0-20,000 ft
Ceiling 20,000-40,000 ft
Ceiling 40,000ft plus
Range 0-1,000 miles
Range 1,000-3,000 miles
Range 3,000 miles plus

**Weapons**
Air-to-air missiles
Air-to-surface missiles
Cruise missiles
Cannon
Trainable guns
Naval weapons
Nuclear-capable
Rockets
'Smart' weapon kit
Weapon load 0-4,000 lb
Weapon load 4,000-15,000 lb
Weapon load 15,000 lb plus

**Avionics**
Electronic Counter Measures
Electronic Support Measures
Search radar
Fire control radar
Look-down/shoot-down
Terrain-following radar
Forward-looking infra-red
Laser
Television

# CASA C- 101 Aviojet

*CASA C-101 Aviojet of the Spanish air force.*

## Role

Fighter
Close support
Counter-insurgency
Tactical strike
Strategic bomber
Tactical reconnaissance
Strategic reconnaissance
Maritime patrol
Anti-ship strike
Anti-submarine warfare
Search and rescue
Assault transport
Transport
Liaison
Trainer
Inflight-refuelling tanker
Specialized

## Performance

All-weather capability
Rough field capability
STOL capability
VTOL capability
Airspeed 0-250 mph
Airspeed 250 mph-Mach 1
Airspeed Mach 1 plus
Ceiling 0-20.000 ft
Ceiling 20.000-40.000 ft
Ceiling 40.000ft plus
Range 0-1,000 miles
Range 1,000-3,000 miles
Range 3.000 miles plus

## Weapons

Air-to-air missiles
Air-to-surface missiles
Cruise missiles
Cannon
Trainable guns
Naval weapons
Nuclear-capable
Rockets
'Smart' weapon kit
Weapon load 0-4,000 lb
Weapon load 4,000-15,000 lb
Weapon load 15,000 lb plus

## Avionics

Electronic Counter Measures
Electronic Support Measures
Search radar
Fire control radar
Look-down/shoot-down
Terrain-following radar
Forward-looking infra-red
Laser
Television

Designed by CASA with technical assistance from Northrop and MBB, the **CASA C-101 Aviojet** jet trainer has been rewarded by substantial sales to the EdA (Spanish air force), which calls it the **E.25 Mirlo** (blackbird), and the Chilean air force which uses the T-36 and **A-36 Halcón** (hawk) versions.

Features include a single high-bypass-ratio turbofan good fuel economy, stepped tandem Martin-Baker Mk 10L zero-zero ejector seats, a pressurized cockpit with separate canopies that hinge open to the right, levered-suspension landing gear units with a non-steerable nosewheel, fuel contained in integral tanks in the wings and a flexible cell in the fuselage with pressure fuelling, fixed wing leading edge, slotted flaps, powered ailerons but manual elevators and rudder, and a tailplane with electric variable incidence for trimming.

The most unusual feature is that the provision for external stores under the wings is complemented by the volume of a large fuselage bay beneath the rear cockpit. This can carry armament (see specification) or items such as a reconnaissance camera, ECM jammer, or laser designator. The original version, of which 88 were built, is the **C-101EB** (E.25 Mirlo) that first flew in prototype form on 27 June 1977 with the 1588-kg (3,500-lb) dry thrust Garrett TFE731-2-2J turbofan. The **C-101BB** is the armed export version with the 1678-kg (3,700-lb)dry thrust TFE731-3-1J; production totals four for Honduras and 16 for Chile (T-36), of which all but the first four are being assembled and increasingly manufactured by ENAER in Chile.

The latest production model is the **C-101CC** light attack version with the TFE731-5-1J engine possessing a military power reserve rating of 2132 kg (4,700 lb), and provision for a heavier external load. The prototype flew In November 1983, and of 24 A-36 Halcóns ordered by Chile, 19 were partially made and assembled by ENAER; another 16 were cold to Jordan. In May 1985 CASA flew the first **C-101DD** enhanced trainer with the TFE731-5-1J engine, GEC Ferranti HUD and other new avionics. No orders for this model had been received by the mid-1990s.

## Specification: CASA C-101CC Aviojet

**Origin:** Spain
**Type:** light attack aircraft with advanced flying/weapons training capabilities
**Powerplant:** one 1950-kg (4,300-lb) dry thrust Garrett TFE731-5-1J turbofan
**Performance:** maximum speed 415 kt (769 km/h; 478 mph) at sea level and 450 kt (834 km/h; 518 mph) at 15,000 ft (4570 m); initial rate of climb 5,300 ft (1615 m) per minute; service ceiling 42,000 ft (12800 m); range 3706 km (2,303 miles); combat radius 370 km (230 miles) on a lo-lo-lo close support mission with weapons and 50-minute loiter over target
**Weights:** empty 3340 kg (7,666 lb): maximum take-off 6300 kg (13,889 lb)
**Dimensions:** span 10.60 m (34 ft 9.3 in); length 12.50 m (41 ft 0.1 in); height 4.25 m (13 ft 11.3 in); wing area 20.0 m² (215.29 sq ft)
**Armament:** fuselage bay can house 30-mm DEFA cannon or two 12.7-mm (0.5-in) M3 machine-guns, and six wing pylons can carry up to 2250 kg (4,960 kg) of disposable stores

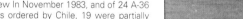

*CASA C-101 Aviojet*

*A camouflaged **CASA C-101EB** Aviojet (E.25 Mirlo) of the Spanish air force, which uses the type for advanced and weapons training. This aircraft is believed to belong to 41 Grupo at Zaragoza.*

*A formation of four **CASA C-101** Aviojet (E.25 Mirlo) trainers of the Academia General del Aire at San Javier. The C-101 has also been exported to Chile, Honduras and Jordan.*

# Cessna Model 318E (A-37 Dragonfly)

*Cessna A-37B Dragonfly of the Chilean air force.*

Around 1960 there was a sharp increase in American interest in light COIN (counter-insurgency) aircraft for so-called brushfire wars. The USAF set up a Special Air Warfare Center and began the evaluation of suitable aircraft, one being the Cessna T-37B trainer. Later two of these machines were re-engined with the General Electric J85 turbojet offering more than twice the power of the original Continental J69 turbojets, and these YAT-37D aircraft were tested with increasing loads of external stores until the maximum take-off weight reached 6350 kg (14,000 lb), well over twice that of the T-37B.

US involvement in Vietnam led to a 1966 contract for the conversion of 39 T-37B trainers to **A-37A Dragonfly** standard with J85-5 engines, a much stronger structure, fixed tip tanks to increase internal fuel to 1920 litres (1,507 US gal), and eight underwing pylons for a great diversity of weapons and other stores. In late 1967 a squadron equipped with 25 A-37As served in Vietnam, and eventually remained in that country.

In 1967 the design was finalized of the definitive **A-37B**, and by 1977 a total of 577

had been delivered. Most were supplied to friendly nations, although moderately large numbers were transferred to the US Air National Guard as **OA-37B** forward air control aircraft. Very economical to operate, the A-37B has a further strengthened and refined airframe, hydraulically operated landing gear, ventral airbrake, slotted flaps, unpressurized cockpit with side-by-side fixed seats, flak curtains of layered nylon in place of armour, very comprehensive night and bad-weather avionics (except for any sensors or night vision devices), an inflight-refuelling probe on the nose, and provision four drop tanks on the inner pylons. All the flight controls are manual, the tailplane being fixed, although all three axes have electric trim tabs.

One of the major recipients was the VNAF (air force of South Vietnam), and captured examples are some of very few US types still flown by the Vietnamese People's air force. Most recipients were in Latin America (Paraguay, Uruguay, Chile, Peru, Ecuador, Guatemala and Honduras among them), and a squadron of 16 was supplied to Thailand.

## Specification: Cessna A-37B Dragonfly
**Origin:** USA
**Type:** light attack and reconnaissance aircraft
**Powerplant:** two 1293-kg (2,850-lb) dry thrust General Electric J85-GE-17A turbojets
**Performance:** maximum speed 440 kt (816 km/h; 507 mph) at 16,000 ft (4875 m); maximum cruising speed 425 kt (787 km/h; 489 mph) at 25,000 ft (7620 m); initial rate of climb 6990 ft (2130 m) per minute; service ceiling 41,765 ft (12730 m); range 740 km (460 miles) with 1860-kg (4,100-lb) warload
**Weights:** empty 2817 kg (6,211 lb); maximum take-off 6350 kg (14,000 lb)
**Dimensions:** span 10.93 m (35 ft 10.3 in) including tip tanks; length 8.62 m (28 ft 3.4 in) excluding probe; height 2.70 m (8 ft 10.3 in); wing area 17.09 m² (183.9 sq ft)
**Armament:** one 7.62-mm (0.3-in) GAU-2 Minigun six-barrel machine-gun, and provision for more than 2268 kg (5,000 lb) of bombs, rocket-launcher pods, gun pods and other tactical stores on eight underwing hardpoints

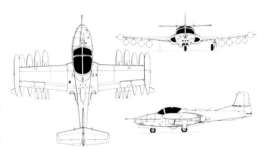

**Cessna Model 318E (A-37B Dragonfly)**

*A Cessna A-37B Dragonfly of the Chilean air force, a major user of this handy little COIN/attack machine. The aircraft wears the original colour scheme, which has now been replaced.*

*Another Latin American operator of the Cessna A-37B is the Peruvian air force. Thirty-six were delivered, and serve alongside Canberras with Grupo 21 and Mirages with Grupo 13.*

| Role |
| --- |
| Fighter |
| Close support |
| Counter-insurgency |
| Tactical strike |
| Strategic bomber |
| Tactical reconnaissance |
| Strategic reconnaissance |
| Maritime patrol |
| Anti-ship strike |
| Anti-submarine warfare |
| Search and rescue |
| Assault transport |
| Transport |
| Liaison |
| Trainer |
| Inflight-refuelling tanker |
| Specialized |

| Performance |
| --- |
| All-weather capability |
| Rough field capability |
| STOL capability |
| VTOL capability |
| Airspeed 0-250 mph |
| Airspeed 250 mph-Mach 1 |
| Airspeed Mach 1 plus |
| Ceiling 0-20,000 ft |
| Ceiling 20,000-40,000 ft |
| Ceiling 40,000ft plus |
| Range 0-1,000 miles |
| Range 1,000-3,000 miles |
| Range 3,000 miles plus |

| Weapons |
| --- |
| Air-to-air missiles |
| Air-to-surface missiles |
| Cruise missiles |
| Cannon |
| Trainable guns |
| Naval weapons |
| Nuclear-capable |
| Rockets |
| 'Smart' weapon kit |
| Weapon load 0-4,000 lb |
| Weapon load 4,000-15,000 lb |
| Weapon load 15,000 lb plus |

| Avionics |
| --- |
| Electronic Counter Measures |
| Electronic Support Measures |
| Search radar |
| Fire control radar |
| Look-down/shoot-down |
| Terrain-following radar |
| Forward-looking infra-red |
| Laser |
| Television |

# Cessna O-2 and Model 337 Skymaster

**Cessna O-2A of the Sri Lankan air force.**

### Role
Fighter
Close support
Counter-insurgency
Tactical strike
Strategic bomber
Tactical reconnaissance
Strategic reconnaissance
Maritime patrol
Anti-ship strike
Anti-submarine warfare
Search and rescue
Assault transport
Transport
Liaison
Inflight-refuelling tanker
Trainer
Specialized

### Performance
All-weather capability
Rough field capability
STOL capability
VTOL capability
Airspeed 0-250 mph
Airspeed 250 mph-Mach 1
Airspeed Mach 1 plus
Ceiling 0-20,000 ft
Ceiling 20,000-40,000 ft
Ceiling 40,000ft plus
Range 0-1,000 miles
Range 1,000-3,000 miles
Range 3,000 miles plus

### Weapons
Air-to-air missiles
Air-to-surface missiles
Cruise missiles
Cannon
Trainable guns
Naval weapons
Nuclear-capable
Rockets
'Smart' weapon kit
Weapon load 0-4,000 lb
Weapon load 4,000-15,000 lb
Weapon load 15,000 lb plus

### Avionics
Electronic Counter Measures
Electronic Support Measures
Search radar
Fire control radar
Look-down/shoot-down
Terrain-following radar
Forward-looking infra-red
Laser
Television

On 28 February 1961 there flew the prototype Cessna Model 336 Skymaster, which was the company's attempt to produce a twin that could be easily and safely flown by any private pilot, without needing a twin rating. The unusual push/pull layout did not significantly degrade flight performance or increase cabin noise, and the Model 336 and later **Cessna Model 337 Skymaster** (largely redesigned and fitted with retractable landing gear) sold well into the 4/6-seat civil market, a proportion being made by Reims Aviation in France. The Model 337 is an all-metal machine with single wing bracing struts, manual flight controls (with twin rudders), electric flaps, hydraulic landing gear and optional pneumatic de-icers on the wings and tail.

In 1967-70 Cessna delivered to the USAF 501 of a FAC (forward air control) version designated **O-2A**; another 12 were supplied to the Iranian air force. The O-2A was equipped for reconnaissance, target identification and marking, ground/air co-ordination and damage assessment. Comprehensive radio equipment was fitted, as well as four wing pylons for a wide range of stores and equipment including light weapons.

In 1968 Cessna also delivered 31 **O-2B** psy-war (psychological warfare) aircraft. These were unused ex-civil machines equipped with a massive broadcasting system with three highly directional 600-watt speakers. Other equipment included a leaflet dispenser. Almost all the O-2s saw combat duty in Vietnam.

Only prototypes were made of the twin-turboprop O-2TT with Allison 250 (T63) engines. Among numerous Model 337 variants produced by Reims was the **FTMA Milirole**, first flown on 26 May 1970. This was a versatile military aircraft able to carry two pilots side-by-side (as in the O-2) and either four passengers or two litters. It had four underwing pylons, and STOL performance with special high-lift flaps. Small numbers of commercial Model 337s were sold to foreign air forces and navies, various sub-species having different designations.

## Specification: Cessna O-2A
**Origin:** USA
**Type:** FAC and observation aircraft
**Powerplant:** two 157-kW (210-hp) Teledyne Continental IO-360-C/D six-cylinder horizontally opposed air-cooled piston engines
**Performance:** maximum speed 173 kt (320 km/h; 199 mph) at sea level; initial rate of climb 1,100 ft (334 m) per minute; service ceiling 18,000 ft (5490 m); range 1705 km (1,060 miles)
**Weights:** empty 1291 kg (2,848 lb); maximum take-off 2450 kg (5,400 lb)
**Dimensions:** span 11.63 m (38 ft 2 in); length 9.07 m (29 ft 9 in); height 2.84 m (9 ft 4 in); wing area 18.81 m² (202.5 sq ft)
**Armament:** four underwing pylons can carry 7.62-mm (0.3-in) Minigun pods and/or a variety of rocket-launcher pods

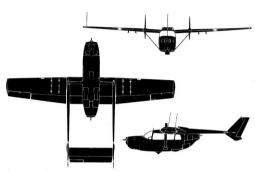

**Cessna O-2A**

**A Cessna O-2A of VA-122, US Navy. The US Navy's O-2As were used for a variety of support and liaison tasks, but only a small number were operated.**

**The Portuguese air force operated the Cessna FTB 337G mainly with Esquadra 401 of Grupo 12 and Esquadrons 701 and 702 of Grupo 21.**

# Convair QF-106 Delta Dart

*Convair F-106A Delta Dart of the 87th Fighter interceptor Squadron, USAF.*

During the frantic redesign of the F-102 Delta Dagger all-weather interceptor in 1954, it became obvious that a much better aircraft could be created. Instead of modifying an imperfect shape to conform to the area rule (a newly discovered formula for minimum transonic drag) the aircraft could be designed to obey the rule from the start, and with the more powerful J75 turbojet the maximum speed might be twice as high as the Mach 1.25 limit of the F-102. Accordingly, in 1955, the USAF ordered the F-102B. but this emerged as a totally new aircraft and was redesignated as the **Convair F-106A Delta Dart**.

Compared with the F-102A, the F-106A had a similar wing but a new fuselage with slimmer lines, completely new engine inlets moved right back to the wing root leading edges, a broad square-topped fin, twin steerable nosewheels, and, most important of all, a new-generation radar, fire-control and missile system. Unlike that of its predecessor, the F-106A's development programme went very well. The first F-106A (there was no prototype) flew on 26 December 1956, and

by far the largest development task was clearing bugs in the Hughes MA-1 integrated fire-control system and linking this with the nation-wide SAGE (Semi-Automatic Ground Environment) air- defence system. Deliveries to USAF Air (later Aerospace) Defense Command began in July 1959, and Convair delivered 277 F-106A interceptors as well as 63 **F-106B** tandem dual-control trainers with full combat capability.

In the event this total was not enough to meet the demands of an unexpected service life of almost 30 years. Almost continuous updating gave the F-106 a new ejector seat, vertical-tape instruments, new onboard systems, an upgraded MA-1 fire-control system, an internal gun and sensitive IR seeker. The last aircraft were retired in the later 1980s, and numbers have been converted to the **Honeywell/Convair QF-106A** standard as ground-controlled target drones for missile trials with two propane burners under the wing to increase the type's IR signature. The first QF-106A was completed in 1990, and the USAF plans the conversion of an eventual 194 aircraft to this standard.

**Specification:** Honeywell/Convair QF-106A Delta Dart
**Origin:** USA
**Type:** pilotable or remotely controlled target drone
**Powerplant:** one 11113-kg (24,500-lb) afterburning thrust Pratt & Whitney J75-P-17 turbojet
**Performance:** maximum speed 2.31 or 1,290 kt (2390 km/h: 1,485 mph) at high altitude; initial rate of climb 30,000 ft (9145 m) per minute; service ceiling 58,000 ft (17680 m)
**Weight:** normal take-off 16012 kg (35,500 lb)
**Dimensions:** span 11.67 m (38 ft 3.5 in); length 21.56 m (70 ft 9.75 in); height 6.18 m (20 ft 3.2 in); wing area 64.83 m² (697.83 sq ft)
**Armament:** now not used, but did comprise four Hughes AIM-4F (radar) or AIM-4G (IR) Falcon AAMs and either two AIR-2A Genie or AIR-2B Super Genie nuclear rockets or one 20-mm M61 cannon in an internal bay

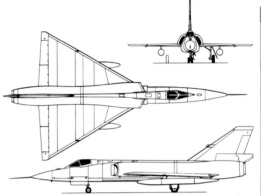

**Convair F-106A Delta Dart**

*The Air Defense Weapons Center at Tyndall AFB, Florida, used the F-106 in small numbers. An F-106B of the 96th Fighter Interceptor Training Squadron is seen here.*

*One of the last operators of the F-106 was the New Jersey Air National Guard. The 119th Fighter Interceptor Squadron, 177th Fighter Interceptor Group, flew the type from Atlantic City Airport.*

## Role
Fighter
Close support
Counter-insurgency
Tactical strike
Strategic bomber
Tactical reconnaissance
Strategic reconnaissance
Maritime patrol
Anti-ship strike
Anti-submarine warfare
Search and rescue
Assault transport
Transport
Liaison
Trainer
Inflight-refuelling tanker
Specialized

## Performance
All-weather capability
Rough field capability
STOL capability
VTOL capability
Airspeed 0-250 mph
Airspeed 250 mph-Mach 1
Airspeed Mach 1 plus
Ceiling 0-20,000 ft
Ceiling 20,000-40,000 ft
Ceiling 40,000ft plus
Range 0-1,000 miles
Range 1,000-3,000 miles
Range 3,000 miles plus

## Weapons
Air-to-air missiles
Air-to-surface missiles
Cruise missiles
Cannon
Trainable guns
Naval weapons
Nuclear-capable
Rockets
'Smart' weapon kit
Weapon load 0-4,000 lb
Weapon load 4,000-15,000 lb
Weapon load 15,000 lb plus

## Avionics
Electronic Counter Measures
Electronic Support Measures
Search radar
Fire control radar
Look-down/shoot-down
Terrain-following radar
Forward-looking infra-red
Laser
Television

# Dassault Br.1150 Atlantic 1

*Dassault Br.1150 Atlantic 1 of the Pakistani navy.*

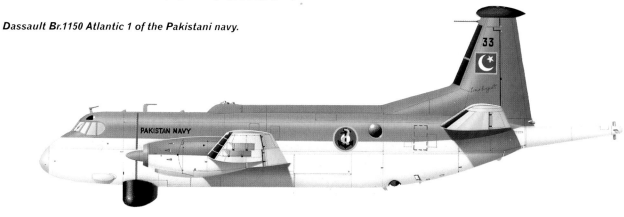

### Role
Fighter
Close support
Counter-insurgency
Tactical strike
Strategic bomber
Tactical reconnaissance
Strategic reconnaissance
Maritime patrol
Anti-ship strike
Anti-submarine warfare
Search and rescue
Assault transport
Transport
Liaison
Trainer
Inflight-refuelling tanker
Specialized

### Performance
All-weather capability
Rough field capability
STOL capability
VTOL capability
Airspeed 0-250 mph
Airspeed 250 mph-Mach 1
Airspeed Mach 1 plus
Ceiling 0-20,000 ft
Ceiling 20,000-40,000 ft
Ceiling 40,000ft plus
Range 0-1,000 miles
Range 1,000-3,000 miles
Range 3,000 miles plus

### Weapons
Air-to-air missiles
Air-to-surface missiles
Cruise missiles
Cannon
Trainable guns
Naval weapons
Nuclear-capable
Rockets
'Smart' weapon kit
Weapon load 0-4,000 lb
Weapon load 4,000-15,000 lb
Weapon load 15,000 lb plus

### Avionics
Electronic Counter Measures
Electronic Support Measures
Search radar
Fire control radar
Look-down/shoot-down
Terrain-following radar
Forward-looking infra-red
Laser
Television

Whereas all other widely used long-range land-based maritime patrol and ASW aircraft are mere conversions of civil airliners, the **Breguet Br.1150** was a 'clean sheet of paper' aircraft designed, before Breguet's merger with Dassault, specifically for these roles. It was the winner of a NATO competition in 1958 which attracted 27 designs from seven nations. A consortium called SECBAT was formed to share manufacturing work, with companies in France, West Germany, the Netherlands and Belgium being the original members, and with the UK and the USA sharing in the engines and equipment. Later Italian industry also received some work; on the other hand, Belgium never bought any.

A design of great merit, the Br.1150 uses a high proportion of light-alloy honeycomb sandwich to give a smooth skin devoid of irregularities. The capacious fuselage houses two pilots, three observers and, in the central tactical compartment, a tactical co-ordinator, a navigator, two sonics (sonobuoy) operators, a radar operator, a radio operator and MAD/ECM operator. The MAD sensor is at the tip of the long tail boom, an ESM receiver installation is housed in the prominent fin cap, and the Thomson-CSF radar is extended in a retractable 'dustbin' ahead of the very large weapons bay.

Production comprised 40 for the French Aéronavale, 20 for the West German Marineflieger, and (in a slightly modified second batch) nine for the Dutch Marine Luchtvaartdienst and 18 for the Italian Marinavia. Subsequently three of the French Atlantics were transferred to Pakistan. In service the Atlantic proved most efficient, and was able to undertake a great variety of tasks, although those of the Dutch MLD have been replaced by Lockheed Orions. Surviving Atlantics have been subjected to varying amounts of updating, and MFG 3 of the Marineflieger put its remaining 15 through a major revision with new search radar and extensive Loral ESM/ECM (five becoming special ESM platforms). France is buying the 'new-generation' Atlantique, the original type as a consequence being redesignated **Atlantic 1**.

## Specification: Dassault Br.1150 Atlantic 1
**Origin:** France but built by five-nation SECBAT consortium
**Type:** maritime patrol and ASW aircraft
**Powerplant:** two 4638-ekW (6,220-ehp) Rolls-Royce Tyne Mk 21 turboprops
**Performance:** maximum speed 355 kt (658 km/h; 409 mph); patrol speed 169 kt (315 km/h; 195 mph); service ceiling 32,810 ft (10000 m); endurance 18 hours; range 7970 km (4,950 miles) with 10 per cent reserve
**Weights:** empty 24000 kg (52,900 lb); maximum take-off 43500 kg (95,900 lb)
**Dimensions:** span 36.30 m (119 ft 1 in); length 31.75 m (104 ft 2 in); height 11.33 m (37 ft 2 in); wing area 120.34 m² (1,295.3 sq ft)
**Armament:** internal bay carries up to nine torpedoes of various kinds, or depth charges and other stores; four underwing pylons carry rockets or ASMs

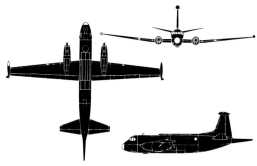

*Dassault Br.1150 Atlantic 1*

*Germany's MFG 3, based at Nordholz, uses the Atlantic 1 for ASW and patrol duties, but also has a small flight of Sigint-configured machines. This aircraft may be a Sigint trainer.*

*Flottilles 21F, 22F, 23F and 24F are the Aéronavale's front-line Atlantic 1 units, and are based at Nimes-Garons and Lann-Bihoué. This Atlantic is seen on a visit to RNAS Yeovilton.*

# Dassault-Breguet Atlantique 2

*Dassault Atlantique 2 prototype.*

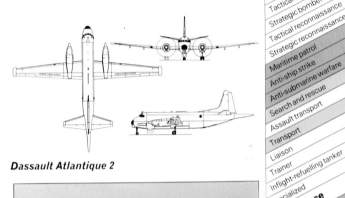

Originally called the ANG (Atlantic Nouvelle Génération, or new-generation Atlantic), the **Dassault Atlantique 2** was intended as a multi-national programme to replace the Atlantic (now Atlantic 1) with its various users. At present it seems that France will remain the only customer, although that country's requirement for 42 aircraft makes the project viable even if the rate of manufacture is too low for competitive costing.

After very prolonged studies, the Atlantique 2 was planned as a minimum-change aircraft with totally new avionics, systems and equipment packaged into an airframe/powerplant combination differing only in ways to improve life, reduce costs and minimize maintenance. Structural changes include detail redesign to achieve a 30,000-hour fatigue life, improved bonding and anti-corrosion protection, and better inter-panel sealing. An Astadyne gas turbine auxiliary power unit is fitted, and production machines may later have new Ratier-Figeac

propellers with larger composite blades to replace the British design adopted for the Atlantic 1.

Sensors include the Thomson-CSF Iguane frequency-agile radar with a new interrogator and decoder, a SAT/TRT FLIR in a chin turret, over 100 sonobuoys in the rear fuselage, a new Crouzet MAD in the long tailboom, and the Thomson-CSF ARAR 13 ESM installation with frequency analysis at the top of the fin and D/F in the new wingtip nacelles. All processors, databuses and sensor links are of standard digital form, navaids include an inertial system and Navstar satellite receiver, and every part of the avionics and communications has been upgraded. It is difficult to compare the ATL 1 and ATL 2 numerically, but with minimal airframe changes the new aircraft might be said to do five times as good a job. The first ATL flew in May 1981 and production deliveries began in October 1988 for the type to become operational in February 1991.

**Specification:** Dassault Atlantique 2
**Origin:** France
**Type:** maritime patrol and ASW aircraft
**Powerplant:** two 4638-ekW (6,220-ehp) Rolls-Royce Tyne Mk 21 turboprops
**Performance:** maximum speed 350 kt (648 km/h; 402 mph) at optimum altitude; low-level patrol speed 170 kt (315 km/h; 195 mph); initial rate of climb 2,900 ft (884 m) per minute; service ceiling 30,000 ft (9145 m); maximum endurance 18 hours; ferry range 9075 km (5,635 miles)
**Weights:** empty 25600 kg (56,438 lb); maximum take-off 46200 kg (101,850 lb)
**Dimensions:** span 37.42 m (122 ft 9.2 in) including ESM pods; length 32.63 m (107 ft 0.6 in); height 10.89 m (35 ft 8.7 in); wing area 120.34 m² (1,295.3 sq ft)
**Armament:** internal bay can house eight Mk 46 torpedoes and all NATO bombs and depth charges, one load being an AM.39 Exocet and three torpedoes; up to 3500 kg (7,717 lb) of stores can also be carried on four underwing pylons

**Dassault Atlantique 2**

*The second prototype Atlantique 2 is seen landing at Farnborough after an SBAC display. No foreign orders have been received for the aircraft, but it will see widespread use with the Aéronavale.*

*The Atlantique 2, originally dubbed the ANG (Atlantic Nouvelle Génération), first flew in May 1981. Production deliveries began in 1989 and the type became operational in 1991.*

91

**Role**
Fighter
Close support
Counter-insurgency
Tactical strike
Strategic bomber
Tactical reconnaissance
Strategic reconnaissance
Maritime patrol
Anti-ship strike
Anti-submarine warfare
Search and rescue
Assault transport
Transport
Liaison
Trainer
Inflight-refuelling tanker
Specialized

**Performance**
All-weather capability
Rough field capability
STOL capability
VTOL capability
Airspeed 0-250 mph
Airspeed 250 mph-Mach 1
Airspeed Mach 1 plus
Ceiling 0-20,000 ft
Ceiling 20,000-40,000 ft
Ceiling 40,000 ft plus
Range 0-1,000 miles
Range 1,000-3,000 miles
Range 3,000 miles plus

**Weapons**
Air-to-air missiles
Air-to-surface missiles
Cruise missiles
Cannon
Trainable guns
Naval weapons
Nuclear-capable
Rockets
'Smart' weapon kit
Weapon load 0-4,000 lb
Weapon load 4,000-15,000 lb
Weapon load 15,000 lb plus

**Avionics**
Electronic Counter Measures
Electronic Support Measures
Search radar
Fire control radar
Look-down/shoot-down
Terrain-following radar
Forward-looking infra-red
Laser
Television

# Dassault Etendard IV

*Dassault Etendard IVP of the Aéronavale.*

**Role**
- Fighter
- Close support
- Counter-insurgency
- Tactical strike
- Strategic bomber
- Tactical reconnaissance
- Strategic reconnaissance
- Maritime patrol
- Anti-ship strike
- Anti-submarine warfare
- Search and rescue
- Assault transport
- Transport
- Liaison
- Trainer
- Inflight-refuelling tanker
- Specialized

**Performance**
- All-weather capability
- Rough field capability
- STOL capability
- VTOL capability
- Airspeed 0-250 mph
- Airspeed 250 mph-Mach 1
- Airspeed Mach 1 plus
- Ceiling 0-20,000 ft
- Ceiling 20,000-40,000 ft
- Ceiling 40,000ft plus
- Range 0-1,000 miles
- Range 1,000-3,000 miles
- Range 3,000 miles plus

**Weapons**
- Air-to-air missiles
- Air-to-surface missiles
- Cruise missiles
- Cannon
- Trainable guns
- Naval weapons
- Nuclear-capable
- Rockets
- 'Smart' weapon kit
- Weapon load 0-4,000 lb
- Weapon load 4,000-15,000 lb
- Weapon load 15,000 lb plus

**Avionics**
- Electronic Counter Measures
- Electronic Support Measures
- Search radar
- Fire control radar
- Look-down/shoot-down
- Terrain-following radar
- Forward-looking infra-red
- Laser
- Television

The original Etendard (standard, or national flag) was Dassault's entry in a 1955 NATO competition for a light attack fighter able to operate from unpaved strips. It was developed with various engines and finally entered production in 1960 as the **Dassault Etendard IVM** carrierborne attack fighter with a powerplant of one SNECMA Atar non-afterburning turbojet. A conventional subsonic machine, the Etendard IVM stands high on tricycle landing gear stressed for carrier landings, the main wheels folding inwards to be housed in the fuselage. The engine is fed by plain lateral inlets on each side of the pressurized cockpit, which has an upward-hinged canopy and French-built Martin- Baker Mk N4A ejector seat. The almost untapered swept wing has slight anhedral, drooping leading edges with dog-toothed notches, and rather small flaps and ailerons all inboard of the power-folding tips. The variable-incidence tailplane with inset elevators is mounted well up the fin, and all the flight controls are powered.

Despite its limited flight performance, the Etendard IVM proved a popular and useful machine. The slim nose housed only a simple ESD Aïda radar with a fixed antenna aimed with the whole aircraft to provide detection and ranging of targets within a narrow cone dead ahead. Under the nose is a unique underfin blade containing the guidance aerial for the now-obsolete AS.20 radio-commanded missile.

Dassault delivered 69 aircraft in 1962-4, these serving with Flottilles 15F (training unit) and 11F and 17F. A further 21 Etendards were delivered to the somewhat revised **Etendard IVP** photo-reconnaissance standard in which three OMERA cameras replaced the Etendard IVM's Aïda radar and Saab toss-bombing computer, while two more replaced the Etendard IVM's guns. The Etendard IVM has been replaced by the Super Etendard, but the Etendard IVP remains in service with Flottille 16F. The Etendard IVP had an inflight-refuelling probe and can also carry a 'buddy' refuelling pack, allowing about half of the current force of 20 aircraft to operate in the tanker role.

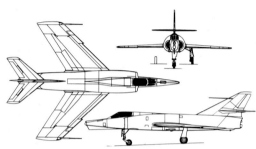

*Dassault Etendard IVM*

*A Dassault Etendard IVM of Flottille 16F takes the wire on board the aircraft-carrier Foch; 16F is the only remaining Etendard unit, operating the unarmed Etendard IVP.*

*A Dassault Etendard IVP shows its blunt camera nose, refuelling probe and the optional buddy refuelling pod. About 20 Etendards remain in service.*

## Specification: Dassault Etendard IVP
**Origin:** France
**Type:** carrier-based photo-reconnaissance aircraft
**Powerplant:** one 4400-kg (9,700-lb) dry thrust SNECMA Atar 8B turbojet **Performance:** maximum speed 593 kt (1099 km/h; 683 mph) at sea level; initial rate of climb 19,685 ft (6000 m) per minute; service ceiling 50,850 ft (15500 m); tactical radius 300 km (186 miles) at sea level; ferry range 2816 km (1,750 miles)
**Weights:** empty 5900 kg (13,000 lb); maximum take-off 10200 kg (22,486 lb)
**Dimensions:** span 9.60 m (31 ft 6 in); length 14.53 m (47 ft 8 in); height 4.30m (14 ft 2 in); wing area 29.0 m² (312.0 sq ft)
**Armament:** none

# Dassault Falcon 20, 200 and Gardian

*Dassault Falcon 20 of 335 Skvadron, Norwegian air force.*

Originally called the Dassault Mystère 20, the Falcon 20 twin-engined business jet first flew on 7 May 1963. From the start it was a 'top of the market' aircraft with extensive integral tankage, fully powered controls and General Electric CF700 aft-fan engines each flat-rated at 1905-kg 14,200-lb) dry thrust and fitted with target-type reversers. The cabin, about 1.75 m (5 ft 9 in) wide and high, could be furnished for anything up to 12 passengers, although corporate versions seated nine or ten. Large US sales resulted from a link with PanAm (later Dassault's Falcon Jet Corporation subsidiary), and this helped sales of many specially-equipped versions for military purposes. In January 1977 a sale of 41 **Falcon 20G** aircraft to the US Coast Guard, which calls the type **HU-25A Guardian**, introduced the unique three-spool ATF3 engine, and this became standard from 1983 in the **Falcon 200** that was built up to 1988. This type also has extra rear-fuselage tankage as well as major aerodynamic and system changes.

All versions have a conventional metal fail-safe structure, manufacture of which was shared with other companies in France and Spain. The leading-edge slats, slotted flaps, wing-mounted airbrakes, flight control surfaces, and twin-wheel landing gear units are all actuated hydraulically. Engine bleed air is used to de-ice the wings and engine inlets.

The specification below is for the **Gardian** maritime surveillance version used by the French Aéronavale in the Pacific. It has extremely comprehensive avionics including Thomson-CSF Varan radar and VLF Omega navigation. The **Gardian 2** is a simplified export version that was marketed for the Exocet attack, light (gun/bomb) attack, ESM/ECM, target designation and target towing roles. The basic Falcon 200 was offered with equipment for every kind of specialized role. Libya and the Armée de l'Air use the **Falcon 20 SNA** version with Mirage radar and electronics for training in low-level attack, while the UK (Royal Navy), Norway and Canada are among seven users of EW/ECM versions, Total sales exceeded 500 aircraft.

## Specification: Dassault Gardian and Gardian 2
**Origin:** France
**Type:** maritime surveillance and multi-role attack/EW aircraft
**Powerplant:** two 2468-kg (5,440-lb) dry thrust Garrett ATF3-6A-3C turbofans
**Performance:** maximum cruising speed 470 kt (870 km/h; 541 mph) at 30,000 ft (9145 m); maximum patrol speed 150 kt (278 km/h; 173 mph) at sea level; service ceiling 45,000 ft (13715 m); range 4490 km (2,790 miles) with six crew, full avionics and full fuel reserves at sea level
**Weights:** empty 8700 kg (19,180 lb); maximum take-off 15200 kg (33,510 lb)
**Dimensions:** span 16.30 m (53 ft 6 in); length 17.15 m (56 ft 3 in); height 5.32 m (17 ft 5 in); wing area 41.0 m² (440.3 sq ft)
**Armament:** provision for AM.39 Exocet anti-ship missiles, cannon or machine-gun pods, rocket-launcher pods, bombs, ECM equipment and other stores carried on four underwing hardpoints

**Dassault Falcon 20**

*In US Coast Guard service the Falcon 20 is known as the HU-25A Guardian, of which 41 were acquired. This aircraft is operated from Elizabeth City.*

*This Falcon 20 SNA radar trainer is used by 339 Centre Prédiction et Instruction Radar at Luxeuil for interception training by Mirage fighter squadrons.*

**Role**

Fighter
Close support
Counter-insurgency
Tactical strike
Strategic bomber
Tactical reconnaissance
Strategic reconnaissance
Maritime patrol
Anti-ship strike
Anti-submarine warfare
Search and rescue
Assault transport
Transport
Liaison
Trainer
Inflight-refuelling tanker
Specialized

**Performance**

All-weather capability
Rough field capability
STOL capability
VTOL capability
Airspeed 0-250 mph
Airspeed 250 mph-Mach 1
Airspeed Mach 1 plus
Ceiling 0-20,000 ft
Ceiling 20,000-40,000 ft
Ceiling 40,000ft plus
Range 0-1,000 miles
Range 1,000-3,000 miles
Range 3,000 miles plus

**Weapons**

Air-to-air missiles
Air-to-surface missiles
Cruise missiles
Cannon
Trainable guns
Naval weapons
Nuclear-capable
Rockets
'Smart' weapon kit
Weapon load 0-4,000 lb
Weapon load 4,000-15,000 lb
Weapon load 15,000 lb plus

**Avionics**

Electronic Counter Measures
Electronic Support Measures
Search radar
Fire control radar
Look-down/shoot-down
Terrain-following radar
Forward-looking infra-red
Laser
Television

# Dassault Mirage IIIR and 5R

*Dassault Mirage IIIR2Z of No.2 Squadron, South African Air Force.*

At the start of the Mirage III fighter programme the Armée de l'Air was interested in the possibility of developing a reconnaissance version to replace the obsolete Republic RF-84F in the 33e Escadre. This proved a straightforward task, the first of two converted Mirage IIIA pre-series aircraft flying on 31 October 1961, and after further refinement the first production **Dassault Mirage IIIR** flew on 1 February 1963. An initial series of 50 was delivered for the 'Moselle' and 'Savoie' squadrons (3/33 and then 2/33) in 1964-5.

The chief new feature of the Mirage IIIR was the nose, longer than any other variant and filled with cameras instead of the Cyrano radar. The original Armée de l'Air version carried five OMERA Type 31 cameras, as well as a CSF radar altimeter which automatically adjusted the camera framing (picture-taking) rate according to height above ground, a removable flare launcher and a removable photo-electric cell which triggered the cameras at night as soon as flares are ignited. The optional twin-cannon pack was usually carried, and other options for armed reconnaissance included a SFOM

reflector sight and LABS (low-altitude bombing system) for toss delivery of nuclear bombs that were, in fact, never carried. The cameras could be angled to give optimum overlap in low-, medium- or high-altitude runs, or for night photography. All Mirage IIIRs later had a self-contained navigation system, normally comprising a Doppler radar and twin-gyro platform.

Export orders were received from Switzerland (**Mirage IIIRS** with many differences, licence built in Switzerland) and South Africa (**Mirage IIIRZ**). The **Mirage IIIRD** introduced a new Doppler in a large chin blister, automatic camera installation with OMERA Types 40 and 33 cameras, and a gyro sight. The 20 Armée de l'Air Mirage IIIRDs were followed by a batch of **Mirage IIIRP** aircraft for Pakistan with Vinten cameras. After 1973 French Mirage IIIRDs carried SAT Cyclope infra-red linescan equipment in a ventral fairing. The **Mirage IIIR2Z** series delivered to South Africa from 1974 possibly have the uprated Atar 9K-50 engine. Abu Dhabi, Belgium, Colombia and Libya fly **Mirage 5R** versions of the longer-range Mirage 5, bringing total deliveries of all R versions to 159.

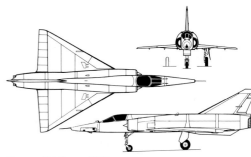

**Dassault Mirage IIIR**

*This Mirage **IIIRD** of ER3/33 carries a shark-mouthed fuel tank on the centreline, and rocket launchers in the noses of its underwing drop tanks.*

*This **Swiss** air force Mirage **IIIRS** carries the eagle-head badge of Fliegerstaffel 10 on its fin. This squadron, based at Dübendorf, is the only Swiss reconnaissance unit.*

## Specification: Dassault Mirage IIIR
**Origin:** France
**Type:** tactical reconnaissance aircraft with attack capability
**Powerplant:** one 6200-kg (13,668-lb) afterburning thrust SNECMA Atar9C turbojet
**Performance:** maximum speed 750 kt (1390 km/h; 863 mph) at sea level; cruising speed Mach 0.9 or 516 kt (956 km/h; 594 mph) at 36,000 ft (10975 m); service ceiling 55,775 ft (17000 m); mission radius about 685 km (425 miles) on a low-level mission with maximum external fuel
**Weights:** empty 6600 kg (14,550 lb); maximum take-off 13700 kg (30,203 lb)
**Dimensions:** span 8.22 m (26 ft 11.6 in); length 15.50 m (50 ft 10.2 in); height 4.50 m (14 ft 9 in); wing area 35.0 m² (376.7 sq ft)
**Armament:** option of carrying two 30-mm DEFA 552A cannon with 125rounds per gun and, in exceptional circumstances, air-to-surface armament

# Dassault Mirage III trainers

*Dassault Mirage IIIOD of the Aircraft Research & Development Unit, Royal Australian Air Force.*

Back in the early days of the Mirage III programme, it was decided to complete one of the Mirage IIIA development aircraft as a tandem-seat dual-control conversion trainer. The resulting **Dassault Mirage IIIB** made its first flight on 21 October 1959. Compared with the single-seater, the Mirage IIIB had its fuselage lengthened by some 0.6 m (1 ft 11.6 in), putting the front cockpit in the same position relative to the engine air inlets as in the single-seat Mirage IIIE, although both cockpits are enclosed by a single giant canopy. The rear cockpit occupies the volume normally used to house avionics (communication and navigation equipment, for example) and so in almost all two-seat Mirage III versions this equipment is located to the nose in place of radar. With few exceptions, therefore, Mirage III trainers cannot fly interception missions although they do retain a limited ground-attack and limited attack training capability.

The first production Mirage IIIB for the Armée de l'Air flew on 19 July 1962. As supplied to this customer, the Mirage IIIB was unarmed and, despite its use of the original Atar 9B turbojet, its light weight resulted in sprightly performance. other customers for the Mirage IIIB were Israel (**Mirage IIIBJ**), Lebanon (**Mirage IIIBL**), South Africa (**Mirage IIIBZ**) and Switzerland (**Mirage IIIBS**), mostly with cannon armament installed. The Armée de l'Air's **Mirage IIIB2** (**Mirage IIIB-RV**) had a dummy refuelling probe for tanker training.

The need for a trainer equivalent to the upgraded Mirage IIIE was obvious, and this is designated **Mirage IIID** except for the Armée de l'Air's own version, which was designated **Mirage IIIBE**. The Mirage IIID was initially built in Australia as the **Mirage IIIOD** by Commonwealth Aircraft, but was soon ordered by many other export customers, and later Dassault built a further six aircraft for the RAAF. Distinguished chiefly by its Atar 9C engine, the Mirage IIID has the same cockpit arrangement and fuselage length as the Mirage IIIB Radio beacon equipment but not radar is fitted, although some sub-types (**Mirage IIIDBR** for Brazil and **Mirage IIIDS** for Switzerland) have the dorsal fin with extra radio aerials. One version, the **Mirage IIID2Z** of South Africa, has the uprated Atar 9K-50 engine. Altogether 186 tandem two-seat Mirage III and equivalent **Mirage 5D** aircraft were sold to 20 air forces.

**Specification:** Dassault Mirage IIIB
**Origin:** France
**Type:** advanced and conversion trainer
**Powerplant:** one 6000-kg (13,228-lb) afterburning thrust SNECMA Atar 9B turbojet
**Performance:** maximum speed Mach 1.8 or 1,030 kt (1912 km/h; 1,188 mph) at 40,000 ft (12190 m); service ceiling 57,000 ft (17375 m); tactical radius 250 km (155 miles) at 36,000 ft (10975 m)
**Weights:** empty 6270 kg (13,823 lb); maximum take-off 12000 kg (26,455 lb)
**Dimensions:** span 8.22 m(26 ft 11.6 in); length 15.40 m (50 ft 6.3 in); height 4.25 m (13ft 11.3 in); wing area 34.85 m² (375.1 sq ft)
**Armament:** provision for carrying two 30-mm DEFA 552A or similar cannon, and (seldom fitted) underwing pylons for ground-attack ordnance

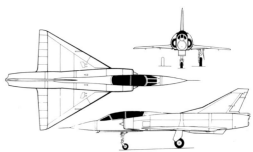

*Dassault Mirage IIIB*

*Swiss air force Mirage two-seaters are designated Mirage IIIBS, and are used for training by the two Mirage fighter units and by the reconnaissance squadron.*

*Some Mirage IIIBs remained in service with the French air force, mainly for conversion and continuation training, into the mid-1980s.*

**Role**
Fighter
Close support
Counter-insurgency
Tactical strike
Strategic bomber
Tactical reconnaissance
Strategic reconnaissance
Maritime patrol
Anti-ship strike
Anti-submarine warfare
Search and rescue
Assault transport
Transport
Liaison
Trainer
Inflight-refuelling tanker
Specialized

**Performance**
All-weather capability
Rough field capability
STOL capability
VTOL capability
Airspeed 0-250 mph
Airspeed 250 mph-Mach 1
Airspeed Mach 1 plus
Ceiling 0-20,000 ft
Ceiling 20,000-40,000 ft
Ceiling 40,000ft plus
Range 0-1,000 miles
Range 1,000-3,000 miles
Range 3,000 miles plus

**Weapons**
Air-to-air missiles
Air-to-surface missiles
Cruise missiles
Cannon
Trainable guns
Naval weapons
Nuclear-capable
Rockets
'Smart' weapon kit
Weapon load 0-4,000 lb
Weapon load 4,000-15,000 lb
Weapon load 15,000 lb plus

**Avionics**
Electronic Counter Measures
Electronic Support Measures
Search radar
Fire control radar
Look-down/shoot-down
Terrain-following radar
Forward-looking infra-red
Laser
Television

# Dassault Mirage III/5 upgrades

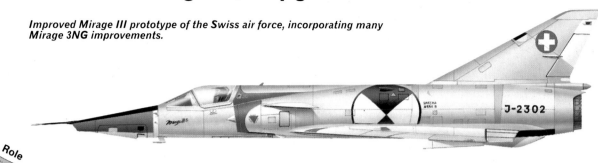

*Improved Mirage III prototype of the Swiss air force, incorporating many Mirage 3NG improvements.*

**Role**
Fighter
Close support
Counter-insurgency
Tactical strike
Strategic bomber
Tactical reconnaissance
Strategic reconnaissance
Maritime patrol
Anti-ship strike
Anti-submarine warfare
Search and rescue
Assault transport
Transport
Liaison
Trainer
Inflight-refuelling tanker
Specialized

**Performance**
All-weather capability
Rough field capability
STOL capability
VTOL capability
Airspeed 0-250 mph
Airspeed 250 mph-Mach 1
Airspeed Mach 1 plus
Ceiling 0-20,000 ft
Ceiling 20,000-40,000 ft
Ceiling 40,000ft plus
Range 0-1,000 miles
Range 1,000-3,000 miles
Range 3,000 miles plus

**Weapons**
Air-to-air missiles
Air-to-surface missiles
Cruise missiles
Cannon
Trainable guns
Naval weapons
Nuclear-capable
Rockets
'Smart' weapon kit
Weapon load 0-4,000 lb
Weapon load 4,000-15,000 lb
Weapon load 15,000 lb plus

**Avionics**
Electronic Counter Measures
Electronic Support Measures
Search radar
Fire control radar
Look-down/shoot-down
Terrain-following radar
Forward-looking infra-red
Laser
Television

Since 1977 Dassault has been awarded several contracts the Mirage III and Mirage 5 fighters of client air force. These developments were developed for the planned Mirage 3NG (Nouvelle Génération) fighter that first flew in prototype form in December 1982 but failed to secure orders for new-build aircraft. The programme involves the installation of any or all of the following features: the uprated Atar 9K-50 turbojet, fixed canard foreplanes on the inlets for an increase of 1000 kg (2,205 lb) in maximum take-off weight without detriment to field performance and with benefit to agility even at high weights, revised flight controls and instruments, new Martin-Baker Mk 6 or Mk 10 zero-zero ejector seat, new radio com/nav systems, inertial navigation system, modernized radar, HUD, laser ranger, digital computer, new EW (radar warning receivers and ECM/IRCM dispensers and jammers), and inflight-refuelling kit. This programme has been adopted in part by many customers, and operators such as Argentina, Belgium, Brazil, Chile, Colombia, Egypt, Pakistan, Peru, South Africa, Spain, Switzerland and Venezuela have also considered or implemented their own upgrades.

The upgrade offered by IAI and adopted in part by several countries undertaking their own upgrades, with Israeli technical assistance, includes fixed canard foreplanes, strengthened landing gear, an additional fuel tank aft of the cockpit, extended nose for avionics such as a control and stability augmentation system, radar warning system, inertial navigation and weapon-delivery system, Martin-Baker Mk 10 seat, missiles or ECM pods on wingtip rails, two or four additional hardpoints, and chaff/flare dispenser(s) under the rear fuselage.

The Swiss Federal Aircraft Factory (F+W) at Emmen, which licence built 30 Mirage IIIS, 18 Mirage IIIRS, two Mirage IIIBS and two Mirage IIIDS aircraft, is putting these aircraft though its own upgrade with fixed foreplanes, small strakes under the nose, Martin-Baker Mk 6 seats, IR and active/passive ECM dispensers and jammer, VHF radio, aural and visual angle of attack monitoring and warning systems, and the ability to carry a 730-litre (160.5-Imp gal) centreline and two 500-litre (110-Imp gal) underwing tanks.

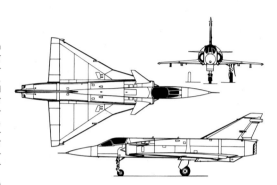

***Dassault Mirage 3NG***

***The Mirage 3NG is powered by the same SNECMA Atar 9K-50 engine as is used by the Mirage 50, and Mirage F1. Aerodynamic improvements, modern avionics and systems combine to make the Mirage 3NG a much more capable machine than the Mirage III.***

***Below: This Venezuelan Mirage 50EV is typical of upgraded Mirage Deltas now in service with canard foreplanes and other improvements.***

## Specification: Dassault Mirage 3NG
**Origin:** France
**Type:** multi-role fighter based on upgrade of the Mirage III/5
**Powerplant:** one 7200-kg (15,873-lb) afterburning thrust SNECMA Atar 9K-50 turbojet
**Performance:** maximum speed Mach 2.2 or 1,269 kt (2350 km/h; 1,460 mph) at high altitude; service ceiling 54,000 ft (16460 m); range not published but similar to that of the Mirage IIIE
**Weight:** maximum take-off 14700 kg (32,407 lb)
**Dimensions:** span 8.22 m (26 ft 11.6 in); length 15.65 m (51 ft 4.1 in); height 4.50 m (14 ft 9 in); wing area 35.0 m² (376.7 sq ft); canard foreplane area 1.0 m² (10.8 sq ft)
**Armament:** two 30-mm DEFA cannon, and provision for an external load similar to that of the Mirage IIE/5 augmented in type and also, through the addition of four lateral stores stations under the fuselage, in weight

# Dassault Mirage IV

*Dassault Mirage IVA of Escadre de Bombardement 94.*

In 1954 the France decided to create a nuclear deterrent capability as the Force de Frappe, one element of which would be a manned bomber. Originally planned as a larger aircraft with more powerful Pratt & Whitney engines, the **Dassault Mirage IV** was finally scaled down as the **Mirage IVA** with two SNECMA Atar turbojets, which meant that the type could not fly two-way missions against Soviet targets. The prototype first flew on 17 June 1959, and following considerable further development authorization was issued for a production run of 50 aircraft, later supplemented by a further 12 machines. The force was completed in March 1968, and was then subjected to a steady programme of improvement.

Aerodynamically, the Mirage IVA is broadly a scaled-up Mirage III revised with side-by-side engines, pilot and navigator in tandem cockpits with upward-hinged canopies, four-wheel bogie main landing gears, tall steerable twin-wheel nose gear and a slender nose terminating in an inflight-refuelling probe. This probe is vital to any mission, because virtually all combat sorties are planned on the basis of one or more refuellings from a Boeing C-135FR tanker or via a buddy pack from an accompanying Mirage IVA. Navigation is by a CSF surveillance radar under the belly, Marconi Doppler,

Dassault computer and SFENA autopilot, later upgraded by the installation of dual inertial systems. OMERA Robot strike cameras are fitted, and the original weapon load comprised a 60-kiloton nuclear bomb semi-recessed into the rear fuselage, although by removing the large drop tanks it was possible to carry six conventional bombs or four AS.37 Martel anti-radar missiles. For many years the force at readiness comprised 36 aircraft (of 50 bombers available) assigned to EB91 and EB94, and dispersed in small groups around seven bases. In emergency further dispersal was possible, using chemicals to harden tracts of farmland and six RATO units to blast the aircraft into the air. The last aircraft were retired in the late 1980s.

At Bordeaux were based 12 **Mirage IVR** reconnaissance aircraft with special navaids, sensors and EW systems. Some 18 of the bombers have been rebuilt to **Mirage IVP** standard with the ASMP stand-off nuclear missile, Thomson-CSF Arcana pulse-Doppler radar, new EW internal systems and new dispensing and jamming pods on the outer wing pylons. The Mirage IVP became operational in the late 1980s, but the associated missile was not available until a later date, and the last of these aircraft are due for retirement in 1996.

## Specification: Dassault Mirage IVP

**Origin:** France
**Type:** stand-off missile launch platform
**Powerplant:** two 7000-kg (15,432-lb) afterburning thrust SNECMA Atar 9K turbojets
**Performance:** maximum sustained speed Mach 1.8 or 1,030 kt (1912 km/h; 1,188 mph) at high altitude; climb t0 36,090 ft (11000 M0 in 4 minutes 15 seconds; service ceiling 65,615 ft (20000 m); combat radius 1240 km (771 miles) without inflight refuelling; ferry range 4000 km (2,486 miles)
**Weights:** empty 14500 kg (31,967 lb); maximum take-off 33475 kg (73,779 lb)
**Dimensions:** span 11.85 m (38 ft 10.5 in); length 23.50 m (77 ft 1 in); height 5.40 m (17 ft 8.5 in); wing area 78.0 m² (839.6 sq ft)
**Armament:** one ASMP stand-off nuclear missile carried under the fuselage

**Dassault Mirage IVA with semi-recessed bomb**

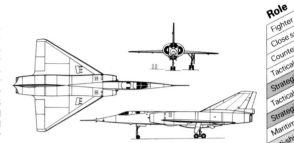

*The French Force de Frappe, later known as the Forces Aériennes Stratégiques, contained two Mirage IV wings, whose aircraft now have the ASMP missile.*

*A Mirage IVP, with an ASMP under the belly, makes a rocket-assisted take-off. The Mirage IVP attain an initial operational capability in the later 1980s.*

**Role**
Fighter
Close support
Counter-insurgency
Tactical strike
Strategic bomber
Tactical reconnaissance
Strategic reconnaissance
Maritime patrol
Anti-ship strike
Anti-submarine warfare
Search and rescue
Assault transport
Transport
Liaison
Trainer
Inflight-refuelling tanker
Specialized

**Performance**
All-weather capability
Rough field capability
STOL capability
VTOL capability
Airspeed 0-250 mph
Airspeed 250 mph-Mach 1
Airspeed Mach 1 plus
Ceiling 0-20,000 ft
Ceiling 20,000-40,000 ft
Ceiling 40,000ft plus
Range 0-1,000 miles
Range 1,000-3,000 miles
Range 3,000 miles plus

**Weapons**
Air-to-air missiles
Air-to-surface missiles
Cruise missiles
Cannon
Trainable guns
Naval weapons
Nuclear-capable
Rockets
'Smart' weapon kit
Weapon load 0-4,000 lb
Weapon load 4,000-15,000 lb
Weapon load 15,000 lb plus

**Avionics**
Electronic Counter Measures
Electronic Support Measures
Search radar
Fire control radar
Look-down/shoot-down
Terrain-following radar
Forward-looking infra-red
Laser
Television

# Dassault Mirage 5

*Dassault Mirage 5BR of 42 Smaldeel of the Belgian air force at Florennes.*

## Role
Fighter
Close support
Counter-insurgency
Tactical strike
Strategic bomber
Tactical reconnaissance
Strategic reconnaissance
Maritime patrol
Anti-ship strike
Anti-submarine warfare
Search and rescue
Assault transport
Transport
Liaison
Trainer
Inflight-refuelling tanker
Specialized

## Performance
All-weather capability
Rough field capability
STOL capability
VTOL capability
Airspeed 0-250 mph
Airspeed 250 mph-Mach 1
Airspeed Mach 1 plus
Ceiling 0-20,000 ft
Ceiling 20,000-40,000 ft
Ceiling 40,000ft plus
Range 0-1,000 miles
Range 1,000-3,000 miles
Range 3,000 miles plus

## Weapons
Air-to-air missiles
Air-to-surface missiles
Cruise missiles
Cannon
Trainable guns
Naval weapons
Nuclear-capable
Rockets
'Smart' weapon kit
Weapon load 0-4,000 lb
Weapon load 4,000-15,000 lb
Weapon load 15,000 lb plus

## Avionics
Electronic Counter Measures
Electronic Support Measures
Search radar
Fire control radar
Look-down/shoot-down
Terrain-following radar
Forward-looking infra-red
Laser
Television

In 1966 the Israeli air force asked Dassault to build a simplified version of its Mirage IIIE attack fighter optimized for the daytime VFR (visual flight rules) ground-attack mission. The first **Dassault Mirage 5** flew on 19 May 1967 as the first of 50 ordered and paid for by the Israeli government. On President de Gaulle's orders these were never delivered, and eventually entered service as **Mirage 5F** aircraft with the French Armée de l'Air. Meanwhile this cheaper, longer-range version of the Mirage III proved a smash hit, and 11 other air forces took 525 aircraft including the baseline Mirage 5, reconnaissance Mirage 5R and two-seat Mirage 5D.

The basic changes effected in the Mirage 5 were the relocation of the main avionics racking from behind the cockpit into the nose volume previously occupied by the radar: this made the nose slimmer and more perfectly conical, and allowed the addition of tankage for an extra 470 litres (103 Imp gal) of fuel in the volume to the rear of the cockpit. Two extra outward-splayed fuselage pylons were added, increasing the theoretical disposable load to 4000 kg (8,818 lb) excluding up to 1000 litres (220 Imp gal) of external fuel. Alternatively, the Mirage 5 can operate as a VFR interceptor with two small AAMs and 4700 litres (1,034 Imp gal) of external fuel, but all missions flown at high weight demand a very long runway. It was partly to overcome this handicap that Dassault, in partnership with the Swiss F+W company, in 1969 fitted one example of the Mirage 5 with retractable 'moustache' foreplanes, but this Mirage Milan did not enter production.

Later Mirage 5s were offered with options such as Agave or Aïda II lightweight radar, installed either in the nose or in an underwing pod, inertial navigation system, HUD and laser ranger.

## Specification: Dassault Mirage 5
**Origin:** France
**Type:** day visual fighter-bomber
**Powerplant:** one 6200-kg (13,668-lb) afterburning thrust SNECMA Atar 9C turbojet
**Performance:** maximum sustained speed, clean Mach 1.8 or 1,030 kt (1912 km/h; 1,188 mph) at high altitude; maximum speed with external stores typically 500 kt (926 km/h; 575 mph) at sea level; climb to 36,090 ft (11000 m) in 3 minutes; service ceiling 55,755 ft (17000 m); combat radius 650 km (404 miles) on a lo-lo-lo mission with a 907-kg (2,000-lb) warload; ferry range 4000 km (2,485 miles)
**Weights:** empty 6600 kg (14,550 lb); maximum take-off 13700 kg (30,203 lb)
**Dimensions:** span 8.22 m (26 ft 11.6 in); length 15.55 m (51 ft 0.2 in); height 4.50 m (14 ft 9 in); wing area 35.0 m² (376.7 sq ft)
**Armament:** two 30-mm DEFA 552A cannon with 125 rounds per gun, plus provision for up to 4000 kg (8,818 lb) of disposable stores carried on seven external pylons for various combinations of weapons and/or tanks, including Magic or Sidewinder AAMs

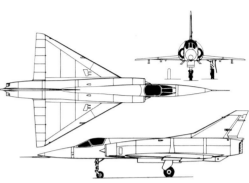

*Dassault Mirage 5*

*Venezuela's Mirage 5Vs and 5DVs are operated by Escuadron de Caza No. 36, and were delivered during the 1970s. They are augmented by Northrop F-5s obtained from Canada.*

*The handful of Mirage 5s operated by the Gabonese air force includes at least one two-seater and one reconnaissance variant.*

# Dassault Mirage 50

*Dassault Mirage 50 of Grupo No. 4, Fuerza Aerea de Chile.*

In 1966 the French SNECMA engine company pulled out all the stops to develop the most powerful possible version of the Atar afterburning turbojet as the Atar 9K-50. This engine was needed for the Mirage F1 and Mirage G4, then soon to fly. Some customers. however, recognized that this more powerful engine would enhance the performance of the standard delta-winged Mirage variants, and accordingly specified it for these basically earlier-generation aircraft: one example is South Africa for its Mirage IIIR2Z reconnaissance aircraft.

This eventually prompted Dassault to develop an upgraded version of the Mirage III/5 powered by the Atar 9K-50 engine. The resulting **Dassault Mirage 50** can be regarded as an upgraded version of the Mirage III or Mirage 5 as the basic airframes is common to both. The Mirage 50 was offered with any of the upgrades studied by Dassault since 1977, with one or two seats and with a reconnaissance nose, or a larger nose housing Cyrano

IVM-3 radar, or a slim conical nose housing the small Agave radar. Other options included an inertial navigation system and HUD. The type was offered as a multi-mission fighter with the ability to fly day interception and dogfight missions, day visual ground-attack or (with camera nose) reconnaissance missions and, depending on the radar and other sensors chosen, night and bad-weather missions With long nose and Agave radar, the internal fuel capacity is 3410 litres (750 Imp gal), the same as most Mirage 5s. This figure can be doubled with external tanks.

The prototype Mirage 50, with Agave radar, flew on 15 April 1979. The only countries to take the type were Chile (16) and Venezuela (7), the completion of the latter's order in the early 1990s ending production of the Mirage III, 5 and 50 series after 1,422 aircraft. With the assistance of IAI, ENAER is upgrading the Chilean aircraft to **Pantera 50** standard with canard foreplanes and more advanced avionics.

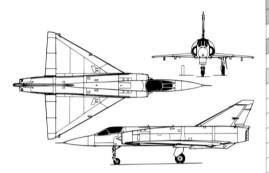

**Dassault Mirage 50**

*Chile's order for Mirage 50s was approved in 1979. The first were delivered in that year, and a group of pilots underwent conversion in France.*

## Specification: Dassault Mirage 50

**Origin:** France

**Type:** multi-role warplane (fighter, fighter-bomber, reconnaissance aircraft and trainer variants)

**Powerplant:** one 7200-kg (15,873-lb) afterburning thrust SNECMA Atar 9K-50 turbojet

**Performance:** maximum speed Mach2.2 or 1,268 kt (2350km/h; 1,460 mph) at high altitude; initial rate of climb 36,600 ft (11156 m) per minute; service ceiling 59,055 ft (18000 m); combat radius 685 km (425 miles) on a low-altitude mission with two 400-kg (882-lb) bombs and external fuel

**Weights:** empty 7150 kg (15, 763 lb); maximum take-off 13700 kg (30,203 lb)

**Dimensions:** span 8.22 m (26 ft 11. 6 in); length 15.56 m (51 ft 0.6 in); height 4.50 m (14 ft 9 in); wing area 35.0 m² (376.7 sq ft)

**Armament:** two 30-mm DEFA 552A cannon with 125 rounds per gun, and (with Agave radar) Magic or (Cyrano radar) R.530 AAMs and various attack loads including 454-kg (l,000-lb) bombs, AS.30 or AS.30L missiles, rocket-launcher pods and combined tank/launchers, and many other stores

*The Mirage 50 retains the same basic airframe as the Mirage 111 and Mirage 5, but is fitted with the more powerful engine of the Mirage F1.*

## Role
Fighter
Close support
Counter-insurgency
Tactical strike
Strategic bomber
Tactical reconnaissance
Strategic reconnaissance
Maritime patrol
Anti-ship strike
Anti-submarine warfare
Search and rescue
Assault transport
Transport
Liaison
Trainer
Inflight-refuelling tanker
Specialized

## Performance
All-weather capability
Rough field capability
STOL capability
VTOL capability
Airspeed 0-250 mph
Airspeed 250 mph-Mach 1
Airspeed Mach 1 plus
Ceiling 0-20,000 ft
Ceiling 20,000-40,000 ft
Ceiling 40,000ft plus
Range 0-1,000 miles
Range 1,000-3,000 miles
Range 3,000 miles plus

## Weapons
Air-to-air missiles
Air-to-surface missiles
Cruise missiles
Cannon
Trainable guns
Naval weapons
Nuclear-capable
Rockets
'Smart' weapon kit
Weapon load 0-4,000 lb
Weapon load 4,000-15,000 lb
Weapon load 15,000 lb plus

## Avionics
Electronic Counter Measures
Electronic Support Measures
Search radar
Fire control radar
Look-down/shoot-down
Terrain-following radar
Forward-looking infra-red
Laser
Television

# Dassault Mirage F1A and F1E

*Dassault Mirage F1E of the Iraqi air force.*

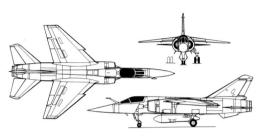

While most export customers for the Mirage F1 series were content to specify aircraft based on the original Armée de l'Air Mirage F1C, the South African Air Force recognized the advantages of a simplified version for day visual attack missions. This exactly parallels the Mirage 5 simplified version of the Mirage III. Like the Mirage 5, the resulting **Dassault Mirage F1A** is visually distinguishable by its slender conical nose, resulting from removal of the large Cyrano IVM radar. In its place is a small ranging radar, which is almost certainly the ESD Aïda II as fitted to some Mirage 5 versions. Again like these Mirage 5s, the large instrument boom housing the pitot/static heads is attached on the underside of the nose, out of the way of the fixed forward-pointing axis of this radar.

The main advantages of the Mirage F1A are cheapness and extra range or weapon load. The main avionics racking is moved from behind the cockpit to the nose, making room for an extra fuselage tank. Another addition is a Doppler navigation system housed in a fairing on the underside of the nose The customers for the Mirage F1A were Libya and South Africa, the latter's subtype being the **Mirage F1AZ**, and a licence

to build this type was granted to Armscor, although the company's Atlas Aircraft division, the main South African manufacturer of aircraft, never announced more than the manufacture of parts.

On 22 December 1974 Dassault flew the Mirage F1E prototype powered by the then-new M53 engine. This aircraft failed to win large orders from four European NATO countries, and the M53-powered version was abandoned. Instead, and repeating the practice established with the Mirage III, the designation was then applied to an upgraded multi-role fighter/attack version for export customers. Outwardly resembling the Mirage F1C, this **Mirage F1E** has a SAGEM inertial system, EMD.182 central digital computer, VE.120C HUD, Crouzet air data computer, and digital armament/navigation controls. Like all Mirage F1 versions, the Mirage F1E can be fitted with comprehensive radar-warning receivers, chaff/flare dispensers and active ECM jammer pods, the most important of the latter being the Thomson-CSF Remora and Caiman. Customers for the Mirage F1E are Ecuador, Iraq (with Exocet), Jordan, Libya, Morocco, Qatar and Spain.

## Specification: Dassault Mirage F1E
**Origin:** France
**Type:** multi-role fighter and attack aircraft
**Powerplant:** one 7200-kg (15,873-lb) afterburning thrust SNECMA Atar 9K-50 turbojet
**Performance:** maximum speed about Mach 2 or 1,150 kt (2124 km/h; 1,320 mph) at high altitude; initial rate of climb about 39,400 ft (12000 m) per minute; combat radius similar to that of the Mirage F1C; combat air patrol endurance 2 hours 15 minutes
**Weights:** empty 7600 kg (16,755lb); maximum take-off 16200 kg (35,714 lb)
**Dimensions:** span 9.32 m (30 ft 6.9 in) including AAMs; length 15.30 m (50 ft 2.4 in); height 4.50 m (14 ft 9 in); wing area 25.0 m² (269.1 sq ft)
**Armament:** two 30-mm DEFA 553 cannon with 135 rounds per gun, plus Matra Super 530 and Matra Magic or sidewinder AAMs and attack loads as described for the Mirage F1C

*Dassault Mirage F1E*

*This Mirage F1E demonstrator carries an Aérospatiale Exocet on the centreline. Exocet-armed Mirage F1s have been used in anger by Iraq.*

*This Mirage F1EE is one of 22 delivered to supplement the 45 air defence-configured Mirage F1CEs also procured by the Spanish air force, which knows the F1EE as the C. 14B.*

### Role
Fighter
Close support
Counter-insurgency
Tactical strike
Strategic bomber
Tactical reconnaissance
Strategic reconnaissance
Maritime patrol
Anti-ship strike
Anti-submarine warfare
Search and rescue
Assault transport
Transport
Liaison
Trainer
Inflight-refuelling tanker
Specialized

### Performance
All-weather capability
Rough field capability
STOL capability
VTOL capability
Airspeed 0-250 mph
Airspeed 250 mph-Mach 1
Airspeed Mach 1 plus
Ceiling 0-20,000 ft
Ceiling 20,000-40,000 ft
Ceiling 40,000ft plus
Range 0-1,000 miles
Range 1,000-3,000 miles
Range 3,000 miles plus

### Weapons
Air-to-air missiles
Air-to-surface missiles
Cruise missiles
Cannon
Trainable guns
Naval weapons
Nuclear-capable
Rockets
'Smart' weapon kit
Weapon load 0-4,000 lb
Weapon load 4,000-15,000 lb
Weapon load 15,000 lb plus

### Avionics
Electronic Counter Measures
Electronic Support Measures
Search radar
Fire control radar
Look-down/shoot-down
Terrain-following radar
Forward-looking infra-red
Laser
Television

# Dassault Mirage F1C

*Dassault Mirage F1CK of the Kuwait air force.*

This attractive fighter was planned 35 years ago (although on a bigger scale of size and with a TF306 afterburning turbofan) to replace the Mirage III family. Nobody at that time could predict that the tailless delta version would remain in production for a further 25 years! The big Mirage F2 was flown in June 1966, but by this time (as a result of getting out of the Anglo- French Variable-Geometry project) Dassault had designed a smaller version powered by a single Atar engine. This prototype, the **Dassault Mirage F1**, flew on 23 December 1966.

Compared with the Mirage III, the Mirage F1 has a very much higher aerodynamic efficiency, much greater maximum lift/drag ratio, and 40 per cent greater internal fuel capacity despite the fact that the external skin area is considerably less. Although the wing had a gross area reduced from 35 m² (377 sq ft) to only 25 m² (269 sq ft), it was so much more efficient, with full-span leading-edge drooping slats and powerful double-slotted trailing-edge flaps, that approach speed was reduced 25 per cent and landing

run by 35 per cent, while dogfight manoeuvrability was greatly enhanced and also escaped the severe loss of speed and energy in turns suffered by the Mirage III family. Thanks to integral tankage in the fuselage, internal fuel capacity was raised from 2937 to 4300 litres (646 to 946 Imp gal), and a further 4455 litres (980 Imp gal) could be carried in three external tanks The **Mirage F1C-200** standard, to which most of the Armée de l'Air's 166 **Mirage F1C** fighters have been modified, has a fixed inflight-refuelling probe above the right side of the nose.

The first production Mirage F1C flew on 15 February 1973 and was officially delivered a month later. The first combat unit was the 30e Escadre de Chasse (fighter wing) at Reims followed by EC5 at Orange, EC12 at Cambrai and EC10 at Creil. Many overseas customers also purchased Mirage F1Cs, usually with the Cyrano IV radar that is simpler than the Cyrano IVM of the French fighters. Some 55 of the fighters are being upgraded to the **Mirage F1CT** standard for enhanced ground-attack capability.

**Specification:** Dassault Mirage F1C
**Origin:** France
**Type:** interceptor and fighter-bomber
**Powerplant:** one 7200-kg (15,873-lb) afterburning thrust SNECMA Atar 9K-50 turbojet
**Performance:** maximum speed Mach 2.2 or 1,259 kt (2335 km/h; 1450 mph) at high altitude; initial rate of climb 41,390 ft (12780 m) per minute; service ceiling 65,615 ft (20000 m); combat radius 425 km (265 miles) on a hi-lo-hi mission with 14 250-kg (551-lb) bombs and maximum internal fuel
**Weights:** empty 7400 kg (16,314 lb) maximum take-off 16200 kg (35,714 lb)
**Dimensions:** span 9.32 m (30 ft 6.69in) over AAMs; length 15.30 m (50 ft 2.4 in); height 4.50 m (14 ft 9 in); wing area 25.0 m² (269.1 sq ft)
**Armament:** two 30-mm DEFA 553 cannon with 135 rounds per gun, plus provision for a maximum external load of 6300 kg (13,889 lb) carried on five pylons, and Magic AAMs on wingtip rails; weapons include Matra Super 530 AAMs and all normal tactical bombs and rockets or laser-guided bombs, AS.30L laser-guided ASMs, AM.39 Exocet anti-ship missiles, ARMAT ARMs, or Durandal, Belouga or BAP anti-runway weapons

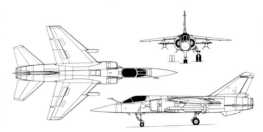

*Dassault Mirage F1C-200*

*The Moroccan air force uses both the Mirage F1CH and the Mirage F1EH for interception and ground- attack duties. This aircraft is an F1CH.*

*This Matra R530-armed Mirage F1C wears the markings of EC2/12 'Cornouaille', which began to work up on the Mirage F1 during 1976.*

**Role**
Fighter
Close support
Counter-insurgency
Tactical strike
Strategic bomber
Strategic reconnaissance
Tactical reconnaissance
Strategic reconnaissance
Maritime patrol
Anti-ship strike
Anti-submarine warfare
Search and rescue
Assault transport
Transport
Liaison
Trainer
Inflight-refuelling tanker
Specialized

**Performance**
All-weather capability
Rough field capability
STOL capability
VTOL capability
Airspeed 0-250 mph
Airspeed 250 mph-Mach 1
Airspeed Mach 1 plus
Ceiling 0-20,000 ft
Ceiling 20,000-40,000 ft
Ceiling 40,000ft plus
Range 0-1,000 miles
Range 1,000-3,000 miles
Range 3,000 miles plus

**Weapons**
Air-to-air missiles
Air-to-surface missiles
Cruise missiles
Cannon
Trainable guns
Naval weapons
Nuclear-capable
Rockets
'Smart' weapon kit
Weapon load 0-4,000 lb
Weapon load 4,000-15,000 lb
Weapon load 15,000 lb plus

**Avionics**
Electronic Counter Measures
Electronic Support Measures
Search radar
Fire control radar
Look-down/shoot-down
Terrain-following radar
Forward-looking infra-red
Laser
Television

# Dassault Mirage F1R

*Dassault Mirage F1CR of ER33, French air force.*

### Role

Fighter
Close support
Counter-insurgency
Tactical strike
Strategic bomber
Tactical reconnaissance
Strategic reconnaissance
Maritime patrol
Anti-ship strike
Anti-submarine warfare
Search and rescue
Assault transport
Transport
Liaison
Trainer
Inflight-refuelling tanker
Specialized

### Performance

All-weather capability
Rough field capability
STOL capability
VTOL capability
Airspeed 0-250 mph
Airspeed 250 mph-Mach 1
Airspeed Mach 1 plus
Ceiling 0-20,000 ft
Ceiling 20,000-40,000 ft
Ceiling 40,000 ft plus
Range 0-1,000 miles
Range 1,000-3,000 miles
Range 3,000 miles plus

### Weapons

Air-to-air missiles
Air-to-surface missiles
Cruise missiles
Cannon
Trainable guns
Naval weapons
Nuclear-capable
Rockets
'Smart' weapon kit
Weapon load 0-4,000 lb
Weapon load 4,000-15,000 lb
Weapon load 15,000 lb plus

### Avionics

Electronic Counter Measures
Electronic Support Measures
Search radar
Fire control radar
Look-down/shoot-down
Terrain-following radar
Forward-looking infra-red
Laser
Television

As soon as it was clear that the Mirage F1 would support a major production programme, Dassault studied a dedicated reconnaissance version, one of the main potential customers being the French air force (Armée de l'Air), which would eventually need a replacement for the Mirage IIIR in the 33e Escadre de Reconnaissance at Strasbourg. Given the escalating unit price of combat aircraft, there was a strong case for not building such a variant, but instead concentrating on the procurement of multi-sensor reconnaissance pods which could be carried by otherwise fully combat capable Mirage F1 versions.

In fact export customers, as well as EC5 of the Armée de l'Air at Orange, have installed various reconnaissance pods on the centreline pylon of the Mirage F1 fighter/attack aircraft. These pods include one combining a SAT Cyclope IRLS (infra-red linescan) and an EMI SLAR (side-looking airborne radar), another combining SAT Cyclope and four cameras, and a third having an unspecified mix of equipment for high-altitude long-distance coverage.

In February 1979 it was announced that the Armée de l'Air would replace the Mirage IIIR with a dedicated **Dassault Mirage F1CR-200** as the initial member of

the planned Mirage F1R family. The first of two prototypes, converted from Mirage F1C-200 fighters, flew on 20 November 1981. Prolonged testing was needed to debug the advanced software and SNAR navigation system, which was derived from that of the Mirage 2000 and built around a high-power ESD computer, Uliss 47 inertial system and Cyrano IVM-R radar with ground-map and DBS (Doppler beam sharpening) modes. Internal equipment includes an OMERA 33 vertical medium-altitude camera, OMERA 40 panoramic horizon-to-horizon camera, OMERA 400 sight/recorder, photoflash installation, SAT Super Cyclope WCM 2400 IRLS, and Thomson-CSF Raphaël SLAR. External equipment, usually carried on the centreline, can include the Harold pod, a new SLAR, a Nora pod with optronic sensor for imagery at Mach 1 at low (or high) level, and the Thomson-CSF Syrel Elint pod for recording and analysing hostile radiations.

The Armée de l'Air Mirage F1CR-200 has no guns but possesses an inflight-refuelling probe. Including the two prototypes, 64 such aircraft were delivered: the first production machine flew on 10 November 1982, and ER2/33 became operational in July 1983. No export order was received.

**Dassault Mirage F1CR**

**One of ER33's Dassault Mirage F1CRs is seen outside a HAS (Hardened Aircraft Shelter) at RAF Alconbury. Underwing fuel tanks are almost invariably carried.**

**This Dassault-operated Mirage F1CR carries underwing fuel tanks and jammer pods, wingtip-mounted Magic AAMs and a sensor pod under the belly.**

**Specification:** Dassault Mirage F1CR-200
**Type:** tactical and strategic all-weather reconnaissance aircraft
**Powerplant:** one 7200-kg (15,873-lb) afterburning thrust SNECMA Atar 9K-50 turbojet
**Performance:** maximum speed about Mach 1.8 or 1,033 kt (1915 km/h; 1,190 mph) at high altitude with centreline pod; combat radius 1390 km (863 miles) on a hi-lo-hi mission with one external pod and two drop tanks
**Weights:** empty about 7900 kg (17,416 lb); maximum take-off 16200 kg (35,714 lb)
**Dimensions:** span 9.32 m (30 ft 6.9in) including AAMs; length 15.30 m (50 ft 2.4 in); height 4.50 m (14 ft 9 in); wing area 25.0 m² (269.1 sq ft)
**Armament:** not carried except self-defence Magic AAMs on the wingtips

# Dassault Mirage 2000B

*Dassault Mirage 2000B of EC1/2, Armée de l'Air.*

Although it had specified a two-seat model of the Mirage F1 almost as an afterthought, the Armée de l'Air decided that a dual-control trainer version of its next-generation Mirage should be delivered in parallel with the Mirage 2000C interceptor to assist pilots' conversion. The fifth Mirage 2000 prototype, flown for the first time on 11 October 1980, was thus the initial **Dassault Mirage 2000B** trainer, and it was followed into the air from 7 October 1983 by production aircraft of the same variant. In order to accommodate the additional cockpit with its Martin-Baker ejector seat the internal cannon are removed. there is an increase in fuselage length of 0.19 m (7.5 in), and a reduction of internal fuel capacity from 3980 to 3870 litres (875 to 851 Imp gal). The Mirage 2000B is otherwise similar to its single-seat counterpart and, of course, is able to rectify some of its operational shortcomings through carriage of a podded 30-mm cannon and external fuel tanks, as well as the full range of operational equipment found on the Mirage 2000C. Radar is fitted as standard, and one Mirage 2000B was heavily involved in development of the definitive RDI radar.

France is acquiring 22 examples of the Mirage 2000B, and the aircraft were first allocated to the three squadrons of 2e

Escadre de Chasse at Dijon. Dual-control aircraft have been included in the first five export contracts for the Mirage 2000 series, although not all of these two-seaters have the suffix B in their designation. India, whose first aircraft were delivered in June 1985, has received seven **Mirage 2000TH** trainers with its 42 Mirage 2000H attack aircraft (see Mirage 2000C and Mirage 2000N), both types having the local name **Vajra** (divine thunderbolt). Only the last 10 of the initial 40 aircraft were delivered with the uprated SNECMA M53-P2 engine, although the M53-5 turbofans of the first 30 were later upgraded.

Peru, the next recipient, ordered two **Mirage 2000DP** trainers and 24 Mirage 2000P fighters, but later reduced the order to two and 10 aircraft respectively for financial reasons. Egypt's order comprised four **Mirage 2000BM** trainers with 16 Mirage 2000EM fighters, but nothing came of a plan to assemble a repeat batch locally from French components. Also in the Middle East, Abu Dhabi doubled an initial order to a total 36 aircraft including six **Mirage 2000DAD** trainers, eight Mirage 2000RAD reconnaissance models and 22 Mirage 2000EAD attack/interceptors. Deliveries to Greece included four **Mirage 2000BGM** trainers and 36 Mirage 2000EGM multi-role aircraft.

**Specification:** Dassault Mirage 2000B
**Origin:** France
**Type:** combat-capable two-seat trainer
**Powerplant:** one 9700-kg (221,834-lb) afterburning thrust SNECMA M53-P2 turbofan
**Performance:** maximum speed Mach2.2 or 1,261 kt (2338 km/h; 1,453 mph) at high altitude; initial rate of climb 56,000 ft (17069 m) per minute; service ceiling 59,055 ft (18000 m ); range 1850 km (1,150 miles ) with two 1700-litre (374-lmp gal) drop tanks
**Weights:** empty 7600 kg (16,755 lb), maximum take-off 17000 kg (37,478 lb)
**Dimensions:** span 9.26 m (30 ft 4.5 in); length 14.55 m (47 ft 9 in); height 5.15 m (l6 ft 10.75in); wing area 41.0 m² (441.3 sq ft)
**Armament:** provision for up to 6300 kg (13,889 lb) of stores on nine external hardpoints, including cannon pods, AAMs, ASMs, bombs. rockets and ECM pods

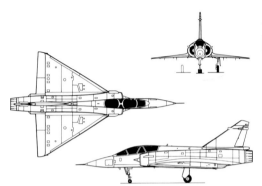

*Dassault Mirage 2000B*

*This unmarked Mirage 2000 is actually one of the Mirage 2000DPs built for the Peruvian air force; Peru ordered two two-seat aircraft to serve alongside its eventual 10 single-seaters.*

*EC1/2 operates Mirage 2000Bs from Dijon. The unit's aircraft proudly wear the stork insignia of 'Les Cigognes', carrying on a tradition dating from World War I.*

## Role

Fighter
Close support
Counter-insurgency
Tactical strike
Strategic bomber
Tactical reconnaissance
Strategic reconnaissance
Maritime patrol
Anti-ship strike
Anti-submarine warfare
Search and rescue
Assault transport
Transport
Liaison
Trainer
Inflight-refuelling tanker
Specialized

## Performance

All-weather capability
Rough field capability
STOL capability
VTOL capability
Airspeed 0-250 mph
Airspeed 250 mph-Mach 1
Airspeed Mach 1 plus
Ceiling 0-20,000 ft
Ceiling 20,000-40,000 ft
Ceiling 40,000ft plus
Range 0-1,000 miles
Range 1,000-3,000 miles
Range 3,000 miles plus

## Weapons

Air-to-air missiles
Air-to-surface missiles
Cruise missiles
Cannon
Trainable guns
Naval weapons
Nuclear-capable
Rockets
'Smart' weapon kit
Weapon load 0-4,000 lb
Weapon load 4,000-15,000 lb
Weapon load 15,000 lb plus

## Avionics

Electronic Counter Measures
Electronic Support Measures
Search radar
Fire control radar
Look-down/shoot-down
Terrain-following radar
Forward-looking infra-red
Laser
Television

# Dassault Mirage 2000C/N

*Dassault Mirage 2000H Vajra of No.225 Squadron, Indian Air Force.*

## Role
Fighter
Close support
Counter-insurgency
Tactical strike
Strategic bomber
Tactical reconnaissance
Strategic reconnaissance
Maritime patrol
Anti-ship strike
Anti-submarine warfare
Search and rescue
Assault transport
Transport
Liaison
Trainer
Inflight-refuelling tanker
Specialized

## Performance
All-weather capability
Rough field capability
STOL capability
VTOL capability
Airspeed 0-250 mph
Airspeed 250 mph-Mach 1
Airspeed Mach 1 plus
Ceiling 0-20,000 ft
Ceiling 20,000-40,000 ft
Ceiling 40,000ft plus
Range 0-1,000 miles
Range 1,000-3,000 miles
Range 3,000 miles plus

## Weapons
Air-to-air missiles
Air-to-surface missiles
Cruise missiles
Cannon
Trainable guns
Naval weapons
Nuclear-capable
Rockets
'Smart' weapon kit
Weapon load 0-4,000 lb
Weapon load 4,000-15,000 lb
Weapon load 15,000 lb plus

## Avionics
Electronic Counter Measures
Electronic Support Measures
Search radar
Fire control radar
Look-down/shoot-down
Terrain-following radar
Forward-looking infra-red
Laser
Television

For its third generation of the Mirage fighter family, Dassault-Breguet returned to the delta wing configuration. By the time it appeared, fly-by-wire (FBW) technology and advances in aerodynamics had obviated many of the disadvantages associated with earlier deltas (notably a lack of low-speed manoeuvrability) making the **Dassault Mirage 2000** a highly agile aircraft. Adopted by the French government in December 1975, the Mirage 2000 stems from the Delta 1000 study of three years earlier. By the time of the prototype's first flight on 10 March 1978, plans had been laid for large-scale production for the Armée de l'Air of at least 127 (later 146) **Mirage 2000C** interceptors.

In addition to being the first French combat aircraft with relaxed stability and FBW, the Mirage 2000C incorporates a new powerplant and advanced avionics. The SNECMA M53 turbofan equipped early aircraft in its 9000-kg (19,8410-lb) afterburning thrust M53-5 form, but this was then replaced by the uprated M53-P2. First available in export aircraft, the M53-P2 has been fitted in new Armée de l'Air Mirage 2000B trainers and Mirage 2000C interceptors from June 1986.

At about the same time, the Mirage 2000C's radar was changed from the original Thomson-CSF RDM (Radar Doppler Multifonction) derived from the Mirage F1's air-to-air/air-to-ground Cyrano to the more advanced Thomson-CSF/ESD RDI (Radar Doppler à Impulsions) optimized for interception of opposing aircraft. It is integrated with the equally new medium-range Matra Super 530D semi-active radar-homing AAM, although the shorter-range Magic 2 IR-homing AAM is also carried for close combats.

In addition to two internal 30-mm DEFA 554 cannon, the Mirage 2000C has four underwing and five underfuselage attachments for armament and ECM equipment. In the case of the **Mirage 2000RAD** ordered by Abu Dhabi, a reconnaissance pod is carried on the centreline position. The first production Mirage 2000C flew on 20 November 1982, and the type formally entered French service on 2 July 1984. Export contracts were received from Abu Dhabi, Egypt, Greece, India and Peru for the **Mirage 2000EAD, Mirage 2000EM, Mirage 2000EGM, Mirage 2000H** and **Mirage 2000P**.

First flown on 3 February 1983, the **Mirage 2000N** is a specialized low-level strike fighter based on the airframe of the Mirage 2000B with the rear cockpit adapted for the weapons system officer, whose primary equipment includes the Antilope 5 terrain-following radar and the Integrated Countermeasures System based on a Serval radar warner, Sabre jammer and Spirale automatic chaff/flare dispenser. The first 31 aircraft are **Mirage 2000N-K1** machines with the ASMP nuclear stand-off missile but the following 39 **Mirage 2000N-K2** machines have provision for conventional weapons.

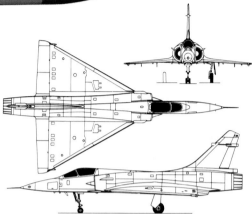

*Dassault Mirage 2000C*

## Specification: Dassault Mirage 2000C (from 1987)
**Origin:** France
**Type:** single-seat air-superiority and attack fighter
**Powerplant:** one 9700-kg (21,834-lb) afterburning thrust SNECMA M53-P2 turbofan
**Performance:** maximum speed Mach2.2 or 1,261 kt (2338 km/h; 1,453 mph) at high altitude; initial rate of climb 56,000 ft (17069 m) per minute; service ceiling 59,055 ft (18000 m); range 1480+ km (920+ miles) with a 1000-kg (2,205-lb) bombload
**Weights:** empty 7500 kg (16,534 lb); maximum take-off 17000 kg (37,478 lb)
**Dimensions:** span 9.13 m (29 ft 11.5 in); length 14.36 m (47 ft 1.25 in); height 5.20 m (17 ft 0.75 in); wing area 41.0 m² (441.3 sq ft)
**Armament:** two 30-mm DEFA 554 cannon with 125 rounds per gun, plus provision for up to 6300 kg (13,889 lb) of external stores including AAMs, ASMs, bombs, rockets, ECM pods and reconnaissance pods

*This EC1/2 'Les Cicognes' Mirage 2000C carries Matra Magic missiles outboard and Super 530s inboard, a potent mix for air-to-air combat. Air-to-surface weapons can also be carried.*

*Sitting outside its Hardened Aircraft Shelter, this French air force Mirage 2000C carries a pair of Matra Magic practice rounds. A superb fly-by-wire control system makes the aircraft versatile.*

# Dassault Rafale

*One of two prototypes of the navalised Dassault Rafale M.*

Intended to meet requirements for an Avion de Combat Tactique (ACT) to supersede the Armée de l'Air's SEPECAT Jaguars in the 1990s, and an Avion de Combat Marine (ACM) for deployment on the navy's forthcoming nuclear-powered carriers, the ACX (advanced combat experimental) design was finally committed as an all-French effort. The new type was required to offer a multi-role capability: for air combat the carriage of at least six AAMs was requested, and for attack the demand was for a radius of 650 km (404 miles) with a 3500-kg (7,716-lb) bombload.

The company decided to go ahead with the **Dassault Rafale** (squall) project in early 1983. Work on the single **Rafale** technology demonstrator in March 1984, and the aircraft was rolled out on 14December 1985. It has a compound delta mid-set monoplane wing incorporating full-span leading-edge slats linked to full-span trailing- edge elevons, all made mainly of carbon fibre as are the shoulder-mounted, all-moving swept foreplanes located just forward of the junction of the wing leading edges and the fuselage. The swept vertical tail surfaces and some 50 per cent of the fuselage are also constructed of composites. Power was provided in the prototype by two General Electric F404-GE-400 afterburning turbofans. The pilot relied on an advanced-technology FBW system to control the aircraft safely to the full limits of its flight envelope. The armament included a single 30-mm cannon and there were 12 external stores attachments. First flown on 4

July 1986, the Rafale A soon demonstrated its potential, achieving Mach 1.3 during its maiden flight and Mach 1.8 only a few days later. As development of the Rafale A continued, the French ministry of defence in April 1988 ordered the development of the planned production model in an initial three variants with slightly smaller dimensions and reduced weights for propulsion by two SNECMA M88-2 turbofans that will be replaced in production aircraft by 8875-kg (19,566-lb) afterburning thrust M88-3 turbofans. These three radar-equipped variants are the Rafale B tandem two-seat trainer for the Armée de l'Air, the **Rafale C** single-seat operational aircraft for the Armée de l'Air, and the **Rafale M** for the Aéronavale. Although the program has progressed satisfactorily in technical terms, the first prototypes of the three variants flying in May 1991, February 1993 and December 1991 respectively, its political and economic progress has been affected by the end of the 'Cold War': the navy still needs 78 aircraft for service from 2000, and the air force requires 334 aircraft from a time shortly after this, but for financial reasons the French government wants to stretch the programme and reduce its numbers. At the same time the air force is concerned about its blend of single- and two-seat aircraft, and now wants 239 Rafale B multi-role warplanes, together with 95 examples of the Rafale C single-seater operating mainly in the reconnaissance role.

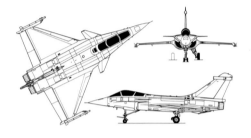

**Dassault Rafale M**

**The Rafale was developed as a highly agile tactical fighter for the 1990s and beyond, and is intended to replace Armée de l'Air Jaguars and Aéronavale Crusaders.**

**Specification:** Dassault Rafale C (estimated)
**Origin:** France
**Type:** multi-role combat aircraft
**Powerplant:** two 7450-kg (16,424-lb) afterburning thrust SNECMA M88-2 turbofans
**Performance:** maximum speed Mach 2 or 1,150 kt (2130 km/h; 1,324 mph) at high altitude; combat radius 1093 km (679 miles) on a low-level mission with 12 551-lb (250-kg) bombs and four Mica AAMs
**Weights:** empty 9060 kg (19,973 lb); maximum 19500 kg (42,990 lb)
**Dimensions:** span 10.90 m (35 ft 9.125 in) including AAMs; length 15.30 m (50 ft 2.375 in); height 5.34 m (17 ft 6.25 in); wing area 46.0 m² (495.1 sq ft)
**Armament:** one 30-mm DEFA 791B cannon, plus provision for up to 6000 kg (13,228 lb) of disposable stores carried on 14 external hardpoints

**The production version of the Rafale will be slightly smaller than the Rafale A technology demonstrator. The naval version should enter service slightly before the air force models.**

## Role
Fighter
Close support
Counter-insurgency
Tactical strike
Strategic bomber
Tactical reconnaissance
Strategic reconnaissance
Maritime patrol
Anti-ship strike
Anti-submarine warfare
Search and rescue
Assault transport
Transport
Liaison
Trainer
Inflight-refuelling tanker
Specialized

## Performance
All-weather capability
Rough field capability
STOL capability
VTOL capability
Airspeed 0-250 mph
Airspeed 250 mph-Mach 1
Airspeed Mach 1 plus
Ceiling 0-20,000 ft
Ceiling 20,000-40,000 ft
Ceiling 40,000ft plus
Range 0-1,000 miles
Range 1,000-3,000 miles
Range 3,000 miles plus

## Weapons
Air-to-air missiles
Air-to-surface missiles
Cruise missiles
Cannon
Trainable guns
Naval weapons
Nuclear-capable
Rockets
'Smart' weapon kit
Weapon load 0-4,000 lb
Weapon load 4,000-15,000 lb
Weapon load 15,000 lb plus

## Avionics
Electronic Counter Measures
Electronic Support Measures
Search radar
Fire control radar
Look-down/shoot-down
Terrain-following radar
Forward-looking infra-red
Laser
Television

# Dassault Super Etendard

*Dassault Super Etendard of the Aéronavale.*

Developed from the Etendard carrierborne attack aircraft, the **Dassault Super Etendard** is a multi-role fighter equipped for interception as well as maritime strike/attack. The Super Etendard programme was officially launched in January 1973 after the French navy had rejected a maritime version of the SEPECAT Jaguar as its replacement for both the Etendard and LTV F-8E(FN) Crusader fighter.

Considerable improvements in avionics and aerodynamics are to be found in the Super Etendard, the latter including a revised wing with additional high-lift devices. This allows retention of handling characteristics similar to those of the original aircraft despite a higher all-up weight, and even reduces the approach speed. Available power is also increased as the result of a change to the Atar 8K-50 non-afterburning turbojet. An inertial navigation system (the first fitted in a French combat aircraft) provides a high degree of accuracy during sorties over featureless ocean. The Super Etendard also benefits from the addition of radar in the form of the Thomson-CSF/ESD Agave multi-mode unit that provides for surface attack as well as air-to-air interception. The formidable sea-skimming Aérospatiale AM.39 Exocet is the prime anti-shipping weapon (one being carried on the starboard inner pylon), whilst the Matra Magic IR-homing AAM is employed for air defence. From 1987 onward, Super Etendards have exchanged their AN-52 free-fall nuclear bombs for the Aérospatiale ASMP stand-off nuclear missile carried by 50 of the aircraft.

Features of the Super Etendard's revised design and systems were flown separately in three converted Etendards from October 1974 onward, although it was not until 3 October 1975 that a true prototype took to the air. Deliveries of 71 Super Etendards to the French navy began in June 1978, and were completed in March 1983, but five were loaned to the Iraqi air force for a two-year period soon after this. The latter made numerous Exocet attacks in the Gulf as part of Iraq's war effort against Iran, claiming several oil tankers destroyed or damaged. A further 14 Super Etendards were supplied to Argentina from November 1981 onward, although only five had been received by the time of the Falklands war of 1982, during which they sank two British ships for no loss to themselves. These operations were undertaken from land bases, and it was not until April 1983 that the aircraft began flying from the carrier *Veinticinco de Mayo*. France's Super Etendards are operated by Flottilles 11F, 14F and 17F aboard *Foch* and *Clemenceau*.

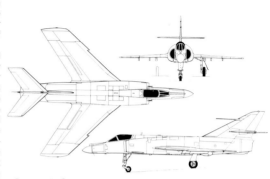

**Dassault Super Etendard**

## Specification: Dassault Super Etendard
**Origin:** France
**Type:** carrierborne strike/attack and interceptor fighter
**Powerplant:** one 5000-kg (11,023-lb) dry thrust SNECMA Atar 8K-50 turbojet
**Performance:** maximum speed 637 kt (1180 km/h;733 mph) at low level, or Mach 1.3 or 734 kt (1380 km/h; 857 mph) at 36,000 ft (10975 m); initial rate of climb 19,685 ft (6000 m) per minute; service ceiling 44,950 ft (13700 m); combat radius 850 km (528 miles) on a hi-lo-hi mission with one Exocet and two external tanks
**Weights:** empty 6500 kg (14,330 lb); maximum take-off 12000 kg (26,455 lb)
**Dimensions:** span 9.60 m (31 ft 6 in); length 14.31 m (46 ft 11.2 in); height 3.86 m (12 ft 8 in); wing area 28.4 m² (305.7 sq ft)
**Armament:** two 30-mm DEFA 553 cannon with 125 rounds per gun, plus provision for up to 2100 kg (4,630 lb) of stores carried on five external pylons, including AN-52 and ASMP nuclear weapons, Exocet and (Argentina only) Martin Pescador ASMs, Magic AAMs, bombs and rockets, and refuelling and reconnaissance pods

*This is one of 14 Super Etendards supplied to the Argentine navy, and used by that service during the Falklands war of 1982.*

*A Super Etendard of Flotille 11F is catapult-launched from the deck of a French carrier. The squadron's land base is Landivisiau in Brittany.*

# Dassault/Dornier Alpha Jet
# Close Support Version

Although West Germany joined with France in the Alpha Jet programme intending to acquire an advanced trainer similar to that of its partner, although in a form powered by General Electric J85 turbojets, its plans were radically altered in 1971 by the decision to adopt a light attack model. This resulted in the construction of 175 **Dornier Alpha Jet A** (for Attaque, or attack) aircraft of the **Alpha Jet Close Support Version** readily identifiable by its sharply pointed nose. Despite considerable avionics changes, the Alpha Jet A moved closer to its French brother when Larzac turbofans were adopted for reasons of cost-saving commonality.

Additional combat equipment in the Alpha Jet A includes a HUD, radar-warning receiver, Doppler navigation, attitude and heading reference system, and Stencel SIII rather than Martin-Baker ejector seats. Most aircraft are flown by the pilot only, however, and those with rear seats are dual-control models used for operational training. The Alpha Jet A carries a ventral 27-mm cannon pack and a typical underwing load of four Hunting BL755 cluster bombs. The cannon was intended for use in the secondary role of anti-helicopter attack. The aircraft were delivered in 1979-82, initially to the OCU, Jagdbombergeschwader 49 (JBG 49) at Fürstenfeldbruck during January 1980.

Further aircraft were supplied to JBG 41 at Husum, JBG 43 at Oldenburg and the armament training establishment (Ubungsplatzkommando) at Beja in Portugal.

In 1987 West Germany announced its intention to upgrade the Alpha Jet A force between 1990 and 1995 in the ICE (Improved Combat Efficiency) programme that would introduce a new nav/attack system for night and poor weather operations; improved ECM, HUD and AHARS; laser rangefinder; improved weapons such as the AGM-65 Maverick air-to-surface missile; and 1440-kg (3,175-lb) dry thrust Larzac 04-C20 engines. Self-defence and anti-helicopter provision would also be upgraded through wingtip provision for AIM-9L Sidewinder AAMs. In 1988 this programme was curtailed drastically to the Sidewinders, improved navigation and air data sensors, and the Larzac 04-C20 engines, but the end of the communist threat in the late 1980s with the collapse of the USSR and the later dissolution of the Warsaw Pact meant that even this programme was cancelled and it was decided to retire the Alpha Jet As as rapidly as possible though grounding or transfer to friendly nations such as Portugal (50 aircraft) and possibly Turkey. All but 35 aircraft had been retired from German service by 1995.

**Specification:** Dornier Alpha Jet A
**Origin:** West Germany (and France)
**Type:** light attack aircraft with weapons training capability
**Powerplant:** two 1350-kg (2,976-lb) dry thrust SNECMA/Turbomeca Larzac 04-C6 turbofans
**Performance:** maximum speed 539 kt (1000 km/h; 621 mph) at sea level, or Mach 0.85 or 494 kt (916 km/h; 569 mph) at 32,810 ft (10,000 m); initial rate of climb 11,220 ft (3420 m) per minute; service ceiling 48,000 ft (14630 m); combat radius 583 km (363 miles) on a hi-lo-hi mission including a 100-km (62-mile) dash on internal fuel or 1075 km (668 miles) with external tanks
**Weights:** 3515 kg (7,749 lb); maximum take-off 8000kg (17,637 lb)
**Dimensions:** span 9.11 m (29 ft 10.75 in); length 13.23 m (43 ft 4.9 in) including probe; height 4.19 m (13 ft 9 in); wing area 17.50 m² (188.37 sq ft)
**Armament:** one 27-mm IWKA-Mauser cannon, plus provision for up to 2500 kg (5,511 lb) of external stores on five attachment points, and including Hunting BL755 CBUs

*Dassault/Dornier Alpha Jet A of JBG 49, Luftwaffe, based at Fürstenfeldbruck.*

*Dornier Alpha Jet A*

*One of JBG 49's Alpha Jet As is seen at RAF Abingdon, in company with an example of its great rival, the British Aerospace Hawk T.Mk 1.*

*A Dornier Alpha Jet A of JBG 43 is shown on approach to its base at Oldenburg. Luftwaffe Alpha Jets are used in the light attack role.*

**Role**
Fighter
Close support
Counter-insurgency
Tactical strike
Strategic bomber
Tactical reconnaissance
Strategic reconnaissance
Maritime patrol
Anti-ship strike
Anti-submarine warfare
Search and rescue
Assault transport
Transport
Liaison
Trainer
Inflight-refuelling tanker
Specialized

**Performance**
All-weather capability
Rough field capability
STOL capability
VTOL capability
Airspeed 0-250 mph
Airspeed 250 mph-Mach 1
Airspeed Mach 1 plus
Ceiling 0-20,000 ft
Ceiling 20,000-40,000 ft
Ceiling 40,000ft plus
Range 0-1,000 miles
Range 1,000-3,000 miles
Range 3,000 miles plus

**Weapons**
Air-to-air missiles
Air-to-surface missiles
Cruise missiles
Cannon
Trainable guns
Naval weapons
Nuclear-capable
Rockets
'Smart' weapon kit
Weapon load 0-4,000 lb
Weapon load 4,000-15,000 lb
Weapon load 15,000 lb plus

**Avionics**
Electronic Counter Measures
Electronic Support Measures
Search radar
Fire control radar
Look-down/shoot-down
Terrain-following radar
Forward-looking infra-red
Laser
Television

# de Havilland Canada DHC-6 Twin Otter

de Havilland Canada DHC-6 Twin Otter of the Fuerza Aérea de Chile.

### Role
Fighter
Close support
Counter-insurgency
Tactical strike
Strategic bomber
Tactical reconnaissance
Strategic reconnaissance
Maritime patrol
Anti-ship strike
Anti-submarine warfare
Search and rescue
Assault transport
Transport
Liaison
Trainer
Inflight-refuelling tanker
Specialized

### Performance
All-weather capability
Rough field capability
STOL capability
VTOL capability
Airspeed 0-250 mph
Airspeed 250 mph-Mach 1
Airspeed Mach 1 plus
Ceiling 0-20,000 ft
Ceiling 20,000-40,000 ft
Ceiling 40,000ft plus
Range 0-1,000 miles
Range 1,000-3,000 miles
Range 3,000 miles plus

### Weapons
Air-to-air missiles
Air-to-surface missiles
Cruise missiles
Cannon
Trainable guns
Naval weapons
Nuclear-capable
Rockets
'Smart' weapon kit
Weapon load 0-4,000 lb
Weapon load 4,000-15,000 lb
Weapon load 15,000 lb plus

### Avionics
Electronic Counter Measures
Electronic Support Measures
Search radar
Fire control radar
Look-down/shoot-down
Terrain-following radar
Forward-looking infra-red
Laser
Television

The last production version of the **de Havilland Canada DHC-6 Twin Otter** was the **DHC-6 Series 300**, which was bought by 22 air forces. Originally developed in the 1960s and first flown on 20 May 1965, the Twin Otter was first powered by two 432-kW (579-ehp) PT6A-6 turboprops and was intended to extend the transport potential of the popular single-engine DHC-3 Otter while retaining the efficient high-lift wing for STOL. Indeed the new 13/18-seat transport retained no more than the original basic wing structure with its full-span double-slotted flaps and ailerons, and from the fourth aircraft onwards the **DHC-6 Series 100** adopted PT6A-20 engines. Optional conversion from fixed tricycle wheeled landing gear to floats or skis was available

FAA type approval was gained in 1966 and led quickly to commercial orders, but military interest was slow to materialize: nevertheless eight aircraft were delivered to the Canadian Armed Forces as **CC-138** search and rescue machines. After 115 Series 100 aircraft had been completed, production switched to the **DHC-6 Series 200** with a lengthened nose and increased baggage capacity. Some 115 of this version were produced (a few of them for military customers) before DHC embarked on the Series 300. In this adoption of the more powerful PT6A-27 engine allowed the accommodation to be increased to 20 and the maximum take-off weight to rise by some 454 kg (1,000 lb).

Military customers have included Argentina (seven transports for the air force, three liaison aircraft for the army and a liaison aircraft for the navy), Afghanistan (two transports), Chile (12 transports), Colombia (four coastal patrol aircraft), Ecuador (two transports), Ethiopia (three transports), France (eight for the army and three for the air force), Jamaica (one for VIP use), Nepal (three transports), Norway (five for search and rescue/liaison), Panama (two transports), Paraguay (two transports), Peru (11 transports, including some float-equipped Series 100s), Sudan (one Series 300 for survey work) and Uganda (one transport for the police wing). A total of 10 was supplied to the USA, two and three being flown by the US Army and USAF Academy as **UV-18A** aircraft, and five by the Alaska Air National Guard as **UV-18B** aircraft.

In 1982 DHC offered three dedicated military versions of the Twin Otter: the DHC-6-300M was a 15-troop transport convertible to 20-seater or with paratroop or ambulance layout; the DHC-6-300M (COIN) was a counter-insurgency variant with provision for armour protection, a cabin-mounted machine-gun and underwing ordnance; and the DHC-6300MR was a maritime reconnaissance model with search radar under the nose and underwing searchlight pod. The only sale was one of the last variant, purchased by the Senegal Department of Fisheries.

**Specification:** de Havilland Canada DHC-6 Twin Otter Series 300
**Origin:** Canada
**Type:** 13/18-seat STOL utility transport
**Powerplant:** two 486-ekW (652-ehp) Pratt & Whitney Canada PT6A-27 turboprops
**Performance:** maximum speed 182 kt (338 km/h; 210 mph) at 10,000 ft (3050 m); service ceiling 26,700 ft (8140 m); range 1297 km (806 miles) with a 1134-kg (2,500-lb) payload
**Weights:** empty 3363 kg (7,415 lb); maximum take-off 5670 kg (12,500 lb)
**Dimensions:** span 19.81 m (65 ft 0 in); length 15.77 m (51 ft 9 in); height 5.94 m (19 ft 6 in); wing area 39.02 m² (420.0 sq f t)
**Armament:** the DHC-6-300M (COIN) was offered with provision for light ordnance on underwing hardpoints and a single machine-gun in the cabin

de Havilland Canada DHC-6 Twin Otter

*This aircraft was the first of at least three Twin Otters delivered to the Fuerza Aérea Panamena. It is understood to have been written off since it was delivered in 1970.*

*Many Twin Otters of the Canadian Armed Forces are painted in high-conspicuity yellow for search and rescue duties. Some aircraft are ski-equipped; this machine has a nosewheel ski only.*

# Dornier Do 28/28D Skyservant and Do 128 TurboSky

*Dornier Do 28D of the Marineflieger.*

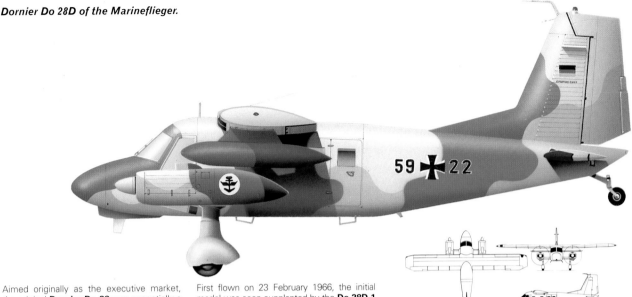

Aimed originally as the executive market, the original **Dornier Do 28** was essentially a twin-engined derivative of the Do 27, with a pair of Lycoming engines mounted at the tips of stub wings beside the cabin. The wings, rear fuselage and tail unit were unchanged, but the cabin was enlarged to seat eight, and a new wide-track landing gear was fitted beneath the engine nacelles. The prototype first flew on 29 April 1959, and was followed by 60 **Do 28A** and then by 60 Do 28B aircraft with more powerful engines and other improvements. Three Do 28As were delivered to the Luftwaffe, but the only **Do 28A** and Do 28B series aircraft to survive into the 1980s were those of Somalia, Turkey and Zambia.

The Do 28B was superseded by the **Do 28D Skyservant**, which was redesignated at the **Do 128** in 1980 and was a virtually complete redesign of the basic aircraft incorporating a new fuselage, wing, tail unit and powerplant.

First flown on 23 February 1966, the initial model was soon supplanted by the **Do 28D-1** with a wing of increased span. Production of the Do 28D series totalled 49 aircraft. The **Do 28D-2** introduced aerodynamic improvements, extra fuel capacity and underwing hardpoints, and was exported to eight countries as well as being procured in large number for the Luftwaffe and Marineflieger. The German aircraft were powered by Lycoming IGSO-540 engines, most being uprated to TGIO-540 standard during the 1980s.

First flown on 9 April 1978 as the Do 126D-5X prototype, the **Do 128-6 TurboSky** was a comparatively radical update of the Do 128 with a turboprop powerplant of two 298-kW (400-shp) Pratt & Whitney Canada PT6A-110 engines. The only military operators of the type in its Do 128-6 baseline and **Do 128-6MPA** maritime patrol forms were Cameroun and Nigeria, which took 18 Do 128-6 and a few Do 128-6MPA aircraft respectively.

**Specification:** Dornier Do 28B-1
**Origin:** West Germany
**Type:** eight-seat general-purpose STOL transport
**Powerplant:** two 216-kW (290-shp) Avco Lycoming IO-540A flat-six piston engines
**Performance:** maximum speed 156 kt (290 km/h; 180 mph) at sea level; initial rate of climb 1,400 ft (427 m) per minute; service ceiling 20,700 ft (6300 m); range 1235 km (768 miles) with maximum payload
**Weights:** empty 1730 kg (3,814 lb); maximum take-off 2720 kg (5,996 lb)
**Dimensions:** span 13.80 m (45 ft 3.5 in); length 9.00 m (29 ft 6 in); height 2.80 m (9 ft 2 in); wing area 22.40 m² (241.1 sq ft)
**Armament:** none

**Dornier Do 28D (Do 128D Skyservant since 1980)**

*Every Luftwaffe wing had a number of Do 128s on strength for support and communications duties. This example is seen in the markings of JBG 31 'Boelcke', a fighter-bomber unit.*

*This attractively camouflaged Do 128 Skyservant belongs to MFG 5, based at Kiel with a mixture of types including the Westland Lynx and Westland Sea king helicopters. It also evaluated the Do 228.*

**Role**
Fighter
Close support
Counter-insurgency
Tactical strike
Strategic bomber
Tactical reconnaissance
Strategic reconnaissance
Maritime patrol
Anti-ship strike
Anti-submarine warfare
Search and rescue
Assault transport
Transport
Liaison
Trainer
Inflight-refuelling tanker
Specialized

**Performance**
All-weather capability
Rough field capability
STOL capability
VTOL capability
Airspeed 0-250 mph
Airspeed 250 mph-Mach 1
Airspeed Mach 1 plus
Ceiling 0-20,000 ft
Ceiling 20,000-40,000 ft
Ceiling 40,000ft plus
Range 0-1,000 miles
Range 1,000-3,000 miles
Range 3,000 miles plus

**Weapons**
Air-to-air missiles
Air-to-surface missiles
Cruise missiles
Cannon
Trainable guns
Naval weapons
Nuclear-capable
Rockets
'Smart' weapon kit
Weapon load 0-4,000 lb
Weapon load 4,000-15,000 lb
Weapon load 15,000 lb

**Avionics**
Electronic Counter Measures
Electronic Support Measures
Search radar
Fire control radar
Look-down/shoot-down
Terrain-following radar
Forward-looking infra-red
Laser
Television

# Dornier Do 228

*Dornier Do 228 under evaluation by the Marineflieger.*

## Role

Fighter
Close support
Counter-insurgency
Tactical strike
Strategic bomber
Tactical reconnaissance
Strategic reconnaissance
Maritime patrol
Anti-ship strike
Anti-submarine warfare
Search and rescue
Assault transport
Transport
Liaison
Inflight-refuelling tanker
Trainer
Specialized

## Performance

All-weather capability
Rough field capability
STOL capability
VTOL capability
Airspeed 0-250 mph
Airspeed 250 mph-Mach 1
Airspeed Mach 1 plus
Ceiling 0-20,000 ft
Ceiling 20,000-40,000 ft
Ceiling 40,000ft plus
Range 0-1,000 miles
Range 1,000-3,000 miles
Range 3,000 miles plus

## Weapons

Air-to-air missiles
Air-to-surface missiles
Cruise missiles
Cannon
Trainable guns
Naval weapons
Nuclear-capable
Rockets
'Smart' weapon kit
Weapon load 0-4,000 lb
Weapon load 4,000-15,000 lb
Weapon load 15,000 lb plus

## Avionics

Electronic Counter Measures
Electronic Support Measures
Search radar
Fire control radar
Look-down/shoot-down
Terrain-following radar
Forward-looking infra-red
Laser
Television

In producing a larger successor to the popular Do 128 Skyservant, Dornier expended great effort in developing its Tragflügel Neue Technologie (TNT, or new-technology wing) as a means of obtaining efficient STOL performance. With the accent on a new aerodynamic profile allied to novel methods of construction employing composite materials, the TNT first took to the air on a converted Skyservant on 14 June 1979. The designations Dornier Do 28E-1 and Do 28E-2 were assigned to projected 15- and 19-passenger aircraft featuring the newly proved Dornier A-5 supercritical aerofoil, but in 1980 the designations were changed to **Do 228-100** and **Do 228-200** respectively. Prototypes of the standard and 'stretched' Do 228s flew on 28 March 1981 and 9 May 1981 respectively, and production deliveries began in February of the following year after a short and trouble-free certification period. In 1984, the **Do 228-101** and **Do 228-201** were introduced, having a strengthened structure and different mainwheel tyres to permit a 280 kg (617 lb) increase in maximum take-off weight in both versions.

Early Do 228 production was principally for civilian operators, although the Nigerian government bought three for VIP use, then followed with a military contract for three more late in 1985. At the same time, Malawi con-tracted for three for its army air wing, and Niger ordered one for possible military operation. At home, the Marineflieger leased a Do 228-201 for six months of trials early in 1986, using it to support pollution patrols by Skyservants. This was followed by a six-month evaluation by the Luftwaffe as a VIP transport.

The greatest commitment to the Do 228 has been made by India, which selected the aircraft in 1983 as the winner of its Light Transport Aircraft competition. Apart from a small number to be supplied directly by Dornier, the balance of some 150 needed by the sub-continent is being produced by Hindustan Aeronautics Ltd. Two-thirds of the total will be for military use, including 36 for the newly established Coast Guard air arm, which are to **Do 228-I00MPB-A** standard with chin-mounted MEL Marec 2 search radar. This Maritime Patrol Version-A is optimized for fisheries and oilfields surveillance, territorial water patrol and security, but another model, the **Do 228-I00MPV-B** (now **Do 228 Maritime Pollution Control**) is available with an Ericsson/Swedish Space Corporation SLAR (side-looking airborne radar) as its prime sensor for the being location of oil spillage and other pollution, as well as sea traffic observation and protection of oil exploitation areas and fishing grounds.

## Specification: Dornier Do 228-101

**Origin:** Germany
**Type:** utility transport
**Powerplant:** two 533-kW (715-shp) Garrett TPE331-5-252D turboprops
**Performance:** maximum cruising speed 231 kt (428 km/h; 266 mph) at 10,000 ft (3050 m); initial rate of climb 1,919 ft (585 m) per minute; service ceiling 28,000 ft (8535 m); range 1740 km (1,081 miles) with 15 passengers
**Weights:** empty 2990 kg (6,592 lb); maximum take-off 5980 kg (13,183 lb)
**Dimensions:** span 16.97 m (55 ft 8 in); length 15.04 m (49 ft 4.1 in); height 4.86 m (15 ft 11.5 in); wing area 32.0 m² (344.3 sq ft)
**Armament:** none

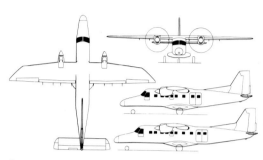

*Dornier Do 228-100 (lower side view: Do228-200)*

*The Omani Police Air Wing has taken delivery of a number of Dornier Do 228 aircraft. Some are painted in an eye-catching blue and white scheme, others in overall sand.*

*A desert-camouflaged Dornier Do 228 of the Omani Police Air Wing. The paramilitary nature of the force is shown in this view by the armed policeman in the foreground.*

# Douglas C-47 Skytrain/Dakota

*Douglas C-47 of SATENA, the Colombian military airline.*

Arguably the most famous aircraft of all time, the Douglas Dakota began life as a civil transport, making its debut in 1935 as the DC-3 day-plane and quickly finding favour with US and world airlines. Although clearly destined to achieve considerable success as an airliner, the DC-3 found true greatness as a result of wartime exigencies, the type successfully making the transition to more demanding military duties as the C-47 Skytrain during World War II.

In the event, huge quantities of C-47 and R4D aircraft were acquired by the US armed forces during the course of that conflict while, in addition, the type was produced in the USSR as the Lisunov Li-2 and in Japan as the Showa L2D. During the post-war era, the large number of surplus aircraft meant that it was available at modest cost and it duly found favour with air arms around the world, probably being the most widely-used military cargo aircraft of all time. Production by Douglas totalled 10,654.

Celebrating in 1995 the 60th anniversary of its maiden flight, the ubiquitous 'Dak' continues to soldier on in considerable numbers, and it is quite likely that some aircraft of this type will still be serving a useful military role at the end of this century.

In the years since it made its debut, the Dakota has proved equal to a bewildering variety of tasks. Naturally, airlift-related duties such as troop transport and cargo hauling have featured heavily, but the Dakota has also undertaken such diverse functions as navigation training, search-and-rescue (with a paradropped lifeboat carried beneath the fuselage), glider-towing, radar countermeasures, staff transport and gunship, use in the last role as the AC-47 coming when the type was well past the first flush of youth. Despite its age, the AC-47 proved a particularly valuable weapon, Minigun-equipped AC-47D aircraft being extensively used in combat by the US Air Force during the first few years of the Vietnam War.

Today most of the Dakotas that remain active in a military capacity are principally concerned with duties of a rather less hostile nature, but it is still remarkably versatile, being employed (for instance) to perform test tasks, airlift duties and the checking and calibration of navigational aids.

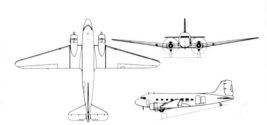

**Douglas C-47**

*Most active military Dakotas are to be found in Third World air forces, although a surprising number soldier on with European nations. The Greek air force is still a major user.*

*The C-47 serves with the Senegal air force in small numbers, augmenting a similar number of Fokker F-27s. Most Senegalese C-47s are ex-French air force machines.*

**Specification:** Douglas C-47A Skytrain
**Origin:** USA
**Type:** troop/cargo transport
**Powerplant:** two 895-kW (1,200-hp) Pratt & Whitney R-1830-92 Twin Wasp radial piston engines
**Performance:** maximum speed 200 kt (370 km/h; 230 mph) at 8,800 ft (2680 m); cruising speed 139 kt (257 km/h; 160 mph); climb to 10,000 ft (3050 m) in 9 minutes 36 seconds; service ceiling 24,000 ft (7315 m); range 2575 km (1,600 miles) with standard payload
**Weights:** empty 8103 kg (17,865 lb) maximum take-off 11793 kg (26,000 lb)
**Dimensions:** span 29.11 m (95 ft 6 in); length 19.43 m (63 ft 9 in); height 5.18 m (17 ft 0 in); wing area 91.695 m² (987.0 sq ft)
**Armament:** AC-47D gunship version employed three General Electric MXU-470/A 7.62-mm (0.3-in) Miniguns firing through fuselage door and port-side windows, complete with 21,000 rounds of ammunition

Role
Fighter
Close support
Counter-insurgency
Tactical strike
Strategic bomber
Tactical reconnaissance
Strategic reconnaissance
Maritime patrol
Anti-ship strike
Anti-submarine warfare
Search and rescue
Assault transport
Transport
Liaison
Trainer
Inflight-refuelling tanker
Specialized
Performance
All-weather capability
Rough field capability
STOL capability
VTOL capability
Airspeed 0-250 mph
Airspeed 250 mph-Mach 1
Airspeed Mach 1 plus
Ceiling 0-20,000 ft
Ceiling 20,000-40,000 ft
Ceiling 40,000 ft plus
Range 0-1,000 miles
Range 1,000-3,000 miles
Range 3,000 miles plus
Weapons
Air-to-air missiles
Air-to-surface missiles
Cruise missiles
Cannon
Trainable guns
Naval weapons
Nuclear-capable
Rockets
'Smart' weapon kit
Weapon load 0-4,000 lb
Weapon load 4,000-15,000 lb
Weapon load 15,000 lb plus
Avionics
Electronic Counter Measures
Electronic Support Measures
Search radar
Fire control radar
Look-down/shoot-down
Terrain-following radar
Forward-looking infra-red
Laser
Television

# EH Industries EH 101

*EH 101 Merlin as it might appear in Royal Navy markings.*

The origins of the Anglo-Italian shipboard helicopter are to be found in the 1977 issue by the Royal Navy of Naval Staff Requirement 6646, calling for a machine capable of operating from the stern platforms of frigates, principally the forthcoming 'Type 23' class. Westland's response was the WG 34, a three-engined helicopter, slightly smaller than the Sikorsky Sea King, yet having a far greater warload. Italian interest in an eventual successor to Sea Kings of the Marinavia resulted in agreement on joint development of the WG 34 with Agusta during 1979. In June 1980, the two firms established European Helicopter Industries Ltd in the UK to manage the programme, their governments also undertaking to assist in funding of additional civilian and utility transport versions of the design.

The first of nine **EH Industries EH 101** flying prototypes began its test programme on 9 October 1987, powered by three 1289-kW (1,729-shp) General Electric CT7-2A turboshafts. CT7-6s are to be installed in the planned 30-passenger civilian EH 101, but Italian military models have the 1278-kW (1,714-shp) General Electric T700-GET6A turboshafts while British helicopters have a Rolls-Royce/Turbomeca turboshaft. Both partners are developing the naval version,

whilst Westland takes the lead with the civil model and Agusta with the utility variant. Two production lines have been established for assembly of single-sourced components. In the area of design, Westland is handling the front fuselage and five main rotor blades, the latter with an advanced aerofoil section and high-speed tips stemming from a UK research programme. Agusta designers are allocated the rear fuselage, rotor head and hydraulic system.

The first navalized EH 101, which has the designation **Merlin HAS.Mk 1** in British service, will enter service in 1998 with the British and Italian navies. Although the Italian machines are to be mostly shore-based, both will have the primary task of anti-submarine warfare, anti-ship surveillance and tracking, amphibious support and SAR. Small enough to be stowed in a frigate's hangar, the EH 101 is nevertheless able to carry a comprehensive array of operational equipment and armament, and can also be used in secondary roles such as AEW and ECM. Tactical transport roles are the forte of the utility version of the EH 101, which has a rear loading ramp and a disposable load capability of 6548 kg (14,436 lb) or 28 troops. The utility version was ordered into production for the RAF in March 1995.

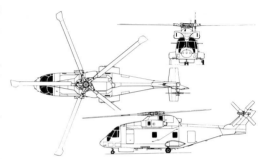

**EH Industries EH 101**

**Specification:** EH Industries EH 101 Merlin HAS.Mk 1
**Origin:** UK and Italy
**Type:** shipborne and land-based multi-role naval helicopter
**Powerplant:** three Rolls-Royce/Turbomeca RTM 322 turboshafts each rated at 1724-kW (2,312-shp) maximum contingency power and 1566-kW (2,100-shp) intermediate contingency power
**Performance:** maximum cruising speed 150 kt (278 km/h; 173 mph); time on station 5 hours with dunking sonar and weapons
**Weights:** empty about 7121 kg (15,700 lb); maximum take-off 13530 kg (29,830 lb)
**Dimensions:** main rotor diameter 18.59 m (61 ft 0 in); length, rotors turning 22.81 m (74 ft 10 in); height, rotors turning 6.65 m (21 ft 10 in); main rotor disc area 271.51 m² (2,955.5 sq ft)
**Armament:** external provision for up to 960 kg (2,112 lb) of weapons such as four lightweight homing torpedoes

*Most Italian EH 101s will be shore-based, although the helicopter is small enough to be stowed in a frigate's hangar. The primary role of the EH 101 is anti-submarine warfare.*

*The EH 101 first prototype made its maiden flight 9 October 1987, with production deliveries scheduled for 1990 but not in fact beginning until 1998.*

**Role**
Fighter
Close support
Counter-insurgency
Tactical strike
Strategic bomber
Tactical reconnaissance
Strategic reconnaissance
Maritime patrol
Anti-ship strike
Anti-submarine warfare
Search and rescue
Assault transport
Transport
Liaison
Trainer
Inflight-refuelling tanker
Specialized

**Performance**
All-weather capability
Rough field capability
STOL capability
VTOL capability
Airspeed 0-250 mph
Airspeed 250 mph-Mach 1
Airspeed Mach 1 plus
Ceiling 0-20,000 ft
Ceiling 20,000-40,000 ft
Ceiling 40,000 ft plus
Range 0-1,000 miles
Range 1,000-3,000 miles
Range 3,000 miles plus

**Weapons**
Air-to-air missiles
Air-to-surface missiles
Cruise missiles
Cannon
Trainable guns
Naval weapons
Nuclear-capable
Rockets
'Smart' weapon kit
Weapon load 0-4,000 lb
Weapon load 4,000-15,000 lb
Weapon load 15,000 lb plus

**Avionics**
Electronic Counter Measures
Electronic Support Measures
Search radar
Fire control radar
Look-down/shoot-down
Terrain-following radar
Forward-looking infra-red
Laser
Television

# EMBRAER EMB-110 Bandeirante

*EMBRAER EMB-110C of the Chilean navy.*

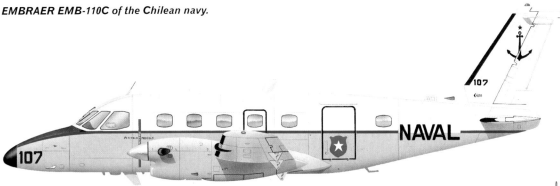

The aircraft which launched EMBRAER as a significant force amongst world aerospace manufacturers was first flown on 19 August 1972. in response to a light transport requirement by the Brazilian air force and the country's regional airlines. A nine-seat predecessor powered by the same Pratt & Whitney Canada PT6A engines had been tested in prototype form (as the YC-95 or EMB-1001), but the **EMBRAER EMB-110 Bandeirante** (pioneer) featured a much larger cabin which found favour with civil operators overseas. as well as with the Brazilian military.

Described by its designers as a perfectly balanced combination of performance and utility, the versions of this unpressurized 12/18- seater can alternatively carry up to 1631 kg (3,706 lb) of freight.

The first three of 80 Bandeirantes originally ordered by the Brazilian air force were delivered in February 1973. The type is now the mainstay of the transport force, serving in one squadron of the Rio-based 2° Grupo and several others allocated to the regional

air commands, and also in a transport conversion unit. The 60 **C-95** models were 12-passenger versions, and were supplemented by 20 **C-95A (EMB-110K1)** freighters with enlarged fuselage doors. Then came 31 examples of the **C-95B**, military version of the improved **EMB-110P** civil model. Four specialized versions have also entered Brazilian military service.

None of the Brazilian air force Bandeirante units is equipped exclusively with the C-95. In 2° Grupo de Transporte at Galeao they are augmented by a handful of older, larger BAe 748s, while the regional air command units operate their Bandeirantes alongside Piper Senecas. The regional units are 1 ETA at Belem, 2 ETA at Recife, 3 ETA at Galeao, 4 ETA at Cumbica, 5 ETA at Brasilia and 6 ETA at Porto Alegre.

The Uruguayan air force took delivery of five **EMB-110C** 15-seater transports. In 1975, and the Chilean navy bought three navalized EMB-110Cs in the following year.

**Specification:** EMBRAER EMB-110P1K (C-95B) Bandeirante
**Origin:** Brazil
**Type:** 14-seat utility transport
**Powerplant:** two 559-kW (750-shp) Pratt & Whitney Canada PT6A-34 turboprops
**Performance:** maximum speed 240 kt (445 km/h; 277 mph); cruising speed 222 kt (430 km/h; 267 mph); initial rate of climb 1,640 ft (500 m) per minute; service ceiling 21,500 ft (6555 m); range 1964 km (1,220 miles) with maximum fuel and 45-minute reserves
**Weights:** empty 3393 kg (7,480 lb); maximum take-off 5400 kg (13,007 lb)
**Dimensions:** span 15.32 m (50 ft 3.5 in); length 14.91 m (46 ft 11 in); height 4.92 m (16 ft 1.7 in); wing area 29.10 m² (313.24 sq ft)
**Armament:** none

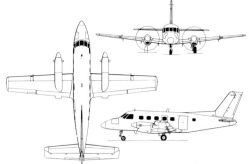

**EMBRAER EMB-110 Bandeirante (C-95B)**

*Five EMB-110Cs were procured by the Uruguayan air force in 1975. They are jointly operated by TAMA and the civil airline PLUNA, and therefore carry both military serials and civil registrations.*

*Two EMB-110P Bandeirantes are used by the Gabonese air force for transport and liaison duties, and serve alongside a single maritime patrol EMB-111 Bandeirulha.*

**Role**
Fighter
Close support
Counter-insurgency
Tactical strike
Strategic bomber
Tactical reconnaissance
Strategic reconnaissance
Maritime patrol
Anti-ship strike
Anti-submarine warfare
Search and rescue
Assault transport
Transport
Liaison
Trainer
Inflight-refuelling tanker
Specialized

**Performance**
All-weather capability
Rough field capability
STOL capability
VTOL capability
Airspeed 0-250 mph
Airspeed 250 mph-Mach 1
Airspeed Mach 1 plus
Ceiling 0-20,000 ft
Ceiling 20,000-40,000 ft
Ceiling 40,000ft plus
Range 0-1,000 miles
Range 1,000-3,000 miles
Range 3,000 miles plus

**Weapons**
Air-to-air missiles
Air-to-surface missiles
Cruise missiles
Cannon
Trainable guns
Naval weapons
Nuclear-capable
Rockets
'Smart' weapon kit
Weapon load 0-4,000 lb
Weapon load 4,000-15,000 lb
Weapon load 15,000 lb plus

**Avionics**
Electronic Counter Measures
Electronic Support Measures
Search radar
Fire control radar
Look-down/shoot-down
Terrain-following radar
Forward-looking infra-red
Laser
Television

# EMBRAER EMB-110/111 Bandeirante

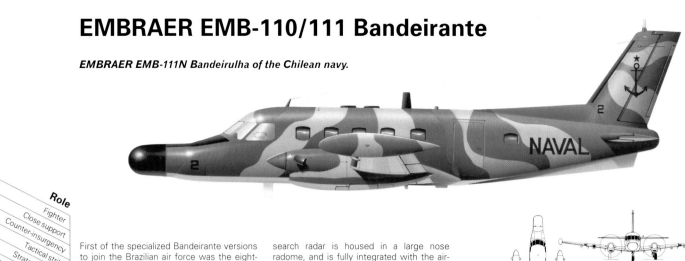

*EMBRAER EMB-111N Bandeirulha of the Chilean navy.*

### Role
Fighter
Close support
Counter-insurgency
Tactical strike
Strategic bomber
Tactical reconnaissance
Strategic reconnaissance
Maritime patrol
Anti-ship strike
Anti-submarine warfare
Search and rescue
Assault transport
Transport
Liaison
Inflight-refuelling tanker
Specialized

### Performance
All-weather capability
Rough field capability
STOL capability
VTOL capability
Airspeed 0-250 mph
Airspeed 250 mph-Mach 1
Airspeed Mach 1 plus
Ceiling 0-20,000 ft
Ceiling 20,000-40,000 ft
Ceiling 40,000ft plus
Range 0-1,000 miles
Range 1,000-3,000 miles
Range 3,000 miles plus

### Weapons
Air-to-air missiles
Air-to-surface missiles
Cruise missiles
Cannon
Trainable guns
Naval weapons
Nuclear-capable
Rockets
'Smart' weapon kit
Weapon load 0-4,000 lb
Weapon load 4,000-15,000 lb
Weapon load 15,000 lb plus

### Avionics
Electronic Counter Measures
Electronic Support Measures
Search radar
Fire control radar
Look-down/shoot-down
Terrain-following radar
Forward-looking infra-red
Laser
Television

First of the specialized Bandeirante versions to join the Brazilian air force was the eight-seat **EC-95** for checking and calibration of navigation aids. Four of these (designated **EMB-110A** by the manufacturer) are in service with the Grupo Especial de Inspecao e Vigilancia (GFIV, or Special Inspection and Checking Group) at Rio de Janeiro, initially alongside a handful of ageing EC-47 Dakotas.

They were followed by six seven-seat **R-95 (EMB-110B)** photographic survey versions. These have apertures in the cabin floor to accommodate a Zeiss camera and associated equipment; Doppler and inertial navigation systems are also fitted. The aircraft serve with 6° Grupo of the Coastal Command (COMCAS) at Recife. The R-95s supplement a handful of RC-130E Hercules also in service with the 6° Grupo.

COMCAS also operates the **P-95** maritime surveillance version which the company designates **EMB-111 Bandeirulha**. In 1978 12 of these joined the two squadrons of 7° Grupo, which had been inactive since its last Lockheed P-2 Neptunes were retired in 1976. An Eaton-AIL APS-128 Sea Patrol search radar is housed in a large nose radome, and is fully integrated with the aircraft's inertial navigation system. A high-power searchlight, signal cartridge launcher and an ESM system are also carried, and rockets can be launched from four under-wing pylons Wingtip fuel tanks increase the aircraft's endurance to nine hours. All the Brazilian P-95s have been individually named after Brazilian sea birds. 1 Esquadrao of 7° Grupo de Aviacao is based at Salvador, while 2 Esquadrao flies from Florianopolis. Six **EMB111N** aircraft were delivered to the Chilean navy, and a single example to the Gabonese air force. The Chilean navy EMB-111Ns were delivered in lieu of four surplus SP-2E Neptunes embargoed by the US government, and are used by VP-3 in the maritime patrol role.

A search-and-rescue version of the Bandeirante is designated **SC-95B**, or **EMB110P1(K)**. Deliveries of eight to 10° Grupo of COMCAS at Campo Grande began in late 1981. Six stretchers can be accommodated alongside observation and rescue personnel. Two bubble windows are fitted on each side of the fuselage.

**EMBRAER EMB-111 Bandeirulha (P-95)**

**Specification:** EMBRAER EMB-111 Bandeirulha (P-95)
**Origin:** Brazil
**Type:** seven-seat maritime surveillance and patrol aircraft
**Powerplant:** two 559-kW (750-shp) Pratt & Whitney Canada PT6A-34 turboprops
**Performance:** maximum cruising speed 194 kt (360 km/h; 223 mph); economical cruising speed 187 kt (347 km/h; 216 mph); initial rate of climb 1,190 ft (363 m) per minute; service ceiling 25,500 ft (7770 m); range 2945 km (1,830 miles) at 10,000 ft (3050 m) with maximum fuel
**Weights:** empty 3900 kg (8,598 lb); maximum take-off 7000 kg (15,432 lb) **Dimensions:** span 15.95 m (52 ft 4 in); length 14.91 m (48 ft 11 in); height 4.91 m (16 ft 1.7 in); wing area 29.1 m² (313.24 sq ft)
**Armament:** 2.75-in (70-mm) FFAR or 5-in (127-mm) HVAR rockets, smoke grenades, flares, chaff etc.

*Two **EMBRAER EMB-111 Bandeirulhas**, designated P-95 by the Brazilian air force, are seen at low level over the sea. The P-95s are operated by 1 Esquadrao of 7° Grupo at Salvador, and each carries a sea-bird name.*

*The **EMB-110P1K** was developed for search and rescue duties. The Brazilians use Bandeirante variants in a variety of roles.*

# EMBRAER EMB-312 Tucano

*EMBRAER EMB-312 (T-27) Tucano of the Brazilian air force*

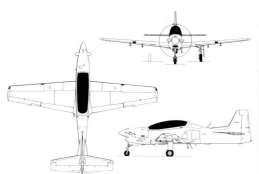

Development of the **EMBRAER EMB-312 Tucano** (toucan) high-performance turbo-prop trainer started in 1978 in response to a Brazilian air force specification for a Cessna T-37 replacement. First flown on 16 August 1980, the initial **T-27** trainer was delivered to the Air Force Academy near Sao Paulo in September 1983. Most of the Brazilian air force's 128 aircraft are operated from here, although some also serve in a conversion unit. The famous Brazilian air force formation aerobatic team, the Escuadron de Fumaca (smoke squadron), received T-27 Tucanos to replace its ageing North American Harvards. These have given impressive displays over a large portion of the American continent.

Designed from the outset to provide a jet-like flying experience, the Tucano has a single control lever governing both propeller pitch and engine throttling, ejector seats, and a staggered tandem-place cockpit.

An export order for 120 Tucanos was concluded with Egypt in September 1983. All except the first 10 of these are being licence-assembled at Helwan, with the first 80 destined for the Iraqi air force, Options on a further 60 are held by Egypt, of which 20 would be for Iraq.

The next customer was the Honduran air force (12 ordered), with Venezuela and Argentina following in South America with 31 and 30 aircraft respectively, and then two other South American countries. The Tucano's export success has continued, the most notable order coming in March 1985, when it won the hotly-contested British order for 131 aircraft to replace the RAF's BAe (Hunting) Jet Provosts. In order to clinch the deal, however, the aircraft had to be considerably revised in its airframe and engine, which became the considerably more powerful 820-kW (1,100-shp) Garrett TPE331-12B. RAF Tucanos were produced under licence by Shorts in Belfast, and this variant has also been exported in modest numbers.

The Tucano was selected only after a long and hotly-fought evaluation, but there has been much criticism that the eventual choice was made largely on political rather than operational grounds. Many sources have suggested that the RAF preferred the Swiss contender, the Pilatus PC-9, while others believe that the indigenous Hunting-backed Turbo Firecracker was the best aircraft. Another European order for the Tucano, albeit in its original form, was placed by France for 80 aircraft for service with the Armée de l'Air.

*EMBRAER EMB-312 (T-27) Tucano*

**The Brazilian air force is the second largest operator of the Tucano, and important export orders have been placed, including one by the UK for a version licence-built by Shorts.**

**Five EMB-312 Tucanos are used by the Brazilian air force aerobatic team. The aircraft's powerful turboprop and viceless handling make it a superb aerobatic mount.**

## Specification: EMBRAER EMB-312 Tucano

**Origin:** Brazil
**Type:** two-seat basic trainer
**Powerplant:** one 559-kW (750-shp) Pratt & Whitney Canada PT6A-25C turboprop
**Performance:** maximum speed 242kt (448 km/h; 278 mph)at 10,000 ft (3050 m); economical cruising speed 172 kt (319 km/h; 198 mph); initial rate of climb 2,230 ft (680 m) per minute; service ceiling 30,000 ft (9145 m); range 1944 km (1,146 miles) at 20,000 ft 6095 m)
**Weights:** empty 1810 kg (3,990 lb); maximum take-off 3175 kg (7,000 lb) **Dimensions:** span 11.14 m (36 ft 6.6 in); length 9.86 m (32 ft 4.2 in); height 3.40 m (11 ft 1.9 in); wing area 19.4 m² (208.8 sq ft)
**Armament:** provision for up to 1000 kg (2,205 lb) of disposable stores carried on four underwing hardpoints, and generally comprising 113-kg (250-lb) bombs, Avibras rocket-launcher pods, machine-gun pods, practice bombs etc

**Role**
Fighter
Close support
Counter-insurgency
Tactical strike
Strategic bomber
Tactical reconnaissance
Strategic reconnaissance
Maritime patrol
Anti-ship strike
Anti-submarine warfare
Search and rescue
Assault transport
Transport
Liaison
Trainer
Inflight-refuelling tanker
Specialized

**Performance**
All-weather capability
Rough field capability
STOL capability
VTOL capability
Airspeed 0-250 mph
Airspeed 250 mph-Mach 1
Airspeed Mach 1 plus
Ceiling 0-20,000 ft
Ceiling 20,000-40,000 ft
Ceiling 40,000ft plus
Range 0-1,000 miles
Range 1,000-3,000 miles
Range 3,000 miles plus

**Weapons**
Air-to-air missiles
Air-to-surface missiles
Cruise missiles
Cannon
Trainable guns
Naval weapons
Nuclear-capable
Rockets
'Smart' weapon kit
Weapon load 0-4,000 lb
Weapon load 4,000-15,000 lb
Weapon load 15,000 lb plus

**Avionics**
Electronic Counter Measures
Electronic Support Measures
Search radar
Fire control radar
Look-down/shoot-down
Terrain-following radar
Forward-looking infra-red
Laser
Television

# Eurofighter EF-2000

*The second prototype Eurofighter (DA2), the first to be built and flown at Warton.*

## Role
Fighter
Close support
Counter-insurgency
Tactical strike
Strategic bomber
Tactical reconnaissance
Strategic reconnaissance
Maritime patrol
Anti-ship strike
Anti-submarine warfare
Search and rescue
Assault transport
Transport
Liaison
Trainer
Inflight-refuelling tanker
Specialized

## Performance
All-weather capability
Rough field capability
STOL capability
VTOL capability
Airspeed 0-250 mph
Airspeed 250 mph-Mach 1
Airspeed Mach 1
Ceiling 0-20,000 ft
Ceiling 20,000-40,000 ft
Ceiling 40,000ft plus
Range 0-1,000 miles
Range 1,000-3,000 miles
Range 3,000 miles plus

## Weapons
Air-to-air missiles
Air-to-surface missiles
Cruise missiles
Cannon
Trainable guns
Naval weapons
Nuclear-capable
Rockets
'Smart' weapon kit
Weapon load 0-4,000 lb
Weapon load 4,000-15,000 lb
Weapon load 15,000 lb plus

## Avionics
Electronic Counter Measures
Electronic Support Measures
Search radar
Fire control radar
Look-down/shoot-down
Terrain-following radar
Forward-looking infra-red
Laser
Television

The initial agreement to develop what has until recently been called the **European Fighter Aircraft** was signed between Italy, the UK and West Germany in May 1988, with Spain joining the organization in November 1988. This important tactical combat aircraft was planned as an extremely agile STOL fighter with a primary air-to-air tasking and secondary air-to-surface role, and in concept is a close-coupled canard design using a high proportion of composites and advanced alloys in the airframe, an advanced sensor and mission avionics suite integrated via a digital databus system, and a combination of a HOTAS cockpit and an advanced fly-by-wire control system to wring maximum agility out of the relaxed-stability airframe. The organization of the program is similar to that for the Panavia Tornado, though in this instance the Eurofighter airframe consortium comprises Alenia (previously Aeritalia) for Italy, British Aerospace for the UK, CASA for Spain and DASA (MBB and Dornier) for Germany, while the Eurojet engine consortium comprises Fiat Aviazione for Italy, MTU for Germany,

Rolls-Royce for the UK and SENER for Spain.

The first of eight prototypes was due to fly in 1991 with a powerplant of two Turbo-Union RB.199-122 turbofans, but the programme suffered a number of delays stemming largely from political and financial indecisions, and to a lesser extent from nationalist arguments about the design and development of major subsystems such as the radar and integrated EW suite. As a result of the easing of tensions in Europe after the collapse of the USSR, and the economic burden imposed on it by its reunification, Germany in 1992 announced its decision to proceed with the programme no further than the flight development phase. Germany's position has been weakened considerably by the other partners' decision to stretch out the whole program and reduce its level of technical sophistication, but the overall future of what is now called the **Eurofighter EF-2000** is still troubled.

The first prototype flew in 1994, and the first of a possible 800 production aircraft should fly late in the decade for service early in the forthcoming century.

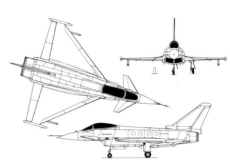

***Eurofighter EF-2000 (DA-2)***

***Service introduction of the Eurofighter will give the RAF its first single-seat fighter since the English Electric Lightning.***

*The first British-built Eurofighter prototype in approach configuration. The flight test programme has been delayed by flight control system software problems.*

## Specification: Eurofighter EF-2000
**Origin:** Germany, Italy, Spain and UK
**Type:** multi-role fighter
**Powerplant:** two 9185-kg (20,250-lb) afterburning thrust Eurojet EJ200 turbofans
**Performance:** maximum speed Mach 2.0 or 1,147 kt (2125 km/h; 1,321 mph) at 36,090 ft (11000 m); combat radius between 463 and 556 km (anos are used by )
**Weights:** empty 9750 kg (21,495 lb); maximum take-off 21000 kg (46,297 lb)
**Dimensions:** span 10.50 m (34 ft 5.5 in); length 14,50 m (47 ft 7 in); height about 4.00 m (13 ft 1.5 in); wing area 52.4 m² (564.05 sq ft) including canard surfaces
**Armament:** one 27-mm Mauser BK27 cannon on the starboard side
of the forward fuselage, and provision for up to 6500 kg (14,330 lb) of stores on four semi-recessed underfuselage missile stations and nine hardpoints (one centreline, six under the wings, and two at the wing tips); typical weapons are short- and medium-range AAMs, and a wide assortment of ASMs, anti-radar missiles, and guided and unguided bombs

# FMA IA 58A Pucará

*FMA IA 58A Pucará of the Argentine air force.*

Originally intended as a COIN aircraft to quell dissidents in northern Argentina, the **FMA IA 58A Pucará** suddenly became front-page news when it went into action during the Falklands conflict of 1982. It was the biggest design and production job ever attempted by the unaided Argentine aircraft industry. Work initially led to a full-scale glider flown on 26 December 1967, followed by a Garrett-engined prototype flown on 20 August 1969. Because France seemed a more reliable source, the engines and propellers were changed to that country for production aircraft, the guns being French and Belgian. Ordnance is almost entirely of Argentine origin.

In design the Pucará (named for a type of native stone fortress) is unique because it is a modern tactical attack aircraft with a twin-turboprop powerplant. Features include all-metal construction to high load factors for operation from rough fields and the ability to undertake tight turns and dive pullouts with heavy weapon loads, manual controls but hydraulic operation of the slotted flaps, tall landing gear units with twin main wheels, nosewheel steering and brakes, usable internal fuel capacity of 1280 litres (281 Imp gal) in fuselage and wing flexible cells, and well-protected staggered tandem cockpits with dual controls, Martin-Baker Mk AP6A zero-zero seats, and single upward-opening clamshell canopy.

The first production IA 58A flew on 8 November 1974. Initial batches for the FAA (Argentine air force) totalled 60, plus six for Uruguay. In the Falklands conflict 24 were lost, two being brought to the UK for evaluation. About 70 more were then ordered, most of which had been delivered by 1986, with 30 available for export. A single IA 58B was built with 30-mm cannon, as well as a single IA 66 with 746-kW (1,000-shp) Garrett engines and four-blade propellers. Future production could have been of the upgraded IA 58C type with totally new avionics and many other changes, including removal of the front cockpit and addition of a 30-mm DEFA cannon and wingtip air-to-air missile launchers.

**Specification:** FMA IA 58A Pucará
**Origin:** Argentina
**Type:** close-support and light attack aircraft
**Powerplant:** two 729-kW (978-shp) Turbomeca Astazou XVIG turboprops
**Performance:** maximum speed 270 kt (500 km/h; 311 mph) at 9,845 ft (3000 m); cruising speed 232 kt (430 km/h; 267 mph); maximum rate of climb 3,543 ft (1080 m) per minute; service ceiling 32,810 ft (10000 m); combat radius 350 km (217 miles) on a hi-lo-hi mission with a 1500-kg (3,307-lb) weapon load
**Weights:** empty 4020 kg(8,862 lb); maximum take-off 6800 kg (14,991 lb)
**Dimensions:** span 14.50 m (47 ft 6.9 in); length 14.253 m (46 ft 9 in); height 5.362 m (17 ft 7 in); wing area 30.3 m² (326.1 sq ft)
**Armament:** two 20-mm Hispano HS 804 cannon with 270 rounds per gun and four 7.62-mm (0.3in) FN M2-30 machine-guns with 900 rounds per gun, plus provision for up to 1500 kg (3,307 lb) of disposable stores carried on three hardpoints

**FMA IA 58A Pucará**

*Before the 1982 Falklands conflict, Pucarás were frequently seen at the Farnborough and Paris air shows, but few of these useful COIN machines have been exported.*

*This Argentine air force IA 58A Pucará was captured intact on the Falklands and was shipped back to Britain for technical evaluation and display.*

### Role
Fighter
Close support
Counter-insurgency
Tactical strike
Strategic bomber
Tactical reconnaissance
Strategic reconnaissance
Maritime patrol
Anti-ship strike
Anti-submarine warfare
Search and rescue
Assault transport
Transport
Liaison
Trainer
Inflight-refuelling tanker
Specialized

### Performance
All-weather capability
Rough field capability
STOL capability
VTOL capability
Airspeed 0-250 mph
Airspeed 250 mph-Mach 1
Airspeed Mach 1 plus
Ceiling 0-20,000 ft
Ceiling 20,000-40,000 ft
Ceiling 40,000ft plus
Range 0-1,000 miles
Range 1,000-3,000 miles
Range 3,000 miles plus

### Weapons
Air-to-air missiles
Air-to-surface missiles
Cruise missiles
Cannon
Trainable guns
Naval weapons
Nuclear-capable
Rockets
'Smart' weapon kit
Weapon load 0-4,000 lb
Weapon load 4,000-15,000 lb
Weapon load 15,000 lb plus

### Avionics
Electronic Counter Measures
Electronic Support Measures
Search radar
Fire control radar
Look-down/shoot-down
Terrain-following radar
Forward-looking infra-red
Laser
Television

# FMA IA 63 Pampa

*First prototype FMA IA 63 Pampa with Paris Air Show number.*

## Role
Fighter
Close support
Counter-insurgency
Tactical strike
Strategic bomber
Tactical reconnaissance
Strategic reconnaissance
Maritime patrol
Anti-ship strike
Anti-submarine warfare
Search and rescue
Assault transport
Transport
Liaison
Trainer
Inflight-refuelling tanker
Specialized

## Performance
All-weather capability
Rough field capability
STOL capability
VTOL capability
Airspeed 0-250 mph
Airspeed 250 mph-Mach 1
Airspeed Mach 1 plus
Ceiling 0-20,000 ft
Ceiling 20,000-40,000 ft
Ceiling 40,000ft plus
Range 0-1,000 miles
Range 1,000-3,000 miles
Range 3,000 miles plus

## Weapons
Air-to-air missiles
Air-to-surface missiles
Cruise missiles
Cannon
Trainable guns
Naval weapons
Nuclear-capable
Rockets
'Smart' weapon kit
Weapon load 0-4,000 lb
Weapon load 4,000-15,000 lb
Weapon load 15,000 lb plus

## Avionics
Electronic Counter Measures
Electronic Support Measures
Search radar
Fire control radar
Look-down/shoot-down
Terrain-following radar
Forward-looking infra-red
Laser
Television

Although by no means the first jet designed in Argentina, the FMA IA 63 Pampa is the first to go into production. Design, assisted by Dornier of Germany which also supplied the wings and tailplanes for all test and prototype purposes, was undertaken from 1979 to provide a modern jet trainer to replace the Morane-Saulnier MS.760 Paris. Dornier started with a configuration resembling that of the Alpha Jet, but with an unswept wing of supercritical aerofoil profile, and a single engine.

The new wing benefited from research carried out by the TST (Transsonik Tragflugel) Alpha Jet, a standard aircraft fitted with a supercritical transonic wing by Dornier and first flown on 12 December 1980. In many ways the Pampa can be seen as a radical redesign of the Alpha Jet, embodying operational experience and improvements in aerodynamic and engineering technology as well as features to make the aircraft more attractive to developing nations. These features included the aircraft's single-engined configuration, and the incorporation of simple and easily maintainable systems. Above all the Pampa is cheap to operate. This is because its small turbofan gives much less power than the engines fitted to the Alpha Jet, but with a

relatively small performance penalty.

Features include conventional metal construction, powered controls (the anhedralled tailplane being slabs), slotted flaps hinged well below the wing, hydraulically operated levered-suspension landing gear units designed for rough airstrips and supplied from Israel, twin door-type airbrakes which open upwards from the top of the rear fuselage, up to 1383 litres (304 Imp gal) of fuel in wing and fuselage tanks, and staggered Martin-Baker Mk AR8LM automatic zero-zero seats (preselected or fired from either cockpit) under a rear-hinged clamshell canopy.

The first of three prototypes flew on 6 October 1984, and a relatively trouble-free development programme allowed the type to enter service with the IV Brigada Aérea in April 1988. Argentina has ordered 100 aircraft, and in-service aircraft are being retrofitted with the HUD and weapon-delivery system that is being installed as standard in later production aircraft. A navalized variant is under development, but an export effort has yielded no tangible results, and Argentina's intention to development a dedicated attack model as successor to the FMA IA 58A Pucará may be stymied by lack of financial resources.

**FMA IA 63 Pampa**

**Two prototype FMA IA 63 Pampas are seen in formation over Argentina. The first prototype wears a smart black, white and red colour scheme, while the other wears Fuerza Aérea Argentina colours.**

**The first FMA IA 63 Pampa trainers were delivered in April 1988. Several countries have expressed interest in the type, but no export orders have materialized as yet.**

## Specification: FMA IA 63 Pampa
**Origin:** Argentina, with German assistance
**Type:** advanced pilot trainer with combat capability
**Powerplant:** one 1588-kg (3,500-lb) dry thrust Garrett TFE731-2-2N turbofan
**Performance:** maximum speed 405 kt (750 km/h; 466 mph) at sea level; initial rate of climb 5,120 ft (1560 m); service ceiling 42,325 ft(12 900m); combat radius 360 km (223 miles) on a hi-lo-hi mission with a 1000-kg (2,205-lb) weapon load; ferry range 1853 km (1,151 miles) with maximum internal and external fuel
**Weights:** empty 2821 kg (6,219 lb); maximum take-off 5000 kg (11,023 lb)
**Dimensions:** span 9.686 m (31 ft 9.3 in); length 10.93 m (35 ft 10.25 in) excluding probe; height 4.29 m (14 ft 1 in); wing area 15.63 m² (168.2 sq ft)
**Armament:** provision for a 30-mm DEFA cannon pod and up to 1160 kg (2,557 lb) of disposable stores carried on four underwing hardpoints

# Fairchild Republic A-10A Thunderbolt II

*Fairchild Republic A-10A Thunderbolt II of the 23d Tactical Fighter Wing, US Air Force, England AFB, Louisiana.*

Designed from the outset to perform the battlefield interdiction and close air support missions, the **Fairchild Republic A-10A Thunderbolt II** is undoubtedly one of the most grotesque warplanes to have made its debut in the years since World War II. More or less built around the fearsome 30-mm GAU-8/A Avenger Gatling-type rotary cannon, the A-10A was one of two candidates for the USAF's A-X (Attack, Experimental) design competition and eventually fought off the challenge posed by the Northrop A-9A, two prototypes of each type having been completed for a comparative evaluation conducted during the early 1970s. Eventually, in January 1973, the Fairchild submission was adjudged more suitable and was ordered into quantity production.

Subsequently the type was introduced to Europe in 1978 when the 81st Tactical Fighter Wing received the first of more than 100 aircraft, and after that the Thunderbolt II was assigned to elements of the Alaskan Air Command, Air National Guard and Air Force Reserve, production terminating in February

1984 when the 713th example was handed over to the USAF.

Powered by a pair of General Electric TF34 turbofans, the A-10A possesses remarkable payload capability, being able to operate with up to 7258 kg (16,000 lb) of ordnance, although in this configuration it cannot carry a full fuel load. As far as internal systems are concerned, the A-10A was relatively unsophisticated in its original form. The type was later earmarked for major improvement starting in 1987, this involving fitment of a wide-angle HUD and the LANTIRN night nav/attack pod system incorporating FLIR and laser sensors as well as terrain-following radar, but this programme was not undertaken and the sole upgrade was the 'Pave Penny' laser-guidance pod. From the late 1980s the aircraft were adapted as **OA-10A** aircraft for the forward air control mission and, despite its excellent showing in the 1991 UN war with Iraq, the Thunderbolt II now numbers only some 125 aircraft in US service with others released for export to friendly countries.

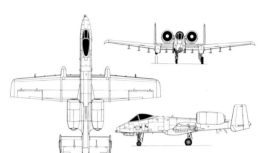

**Fairchild Republic A-10A Thunderbolt II**

**Specification:** Fairchild Republic A-10AThunderbolt II
**Origin:** USA
**Type:** single-seat close air support and battlefield interdiction aircraft
**Powerplant:** two 4112-kg (9,065-lb) dry thrust General Electric TF34-GE-100 turbofans
**Performance:** maximum speed 381 kt (706km/h; 439 mph) at sea level; cruising speed 336 kt (623 km/h; 387 mph) at 5,000 ft(1525 m); combat radius 402 km (250 miles) for a 2-hour loiter with 18 Mk 82 bombs plus 750 rounds of cannon ammunition
**Weights:** operating empty 11321 kg (24,959 lb); forward airstrip 14865 kg (32,771 lb); maximum take off 22680 kg (50,000 lb)
**Dimensions:** span 17.53 m (57 ft 6 in); length 16.26 m (53 ft 4 in); height 4.47 m (14 ft 8 in); wing area 47.01 m² (506.0 sq ft)
**Armament:** one 30-m GAU-8/A rotary cannon with capacity for up to 1,350 rounds of ammunition, plus provision for up to 7258 kg ( 16,000 lb) of disposable stores carried on 11 hardpoints; weapons options include conventional bombs, incendiary bombs, Rockeye cluster bombs, AGM-65 Maverick air-to-surface missiles, laser and optronically guided bombs and SUU-23 20-mm cannon pods

*This 81st TFW A-10A is seen manoeuvring hard at low level. The 81st TFW was based until recently at Bentwaters and Woodbridge, England, with forward operating locations in Germany.*

*An A-10A of the 81st TFW is about to edge in and refuel from a SAC KC-135 high above the North Sea. The A-10 force routinely practised air-to-air refuelling and forward deployments.*

Role
Fighter
Close support
Counter-insurgency
Tactical strike
Strategic bomber
Tactical reconnaissance
Strategic reconnaissance
Maritime patrol
Anti-ship strike
Anti-submarine warfare
Search and rescue
Assault transport
Transport
Liaison
Trainer
Inflight-refuelling tanker
Specialized
Performance
All-weather capability
Rough field capability
STOL capability
VTOL capability
Airspeed 0-250 mph
Airspeed 250 mph-Mach 1
Airspeed Mach 1 plus
Ceiling 0-20,000 ft
Ceiling 20,000-40,000 ft
Ceiling 40,000ft plus
Range 0-1,000 miles
Range 1,000-3,000 miles
Range 3,000 miles plus
Weapons
Air-to-air missiles
Air-to-surface missiles
Cruise missiles
Cannon
Trainable guns
Naval weapons
Nuclear-capable
Rockets
'Smart' weapon kit
Weapon load 0-4,000 lb
Weapon load 4,000-15,000 lb
Weapon load 15,000 lb plus
Avionics
Electronic Counter Measures
Electronic Support Measures
Search radar
Fire control radar
Look-down/shoot-down
Terrain-following radar
Forward-looking infra-red
Laser
Television

119

# Fokker F.27 (surveillance versions)

*Fokker F.27-400MPA of the Peruvian naval air service.*

## Role
Fighter
Close support
Counter-insurgency
Tactical strike
Strategic bomber
Tactical reconnaissance
Strategic reconnaissance
Maritime patrol
Anti-ship strike
Anti-submarine warfare
Search and rescue
Assault transport
Transport
Liaison
Inflight-refuelling tanker
Trainer
Specialized

## Performance
All-weather capability
Rough field capability
STOL capability
VTOL capability
Airspeed 0-250 mph
Airspeed 250 mph-Mach 1
Airspeed Mach 1 plus
Ceiling 0-20,000 ft
Ceiling 20,000-40,000 ft
Ceiling 40,000ft plus
Range 0-1,000 miles
Range 1,000-3,000 miles
Range 3,000 miles plus

## Weapons
Air-to-air missiles
Air-to-surface missiles
Cruise missiles
Cannon
Trainable guns
Naval weapons
Nuclear-capable
Rockets
'Smart' weapon kit
Weapon load 0-4,000 lb
Weapon load 4,000-15,000 lb
Weapon load 15,000 lb plus

## Avionics
Electronic Counter Measures
Electronic Support Measures
Search radar
Fire control radar
Look-down/shoot-down
Terrain-following radar
Forward-looking infra-red
Laser
Television

In 1975 Fokker completed definition of a specialized maritime patrol version of the F.27 that was subsequently sold to Peru, Angola, the Netherlands, Spain, Nigeria, the Philippines and Thailand as the **Fokker F.27 Maritime**. Intended for all forms of coastal surveillance, SAR and environmental control, the Maritime has a crew of up to six and twelve-hour endurance whilst carrying Litton APS-504 search radar (belly blister), Bendix weather radar (nose) and extremely comprehensive navigation systems, as well as a fully equipped tactical compartment, crew rest areas and bulged observation windows to the flight deck and rear of the cabin.

Thailand's aircraft are armed, but otherwise not to the standard of the **Maritime Enforcer** for armed surveillance, ASW, anti-ship attack and other combat roles, with LAPADS processor system for active and passive sonobuoys, MAD and comprehensive ESM and IR detection systems, plus optional underwing searchlight. The **Maritime Enforcer 2** is based on the next-generation Fokker 50, with PW124 engines, six-blade propellers and completely new systems. Fokker also offers its other special-mission variants in Fokker 50 forms.

The **Fokker Sentinel** is a border surveillance and stand-off reconnaissance version, fitted with Motorola APS-135(V) SLAR in a belly pod Fitted with MTI (moving-target indication), this can display on colour screens targets up to 148 km (92 miles) distant. Other equipment includes long-range oblique cameras, IR linescan and Comint (communications intelligence) gear. The **Kingbird** is a proposed AEW version with Hughes AWG-9 pulse-Doppler radar (as fitted to the Grumman F-14 Tomcat) in a retractable belly radome, working in conjunction with ESM equipment to identify all radar-emitting targets.

**Specification:** Fokker Maritime Enforcer
**Origin:** Netherlands
**Type:** armed maritime multi-role patrol aircraft
**Powerplant:** two 1738-ekW (2,330-eshp) Rolls-Royce Dart Mk 552 turboprops
**Performance:** cruising speed 250 kt (463 km/h; 287 mph) at 20,000 ft (6095 m); patrol speed 145-175 kt (268-324 km/h; 167-201 mpg) at low level; climb to 20,000 ft (6095 m) in 27 minutes; service ceiling 25,000 ft(7620 m); maximum range 5000 km (3,107 miles) with 30-minute reserve
**Weights:** empty 13725 kg (30,258 lb); normal take-off 20410 kg (45,000 lb); maximum take-off 22680 kg (50,000 lb)
**Dimensions:** span 29.00 m (95 ft 1.7 in); length 23.56 m (77 ft 3.6 in); height 8.70 m (28 ft 6.5 in); wing area 70.0 m² (753.55 sq ft)
**Armament:** provision for up to 3930 kg (8,664 lb) of disposable stores carried on two fuselage pylons and six underwing hardpoints; typical weapons include up to four AS torpedoes, or AM.39 Exocet, Sea Eagle, Harpoon, Maverick or Sea Skua anti-ship missiles

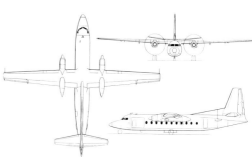

*Fokker F.27 MPA*

*This Fokker F.27-400MPA is used by the Forca Aérea Popular de Angola e Defesa Anti-Avioes for coastal patrol duties, and is supplemented by a single F.27.*

*The Fokker F.27MPA is equipped with Litton APS-504 search radar, Bendix weather radar and comprehensive navigational equipment. This aircraft wears Spanish markings.*

# Fuji T-1

*Fuji T-1A of the Japanese Air Self-Defence Force's 13th Flying Training Wing at Gifu.*

When the Japanese aircraft industry was resurrected in 1953 the greatest recipient of initial government contracts was Fuji Heavy Industries. This company had already begun the design of a small axial turbojet, the JO-1, and then additionally emerged the winner of an industry competition for a dual-control jet trainer with fighter capabilities, to replace the piston-engined North American T-6. An order was placed for seven **Fuji T1F1** aircraft, the first to fly in 1957 with an imported Bristol Orpheus engine but soon to switch to the JO-1 or a successor.

The JO-1 ran in 1954 and led to the more powerful J3. This first ran in July 1956 and was subsequently transferred to the Japan Jet Engine Co.: the inevitable delay meant that the Orpheus was used in the **T1F2** production trainer, first flown on 8 January 1958. Obviously strongly influenced by the North American F-86 Sabre, the T1F2 was designated **T-1A** by the Japan Air Self-

Defence Force, and 40 had been delivered by 1962. Fuji then also built 20 **T-1B (T1F3)** trainers with the 1200-kg (2,646-lb) dry thrust J3-3, although performance was naturally lower. Three T-1Bs were re-engined with the 1400-kg (3,086-lb) thrust J3-7, but plans for further conversions were dropped.

Looking almost exactly like the tandem-seat TF-86 Sabre, the T-1A and T-1B have had a long and successful career with the 13th Flying Training Wing of the JASDF at Gifu and Ashiya, and continue in full service in the mid-1990s, although they and the remaining Lockheed T-33As are being complemented by a the first 50 Kawasaki T-4s from the early 1990s. The T-1s always fly with their Sabre-style twin-finned drop tanks, but do not normally carry any of the weapon options. Instead pupil pilots spend 70 hours on the T-1 as an intermediate aircraft between the piston-engined T-34 and the supersonic Mitsubishi T-2.

## Specification: Fuji T-1A

**Origin:** Japan
**Type:** intermediate jet trainer
**Powerplant:** one 1814-kg (4,000-lb) dry thrust Rolls-Royce (formerly Bristol) Orpheus Mk 805 turbojet
**Performance:** maximum speed 500 kt (925 km/h; 575 mph) at high altitude, but in practice limited to 463 kt (859 km/h; 534 mph); initial rate of climb 6,500 ft(1981 m) per minute; service ceiling 47,250 ft (14400 m); range 1860 km (1,156 miles) at high altitude with drop tanks
**Weights:** empty 2420 kg(5,335 lb); maximum take-off 5000 kg (11,023 lb)
**Dimensions:** span 10.49 m (34 ft 5 in); length 12.12 m (39 ft 9.2in); height 4.08 m (13 ft 4.6 in); wing area 22.22 m² (239.2sq ft)
**Armament:** provision for one 12.7-mm (0.5-in) Browning M53-2 gun in nose and for up to 680 kg (1,500 lb) of disposable stores carried on two underwing pylons; typical weapons are bombs, Sidewinder AAMs or gun pods, but in practice used only for tanks

*Fuji T-1A*

*The tandem-seat T-1 looks very like the North American Sabre, but uses a licence-built British engine, the Orpheus. This T-1A serves with the 13th Wing.*

*The T-1B is powered by a slightly less powerful version of the J-3 turbojet, but is externally indistinguishable from the T-1A. T-1s seldom fly without underwing fuel tanks.*

### Role

Fighter
Close support
Counter-insurgency
Tactical strike
Tactical bomber
Strategic bomber
Tactical reconnaissance
Strategic reconnaissance
Maritime patrol
Anti-ship strike
Anti-submarine warfare
Search and rescue
Assault transport
Transport
Liaison
Trainer
Inflight-refuelling tanker
Specialized

### Performance

All-weather capability
Rough field capability
STOL capability
VTOL capability
Airspeed 0-250 mph
Airspeed 250 mph-Mach 1
Airspeed Mach 1 plus
Ceiling 0-20,000 ft
Ceiling 20,000-40,000 ft
Ceiling 40,000ft plus
Range 0-1,000 miles
Range 1,000-3,000 miles
Range 3,000 miles plus

### Weapons

Air-to-air missiles
Air-to-surface missiles
Cruise missiles
Cannon
Trainable guns
Naval weapons
Nuclear-capable
Rockets
'Smart' weapon kit
Weapon load 0-4,000 lb
Weapon load 4,000-15,000 lb
Weapon load 15,000 lb plus

### Avionics

Electronic Counter Measures
Electronic Support Measures
Search radar
Fire control radar
Look-down/shoot-down radar
Terrain-following radar
Forward-looking infra-red
Laser
Television

# GAF Nomad

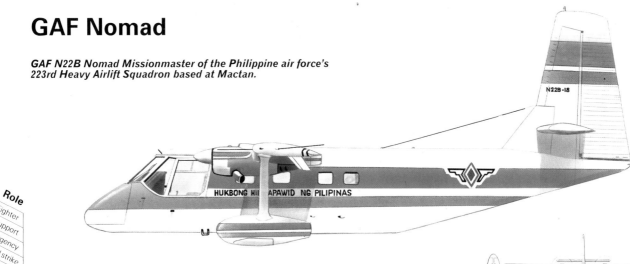

*GAF N22B Nomad Missionmaster of the Philippine air force's 223rd Heavy Airlift Squadron based at Mactan.*

One of the most important all-Australian aircraft since World War II, the **GAF Nomad** was intended to be a large and globally successful programme, but for a variety of reasons unconnected with the engineering or quality of the product it was less than successful. First flown in prototype form on 23 July 1971, the Nomad had been built to the extent of only 170 when manufacture was terminated in 1984. The type is now an ASTA (AeroSpace Technologies of Australia) product since this organization's take-over of the Government Aircraft Factories)

The original version, designated **Nomad N22**, is an all-metal machine with a strut-braced high wing featuring powerful double-slotted flaps and drooping ailerons to give outstanding short-field performance. The fuselage has a forward cockpit seating one or two, with optional dual controls, and a rear cabin which can seat up to 12 passengers. Production began with 298-kW (400-shp) engines, but switched to the **N22B** version with the more powerful version of the

same engine (see specification). A total of 33 civil N22Bs was built, plus two Floatmaster seaplanes, and special Medicmaster and Surveymaster variants. Most Nomads are military. Australia, the Philippines, Thailand and Papua-New Guinea bought the basic **Missionmaster** short-body version as a multi-role transport. Indonesia, Thailand, the Marshall Islands and civil operators bought the Searchmaster B with Bendix nose radar for coastal patrol. Indonesia was the only military customer for the more costly **Searchmaster L** with Litton APS-504(V)2 radar in a guppy radome under the nose.

The **N24A** is a stretched civil model seating 17 passengers, with increased space for baggage. A total of 40 was sold, including several special-role versions. None was fitted with the Missionmaster's military equipment, which apart from the provisions listed under Armament can include armour, self-sealing tanks and surveillance and night-vision equipment in the nose.

### Specification: GAF Nomad N22B
**Origin:** Australia
**Type:** multi-role utility transport
**Powerplant:** two 313-kW (420-shp) Allison 250-B17C turboprops
**Performance:** (landplane at maximum weight) cruising speed 168 kt (311 km/h; 193 mph); initial rate of climb 1,460 ft (445 m) per minute; service ceiling 21,000 ft (6400 m); maximum range 1352 km (840 miles) with standard fuel
**Weights:** empty 2092 kg (4,613 lb) or Missionmaster 2290kg (5,050 lb); maximum take-off 3855 kg (8,500 lb) or N24A 4264 kg (9,400 lb)
**Dimensions:** span 16.51 m (54 ft 2 in); length 12.57 m (41 ft 3 in) or N24A 14.35 m (47 ft 1 in); height 5.54 m(18 ft 2 in); wing area 30.1 m² (324.0 sq ft)
**Armament:** (Missionmaster only) four underwing hardpoints each rated at 227 kg (500 lb) can carry gun pods, rocket-launcher pods, and other stores

**GAF N22B Nomad Missionmaster**

*This GAF N22B Nomad Missionmaster is used by the Papua New Guinea Defence Force for general transport duties.*

*A total of about 10 GAF Nomads serve with No.171 Squadron at Holsworthy, and with No.173 Squadron and the School of Army Aviation at Oakey, all part of the Australian Army Aviation Corps.*

# General Dynamics F-16A/C/N Fighting Falcon

The **General Dynamics (now Lockheed) F-16 Fighting Falcon** is a direct descendant of the successful General Dynamics submission in the 1972 USAF Light-Weight Fighter (LWF) competition. Two YF-16 prototypes were built for trials and for evaluation against the competing Northrop YF-17 prototypes. The first F-16 made an unscheduled and unplanned initial flight when test pilot Philip Oestricher took off following an incident during a high-speed taxi run. An official first flight followed on 2 February 1974.

During January 1975 it was announced that the YF-16 had been selected for full-scale engineering development, largely on account of its superb manoeuvrability and its use of an existing engine. Although the LWF programme had been undertaken to produce a cheap, simple, clear-air air-superiority fighter, the role of the production F-16 has widened considerably to include a significant all-weather and air-to-surface capability. Eight pre-production aircraft, six of them single-seat **F-16A** fighters, were procured from July 1975 with a powerplant of one 10810-kg (23,450-lb) afterburning thrust Pratt & Whitney F100-PW-220 turbofan.

When the USAF announced its F-16 requirement it was for some 1,388 aircraft to replace the McDonnell Douglas F-4 Phantom (and other types) in the active and reserve inventories. The USAF now plans to procure

some 2,800 F-16s and production continued at an initial rate of 150 per year. In June 1975 Belgium, Denmark, the Netherlands and Norway selected the F-16 to replace their ageing Lockheed F-104 Starfighters. The four nations initially ordered a combined total of 348 aircraft, with final assembly of these NATO aircraft undertaken in Belgium and the Netherlands. Other foreign orders for the F-16 have been placed by Bahrain, Egypt, Greece, Indonesia, Israel, Pakistan, Portugal, Singapore, South Korea, Thailand, Turkey and Venezuela.

The **F-16C** is basically an improved development of the F-16A incorporating various structural, systems and avionics changes (including APG-68 radar) developed under the Multi-national Staged Improvement Program. The **F-16N** is a more specialized variant, a derivative of the F-16C modified for use by the US Navy as a land-based aggressor aircraft. Modifications for this role include the deletion of the cannon, underwing missile launchers and pylons, airborne self-protection jammer and global positioning system. The older APG-66 radar of the F-16A is retained, and the General Electric F110-GE-100 afterburning turbofan is used. The wings are structurally strengthened to meet the increased frequency of g loading in the adversary role. The delivery of 26 aircraft was completed in 1987 and 1988.

*General Dynamics F-16A Fighting Falcon of the 4th TFS, 388th TFW, Hill AFB, Utah.*

*General Dynamics (Lockheed) F-16A Fighting Falcon*

**This Belgian air force General Dynamics F-16A is fitted with twin AIM-9 Sidewinder launchers on its wingtips. European F-16s are assembled in Belgium and the Netherlands.**

*Egypt is one of the many overseas operators of the F-16 Fighting Falcon, using the aircraft to replace its ageing Soviet-built MiGs, primarily in the air defence role.*

**Specification:** General Dynamics F-16C Fighting Falcon
**Origin:** USA
**Type:** single-seat air-combat and multi-role fighter
**Powerplant:** one 13154-kg (29,000-lb) afterburning thrust Pratt & Whitney F100-PW-229 or General Electric F110-GE-129 turbofan
**Performance:** maximum speed more than Mach 2 or 1,146 kt (2124 km/h; 1,320 mph) at 40,000 ft (12190 m); service ceiling more than 50,000 ft (15240 m); combat radius more than 925 km (575 miles); ferry range 3886 km (2,415 miles) with maximum internal and external fuel
**Weights:** (F100 engine) empty 8273 kg (18,218 lb); maximum take-off 19187 lb (42,300 lb)
**Dimensions:** span 10.00 m (32 ft 9.75 in) including AAMs; length 15.03 m (49 ft 4in); height 5.09 m (16 ft 8.5 in); wing area 27.87 m² (300.0 sq ft)
**Armament:** one 20-mm M61A1Vulcan cannon with 500 rounds, plus provision for up to 9276 kg (20,450 lb) of external ordnance on one underfuselage, six underwing and two tip hardpoints, this total declining to 5420 kg (11,950 lb) for sorties including 9-g manoeuvres; the ordnance can include AIM-9 Sidewinder and AIM-120 AMRAAM air-to-air missiles, a wide range of disposable ordnance (free-tall and guided), drop tanks and electronic pods (ECM, reconnaissance and targeting)

**Role**
Fighter
Close support
Counter-insurgency
Tactical strike
Strategic bomber
Tactical reconnaissance
Strategic reconnaissance
Maritime patrol
Anti-ship strike
Anti-submarine warfare
Search and rescue
Assault transport
Transport
Liaison
Trainer
Inflight-refuelling tanker
Specialized

**Performance**
All-weather capability
Rough field capability
STOL capability
VTOL capability
Airspeed 0-250 mph
Airspeed 250 mph-Mach 1
Airspeed Mach 1 plus
Ceiling 0-20,000 ft
Ceiling 20,000-40,000 ft
Ceiling 40,000ft plus
Range 0-1,000 miles
Range 1,000-3,000 miles
Range 3,000 miles plus

**Weapons**
Air-to-air missiles
Air-to-surface missiles
Cruise missiles
Cannon
Trainable guns
Naval weapons
Nuclear-capable
Rockets
'Smart' weapon kit
Weapon load 0-4,000 lb
Weapon load 4,000-15,000 lb
Weapon load 15,000 lb plus

**Avionics**
Electronic Counter Measures
Electronic Support Measures
Search radar
Fire control radar
Look-down/shoot-down
Terrain-following radar
Forward-looking infra-red
Laser
Television

# General Dynamics F-16B/D Fighting Falcon

*General Dynamics F-16B Fighting Falcon of the Volkel-based 311 Squadron, Netherlands air force.*

## Role
Fighter
Close support
Counter-insurgency
Tactical strike
Strategic bomber
Tactical reconnaissance
Strategic reconnaissance
Maritime patrol
Anti-ship strike
Anti-submarine warfare
Search and rescue
Assault transport
Transport
Liaison
Trainer
Inflight-refuelling tanker
Specialized

## Performance
All-weather capability
Rough field capability
STOL capability
VTOL capability
Airspeed 0-250 mph
Airspeed 250 mph-Mach 1
Airspeed Mach 1 plus
Ceiling 0-20,000 ft
Ceiling 20,000-40,000 ft
Ceiling 40,000ft plus
Range 0-1,000 miles
Range 1,000-3,000 miles
Range 3,000 miles plus

## Weapons
Air-to-air missiles
Air-to-surface missiles
Cruise missiles
Cannon
Trainable guns
Naval weapons
Nuclear-capable
Rockets
'Smart' weapon kit
Weapon load 0-4,000 lb
Weapon load 4,000-15,000 lb
Weapon load 15,000 lb plus

## Avionics
Electronic Counter Measures
Electronic Support Measures
Search radar
Fire control radar
Look-down/shoot-down
Terrain-following radar
Forward-looking infra-red
Laser
Television

Two of the eight pre-production F-16s were two-seaters, designated **General Dynamics F-16B Fighting Falcon**, and the first of these made its maiden flight on 8 August 1977. The F-16B retained full operational equipment and capability, with the second cockpit taking the place of one fuselage fuel tank, reducing internal fuel capacity by about 17 per cent.

Some 204 of the 1,388 F-16s originally ordered by the USAF were to be two-seat F-16Bs, and the proportion of two-seaters has remained constant with each increase in total F-16 procurement. Most foreign F-16 operators have opted for a similar mix of single- and two-seat F-16s. USAF F-16Bs have been given the same Multi-national Staged Improvement Program (MSIP) modifications as the F-16As, and production MSIP two-seaters are designated **F-16D**. There are three basic stages to the MSIP programme, which is being undertaken to allow the F-16 to remain a viable front-line fighter well into the next century. Stage I of the programme covers the installation of structural and wiring provisions for future systems to production F-16As and F-16Bs delivered between November 1981 and March 1985. Stage II began in July 1984, when production F-16Cs and F-16Ds started being delivered, and these aircraft incorporated core avionics, cockpit and airframe provisions to accommodate new systems. Stage III cov-

ers the installation, during production or as a retrofit, of advanced systems as they become available.

MSIP F-16s incorporate a Westinghouse APG-68 radar in place of the earlier APG-66, giving increased range, sharper resolution and expanded air-to-air and air-to-surface modes. MSIP-configured aircraft also have an advanced versatile cockpit with a GEC wide-angle HUD, and structural improvements to allow an higher maximum take-off weight and increased gross weight limitations for the application of maximum g. Advanced weapons and systems will be added, including AMRAAM, LANTIRN and PLSS, significantly increasing the F-16's multi-role capability and survivability. The adoption of a common engine bay by F-16Cs and F-16Ds also permits the installation of either the Pratt & Whitney F100 or General Electric F110 turbofan in any aircraft.

During September 1984 the USAF placed a contract with General Dynamics to develop a reconnaissance variant of the F-16D as a potential replacement for the USAF's ageing McDonnell Douglas RF-4C Phantoms. The reconnaissance equipment, including a video camera to provide display information to the crew and for real-time transmission to ground stations, will be housed in an underfuselage ATARS pod. There have been considerable problems in development of this pods, however.

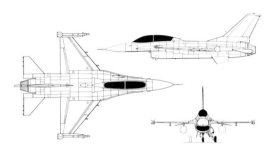

*General Dynamics (Lockheed) F-16B Fighting Falcon*

## Specification: General Dynamics F-16D Fighting Falcon
**Origin:** USA
**Type:** two-seat operational trainer and multi-role fighter
**Powerplant:** one 13154-kg (29,000-lb) afterburning thrust Pratt & Whitney F100-PW-229 or General Electric F110-GE-129 turbofan
**Performance:** maximum speed more than Mach 2 or 1,146 kt (2124 km/h; 1,320 mph) at 40,000 ft (12190 m); service ceiling more than 50,000 ft (15240 m); combat radius more than 925 km (575 miles); ferry range 3886 km (2,415 miles) with maximum internal and external fuel
**Weights:** (F100 engine) empty 8494 kg (18,726 lb); maximum take-off 19187 lb (42,300 lb)
**Dimensions:** span 10.00 m (32 ft 9.75 in) including AAMs; length 15.03 m (49 ft 4in); height 5.09 m (16 ft 8.5 in); wing area 27.87 m² (300.0 sq ft)
**Armament:** one 20-mm M61A1Vulcan cannon with 500 rounds, plus provision for up to 9276 kg (20,450 lb) of external ordnance on one underfuselage, six underwing and two tip hardpoints, this total declining to 5420 kg (11,950 lb) for sorties including 9-g manoeuvres; the ordnance can include AIM-9 Sidewinder and AIM-120 AMRAAM air-to-air missiles, a wide range of disposable ordnance (free-tall and guided), drop tanks and electronic pods (ECM, reconnaissance and targeting)

*An early F-16B fires an AGM-65 Maverick air-to-surface missile. Two-seat F-16s retain full mission equipment and combat capability, with slightly reduced fuel tankage.*

*The Israeli air force has used its F-16s over Lebanon, and on the raids on Tunis and the Iraqi nuclear plant at Baghdad. F-16Bs participated in these attacks.*

# General Dynamics F-111

The remarkable **General Dynamics F-111** was the first tactical aircraft in the world with variable-geometry and also the first in the world with afterburning turbofans. Despite a troubled and controversial birth, the type has also set a new standard of tactical strike capability. Combat experience in Vietnam and more recently in the USAF's April 1985 night attack on Libya proved it to be an unbeatable all-weather precision tactical bomber which has fully overcome its early faults and weaknesses.

The F-111 was developed to fulfil two separate but superficially similar requirements, one from the USAF for a long-range interdictor and strike aircraft, and one from the US Navy for a carrierborne long-range interceptor. The first YF-111A made its maiden flight on 21 December 1964 and it was followed by 17 pre-series aircraft and 141 production **F-111A** aircraft. The F-111B fleet fighter variant was an almost unmitigated disaster, and was cancelled after only nine had been built.

The only export customer for the F-111 has been the Royal Australian Air Force, which received an initial 24 aircraft designated **F-111C**. These aircraft were similar to the USAF's F-111As but with the longer-span wing of the F-111B, strengthened landing gear and eight rather than four wing pylons. These were delivered in 1978 after a 10-year delay. The next USAF variant should have been the **F-111D** with more powerful TF30-

P-9 engines in place of the TF30-P-3 engines used by earlier variants. It also featured new engine air inlets and sophisticated new avionics, the analog computer of the F-111A being replaced by a new digital computer, and the original radar replaced by an Autonetics APQ-130 multi-mode radar. Development problems plagued the F-111D, but 96 eventually entered service with the 27th TFW at Cannon AFB .

Delays with the F-111D led to the development of an interim machine, the **F-111E**. This was basically the F-111A with the new inlets, and various ECM and avionics improvements, as well as a new weapon-management system. The F-111E, of which 94 were built, served with the 20th TFW at RAF Upper Heyford. The advanced F-111D was replaced in production by the **F-111F**, which combined new avionics with the vastly more reliable and considerably more powerful TF30-P-100 turbofan, which also gave improved fuel economy. The F-111F also introduced strengthened wing pivots, and the aircraft are today equipped with the 'Pave Tack' laser acquisition and designating system in a removable belly pod. Production of the F-111F amounted to 106 aircraft, and the type served with the 48th TFW at RAF Lakenheath. The designation **F-111G** was allocated to ex-SAC FB-111As revised for tactical use with conventional weapons.

**Specification:** General Dynamics F-111F
**Origin:** USA
**Type:** two-seat all-weather tactical strike and attack aircraft
**Powerplant:** two 11385-kg (25,100-lb) afterburning thrust Pratt & Whitney TF30-P-100 turbofans
**Performance:** maximum speed Mach 2.5 or 1433 kt (2655 km/h; 1,650 mph) at high altitude, or Mach 1.2 or 792 kt (1468 km/h; 912 mph) at low altitude; service ceiling 60,000 ft (18290 m); range more than 4707 km (2,925 miles) with internal fuel
**Weights:** empty 21398 kg (47,175 lb); maximum take-off 45359 kg (100,000 lb)
**Dimensions:** span 19.20 m (63 ft 0 in) spread and 9.74 m (31 ft 11.4 in) swept; length 22.40 m (73 ft 6 in); height 5.22 m (17 ft 1.4 in); wing area 48.77m² (525.0 sq ft) spread
**Armament:** provision for up to 14228 kg (31,500 lb) of disposable stores carried in an internal bay and on four underwing hardpoints; typical weapons include nuclear or conventional bombs, guided bombs and air-to-surface missiles

*General Dynamics F-111F of the 48th TFW.*

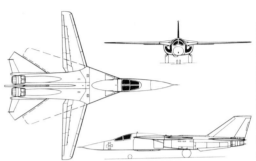

*General Dynamics F-111A*

*Photographed when based at Lakenheath, this F-111F belongs to the 494th Tactical Fighter Squadron, and carries 'Pave Tack', four laser-guided bombs, and an ALQ-131(V) jamming pod.*

*The blue and white chequered fin-cap identifies this F-111E as an aircraft of the 55th Tactical Fighter Squadron, part of the 20th TFW then based at RAF Upper Heyford.*

## Role
- Fighter
- Close support
- Counter-insurgency
- **Tactical strike**
- Strategic bomber
- Tactical reconnaissance
- Strategic reconnaissance
- Maritime patrol
- Anti-ship strike
- Anti-submarine warfare
- Search and rescue
- Assault transport
- Transport
- Liaison
- Trainer
- Inflight-refuelling tanker
- Specialized

## Performance
- All-weather capability
- Rough field capability
- STOL capability
- VTOL capability
- Airspeed 0-250 mph
- Airspeed 250 mph-Mach 1
- Airspeed Mach 1 plus
- Ceiling 0-20,000 ft
- Ceiling 20,000-40,000 ft
- Ceiling 40,000ft plus
- Range 0-1,000 miles
- Range 1,000-3,000 miles
- Range 3,000 miles plus

## Weapons
- Air-to-air missiles
- Air-to-surface missiles
- Cruise missiles
- Cannon
- Trainable guns
- Naval weapons
- Nuclear-capable
- Rockets
- 'Smart' weapon kit
- Weapon load 0-4,000 lb
- Weapon load 4,000-15,000 lb
- Weapon load 15,000 lb plus

## Avionics
- Electronic Counter Measures
- Electronic Support Measures
- Search radar
- Fire control radar
- Look-down/shoot-down
- Terrain-following radar
- Forward-looking infra-red
- Laser
- Television

# Grumman A-6 Intruder

*Grumman A-6E Intruder of VMA(AW)-533, US Marine Corps, based at MCAS El Toro, California.*

**Role**
Fighter
Close support
Counter-insurgency
Tactical strike
Strategic bomber
Tactical reconnaissance
Strategic reconnaissance
Maritime patrol
Anti-ship strike
Anti-submarine warfare
Search and rescue
Assault transport
Transport
Liaison
Trainer
Inflight-refuelling tanker
Specialized

**Performance**
All-weather capability
Rough field capability
STOL capability
VTOL capability
Airspeed 0-250 mph
Airspeed 250 mph-Mach 1
Airspeed Mach 1 plus
Ceiling 0-20,000 ft
Ceiling 20,000-40,000 ft
Ceiling 40,000ft plus
Range 0-1,000 miles
Range 1,000-3,000 miles
Range 3,000 miles plus

**Weapons**
Air-to-air missiles
Air-to-surface missiles
Cruise missiles
Cannon
Trainable guns
Naval weapons
Nuclear-capable
Rockets
'Smart' weapon kit
Weapon load 0-4,000 lb
Weapon load 4,000-15,000 lb
Weapon load 15,000 lb plus

**Avionics**
Electronic Counter Measures
Electronic Support Measures
Search radar
Fire control radar
Look-down/shoot-down
Terrain-following radar
Forward-looking infra-red
Laser
Television

In production from the late 1950s to the mid-1990s, the **Grumman A-6 Intruder** has a record of production longevity record unlikely to be equalled by many combat aircraft types manufactured in the West.

Development of the Intruder dates back to 1957, when 11 companies responded to a US Navy request for proposals for a new jet-powered attack aircraft capable of operating at night or in the worst conceivable weather conditions. Close study of the various contenders resulted in Grumman's G-128 being selected at the end of 1957 for further development as the A2F and eight development examples of the **A2F-1** (**A-6A** from late 1962) were duly ordered, the first making a successful maiden flight on 19 April 1960.

Its distinctly utilitarian appearance perhaps belied the fact that the A-6 was indeed a most sophisticated machine, effectively marrying computer technology with a sturdy airframe to produce a remarkably effective warplane. Despite teething troubles with the early avionics systems, the A-6A eventually went on to compile an impressive combat record in Vietnam, often being the only aircraft able to fly and fight effectively in that theatre.

Production of the basic A-6A ceased in late 1969 after just under 500 had been built, but by then plans were well in hand for the next major attack-dedicated model, this being the **A-6E** which took full advantage of

progress made in the field of avionics, being fitted with Norden APQ-148 multi-mode nav/attack radar and numerous other items new kit.

The A-6E has been progressively modernized since attaining operational status in the early 1970s, visible evidence of this process being best exemplified by the traversable TRAM (Target Recognition Attack Multi-sensor) turret beneath the nose radome. Basically, TRAM consists of FLIR (Forward-Looking Infra-Red) and laser detection gear to provide great accuracy in target acquisition and weapons delivery under all weather conditions.

Other Intruder models, most of them conversions of existing airframes, have included the **EA-6A** ECM platform for the Marine Corps, the **A-6B** for SAM suppression, the **A-6C** with improved night attack capability, and the **KA-6D** inflight-refuelling tanker. Of these models, only the KA-6D remains active in a truly operational capacity with the US Navy.

Now cancelled, the planned A-6F would have been the third-generation Intruder, and was to have entered production in 1989-90 with the General Electric F404 turbofan and fully digital avionics including Norden APQ-177 high-resolution radar of the synthetic-aperture type, a HUD, and five coloured head-down displays. All surviving A-6 aircraft are scheduled for retirement in 1997.

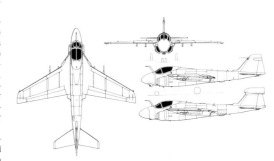

**Grumman A-6E/TRAM Intruder**
*(lower side view: EA-6A)*

*An unmarked A-6E Intruder takes off from USS Coral Sea during operations off Libya, which culminated in the bombing of Benghazi by US Navy A-6s.*

*A KA-6D of VA-55 takes off from USS Coral Sea, with underwing tanks and an underfuselage refuelling pod clearly visible. A-6 attack units usually go to sea with four of these useful tankers.*

## Specification: Grumman A-6E Intruder

**Origin:** USA
**Type:** two-seat carrierborne and land-based all-weather medium strike and attack aircraft
**Powerplant:** two 4218-kg (9,300-lb) dry thrust Pratt & Whitney J52-P-8A turbojets
**Performance:** maximum speed 563 kt (1043 km/h; 648 mph) at sea level; initial rate of climb 7,620 ft (2322 m) per minute; service ceiling 47,500 ft (14480 m); range 1627 km (1,011 miles) with full weapon load
**Weights:** empty 12132 kg (26,746 lb); maximum take-off 26581 kg (58,600 lb) for a catapult launch or 27397 kg (60,400 lb) for a field take-off
**Dimensions:** span 16.15 m (53 ft 0 in); length 16.69 m (54 ft 9 in); height 4.93 m (16 ft 2 in); wing area 49.13 m² (528.9 sq ft)
**Armament:** provision for up to 8165 kg (18,000 lb) of disposable stores carried on five external hardpoints, and generally comprising nuclear weapons, free-fall bombs, guided bombs, air-to-surface missiles such as Harpoon, and drop tanks

# Grumman EA-6 Prowler

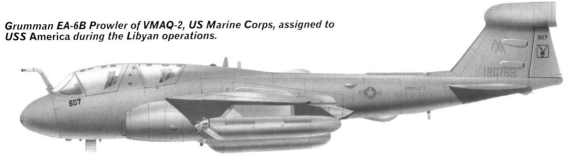

*Grumman EA-6B Prowler of VMAQ-2, US Marine Corps, assigned to USS America during the Libyan operations.*

Inheriting responsibility for electronic countermeasures duties from the veteran Douglas EKA-3B Skywarrior at the beginning of the 1970s, the **Grumman EA-6B Prowler** was evolved from the highly successful A-6 Intruder. Although produced in relatively modest quantities, the Prowler nevertheless forms an important part of the modern carrier air wing, fulfilling functions which range from riding shotgun for US Navy strike aircraft intent on penetrating enemy defences, via provision of a protective screen around carrier task forces to acquisition of electronic intelligence.

Development of the Prowler began in the latter half of the 1960s when it was decided to purchase a new-build aircraft to perform this increasingly important role. The A-6 seemed to provide a good starting point for an ECM-dedicated type and was duly selected to provide the basis for the Prowler, which eventually appeared as a four-seater with a crew consisting of a pilot to fly the aircraft and three electronic warfare officers (EWOs) to manage the sophisticated array of ECM and electronic support measures (ESM) systems.

At the heart of the EA-6B is the ALQ-99 tactical jamming system, this being basically a package capable of detecting, sorting, classifying and dealing with electronic threats across a broad spectrum of frequency bands. Operation may be accomplished automatically, semi-automatically or manually, various antennae located around the airframe being employed to detect electronic emissions whilst up to five external pods can be carried to generate 'noise' jamming signals designed to render enemy radar ineffective.

Not surprisingly, the Prowler's capabilities have been steadily enhanced since the type first attained operational status with VAQ-132 in the summer of 1972. Early production machines were to Basic standard and these have since been followed by EXCAP (Expanded Capability), ICAP (Improved Capability) and ICAP-2, DECM (Defensive Electronic Counter-Measures) and ADVCAP (Advanced Capability) aircraft, the last being the final production model. The ADVCAP version features a number of improvements, including better communications jamming equipment, increased jamming power and electronically steered antennae.

In the mid-1990s some 80 EA-6Bs of various subtypes are to be found in the US Navy and US Marine Corps inventories. In addition to new-build Prowlers, the US Navy has also been pursuing the CILOP (Conversion In Lieu Of Procurement) policy with regard to the EA-6B, many older aircraft having been updated to late-standard configuration, and this process also looks likely to continue.

**Grumman EA-6B Prowler**

**Specification:** Grumman EA-6B Prowler (with five jamming pods)
**Origin:** USA
**Type:** electronic countermeasures platform
**Powerplant:** two 5080-kg (11,200-lb) dry thrust Pratt & Whitney J52- P-408 turbojets
**Performance:** maximum speed 530 kt (982 km/h: 610 mph) at sea level; cruising speed 418 kt (774 km/h; 481 mph); initial rate of climb 10,030 ft (3057 m) per minute; service ceiling 38,000 ft (11580 m); combat range 1769 km (1,099 miles) with maximum external fuel
**Weights:** empty 14588 kg (32,162 lb); take-off in stand-off jamming configuration 24703 kg (54,461 lb); maximum take-off 29484 kg (65,000 lb)
**Dimensions:** span 16.15 m (53 ft 0 in); length 18.24 m (59 ft 10 in); height 4.95 m (16 ft 3 in); wing area 49.13m² (528.9 sq ft)
**Armament:** initially none but retrofitted with capability for the underwing carriage of four or six AGM-88 HARM anti-radar missiles on the ICAP-2 and ADVCAP aircraft respectively

*This US Navy Grumman EA-6B is seen in an unfamiliar environment, in front of a HAS at Zweibrücken in Germany during a rare offship deployment from USS Nimitz.*

*Grumman EA-6Bs, in common with most front-line US Navy aircraft, have received toned-down overall grey colour schemes, although many still carry white underwing ECM pods.*

# Grumman E-2 Hawkeye

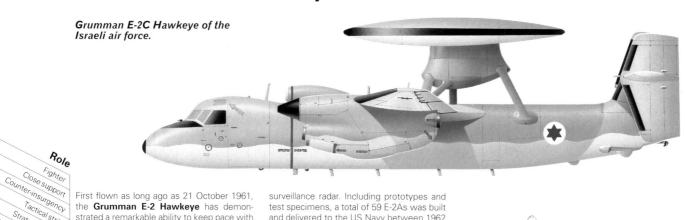

*Grumman E-2C Hawkeye of the Israeli air force.*

## Role
Fighter
Close support
Counter-insurgency
Tactical strike
Strategic bomber
Tactical reconnaissance
Strategic reconnaissance
Maritime patrol
Anti-ship strike
Anti-submarine warfare
Search and rescue
Assault transport
Transport
Liaison
Trainer
Inflight-refuelling tanker
Specialized

## Performance
All-weather capability
Rough field capability
STOL capability
VTOL capability
Airspeed 0-250 mph
Airspeed 250 mph-Mach 1
Airspeed Mach 1 plus
Ceiling 0-20,000 ft
Ceiling 20,000-40,000 ft
Ceiling 40,000ft plus
Range 0-1,000 miles
Range 1,000-3,000 miles
Range 3,000 miles plus

## Weapons
Air-to-air missiles
Air-to-surface missiles
Cruise missiles
Cannon
Trainable guns
Naval weapons
Nuclear-capable
Rockets
'Smart' weapon kit
Weapon load 0-4,000 lb
Weapon load 4,000-15,000 lb
Weapon load 15,000 lb plus

## Avionics
Electronic Counter Measures
Electronic Support Measures
Search radar
Fire control radar
Look-down/shoot-down
Terrain-following radar
Forward-looking infra-red
Laser
Television

First flown as long ago as 21 October 1961, the **Grumman E-2 Hawkeye** has demonstrated a remarkable ability to keep pace with developments in the airborne early warning field, being perhaps a classic example of cramming a quart into a pint pot In its latest guise as the **E-2C**, it is infinitely superior to the original **E-2A** model which entered service with the US Navy's VAW-11 squadron at the beginning of 1964 and which played an important role in controlling US Navy strike packages during the Vietnam War.

Early AEW-dedicated aircraft such as the Grumman TBF Avenger and Grumman WF-2 Tracer were adequate for their times, but were unable to cope with more than a handful of targets at any one time. It gradually became clear, therefore, that computerization was required in some form if radar system operators were to take full advantage of all information at their disposal. However, it was not until the late 1950s that miniaturization of computers reached the stage at which it was possible to install such devices in an airframe small enough for operation from US Navy carriers.

What resulted was the **W2F-1** (E-2A from late 1962), instantly recognizable by the pancake-shaped dorsal radome which housed the antenna for the General Electric APS-96

surveillance radar. Including prototypes and test specimens, a total of 59 E-2As was built and delivered to the US Navy between 1962 and 1967, most being later modified to **E-2B** standard through installation of a Litton L-304 general-purpose computer. A few E-2Bs remained operational until the later 1980s.

Further upgrading of the avionics systems led to the appearance of the E-2C, with General Electric APS-120 radar, since replaced by the even more effective APS-125. Data-processing capability was also improved so that the aircraft could automatically track more than 250 targets at once whilst also controlling 30 nterceptions.

Flown for the first time in prototype form on 20 January 1971, the E-2C became operational with VAW-123 aboard USS Saratoga in the autumn of 1974, and variants of the type now equip all US Navy AEW squadrons. In addition, small quantities have also been purchased by Egypt (6), France (4), Israel (4), Japan (13), Singapore (4) and Taiwan (4), whilst production continues for the US Navy, which plans to buy no fewer than 139 up to 1996, later examples benefiting from installation of the more recent APS-138, APS-139 and APS-145 surveillance radars able to track larger numbers of targets at longer range under poorer electro-magnetic conditions.

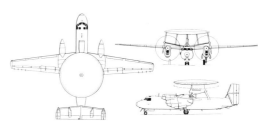

**Grumman E-2C Hawkeye**

**Specification:** Grumman E-2C Hawkeye
**Origin:** USA
**Type:** carrierborne and land-based airborne early warning and control aircraft
**Powerplant:** two 3661-ekW (4,910-ehp) Allison T56-A-425 turboprops
**Performance:** maximum speed 325 kt (602 km/h; 374 mph); economical cruising speed 269 kt (499 km/h; 310 mph); service ceiling 30,800 ft (9390 m); patrol endurance 6 hours; ferry range 2583 km (1,605 miles)
**Weights:** empty 17265 kg (38,063 lb); maximum take-off 23556 kg (51,933 lb)
**Dimensions:** span 24.56 m (80 ft 7 in); length 17.54 m (57 ft 6.75 in); height 5.58 m (18 ft 3.75 in); wing area 65.03 m² (700.0 sq ft)
**Armament:** none

*A Grumman E-2C Hawkeye of VAW-126 is seen during a Pacific fleet deployment on board USS Constellation as a part of CVW-9. The Hawkeye provides fleet airborne early warning control.*

*This E-2C of VAW-124 'Bear Aces' is seen back on an Atlantic Fleet carrier. The Hawkeye's turboprop powerplant confers great economy and thus excellent patrol endurance.*

# Grumman (General Dynamics) EF-111A Raven

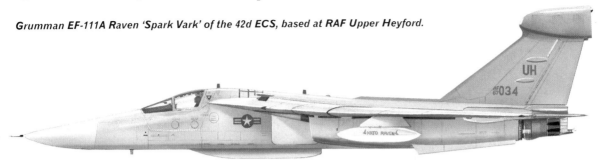

*Grumman EF-111A Raven 'Spark Vark' of the 42d ECS, based at RAF Upper Heyford.*

The importance of aircraft able to provide wide-area ECM jamming coverage for the support of attacking forces was underlined by events in the air war over Vietnam during the late 1960s and early 1970s. Thus in 1974 the USAF awarded study contracts to General Dynamics and Grumman for the development of a suitable conversion of the General Dynamics F-111A tactical strike fighter. Evaluation of the proposals led to Grumman's receipt of a 1975 contract for the conversion of two F-111As as **Grumman (General Dynamics) EF-111A** ECM jamming prototypes. The first of these was flown on 15 December 1975, and the second was the first fully aerodynamic prototype, flown on 10 March 1977 and incorporating the reinforced fin with large fin-tip pod housing the jamming system's receiver and antennae, a conspicuous identification feature. The whole system was flown initially on 10 March 1977. Three operational modes are possible: stand-off with the EF-111A staying in its own airspace to screen the routes of its attack aircraft; escort with the EF-111A accompanying the attack aircraft in penetration of the enemy defences; and neutralization of enemy radars in the close air support role.

Primary role equipment of the EF-111A is the Eaton Corporation ALQ-99E tactical jamming system (housed in the weapons bay), which is claimed to have sufficient power to allow the aircraft to penetrate the most concentrated electronic defences. The ALQ-99E's advanced configuration permits the electronic warfare officer to counter differing threats as they develop. and with the aid of an IBM 4 Pi computer to cope with a workload that previously required several operators. Essential accuracy of navigation is ensured by INS, TACAN, UHF/DF and terrain-following radar, and the ALQ-99E system is backed by electronic countermeasures dispenser, radar countermeasures receiver, self-protection and terminal threat-warning systems.

Development and comprehensive testing of the complete electronics system occupied more than four years, the first fully operational EF-111A, by then named **Raven**, entering service with TAC in November 1981. In December 1983, the 390th Electronic Combat Squadron became the first fully operational unit. In all, 42 EF-111As were produced as F-111A conversions, the last of them being delivered to the USAF during 1985.

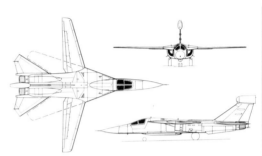

**Grumman (General Dynamics) EF-111A Raven**

*The EF-111A Raven carries its sensitive ALQ-99E emission receiver system in its fin-top fairing. This system's inputs activate the 10 powerful jammers mounted in the weapons bay.*

*Twenty-four of the USAF's EF-111As are based at Mountain Home AFB with the 388th ECS, while 12 serve with the 42nd ECS at Upper Heyford, and six are held in reserve as attrition replacements.*

**Specification:** Grumman (General Dynamics) EF-111A Raven (penetration role)
**Origin:** USA
**Type:** two-seat ECM tactical jamming aircraft
**Powerplant:** two 8391-kg (18,500-lb) afterburning thrust Pratt & Whitney TF30-P-3 turbofans
**Performance:** (estimated) maximum speed Mach 2.14 or 1227 kt (2272 km/h; 1,412 mph) at high altitude; speed in combat area 507 kt (940 km/h; 584 mph); initial rate of climb 3,300 ft (1006m) per minute; service ceiling 45,000 ft (13715 m); combat radius 1495 km (929 miles); unrefuelled endurance more than 4 hours
**Weights:** empty 25072 kg (55,275 lb); maximum take-off 40346 kg (88,948 lb)
**Dimensions:** span 19.20 m (63 ft 0 in) spread and 9.74 m (31 ft 11.4 in) swept; length 23.16 m (76 ft 0 in); height 6.10 m (20 ft 0 in); wing area 48.77 m² (525.0 sq ft) spread
**Armament:** none

**Role**

Fighter
Close support
Counter-insurgency
Tactical strike
Strategic bomber
Tactical reconnaissance
Strategic reconnaissance
Maritime patrol
Anti-ship strike
Anti-submarine warfare
Search and rescue
Assault transport
Transport
Liaison
Trainer
Inflight-refuelling tanker
Specialized

**Performance**

All-weather capability
Rough field capability
STOL capability
VTOL capability
Airspeed 0-250 mph
Airspeed 250 mph-Mach 1
Airspeed Mach 1 plus
Ceiling 0-20,000 ft
Ceiling 20,000-40,000 ft
Ceiling 40,000ft plus
Range 0-1,000 miles
Range 1,000-3,000 miles
Range 3,000 miles plus

**Weapons**

Air-to-air missiles
Air-to-surface missiles
Cruise missiles
Cannon
Trainable guns
Naval weapons
Nuclear-capable
Rockets
'Smart' weapon kit
Weapon load 0-4,000 lb
Weapon load 4,000-15,000 lb
Weapon load 15,000 lb plus

**Avionics**

Electronic Counter Measures
Electronic Support Measures
Search radar
Fire control radar
Look-down/shoot-down
Terrain-following radar
Forward-looking infra-red
Laser
Television

129

# Grumman F-14A Tomcat

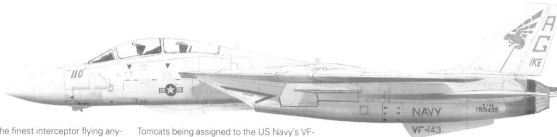

Arguably still the finest interceptor flying anywhere in the world today, the **Grumman F-14 Tomcat** would probably not even have existed had it not been for the failure of the General Dynamics F-111B. Nevertheless, although it fared significantly better than the General Dynamics machine, the **F-14A** variant has not steered entirely clear of trouble, engine-related problems probably being responsible for most of the headaches as well as a substantial proportion of the aircraft lost in accidents. However, more recent developments (described more fully in the separate F-14B/D entry) have addressed and overcome most of these engine-related shortcomings.

What eventually evolved into the Tomcat was already well established on Grumman's drawing boards even before the ill-fated F-111B was cancelled, and the company was therefore well placed to bid for the US Navy's new fighter competition launched soon after the General Dynamics' machine passed into history. Competing against three other proposals, the G-303 design was duly selected by the US Navy in January 1969, an initial contract for six (later increased to 12) development aircraft being placed later in the same year.

The first F-14A eventually became airborne on 21 December 1970 but was destroyed only nine days later on only its second flight after suffering a catastrophic hydraulic system failure. Despite this major setback, the development programme seems to have gone well and culminated in production

Tomcats being assigned to the US Navy's VF-125 training squadron at NAS Miramar, California, during October 1972.

Thereafter, a fairly lengthy period of training followed before the type made its operational debut aboard USS *Enterprise* with VF-1 and VF-2 in September 1974. Since then, the F-14A has gone on to become the US Navy's premier fleet defence fighter, progressive re-equipment allowing it to replace both the McDonnell Douglas F-4 Phantom II and Vought F-8 Crusader, and the type soon equipped 26 front-line and reserve squadrons of the US Navy.

In addition to the 478 F-14As supplied to the US Navy, another 79 were delivered to Iran during the rule of the last Shah, although it seems that only a very few of these now remain serviceable, Iran lacking the technical resources to overcome the embargo on spares imposed by the USA after the overthrow of the Shah.

As far as weaponry is concerned, it is the Hughes AIM-54 Phoenix air-to-air missile that undoubtedly gives the F-14A its edge over other contemporary interceptors, the combination of this AAM and the Hughes AWG-9 radar and weapon-control system providing the ability to destroy aircraft at ranges far in excess of that of any other system. However, in the event of combat being conducted at medium and close ranges, the tomcat can also carry both the radar-guided AIM-7 Sparrow and IR-guided AIM-9 Sidewinder AAMs. A single 20-mm M61A1 Vulcan cannon completes the F-14A's arsenal.

*Grumman F-14A Tomcat of VF-143 'Pukin' Dogs', US Navy.*

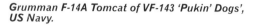

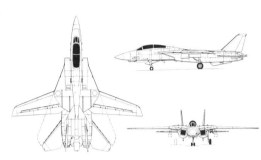

*Grumman F-14A Tomcat*

*This Grumman F-14A Tomcat, seen on the deck of USS America wears the markings of VF-33 'Tarsiers'. The aircraft in the background is from VF-102 'Diamondbacks'.*

*VF-102 'Diamondbacks' is one of the many squadrons trained to use the TARPS pod for operational and tactical reconnaissance. The F-14A/TARPS combination should be succeeded by a derivative of the McDonnell Douglas F/A-18 Hornet.*

**Specification:** Grumman F-14A Tomcat
**Origin:** USA
**Type:** two-seat carrierborne fleet defence fighter
**Powerplant:** two 9480-kg (20,900-lb) afterburning thrust Pratt & Whitney TF30-P-412A turbofans
**Performance:** maximum speed Mach 2.37 or 1,359 kt (2517 km/h; 1,564 mph) at high altitude; initial rate of climb more than 30,000 ft (9145 m) per minute; service ceiling more than 56,000 ft (17070 m); range about 3220 km (2,000 miles) in interceptor configuration with external fuel
**Weights:** empty 18191 kg (40,104 lb); normal take-off 32098 kg (70,764 lb) with six Phoenix AAMs; maximum take-off 33724 kg (74,349 lb)
**Dimensions:** span 19.55 m (64 ft 1.5 in) spread and 11.65 m (38 ft 2.5 in) swept; length 19.10 m (62 ft 8 in); height 4.88 m (16 ft 0 in); wing area 52.49 m² (565.0 sq ft)
**Armament:** one 20-mm M61A1 Vulcan rotary cannon with 675 rounds, and provision for various combinations of AIM-7 Sparrow, AIM-9 Sidewinder and AIM-54 Phoenix AAMs carried under the fuselage and inner parts of the wings

## Role

Fighter
Close support
Counter-insurgency
Tactical strike
Strategic bomber
Tactical reconnaissance
Strategic reconnaissance
Maritime patrol
Anti-ship strike
Anti-submarine warfare
Search and rescue
Assault transport
Transport
Liaison
Trainer
Inflight-refuelling tanker
Specialized

## Performance

All-weather capability
Rough field capability
STOL capability
VTOL capability
Airspeed 0-250 mph
Airspeed 250 mph-Mach 1
Airspeed Mach 1 plus
Ceiling 0-20,000 ft
Ceiling 20,000-40,000 ft
Ceiling 40,000ft plus
Range 0-1,000 miles
Range 1,000-3,000 miles
Range 3,000 miles plus

## Weapons

Air-to-air missiles
Air-to-surface missiles
Cruise missiles
Cannon
Trainable guns
Naval weapons
Nuclear-capable
Rockets
'Smart' weapon kit
Weapon load 0-4,000 lb
Weapon load 4,000-15,000 lb
Weapon load 15,000 lb plus

## Avionics

Electronic Counter Measures
Electronic Support Measures
Search radar
Fire control radar
Look-down/shoot-down
Terrain-following radar
Forward-looking infra-red
Laser
Television

# Grumman F-14B/D Tomcat

*A Grumman F-14D of VF-2 'Bounty Hunters'.*

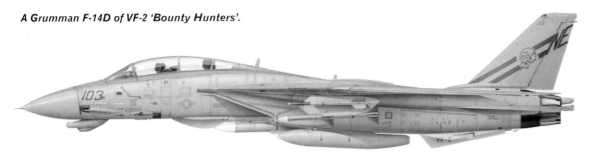

Anyone who has followed the F-14's career closely is well aware that the type has been plagued by engine-related problems for much of Its life. Attempts to eliminate some of the TF30's worst vices have met with a measure of success, but the Pratt & Whitney engine was still a source of major concern in July 1984, when it was decided to install a version of the General Electric F110 turbofan in a new variant of the fighter to be known as the **Grumman F-14D Super Tomcat**.

In fact, the TF30 had initially been viewed only as an interim powerplant, derived from that of the abortive General Dynamics F-111B, pending the availability of a definitive engine which would be installed in a version to be known as the F-14B. But largely as a result of financial restraints, the TF30-engined 'interim' model became the main production model.

Several years later, the question of re-engining the Tomcat re-emerged, and this time the proposal met with greater success. The General Electric F101 turbofan (selected to power the Rockwell B-1) served as the basis for the F101DFE (Derivative Fighter Engine) and was test flown in the sole F-14B for the first time in July 1981.

Now known to the parent company the **Super Tomcat**, the re-engined prototype demonstrated remarkable performance benefits, and this eventually prompted the deci-sion in October 1982 to proceed with full-scale development of the F110. Even then, it was to be another couple of years before the US Navy put its full weight behind this engine, the service first adopting a 'belt and braces' approach by carefully monitoring progress made with the basically similar Pratt & Whitney PW1128N turbofan.

Finally, in early 1984, the US Navy came down in favour of the F110-GE-400, select-ing this engine to power the F-14D that was also to benefit from a major updating of the Hughes AWG-9 weapon control system into the APG-71 radar system drawing on experi-ence with the same company's APG-70 radar used in the McDonnell Douglas F-15 Eagle Multi-Stage Improvement Program. Other changes demanded included a major design of cockpit instrumentation and the installation of improved Pentagon-sponsored items such as the ALQ-165 Airborne Self-Protection Jammer and the Joint Tactical Information Distribution System.

The new engine made its debut in the **F-14B** that was designated as the **F-14A(Plus)** up to May 1991. The whole Tomcat upgrade programme has been trimmed by the end of the 'Cold War', and amounted to 38 and 37 new-build F-14B and F-14D aircraft respec-tively, plus a numbers of conversions. The two variants entered service in late 1988 and November 1990 respectively.

**Grumman F-14D Tomcat**

**Specification:** Grumman F-14D Super Tomcat
**Origin:** USA
**Type:** two-seat carrierborne fleet defence fighter
**Powerplant:** two 12247-kg (27,000-lb) afterburning thrust General Electric F110-GE-400 turbofans
**Performance:** maximum speed Mach 1.88 or 1,078 kt (1998 km/h; 1,241 mph) at high altitude; service ceiling more than 53,000 ft (16150 m); combat radius 1994 km (1,239 miles) for a CAP with six AIM-7 and four AIM-9 AAMs
**Weights:** empty 18951 kg (41,780 lb); normal take-off 29072 kg (64,093 lb) in the fighter/escort mission; maximum take-off 33724 kg (74,349 lb)
**Dimensions:** span 19.54 m (64 ft 1.5 in) spread and 11.65 m (38 ft 2.5 in) swept; length 19.10 m (62 ft 8 in); height 4.88 m (16 ft 0 in); wing area 52.49 m² (565.0 sq ft)
**Armament:** one 20-mm M61A1 Vulcan rotary cannon with 675 rounds, and provision for up to 6577 kg (14,500 lb) of various combinations of AIM-7M Sparrow, AIM-9M Sidewinder and AIM-54A/B/C Phoenix AAMs carried under the fuselage and inner parts of the wings; the type is also being qualified for the carriage of a substantial load of free-fall weapons

*VF-31 Tomcatters are one of three squadrons equipped with the top-of-the-range F-14D. All are based on the West Coast, deploying aboard Pacific Fleet carriers.*

*The F-14D is a considerably more capable fighting machine than the F-14A, with improved avionics and instrumentation as well as more powerful engines and the latest version of the Phoenix AAM. This one wears the insignia of VF-2 aboard the USS Ranger.*

| Role |
| --- |
| Fighter |
| Close support |
| Counter-insurgency |
| Tactical strike |
| Strategic bomber |
| Tactical reconnaissance |
| Strategic reconnaissance |
| Maritime patrol |
| Anti-ship strike |
| Anti-submarine warfare |
| Search and rescue |
| Assault transport |
| Transport |
| Liaison |
| Trainer |
| Inflight-refuelling tanker |
| Specialized |

| Performance |
| --- |
| All-weather capability |
| Rough field capability |
| STOL capability |
| VTOL capability |
| Airspeed 0-250 mph |
| Airspeed 250 mph-Mach 1 |
| Airspeed Mach 1 plus |
| Airspeed 0-20,000 ft |
| Ceiling 0-20,000 ft |
| Ceiling 20,000-40,000 ft |
| Ceiling 40,000ft plus |
| Range 0-1,000 miles |
| Range 1,000-3,000 miles |
| Range 3,000 miles plus |

| Weapons |
| --- |
| Air-to-air missiles |
| Air-to-surface missiles |
| Cruise missiles |
| Cannon |
| Trainable guns |
| Naval weapons |
| Nuclear-capable |
| Rockets |
| 'Smart' weapon kit |
| Weapon load 0-4,000 lb |
| Weapon load 4,000-15,000 lb |
| Weapon load 15,000 lb plus |

| Avionics |
| --- |
| Electronic Counter Measures |
| Electronic Support Measures |
| Search radar |
| Fire control radar |
| Look-down/shoot-down radar |
| Terrain-following radar |
| Forward-looking infra-red |
| Laser |
| Television |

# Grumman OV-1 Mohawk

*Grumman OV-1C Mohawk of the US Army.*

## Role

Fighter
Close support
Counter-insurgency
Tactical strike
Strategic bomber
Tactical reconnaissance
Strategic reconnaissance
Maritime patrol
Anti-ship strike
Anti-submarine warfare
Search and rescue
Assault transport
Transport
Liaison
Trainer
Inflight-refuelling tanker
Specialized

## Performance

All-weather capability
Rough field capability
STOL capability
VTOL capability
Airspeed 0-250 mph
Airspeed 250 mph-Mach 1
Airspeed Mach 1 plus
Ceiling 0-20,000 ft
Ceiling 20,000-40,000 ft
Ceiling 40,000ft plus
Range 0-1,000 miles
Range 1,000-3,000 miles
Range 3,000 miles plus

## Weapons

Air-to-air missiles
Air-to-surface missiles
Cruise missiles
Cannon
Trainable guns
Naval weapons
Nuclear-capable
Rockets
'Smart' weapon kit
Weapon load 0-4,000 lb
Weapon load 4,000-15,000 lb
Weapon load 15,000 lb plus

## Avionics

Electronic Counter Measures
Electronic Support Measures
Search radar
Fire control radar
Look-down/shoot-down
Terrain-following radar
Forward-looking infra-red
Laser
Television

During the operational lifetime of the **Grumman OV-1 Mohawk**, tremendous strides have been taken in the realm of army airborne reconnaissance, and what began as a traditional visual and photographic aircraft is today packed with sophisticated sensors. The G-134, unusual for its time in being an army aviation type with a turboprop power-plant, in the form of two 708-kW (950-shp) Lycoming T53-L-3 engines, was initially designated YAO-1 when the first of nine development aircraft flew on 14 April 1959, these later being redesignated YOV-1A. A further four were ordered to meet US Marine Corps requirements, but this proposed OF-1 model was cancelled before the aircraft were completed. A comprehensive array of avionics was included in the initial production **OV-1A** to enable the aircraft to meet the all-weather battlefield surveillance requirement, and two underwing stores pylons enabled up to 1225 kg (2,700 lb) of ordnance to be carried. Grumman built 64 OV-1As, equipped with KA-30 high-resolution camera systems and removable pods above the wing roots for 52 upward-firing night photography flares

The **OV-1B** (90 built) introduced APS-94 side-looking airborne radar (SLAR) in a large underfuselage container, an AKT-16 VHF data link, and a further 1.83 m (6 ft 0 in) of wing span. Fuselage airbrakes were deleted, as was provision for dual controls for the two-man crew in their armour-protected, Martin-Baker Mk J5 ejector seats. Later OV-1Bs had 858-kW (1,150-hp) T53-L-15s. Built in parallel, the **OV-1C** was an updated OV-1A with short-span wings and UAS-4 infra-red ground surveillance equipment in the underside of the rear fuselage, and late models of the 129 built also progressed to T53-L-15 engines. In the four YOV-1D and 37 **OV-1D** large-span aircraft which followed up to the end of production in December 1970, the SLAR could be exchanged for IR sensors within an hour, thereby combining OV-1B/C functions in an airframe powered by further uprated engines. In addition, 72 OV-1B/C aircraft were converted to OV-1D standard by 1984, with equipment including new APS-94F SLAR. All retain 180° visual spectrum photographic capability. The US Army will operate 110 OV-1Ds, plus 36 **RV-1D** conversions with ALQ-133 'Quick Look II' equipment for pinpointing enemy radars, up to the end of the century. At least two OV-1Ds were supplied to Israel in mid-1976.

**Grumman OV-1B Mohawk**

*A Grumman **RV-1D** of the 73d **Combat Intelligence Company**, US Army, based at **Stuttgart** in the Federal Republic of Germany. The RV-1D is equipped with the **ALQ**-133 'Quick Look III' system.*

*The OV-1D carries an **APS-94 SLAR** in its underfuselage pod, and this can be augmented by photographic and infra-red sensors. Some 110 will remain in service into the next century.*

## Specification: Grumman OV-1 D Mohawk
**Origin:** USA
**Type:** tactical reconnaissance aircraft
**Powerplant:** two 1044-kW (1,400-shp) Lycoming T53-L-701 turboprops
**Performance:** maximum speed 265 kt (491 km/h; 305 mph) with IR sensors, or 251 kt (465 km/h; 289 mph) with SLAR; cruising speed 210kt (389 km/h; 242 mph); service ceiling 25,000 ft (7620 m); range 1738 km (1,080 miles) with IR or 1653 km (1,027 miles) with SLAR
**Weights:** empty 5333 kg (11,757 lb); maximum take-off 8085 kg (17,826 lb) with IR or 8164 kg (18,000 lb) with SLAR
**Dimensions:** span 14.63 m (48 ft 0 in); length 13.69 m (44 ft 11 in); height 3.86 m (12 ft 8 in); wing area 33.45 m² (360.0 sq ft)
**Armament:** generally none

# Grumman S-2 Tracker

*Grumman S-2A Tracker of the Royal Thai navy.*

Making its maiden flight as long ago as December 1952, the **Grumman S-2 Tracker** is still used by a respectable number of air arms throughout the world, although it no longer remains operational with he US Navy since its replacement by the Lockheed S-3A Viking during the course of the 1970s.

A successful marriage of the previously separate search and destroy aspects of anti-submarine warfare, the Tracker can be said to have revolutionized carrierborne ASW and was produced in large numbers for the US Navy, successive updating of the basic G-89 design keeping it abreast of developments in this vital field and, incidentally, ensuring that it remained in production until well into the 1960s.

Powered by a pair of Wright Cyclone radial engines, the first model of the Tracker to enter quantity production was the **S2F-1 (S-2A** from late 1962), this being by far the most numerous subtype with well over 700 completed for service with the US Navy and a number of friendly nations including Italy, Japan and the Netherlands.

Later updating of the S2F-1 led to the appearance of the **S2F-1S (S-2B)** and **S2F-1S1 (S-2F)**, modification work mainly entailing addition of Julie and Jezebel active and passive detection equipment but, following

the advent of later and more modern ASW models of the Tracker, a substantial number of these aircraft were reconfigured for utility missions as the **US-2A** and **US-2B**. Many more were reassigned lo multi-engine training duties as the **S2F-1T (TS-2A)**, and some of these claimed the distinction of being amongst the last Trackers to be employed by the US Navy.

In addition to the initial production model, subsequent new-build versions of the Tracker comprised the **S2F-2 (S-2C)**, **S2F-3 (S-2D)** and **S2F-3S (S-2E)**, retrospective modification of these subtypes leading to the appearance of specialized aircraft engaged in a variety of tasks including target towing and utility functions (**US-2C** and **US-2D**), photo-reconnaissance (**RS-2C**) and telemetry relay/electronic missions (**ES-2D**).

The last anti-submarine model used by the US Navy was the **S-2G** which was essentially an S-2E with enhanced electronics. Indeed, the S-2G was not produced as such, those aircraft which existed being simply conversions of S-2Es. Following service with the US Navy, many of the survivors have found their way overseas examples of the S-2G being supplied to Australia and Uruguay. In recent years a number of the aircraft have been upgraded with a turboprop powerplant and other modern features.

## Specification: Grumman S-2E Tracker
**Origin:** USA
**Type:** carrierborne and land-based anti-submarine warfare aircraft
**Powerplant:** two 1137-kW (1,525-hp) Wright R-1820-82WA Cyclone radial piston engines
**Performance:** maximum speed 230 kt (426 km/h; 265 mph) at sea level; patrol speed 130 kt (241 km/h; 150 mph) at 1,500 ft (460 m); ferry range 2092 km (1,300 miles); endurance 9 hours with maximum fuel and reserves
**Weights:** empty 8505 kg (18,750 lb); maximum take-off 13222 kg (29,150 lb)
**Dimensions:** span 22.12 m (72 ft 7 in); length 13.26 m (43 ft 6 in); height 5.05 m (16 ft 7 in); wing area 46.08 m² (496.0 sq ft)
**Armament:** one Mk 47 or Mk 101 nuclear depth bomb or similar store in the weapons bay plus a variety of bombs, rockets or torpedoes on six underwing stores stations; search devices include 60 echo-sounding depth charges in fuselage and 32 sonobuoys in engine nacelles

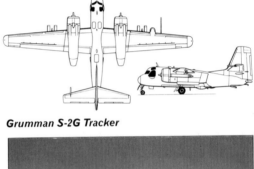

*Grumman S-2G Tracker*

*The Japanese Maritime Self-Defence Force operated a number of S-2F Trackers with its 11 Kokutai, part of 1 Kokugun based at Kanoya, on the southern island of Kyushu.*

*The Canadian Armed Forces was a major user of the Tracker, 18 aircraft equipping No.880 Squadron at Summerside. Canada's Trackers acted as a short-range supplement to the more capable Lockheed CP-140 Auroras.*

**Role**
Fighter
Close support
Counter-insurgency
Tactical strike
Strategic bomber
Tactical reconnaissance
Strategic reconnaissance
Maritime patrol
Anti-ship strike
Anti-submarine warfare
Search and rescue
Assault transport
Transport
Liaison
Trainer
Inflight-refuelling tanker
Specialized

**Performance**
All-weather capability
Rough field capability
STOL capability
VTOL capability
Airspeed 0-250 mph
Airspeed 250 mph-Mach 1
Airspeed Mach 1 plus
Ceiling 0-20,000 ft
Ceiling 20,000-40,000 ft
Ceiling 40,000ft plus
Range 0-1,000 miles
Range 1,000-3,000 miles
Range 3,000 miles plus

**Weapons**
Air-to-air missiles
Air-to-surface missiles
Cruise missiles
Cannon
Trainable guns
Naval weapons
Nuclear-capable
Rockets
'Smart' weapon kit
Weapon load 0-4,000 lb
Weapon load 4,000-15,000 lb
Weapon load 15,000 lb plus

**Avionics**
Electronic Counter Measures
Electronic Support Measures
Search radar
Fire control radar
Look-down/shoot-down
Terrain-following radar
Forward-looking infra-red
Laser
Television

# Grumman U-16 Albatross

*Grumman HU-16B Albatross of the Greek air force.*

**Role**
Fighter
Close support
Counter-insurgency
Tactical strike
Strategic bomber
Tactical reconnaissance
Strategic reconnaissance
Maritime patrol
Anti-ship strike
Anti-submarine warfare
Search and rescue
Assault transport
Transport
Liaison
Trainer
Inflight-refuelling tanker
Specialized

**Performance**
All-weather capability
Rough field capability
STOL capability
VTOL capability
Airspeed 0-250 mph
Airspeed 250 mph-Mach 1
Airspeed Mach 1 plus
Ceiling 0-20,000 ft
Ceiling 20,000-40,000 ft
Ceiling 40,000ft plus
Range 0-1,000 miles
Range 1,000-3,000 miles
Range 3,000 miles plus

**Weapons**
Air-to-air missiles
Air-to-surface missiles
Cruise missiles
Cannon
Trainable guns
Naval weapons
Nuclear-capable
Rockets
'Smart' weapon kit
Weapon load 0-4,000 lb
Weapon load 4,000-15,000 lb
Weapon load 15,000 lb plus

**Avionics**
Electronic Counter Measures
Electronic Support Measures
Search radar
Fire control radar
Look-down/shoot-down
Terrain-following radar
Forward-looking infra-red
Laser
Television

Affectionately known as the 'Goat', the **Grumman U-16 Albatross** has declined in numbers during recent years and the type is no longer operated by the US forces although quite a few are still active overseas, most notably in Greece, Indonesia, Mexico and Taiwan.

Development of the U-16 can be traced back to 1944 when, building on experience gained with the highly successful JRF Goose, Grumman began to design a new amphibian, allocating company designation G-64 to this project. Initially designated XJRF-1, the prototype made its maiden flight on 24 October 1947 and was soon ordered into production for the US Navy as the **UF-1** utility amphibian, this model redesignated **HU-16C** in 1962 when the unified nomenclature system was adopted by the US armed forces.

Later refinement of the basic design led to the appearance of the **UF-2** (**HU-16D**) in the early 1950s, this model featuring increased wing span, cambered wing leading edges, larger ailerons and tail surfaces, and more effective de-icing equipment on wing, tail and fin leading edges. Most UF-2s were produced by the simple expedient of remanu-facturing existing UF-1s, but a modest number of new-build examples did also appear at this time.

In addition to the two basic variants, a small number of sub-types were produced, these including the **UF-1L** (**LU-16C**) which was a winterized model for service in the Antarctic,

and the **UF-1T** (**TU-16C**) dual-control trainer model. Another version (the **UF-1G**) was operated solely by the Coast Guard as a rescue aircraft, a handful of new-build examples supplemented by redundant US Navy air-frames, and all of the survivors were later modified to **UH-2G** (**HU-16E**) configuration.

The Albatross also found favour with the US Air Force which employed it on rescue duties, receiving approximately 300 aircraft of two basic subtypes. The first of these was the **SA-16A** (later **HU-16A**) which closely corresponded to the initial US Navy model, whilst the **SA-16B** (later **HU-16B**) featured the structural changes introduced on the UF-2 in the early 1950s. Availability of turbine-engined helicopters heralded the demise of the USAF aircraft, although a few did see combat action in South East Asia during the Vietnam War.

Much later in the career of the 'Goat', a number of HU-16Bs were reconfigured for anti-submarine warfare duties, mission-relat-ed equipment including nose-mounted search radar, a retractable magnetic anomaly detector boom, a searchlight and external stores stations permitting carriage of up to four torpedoes, mines, depth charges or rocket-launcher pods. ASW-configured examples of the Albatross were operated by Greece, Norway and Spain, but today only the first nation still uses this model, its air-craft being extensively rebuilt to prolong ser-vice life and capability.

**Specification:** Grumman HU-16D Albatross
**Origin:** USA
**Type:** utility/air-sea rescue amphibian
**Powerplant:** two 1063-kW (1,425-hp) Wright R-1820-76A/76B Cyclone radial piston engines
**Performance:** maximum speed 205 kt (380 km/h; 236 mph) at sea level; cruising speed 130 kt (241 km/h; 150 mph); range 4587 km (2,850 miles) with maximum fuel; endurance 22 hours 54 minutes
**Weights:** empty 10379 kg (22,883 lb); maximum take-off 7009 kg (37,500 lb)
**Dimensions:** span 29.46 m (96 ft 8 in); length 18.67 m (61 ft 3 in); height 7.87 m (25 ft 0 in); wing area 96.15 m² (1,045.0 sq ft)
**Armament:** none

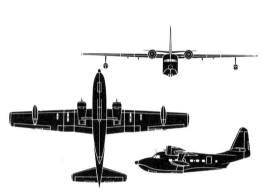

**Grumman HU-16B Albatross**

*About a dozen HU-16Bs are still in use with the Greek air force for maritime reconnaissance, SAR and miscellaneous transport duties. A search radar is fitted in the nose.*

*The Aviación de la Armada de Mexico flew 14 ageing Grumman Albatross amphibians for anti-smuggling, SAR and liaison duties.*

# Harbin Y-8

*Harbin Y-8 of the Chinese People's Army air force.*

Originally regarded as a Harbin project, but now in production at Hanzhong in the Shaanxi province of China, the **Y-8** (Yunshuji-8, or transport aircraft 8) is a slightly modified version of the Antonov An-12BP civil/military transport, and both the An-12 and Y-8 have the NATO reporting name 'Cub'. In their country of origin, the several variants of the An-12 fulfil many roles similar to those which the ubiquitous Lockheed C-130 Hercules carries out for the services of the USA and many other nations.

Manufacture of the Y-8 did not start until the early 1980s, and even then the programme appears to have been at a fairly low key with only 31 reported to have been built by February 1989. The aircraft are generally very similar to the An-12BP, but have a revised nose structure that increases the overall fuselage length by just over 0.91 m (3 ft). There would also appear to be some changes to the flight deck, as the fuselage has different nose contours and modifications to the shape of the windscreens and side transparencies. The powerplant also has a slightly greater output than the 2983-ekW (4,000-eshp) Ivchyenko AI-20K turboprops powering the An-12, the engine used in the

Chinese type being the Wojiang-6, which is a version of the AI-20K developed in China.

The comparatively few Y-8s in service are reported to have been deployed as **Y-8A** long-range helicopter transports with the height of the main hold increased by deletion of the internal gantry. There are a number of other variants for civil as well as military use, however, and the military models include the **Y-8C** pressurized model developed with assistance from Lockheed and also including a redesigned cargo loading door, the **Y-8E** drone carrier with a controller station and provision for two remotely piloted vehicles under the wings, the **Y-8X** maritime patrol model and, currently under development with GEC-Marconi assistance, an AEW model. Other possibilities are the introduction of improved avionics (Doppler and weather radar, and also an inertial navigation system) and the development of an inflight-refuelling model.

The Y-8X maritime patrol variant is understood to have made its first flight on 4 September 1985. It has a Tu-16/H-6 type nose, with extensive glazing, and an under-nose radome which probably contains a Litton search radar.

## Specification: Harbin Y-8A

**Origin:** USSR and China
**Type:** helicopter and utility transport
**Powerplant:** four 3169-ekW (4,250-eshp) SMPMC (Zhuzhou) WJ-6 turboprops
**Performance:** maximum speed 357 kt (662 km/h; 411 mph) at 22,965 ft (700 m); economical cruising speed 286 kt (530 km/h; 329 mph) at 26,250 ft (8000 m); initial rate of climb 1,552 ft (473 m) per minute; service ceiling 34,120 ft (10400 m); range 1273 km (791 miles) with maximum payload or 5615 km (3,490 miles)m with maximum fuel
**Weights:** empty 35500 kg (78,264 lb); maximum take-off 61000 kg (134,480 lb)
**Dimensions:** span 38.00 m (124 ft 8 in); length 34.022 m (111 ft 7.5 in); height 11.16 m (36 ft 11.5 in); wing area 121.86 m² (1,311.7 sq ft)
**Armament:** none

**Harbin Y-8A 'Cub'**

*The Harbin Y-8 has spawned several interesting derivatives, including a study for an inflight-refuelling tanker and a prototype maritime patrol aircraft, shown here.*

*Only a small number of Harbin Y-8s have been built to date, but the aircraft remains in small-scale production and serves alongside Soviet-built Antonov An-12s with CAAC and the PLA.*

### Role

Fighter
Close support
Counter-insurgency
Tactical strike
Strategic bomber
Strategic reconnaissance
Tactical reconnaissance
Strategic reconnaissance
Maritime patrol
Anti-ship strike
Anti-submarine warfare
Search and rescue
Assault transport
Transport
Liaison
Trainer
Inflight-refuelling tanker
Specialized

### Performance

All-weather capability
Rough field capability
STOL capability
VTOL capability
Airspeed 0-250 mph
Airspeed 250 mph-Mach 1
Airspeed Mach 1 plus
Ceiling 0-20,000 ft
Ceiling 20,000-40,000 ft
Ceiling 40,000ft plus
Range 0-1,000 miles
Range 1,000-3,000 miles
Range 3,000 miles plus

### Weapons

Air-to-air missiles
Air-to-surface missiles
Cruise missiles
Cannon
Trainable guns
Naval weapons
Nuclear-capable
Rockets
'Smart' weapon kit
Weapon load 0-4,000 lb
Weapon load 4,000-15,000 lb
Weapon load 15,000 lb plus

### Avionics

Electronic Counter Measures
Electronic Support Measures
Search radar
Fire control radar
Look-down/shoot-down
Terrain-following radar
Forward-looking infra-red
Laser
Television

# Harbin Y-11 and Y-12

*Harbin Y-12 early development model.*

To meet a requirement for a twin-engine utility transport to replace the Antonov An-2 being built in China under the designation Harbin Y-5, work began in the early 1970s on the **Y-11** (Yanshuji-11, or transport aircraft 11). This is a braced high-wing monoplane with a wing of constant chord with a NACA (predecessor of NASA) aerofoil section, automatic leading-edge slats outboard and fixed slats inboard of the underwing mounted engines, double-slotted wide-span trailing-edge flaps and drooping ailerons giving excellent STOL performance, with a take-off or landing run of only 140 m (460 ft). The fuselage cross-section is basically rectangular, and the aeroplane is carried on fixed tricycle landing gear. The flight deck accommodates a crew of two and the cabin normally takes seven passengers, but a folding jump seat can stretch this to eight: instead of passengers a cargo payload of 870 kg (1,918 lb) can be carried. Believed to have flown for the first time during 1975, the Y-11 entered production two years later with a powerplant of two 213-kW (285-hp) SMPMX (Zhuzhou) HS-6A radial piston engines, and has been built in modest numbers, primarily for use in agricultural,

forestry, survey, and a variety of other roles.

Looking for improved performance, especially in single-engined flight, the Chinese then evolved the **Y-11B(I)** with a powerplant of two 261-kW (350-hp) Continental TSIO-550-B flat-six piston engines.

The demand for greater capacity paved the way for the **Y-12**, which began life as the **Y-12 I** development of the Y-11 with a powerplant of two 373-kW (500-shp) Pratt & Whitney Canada PT6A-11 turboprops, and a wider and longer fuselage for a crew of two and a maximum 17 passengers. Three Y-12 I aircraft were built (two for flight test and one as a static airframe) and the first of them was flown on 14 July 1982. Production of some 30 aircraft followed before the advent of the **Y-12 II** aircraft with more powerful PT6A-27 turboprops. Other significant changes from the Y-11 include the use of a more efficient wing aerofoil section, deletion of the wing leading-edge slats, increased wing fuel capacity and a larger passenger/cargo door Apart from civil agricultural, firefighting, passenger/cargo transport and survey roles, the Y-12 II is seen as a useful light transport for military use, carrying up to 14 parachutists or 1700 kg (3,748 lb) of cargo.

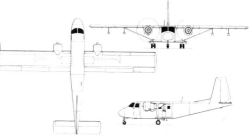

**Harbin Y-11**

*The piston-engined Harbin Y-11 was designed originally as a replacement for the An-2/Y-5, and though successful has been largely replaced in production by the turboprop Y-12.*

*The Y-12 can fulfil a number of military roles, and is thought to be in service with the People's Liberation Army in modest numbers. Seventeen passengers or 14 paratroops can be accommodated.*

**Specification:** Harbin Y-12 II
**Origin:** China
**Type:** utility STOL transport
**Powerplant:** two 462-kW (620-shp) Pratt & Whitney Canada PT6A-27 turboprops
**Performance:** maximum speed 163 kt (302 km/h; 188 mph) at 9,845 ft (3000 m); cruising speed 129 kt (240 km/h;149 mph); initial rate of climb 1,575 ft (480 m) per minute; range 410 km (255 miles0 with 17 passengers
**Weights:** empty 3000 kg (6,614 lb); maximum take-off 5500 kg (12,125 lb)
**Dimensions:** span 17.24 m (56 ft 6.7 in); length 14.86 m (48 ft 9 in); height 5.28 m (17 ft 3.9 in); wing area 34.27 m² (368.89 sq ft)
**Armament:** none

# Ilyushin Il-18 'Coot'

*Ilyushin Il-18 'Coot' of the Algerian government.*

First flown in July 1957, the **Ilyushin Il-18** was intended to introduce a sophisticated turboprop airliner to Aeroflot's domestic and international routes although it was of much the same size as the contemporary Antonov An-10. Initially powered by Kuznetsov NK-4 turboprops, the early aircraft carried 84 passengers, but from the 21st production **Il-18B** power was provided by Ivchyenko AI-20K engines, and accommodation was increased to 110 passengers in the **Il-18V**. Of exceptionally efficient aerodynamic design, the Il-18 employed a high-aspect-ratio wing with three main spars in the centre section reducing to two outboard of the engines. A strange anachronism, however, was the retention of fully manually operated flying controls.

From the outset the Soviet air force's military transport aviation command (VT-A) displayed interest in the Il-18 (NATO reporting name **'Coot'**) although it is likely that the only examples set aside for exclusive military use were those employed for use by VIPs and senior staffs. Instead, as is customary, Aeroflot aircraft were 'borrowed' in the event that a requirement arose to move military personnel in circumstances where dedicated trooping aircraft were considered inappropriate. A developed version, the **Il-18I** with

3169-ekW (4,250-ehp) AI-20M turboprops, was introduced early in the 1960s and, soon redesignated **Il-18D**, this was capable of simple conversion from 110- to 122-seat accommodation. Produced in parallel was the **Il-18Ye**, which lacked the Il-18D's four centre-section fuel tanks for an additional 6300 litres (1,386 Imp gal) of fuel.

Outside the USSR fewer than 20 Il-18Ye and Il-18D aircraft were supplied to foreign air forces, Syria and Algeria each receiving four Il-18D military VIP transports, Guinea, North Korea and East Germany two each, and single examples serving in Poland, Romania and Yugoslavia. At the time of the Soviet intervention in Afghanistan, the Afghan air force operated two Il-18Ds as VIP transports.

By the mid-1970s the great majority of the 500-odd Il-18s retained in the USSR had been withdrawn from commercial and military transport service and were the subject of development for other military roles (see separate Il-20 and Il-38 entries). A few redundant passenger-appointed transports have undergone conversion for freighting, being provided with strengthened cabin floor and a freight-loading door in the side of the rear fuselage. It is not known whether these aircraft are identified by a separate designation.

## Specification: Ilyushin Il-18D 'Coot'

**Origin:** USSR
**Type:** 110/122-seat long-range transport
**Powerplant:** four 3169-ekW (4,250-ehp) Ivchyenko AI-20M turboprops
**Performance:** maximum cruising speed 364 kt (675 km/h; 419 mph) at 27,890 ft (8500 m); normal operating altitude 26,245-32,810 ft (8000 to 10000 m); range 3700 km (2,299 miles) with 13500-kg (29,762-lb) maximum payload
**Weights:** empty 35000 kg (77,162 lb); maximum take-off 64000 kg (141,096 lb)
**Dimensions:** span 37.40 m (122 ft 8.4 in); length 35.90 m (117 ft 9.4 in); height 10.17 m (33 ft 4.4 in); wing area 140.0 m² (1,507.0 sq ft)
**Armament:** none

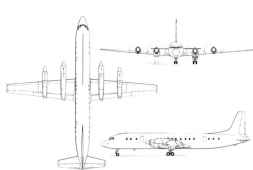

*Ilyushin Il-18*

**Small numbers of Il-18 'Coots' remain in service with various air forces. This aircraft belonged to the Polish air force, which used the type alongside older Il-14s.**

**This Yugoslav Il-18 was used primarily in the VIP transport role. The Il-18 is similar in size, concept and performance to the Bristol Britannia, but has outlasted its Western counterparts.**

**Role**
Fighter
Close support
Counter-insurgency
Tactical strike
Strategic bomber
Tactical reconnaissance
Strategic reconnaissance
Maritime patrol
Anti-ship strike
Anti-submarine warfare
Search and rescue
Assault transport
Transport
Liaison
Trainer
Inflight-refuelling tanker
Specialized

**Performance**
All-weather capability
Rough field capability
STOL capability
VTOL capability
Airspeed 0-250 mph
Airspeed 250 mph-Mach 1
Airspeed Mach 1 plus
Ceiling 0-20,000 ft
Ceiling 20,000-40,000 ft
Ceiling 40,000ft plus
Range 0-1,000 miles
Range 1,000-3,000 miles
Range 3,000 miles plus

**Weapons**
Air-to-air missiles
Air-to-surface missiles
Cruise missiles
Cannon
Trainable guns
Naval weapons
Nuclear-capable
Rockets
'Smart' weapon kit
Weapon load 0-4,000 lb
Weapon load 4,000-15,000 lb
Weapon load 15,000 lb

**Avionics**
Electronic Counter Measures
Electronic Support Measures
Search radar
Fire control radar
Look-down/shoot-down
Terrain-following radar
Forward-looking infra-red
Laser
Television

# Ilyushin Il-20 'Coot-A'

*Ilyushin Il-20 'Coot-A' of the Soviet navy.*

**Role**
Fighter
Close support
Counter-insurgency
Tactical strike
Strategic bomber
Tactical reconnaissance
Strategic reconnaissance
Maritime patrol
Anti-ship strike
Anti-submarine warfare
Search and rescue
Assault transport
Transport
Liaison
Trainer
Inflight-refuelling tanker
Specialized

**Performance**
All-weather capability
Rough field capability
STOL capability
VTOL capability
Airspeed 0-250 mph
Airspeed 250 mph-Mach 1
Airspeed Mach 1 plus
Ceiling 0-20,000 ft
Ceiling 20,000-40,000 ft
Ceiling 40,000ft plus
Range 0-1,000 miles
Range 1,000-3,000 miles
Range 3,000 miles plus

**Weapons**
Air-to-air missiles
Air-to-surface missiles
Cruise missiles
Cannon
Trainable guns
Naval weapons
Nuclear-capable
Rockets
'Smart' weapon kit
Weapon load 0-4,000 lb
Weapon load 4,000-15,000 lb
Weapon load 15,000 lb plus

**Avionics**
Electronic Counter Measures
Electronic Support Measures
Search radar
Fire control radar
Look-down/shoot-down
Terrain-following radar
Forward-looking infra-red
Laser
Television

First identified by Western observers in 1978, the **Ilyushin Il-20** is an electronic intelligence aircraft now accorded the NATO reporting name **'Coot-A'**. Almost certainly the result of extensive reworking of redundant Il-18 airliners, the Il-20 appears to retain the former aircraft's wings, Ivchyenko AI-20M turboprops, landing gear and tail unit, while the fuselage has been extensively modified to accommodate a team of signals specialists and operators.

Externally the Il-20 is readily identifiable by a large container beneath the forward fuselage, about 10.25 m long and 1.15 m deep (33 ft 7.5 in by 3 ft 9 in), which is assumed to contain a side-looking radar. Additional fairings, each about 4.4 m long and 0.88 m deep (14 ft 5 in by 2 ft 10.5 in), are located on each side of the forward fuselage immediately aft of the flight deck; panels on these fairings are assumed to cover cameras or other sensors. There is a pair of large blade antennae on top of the forward fuselage as well as a number of smaller radomes and sensors under the rear fuselage. Apart from extensive navigation equipment, it seems certain that the internal avionics include sophisticated amplifiers as well as a comprehensive satellite data link.

Periodic sightings of 'Coot-As' over the Baltic and North Seas clearly suggest that the type's operational role is Elint (more particularly Sigint) along NATO's northern flank defences, as well as those of Sweden, and this is a task for which the 'Coot-A' is espe-

cially suited as a result of its good range performance. Moreover, it is not unlikely that the aircraft possesses increased internal fuel capacity, like some of the airliner models, to improve this performance still further.

Some of the Il-20's time is spent on Elint missions targeted at NATO warships, the object being the development of a catalogue of radar types carried by each vessel. This overall 'fingerprint' allow Russian naval planners quickly to identify and electronically counter any vessel encountered. Lockheed EP-3E Orions perform a similar task for the US Navy in the investigation of Russian ships. The Il-20 is also used in other tasks, and may possess an active jamming capability. Probably Comint (communications intelligence) gear is also carried, together with foreign language operators.

The 'Coot-A' is operated primarily by the AVMF (Russian naval air arm) for a variety of intelligence-gathering functions in collaboration with the Antonov An-12 'Cub-B' and converted Tupolev Tu-16 'Badger', Tu-95 'Bear and Myasishchyev M-4 'Bison' bombers. The aircraft may also have an important communications relay role.

As the Il-18 was phased out of transport service, additional airframes have become available for conversion to other tasks, so it is not impossible that new variants of the 'Coot-A' may yet appear. What is certain, however, is that the 'Coot-A' had completely replaced the aged Ilyushin Il-14 'Crate' previously operated by the AVMF in the Elint role.

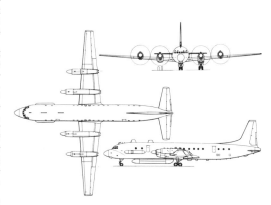

*Ilyushin Il-20 'Coot-A'*

*This Il-20 'Coot-A' was intercepted and photographed by RAF Phantoms from Leuchars in Scotland. The type is in widespread use, and until recently was encountered quite frequently.*

*Ilyushin Il-20s are most often found over the Baltic and North Seas, gathering Sigint and SLAR imagery, and probably transmitting by satellite the intelligence thus gleaned.*

**Specification:** Ilyushin Il-20 'Coot-A'
**Origin:** USSR (now CIS)
**Type:** Elint reconnaissance aircraft
**Powerplant:** four 3169-ekW (4,250-ehp) Ivchyenko AI-20M turboprops
**Performance:** maximum cruising speed 356 kt (660 km/h; 410 mph); economical cruising speed 330 kt (611 km/h; 380 mph); operating altitude 26,245-32,810 ft (8000-10000 m); range 3540 km (2,200 miles) with maximum military load
**Weights:** maximum take-off 64000 kg (141,096 lb)
**Dimensions:** span 37.42 m (122 ft 9.2 in); length 35.90 m (117 ft 9.4 in); height 10.17 m (33 ft 4.4 in); wing area 140.0 m² (1,507.0 sq ft)
**Armament:** none

# Ilyushin Il-28 'Beagle'

*Ilyushin Il-28 'Beagle ' of the Polish air force.*

Although the **Ilyushin Il-28 'Beagle'** dates back to the years immediately following World War II, when Soviet jet engine technology lagged several years behind that of the West, this twin-jet, shoulder-wing tactical bomber has enjoyed a long career among the air forces of the client nations of the former USSR. With a crew of three (pilot and navigator in the nose, and radio operator/gunner in the extreme tail), the aircraft is powered by two Klimov VK-1 centrifugal-flow turbojets (developed directly from the Rolls-Royce Nene), whose bulk demanded nacelles of similar diameter to that of the fuselage.

The unswept wing contrasted with the swept tailplane but ensured that Mach buffet on the tail surfaces would be delayed after that on the wing, thereby allowing pitch control to be maintained in high Mach dives. All fuel is contained in the fuselage except in the **Il-28R**, which introduced auxiliary wingtip tanks. The impression of an unusually long nose is in fact created by the need to mount the wings well aft to reduce the moment caused by the weight of the fuel tanks in the rear fuselage and of the rear gun/radio compartment position.

First flown on 8 August 1948, the Il-28 entered service with V-VS bomber squadrons before the end of 1950 and remained in service and production for many years, being joined by a dual control conversion trainer, the **Il-28U 'Mascot'**, and the **Il-28T** torpedo-armed anti-shipping variant flown by the Soviet navy over the Baltic. Contrary to popular belief, the Il-28R was not a tactical reconnaissance version with optical or reconnaissance sensors mounted in the weapons bay, although these was a version of the Il-28 used for this role.

Licence production of the **H-5** version was undertaken in the 1950s by China, which nation also received more than 500 examples from the USSR. Among other early recipients of the jet bomber were Czechoslovakia, which built a small number of **B-228** aircraft) and Poland. They were followed by more than 20 other nations, and even by the mid-1990s the Il-28 is still in service with a number of ex-Soviet allies and clients, and more than 300 of the type are still operational with the Chinese air arms, most notably the People's Liberation Army air force.

*Ilyushin Il-28 'Beagle'*

*In its heyday, the Il-28 'Beagle' was a front-line bomber with the Soviet air force and navy, equalling the Canberra with its versatility and dependability.*

*Small numbers of Il-28s remained in service with the Soviet air force into the late 1980s, mainly for second-line duties such as target-towing. Some client states, however, still use the type as a bomber.*

## Specification: Ilyushin Il-28 'Beagle'

**Origin:** USSR (now CIS)
**Type:** three-crew tactical day bomber
**Powerplant:** two 2700-kg (5,952-lb) dry thrust Klimov VK-1 turbojets
**Performance:** maximum speed 486 kt (902 km/h; 560 mph) at 14,765 ft (4500 m); climb to 16,405 ft (5000 m) in 6.5 minutes; service ceiling 40,355 ft(12300 m); range 2180 km (1,355 miles)
**Weights:** empty 12890 kg (28,418 lb); maximum take-off 21200 kg(46,738 lb)
**Dimensions:** span 21.45 m(70 ft 4.5 in); length 17.65 m (57 ft 10.9 in); height 6.70 m (21 ft 11.8 in); wing area 60.80 m² (654.47 sq ft0
**Armament:** two 23-mm NR-23 fixed cannon in the nose and two 23-mm NR-23 trainable cannon in a tail turret, plus a bombload of up to 3000 kg (6,614 lb)

### Role
Fighter
Close support
Counter-insurgency
Tactical strike
Strategic bomber
Tactical reconnaissance
Strategic reconnaissance
Maritime patrol
Anti-ship strike
Anti-submarine warfare
Search and rescue
Assault transport
Transport
Liaison
Trainer
Inflight-refuelling tanker
Specialized

### Performance
All-weather capability
Rough field capability
STOL capability
VTOL capability
Airspeed 0-250 mph
Airspeed 250 mph-Mach 1
Airspeed Mach 1 plus
Ceiling 0-20,000 ft
Ceiling 20,000-40,000 ft
Ceiling 40,000ft plus
Range 0-1,000 miles
Range 1,000-3,000 miles
Range 3,000 miles plus

### Weapons
Air-to-air missiles
Air-to-surface missiles
Cruise missiles
Cannon
Trainable guns
Naval weapons
Nuclear-capable
Rockets
'Smart' weapon kit
Weapon load 0-4,000 lb
Weapon load 4,000-15,000 lb
Weapon load 15,000 lb

### Avionics
Electronic Counter Measures
Electronic Support Measures
Search radar
Fire control radar
Look-down/shoot-down
Terrain-following radar
Forward-looking infra-red
Laser
Television

# Ilyushin Il-38 'May'

*Ilyushin Il-38 'May' of the Soviet navy.*

## Role

Fighter
Close support
Counter-insurgency
Tactical strike
Strategic bomber
Tactical reconnaissance
Strategic reconnaissance
Maritime patrol
Anti-ship strike
Anti-submarine warfare
Search and rescue
Assault transport
Transport
Liaison
Trainer
Inflight-refuelling tanker
Specialized

## Performance

All-weather capability
Rough field capability
STOL capability
VTOL capability
Airspeed 0-250 mph
Airspeed 250 mph-Mach 1
Airspeed Mach 1 plus
Ceiling 0-20,000 ft
Ceiling 20,000-40,000 ft
Ceiling 40,000 ft plus
Range 0-1,000 miles
Range 1,000-3,000 miles
Range 3,000 miles plus

## Weapons

Air-to-air missiles
Air-to-surface missiles
Cruise missiles
Cannon
Trainable guns
Naval weapons
Nuclear-capable
Rockets
'Smart' weapon kit
Weapon load 0-4,000 lb
Weapon load 4,000-15,000 lb
Weapon load 15,000 lb plus

## Avionics

Electronic Counter Measures
Electronic Support Measures
Search radar
Fire control radar
Look-down/shoot-down
Terrain-following radar
Forward-looking infra-red
Laser
Television

The Ilyushin **Il-38 'May'** long-range maritime patrol and anti-submarine aircraft underwent a development which followed much the same pattern as the evolution of the US Navy's Lockheed P-3 Orion from the Electra airliner. With a powerplant of four turboprops, the Il-38 was first identified by Western observers as long ago as 1971, since when it has achieved standard equipment status with the Soviet navy. Unlike the Il-20 Elint aircraft, the Il-38 has undergone considerable structural alteration to accommodate specialized ASW equipment. Externally prominent is a large search radome (located immediately aft of the nose landing gear), with which is probably associated considerable equipment of such weight that the entire wing is now located about 2.0 m (6 ft 6 in) farther forward on the fuselage to counter the shift in aircraft centre of gravity. The rear fuselage has been lengthened to accommodate radar operating stations, while almost all the former airliner's windows have been discarded or faired over. A magnetic anomaly detector boom is faired into the extreme tail. The operating team is said to number about nine members in addition to the three-man flight crew.

Most of the flight avionics of the former airliner have been retained, including the navigation and weather radar and the automatic navigation equipment, but a ventral weapons bay has been incorporated in place of the former baggage stowage area. More recently a new variant has been seen with a second ventral radome replacing the forward pair of weapons bay doors.

About 50 Il-38s are currently estimated to serve with the Russian navy and these aircraft fly long patrols over the Atlantic, Mediterranean and Indian Ocean, being deployed to bases in Libya, Syria, Yemen and Ethiopia. In 1975 an order for five ex-Soviet navy Il-38s was placed for the Indian navy, and these aircraft equipped No.315 Squadron at Goa-Dabolim into the later part of the 1980s to keep watch for submarine activity in the Indian Ocean.

Production of the Il-38 'May' is thought to be continuing, and the aircraft now forms the backbone of the CIS's dedicated maritime reconnaissance force, although it is augmented by large numbers of converted Tupolev Tu-16 'Badgers' and new-build Tu-142 'Bears'. This useful aircraft will be in service for many years to come, and is sure to be the subject of regular equipment and avionics updates if and when financial considerations permit.

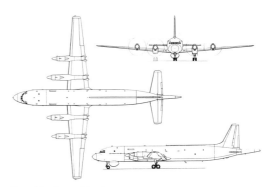

*Ilyushin Il-38 'May'*

**The Il-38 is essentially a maritime reconnaissance derivative of the elderly Il-18 'Coot' airliner. It is equipped with a wide range of reconnaissance and detection sensors.**

**The Ilyushin Il-38 is in service with the Russian navy, which operates aircraft from Yemen, Libya, Syria and Vietnam, covering a huge area of the world's oceans.**

**Specification:** Ilyushin Il-38 'May'
**Origin:** USSR (now CIS)
**Type:** maritime reconnaissance/anti-submarine patrol aircraft
**Powerplant:** four 3169-ekW (4,250-ehp) IvchyenkoAl-20M turboprops
**Performance:** maximum speed 348 kt (645 km/h; 401 mph) at 27,000 ft (8230 m); maximum cruising speed 321 kt (595 km/h; 370 mph); maximum range 7200 km (4,474 miles)
**Weights:** empty 36000 kg (79,366 lb); maximum take-off 63500 kg (139,994 lb)
**Dimensions:** span 37.42 m (122 ft 9.2 in); length 39.60 m (129 ft 11.1 in); height 10.16 m (33 ft 4 in); wing area 140.0 m² (1,507.0 sq ft)
**Armament:** weapons bay in fuselage to accommodate anti-submarine weapons and sonobuoys

# Ilyushin Il-76 'Candid', Il-78 'Midas' and A-40 'Mainstay'

*Ilyushin 1l-76 'Candid', locally dubbed Gajaraj, of No.44 Squadron, Indian Air Force.*

In much the same manner that the American Lockheed C-141 was conceived to complement the Lockheed C-130, so the high-wing four-turbofan **Ilyushin Il-76 'Candid'** extended the capabilities of the Soviet transport fleet, formerly heavily dependent on the Antonov An-12. As usual, the commercial requirement for an aircraft nominally capable of lifting 40 tonnes of freight over a distance of 5000 km (3,107 miles) in under six hours was compatible with military needs, and following the Il-76's first flight on 25 March 1971, four years of testing confirmed excellent operating characteristics in the harsh, primitive conditions of central Siberia no less than the hot-and-high environment of the Middle East.

As early as 1974 a small number of military **Il-76T 'Candid-A'** aircraft (with a tail turret and twin guns) was being evaluated by the Soviet air forces: within two years the military transport was being delivered as the **Il-76M 'Candid-B'** with the ability to carry tracked and wheeled vehicles, palletized freight containers or 90 fully-equipped troops in three modules. Military equipment includes passive ECM whose sensors are located on the sides of the fuselage. Exported 11-76Ms have been

supplied to Iraq, Czechoslovakia, India and Poland (not all of these with the tail gun turret). A follow-up military version, the **Il-76MD**, started delivery late in 1982 with uprated Soloviev turbofans to maintain full take-off power up to ISA +27°C compared with the ISA +15°C figure of the earlier versions. To date more than 550 military Il-76, Il-76M and Il-76MD aircraft have been delivered, more than 500 of them serving with the CIS air force. Numerous examples were sighted during the Afghanistan war of the 1980s.

Among the known developments of the Il-76 are a tanker and an AEW & C version. The tanker is the **Il-78 'Midas'** with three HDUs, while the AEW model is the **A-50 'Mainstay'**. Featuring a prominent saucer radome mounted above the rear fuselage and a lengthened nose, the 'Mainstay' is said to have been developed to detect cruise missiles approaching Soviet territory as well as to provide airborne control for intercepting fighters According to Western intelligence estimates, deliveries up to the mid-1990s amounted to some 25: all are provided with a nose-mounted inflight-refuelling probe, and it may be that the Il-78's main task is support of the A-50 force.

**Specification:** Ilyushin Il-76T 'Candid-A'
**Origin:** USSR (now CIS)
**Type:** heavy freight transport
**Powerplant:** four 12000-kg (26,455-lb) dry thrust Soloviev D-30KP turbofans
**Performance:** maximum speed 459 kt (850 km/h; 528 mph) at 36,090 ft (11000 m); maximum cruising speed 432 kt (800 km/h; 497 mph); maximum cruising altitude 39,370 ft (12000 m); range 5000 km (3,107 miles) with a 40000-kg (88,185-lb) payload
**Weights:** empty about 75000 kg (165,347 lb); maximum take-off 170000 kg (374,786 lb)
**Dimensions:** span 50.50 m (165 ft 8.2 in); length 46.59 m (152 ft 10.25 in); height 14.76 m (48 ft 5.1 in); wing area 300.0 m² (3,229.28 sq ft)
**Armament:** provision for two 23-mm cannon in a tail turret

*Ilyushin Il-76 'Candid'*

*Aeroflot Il-76 'Candids' saw extensive service in Afghanistan, where they resupplied the Soviet garrison and served in the troop transport role.*

**The Il-76MD is fitted with Soloviev D-30KP-1 turbofans which give improved hot-and-high take-off performance. India is one of the latest military customers for the aircraft.**

**Role**
Fighter
Close support
Counter-insurgency
Tactical strike
Strategic bomber
Tactical reconnaissance
Strategic reconnaissance
Maritime patrol
Anti-ship strike
Anti-submarine warfare
Search and rescue
Assault transport
Transport
Liaison
Trainer
Inflight-refuelling tanker
Specialized

**Performance**
All-weather capability
Rough field capability
STOL capability
VTOL capability
Airspeed 0-250 mph
Airspeed 250 mph-Mach 1
Airspeed Mach 1 plus
Ceiling 0-20,000 ft
Ceiling 20,000-40,000 ft
Ceiling 40,000ft plus
Range 0-1,000 miles
Range 1,000-3,000 miles
Range 3,000 miles plus

**Weapons**
Air-to-air missiles
Air-to-surface missiles
Cruise missiles
Cannon
Trainable guns
Naval weapons
Nuclear-capable
Rockets
'Smart' weapon kit
Weapon load 0-4,000 lb
Weapon load 4,000-15,000 lb
Weapon load 15,000 lb plus

**Avionics**
Electronic Counter Measures
Electronic Support Measures
Search radar
Fire control radar
Look-down/shoot-down
Terrain-following radar
Forward-looking infra-red
Laser
Television

# Jodel D.140 Mousquetaire

*Jodel D.140E Mousquetaire of the Armée de l'Air.*

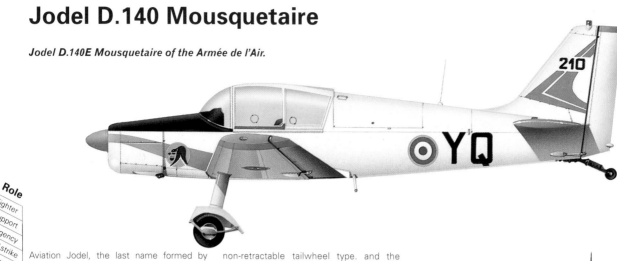

### Role
Fighter
Close support
Counter-insurgency
Tactical strike
Strategic bomber
Tactical reconnaissance
Strategic reconnaissance
Maritime patrol
Anti-ship strike
Anti-submarine warfare
Search and rescue
Assault transport
Transport
Liaison
Trainer
Inflight-refuelling tanker
Specialized

### Performance
All-weather capability
Rough field capability
STOL capability
VTOL capability
Airspeed 0-250 mph
Airspeed 250 mph-Mach 1
Airspeed Mach 1 plus
Ceiling 0-20,000 ft
Ceiling 20,000-40,000 ft
Ceiling 40,000 ft plus
Range 0-1,000 miles
Range 1,000-3,000 miles
Range 3,000 miles plus

### Weapons
Air-to-air missiles
Air-to-surface missiles
Cruise missiles
Cannon
Trainable guns
Naval weapons
Nuclear-capable
Rockets
'Smart' weapon kit
Weapon load 0-4,000 lb
Weapon load 4,000-15,000 lb
Weapon load 15,000 lb plus

### Avionics
Electronic Counter Measures
Electronic Support Measures
Search radar
Fire control radar
Look-down/shoot-down
Terrain-following radar
Forward-looking infra-red
Laser
Television

Aviation Jodel, the last name formed by combining letters from the surnames of the founders Edouard Joly and Jean Delmontez, was established at Beaune, France in March 1946. This company breathed new life into the post-war French light aviation scene with a number of highly successful lightplane designs, many of them later licence-built by other European companies. In France, the Société Aéronautique Normande (SAN), founded in 1948, was one that began construction of Jodel designs, later becoming known as SAN Jodel. From the two-seat line established first by the Jodel D.9 Bébé, SAN developed a new four-seat version designated Jodel D.140, first flown in prototype form on 4 July 1958 by the time that the first production D.140A took to the air for its maiden flight on 1 November 1958 the name Mousquetaire (musketeer) had been adopted. As flown initially, the D.140 was a conventional low-wing monoplane of basic wooden construction with fabric covering. Power was provided by a reliable Avco Lycoming flat-four engine of 134 kW (180 hp), the landing gear was of uncomplicated

non-retractable tailwheel type. and the enclosed cabin seated four in two side-by-side pairs. It was also possible to use the D.140 in an ambulance role, a single stretcher being loaded through the baggage door.

SAN Jodel soon found a keen demand for the D.140A, especially when the French government began procurement for the Service d'Aviation Légère et Sportive. Development continued for some years, producing a number of variants. These include the **D.140B Mousquetaire II** with foot-operated brakes and some internal revisions, followed by the easily recognized **D.140C Mousquetaire III** which had swept vertical tail surfaces but was otherwise unchanged; some D.140As retrofitted with these improved tail surfaces were redesignated **D.140AC.** The French Armée de l'Air acquired 18 of the ensuing **D.140E Mousquetaire IV** for use by the Ecole de l'Air at Salon, this version having extensive revision of control surfaces and introducing an all-moving tailplane. The final four-seat variant was the **D.140R Abeille** (bee) developed as a glider tug, and 15 of this version were also built for the Armée de l'Air.

*Jodel D. 140 Mousquetaire*

*French military Jodel D. 140s are used both for basic training and for glider towing. This D.140E is a training machine from the Ecole de l'Air at Salon. Many more are used by flying clubs.*

*This Jodel D.140E Mousquetaire is one of 18 delivered to the flying school at Salon. A further 15 hook-equipped aircraft are also in service, used for glider towing by the Armée de l 'Air.*

## Specification: SAN Jodel D.140E Mousquetaire IV
**Origin:** France
**Type:** four-seat lightplane
**Powerplant:** one 134-kW (180-hp) Avco Lycoming O-360-A2A flat-four piston engine
**Performance:** maximum speed 173 kt (255 km/h; 158 mph) at sea level; economical cruising speed 108 kt (200 km/h; 124 mph) at 9,025 ft (2750 m); initial rate of climb 755 ft (230 m) per minute; service ceiling 16,405 ft (5000 m); range 1400 km (870 miles) with maximum fuel
**Weights:** empty 620 kg (1,367 lb); maximum take-off 1200 kg (2,645 lb)
**Dimensions:** span 10.27 m (33 ft 8.3 in); length 7.82 m (25 ft 7.9 in); height 2.05 m (6 ft 8.7 in); wing area 18.50 m² (199.14 sq ft)
**Armament:** none

# Kaman H-2 Seasprite

*Kaman SH-2F Seasprite of HSL-33, US Navy.*

**Role**
Fighter
Close support
Counter-insurgency
Tactical strike
Strategic bomber
Tactical reconnaissance
Strategic reconnaissance
Maritime patrol
Anti-ship strike
Anti-submarine warfare
Search and rescue
Assault transport
Transport
Liaison
Trainer
Inflight-refuelling tanker
Specialized

**Performance**
All-weather capability
Rough field capability
STOL capability
VTOL capability
Airspeed 0-250 mph
Airspeed 250 mph-Mach 1
Airspeed Mach 1 plus
Ceiling 0-20,000 ft
Ceiling 20,000-40,000 ft
Ceiling 40,000ft plus
Range 0-1,000 miles
Range 1,000-3,000 miles
Range 3,000 miles plus

**Weapons**
Air-to-air missiles
Air-to-surface missiles
Cruise missiles
Cannon
Trainable guns
Naval weapons
Nuclear-capable
Rockets
'Smart' weapon kit
Weapon load 0-4,000 lb
Weapon load 4,000-15,000 lb
Weapon load 15,000 lb plus

**Avionics**
Electronic Counter Measures
Electronic Support Measures
Search radar
Fire control radar
Look-down/shoot-down
Terrain-following radar
Forward-looking infra-red
Laser
Television

Originating in the YHU2K-1 powered by a single General Electric T58-GE-8B turboshaft and first flown on 2 July l959, the **Kaman H-2 Seasprite** naval rescue and utility helicopter has undergone continuous development and today represents a highly sophisticated anti-submarine weapon in the US Navy's inventory.

From the original single-turboshaft **UH-2A** and **UH-2B** of the early 1960s was developed the **UH-2C** with twin T58-GE-8B engines geared to drive a single rotor, and this in turn led to the combat search-and-rescue **HH-2C** armed with a Minigun chin turret, four-blade tail rotor and extensive armour protection around the cockpit, engines and fuel tanks; this version served in the latter stages of the Vietnam War.

A major development phase was initiated with the acceptance of Kaman's Light Airborne Multi-Purpose System (LAMPS) in 1969-70. This integrated avionics package comprises the Canadian Marconi LN-66HP surveillance radar, ALR-66 passive radiation detection receivers and ASN-123 tactical navigation system operating in conjunction with ASQ-81(V)2 magnetic anomaly detector, ARR-75 sonobuoy receiver, ASA-26B

sonobuoy recorder and AKT-22(V)6 sonobuoy data link. Thus equipped, the SH-2F started deliveries to the US Navy in May 1973 and continued for two years, while earlier SH-2D helicopters were updated to include LAMPS Mk I in a programme that was completed in 1982. After initial production of 88 SH-2Fs and updating of 16 SH-2Ds had been completed, further orders for 54 SH-2Fs were all delivered by December 1989. Between 1971 and 1985 400,000 flight hours had been accumulated by the LAMPS-equipped Seasprite helicopters during long-cruise assignments by US Navy warships.

In October 1985 authorization was given for an increase in the SH-2F's gross weight to 6123 kg (13,500 lb), enabling larger auxiliary fuel tanks to be carried to extend the helicopter's patrol endurance, while a single YSH-2G prototype was being evaluated with new 1285-kW (1,723-shp) T700-GE-401 fuel-efficient turboshafts and composite main rotor blades. Six new helicopters were delivered to this **SH-2G Super Seasprite** standard, to which many SH-2Fs are also being upgraded. A number of SH-2Fs have been exported to country's such as Pakistan and Taiwan together with ex-US Navy frigates.

**Specification:** Kaman SH-2F Seasprite
**Origin:** USA
**Type:** naval light multi-purpose helicopter
**Powerplant:** two 1007-kW (1,350-shp) General Electric T58-GE-8F turboshafts
**Performance:** maximum speed 130 kt (241 km/h; 150 mph) at sea level; normal cruising speed 120 kt (222 km/h; 138 mph); service ceiling 22,500 ft (6860 m); normal range 661 km (411 miles)
**Weights:** empty 3193 kg (7,040 lb); maximum take-off 6123 kg (13,500 lb)
**Dimensions:** main rotor diameter 13.41 m (44 ft 0 in); length, rotors turning 16.03 m (52 ft 7 in); height 4.72 m (15 ft 6 in); main rotor disc area 141.26 m² (1,520.53 sq ft)
**Armament:** up to two Mk 46 torpedoes and combinations of DIFAR and/or DICASS sonobuoys, and eight Mk 25 marine smoke markers

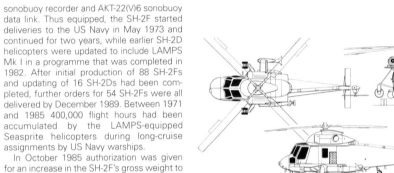

**Kaman SH-2F Seasprite**

**This Seasprite is a *LAMPS*-configured SH-2F of HSL-33 'Snakes', whose shore-base is NAS North Island, California. This helicopter was assigned to USS Bagley, a 'Knox' class frigate.**

*These NAS North Island-based SH-2Fs were assigned to HSL-35. US Navy Seasprites have received a low-visibility grey colour scheme. Sonobuoys are ejected from the side panels.*

143

# Kaman K-MAX

*A Kaman K-MAX of Erickson Air Crane.*

## Role

Fighter
Close support
Counter-insurgency
Tactical strike
Strategic bomber
Tactical reconnaissance
Strategic reconnaissance
Maritime patrol
Anti-ship strike
Anti-submarine warfare
Search and rescue
Assault transport
Transport
Liaison
Trainer
Inflight-refuelling tanker
Specialized

## Performance

All-weather capability
Rough field capability
STOL capability
VTOL capability
Airspeed 0-250 mph
Airspeed 250 mph-Mach 1
Airspeed Mach 1 plus
Ceiling 0-20,000 ft
Ceiling 20,000-40,000 ft
Ceiling 40,000ft plus
Range 0-1,000 miles
Range 1,000-3,000 miles
Range 3,000 miles plus

## Weapons

Air-to-air missiles
Air-to-surface missiles
Cruise missiles
Cannon
Trainable guns
Naval weapons
Nuclear-capable
Rockets
'Smart' weapon kit
Weapon load 0-4,000 lb
Weapon load 4,000-15,000 lb
Weapon load 15,000 lb plus

## Avionics

Electronic Counter Measures
Electronic Support Measures
Search radar
Fire control radar
Look-down/shoot-down
Terrain-following radar
Forward-looking infra-red
Laser
Television

In the first part of the 1980s, the Kaman Aerospace Corporation decided that there was considerable market potential for a light flying crane optimized for tasks such as the movement of medium-weight logs out of logging sites, and comparable tasks involving the movement of loads weighing up to 2722 kg (6,000 lb) that could be carried as a single load from an external hook. Several types of general-purpose light and medium helicopters were currently employed in this task, but Kaman felt that any conversion to the flying crane role must be inferior to a type designed specifically for the task. The key to success, it was felt, lay with a small but strong airframe sized down to the task and therefore providing the design team with the chance to evolve a helicopter offering and excellent lift/weight ratio for maximization of payload potential.

Design of such a type was put in hand as the Multi-Mission Intermeshing Rotor Aircraft based on Kaman's long experience with a side-by-side pair of two-blade rotors on outward-canted pylons that permitted the blades of the counter-rotating rotors to intermesh without touching. The type is based on a thoroughly utilitarian fuselage of light alloy construction with a fully enclosed cockpit for the single pilot, fixed tricycle landing gear with provision for skis fitting round the single wheels, and a powerplant of one T5317 turboshaft (the civil version of the well proved and highly reliable T53 military engine) in a derated form located between and behind the common transmission powering the two rotors, which have blades of carbonfibre-reinforced plastics construction for strength and lightness.

Careful consideration was given to reduction of drag and maximization of controllability so that the helicopter could be operated safely in confined spaces and also under the adverse flying conditions likely to be encountered round mountains. The first of three prototypes made its maiden flight on 23 December 1993, and initial development trials soon confirmed that the design team had succeeded in all its primary objectives. Kaman offers the type primarily for forest operations (logging and firefighting, the latter with a Bambi firefighting bucket), but patrol and similar paramilitary tasks are also possible.

## Specification: Kaman K-MAX
**Origin:** USA
**Type:** multi-role flying crane
**Powerplant:** one 1343-kW (1,800-shp) Avco Lycoming T5317A turboshaft flat-rated at 1119 kW (1,500 shp)
**Performance:** maximum speed 100 kt (185 km/h; 115 mph)
**Weights:** empty 1859 kg (4,100 lb); maximum take-off 5216 kg (11,500 lb)
**Dimensions:** rotor diameter, each 14.32 m (47 ft 0 in); length, rotor turning 15.39 m (50 ft 6 in); rotor disc area, total 322.35 m² (3,469.89 sq ft)
**Armament:** none

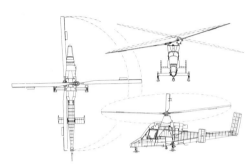

*Kaman K-MAX*

*Although primarily designed as a lightweight flying crane for civil applications, Kaman anticipate several military and para-military roles for K-MAX.*

*The K-MAX uses a pair of intermeshing side-by-side main rotors, like the earlier generation Kaman H-43 Huskie.*

# Kamov Ka-25 'Hormone'

From the mid-1950s there were reports of the efforts being made by the US Navy to develop strategic ballistic missiles which could be launched by submerged submarines, and this was immediately seen by the USSR as a new and serious threat. This was just one facet of the potential of a completely new generation of submarines, and highlighted the need to develop as, quickly as possible, genuinely effective ASW measures. High on the list of priorities was a ship-based helicopter to be equipped specifically for the ASW role, and the Kamov and Mil design bureaux soon found themselves in competition to meet the requirement. The first bureau was the winner, demonstrating a new helicopter with co-axial twin rotors in the Aviation Day display at Tushino in July 1961. This, thought to have the designation **Ka-20**, was allocated the NATO reporting name **'Harp'**, and clearly possessed a kinship with the earlier piston-engined Kamov Ka-15 'Hen' and Ka-18 'Hog'. However, the Ka-20 was much larger and powered by two turboshafts mounted above the cabin.

Nothing more was apparently heard of this helicopter until, at the 1967 Paris Air Show, Kamov demonstrated a civil flying crane heli-copter designated **Ka-25K**. Its similarity to the Ka-20 prototype seen at Tushino was immediately noted, and that the Ka-25 had entered production was confirmed later in the year when the Soviet cruiser/helicopter carriers Leningrad and Moskva were each seen to be carrying a number of these machines. The types was subsequently identified as the **Kamov Ka-25** and given the reporting name **'Hormone'**.

Between 1966 and 1975 an estimated 460 were built, and of those remaining in service three versions were identified. First is the ship-based **Ka-25BSh 'Hormone-A'** ASW type with search radar and dipping sonar, some equipped to carry guided torpedoes. The **Ka-25 'Hormone-B'**, also ship-based, is an electronic warfare helicopter equipped to provide target acquisition and mid-course guidance for ship-launched long-range cruise missiles. Last is the **Ka-25PS 'Hormone-C'** search and rescue/utility helicopter, basically similar to the 'Hormone-A' but with all non-essential equipment removed to give maximum interior capacity. About 100 remained in Russian service in the mid-1990s, and others are used by India, Syria and Vietnam.

**Specification:** Kamov Ka-25BSh 'Hormone-A'
**Origin:** USSR (now CIS)
**Type:** ASW helicopter
**Powerplant:** two 671-kW (900-shp) Glushenkov GTD-3F turboshafts
**Performance:** maximum speed 113 kt (209 km/h; 130 mph); cruising speed 104 kt (193 km/h; 120 mph); service ceiling 11,480 ft (3500 m); range 400 km (249 miles) with standard fuel and reserves
**Weights:** empty 4765 kg (10,505 lb); maximum take-off 7500 kg (l6,535 lb)
**Dimensions:** rotor diameter, each 15.74 m (51 ft 7.7 in); length, fuselage 9.75 m (31 ft 11.9 in); height 5.37 m (17 ft 7.4 in); rotor disc area total 389.16 m² (4,189.03 sq ft)
**Armament:** some have an underfuselage weapons bay for two ASW torpedoes, nuclear depth charges or other weapons; some may carry guided torpedoes or be armed with small air-to-surface missiles

*Kamov Ka-25BSh 'Hormone-A' of the Soviet navy.*

*Kamov Ka-25BSh 'Hormone-A'*

*A rather battered Ka-25BSh 'Hormone-A' conducts anti-submarine operations from the helicopter cruiser Moskva in 1983. The type is also carried by the 'Kiev' class carriers.*

*A crewman leans out of the cabin door of this 'Hormone-A' to take a photograph of a NATO vessel. The 'Hormone' can carry weapons in an external weapons bay, when fitted.*

**Role**
Fighter
Close support
Counter-insurgency
Tactical strike
Strategic bomber
Tactical reconnaissance
Strategic reconnaissance
Maritime patrol
Anti-ship strike
Anti-submarine warfare
Search and rescue
Assault transport
Transport
Liaison
Trainer
Inflight-refuelling tanker
Specialized

**Performance**
All-weather capability
Rough field capability
STOL capability
VTOL capability
Airspeed 0-250 mph
Airspeed 250 mph-Mach 1
Airspeed Mach 1 plus
Ceiling 0-20,000 ft
Ceiling 20,000-40,000 ft
Ceiling 40,000 ft plus
Range 0-1,000 miles
Range 1,000-3,000 miles
Range 3,000 miles plus

**Weapons**
Air-to-air missiles
Air-to-surface missiles
Cruise missiles
Cannon
Trainable guns
Naval weapons
Nuclear-capable
Rockets
'Smart' weapon kit
Weapon load 0-4,000 lb
Weapon load 4,000-15,000 lb
Weapon load 15,000 lb plus

**Avionics**
Electronic Counter Measures
Electronic Support Measures
Search radar
Fire control radar
Look-down/shoot-down
Terrain-following radar
Forward-looking infra-red
Laser
Television

# Kamov Ka-26 'Hoodlum'

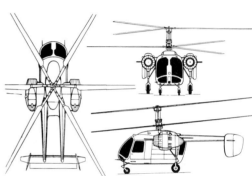

*Kamov Ka-26 'Hoodlum' of Aeroflot.*

**Role**
Fighter
Close support
Counter-insurgency
Tactical strike
Strategic bomber
Tactical reconnaissance
Strategic reconnaissance
Maritime patrol
Anti-ship strike
Anti-submarine warfare
Search and rescue
Assault transport
Transport
Liaison
Trainer
Inflight-refuelling tanker
Specialized

**Performance**
All-weather capability
Rough field capability
STOL capability
VTOL capability
Airspeed 0-250 mph
Airspeed 250 mph-Mach 1
Airspeed Mach 1 plus
Ceiling 0-20,000 ft
Ceiling 20,000-40,000 ft
Ceiling 40,000ft plus
Range 0-1,000 miles
Range 1,000-3,000 miles
Range 3,000 miles plus

**Weapons**
Air-to-air missiles
Air-to-surface missiles
Cruise missiles
Cannon
Trainable guns
Naval weapons
Nuclear-capable
Rockets
'Smart' weapon kit
Weapon load 0-4,000 lb
Weapon load 4,000-15,000 lb
Weapon load 15,000 lb plus

**Avionics**
Electronic Counter Measures
Electronic Support Measures
Search radar
Fire control radar
Look-down/shoot-down
Terrain-following radar
Forward-looking infra-red
Laser
Television

The **Kamov Ka-26**, first announced in early 1964 and later given the NATO reporting name **'Hoodlum-A'**, was designed specifically as a multi-role utility helicopter which could be converted easily to fulfil a maximum number of mainly civil roles. Particular emphasis, however, was placed on its suitability for use in a variety of agricultural roles.

When the prototype was flown in 1965 it was soon seen to be of unusual configuration, with a short light alloy fuselage above which is mounted a mast for the co-axial rotors, and having a small span stub wing with a podded radial piston engine located at each wingtip. Slender twin tailbooms extend aft and are linked at the rear by a tailplane which carries twin endplate fins and rudders. The non-retractable quadricycle landing gear consists of twin shock struts each with a castoring nosewheel, and two main struts each with a braked mainwheel. Below the forward end of the fuselage a two-seat fully enclosed cabin is attached so that in the space formed behind the cabin, between the main landing gear legs and beneath the rotor mast, there is ample room to accommodate a variety of pay-

loads. These loads, suitably attached, are thus carried in an ideal position, almost directly on the helicopter's centre of gravity.

For the primary role of the Ka-26 a chemical hopper and spraybars/dust spreader can be carried, but these can be quickly removed for the installation of an open platform to transport freight, or a six-seat passenger/cargo pod which, if required, can receive heat from the cabin heating system. This pod has a variety of uses, including casevac with two stretchers, two seated casualties and a medical attendant; firefighting with firemen or retardant chemicals; aerial survey with camera and operator; as a housing for an electromagnetic pulse generator for geophysical survey; and to mount a 150-kg (331-lb) capacity hoist that makes the helicopter suitable for use in the SAR role. It is in the last capacity that the majority of Ka-26s have seen military service.

Accurate production figures for this useful little helicopter are not known, but it was believed that 850 had been built by 1994. The **'Hoodlum-B'** is the Romanian **IAR Ka-126** development with a single 537-kW (720-shp) Kobchyenko TV-O-100 turboshaft.

*Kamov Ka-26 'Hoodlum'*

## Specification: Kamov Ka-26 'Hoodlum-A'
**Origin:** USSR (now CIS)
**Type:** multi-role light helicopter
**Powerplant:** two 242-kW (325-shp) Vedeneyev M-14V-26 radial piston engines
**Performance:** maximum speed 92 kt (170 km/h; 106 mph); economical cruising speed 49-59 kt (90-110km/h; 56-68 mph); service ceiling 9,845 ft (3000 m); range 400 km (249 miles) with pilot, seven passengers and reserves
**Weights:** empty1950 kg (4,299 lb); maximum take-off 3250kg (7,165 1b)
**Dimensions:** rotor diameter, each 13.00 m (42 ft 7.8 in); length, fuselage 7.75 m (25 ft 5.1 in); height 4.05 m (13 ft 3.4 in); rotor disc area, total 265.46 m² (2,857.53 sq ft)
**Armament:** none

*The Bulgarian and Hungarian air forces may still use the diminutive 'Hoodlum', but larger numbers remain in semi-civil use for SAR and police support duties.*

*Even agricultural Ka-26 'Hoodlums' would be hastily requisitioned by the Russian military in the event of war, and used for a variety of support duties.*

# Kamov Ka-27 'Helix'

*Kamov Ka-27PL 'Helix-A' of the Soviet navy.*

The introduction of a new Soviet aircraft frequently brought problems of identification and designation in the West, and this was the case with the Kamov helicopter which in its civil form is known as the Ka-32. Only more recently was it established that there is a military version with the designation **Kamov Ka-27**, at one time thought to be a variant of the Ka-25 'Hormone', and this was allocated the NATO reporting name **'Helix'**.

Intended as a replacement for the ship-based Ka-25, it is of generally similar configuration and size so that it can utilize the same on-board hangars and deck lifts. Apart from having a revised tail unit with only two fins, the Ka-27 differs from its predecessor in two most important ways: it has more than double the power for operation at a much higher gross weight, and this has allowed the fuselage to be redesigned to provide a much more spacious cabin. This last advantage is seen as providing a vertical replenishment capability at sea, as well as an assault transport for 16 fully equipped troops.

Three versions of the helicopter have been positively identified in the West and accordingly have been allocated NATO reporting names The first, which has been seen in service since 1982 and is clearly a replacement for the 'Hormone-A', is the **Ka-27PL 'Helix-A'** for the ASW role. The **Ka-29TB 'Helix-B'** is the 16-troop assault transport. The Ka-27PS 'Helix-D' is the SAR and planeguard version: like the civil Ka-32 'Helix-C', this has external fuel tanks, one on each side of the fuselage, and a 300-kg (661-lb) capacity rescue hoist. In the early 1990s it was also revealed that there is an EW version of the 'Helix' whose designation is not yet known.

There are, so far, no accurate details of the weapons carried by the Ka-27PL. Presumably they are similar to those of the Ka-25BSh, with an underfuselage weapons bay for torpedoes and other stores, together with stowage for sonobuoys and possibly wire-guided torpedoes. The specification which follows is that of the Ka-32, but the Ka-27/Ka-29 are believed to be generally similar.

**Specification:** Kamov Ka-27PL 'Helix-A'
**Origin:** USSR (now CIS)
**Type:** ship-borne anti-submarine helicopter
**Powerplant:** two 1660-kW (2,225-shp) Isotov TV3-117V turboshafts
**Performance:** maximum speed 135 kt (250 km/h;155 mph); maximum cruising speed 124 kt (230 km/h; 143 mph); service ceiling 19,685 ft (6000 m); range 800 km (497 miles) with maximum fuel
**Weights:** normal take-off 11000 kg (24,251 lb); maximum take-off 12600 kg (27,778 lb)
**Dimensions:** rotor diameter, each 15.90 m (52 ft 2 in); length, fuselage 11.30 m (37 ft 0.9 in); height 5.40 m (17 ft 8.6 in); rotor disc area, total 397.11 m² (4,274.63 sq ft)
**Armament:** see text

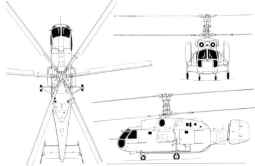

**Kamov Ka-27PL 'Helix-A'**

*This Ka-27 is seen on the helicopter deck of the guided missile destroyer* **Udaloy** *during amphibious exercises in the Baltic.* **Udaloy** *carries a Ka-27 for anti-submarine duties.*

*This Soviet navy Ka-27 'Helix' displays its distinctive co-axial rotors, and the longer fuselage which distinguishes it from the earlier Ka-25 'Hormone'.*

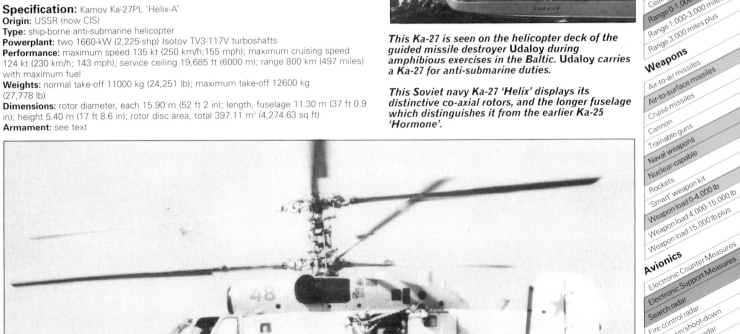

**Role**
Fighter
Close support
Counter-insurgency
Tactical strike
Strategic bomber
Tactical reconnaissance
Strategic reconnaissance
Maritime patrol
Anti-ship strike
Anti-submarine warfare
Search and rescue
Assault transport
Transport
Liaison
Trainer
Inflight-refuelling tanker
Specialized

**Performance**
All-weather capability
Rough field capability
STOL capability
VTOL capability
Airspeed 0-250 mph
Airspeed 250 mph-Mach 1
Airspeed Mach 1 plus
Ceiling 0-20,000 ft
Ceiling 20,000-40,000 ft
Ceiling 40,000ft plus
Range 0-1,000 miles
Range 1,000-3,000 miles
Range 3,000 miles plus

**Weapons**
Air-to-air missiles
Air-to-surface missiles
Cruise missiles
Cannon
Trainable guns
Naval weapons
Nuclear-capable
Rockets
'Smart' weapon kit
Weapon load 0-4,000 lb
Weapon load 4,000-15,000 lb
Weapon load 15,000 lb plus

**Avionics**
Electronic Counter Measures
Electronic Support Measures
Search radar
Fire control radar
Look-down/shoot-down
Terrain-following radar
Forward-looking infra-red
Laser
Television

# Kamov Ka-50 'Hokum'

*The seventh prototype Ka-50 'Hokum', now being marketed as the Werewolf.*

Designed with the co-axial twin rotors typical of Kamov practise and initially known only by the NATO reporting name **'Hokum'** and supposed designation Ka-41, the **Kamov Ka-50 Werewolf** first flew in July 1982 in the form of the V-80 prototype for an advanced battlefield helicopter of which relatively few details are available. In combination with a slim fuselage and retractable landing gear, the rotor design offers a high degree of agility and speed, while the elimination of the tail rotor offers the advantages of a shorter fuselage for reduced battlefield visibility and vulnerability. Though it was originally thought that the type was tasked with the anti-helicopter escort role over the land battlefield in conjunction with offensive operations by Mil Mi-24 'Hind' and Mi-28 'Havoc' helicopters, the Ka-50 was later assessed as a shipborne type designed to provide Naval Infantry amphibious assault forces with close air support

In 1992, however, the Russians finally revealed that the type had indeed been developed in competition with the Mi-28 and had been selected in preference to that type as successor to the Mil Mi-24 'Hind-D'. The Ka-50's cockpit, powerplant and transmission are protected by two layers of load-bearing armour capable of withstanding 20-mm cannon strikes, and a notable feature is the installation of an ejector seat as the main component of an escape system that ensures explosive separation of the two rigid rotors' six blades at the moment of seat initiation.

The Ka-50 is unique as the world's first single-seat attack/anti-tank helicopter to enter full production, and its electronics are optimized for the easing of the pilot's workload. The cannon barbette on the port side of the nose hydraulically elevated and depressed but has no traverse capability, so the complete helicopter is yawed to aim the weapon and then held on target by a tracking system that turns the helicopter on its vertical axis. This cannon is the same weapon as already used in the BMP infantry fighting vehicle, but its resultant high weight is offset by its ruggedness under dusty and hot conditions, and it is a dual-feed weapon able to fire HEI or AP rounds. The whole machine was designed for deployment away from base for at least two weeks without need of maintenance ground equipment as all refuelling and servicing of the avionics and weapons can be undertaken from ground level. There will also be a **'Hokum-B'** two-seat conversion trainer model.

*Kamov Ka-50 'Hokum'*

## Specification: Kamov Ka-50 Werewolf 'Hokum-A'
**Origin:** USSR (now CIS)
**Type:** air-to-air combat/ground-attack helicopter
**Powerplant:** two 1660-kW (2,226-shp) Isotov TV3-117VK turboshafts
**Performance:** maximum speed 188 kt (350 km/h; 217 mph); maximum rate of climb 1,969 ft (600 m) per minute; combat radius 250 km (155 miles)
**Weights:** maximum take-off 7500 kg (16,534 lb)
**Dimensions:** rotor diameter, each 14.50 m (45 ft 6.9 in); length, rotors turning 16.00 m (52 ft 5.9 in); height 5.40 m (17 ft 8.6 in); rotor disc area, total 330.26 m² (3,555.0 sq ft)
**Armament:** one 30-mm 2A42 cannon with 500 rounds in a barbette on the starboard side of the nose, and provision for an unrevealed weight of disposable
stores carried on four hardpoints and generally comprising four multiple launchers each carrying 20 80-mm (3.15-in) rockets, two eight-round clusters of AT-9 'Whirlwind' anti-tank missiles, ASMs and short-range AAMs

*The Ka-50 uses a coaxial contra-rotating main rotor in order to reduce rotor diameter and to do away with the need for a vulnerable, energy-absorbing anti-torque tail rotor.*

*The Kamov Ka-50 'Hokum ' is an extremely advanced, highly manoeuvrable close-support and air-combat helicopter, capable of high speeds and packing a mighty punch, though questions remain as to whether a single pilot can operate successfully in the attack helicopter role, even with advanced automated systems.*

# Kawasaki C-1

*Kawasaki C-1Kai ECM trainer prototype of the Japanese Air Self-Defence Force.*

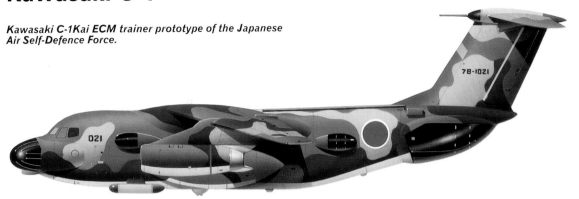

With a need to replace in the early 1970s the Curtiss C-46 Commando transport aircraft then in service, the Japan Air Self-Defence Force drew up its C-X specification for an indigenous replacement. Nihon Aeroplane Manufacturing Company began its design in 1966 and, even before approval of a full-size mockup, was contracted in 1968 to build two CX-1 flying prototypes plus a static test airframe. The first of the prototypes, assembled by Kawasaki, made its maiden flight on 12 November 1970, and the test programme of the two prototypes was completed by the Japan Defence Agency in March 1973. Following construction of two pre-production aircraft, a first contract was placed for 11 production Kawasaki C-1 transports.

Fairly typical of modern military transport aircraft, the C-1 is of high-wing monoplane configuration to maximize cabin volume, has a fuselage with a pressurized and air-conditioned flight deck and cabin/cargo hold, and a rear-loading ramp door. The landing gear is of retractable tricycle type, and the aircraft's two turbofan engines are pylon-mounted beneath the wings. The C-1 is operated by a flight crew of five, and typical loads include 60 fully equipped troops or 45 paratroops, up to 36 litters with attendants, and a variety of equipment or palletized cargo.

A collective project, the C-1 was built by Fuji (outer wings), Mitsubishi (centre/aft fuselage/tail surfaces) and Nihon (control surfaces/engine pods), with Kawasaki responsible for forward fuselage, wing centre-section, final assembly and testing. With the last delivery on 21 October 1981 production totalled 31. including the four prototype and pre-production aircraft. Although built to JASDF requirements, the C-1's maximum payload of 11900kg (26,266 lb) limited its value and plans for variants did not materialize. A C-1 airframe was used by Japan's National Aerospace Laboratory for modification as the Asuka quiet/STOL research aircraft, and one by the JDA as a flying testbed for the Ishikawajima-Harima XF3 and MITI/NAL FJR-710 turbofan engines. More recently Kawasaki modified one aircraft as the **C-1Kai** ECM trainer, giving it a flat bulbous nose and tail radomes, an ALQ-5 ECM system and antennae beneath the fuselage

## Specification: Kawasaki C-1

**Origin:** Japan
**Type:** short-range military transport
**Powerplant:** two 6577-kg (14,500-lb) dry thrust Mitsubishi (Pratt & Whitney) JT8D-M-9 turbofans
**Performance:** maximum speed 435 kt (806 km/h; 501 mph) at 25,000 ft (7620 m); economical cruising speed 354 kt (657 km/h; 408 mph) at 35,000 ft (10670 m); initial rate of climb 3,495 ft (1065 m) per minute; service ceiling 38,000 ft (11580 m); range 1300 km (808 miles) with standard 7900-kg (17,417-lb) payload
**Weights:** empty 23320 kg (51,412 lb); maximum take-off 45000 kg (99,208 lb)
**Dimensions:** span 30.60 m (100 ft 4.7in); length 29.00 m (95 ft 1.7 in); height 10.0 m (32 ft 9.3 in); wing area 120.50 m² (1,297.09 sq ft)
**Armament:** none

**Kawasaki C-1**

*The C-1 is a high-winged, T-tailed, turbofan-powered light transport similar in configuration to the much larger Lockheed C-5 Galaxy. Only 31 have been built.*

*This C-1 is seen in service with Japan's 402nd Hikotai of the 1st Kokutai. The 402nd is based at Iruma, and forms part of the Air Transport Wing (Yuso Kokudan).*

**Role**
Fighter
Close support
Counter-insurgency
Tactical strike
Strategic bomber
Tactical reconnaissance
Strategic reconnaissance
Maritime patrol
Anti-ship strike
Anti-submarine warfare
Search and rescue
Assault transport
Transport
Liaison
Trainer
Inflight-refuelling tanker
Specialized

**Performance**
All-weather capability
Rough field capability
STOL capability
VTOL capability
Airspeed 0-250 mph
Airspeed 250 mph-Mach 1
Airspeed Mach 1 plus
Ceiling 0-20,000 ft
Ceiling 20,000-40,000 ft
Ceiling 40,000ft plus
Range 0-1,000 miles
Range 1,000-3,000 miles
Range 3,000 miles plus

**Weapons**
Air-to-air missiles
Air-to-surface missiles
Cruise missiles
Cannon
Trainable guns
Naval weapons
Nuclear-capable
Rockets
'Smart' weapon kit
Weapon load 0-4,000 lb
Weapon load 4,000-15,000 lb
Weapon load 15,000 lb plus

**Avionics**
Electronic Counter Measures
Electronic Support Measures
Search radar
Fire control radar
Look-down/shoot-down
Terrain-following radar
Forward-looking infra-red
Laser
Television

# Kawasaki (Boeing Vertol) KV-107

*Kawasaki KV-107 of the Japanese Ground Self-Defence Force.*

## Role

Fighter
Close support
Counter-insurgency
Tactical strike
Strategic bomber
Tactical reconnaissance
Strategic reconnaissance
Maritime patrol
Anti-ship strike
Anti-submarine warfare
Search and rescue
Assault transport
Transport
Liaison
Trainer
Inflight-refuelling tanker
Specialized

## Performance

All-weather capability
Rough field capability
STOL capability
VTOL capability
Airspeed 0-250 mph
Airspeed 250 mph-Mach 1
Airspeed Mach 1 plus
Ceiling 0-20,000 ft
Ceiling 20,000-40,000 ft
Ceiling 40,000ft plus
Range 0-1,000 miles
Range 1,000-3,000 miles
Range 3,000 miles plus

## Weapons

Air-to-air missiles
Air-to-surface missiles
Cruise missiles
Cannon
Trainable guns
Naval weapons
Nuclear-capable
Rockets
'Smart' weapon kit
Weapon load 0-4,000 lb
Weapon load 4,000-15,000 lb
Weapon load 15,000 lb plus

## Avionics

Electronic Counter Measures
Electronic Support Measures
Search radar
Fire control radar
Look-down/shoot-down
Terrain-following radar
Forward-looking infra-red
Laser
Television

The Boeing Vertol Model 107 tandem-rotor helicopter proved attractive for civil use in Japan, and in 1962 Kawasaki secured a manufacturing licence for the type. The first **Kawasaki (Boeing Vertol) KV-107** to be built under this arrangement was flown in May 1962 and, following further negotiations, in 1965 the Japanese company acquired from Boeing Vertol world-wide sales rights.

Since then Kawasaki has built several KV107 versions, the **KV-107/II** range being powered by 932-kW (1,250-shp) General Electric CT58-110-1 turboshaft engines or licence-built Ishikawajima-Harima CT58-IHI-110-1 engines of similar output. The range includes the KV-107/II-2 standard 25-passenger airline helicopter and the 6/11-seat KV-107/II-7 VIP transport. The first of the military variants was the **KV-107/II-3**, a mine countermeasures version for the JMSDF (two built). The **KV-107/II-4** tactical cargo/troop carrier for the JGSDF was more extensively produced (42, one of them fitted out as a VIP transport): this version has a strengthened floor, can accommodate 26 equipped troops on foldable seats, or alternatively 15 casualties on litters. For the JASDF Kawasaki developed the **KV-107/II-5** long-range search and rescue helicopter ( 14 built) with an external auxiliary fuel tank on each side, a domed observation window, four searchlights, a rescue hoist and an extensive nav/com system. During 1972-4 Kawasaki supplied eight similar helicopters to the Swedish navy; these are designated **HKP 4C** and have Rolls-Royce Gnome H.1200 powerplants and Decca navigation systems fitted in Sweden.

The later **KV-107/IIA** production version has more powerful turboshafts for improved performance in hot-and-high or VTOL operations. The range includes seven **KV-107/IIA-3**, 18 **KV-107/IIA-4** (four of them with external auxiliary fuel tanks), and 22 KV-107/IIA-5 helicopters, these three versions being comparable respectively to the KV-107/II-3, -4 and -5. For Saudi Arabia Kawasaki has built one **KV-170/IIA-17** long-range passenger/cargo transport, seven **KV-107/IIA-SM-1** firefighting helicopters, four **KV-107/IIA-SM-2** aeromedical and rescue helicopters, two **KV-107/IIA-SM-3** transports, and three **KV-107/IIA-SM-4** air ambulance helicopters.

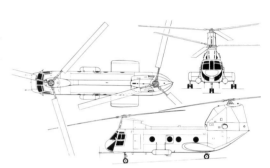

*Kawasaki KV-107 (with auxiliary tanks)*

*Sweden is the only European operator of the Kawasaki KV-107, using the type for anti-submarine, search and rescue and even firefighting duties. All wear splinter camouflage.*

*This attractive KV-107 wears Japanese Ground Self-Defence Force markings, and is probably one of those allocated to the 1st Helicopter Brigade at Kisarazu.*

## Specification: Kawasaki KV-107/IIA-2

**Origin:** Japan (US design)
**Type:** 25-passenger transport helicopter
**Powerplant:** two 1,044-KW (1,400-shp) General Electric CT58-140-1 or Ishikawajima-Harima (General electric) CT58-IHI-140-1 turboshafts
**Performance:** maximum speed 137 kt (254 km/h; 158 mph) at sea level; cruising speed 130 kt (241 km/h; 150 mph) at 5,000 ft (1525 m); initial rate of climb 2,050 ft (625 m) per minute; service ceiling17,000 ft (5180 m); range 1097 km (682 miles) with maximum fuel
**Weights:** empty 5251 kg (11,576 lb); maximum take-off 9707 kg (21,400 lb)
**Dimensions:** rotor diameter, each 15.24 m (50 ft 0 in); length, rotors turning 25.40 m (83 ft 4 in); height 5.13 m (16 ft 10 in); rotor disc area, total 364.82 m² (3,926.99 sq ft)
**Armament:** none

# Lockheed C-5 Galaxy

*Lockheed C-5A Galaxy of Military Airlift Command, US Air Force.*

Designed to meet requirements formulated by the USAF's MATS in 1963 for a very large logistics transport capable of lifting a 56700-kg (125,000-lb) payload over a range of 12875 km (8,000 miles), the **Lockheed C-5 Galaxy** was selected in October 1965, the first C-5A being flown on 30 June 1968. The largest landplane then built, it featured a high-set swept wing with leading-edge slats, wide-span modified Fowler trailing-edge flaps, and aileron-cum-spoilers. Through-loading by means of upward-hingeing nose and drop-down rear fuselage ramps enabled large and heavy vehicles and missiles (such as two M60 tanks or 10 Pershing missiles with launch tractors) to be loaded. Power was provided by four underslung General Electric TF39-GE-1 turbofans specifically designed for this application.

B y the end of 1970 30 C-5As out of an order for 81 aircraft had flown and deliveries made to MAC squadrons in the USA; already heavy-lift services were being flown to Europe and the Far East. In the meantime the entire specification had been extended to include a gross weight of 317515 kg (700,000 lb) and global deployment, calling for flight-refuelling compatibility with the USAF's Boeing KC-135 tankers. Although

the C-5's prime role was and remains heavy freighting, in which its 28-wheel landing gear permits operations from semi-prepared runways in potential combat areas, it is capable of lifting 345 fully equipped troops, the entire upper deck and cargo hold being pressurized and air-conditioned.

In 1978 Lockheed gained authority to proceed with improved wings constructed of 7175-T73511 aluminium alloy for greater strength and corrosion resistance, intended to increase the service life to 30,000 hours, and all surviving C-5As were re-winged by the end of 1987. In 1982 a new production version, the C-5B, was authorized in which all modifications and improvements evolved in the C-5A were to be incorporated, including uprated TF39-GE-1C turbofans, extended-life wing, Bendix colour weather radar, and triple Delco inertial navigation systems.

With C-5As then serving with the USAF's 60th, 436th, 437th and 443d MAWs, as well as the 105th MAG of the New York ANG, the 50 C-5Bs were delivered to the service in a programme that was completed in 1988. For more than 15 years the Galaxy remained the world's largest military aircraft before being eclipsed by the Soviet Antonov An-124 'Condor'.

**Lockheed C-5A Galaxy**

**Specification:** Lockheed C-5B Galaxy
**Origin:** USA
**Type:** heavy logistics transport
**Powerplant:** four 19504-kg (43,000-lb) dry thrust General Electric TF39-GE 1C turbofans
**Performance:** maximum cruising speed 490 kt (908 km/h; 564 mph) at 25,000 ft (7620 m); initial rate of climb 1,725 ft (526 m) per minute; service ceiling 35,750 ft (10895 m) at 278959-kg (615,000-lb) AUW; range 5526 km (3,434 miles) with a 118388-kg (261,000-lb) maximum payload
**Weights:** empty 169644 kg (374,000 lb); maximum take-off 379657 kg (837,000 lb)
**Dimensions:** span 67.88 m (222 ft 8.5 in); length 75.54 m (247 ft 10 in); height 19.85 m (65 ft 1.5 in); wing area 575.98 m² (6,200.0 sq ft)
**Armament:** none

*The prototype C-5B Galaxy is towed into position before making its maiden flight on 10 September 1985 at the Lockheed plant at Marietta, Georgia.*

*A large number of C-5s have received this 'Euro One' camouflage scheme, but it has caused severe overheating problems and a lighter scheme may be adopted.*

## Role

Fighter
Close support
Counter-insurgency
Tactical strike
Strategic bomber
Tactical reconnaissance
Strategic reconnaissance
Maritime patrol
Anti-ship strike
Anti-submarine warfare
Search and rescue
Assault transport
Transport
Liaison
Trainer
Inflight-refuelling tanker
Specialized

## Performance

All-weather capability
Rough field capability
STOL capability
VTOL capability
Airspeed 0-250 mph
Airspeed 250 mph-Mach 1
Airspeed Mach 1 plus
Ceiling 0-20,000 ft
Ceiling 20,000-40,000 ft
Ceiling 40,000ft plus
Range 0-1,000 miles
Range 1,000-3,000 miles
Range 3,000 miles plus

## Weapons

Air-to-air missiles
Air-to-surface missiles
Cruise missiles
Cannon
Trainable guns
Naval weapons
Nuclear-capable
Rockets
'Smart' weapon kit
Weapon load 0-4,000 lb
Weapon load 4,000-15,000 lb
Weapon load 15,000 lb plus

## Avionics

Electronic Counter Measures
Electronic Support Measures
Search radar
Fire control radar
Look-down/shoot-down
Terrain-following radar
Forward-looking infra-red
Laser
Television

# Lockheed C-130A/G Hercules

*Lockheed C-130E of No.16 Squadron, Royal Saudi Air Force, based at Riyadh.*

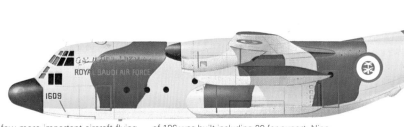

**Role**
Fighter
Close support
Counter-insurgency
Tactical strike
Strategic bomber
Tactical reconnaissance
Strategic reconnaissance
Maritime patrol
Anti-ship strike
Anti-submarine warfare
Search and rescue
Assault transport
Transport
Liaison
Trainer
Inflight-refuelling tanker
Specialized

**Performance**
All-weather capability
Rough field capability
STOL capability
VTOL capability
Airspeed 0-250 mph
Airspeed 250 mph-Mach 1
Airspeed Mach 1 plus
Ceiling 0-20,000 ft
Ceiling 20,000-40,000 ft
Ceiling 40,000 ft plus
Range 0-1,000 miles
Range 1,000-3,000 miles
Range 3,000 miles plus

**Weapons**
Air-to-air missiles
Air-to-surface missiles
Cruise missiles
Cannon
Trainable guns
Naval weapons
Nuclear-capable
Rockets
'Smart' weapon kit
Weapon load 0-4,000 lb
Weapon load 4,000-15,000 lb
Weapon load 15,000 lb plus

**Avionics**
Electronic Counter Measures
Electronic Support Measures
Search radar
Fire control radar
Look-down/shoot-down
Terrain-following radar
Forward-looking infra-red
Laser
Television

There are few more important aircraft flying with the world's air forces than the ubiquitous **Lockheed C-130 Hercules**. In production since 1955, the aircraft has been successively developed to meet changing demands, but so sound was the basic design that current production models differ little externally from the first prototype. Built to a USAF specification for a turboprop-engined tactical transport with good short-field performance from rough airstrips, the YC-130 prototype first flew on 23 August 1954, and among its features were the rear ramp essential to facilitate loading of bulky items and to ensure paradrops with minimum dispersion, and a payload of 11340 kg (25,000 lb) of cargo, 92 infantrymen or 64 paratroops. Other features of the design were sturdy multi-wheel landing gear (the main units retracting into fuselage blisters) to keep the fuselage level at truck-bed height, and a high-set wing above the hold.

The first production **C-130A** flew on 7 April 1955 followed by 192 for the USAF and 12 for the RAAF. First USAF unit to fly the new transport was the 463d Tactical Control Wing at Ardmore AFB from December 1956. Gross weight of the early aircraft was 46266 kg (102,000 lb) and the clear cargo volume was 12.19 by 3.05 by 2.74 m (40 by 10 by 9 ft). The **C-130B** entered production in 1958 and incorporated the Allison T56-A-7 turboprop with a four-blade Hamilton Standard propeller, permitting an increase in gross weight to 61235 kg (135,000 lb) with increased fuel capacity. Speed was increased by 13 kt (24 km/h; 15 mph). A total

of 186 was built including 29 for export. Nine C-130Bs were converted to serve alongside five new-build **WC-130B** aircraft for weather reconnaissance.

The long-range **C-130E** was built to meet a Military Air Transport Service (MATS) requirement for a transoceanic-range interim aircraft pending delivery of the Lockheed C-141. Fitted with two 5148-litre (1,360-US gal) wing tanks on inboard pylons plus increased internal fuel and with a strengthened structure, the C-130 had a gross weight increased to 70307 kg (155,000 lb). Range with a 9072-kg (20,000-lb) payload is 7411 km (4,605 miles), and maximum payload is 20412 kg (45,000 lb). Acquired by Tactical Airlift Command (TAC) from 1963, this model bore the brunt of tactical transport work in Vietnam and was also widely exported. The civil **Hercules L-100** (21 built) is a demilitarized version of the C-130E and is flown by several air forces. Six C-130Es were converted to **WC-130E** aircraft from 1965 to 1969, these featuring increased range and enhanced data-link technology compared with the WC-130Bs.

The C-130 has been developed in many variants and most are covered separately. Of note were the sole NC-130B boundary layer control research conversion (of which the C130C production version was not built) and the ski-equipped **C-130D** variant (12 built) of the C-130A for use in the Antarctic. In US Navy service the C-130B and C-130E became the **C-130F** (originally GV-1U of which seven were built) and **C-130G** (four built) respectively.

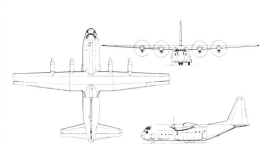

*Lockheed C-130A Hercules (radar not fitted)*

*This C-130B Hercules serves with the Royal Jordanian Air Force, flying with No.8 Squadron based at Amman-King Abdullah air base. This C-130B serves alongside four C-130Hs.*

**Specification:** Lockheed C-130A Hercules
**Origin:** USA
**Type:** tactical transport
**Powerplant:** four 2796-ekW (3,750-eshp) Allison T56-A-1A turboprops
**Performance:** maximum speed 330 kt (612 km/h; 380 mph) at 30,000 ft (9145 m); cruising speed 290 kt (540 km/h; 335 mph); initial rate of climb 1,700 ft (518 m) per minute; service ceiling 41,300 ft (12590 m); range 4667 km (2,900 miles) with a 11703-kg (25,800-lb) payload
**Weights:** empty 26911 kg (59,328 lb); maximum take-off 56336 kg (124,200 lb)
**Dimensions:** span 40.41 m (132 ft 7 in); length 29.79 m (97 ft 9 in); height 11.66 m (38 ft 3 in); wing area 162.11 m² (1,745.0 sq ft)
**Armament:** none

*This is one of the few remaining C-130As still in original configuration with three-bladed propellers and short nose. This aircraft serves with the 105th TAS, 118th TAG, Tennessee Air National Guard.*

# Lockheed C-130H/K Hercules

*Lockheed C-130H Hercules of Eskadrille 721, Royal Danish air force.*

Manufacture of the planned 503 examples of the C-130E version of the Hercules was completed in February 1975, but by then Lockheed already had the next improved model in production with derated T56-A-15 engines, a revised centre- section structure and improved brakes. This was the **Lockheed C-130H Hercules**, the current production transport type still rolling off the Marietta production line in the mid-1990s. The first C-130H variant was the **HC-130H** ordered from 1964 for the Aerospace Rescue and Recovery Service in the task of catching re-entering spacecraft. This specialized type first featured the more powerful 3661-ekW (4,910-eshp) Allison T56-A-15 engines derated to 3362 ekW (4,508 eshp). Ferry range is extended to 8803 km (5,470 miles), and the aircraft enjoys an improved wing and more up-to-date avionics. The first basic transport version followed shortly after the recovery type from 1968. The **LC-130R** is the ski-equipped version for US Navy Antarctic use. A total of 15 **WC-130H** aircraft were produced from C-130H and HC-130H conversions to replace the early WC-130Bs. The WC-130H features an auxiliary fuel tank in the main cabin and an increased crew. One WC-130H has been lost.

Ordered from 1965 for the Royal Air Force was the **C-130K** designated **Hercules C.Mk 1** in British service. Sixty-six were produced from 1966, and these were basically similar to the C130H but with a British avionics fit. Marshall of Cambridge was awarded the UK support contract, and at an early stage con-verted one aircraft, XV208, to **Hercules W.Mk 2** standard for meteorological research.

With more than adequate power available, Lockheed produced a stretched version of the civil L-100 by adding 2.54 m (8 ft 4 in) to the fuselage to produce the **L-100-20**. Among other operators, this model is in service with the Gabonese, Peruvian and Philippine air forces. Dating from 1968, the L-100-20 was followed in 1970 by the **L-100-30** with a total stretch of 4.57 m (15 ft 0 in), increasing capacity to 128 infantrymen or 92 fully equipped paratroops. The type also entered military production as the **C-130H-30**, and 30 of the RAF's Hercules were converted to this standard as the **Hercules C.Mk 3**, later fitted with a flight-refuelling probe as the **Hercules C.Mk 3P**.

The versatility of the Hercules is clearly demonstrated through the specialized entries and there is no doubt that the type will continue to surprise through its longevity and adaptability. In Vietnam the aircraft dropped the USAF's heaviest bombs to create cleared landing zones for helicopter use, and the **C-130-MP** is a maritime patrol variant in service with the Indonesian and Malaysian air forces A high-technology test-bed developed by Lockheed from the L-100-20, the HTTB, flew in June 1984 as a STOL research vehicle, and an AEW version was also planned but not developed to prototype stage. At the time of writing in mid-1995, total sales of all models had passed 2,000 aircraft.

**Specification:** Lockheed C-130H Hercules
**Origin:** USA
**Type:** tactical transport
**Powerplant:** four 3362-ekW (4,508-ehp) Allison T56-A-15 turboprops
**Performance:** maximum speed 333 kt (618 km/h; 384 mph) at 30,000 ft (9145 m); cruising speed 326 kt (603 km/h; 375 mph); initial rate of climb 1,900 ft (579 m) per minute; service ceiling 42,900 ft (13075 m); range 8264 km (5,135 miles) with a 9072-kg (20,000-lb) payload
**Weights:** empty 34827 kg (76,780 lb); maximum take-off 79379 kg (175,000 lb)
**Dimensions:** span 40.41 m (132 ft 7 in); length 29.79 m (97 ft 9 in); height 11.66 m (38 ft 3 in); wing area 162.11 m² (1,745.0 sq ft)
**Armament:** none

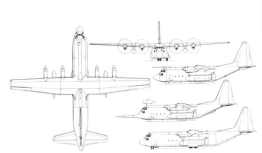

*Lockheed Hercules C.Mk 3 (upper side view: Hercules C.Mk 1P; central side view: Hercules W.Mk 2)*

*This Lockheed C-130H serves with No.36 Squadron, Royal Australian Air Force, flying from Richmond. No.36 is one of two Hercules-equipped units, the other being No.37, also at Richmond.*

*This Hercules C. Mk 3 shows its stretched fuselage to advantage. Thirty RAF Hercules were 'stretched' by Marshall of Cambridge, giving a marked improvement in payload capability.*

**Role**
Fighter
Close support
Counter-insurgency
Tactical strike
Strategic bomber
Strategic reconnaissance
Tactical reconnaissance
Strategic reconnaissance
Maritime patrol
Anti-ship strike
Anti-submarine warfare
Search and rescue
Assault transport
Transport
Liaison
Trainer
Inflight-refuelling tanker
Specialized

**Performance**
All-weather capability
Rough field capability
STOL capability
VTOL capability
Airspeed 0-250 mph
Airspeed 250 mph-Mach 1
Airspeed Mach 1 plus
Ceiling 0-20,000 ft
Ceiling 20,000-40,000 ft
Ceiling 40,000ft plus
Range 0-1,000 miles
Range 1,000-3,000 miles
Range 3,000 miles plus

**Weapons**
Air-to-air missiles
Air-to-surface missiles
Cruise missiles
Cannon
Trainable guns
Naval weapons
Nuclear-capable
Rockets
'Smart' weapon kit
Weapon load 0-4,000 lb
Weapon load 4,000-15,000 lb
Weapon load 15,000 lb plus

**Avionics**
Electronic Counter Measures
Electronic Support Measures
Search radar
Fire control radar
Look-down/shoot-down
Terrain-following radar
Forward-looking infra-red
Laser
Television

# Lockheed AC-130 Hercules

*Lockheed AC-130H 'Pave Spectre' of the 16th SOS, 1st SOW, based at Hurlburt Field, Florida.*

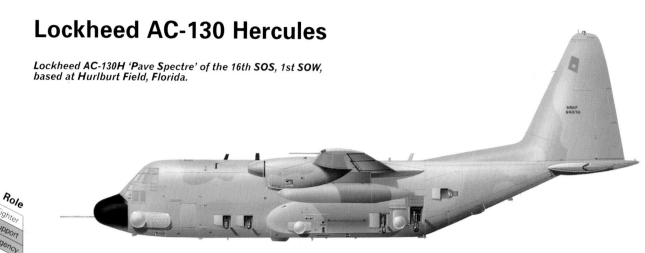

**Role**
Fighter
Close support
Counter-insurgency
Tactical strike
Strategic bomber
Tactical reconnaissance
Strategic reconnaissance
Maritime patrol
Anti-ship strike
Anti-submarine warfare
Search and rescue
Assault transport
Transport
Liaison
Trainer
Inflight-refuelling tanker
Specialized

**Performance**
All-weather capability
Rough field capability
STOL capability
VTOL capability
Airspeed 0-250 mph
Airspeed 250 mph-Mach 1
Airspeed Mach 1 plus
Ceiling 0-20,000 ft
Ceiling 20,000-40,000 ft
Ceiling 40,000ft plus
Range 0-1,000 miles
Range 1,000-3,000 miles
Range 3,000 miles plus

**Weapons**
Air-to-air missiles
Air-to-surface missiles
Cruise missiles
Cannon
Trainable guns
Naval weapons
Nuclear-capable
Rockets
'Smart' weapon kit
Weapon load 0-4,000 lb
Weapon load 4,000-15,000 lb
Weapon load 15,000 lb plus

**Avionics**
Electronic Counter Measures
Electronic Support Measures
Search radar
Fire control radar
Look-down/shoot-down
Terrain-following radar
Forward-looking infra-red
Laser
Television

A need perceived from early USAF experience in Vietnam was quick-reaction concentrated firepower for use against small targets, especially in support of the defenders of isolated areas subject to nocturnal attack. The first solution was the Gunship I conversion of the Douglas C-47 as the AC-47, known informally as 'Puff the Magic Dragon' or 'Spooky'. Initially fitted with three side-firing 7.62-mm (0.3-in) general-purpose machine-guns, they were soon refitted with three 7.62-mm multi-barrelled Miniguns. Developed by the USAF Aeronautical Systems Division (ASD), the gunship applied a principle adopted by bush pilots in South America. This was the use of a weighted bucket suspended on a rope from an aircraft flying a very tight continuous turn to keep the bucket stationary at the tip of an imaginary cone for the collection of mail and the like from inaccessible sites. The gunship pilot was required to bank his aircraft at between 30° and 50° and, when the target was constantly sighted in a left-hand circuit, fire the guns.

With the system operational, there was a need to improve firepower, sensing equipment, targeting and armour. The Fairchild C-119 was adapted as the AC-119G 'Shadow' and AC-119K 'Stinger' with the 17th and 18th Special Operations Squadrons respectively, while ASD began converting the 13th production C-130A to Gunship II standard in 1965. This involved installation of four 20-mm Vulcan cannon, four 7.62-mm Miniguns, flare equipment and improved sighting, This aircraft was tested operationally in Vietnam in late 1967, and LTV Electrosystems was awarded an immediate contract to modify seven JC-130A missile trackers to **Lockheed AC-130A** standard. These aircraft were fitted with a searchlight, sensors, FLIR target acquisition, and direct-view image intensifiers. Four were in service in Vietnam by the end of 1968 with the 14th Air Commando Wing operating from Ubon in Thailand. A further single C-130 was converted in the 'Surprise Package' project with two 40-mm cannon replacing two of the 20mm variety and with computerized fire control.

So successful was the project that 11 C-130E models were converted to **AC-130E** standard in the 'Pave Spectre' programme. The aircraft were given heavier armour, better avionics and provision for more ammunition; from 1973 they were brought up to **AC-130H** standard by the installation of the more powerful T56-A-15 engine. The final developments for use in South East Asia were the fitting of a 105-mm howitzer and laser target designator in the 'Pave Aegis' programme. At the end of the Vietnam War remaining AC-130A/H aircraft returned to the USA to serve with the 1st Special Operations Wing at Eglin AFB. The AC-130 was used operationally against Cuban positions during the US occupation of Grenada in October 1983.

The latest Hercules gunship model is the **AC-130U**, of which 13 are being delivered by Rockwell as C-130H conversions with port-firing armament of one 25-mm GAU-12/U cannon, one 40-mm Bofors gun and one 105-mm (4.13-in) howitzer, and a state-of-the-art target-acquisition and fire-control system.

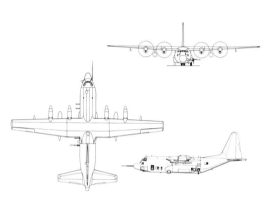

*Lockheed AC-130H 'Spectre'*

**The AC-130Hs of the 16th SOS were used over Grenada during the US invasion in the gunship role, and over Central America as unarmed night reconnaissance aircraft.**

**This Spectre is an AC-130A (note the three-bladed propellers) of the 711th SOS, 919th SOG, AFRes, based at Duke Field AFB, Florida. This unit would be assigned to TAC during time of tension or war.**

**Specification:** Lockheed AC-130E Hercules
**Origin:** USA
**Type:** multi-sensor ground-attack gunship
**Powerplant:** four 3020-ekW (4,050-eshp) Allison T56-A-7 turboprops
**Performance:** maximum speed 330 kt (612 km/h; 380 mph) at 30,000 ft(9145 m); cruising speed 320 kt (592 km/h; 368 mph); initial rate of climb 1,830 ft (558 m) per minute; endurance 5 hours
**Weights:** empty 33063 kg (72,892 lb); maximum take-off 70307 kg (155,000 lb)
**Dimensions:** span 40.41 m (132 ft 7 in); length 29.79 m (97 ft 9 in); height 11.66 m (38 ft 3 in); wing area 162.11 m² (1,745.0 sq ft)
**Armament:** (AC-130H) one 105-mm (4.13-in) howitzer, two 40-mm Bofors cannon, two 20-mm Vulcan cannon and four 7.62-mm (0.3-in) Miniguns

# Lockheed HC-130 Hercules

*Lockheed HC-130H Hercules of the US Coast Guard.*

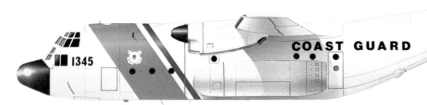

First customer for a search-and-rescue variant of the Hercules was the US Coast Guard, which ordered 12 modified C-130Bs from 1958 with the designation R8V-1G that became **Lockheed SC-130B Hercules** before the first deliveries were made in 1959. Later redesignated **HC130B**, these aircraft featured additional crew posts, two scanner stations offering an unrestricted field of view, and accommodation for 74 litters. The basic avionics of the transport version were retained, including the APS-59 nose radar.

On 8 December 1964 Lockheed flew the first **HC-130H**, a rescue variant powered by Allison T56-A-15s. Forty-five were ordered for the USAF Air Rescue Service, and the Coast Guard also received 23 aircraft. The HC-130H was ordered for a variety of work focusing on the recovery of downed aircrew but also including duties related to the space programme. The HC-130H carried additional equipment and two 6814-litre (1,800-US gal) fuel tanks in the cargo hold. Externally it mounted a large blister above the forward fuselage containing the Cook Electric re-entry tracking system for use in conjunction with Gemini spacecraft. The most remarkable feature, however, is the Fulton recovery system: this features two 4.42-m (14.5-ft) nose-mounted tines that are normally stowed back along the fuselage but arranged to hinge forward to make a V-shaped fork. The aircraft

also carry recovery kits, including rafts and helium balloons. The latter, when inflated, carry aloft a 152-m (500-ft) line which is attached to a body harness. Flying at 122 kt (225 km/h; 140 mph) into wind, the HC-130 snags the line with its recovery yoke, snatching the maximum 227-kg (500-lb) load from the surface. The balloon breaks away at a weak link and the rescued person or load is winched into the aircraft, the line being grappelled to allow recovery into the cargo bay. Teflon lines from nose to fin and wingtips deflect the wire from the propellers in the event of a missed approach. The US Coast Guard's HC-130s do not usually operate with the Fulton gear. Four USAF HC-130Hs were subsequently converted for space capsule recovery as the **JHC-130H** version.

To cope with the increased rescue demands of the Vietnam War, an additional 20 HC-130Hs were built in a variant with outer wing pods for inflight-refuelling of helicopters. Designated **HC-130P**, these aircraft worked most successfully with the Sikorsky HH-3E to save many lives. The last rescue Hercules is the **HC-130N**, which differs from earlier models in having advanced direction-finding equipment but without the Fulton gear and additional fuel tanks. Fifteen were delivered to the USAF from 1969, and with the earlier types these equipped 10 squadrons across the world.

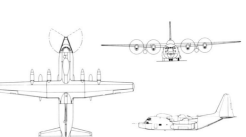

*Lockheed HC-130P Hercules with Fulton gear on nose (now rarely carried)*

**This RAF Woodbridge-based *HC-130P* of the 67th ARRS, US Air Force, is seen refuelling an *HH-3* during a deployment to Keflavik, Iceland. The 67th ARRS was responsible for Europe-wide combat rescue.**

**The US Coast Guard operates a large fleet of HC-130 Hercules for rescue and patrol missions. This HC-130H does not carry the Fulton recovery system, in common with most current examples.**

**Specification:** Lockheed HC-130H Hercules
**Origin:** USA
**Type:** rescue and recovery aircraft
**Powerplant:** four 3362-ekW (4,508-eshp) Allison T56-A-15 turboprops
**Performance:** maximum speed 325 kt (602 km/h; 374 mph) at 30,000 ft (9145 m); initial rate of climb 1,900 ft (579 m) per minute; service ceiling 33,000 ft (10060 m); range 3792 km (2,356 miles) with maximum payload and reserves
**Weights:** empty 32936 kg (72,611 lb); maximum take-off 70307 kg (155,000 lb)
**Dimensions:** span 40.41 m (132 ft 7 in); length 30.73 m (100 ft 10 in); height 11.66 m (38 ft 3 in); wing area 162.16 m²(1,745.0 sq ft)
**Armament:** none

## Role

Fighter
Close support
Counter-insurgency
Tactical strike
Strategic bomber
Tactical reconnaissance
Strategic reconnaissance
Maritime patrol
Anti-ship strike
Anti-submarine warfare
Search and rescue
Assault transport
Transport
Liaison
Trainer
Inflight-refuelling tanker
Specialized

## Performance

All-weather capability
Rough field capability
STOL capability
VTOL capability
Airspeed 0-250 mph
Airspeed 250 mph-Mach 1
Airspeed Mach 1 plus
Ceiling 0-20,000 ft
Ceiling 20,000-40,000 ft
Ceiling 40,000 ft plus
Range 0-1,000 miles
Range 1,000-3,000 miles
Range 3,000 miles plus

## Weapons

Air-to-air missiles
Air-to-surface missiles
Cruise missiles
Cannon
Trainable guns
Naval weapons
Nuclear-capable
Rockets
'Smart' weapon kit
Weapon load 0-4,000 lb
Weapon load 4,000-15,000 lb
Weapon load 15,000 lb plus

## Avionics

Electronic Counter Measures
Electronic Support Measures
Search radar
Fire control radar
Look-down/shoot-down radar
Terrain-following radar
Forward-looking infra-red
Laser
Television

# Lockheed KC-130 Hercules

*Lockheed KC-130H Hercules of Escuadron 312,*
*Spanish air force, from Zaragoza.*

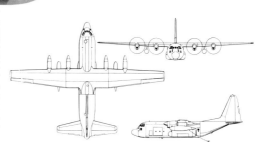

The US Marine Corps required a tactical transport which could double as an inflight-refuelling tanker using the probe and drogue system. In August 1957 two US Air Force C-130As were borrowed and each fitted with two 1915-litre (506-US gal) tanks in the fuselage and two underwing pods containing the hose equipment. So successful were the trials that 46 **Lockheed KC-130F Hercules** were ordered for delivery from 1960. The KC-130F is based on the C-130B airframe, initially with Allison T56-A-7 engines but later re-engined with 3661-ekW (4,910-eshp) T56-A-16s. An easily removable fuselage tank holding 13627 litres (3,600 US gal) is fitted, and the two equipment pods enable fuel transfer at the rate of 1136 litres (300 US gal) per minute. As well as the transfer fuel, the tanker is able to transfer its own surplus fuel. Originally designated GV-1, the first production aircraft flew on 22 January 1960. The type currently equips the US MAC's VMGR-152, VGMR-252, VGRMT-253 and VGMR-352, and the US Navy's VR-22.

To cope with attrition, the USMC ordered 14 **KC-130R** tankers based on the C-130H.

These aircraft feature the T56-A-16 powerplant and pylon-mounted fuel tanks with an extra 10296 litres (2,720 US gal) of fuel. Initial deliveries were to VMGR-352 at MCAS El Toro, California. Although not in service with US forces, the **KC-130H** (similar in most respects to the KC-130R) has been successfully exported to seven countries. The most recent USMC variant is the **KC-130T**, of which 20 (plus two stretched **KC-130T-30** aircraft) were delivered for VMGR-234 and VMGR-452. This model has updated avionics, a new search radar and improved navigation systems

The Falklands war resulted in an urgent RAF demand for increased tanker support. Marshals of Cambridge started work in May 1982 on converting a standard Hercules C.Mk 1 to tanker configuration. Four ex-Andover 4091-litre (900-Imp gal) tanks were fitted in the fuselage and a single Flight Refuelling Mk 17B Hose Drum Unit (HDU) was attached to the ramp door. First flight was on 7 June 1982, and within three months four aircraft had been converted. Designated **Hercules C.Mk 1K**, six such aircraft are operated by the Lyneham Transport Wing.

**Lockheed KC-130H Hercules**

**Specification:** Lockheed KC-130F Hercules
**Origin:** USA
**Type:** inflight-refuelling tanker
**Powerplant:** four 3661-ekW (4,910-eshp) AllisonT56-A-16 turboprops
**Performance:** maximum speed 330 kt (612 km/h; 380 mph) at 30,000 ft (9145 m); refuelling speed 308 kt (571 km/h; 355 mph); range 1609 km (1,000 miles) to transfer 14061 kg (31,000 lb) of fuel
**Weights:** empty 31434 kg (69,300 lb); maximum take-off 61235kg (135,000 lb)
**Dimensions:** span 40.41 m (132 ft 7 in); length 29.79 m (97 ft 9 in); height 11.66 m (38 ft 3 in); wing area 161.16 m² (1,745.0 sq ft)
**Armament:** none

*This KC-130H was operated by Lockheed-Georgia as a demonstrator, and is seen here drumming up interest from the Colombian air force by refuelling a quartet of its Cessna A-37s.*

*A prototype AV-8B, representing the future of USMC air power, refuels from a type that forms the backbone of its current fleet, a Lockheed KC-130R of VMGR-352 based at MCAS El Toro.*

## Role
Fighter
Close-support
Counter-insurgency
Tactical strike
Strategic bomber
Tactical reconnaissance
Strategic reconnaissance
Maritime patrol
Anti-ship strike
Anti-submarine warfare
Search and rescue
Assault transport
Transport
Liaison
Trainer
Inflight-refuelling tanker
Specialized

## Performance
All-weather capability
Rough field capability
STOL capability
VTOL capability
Airspeed 0-250 mph
Airspeed 250 mph-Mach 1
Airspeed Mach 1 plus
Ceiling 0-20,000 ft
Ceiling 20,000-40,000 ft
Ceiling 40,000ft plus
Range 0-1,000 miles
Range 1,000-3,000 miles
Range 3,000 miles plus

## Weapons
Air-to-air missiles
Air-to-surface missiles
Cruise missiles
Cannon
Trainable guns
Naval weapons
Nuclear-capable
Rockets
'Smart' weapon kit
Weapon load 0-4,000 lb
Weapon load 4,000-15,000 lb
Weapon load 15,000 lb plus

## Avionics
Electronic Counter Measures
Electronic Support Measures
Search radar
Fire-control radar
Look-down/shoot-down
Terrain-following radar
Forward-looking infra-red
Laser
Television

# Lockheed MC-130 Hercules

*Lockheed MC-130H Hercules of the Rhein-Main based 7th SOS, US Air Force.*

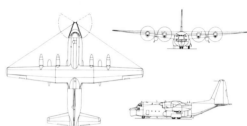

In the late 1970s the USAF began a programme of improving a number of HC-130Es for clandestine work throughout the world. Eventually 14 aircraft were involved and given the designation **Lockheed C-130E-I Hercules**, later changed to **MC-130E**. In the 'Combat Talon' programme the type was equipped for all-weather day/night infiltration and exfiltration of special forces and agents. Additional roles include psychological warfare, resupply, aerial reconnaissance and STAR (Surface To Air Retrievals). The nose suffered yet further indignities with the fitting (to some aircraft) of the Fulton retrieval yoke and also of terrain-following radar. Other equipment included precision ground mapping radar, an inertial navigation system, secure voice UHF/VHF/FM radios, a retractable FLIR pod and an ALQ-87 ECM pod under the port wing. A crew of up to 11 is carried.

From 1979 a number of 'Combat Talon II' aircraft were supplied. These later models are equipped with more advanced avionics

including the ALR-46 radar-warning receiver and ALE-27 chaff dispenser. Importantly, they are also equipped for inflight-refuelling from the Boeing KC-135 or McDonnell Douglas KC-10.The MC-130Es are distributed within three operational units. The 1st Special Operations Squadron, 353d SOW, is based at Kadena AB, Okinawa, while the European operator is the 7th SOS, 39th SOW, at Rhein-Main AB, West Germany and the US operator is the 8th SOS, 1st SOW at Hurlburt Field, Eglin AFB, Florida; this last has both operational and training roles. The latter unit supplied three aircraft, via Egypt, to fly in 90 special force troops for the abortive Iran rescue attempt in April 1980.

The latest standard, based on the C-130H, is the **MC-130H**, of which 25 are being procured in a programme that is seeing the gradual introduction of the significantly improved systems and equipment including multimode radar for enhanced law-level navigation as well as terrain-avoidance/following.

**Specification:** Lockheed MC-130E Hercules
**Origin:** USA
**Type:** special tactical mission support aircraft
**Powerplant:** four 3020-ekW(4,050-eshp) Allison T56-A-7 turboprops
**Performance:** maximum speed 318 kt (589 km/h; 366 mph); speed for personnel airdrop 125 kt (232 km/h; 144 mph) at a minimum height of 50 ft (15 m); initial rate of climb 1,600 ft (488 m) per minute; unrefuelled range 3701 km (2,300 miles)
**Weights:** empty 33063 kg (72,892 lb); maximum take-off 70307 kg(155,000 lb)
**Dimensions:** span 40.41 m (132 ft 7 in); length 30.73 m (100 ft 10 in); height 11.66 m (38 ft 3 in); wing area 162.16 m² (1,745.0 sq ft)
**Armament:** none

*Lockheed MC-130E Hercules (Fulton gear usually not carried)*

**The US Air Force is the only operator of the MC-130, but other users have modified aircraft which are used for clandestine insertion duties. RAF C-130s of No. 47 Squadron's Special Forces Flight are a typical example.**

**An MC-130130E 'Combat Talon' of the 7th Special Operations Squadron. These aircraft are equipped to fly at low level in all weathers, and for inflight-refuelling.**

## Role
Fighter
Close support
Counter-insurgency
Tactical strike
Strategic bomber
Tactical reconnaissance
Strategic reconnaissance
Maritime patrol
Anti-ship strike
Anti-submarine warfare
Search and rescue
Assault transport
Transport
Liaison
Trainer
Inflight-refuelling tanker
Specialized

## Performance
All-weather capability
Rough field capability
STOL capability
VTOL capability
Airspeed 0-250 mph
Airspeed 250 mph-Mach 1
Airspeed Mach 1 plus
Ceiling 0-20,000 ft
Ceiling 20,000-40,000 ft
Ceiling 40,000ft plus
Range 0-1,000 miles
Range 1,000-3,000 miles
Range 3,000 miles plus

## Weapons
Air-to-air missiles
Air-to-surface missiles
Cruise missiles
Cannon
Trainable guns
Naval weapons
Nuclear-capable
Rockets
'Smart' weapon kit
Weapon load 0-4,000 lb
Weapon load 4,000-15,000 lb
Weapon load 15,000 lb plus

## Avionics
Electronic Counter Measures
Electronic Support Measures
Search radar
Fire control radar
Look-down/shoot-down
Terrain-following radar
Forward-looking infra-red
Laser
Television

# Lockheed C-141 StarLifter

*Lockheed C-141B StarLifter of Military Airlift Command, US Air Force.*

### Role

Fighter
Close support
Counter-insurgency
Tactical strike
Strategic bomber
Tactical reconnaissance
Strategic reconnaissance
Maritime patrol
Anti-ship strike
Anti-submarine warfare
Search and rescue
Assault transport
**Transport**
Liaison
Trainer
Inflight-refuelling tanker
Specialized

### Performance

All-weather capability
Rough field capability
STOL capability
VTOL capability
Airspeed 0-250 mph
Airspeed 250 mph-Mach 1
Airspeed Mach 1 plus
Ceiling 0-20,000 ft
Ceiling 20,000-40,000 ft
Ceiling 40,000ft plus
Range 0-1,000 miles
Range 1,000-3,000 miles
Range 3,000 miles plus

### Weapons

Air-to-air missiles
Air-to-surface missiles
Cruise missiles
Cannon
Trainable guns
Naval weapons
Nuclear-capable
Rockets
'Smart' weapon kit
Weapon load 0-4,000 lb
Weapon load 4,000-15,000 lb
Weapon load 15,000 lb plus

### Avionics

Electronic Counter Measures
Electronic Support Measures
Search radar
Fire control radar
Look-down/shoot-down
Terrain-following radar
Forward-looking infra-red
Laser
Television

With an air transport fleet composed almost entirely of piston-engined aircraft in the late 1950s, the USAF's Military Air Transport Service was inadequately equipped for its growing world-wide responsibilities. In May 1960 the USAF's Specific Operational Requirement 182 was drawn up, and Requests for Proposals accordingly circulated to US manufacturers. From submissions received, Lockheed was announced winner and on 13 March 1961 awarded an initial contract for five DT & E aircraft. SOR 182 specified an aircraft to airlift a payload of 27216 kg (60,000 lb) over a range of 6477 km (4,025 miles), and Lockheed's proposal probably gained favour by using proven ideas adopted from the C-130 Hercules. Thus the new design had the C-130's high-wing configuration and main landing gear arrangement with the units retracting into fuselage side fairings to maximize cabin volume, and a similar main loading door/ramp in the rear fuselage for straight-in cargo/vehicle loading. Conspicuous differences, apart from size, were the T-tail and turbofan engines pylon-mounted in pods beneath the wings.

Given the basic designation **Lockheed C-141**, the first example was flown on 17 December 1963: just over 16 months later, on 23 April 1965, the type had become operational with Military Airlift Command, the successor to MATS. Operated by a flight crew of five, these aircraft were soon providing a daily service across the Pacific, outward bound with up to 138 troops or some 28440 kg (62,700 lb) of cargo and returning with the casualties of growing conflict in Vietnam, the main cabin having room for 80 litters and 23 medical attendants. The last of 284 **C-141A StarLifter** aircraft was delivered to the USAF in February 1968

Experience showed that the C-141A frequently ran out of cabin volume long before its maximum payload weight had Ben loaded. This problem was resolved from 1976 onward by a programme that lengthened the fuselage by 7.11 m (23 ft 4 in) and at the same time provided an inflight-refuelling capability. The prototype YC-141B conversion was flown on 24 March 1977, and on 29 June 1982 the last of the 270 surviving C-141As had been converted to the new **C-141B** configuration, ahead of schedule and below projected cost. This programme has, in effect provided MAC with 90 additional transports of C-141A capacity that require no extra crew.

### Specification: Lockheed C-141B StarLifter
**Origin:** USA
**Type:** strategic troop/cargo transport
**Powerplant:** four 9526-kg (21,000-lb) dry thrust Pratt & WhitneyTF33-7 turbofans
**Performance:** maximum cruising speed 492 kt (912 km/h; 567 mph); long-range cruising speed 430 kt (797 km/h; 495mph); initial rate of climb 2,920 ft (890 m) per minute; range 4723 km (2,935 miles) with maximum payload; ferry range 10284 km (6,390 miles)
**Weights:** empty 677186 kg (148,120 lb); maximum take-off 155582 kg (343,000 lb)
**Dimensions:** span 48.74 m (159 ft 11 in); length 51.29 m (168 ft 3.5 in); height 11.96 m (39 ft 3 in); wing area 299.88 m² (3,228.0 sq ft)
**Armament:** none

*Lockheed C-141B StarLifter*

**All surviving C-141As were converted to C-141B standard by stretching the fuselage. This prevents the aircraft 'bulking out' before maximum payload weight is reached.**

**The C-141B has seen active service in Vietnam, the invasion of Grenada and the US-led war against Iraq, as well as providing logistic support for countless smaller operations of equal importance.**

# Lockheed F-117 Night Hawk

*A Lockheed F-117A of the 410th Flight Test Squadron, based at Palmdale for test and trials duties.*

Even now, nearly 20 years after the program's start in 1976, little of a definite nature is known of the **Lockheed F-117 Night Hawk**, the world's first true 'stealth' warplane to reach operational status. The origins of the type can be traced back to the 1973 'Yom Kippur War', in which the Israeli air force initially suffered a number of setbacks with US warplane types in the face of modern Soviet surface-to-air weapon systems operated by its Egyptian and Syrian opponents. An early aspect of the resulting 'Have Blue' observability-reduction effort was the Experimental Stealth Technology requirement. This drew design submissions from Lockheed and Northrop, the former winning with a type spanning 6.86 m (22 ft 6 in) and powered by two General Electric CJ610 turbojets: this was a virtually half-size prototype for the F-117 and flew in December 1977.

Design and development of the full-size F-117 was ordered in November 1978, and the first of five service trials aircraft flew in June 1981. Production was then trimmed from 100 to 59 **F-117A** aircraft for a total of 64 aircraft, and deliveries began in August 1982 for an initial operational capability in October 1983. The F-117A is a highly angular type of flying-wing basic design (based on relaxed stability and controlled via a quadruplex fly-

by-wire control system) with a butterfly tail and elements of lifting-body vehicle design, the whole concept being schemed not so much to trap or absorb incoming electromagnetic energy as to reflect such radiation in all directions except that straight back to the emitter. The type is intended to detect and then destroy high-value targets after undetected penetration of enemy airspace using its low visual, electromagnetic and thermal signatures, the last being aided by the use between the wings and tail of exhaust-spreading slot nozzles that also mix cold air and hot gas. Two of the features that produce a high level of electromagnetic illumination in conventional warplanes are active radars and external carriage of weapons on protruding hardpoints. The F-117A therefore has no active radars (the place of a search radar being taken by an advanced passive system based on IR sensors and that of the Doppler navigation system by a high-quality INS) and has internal accommodation for a small warload of 'smart' weapons in a lower-fuselage weapon bay that is 4.70 m (15 ft 5 in) long and 1.75 m (5 ft 9 in) wide.

The surviving aircraft (three having been lost in accidents) are being upgraded significantly in weapon system capability between 1994 and 2005.

### Specification: Lockheed F-117A Night Hawk
**Origin:** USA
**Type:** 'stealthy' attack warplane
**Powerplant:** two 4899-kg (10,800-lb) dry thrust General Electric F404-GE-F1D2 turbofans
**Performance:** maximum speed possibly more than Mach 1 at high altitude; maximum cruising speed Mach 0.9 at optimum altitude; combat radius about 1112 km (691 miles) with maximum ordnance
**Weights:** empty 13608 kg (30,000 lb); maximum take-off 23814 kg (52,500 lb)
**Dimensions:** span 13.20 m (43 ft 4 in); length 20.08 m (65 ft 11 in); height 3.78 m (12 ft 5 in); wing area about 105.9 m² (1,140.0 sq ft)
**Armament:** provision for 2268 kg (5,000 lb) of disposable stores carried in a lower-fuselage weapon bay; standard weapons are the AGM-88 HARM anti-radar missile, AGM-65 Maverick ASM, GBU-19 and GBU-27 optronically guided bombs, BLU-109 laser-guided bomb, and B61 free-fall nuclear bomb

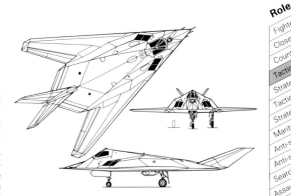

**Lockheed F-117A *Night Hawk***

*An F-117A of the 49th Fighter Wing on approach. The Holloman, New Mexico-based unit is the only frontline operator of the F-117 and has three constituent squadrons.*

*The F-117's unusual faceted exterior has led to the use of a variety of unflattering nicknames, including the 'Cockroach'. It is also responsible for the aircraft's remarkable stealth characteristics.*

### Role
Fighter
Close support
Counter-insurgency
Tactical strike
Strategic bomber
Tactical reconnaissance
Strategic reconnaissance
Maritime patrol
Anti-ship strike
Anti-submarine warfare
Search and rescue
Assault transport
Transport
Liaison
Trainer
Inflight-refuelling tanker
Specialized

### Performance
All-weather capability
Rough field capability
STOL capability
VTOL capability
Airspeed 0-250 mph
Airspeed 250 mph-Mach 1
Airspeed Mach 1 plus
Ceiling 0-20,000 ft
Ceiling 20,000-40,000 ft
Ceiling 40,000ft plus
Range 0-1,000 miles
Range 1,000-3,000 miles
Range 3,000 miles plus

### Weapons
Air-to-air missiles
Air-to-surface missiles
Cruise missiles
Cannon
Trainable guns
Naval weapons
Nuclear-capable
Rockets
'Smart' weapon kit
Weapon load 0-4,000 lb
Weapon load 4,000-15,000 lb
Weapon load 15,000 lb plus

### Avionics
Electronic Counter Measures
Electronic Support Measures
Search radar
Fire control radar
Look-down/shoot-down radar
Terrain-following radar
Forward-looking infra-red
Laser
Television

# Lockheed L-1011 TriStar

*Lockheed TriStar K.Mk 1 of No.216 Squadron, RAF, based at Brize Norton.*

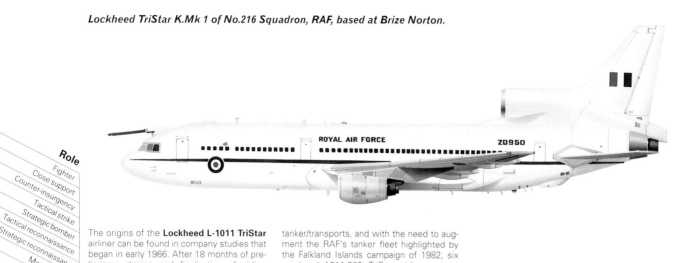

## Role
Fighter
Close support
Counter-insurgency
Tactical strike
Strategic bomber
Tactical reconnaissance
Strategic reconnaissance
Maritime patrol
Anti-ship strike
Anti-submarine warfare
Search and rescue
Assault transport
Transport
Liaison
Trainer
Inflight-refuelling tanker
Specialized

## Performance
All-weather capability
Rough field capability
STOL capability
VTOL capability
Airspeed 0-250 mph
Airspeed 250 mph-Mach 1
Airspeed Mach 1 plus
Ceiling 0-20,000 ft
Ceiling 20,000-40,000 ft
Ceiling 40,000ft plus
Range 0-1,000 miles
Range 1,000-3,000 miles
Range 3,000 miles plus

## Weapons
Air-to-air missiles
Air-to-surface missiles
Cruise missiles
Cannon
Trainable guns
Naval weapons
Nuclear-capable
Rockets
'Smart' weapon kit
Weapon load 0-4,000 lb
Weapon load 4,000-15,000 lb
Weapon load 15,000 lb plus

## Avionics
Electronic Counter Measures
Electronic Support Measures
Search radar
Fire control radar
Look-down/shoot-down
Terrain-following radar
Forward-looking infra-red
Laser
Television

The origins of the **Lockheed L-1011 TriStar** airliner can be found in company studies that began in early 1966. After 18 months of preliminary design and finalization of airline requirements, the most significant change was adoption of a three- rather than two-engine layout as first planned. Production design began in mid-1968 and the first aircraft made the type's maiden flight on 16 November 1970. Within three months the engine manufacturer, Rolls-Royce in the UK, was forced into receivership while Lockheed teetered on the brink of bankruptcy; fortunately, with government aid and consideration from airline customers, both companies survived. In service the TriStar proved successful, but escalating fuel costs and worldwide recession meant that the L-1011, despite its several versions, could not fight off competition from the Boeing family of civil transports. On 7 December 1981 Lockheed stated that production would end when current orders had been met, the 250th and last TriStar being rolled out on 19 August 1983.

There have been several programmes to convert airliners for use as military tanker/transports, and with the need to augment the RAF's tanker fleet highlighted by the Falkland Islands campaign of 1982, six surplus L-1011-500 TriStar airliners were acquired from British Airways. Marshall of Cambridge have converted of them four as **TriStar K.Mk 1** tanker/passenger aircraft and the other two as **TriStar KC.Mk 1** tanker/freight aircraft with a large cargo door on the port side of the fuselage. The primary work involved installation of tanks in the underfloor cargo holds to give an extra 45359 kg (100,000 lb) of fuel for a total capacity of 136078 kg (300,000 lb), twin HDUs in the rear fuselage, and an inflight-refuelling probe above the flight deck, offset to starboard.

The first TriStar K.Mk 1 conversion was flown on 9 July 1985 and transferred to the A&AEE at Boscombe Down in August for service trials, while he first TriStar K.Mk 1 in service was delivered to No.216 Squadron on 24 March 1986. Three more L-1011s were then acquired from Pan Am for conversion as **TriStar K.Mk 2** tanker/passenger aircraft with slightly less fuel than the TriStar K.Mk 1s.

## Specification: Lockheed TriStar K.Mk 1
**Origin:** UK (from a US design)
**Type:** long-range strategic transport and inflight-refuelling tanker
**Powerplant:** three 22680-kg (50,000-lb) dry thrust Rolls-Royce RB .211-524B turbofans
**Performance:** maximum cruising speed 520 kt (964 km/h; 599 mph) at 35,000 ft (10670 m); economical cruising speed 480 kt (890 km/h; 553 mph) at 35,000 ft (10670 m); initial rate of climb 2,820 ft (860 m) per minute. Service ceiling 43,000 ft (13105 m); range 7783 km (4,836 miles) with maximum payload
**Weights:** empty 110163 kg (242,684 lb); maximum take-off 244944 kg (540,000 lb)
**Dimensions:** span 50.09 m (164 ft 4 in); length 50.05 m (164 ft 2.5 in); height 16.87 m (55 ft 4 in); wing area 329.96 m² (3,541.0 sq ft)
**Armament:** none

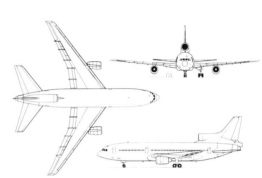

**Lockheed L-1011-500 TriStar**

*This aircraft was the first to be converted to tanker configuration by Marshall of Cambridge, and is designated TriStar K.Mk 1 by the RAF. Tankers and transports are operated by No.216 Squadron.*

*This early McDonnell Douglas Phantom FG.Mk 1 has spent most of its life as a development aircraft. It is seen here during the TriStar's tanker clearance trials, flying from Boscombe Down.*

# Lockheed P-3A and P-3B Orion

*Lockheed P-3B Orion of the Spanish air force.*

In August 1957 Type Specification No.146 was issued by the US Navy, calling for a new anti-submarine aircraft to replace the Lockheed P2V Neptune. The Lockheed proposal was based on the company's L-188 Electra passenger airliner. In May 1958 Lockheed was awarded a contract largely on the basis of the strength of the aircraft's structure and its size, which was sufficient to house an extensive array of detection and tactical processing systems. Lockheed modified the third Electra airframe as the prototype with a tail-mounted magnetic anomaly detector (MAD) boom and a ventral bulge simulating a weapons bay. Following extensive adaptations (including a shortening of the fuselage) the aircraft made a successful maiden flight as the YP3V-1 on 25 November 1959. The navy ordered an initial batch of seven aircraft in October 1960, and the first of these flew in April of the following year. In 1962 the type was redesignated **Lockheed P-3A** and named **Orion**.

The P-3A entered service in the summer of 1962, with Patrol Squadron Eight (VP-8); other units soon followed, and by December 1963 Lockheed had delivered over 50 Orions to eight squadrons. After the production of 109 P-3As, Lockheed incorporated the DELTIC installation in an improvement programme. This doubled sonobuoy information-processing capability and also incorporated redesigned avionics. The first squadron to receive the new **P-3A DELTIC**

was VP-46 at Moffett Field, and within a short time most aircraft had been retrofitted.

In the summer of 1965, after three years experience and with 157 P-3As built, Lockheed started production of a new variant. This **P-3B** was fitted with the more powerful Allison T56-A-14 engine and was heavier than its predecessor, mainly through having provision for the AGM-12 Bullpup ASM, although it maintained basically the same electronics. The P-3B secured the first export orders and became operational with the Royal New Zealand Air force (five **P-3K** aircraft), Norwegian air force (five aircraft) and RAAF (10 aircraft); ex-USN aircraft were later transferred to Portugal (five **P-3P** machines) and Spain (five machines including two upgraded to **P-3N** standard). From 1977 the USN's P-3Bs were updated with improved navigation and acoustic-processing equipment and with provision for the AGM-84 Harpoon anti-ship missile.

Having been continuously improved, the P-3B remains in service with USN reserve units. P-3As were converted to **RP-3A** standard (three aircraft) for oceanographic reconnaissance use by VXN-8, and to **WP-3A** standard (four aircraft) for weather reconnaissance by VW-4. At least five aircraft were refitted for executive transport use as **VP-3A** machines. In 1984 the Lockheed Aircraft Service Company was awarded an initial USN contract for the conversion of 30 aircraft to **CP-3A** transport standard.

## Specification: Lockheed P-3A Orion

**Origin:** USA
**Type:** 10-crew anti-submarine warfare and maritime patrol aircraft
**Powerplant:** four 3356-ekW (4,500-eshp) Allison T56-A-10W turboprops
**Performance:** maximum speed 380 kt (703 km/h; 437 mph) at 15,000 ft (4570 m); patrol speed 198 kt (367 km/h; 228 mph); initial rate of climb 2,175 ft (663 m) per minute; service ceiling 28,300 ft (8625 m); maximum mission radius 4075 km (2,532 miles)
**Weights:** empty 27216 kg (60,000 lb); maximum take-off 57833 kg(127,500 lb)
**Dimensions:** span 30.38 m (99 ft 8 in); length 35.61 m (116 ft 10 in); height 10.27 m (33 ft 8.5 in); wing area 120.77 m² (1,300.0 sq ft)
**Armament:** a combination of mines, depth bombs, torpedoes, sonobuoys and rockets can be carried to maximum weights of 3289 kg (7,250 lb) in the lower-fuselage weapons bay and of 7257 kg (16,000 lb) on the 10 underwing stations

*Lockheed P-3B Orion*

**An interesting view of a US Navy P-3B bearing down on a target submarine. Production of the P-3B ended in 1969, and most US Navy aircraft have been exported, converted or retired.**

*Norwegian Orions wear an overall dark grey colour scheme, with white code letters on each side of the fuselage roundel. This aircraft is a P-3B of 333 Skvadron, based at Andoya.*

### Role

Fighter
Close support
Counter-insurgency
Tactical strike
Strategic bomber
Tactical reconnaissance
Strategic reconnaissance
Maritime patrol
Anti-ship strike
Anti-submarine warfare
Search and rescue
Assault transport
Transport
Liaison
Trainer
Inflight-refuelling tanker
Specialized

### Performance

All-weather capability
Rough field capability
STOL capability
VTOL capability
Airspeed 0-250 mph
Airspeed 250 mph-Mach 1
Airspeed Mach 1 plus
Ceiling 0-20,000 ft
Ceiling 20,000-40,000 ft
Ceiling 40,000ft plus
Range 0-1,000 miles
Range 1,000-3,000 miles
Range 3,000 miles plus

### Weapons

Air-to-air missiles
Air-to-surface missiles
Cruise missiles
Cannon
Trainable guns
Naval weapons
Nuclear-capable
Rockets
'Smart' weapon kit
Weapon load 0-4,000 lb
Weapon load 4,000-15,000 lb
Weapon load 15,000 lb plus

### Avionics

Electronic Counter Measures
Electronic Support Measures
Search radar
Fire control radar
Look-down/shoot-down
Terrain-following radar
Forward-looking infra-red
Laser
Television

# Lockheed P-3C Orion

*Lockheed P-3C Orion of 51 Kokutai, JMSDF, based at Shimofusa.*

Although the P-3B offered superior engine power in comparison with the P-3A, there was a need for an electronically more advanced version of the Orion to counter advances in the technology of nuclear submarines. The result was the **Lockheed P-3C Orion**, first flown on 18 September 1968. This much improved type entered service with VP-56 in 1969. The primary advance was the adoption of the ANEW system of sensors and control equipment, the heart of which was the UNIVAC ASQ-114 digital computer. This produced more easily interpretable data, allowing the crew more time to perform the task of hunting submarines.

Since entering service, the P-3C has also been subjected to several important technological updates. The first produced the **P-3C Update I** in 1974 and involved expansion of the computer's memory and some modifications to the navigation system. The **P-3C Update II** programme, undertaken in 1977, involved the introduction of the ARS-3 sonobuoy system enabling the aircraft to locate buoys without having to overfly them, and of an infra-red detection system (IRDS) allowing the aircraft to track automatically a detected target by day or night. Against this background of further electronic development, Update II also conferred on the P-3C the abili-

ty to operate with the McDonnell Douglas AGM-84 Harpoon anti-ship missile. The third and most extensive modification, incorporated from 1984 in the **P-3C Update III** programme, involved the installation of the IBM Proteus signal processor which works more efficiently than the previous system. Also included were a new sonobuoy receiver and an improved auxiliary power unit. Now on the verge of service is the **P-3C Update IV** with improved radar and the ALR-77 ESM system.

Export successes have been notable for such a complex and expensive aircraft. In 1975 the Imperial Iranian air force acquired six **P-3F** aircraft for long-range surface surveillance and anti-submarine warfare duties: these were basic P-3C models equipped for inflight-refuelling (the only P-3s with such a facility). Other operators include Australia (**P-3W** aircraft), Japan, the Netherlands and Norway, making the Orion one of the most widely used aircraft in its field. In addition two P-3Cs were procured as **WP-3D** weather reconnaissance aircraft for the National Oceanographic and Atmospheric Administration (NOAA). The 51st P-3C was modified with additional fuel capacity for atmospheric research and magnetic survey, and as the sole **RP-3D** this aircraft is operated by VXN-8 in 'Project Magnet'.

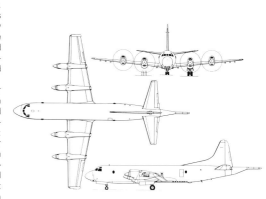

**Lockheed P-3C Orion**

*This is one of two civil-registered WP-3D aircraft operated by the US Department of Commerce on behalf of the National Oceanographic and Atmospheric Administration for long-range weather reconnaissance.*

## Specification: Lockheed P-3C Orion

**Origin:** USA
**Type:** 10-crew anti-submarine warfare and maritime patrol aircraft
**Powerplant:** four 3661-ekW (4,910-eshp) Allison T56-A-14 turboprops
**Performance:** maximum speed 411 kt (761 km/h; 473 mph) at 15,000 ft (4570 m); patrol speed 206 kt (381 km/h; 237 mph); initial rate of climb 1,950 ft (594 m) per minute; service ceiling 28,300 ft (8625 m); maximum mission radius 3835 km (2,383 miles)
**Weights:** empty 27892 kg (61,491 lb); maximum take-off 61235 kg (135,000 lb)
**Dimensions:** span 30.38 m (99 ft 8 in); length 35.61 m (116 ft 10 in); height 10.27 m (33 ft 8.5 in); wing area 120.77 m² (1,300.0 sq ft)
**Armament:** one 907-kg (2,000-lb) or three 454-kg (1,000-lb) mines, or eight depth bombs, or torpedoes, or combinations of these weapons in the lower-fuselage weapons bay, plus up to 7257 kg (16,000 lb) of mines, torpedoes, rockets or AGM-84 Harpoon anti-ship missiles on the 10 underwing stations, and 87 sonobuoys launched from tubes in the lower fuselage

*This Royal Australian Air Force P-3C belongs to No.10 Squadron, based at Edinburgh. Australia's neighbour, New Zealand, operates the earlier P-3B.*

# Lockheed EP-3 Orion

For weapons to be applied most effectively, knowledge of the potential opposition is essential. Nowhere is this more true than in the area of electronics. Modern navies (especially) depend upon a wide range of communications and identification systems in order to function. It therefore follows that detailed information about the characteristics of radars and radios is necessary if they are to be avoided or, better still, neutralized. For this reason, the major navies have long employed a range of electronic intelligence (Elint) vehicles, including aircraft. The US Navy had used the Lockheed EC-121 version of the Constellation airliner, but by the mid-1960s these aircraft were becoming outdated.

Initially the US Navy converted one P-3A to **Lockheed EP-3A Orion** configuration for use by the Naval Air Test Center (NATC), the Naval Weapons Laboratory (NWL) and later Air Test & Evaluation Squadron One (VX-1) at NAS Patuxent River. The aircraft was fitted with additional radomes and used to test a range of electronic surveillance equipment. The magnetic anomaly detector (MAD) boom on the tail was deleted. In 1969 two P-3Bs were converted into **EP-3B** aircraft for use by VQ-1: both were subsequently updated to **EP-3E** standard, but were maintained by the same squadron. Between 1971 and 1975, 10 more powerful **EP-3E 'Aries II'** aircraft entered service with the two operational fleet air reconnaissance countermea-

sures squadrons, VQ-1 and VQ-2, which are assigned the task of giving 'signal warfare support' to various units, particularly to the large aircraft carriers. VQ-1 operates out of NAS Agana on Guam and VQ-2 covers the Mediterranean and Eastern Atlantic from its base at NAS Rota in Spain.

The EP-3E is a modification of the basic patrol P-3A with the anti-submarine warfare equipment replaced by electronic equipment for analysing radar signals The new electronics installed within the EP-3E include the ALQ-110 signals-gathering system from United Technology Laboratory, the ALD-8 radio direction finder from E-Systems, the ALR-52 automatic frequency-measuring receiver from ARGO-Systems, and the ALR-60 from GTE-Sylvania for the multiple recording of radio communications. Externally, the main features which distinguish the EP-3E from the conventional P-3 is a flat, circular radome under the forward fuselage and two oblong black antennae domes on top of and underneath the fuselage. The work of these aircraft involves collecting, storing and analysing signals emitted by radar or radio: major surface vessels employ dozens of separate systems and if the signals are successfully analysed, it is possible to identify the installations, their purpose and range. To make the task of the squadrons as difficult as possible, the Soviet (now Russian) navy frequently alters the radiation patterns of its ships.

## Specification: Lockheed EP-3 Orion
**Origin:** USA
**Type:** Elint platform
**Powerplant:** four 3661-ekW(4,910-eshp) Allison T56-A-15 turboprops
**Performance:** maximum speed 380 kt (703 km/h; 437 mph) at 15,000 ft (4570 m); patrol speed 180 kt (333 km/h; 207 mph); initial rate of climb 2,175 ft (663 m) per minute; service ceiling 28,000 ft (8535m); maximum mission radius 4075 km (2,532 miles)
**Weights:** maximum take-off 64410 kg (142,000 lb)
**Dimensions:** span 30.38 m (99 ft 8 in); length 35.61 m (116 ft 10 in); height 10.27 m (33 ft 8.5 in); wing area 120.77 m² (1,300.0 sq ft)
**Armament:** none

*Lockheed EP-3E Orion of VQ-1, US Navy, based at NAS Agana, Guam.*

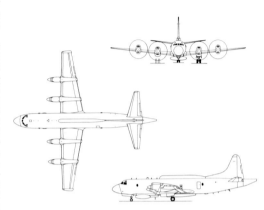

*Lockheed EP-3E Orion*

*This EP-3A is one of those used by the Pacific Missile Test Center, based at Point Mugu, California, for miscellaneous missile tracking and calibration duties.*

*Squatting down on its nosewheel, this EP-3E of VQ-2 winds up to full power before taking off from RAF Wyton, an occasional port of call for this Rota-based Elint unit.*

| | |
|---|---|
| **Role** | |
| Fighter | |
| Close support | |
| Counter-insurgency | |
| Tactical strike | |
| Strategic bomber | |
| Tactical reconnaissance | |
| Strategic reconnaissance | |
| Maritime patrol | |
| Anti-ship strike | |
| Anti-submarine warfare | |
| Search and rescue | |
| Assault transport | |
| Transport | |
| Liaison | |
| Trainer | |
| Inflight-refuelling tanker | |
| Specialized | |
| **Performance** | |
| All-weather capability | |
| Rough field capability | |
| STOL capability | |
| VTOL capability | |
| Airspeed 0-250 mph | |
| Airspeed 250 mph-Mach 1 | |
| Airspeed Mach 1 plus | |
| Ceiling 0-20,000 ft | |
| Ceiling 20,000-40,000 ft | |
| Ceiling 40,000ft plus | |
| Range 0-1,000 miles | |
| Range 1,000-3,000 miles | |
| Range 3,000 miles plus | |
| **Weapons** | |
| Air-to-air missiles | |
| Air-to-surface missiles | |
| Cruise missiles | |
| Cannon | |
| Trainable guns | |
| Naval weapons | |
| Nuclear-capable | |
| Rockets | |
| 'Smart' weapon kit | |
| Weapon load 0-4,000 lb | |
| Weapon load 4,000-15,000 lb | |
| Weapon load 15,000 lb plus | |
| **Avionics** | |
| Electronic Counter Measures | |
| Electronic Support Measures | |
| Search radar | |
| Fire control radar | |
| Look-down/shoot-down | |
| Terrain-following radar | |
| Forward-looking infra-red | |
| Laser | |
| Television | |

# Lockheed Orion AEW & C

*Lockheed Orion AEW & C prototype.*

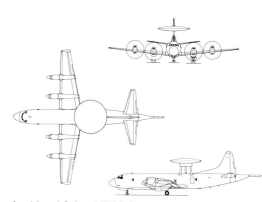

**Lockheed Orion AEW & C**

*The Lockheed Orion AEW & C prototype was converted from an ex-Australian P-3B airframe, and was displayed, albeit without its radar fitted, at the 1985 Paris Air Salon.*

*At one time, the Orion AEW & C was a contender for the RAF's requirement for an AEW aircraft to replace its ageing Shackletons, in the face of serious problems with the Nimrod AEW.Mk 3.*

**Role**
Fighter
Close support
Counter-insurgency
Tactical strike
Strategic bomber
Tactical reconnaissance
Strategic reconnaissance
Maritime patrol
Anti-ship strike
Anti-submarine warfare
Search and rescue
Assault transport
Transport
Liaison
Trainer
Inflight-refuelling tanker
Specialized

**Performance**
All-weather capability
Rough field capability
STOL capability
VTOL capability
Airspeed 0-250 mph
Airspeed 250 mph-Mach 1
Airspeed Mach 1 plus
Ceiling 0-20,000 ft
Ceiling 20,000-40,000 ft
Ceiling 40,000ft plus
Range 0-1,000 miles
Range 1,000-3,000 miles
Range 3,000 miles plus

**Weapons**
Air-to-air missiles
Air-to-surface missiles
Cruise missiles
Cannon
Trainable guns
Naval weapons
Nuclear-capable
Rockets
'Smart' weapon kit
Weapon load 0-4,000 lb
Weapon load 4,000-15,000 lb
Weapon load 15,000 lb plus

**Avionics**
Electronic Counter Measures
Electronic Support Measures
Search radar
Fire control radar
Look-down/shoot-down
Terrain-following radar
Forward-looking infra-red
Laser
Television

By the early 1960s air-defence equipment had so improved that the high-flying attack aircraft was no longer safe. Air forces then turned their attention to low-flying penetration, which delayed detection to the last minute. This new threat then had to be countered and the response was the development of specialized aircraft of the flying radar picket type long used by navies. The size of the radars involved had grown to such an extent that in 1957 Grumman tested the first aerodynamic prototype of the E-1B Tracer with a remarkable 9.14 m (30 ft) by 6.10 m (20 ft) 'rotodome' mounted above the fuselage. Other types featuring rotodomes followed, and as radar technology improved the ability to control air defence fighters and other aircraft added to the radar picket's role.

Although many air forces have a requirement for an airborne warning (and ideally control) aircraft, they are needed in relatively small numbers. Aircraft as complex and specialized as the Boeing E-3A Sentry and Ilyushin A-50 'Mainstay' are beyond the pockets (and indeed requirements) of all but a few, so in recent years manufacturers have looked at the possibility of adapting existing types. The attraction to potential purchasers is the wider availability of spares and, if the basic type is already operated, economy of spares stockholdings. A further attraction to air forces operating the original design is the much reduced costs of training. Lockheed has suggested two developments, of the C-130 Hercules and the P-3 Orion, both of which have obvious attraction. The **Lockheed P-3 AEW & C** flew in aerodynamic prototype form from the company's Palmdale works on 14 June 1984. Rebuilt from an ex-RAAF P-3B, the aircraft featured a 7.32-m (24-ft) diameter Randtron APA-171 rotodome above the rear fuselage. Testing of the complete system, with the General Electric APS-138/139 radar (as on the Grumman E-2C Hawkeye) and MIL-1553A communications and data handling system, began in 1988.

Although it uses the same radar as the smaller E-2C Hawkeye, the Orion AEW & C is a very much more capable aircraft, with greater endurance and range capabilities and with a larger cabin, which allows a larger number of operators and flight crew to be carried. Two operating crews can be put aboard, dramatically extending sortie endurance.

The same equipment has been proposed for an AEW & C variant of the C-130 Hercules, and this aircraft would offer similar advantages over the smaller Grumman aircraft. Both the Hercules and the Orion are in widespread service over the world.

Lockheed claims a 14-hour endurance for the Orion AEW & C, extendible with inflight refuelling. Several countries have expressed interest, but so far the only customer has been the US Coast Guard, which in 1987 ordered one aircraft and took options on another three. The four aircraft were delivered between June 1988 and 1993, and operate within the USCG's element of the USA war on drug smuggling.

**Specification:** Lockheed Orion AEW & C
**Origin:** USA
**Type:** airborne early warning and control platform
**Powerplant:** four 3661-ekW (4,910-eshp) Allison T56-A-14 turboprops
**Performance:** cruising speed 200 kt (370 km/h; 230 mph) at 30,000 ft (9145 m); endurance 14 hours
**Weights:** maximum take-off 57833 kg (127,500 lb)
**Dimensions:** span 30.38 m (99 ft 8 in); length 35.61 m (116 ft 10 in); height 10.27 m (33 ft 8.5in); wing area 120.77 m² (1,300.0 sq ft)
**Armament:** none

# Lockheed S-3 Viking

*Lockheed S-3A Viking of VS-38 'Red Griffins', US Navy.*

The growing capability of the submarines in service with the Soviet navy in the 1960s, plus certain domestic factors, highlighted to the US Navy a need for an advanced carrier-borne ASW aircraft. In late 1966 procurement for this VSX requirement began, with Lockheed gaining in August 1969 an initial contract for development of such an aircraft under the designation **Lockheed S-3**, later named **Viking**.

Lockheed made great efforts to ensure that its design submission, and ultimately the production aircraft, would give the US Navy the aircraft it needed, the company teaming with LTV (Ling-Temco-Vought) to benefit from the latter's experience in carrierborne aircraft, and with Univac Federal Systems for its skills in ASW systems. LTV designed and built the engine pods, landing gear, tail unit and wing; Univac produced the complete ASW system; and Lockheed built the fuselage, integrated the systems and carried out final assembly and test. The first of eight YS-3A pre-production aircraft made the type's maiden flight on 21 January 1972 and the first batch of **S-3A** production aircraft was authorized in April 1972. Just under two years later, on 20 February 1974,

the S-3A entered service with training squadron VS-41 at NAS North Island, San Diego. VS-21, also based at NAS North Island, was the first operational unit and in July 1975 took the S-3A for its first carrier deployment aboard the USS John F Kennedy. When production ended in mid-1978, a total of 187 S-3As had been built.

In early 1980 demonstration examples of a Carrier Onboard Delivery (COD) **US-3A** and a tanker **KS-3A** were evaluated by the Navy but failed to gain orders, although three of the YS-3As and one-off KS-3A were later converted to US-3A configuration. Also in 1980, Lockheed was awarded a WSIP (Weapon System Improvement Program) contract to give the S-3As expanded ASW capability. This introduced a new generation of avionics and provisions to carry the Harpoon anti-ship missile. The first two WSIP conversions, designated **S-3B**, began service trials in 1985 and proved so successful that the US Navy is having large numbers of S-3As modified to this standard in an ongoing programme. Another 16 S-3As have been modified to **ES-3A** standard as replacement for the Douglas EA-3B in the Elint and ECM roles.

**Lockheed S-3A Viking**

**Seen on the flightdeck of USS America is this S-3A Viking of VS-32 'Norsemen', home-based at NAS Cecil Field, Florida, but here forming a component of CVW-1 (Carrier Air Wing One).**

**This VS-29 S-3A is landing on USS Kitty Hawk. VS-29, the 'Vikings', is a Pacific Fleet anti-submarine warfare unit and is home-based at NAS North Island, California.**

## Specification: Lockheed S-3A Viking

**Origin:** USA
**Type:** carrierborne ASW aircraft
**Powerplant:** two 4207-kg (9,275-lb) dry thrust General Electric TF34-2 turbofans
**Performance:** maximum speed 450 kt (834 km/h; 518 mph) at 25,000 ft (7620 m); patrol speed 160 kt (296 km/h; 184 mph); initial rate of climb 4,200 ft (1280 m) per minute; service ceiling 35,000 ft (10670 m); combat range more than 3701 km (2,300 miles)
**Weights:** empty 12088 kg (26,650 lb); maximum take-off 23831 kg (52,539 lb)
**Dimensions:** span 20.93 m (68 ft 8 in); length 16.26 m (53 ft 4 in); height 6.93 m (22 ft 9 in); wing area 55.55 m² (598.0 sq ft)
**Armament:** internal weapons bay for bombs, depth bombs, destructors, mines or torpedoes up to a weight of 1814 kg (4,000 lb), plus two underwing pylons suitable for auxiliary fuel tanks, cluster bombs, flare launchers or rocket pods up to a weight of 1361 kg (3,000 lb)

### Role

Fighter
Close support
Counter-insurgency
Tactical strike
Strategic bomber
Strategic reconnaissance
Tactical reconnaissance
Maritime patrol
Anti-ship strike
Anti-submarine warfare
Search and rescue
Assault transport
Transport
Liaison
Trainer
Inflight-refuelling tanker
Specialized

### Performance

All-weather capability
Rough field capability
STOL capability
VTOL capability
Airspeed 0-250 mph
Airspeed 250 mph-Mach 1
Airspeed Mach 1 plus
Ceiling 0-20,000 ft
Ceiling 20,000-40,000 ft
Ceiling 40,000ft plus
Range 0-1,000 miles
Range 1,000-3,000 miles
Range 3,000 miles plus

### Weapons

Air-to-air missiles
Air-to-surface missiles
Cruise missiles
Cannon
Trainable guns
Naval-capable
Nuclear-capable
Rockets
'Smart' weapon kit
Weapon load 0-4,000 lb
Weapon load 4,000-15,000 lb
Weapon load 15,000 lb plus

### Avionics

Electronic Counter Measures
Electronic Support Measures
Search radar
Fire control radar
Look-down/shoot-down
Terrain-following radar
Forward-looking infra-red
Laser
Television

# Lockheed SR-71

*Lockheed SR-71A of the 9th SRW, US Air Force, based at Beale AFB, California.*

Development of the Lockheed SR-71 was shrouded in secrecy, and much 'information' about this remarkable type is based on assumption and analysis rather than on direct fact. The SR-71 came into service as a result of a decision by the Central Intelligence Agency to acquire an aircraft with both a higher service ceiling and a greater maximum speed than the Lockheed U-2. The new aircraft was to carry out clandestine reconnaissance over the USSR and other sensitive territory, and a contract was awarded to Lockheed in August 1959.

Because of the specific nature of the aircraft's requirements, including a maximum speed of Mach 3 and a ceiling of 85,000 ft (25910 m), unprecedented problems were encountered during design and construction These problems emanated from the need to employ refined aerodynamics and structural materials to withstand the inevitable high temperatures. The airframe had to be constructed from titanium, and engineering problems arose with the propulsion and hydraulic systems, which were also constructed on the basis of new materials and techniques. As long range was also required at the high cruise speed, the aircraft has a highly swept delta wing with a camber on the leading edge for low induced drag.

It is believed that approximately 15 aircraft based on the design and designated **A-12** were delivered to the CIA from 1962: these were single-seaters, although one was mod-ified as a trainer and two had an additional seat for a launch officer for the D-21 drone programme. A further three research proto-types (designated YF-12A) were built as two-seat interceptors in 1963, with Hughes ASG-18 radar. The A-12s, currently in store at Palmdale, were employed by the USAF for the CIA until the **Lockheed SR-71** (originally RS-71) came into service from 1964. The SR-71 has a more efficient airframe, greater fuel capacity and a more complex reconnaissance system, but is not fitted with a missile bay.

The first SR-71s were delivered in 1966 to the 4200th SRW, a new unit based at Beale AFB in California, where the special Boeing KC-135Q tankers of the 100th ARW (required for inflight-refuelling with the spe-cial JP-7 fuel) were also based. Of the initial batch of 29, two were designated **SR-71B** and fitted with dual pilot controls for use as trainer aircraft; another trainer was produced by converting one YF-12A into an **SR-71C**, and one of the 27 **SR-71A** aircraft was redesignated YF-12C for NASA research pur-poses. In June 1966 the 4200th was renum-bered the 9th SRW and the SR-71s were assigned to the 1st SRS: detachments flew regularly from RAF Mildenhall in the UK and Kadena AB in Okinawa. The 'Blackbird' was retired in the early 1990s, but the current shortfall in the USAF's reconnaissance capa-bility resulted in the decision to bring at least three of the stored aircraft back into the active inventory.

## Specification: Lockheed SR-71A
**Origin:** USA
**Type:** strategic reconnaissance aircraft
**Powerplant:** two 14742-kg (32,500-lb) afterburning thrust Pratt & Whitney JT11D-20B (J58) bleed-turbojets
**Performance:** maximum speed more than Mach 3 or 1,737 kt (3219 km/h; 2,000 mph) at 80,000 ft (24385m); ceiling more than 80,000 ft (24385m); unrefuelled range 4800 km (2,983 miles) at maximum speed
**Weights:** empty27216 kg (60,000 lb); maximum take-off 77111 kg (170,000 lb)
**Dimensions:** span 16.94 m (55 ft 7 in); length 32.74 m (107 ft 5 in); height 5.64m (18 ft 6 in); wing area 167.22 m² (1,800.0 sq ft)
**Armament:** none

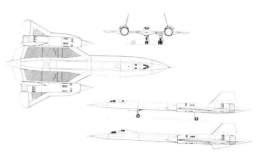

*Lockheed SR-71A (lower side view: SR-71B)*

**There have been three twin-stick SR-71s. Two were purpose-built SR-71Bs, and one SR-71C 'The Bastard' was converted from a YF-12A when one of the original trainers was written off.**

*SR-71 'Blackbirds ' flew from two permanent forward-operating bases, with Detachment One 9th SRW at Kadena AB, Okinawa, and Detachment Four at RAF Mildenhall, Suffolk. KC-135Q tankers were co-deployed.*

# Lockheed/Boeing F-22 Rapier

*The F119-powered second prototype YF-22A, wearing the civilian registration applied for the second phase of its flight trials.*

In April 1991 the US Air Force announced that it had selected the Pratt & Whitney-powered version of the **Lockheed/Boeing F-22** in preference to the rival Northrop/McDonnell Douglas F-23 design to meet its exacting ATF (Advanced Tactical Fighter) requirement for a successor to the McDonnell Douglas F-15 Eagle. Issued in 1981, the ATF requirement called for a fighter combining low-observability or 'stealthy' design, the ability to cruise over long ranges at supersonic speed without afterburning, a very high level of aerial agility and STOL capability with the aid of a two-dimensional thrust vectoring system, a fly-by-light control system (developed by Lear Astronics) for a relaxed-stability airframe, and an advanced nav/attack system using artificial intelligence to filter data and so reduce the pilot's workload while improving his grasp of the tactical situation.

Two prototypes of each twin-engined design were ordered, each powered by examples of the two competing engine designs, namely the Pratt & Whitney F119 and General Electric F120 turbofans. The

first YF-22A prototype flew in September 1990 with YF120 engines and was followed in October 1991 by the second machine with YF119 engines, and revealed the ability to cruise at Mach 1.58 without afterburning and to attain Mach 1.7 with afterburning at 30,000 ft (9145 m).

Key features of the design are an angular but clean external shape with jagged edges on any portion that could reflect electromagnetic energy back toward a hostile radar, three internal weapon bays in place of external hardpoints, and an avionics suite integrated by TRW Inc. on the basis of a VHSIC computer system (operating on the artificial intelligence principles of the Pilot's Associate system) offering three times the memory and 16 times the operating speed of the F-15's system.

The **F-22A Rapier** is due to enter service in the late 1990s, and has a number of alterations from the YF-22A standard including a wing of greater span and a shorter fuselage. The **F-22B Rapier** is the combat-capable two-seat conversion and continuation trainer derivative of the F-22A.

**Lockheed YF-22A Rapier**

*The Pratt and Whitney YF-119-powered second prototype YF-22 crashed at Edwards AFB in 1992, leading to a halt in the flight test programme until the first pre-production F-22 flies in 1996. The first prototype, with its unrepresentative General Electric YF-120 engines, had already been grounded.*

*In order to reduce radar cross section as much as possible, the YF-22 carries its weaponload internally, in missile bays in the intake ducts and lower fuselage.*

## Specification: Lockheed/Boeing F-22A Rapier
**Origin:** USA
**Type:** advanced tactical fighter
**Powerplant:** two 15876-kg (35,000-lb) afterburning thrust Pratt & Whitney F119-P-100 turbofans
**Performance:** not revealed
**Weights:** maximum take-off 27216 kg (60,000 lb)
**Dimensions:** span 13.56 m (44 ft 6 in); length 18.92 m (62 ft 1 in); height 5.00 m (16 ft 5 in); wing area 78.0 m² (840.0 sq ft)
**Armament:** one 20-mm M61A1 Vulcan six-barrel cannon; an unrevealed maximum weight of disposable stores carried in two lateral weapon bays and one lower-fuselage weapon bay; the lateral bays are designed to accommodate short-range AAMs such as the AIM-9 Sidewinder, while the larger lower-fuselage bay is intended for the carriage of medium-range weapons such as the AIM-120 AMRAAM AAM; other weapons projected for the F-22 include the 'Have Sash 2' AAM and 'Have Slick' ASM currently under development

**Role**
Fighter
Close support
Counter-insurgency
Tactical strike
Strategic bomber
Tactical reconnaissance
Strategic reconnaissance
Maritime patrol
Anti-ship strike
Anti-submarine warfare
Search and rescue
Assault transport
Transport
Liaison
Trainer
Inflight-refuelling tanker
Specialized

**Performance**
All-weather capability
Rough field capability
STOL capability
VTOL capability
Airspeed 0-250 mph
Airspeed 250 mph-Mach 1
Airspeed Mach 1 plus
Ceiling 0-20,000 ft
Ceiling 20,000-40,000 ft
Ceiling 40,000ft plus
Range 0-1,000 miles
Range 1,000-3,000 miles
Range 3,000 miles plus

**Weapons**
Air-to-air missiles
Air-to-surface missiles
Cruise missiles
Cannon
Trainable guns
Naval weapons
Nuclear-capable
Rockets
'Smart' weapon kit
Weapon load 0-4,000 lb
Weapon load 4,000-15,000 lb
Weapon load 15,000 lb plus

**Avionics**
Electronic Counter Measures
Electronic Support Measures
Search radar
Fire control radar
Look-down/shoot-down
Terrain-following radar
Forward-looking infra-red
Laser
Television

# Lockheed T-33

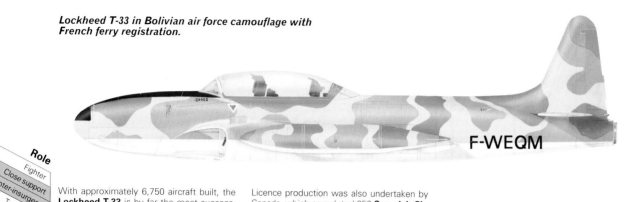

*Lockheed T-33 in Bolivian air force camouflage with French ferry registration.*

With approximately 6,750 aircraft built, the **Lockheed T-33** is by far the most successful jet trainer yet developed for service anywhere in the world, and it says much for the durability of the 'Tee-bird' that many of the aircraft remain airworthy around the world today, more than 40 years after the type first flew.

A logical development of the single-seat F-80 (the first jet-powered fighter to become operational with the US Army Air Forces) the T-33A has a lineage made evident by the fact that it actually began life in the late 1940s as the **TF-80C**, being quite simply a stretched tandem two-seater trainer version of the F-80.

Following introduction to service with the US Air Force in the closing stages of the 1940s, the **T-33A** or 'Tee bird' was soon being built in numbers that far outstripped those of the F-80, and it ultimately became the USAF's standard jet trainer type, equipping flying schools at many US air bases for several years in the 1950s. Just under 700 examples of the T-33A were also diverted to the US Navy, by which it initially became known as the **TO-2** although it was soon redesignated **TV-2** (**T-33B** from late 1962).

In addition to being extensively used by the USAF and US Navy, the T-33A also found a ready market overseas, many of the aircraft built being supplied to friendly nations under the Military Assistance Program. Countries which acquired the T-33A in this way included France, Greece, Italy, the Philippines, Portugal, Spain, Taiwan, Thailand, Turkey and West Germany.

Licence production was also undertaken by Canada, which completed 656 **Canadair CL-30 Silver Star** aircraft, and by Japan, which assembled 210, more than 100 of them still engaged in training duties today

Although viewed basically as a trainer. Lockheed's jet has performed other roles, a modest number of aircraft being fitted with a camera nose and electronic equipment in the aft cockpit in order to perform reconnaissance functions. Designated **RT-33A**, these single-seaters were produced mainly for MAP, operators including France, Italy, the Netherlands, Pakistan, Thailand and Turkey. A version armed for interdiction and close support was the **AT-33A**, of which small numbers are still in service.

Another important role was that of target drone, the US Navy being perhaps the major operator and destroyer of drone-configured 'Tee-birds'. Painted in a garish overall scarlet colour scheme, and often controlled by a **DT-33** director, the **QT-33** took part in numerous weapons test projects, most of the converted aircraft meeting a fiery end over the range areas of the Pacific Missile Test Center and the Naval Weapons Center at Point Mugu and China Lake respectively

More recently a company known as the Skyfox Corporation proposed remanufacturing the T-33A as a twin-turbofan advanced trainer employing externally mounted Garrett TFE731 engines. Extensive redesign of the fuselage and empennage formed part of the modernization process, but so far no orders have been placed for the resulting Skyfox.

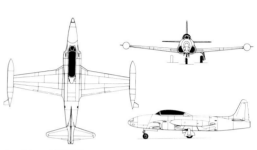

*Lockheed T-33A*

*Several Latin American air arms still use the Lockheed T-33, this one is seen in the markings of the Colombian air force.*

## Specification: Lockheed T-33A
**Origin:** USA
**Type:** two-seat jet trainer
**Powerplant:** one 2449-kg (5,400-lb) dry thrust Allison J33-A-35 turbojet
**Performance:** maximum speed 521 kt (966 km/h; 600 mph) at sea level and 474 kt (879 km/h; 546 mph) at 25,000 ft (7620 m); initial rate of climb 4,870 ft (1484 m) per minute; service ceiling 48,000 ft (14630 m); endurance 3 hours 7 minutes
**Weights:** empty 3667 kg (8,0841b); maximum take-off 6551 kg (14,442 lb)
**Dimensions:** span 11.85 m (38 ft 10.5 in); length 11.51 m (37 ft 9 in); height 3.56 m (11 ft 8 in); wing area 21.81 m² (234.8 sq ft)
**Armament:** none

*This is one of five Canadair CT-133 Silver Stars operated by the 1st Canadian Air Group Target Towing Flight. They are also used for instrument flying training and general liaison flying.*

### Role
Fighter
Close support
Counter-insurgency
Tactical strike
Strategic bomber
Tactical reconnaissance
Strategic reconnaissance
Maritime patrol
Anti-ship strike
Anti-submarine warfare
Search and rescue
Assault transport
Transport
Liaison
Trainer
Inflight-refuelling tanker
Specialized

### Performance
All-weather capability
Rough field capability
STOL capability
VTOL capability
Airspeed 0-250 mph
Airspeed 250 mph-Mach 1
Airspeed Mach 1 plus
Ceiling 0-20,000 ft
Ceiling 20,000-40,000 ft
Ceiling 40,000ft plus
Range 0-1,000 miles
Range 1,000-3,000 miles
Range 3,000 miles plus

### Weapons
Air-to-air missiles
Air-to-surface missiles
Cruise missiles
Cannon
Trainable guns
Naval weapons
Nuclear-capable
Rockets
'Smart' weapon kit
Weapon load 0-4,000 lb
Weapon load 4,000-15,000 lb
Weapon load 15,000 lb plus

### Avionics
Electronic Counter Measures
Electronic Support Measures
Search radar
Fire control radar
Look-down/shoot-down
Terrain-following radar
Forward-looking infra-red
Laser
Television

# Lockheed TR-1

*Lockheed **TR-1A** of the 95th **RS**, 17th **RW**, US Air Force, based at **RAF Alconbury, UK**.*

The **Lockheed U-2** was conceived in response to a call from the US Air Force and Central Intelligence Agency for an aircraft capable of cruising at very high altitudes with advanced optical reconnaissance equipment. Introduced in 1956, the U-2 is essentially a jet-powered glider and fulfilled its role adequately for several years. But by the mid-1960s many had been lost, primarily as a result of the type's notably poor handling characteristics. In August 1966, therefore, the USAF contracted with Lockheed for a more advanced **U-2R** with increased range, improved flying qualities and greater payload. The U-2R was a complete redesign, correcting the original poor engine/airframe match and allowing for greater sensor payload. Handling at low altitude was particularly improved, and in the U-2R the J75-P-13B and the wing aerofoil section were the only features shared with the earlier design. After the first flight on 28 August 1967, six aircraft went to the CIA, the balance going to the 349th SRS, 100th SRW by late 1968.

In 1978 the USAF announced a new tactical reconnaissance programme, and in 1979 the U-2 line reopened for production. On 11 May 1981, the first aircraft took to the air. This was the **ER-2**, a demilitarized version for NASA Ames, and was used for earth resources and other high altitude research.

On 1 August 1981 there followed the first of 32 single-seat operational aircraft (seven U-2R and 25 **TR-1A** machines) and three two-seat trainers (one **U-2RT** and two **TR-1B** machines) for the USAF.

In physical terms, the TR-1A differs only in secondary systems from the original U-2R, and also in its primary role. Battlefield surveillance is undertaken with high-resolution radars such as the Hughes ASARS-2 (Advanced Synthetic Aperture Radar System type 2), which allows the TR-1A to patrol for many hours behind friendly lines, the radar searching for enemy tank concentrations and other installations at long oblique ranges. TR-1As retain the strategic reconnaissance capability of the U-2R, and are sometimes seen with large 'farms' of Comint and Elint gathering antennae or windows for optical sensors. After initial technical problems, the Precision Location Strike System was developed for use with the TR-1A for the location of hostile radar emitters.

In December 1991 the USAF decided to redesignate the TR-1 family in the U-2 series, the TR-1A and TR-1B becoming the U-2R and U-2RT respectively. Further development of the series is centred on a programme to re-engine the aircraft with the General Electric F118 turbofan for increased thrust, greater reliability and reduced fuel consumption.

**Specification:** Lockheed TR-1A
**Origin:** USA
**Type:** single-seat high-altitude reconnaissance aircraft
**Powerplant:** one 7711-kg (17,000-lb) dry thrust Pratt & Whitney J75-P-13B turbojet
**Performance:** maximum cruising speed 373 kt (692 km/h; 430 mph) at more than 70,000 ft (21335 m); initial climb rate about 5,000 ft (1524 m) per minute; operational ceiling 90,000 ft (27430 m); maximum range 10050 km (6,250 miles)
**Weights:** empty 7031 kg (15,500 lb); maximum take-off 18733 kg (41,300 lb)
**Dimensions:** span 31.39 m (103 ft 0 in); length 19.13 m (62 ft 9 in); height 4.88 m (16 ft 0 in); wing area 92.9 m² (1,000.0 sq ft)
**Armament:** none

*Lockheed **TR-1A** (upper side view: **TR-1B**)*

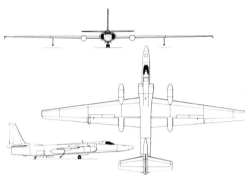

*This underside view of a **TR-1A** shows to advantage its long, slender wings and huge 'superpods' containing mission equipment, as well as the sinister matt-black colour scheme.*

*This 17th **RW** (now absorbed into the 9th **SRW**) aircraft has clearly been operating at high altitude, since ice is still visible under its wings as it comes in to land at **RAF Alconbury**. TR-1s have flown from this base since February 1983.*

**Role**

Fighter
Close support
Counter-insurgency
Tactical strike
Strategic bomber
Tactical reconnaissance
Strategic reconnaissance
Maritime patrol
Anti-ship strike
Anti-submarine warfare
Search and rescue
Assault transport
Transport
Liaison
Trainer
Inflight-refuelling tanker
Specialized

**Performance**

All-weather capability
Rough field capability
STOL capability
VTOL capability
Airspeed 0-250 mph
Airspeed 250 mph-Mach 1
Airspeed Mach 1 plus
Ceiling 0-20,000 ft
Ceiling 20,000-40,000 ft
Ceiling 40,000ft plus
Range 0-1,000 miles
Range 1,000-3,000 miles
Range 3,000 miles plus

**Weapons**

Air-to-air missiles
Air-to-surface missiles
Cruise missiles
Cannon
Trainable guns
Naval weapons
Nuclear-capable
Rockets
'Smart' weapon kit
Weapon load 0-4,000 lb
Weapon load 4,000-15,000 lb
Weapon load 15,000 lb plus

**Avionics**

Electronic Counter Measures
Electronic Support Measures
Search radar
Fire control radar
Look-down/shoot-down
Terrain-following radar
Forward-looking infra-red
Laser
Television

# McDonnell Douglas A-4 Skyhawk

*McDonnell Douglas A-4C Skyhawk of Grupo 4, Argentine air force.*

## Role
Fighter
Close support
Counter-insurgency
Tactical strike
Strategic bomber
Tactical reconnaissance
Strategic reconnaissance
Maritime patrol
Anti-ship strike
Anti-submarine warfare
Search and rescue
Assault transport
Transport
Liaison
Trainer
Inflight-refuelling tanker
Specialized

## Performance
All-weather capability
Rough field capability
STOL capability
VTOL capability
Airspeed 0-250 mph
Airspeed 250 mph-Mach 1
Airspeed Mach 1 plus
Ceiling 0-20,000 ft
Ceiling 20,000-40,000 ft
Ceiling 40,000ft plus
Range 0-1,000 miles
Range 1,000-3,000 miles
Range 3,000 miles plus

## Weapons
Air-to-air missiles
Air-to-surface missiles
Cruise missiles
Cannon
Trainable guns
Naval weapons
Nuclear-capable
Rockets
'Smart' weapon kit
Weapon load 0-4,000 lb
Weapon load 4,000-15,000 lb
Weapon load 15,000 lb plus

## Avionics
Electronic Counter Measures
Electronic Support Measures
Search radar
Fire control radar
Look-down/shoot-down
Terrain-following radar
Forward-looking infra-red
Laser
Television

A classic aeroplane by any criterion, the relatively small, compact and lightweight **Douglas A-4 Skyhawk** single-seat naval attack bomber remained in first-line US Navy and US Marine Corps service from 1956 to the late 1980s and is still an important type in the two services' training schemes. What may be termed the first generation of Skyhawks included those versions based on variants up to and including the A-4F. Of low-set delta wing planform, the Skyhawk first flew in XA4D-1 prototype form on 22 June 1954 with a Wright J65 turbojet. Considerable wing strength derived from the use of single-piece tip-to-tip spars machined from solid planks, and an exceptionally low thickness/ chord ratio gave speed well in excess of that possessed by many contemporary fighters yet, with automatic wing slats, variable-incidence tailplane and long-travel nosewheel landing gear, the Skyhawk remained entirely tractable as a carrierborne high-performance aircraft.

After 165 **A4D-1** aircraft had been built, the **A4D-2** (later redesignated **A-4B**) introduced provision for Martin Bullpup air-to-surface missiles, navigation and bombing computer, powered rudder with unique central 'skin' with external stiffeners, and inflight refuelling (both as buddy tanker and receiver); 542 were produced for the USN and USMC. Of these, 66 were rebuilt in the late 1960s as the **A-4P** and **A-4Q** for the Argentine air force and navy respectively,

being much in evidence during the Falkland campaign of 1982, and 40 others were rebuilt as the **A-4S** for the Singapore Air Defence Command with 30-mm guns in place of the US Navy's 20-mm type.

Some 638 **A-4C** limited all-weather/night attack aircraft were delivered from 1959, introducing an improved autopilot, LABS and terrain-avoidance radar, and gave outstanding service during the Vietnam War: none remain in service. Some 499 **A-4E** aircraft were produced in the early and mid-1960s with a zero/90-kt (167-km/h; 104mph) ejector seat, five store pylons and the J52 turbojet, many of these becoming the first of some 300 Skyhawks of various versions delivered to Israel over some 10 years, the majority of which remain in service today. The **A-4F**, of which 147 examples were built, introduced the dorsal avionics hump into the production line, as well as lift dumpers and spoilers, steerable nosewheel, zero-zero seat and extra cockpit armour. Some of these remain in USN service for aggressor training, while export derivatives included 14 **A-4G** aircraft for the Royal Australian Navy and 10 **A-4K** aircraft for the Royal New Zealand Air Force, the latter machines with a braking parachute and very considerably updated with radar and other modern avionics.

The last version in first-line USMC service was the **A-4M Skyhawk II**, of which 162 were delivered with the uprated J52-P-408A engine and enhanced avionics in a larger dorsal hump.

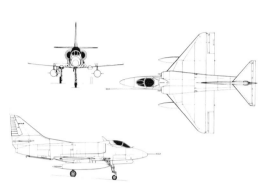

*McDonnell Douglas A-4 Skyhawk*

*The A-4K Skyhawk replaced the Canberra B(I).Mk 12 in RNZAF service and serves with No.75 Squadron at Ohakea. This aircraft carries a full load of bombs and fuel tanks, and a pair of AIM-9Ds.*

## Specification: McDonnell Douglas A-4F Skyhawk
**Origin:** USA
**Type:** carrierborne attack fighter-bomber
**Powerplant:** one 4218-kg (9,300-lb) dry thrust Pratt & Whitney J52-P-8A turbojet
**Performance:** maximum speed 515 kt (954 km/h; 593 mph) at 34,000 ft (10365 m) with a 1814-kg (4,000-lb) bombload; initial rate of climb 5,620 ft (1713 m) per minute; maximum unrefuelled range 3307 km (2,055 miles)
**Weights:** empty 4739 kg (10,448 lb); maximum take-off 12437 kg (27,420 lb)
**Dimensions:** span 8.38 m (27 ft 6 in); length (excluding refuelling probe) 12.27 m (40 ft 3.25 in); height 4.57 m (15 ft 0 in); wing area 24.15 m² (260.0 sq ft)
**Armament:** two 20-mm Mk 12 cannon with 200 rounds per gun; provision for 2268 kg (5,000 lb) of disposable stores, including ASMs, bombs, cluster bombs, dispenser weapons, rocket-launcher pods, cannon pods, drop tanks and ECM pods, carried on five external hardpoints

*The Indonesian air force operated ex-Israeli A-4Es complete with extended IR-suppressing tailpipe and dorsal avionics hump. This aircraft belonged to Skwadron Udara II of No.300 Wing at Maidun.*

# McDonnell Douglas AH-64 Apache

*McDonnell Douglas AH-64A Apache of the US Army.*

Formulated in the early 1970s, the US Army's requirement for an Advanced Attack Helicopter (AAH) visualized a machine that could operate in and fight from a front-line environment, and would be suitable for the day/night/adverse- weather anti-armour role. US manufacturers Bell and Hughes were selected to build competing prototypes as the YAH-64 and YAH-64 respectively, but it was the Hughes submission that on 10 December 1976 was declared winner of the first stage. It was not until 26 March 1982 that final production approval was given with the issue of a US Army contract for an initial batch of 11 **Hughes AH-64A Apache** helicopters. Total planned procurement was 536, a figure which rising costs later cut back to 446, but since then growing confidence in the Apache's capability has brought further revisions and the US Army eventually procured 807 of the type by 1994, built since 1984 by McDonnell after its purchase of Hughes Helicopters.

In formulating its Model 77 design, Hughes began with a fuselage structure to survive fire from weapons up to 23-mm calibre. The fuselage is carried on fixed tail-wheel landing gear, the main units of which fold to reduce height for storage/transport, and has seats in tandem for the co-pilot/gunner and pilot, the latter in a raised seat. There is extensive armour protection, and provision is made for high-impact landings. The main rotor has four wide-chord blades with swept tips, and the blades can be folded or easily removed for transport; the tail rotor is unusual, it four blades being located at an optimum quiet setting of about 55º/125º to each other. The two turboshafts are mounted on the fuselage sides above the removable stub wings that each have two hardpoints. Beneath the fuselage, forward of the mainwheel legs, is a 30-mm McDonnell Douglas M230 Chain Gun. The avionics include the specially developed PNVS and TADS in independent nose-mounted turrets. The Pilot's Night-Vision System incorporates FLIR for night vision, while the Target Acquisition and Designation System combines TV camera, laser tracker and laser ranger/designator. In concert with an inertial attitude/heading reference system, Doppler navigation and other advanced items, these allow the crew to fly nap-of-the-Earth under any and all weather conditions.

The AH-64A proved extremely successful in the 1991 UN-led war with Iraq, and current developments are the **AH-64B** upgrade of 254 AH-64As with target hand-off capability, secure radio, GPS, improved navigation system and new rotor blades, the **AH-64C** upgrade of 308 AH-64As to a standard approximating that of the **AH-64D** with the exception of the Longbow radar, and the AH-64D with uprated T700-GE-701C engines and a MIL-1553B digital databus for integration of a mast-mounted Longbow millimetric-wavelength radar and Hellfire RF missiles.

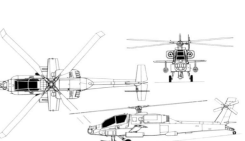

**McDonnell Douglas AH-64A Apache**

*An AH-64A Apache prototype carries clusters of four Rockwell Hellfire anti-tank missiles under each of its stub wings, with rocket pods at the tips. A 30-mm Chain Gun is located under the nose.*

*The AH-64 has entered service in large numbers, but had a troubled gestation, with groundings and restrictions affecting the whole fleet on several occasions.*

**Specification:** McDonnell Douglas AH-64A Apache
**Origin:** USA
**Type:** anti-tank and battlefield support helicopter
**Powerplant:** two 1265-kW (1,696-shp) General Electric T700-GE-701 turboshafts
**Performance:** maximum speed 160 kt (296 km/h; 184mph); initial vertical climb rate 2,500 ft (762 m) per minute; service ceiling 21,000 ft (6400 m); maximum range 483 km (300 miles) with internal fuel
**Weights:** empty 4881 kg (10,760 lb); maximum take-off 9525 kg (21,000 lb)
**Dimensions:** main rotor diameter 14.63 m (48 ft 0 in); length, rotors turning 17.76 m (58 ft 3.1 in); height overall 5.12m (16 ft 9.5 in); main rotor disc area 168.11 m² (1,809.56 sq ft)
**Armament:** one 30-mm M230 Chain Gun with 1,200 rounds, plus four underwing hardpoints for up to 16 Hellfire anti-tank missiles, or 76 2.75-in (70-mm) rockets, or combinations of both weapons

Role

Fighter
Close support
Counter-insurgency
Tactical strike
Strategic bomber
Tactical reconnaissance
Strategic reconnaissance
Maritime patrol
Anti-ship strike
Anti-submarine warfare
Search and rescue
Assault transport
Transport
Liaison
Trainer
Inflight-refuelling tanker
Specialized

Performance

All-weather capability
Rough field capability
STOL capability
VTOL capability
Airspeed 0-250 mph
Airspeed 250 mph-Mach 1
Airspeed Mach 1 plus
Ceiling 0-20,000 ft
Ceiling 20,000-40,000 ft
Ceiling 40,000ft plus
Range 0-1,000 miles
Range 1,000-3,000 miles
Range 3,000 miles plus

Weapons

Air-to-air missiles
Air-to-surface missiles
Cruise missiles
Cannon
Trainable guns
Naval weapons
Nuclear-capable
Rockets
'Smart' weapon kit
Weapon load 0-4,000 lb
Weapon load 4,000-15,000 lb
Weapon load 15,000 lb plus

Avionics

Electronic Counter Measures
Electronic Support Measures
Search radar
Fire control radar
Look-down/shoot-down
Terrain-following radar
Forward-looking infra-red
Laser
Television

171

# McDonnell Douglas C-17 Globemaster III

*McDonnell Douglas C-17A Globemaster III of Air Mobility Command, US Air Force.*

## Role

Fighter
Close support
Counter-insurgency
Tactical strike
Strategic bomber
Tactical reconnaissance
Strategic reconnaissance
Maritime patrol
Anti-ship strike
Anti-submarine warfare
Search and rescue
Assault transport
Transport
Liaison
Trainer
Inflight-refuelling tanker
Specialized

## Performance

All-weather capability
Rough field capability
STOL capability
VTOL capability
Airspeed 0-250 mph
Airspeed 250 mph-Mach 1
Airspeed Mach 1 plus
Ceiling 0-20,000 ft
Ceiling 20,000-40,000 ft
Ceiling 40,000ft plus
Range 0-1,000 miles
Range 1,000-3,000 miles
Range 3,000 miles plus

## Weapons

Air-to-air missiles
Air-to-surface missiles
Cruise missiles
Cannon
Trainable guns
Naval weapons
Nuclear-capable
Rockets
'Smart' weapon kit
Weapon load 0-4,000 lb
Weapon load 4,000-15,000 lb
Weapon load 15,000 lb plus

## Avionics

Electronic Counter Measures
Electronic Support Measures
Search radar
Fire control radar
Look-down/shoot-down
Terrain-following radar
Forward-looking infra-red
Laser
Television

By the end of the 1970s the US Air Force had become acutely aware of the inadequacy of its long-range heavy airlift capability. Various remedies for this situation were examined, and in February 1980 the service issued its CX requirement for a new heavy transport, even though this would by costlier and slower than purchase of an existing type. The requirement demanded an airlifter able to operate in the strategic role yet provide the tactical ability to land close behind the battlefield on semi-prepared or even unprepared airstrips. Boeing, Lockheed and McDonnell Douglas responded, and in August 1981 the McDonnell Douglas design was accepted. The USAF placed a small research and development contract for a type intended to supplement and then supplant the Lockheed C-141B StarLifter from 1987, but impetus was then stripped from the program by the USAF's 1982 decision to procure 50 examples of the Lockheed C-5B Galaxy improved version of the C-5A and 44 (later 60) examples of the McDonnell Douglas KC-10A Extender version of the DC-10-30CF civil transport.

In September 1983 the Airlift Master Plan reinstated the **McDonnell Douglas C-17** as a high-priority programme with design and development to move ahead as rapidly as possible for a planned first flight in August 1990 and production of 210 aircraft. The **C-17A Globemaster III** was designed to what has now become the classical airlifter concept with a large circular-section fuselage accommodating the flightdeck and pressurized hold, tricycle landing gear retracting into external fairings, and high-set flying surfaces.

Various delays pushed construction of the first C-17A back to November 1987, and by the time this machine first took to the air in September 1991, production plans had been trimmed to 120 aircraft. The type became operational in 1994 but has been beset by a number of management and economic problems that may yet result in further curtailment of the procurement total for this highly capable type with the size of the Lockheed C-141 StarLifter, the STOL capability of the Lockheed C-130 Hercules, and the fuselage diameter of the Lockheed C-5 Galaxy for a load that can include 144 troops, or 102 paratroops, or 48 litters and 102 seated casualties plus attendants, or 78108 kg (172,200 lb) of freight.

## Specification: C-17A Globemaster III
**Origin:** USA
**Type:** long-range heavy-lift transport
**Powerplant:** four 18915-kg (41,700-lb) dry thrust Pratt & Whitney F117-P-100 turbofans
**Performance:** maximum cruising speed 447 kt (829 km/h; 515 mph) at 35,000 ft (10670 m); airdrop speed 115-250 kt (213-463 km/h; 132-288 mph) at sea level; service ceiling 45,000 ft (13715 m); ferry range 8710 km (5,412 miles) with maximum fuel and no payload; range 5190 km (3,225 miles) with a payload of 56245 kg (124,000 lb)
**Weights:** empty 122016 kg (269,000 lb); maximum take-off 263083 kg (580,000 lb)
**Dimensions:** span 50.29 m (165 ft 0 in) basic and 52.20 m (171 ft 3 in) between winglet tips; length 53.04 m (174 ft 0 in); height 16.79 m (55 ft 1 in); wing area 353.02 m² (3,800.0 sq ft)
**Armament:** none

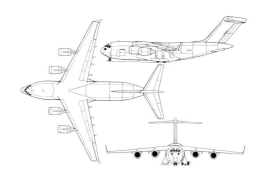

**McDonnell Douglas C-17 Globemaster III**

*The C-17A Globemaster III can deliver heavy and bulky items into primitive, small, forward airfields. As such it serves largely as a C-130 Hercules replacement, although its fuselage diameter rivals that of the giant C-5A Galaxy!*

*Production of the McDonnell Douglas C-17A is now scheduled at 120 aircraft. The type can carry four Sikorsky UH-60 helicopters, or a pair of McDonnell Douglas AH-64 Apaches and three Bell OH-58s.*

# McDonnell Douglas F-4C/D Phantom II

A measure of the advanced operational concept built into the **McDonnell F-4 Phantom II** may be judged from the fact that though production of the USAF's **F-4C** and **F-4D** ended nearly 30 years ago, some of these fighters were still serving in squadrons of the US Air National Guard and with the air forces of Iran, Spain and South Korea in the mid-1980s and still serve with Iran and South Korea in the mid-1990s. Originally adapted from the US Navy's successful F-4B of the early 1960s as an outcome of a current policy for commonality of equipment among the services, the F-4C (635 production examples built) was powered by J79-GE-15 turbojets which bestowed a genuine Mach 2 performance at altitude. The F-4C's equipment fit includes APQ-100 radar, A/A24G central air data computer, ASN-48 inertial navigator, AJB-7 bombing system and ARW-77 missile system. This version saw considerable action in the Vietnam War, being joined by the F-4D in 1967. Like their earlier naval counterparts, these Phantoms carried a normal air combat weapon complement of four AIM-7 Sparrow medium-range AAMs semi-recessed into the fuselage underside and up to four AIM-9 Sidewinder short-range AAMs on underwing pylons in addition to external fuel tanks; for deep penetration sorties extensive use was made of inflight-refuelling.

In the F-4D version, which was more suited to the USAF's own operational roles, a partially solid-state APQ-109 radar giving air-to-ground ranging replaced the F-4C's APQ-100 radar and optical sight, and the ASN-63 replaced the ASN-48 inertial navigator. Despite these changes, Phantom pilots were critical of the lack of inbuilt gun armament (although a ventral gun pod could be carried at the expense of the centreline drop tank), a deficiency not rectified until the appearance of the F-4E. Despite this and other shortcomings (such as the absence of look-down radar), the Phantom proved a formidable opponent over Vietnam.

The replacement of USAF F-4Cs by F-4Es in Europe provided a ready source for supply of 36 to Spain in 1972, these undergoing thorough refurbishing at the CASA plant at Getafe to reappear with the designation **F-4C(S)**. In the late 1960s Iran, then pursuing considerable modernization of its air force with American assistance, acquired 32 ex-USAF F-4Ds and these equipped two squadrons in 1969; most survivors were probably cannibalized to keep later aircraft airworthy after the discontinuation of American support at the end of the 1970s. Eighteen USAF-surplus F-4Ds also equipped a wing of the Republic of Korea Air Force (ROKAF) in 1972, replacing North American F-86s.

**Specification:** McDonnell Douglas F-4C Phantom II
**Origin:** USA
**Type:** two-seat land-based strike/attack fighter
**Powerplant:** two 7711-kg (17,000-lb) afterburning thrust General Electric J79-GE-15 turbojets
**Performance:** maximum speed more than Mach 2 or 1,146 kt (2124 km/h; 1,320 mph) at 40,000 ft (12190 m); service ceiling 61,000 ft (18590 m); unrefuelled combat radius 990 km (615miles)
**Weights:** empty 13245 kg (29,200 lb); maximum take-off 24766 kg (54,600 lb)
**Dimensions:** span 11.71 m (38 ft 5 in); length 17.75 m (58 ft 3 in); height 4.95 m (16 ft 3 in); wing area 49.24 m2 (530.0 sq ft)
**Armament:** basic weapon configuration comprises four AIM-7 Sparrow AAMs semi-recessed under fuselage and up to four AIM-9 Sidewinder AAMs on wing pylons in addition to two drop tanks; 20-mm cannon pod or other stores alternative to AIM-7s, maximum bombload of up to 18 340-kg (750-lb) bombs on multiple carriers under fuselage and wings

*McDonnell Douglas F-4C Phantom II of Ala de Caza 12, Spanish air force.*

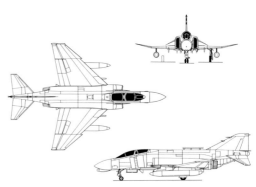

**McDonnell Douglas F-4D Phantom**

*Spain operated the survivors of 40 Phantoms with Escuadrones 121 and 122 from Torrejon, near Madrid. The F-4C was designated C. 12 in Spanish air force service.*

*A small number of F-4Cs remained in service with US Air National Guard Units in the mid-1980s but were then rapidly replaced. This aircraft wears the markings of the 182d TFS, Texas ANG.*

**Role**
Fighter
Close support
Counter-insurgency
Tactical strike
Strategic bomber
Tactical reconnaissance
Strategic reconnaissance
Maritime patrol
Anti-ship strike
Anti-submarine warfare
Search and rescue
Assault transport
Transport
Liaison
Trainer
Inflight-refuelling tanker
Specialized

**Performance**
All-weather capability
Rough field capability
STOL capability
VTOL capability
Airspeed 0-250 mph
Airspeed 250 mph-Mach 1
Airspeed Mach 1 plus
Ceiling 0-20,000 ft
Ceiling 20,000-40,000 ft
Ceiling 40,000ft plus
Range 0-1,000 miles
Range 1,000-3,000 miles
Range 3,000 miles plus

**Weapons**
Air-to-air missiles
Air-to-surface missiles
Cruise missiles
Cannon
Trainable guns
Naval weapons
Nuclear-capable
Rockets
'Smart' weapon kit
Weapon load 0-4,000 lb
Weapon load 4,000-15,000 lb
Weapon load 15,000 lb plus

**Avionics**
Electronic Counter Measures
Electronic Support Measures
Search radar
Fire control radar
Look-down/shoot-down
Terrain-following radar
Forward-looking infra-red
Laser
Television

# McDonnell Douglas F-4E/F Phantom II

Most widely used of all Phantoms has been the **McDonnell Douglas F-4E Phantom II**, of which 1,329 were produced for the USAF, with delivery to squadrons beginning in 1968. The raison d'être of this version had been the APQ-109/CORDS (Coherent On Receive Doppler System), but in the event the CORDS element was cancelled in 1968 and the Westinghouse APQ-120 radar was adopted. With a considerably lengthened nose on which the chin-located IR seeker of earlier F-4s was omitted, the F-4E included an integral 20-mm multi-barrel cannon in a long fairing on the centreline. An additional (seventh) fuel cell was included in the rear fuselage to compensate for centre of gravity movement. Martin-Baker zero-zero ejector seats were also fitted from the outset, and in 1972 (too late to reach operational status over Vietnam) slats were added to the outer wing sections. Avionics updating included the installation in later aircraft of ASX-1 TISEO (Target Identification System, Electro-Optical) and a modified ASG-26 computing sight; a much-enhanced range of weapons became compatible, including the guided bomb family (Mk 84/118 LGB/IR/EO) as well as ALQ-71, -72, -87 and -101 ECM pods.

Numerically, the F-4E continued to dominate the USAF's inventory in all theatres throughout the 1970s despite the arrival in service of the McDonnell Douglas F-15 and the General Dynamics F-16. However, such was the aircraft's unquestioned reputation that a considerable export trade flourished, with the largest number (204) being supplied to Israel, in whose air force the type equipped seven squadrons and took a major part in the 1973 'Yom Kippur' War: much indigenous equipment was added, including the Elta EL/M-2021 multi-mode radar, and it is also said that the Israeli F-4Es were made compatible with the Luz stand-off bomb. Other air forces that used the F-4E included those of Egypt, Greece, Iran (with eight squadrons), South Korea and Turkey. Australia leased a small number in 1970-2 pending the arrival of General Dynamics F-111Cs, and Mitsubishi licence-built 140 **F-4EJ** aircraft to equip five squadrons of the JASDF. West Germany also adopted the aircraft as basic strike/fighter equipment, Luftwaffe crews being trained in the USA on F-4Es before the delivery of 175 new-build **F-4F** aircraft during 1975-6 to equip four Jagdgeschwader and Jagdbombergeschwader in the interception and quick-reaction strike roles respectively, replacing Lockheed F-104Gs.

Representing the latest aerodynamic standard achieved in production (with slatted wings and other refinements), the F-4F featured simplified APQ-100 radar and reduced fuel capacity, and also lacked any inflight-refuelling facility. Most of the airframe was manufactured in West Germany for final assembly in the USA, and upgraded air-defence F-4Fs are still in gainful service during the mid-1990s.

**Specification:** McDonnell Douglas F-4E Phantom II
**Origin:** USA
**Type:** two-seat multi-role strike/attack fighter
**Powerplant:** two 8119-kg (17,900-lb) afterburning thrust General Electric J79-GE-17 turbojets
**Performance:** maximum speed Mach 2.25 or 1,290 kt (2390 km/h; 1,485 mph) at 40,000 ft (12190 m); initial rate of climb 49,800 ft (15180 m) per minute; service ceiling 62,250 ft (18975 m); unrefuelled combat radius 958 km (595 miles)
**Weights:** empty 13397 kg (29,535 lb); maximum take-off 27964 kg (61,651 lb)
**Dimensions:** span 11.71 m (38 ft 5 in); length 19.20 m (63 ft 0 in); height 5.03 m (16 ft 6 in); wing area 49.24 m² (530.0 sq ft)
**Armament:** one 20-mm M61A1 Vulcan six-barrel cannon with 640 rounds and four AIM-7 Sparrow AAMs semi-recessed into fuselage underside or other weapons up to 1370 kg (3,020 lb) on centreline pylon; four underwing hardpoints can carry a load of up to 5888 kg (12,980 lb) of fuel tanks and/or weapons

*McDonnell Douglas F-4E Phantom II of the 3d TFW, US Air Force, based at Clark AB, Philippines.*

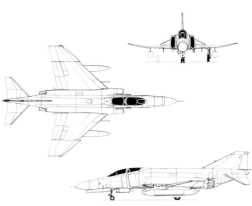

*McDonnell Douglas F-4E Phantom*

*The Hopsten-based Jagdbombergeschwader 36 operated the F-4F Phantom in the quick-reaction strike role, but all the F-4Fs are now operated in the air-defence role.*

*A pair of 301st Hikotai Mitsubishi (McDonnell Douglas) F-4EJs scramble from Hyakuri. Japan's Phantom IIs share their air-defence task with Mitsubishi (McDonnell Douglas) F-15 Eagles.*

**Role**
Fighter
Close support
Counter-insurgency
Tactical strike
Strategic bomber
Tactical reconnaissance
Strategic reconnaissance
Maritime patrol
Anti-ship strike
Anti-submarine warfare
Search and rescue
Assault transport
Transport
Liaison
Trainer
Inflight-refuelling tanker
Specialized

**Performance**
All-weather capability
Rough field capability
STOL capability
VTOL capability
Airspeed 0-250 mph
Airspeed 250 mph-Mach 1
Airspeed Mach 1 plus
Ceiling 0-20,000 ft
Ceiling 20,000-40,000 ft
Ceiling 40,000ft plus
Range 0-1,000 miles
Range 1,000-3,000 miles
Range 3,000 miles plus

**Weapons**
Air-to-air missiles
Air-to-surface missiles
Cruise missiles
Cannon
Trainable guns
Naval weapons
Nuclear-capable
Rockets
'Smart' weapon kit
Weapon load 0-4,000 lb
Weapon load 4,000-15,000 lb
Weapon load 15,000 lb plus

**Avionics**
Electronic Counter Measures
Electronic Support Measures
Search radar
Fire control radar
Look-down/shoot-down
Terrain-following radar
Forward-looking infra-red
Laser
Television

# McDonnell Douglas F-4G 'Wild Weasel'

*McDonnell Douglas **F-4G** 'Wild Weasel' of the 81st **TFS**, 52d **TFW**, US Air Force, based at Spangdahlem, Germany.*

Widespread use by the communist forces in Vietnam of Soviet-supplied SA-2 'Guideline' SAMs was only partly countered by use of aircraft such as the unarmed Douglas EB-66 and Grumman EA-6B by the US Air Force and US Navy respectively. It was perhaps inevitable, therefore, after better success had attended development of the armed North American F-100 and Republic F-105 in the radar-suppression role, that the F-4, with its much higher performance and attack capabilities, should come to be introduced for similar tasks. By 1972 about 12 **McDonnell Douglas F-4C 'Wild Weasel IV'** aircraft were in service. Employing Westinghouse ECM pods in conjunction with AGM-45 Shrike anti-radiation missiles, such aircraft frequently accompanied routine attack missions by standard F-4Cs.

In due course a much more extensive modification programme was undertaken, a total of an initial 116 **F-4G** aircraft (known initially as **'Advanced Wild Weasel'** or **'Wild Weasel V'**) were produced by modifying F-4Es from production Block 42 onwards when they were returned for life-extension programmes; a number of attrition-replacement conversions were added at a later date. Changes included deletion of the integral M61A1 cannon and installation of the McDonnell Douglas APR-38 radar warning, homing and missile management system

(RHAWS), much of whose component avionics are located in a long cylindrical fairing on top of the aircraft's fin. Associated with the APR-38 is a Texas Instruments computer whose purpose is to accommodate varying future circumstances without demands for additional electronic hardware in an already densely packed aircraft (there are no fewer than 52 antennae distributed throughout the airframe). Self-defence weaponry is confined to a pair of AIM-7 Sparrow medium-range AAMs in the rear fuselage recesses; one of the forward missile recesses is normally occupied by an ECM pod such as ALQ-131. The APR-38 is compatible with the AGM-45 Shrike, AGM-65 Maverick optronically guided missile), and features automatic and blind weapon firing. Cockpit displays include annotated threat symbology, while reaction to priority threats is automatically initiated. Most aircraft in service today have been re-equipped with LORAN, while restressing of the fuselage store mounting enables the McDonnell Douglas F-15 type of centreline drop tank to be carried: this is cleared to 5 g when full, compared with 3 g for the F-4's customary tank. The F-4G will remain in front-line service with the USAF until the end of the century, and is sure to be the last variant of the classic Phantom II in first-line service, following the **'Wild Weasel VI'** update with the APR-47 RHAWS.

**Specification:** McDonnell Douglas F-4G 'Wild Weasel'
**Origin:** USA
**Type:** two-seat EW/radar-suppression attack aircraft
**Powerplant:** two 8119-kg (17,900-lb) afterburning thrust General Electric J79-GE-17 turbojets
**Performance:** maximum speed Mach 2.25 or 1,290 kt (2390km/h; 1,485 mph) at 40,000 ft (12190m); service ceiling 62,250 ft (18975m); unrefuelled combat radius 958 km (595 miles)
**Weights:** empty 13300 kg (29,321 lb); maximum take-off 28300 kg (62,390 lb)
**Dimensions:** span 11.71 m (38 ft 5 in); length 19.20 m (63 ft 0 in); height 5.02 m (16 ft 5.5 in); wing area 49.24 m² (530.0 sq ft)
**Armament:** provision to mount two AIM-7 Sparrow self-defence AAMs in rear fuselage recesses; radar suppression weapons include mix of AGM-45 Shrike, AGM-65 Maverick and AGM-88 HARM missiles in conjunction with APR-38 RHAWS integral equipment and podded ALQ-119 ECM

**McDonnell Douglas F-4G 'Wild Weasel'**

*This F-4G 'Wild Weasel' defence-suppression Phantom wears the red fin stripe of the 480th TFS, one of three 'Weasel' that was based at Spangdahlem.*

*The F-4G is used for radar-suppression duties and is equipped with a comprehensive RHAWS and a variety of anti-radar and other air-to-surface missiles.*

Role
Fighter
Close support
Counter-insurgency
Tactical strike
Strategic bomber
Tactical reconnaissance
Strategic reconnaissance
Maritime patrol
Anti-ship strike
Anti-submarine warfare
Search and rescue
Assault transport
Transport
Liaison
Trainer
Inflight-refuelling tanker
Specialized

Performance
All-weather capability
Rough field capability
STOL capability
VTOL capability
Airspeed 0-250 mph
Airspeed 250 mph-Mach 1
Airspeed Mach 1 plus
Airspeed 0-20,000 ft
Ceiling 0-20,000 ft
Ceiling 20,000-40,000 ft
Ceiling 40,000ft plus
Range 0-1,000 miles
Range 1,000-3,000 miles
Range 3,000 miles plus

Weapons
Air-to-air missiles
Air-to-surface missiles
Cruise missiles
Cannon
Trainable guns
Naval weapons
Nuclear-capable
Rockets
'Smart' weapon kit
Weapon load 0-4,000 lb
Weapon load 4,000-15,000 lb
Weapon load 15,000 lb

Avionics
Electronic Counter Measures
Electronic Support Measures
Search radar
Fire control radar
Look-down/shoot-down
Terrain-following radar
Forward-looking infra-red
Laser
Television

# McDonnell Douglas F-15A/C Eagle

*McDonnell Douglas F-15C Eagle of the Israeli air force.*

### Role

Fighter
Close support
Counter-insurgency
Tactical strike
Strategic bomber
Tactical reconnaissance
Strategic reconnaissance
Maritime patrol
Anti-ship strike
Anti-submarine warfare
Search and rescue
Assault transport
Transport
Liaison
Trainer
Inflight-refuelling tanker
Specialized

### Performance

All-weather capability
Rough field capability
STOL capability
VTOL capability
Airspeed 0-250 mph
Airspeed 250 mph-Mach 1
Airspeed Mach 1 plus
Ceiling 0-20,000 ft
Ceiling 20,000-40,000 ft
Ceiling 40,000ft plus
Range 0-1,000 miles
Range 1,000-3,000 miles
Range 3,000 miles plus

### Weapons

Air-to-air missiles
Air-to-surface missiles
Cruise missiles
Cannon
Trainable guns
Naval weapons
Nuclear-capable
Rockets
'Smart' weapon kit
Weapon load 0-4,000 lb
Weapon load 4,000-15,000 lb
Weapon load 15,000 lb plus

### Avionics

Electronic Counter Measures
Electronic Support Measures
Search radar
Fire control radar
Look-down/shoot-down
Terrain-following radar
Forward-looking infra-red
Laser
Television

Representing a logical progression from the F-4, the **McDonnell Douglas F-15 Eagle** was the outcome of a USAF funding request in 1965 for a new air-superiority fighter (at just about the time the US Navy's F-4 was first adopted by the USAF). First flown on 27 July 1972, the F-15A emerged as a single-seat twin-turbofan aircraft featuring broad centre and rear fuselage, fixed-geometry swept wings of low aspect ratio, tall twin vertical tail surfaces and all-moving horizontal tail surfaces with saw-tooth extended leading edges. Pratt & Whitney F100-PW-100 turbofans with external compression inlets bestowed Mach 2.5 performance at high altitude, in turn resulting in extensive use of titanium (more than 20 per cent of airframe weight). Production of the F-15A continued until 1979 with 385 built, including 19 delivered to Israel.

The principal variant thus far is the **F-15C**, whose first production examples appeared in 1979 and had reached 481 before a temporary production halt was called in November 1989; limited production resumed in the first half of the 1990s. Export have been made to Israel and Saudi Arabia. This version, which is now in operational service with USAF tactical fighter wings and fighter interceptor squadrons in the USA (including Alaska), at Kadena (Okinawa), and in Europe, features

provision for a pair of conformal fuel tanks (CFTs) which each contain 3228 litres (853 US gal) of usable fuel and which are fitted 'flush' to the sides of the inlet trunks, thus leaving all store hardpoints available for ordnance (or further fuel tanks). Tangential store mountings have been developed, allowing up to 12 further 454-kg (1,000-lb) stores to be located at the lower shoulders of the CFTs, in all representing an external store load of 10705 kg (23,600 lb). Avionics include Hughes APG-63 or later APG-70 pulse-Doppler radar, General Electric automatic analog flight-control system, IBM central computer, Northrop Enhanced ALQ-135(V) integral automatic jammer, Magnavox EW warning subsystem and DCC stores management system. The inbuilt armament comprises a single 20-mm M61A1 six-barrel cannon with 940 rounds in the right-hand wing root, and a normal missile fit is either four AIM-7F/M Sparrow medium-range AAMs and four AIM-9L/M Sidewinder short-range AAMs, or eight AIM-120A AMRAAMs.

In service F-15Cs have replaced all F-15As with regular wings, the redundant aircraft being introduced into the Air National Guard. The F-15C was selected for licence production by Japan, 14 US-built aircraft preceding the first of a planned 189 **F-15J** fighters manufactured by Mitsubishi.

## Specification: McDonnell Douglas F-15C Eagle
**Origin:** USA
**Type:** air-superiority fighter with secondary strike/attack role
**Powerplant:** two 10782-kg (23,770-lb) afterburning thrust Pratt & Whitney F100-P-220 turbofans
**Performance:** maximum speed more than Mach 2.5 or 1,433 kt (2655km/h; 1,650 mph) at high altitude; service ceiling 60,000 ft (18290 m); maximum unrefuelled ferry range 5745 km (3,570 miles) with conformal fuel tanks
**Weights:** empty 12973 kg (28,600 lb); maximum take-off 30844 kg (68,000 lb)
**Dimensions:** span 13.05 m (42 ft 9.75 in); length 19.43 m (63 ft 9 in); height 5.63 m (18 ft 5.5 in); wing area 56.48 m² (608.0 sq ft)
**Armament:** air-to-air weaponry comprises one 20-mm M61A1 Vulcan six-barrel cannon and provision for four AIM-9L/M Sidewinder and four AIM-7F/M Sparrow AAMs or eight AIM-120A AMRAAMs; when configured for the attack role with five weapon stations (including two on CFTs) up to 10705 kg (23,600 lb) of bombs, rockets and other air-to-surface weapons can be carried

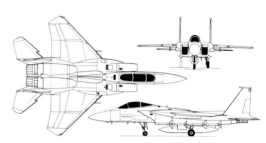

*McDonnell Douglas F-15A Eagle*

*These McDonnell Douglas F-15s of the 32d TFS are based at Camp New Amsterdam, otherwise known as Soesterberg. The unit reports directly to the Netherlands air force, and is assigned to the 2nd ATAF.*

*The 36th TFW at Bitburg consists of three F-15 squadrons; each wears a different coloured finband. Here two F-15Cs of the 22d TFS display their huge dorsal airbrakes on approach.*

# McDonnell Douglas F-15B/D Eagle

*Mitsubishi (McDonnell Douglas) F-15DJ Eagle of the 204 Hikotai, JASDF, based at Hyakuri.*

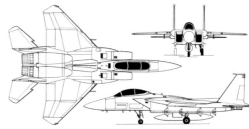

Developed more or less simultaneously with the single-seat F-1 5A Eagle, the first two-seat **McDonnell Douglas F-15B Eagle** (originally termed the **TF-15A**) made its maiden flight on 7 July 1973 and started delivery to the USAF on 14 November the following year, first equipping the 58th Tactical Training Wing at Luke AFB. Inclusion of the second cockpit was effected without extensive structural alteration and without overall airframe dimension change, and involved a structural weight penalty of no more than 363kg (800 lb). The complete avionics equipment and stores fit are retained, enabling full operational conversion training and checkout to be carried out. F-15Bs figured in the establishment of most F-15A tactical squadrons. Two F-15Bs were included in the export package to Israel in 1977, while a total of 58 was completed for the USAF.

As the first F-15Cs appeared in 1979, its **F-15D** two-seat derivative was first flown on 19 June of that year, joining the 18th TFW in December and the 33d TFW in the following March. Like the F-15C single-seater, the F-15D two-seater can also accommodate the CFTs as well as the full fuel load, weapon

range and ECM fit, and features the single-seater's entire range of avionics.

Currently being pursued is a programme to arrive at a version of the F-15D to assume the 'Wild Weasel' air-defence suppression tasks currently undertaken by the F-4G, and early in 1984 a modified F-15D was evaluated with a chin pack capable of housing a variety of sensors, including APR-38 'Wild Weasel' radar-location system, IR search-and-track system and a TV sight; missile fits would include the current ARM and ARM family as well as ECM pods. No production or conversion order has yet been issued, however. The F-15D is not a subject of the Multi-Stage Improvement Program (MSIP), already implemented for the single-seat F-15C, which involves a continuing update of all avionics and, by implication, missiles), but if no trainer version of the F-15E is forthcoming it seems certain that the F-15D two-seater must be kept abreast of the latest single-seaters. Foreign F-15D two-seaters are currently confined to the Japanese **F-15DJ**, of which 12 were delivered, and the two and 19 aircraft delivered to the Israeli and Saudi Arabian air forces respectively.

## Specification: McDonnell Douglas F-15D Eagle

**Origin:** USA
**Type:** air-superiority fighter trainer with full operational capability
**Powerplant:** two 10782-kg) (23,700-lb) afterburning thrust Pratt & Whitney F100-P-220 turbofans
**Performance:** maximum speed Mach 2.5 or 1,433 kt (2655 km/h; 1,650 mph) above 40,000 ft (12190 m); service ceiling 60,000 ft (18290 m); maximum unrefuelled range more than 4631 km (2,878 miles) without conformal fuel tanks
**Weights:** empty 13336 kg (29,400 lb); maximum take-off 30844 kg (68,000 lb)
**Dimensions:** span 13.05 m (42 ft 9.75 in); length 19.43 m (63 ft 9 in); height 5.63 m (18 ft 5.5 in); wing area 56.48 m² (608.0 sq ft)
**Armament:** one 20-mm M61A1 Vulcan six-barrel cannon, and an air-to-air missile load of four AIM-7F/M Sparrow and four AIM-9L/M Sidewinder AAMs or up to eight AIM-120A AMRAAMs; if fitted with CFTs air-to-surface and ECM stores of up to a total of 10705 kg (23,600 lb) can be carried

**McDonnell Douglas F-15D Eagle**

*Dog footprints on the fin and a fierce bulldog's head badge on the engine intake identify this Bitburg-based F-15D as belonging to the 525th TFS, 36th TFW.*

*The 405th TTW at Luke AFB serves as one of two conversion and refresher training units for the F-15 force. The four squadrons include the 550th TFTS, one of whose aircraft is shown here.*

**Role**
Fighter
Close support
Counter-insurgency
Tactical strike
Strategic bomber
Tactical reconnaissance
Strategic reconnaissance
Maritime patrol
Anti-ship strike
Anti-submarine warfare
Search and rescue
Assault transport
Transport
Liaison
Trainer
Inflight-refuelling tanker
Specialized

**Performance**
All-weather capability
Rough field capability
STOL capability
VTOL capability
Airspeed 0-250 mph
Airspeed 250 mph-Mach 1
Airspeed Mach 1 plus
Ceiling 0-20,000 ft
Ceiling 20,000-40,000 ft
Ceiling 40,000ft plus
Range 0-1,000 miles
Range 1,000-3,000 miles
Range 3,000 miles plus

**Weapons**
Air-to-air missiles
Air-to-surface missiles
Cruise missiles
Cannon
Trainable guns
Naval weapons
Nuclear-capable
Rockets
'Smart' weapon kit
Weapon load 0-4,000 lb
Weapon load 4,000-15,000 lb
Weapon load 15,000 lb plus

**Avionics**
Electronic Counter Measures
Electronic Support Measures
Search radar
Fire control radar
Look-down/shoot-down
Terrain-following radar
Forward-looking infra-red
Laser
Television

# McDonnell Douglas F-15E Eagle

*A McDonnell Douglas F-15E Strike Eagle of the 391st Fighter Squadron, the 'Bold Tigers' of the Mountain Home-based 366th Wing.*

## Role

Fighter
Close support
Counter-insurgency
Tactical strike
Strategic bomber
Tactical reconnaissance
Strategic reconnaissance
Maritime patrol
Anti-ship strike
Anti-submarine warfare
Search and rescue
Assault transport
Transport
Liaison
Trainer
Inflight-refuelling tanker
Specialized

## Performance

All-weather capability
Rough field capability
STOL capability
VTOL capability
Airspeed 0-250 mph
Airspeed 250 mph-Mach 1
Airspeed Mach 1 plus
Ceiling 0-20,000 ft
Ceiling 20,000-40,000 ft
Ceiling 40,000ft plus
Range 0-1,000 miles
Range 1,000-3,000 miles
Range 3,000 miles plus

## Weapons

Air-to-air missiles
Air-to-surface missiles
Cruise missiles
Cannon
Trainable guns
Naval weapons
Nuclear-capable
Rockets
'Smart' weapon kit
Weapon load 0-4,000 lb
Weapon load 4,000-15,000 lb
Weapon load 15,000 lb plus

## Avionics

Electronic Counter Measures
Electronic Support Measures
Search radar
Fire control radar
Look-down/shoot-down
Terrain-following radar
Forward-looking infra-red
Laser
Television

Developed initially with commercial funding, the **McDonnell Douglas F-15E Eagle** is a two-seat dual-role deep interdiction strike/attack aircraft which retains the basic type's proven air-to-air combat capabilities. Based on an upgraded F-15B, the 'Strike Eagle' prototype was flown in 1982 and, following successful competitive evaluation with the General Dynamics F-16XL in 1982-3, the USAF announced its intention to proceed with the F-15E, and manufacture of three prototypes started in 1985. The original plan was for the procurement of 392 F-15Es, although this total was later trimmed to 209.

Adoption of the two-seat layout for this adverse-weather deep-penetration strike aircraft represented a *volte face* in the USAF, which had tended to the belief that, with the aid of adequate avionics sophistication, accurate navigation, weapon delivery and mission management were possible for the pilot alone. The F-15E's rear-seat occupant is provided with four multi-purpose CRT displays for radar, weapon management and selection, and threat monitoring; the pilot is provided with wide-angle HUD, CRTs and a moving map display for navigation, precision radar mapping and automatic terrain following. To accommodate the increased avionics volume, one fuselage tank has been reduced in size, but the F-15E can employ the standard conformal tanks, and an important feature is the inclusion of provision for the accommodation of physical and performance growth of new equipment without extensive alteration to the aircraft structure. For instance the engine bay has been redesigned so as to accept either Pratt & Whitney F100 or General Electric F110 turbofans, even when a pair of these or other engines is developed to deliver up to 27215-kg (60,000-lb) thrust. The radar is the Hughes APG-70 radar with a 1,000-K memory and trebled processing speed, and other MSIP avionics are standard. Clearance at a maximum take-off weight of 36741 kg (81,000 lb) has been achieved by local structure strengthening and the introduction of revised landing gear components: during early testing an F-15 took-off at 34019 kg (75,000 lb) carrying two full conformal tanks and three 2,309-litre (610-US gal) external fuel tanks as well as eight 227-kg (500-lb) Mk 82 bombs on the CFTs' tangential racks. Among the weapon delivery systems compatible with the F-15E are the LANTIRN two-pod navigation/targeting system used with GBU-12, -22 and -24 laser-guided weapons, and the AXQ-14 data link pod used with GBU-15 weapon.

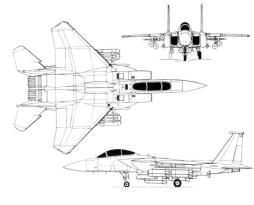

**McDonnell Douglas F-15E Eagle**

### Specification: McDonnell Douglas F-15E Eagle
**Origin:** USA
**Type:** dual-role strike/attack and air-superiority fighter
**Powerplant:** two 13154-kg (29,000-lb) afterburning thrust Pratt & Whitney F100-P-229 turbofans
**Performance:** maximum speed more than Mach2.5 or 1,433 kt (2655 km/h; 1 650 mph) above36,000 ft (10970 m); service ceiling 60,000 ft (18290 m); maximum unrefuelled range 5745 km (3,570 miles) with conformal fuel tanks
**Weights:** empty 14379 kg (31,700 lb); maximum take-off 36741 kg (81,000 lb)
**Dimensions:** span 13.05 m (42 ft 9.75 in); length 19.43 m (63 ft 9 in); height 5.63 m (18 ft 5.5 in); wing area 56.48 m² (608.0 sq ft)
**Armament:** one 20-mm M61A1 Vulcan six-barrel cannon; single centreline store mountings and two underwing pylons for fuel tanks, AIM-7, AIM-9 and/or or AIM-120 AAMs; a tangential rack on each CFT allows carriage of six bomb racks; typical loads include 26 Mk 20 Rockeye cluster bombs, six AGM-65 Maverick air to-surface missiles or nine B61 nuclear weapons

*The wing commander of the 366th Wing at Mountain Home can claim this F-15E as his own. It is seen here laden with four GBU-10 laser-guided bombs.*

*Two McDonnell Douglas F-15E Strike Eagles of the Nellis-based 57th Wing, whose 422nd Test and Evaluation Squadron has a primary role of developing tactics and training weapons instructors for the frontline force.*

# McDonnell Douglas FA-18A/C Hornet

*McDonnell Douglas CF-18A of the Canadian Armed Forces.*

The **McDonnell Douglas F/A-18 Hornet** was designed to fulfil the distinct fighter and attack roles, and consequently is produced in a form easily adaptable to either of them through a change in mission computer software. The first role resulted from the increasing realization in the USA during the early 1970s that there existed the requirement for an aircraft which was inexpensive, straightforward to produce and light in weight as replacement for the McDonnell Douglas F-4 Phantom II and to operate in combination with the more sophisticated, but heavier and more expensive Grumman F-14 and McDonnell Douglas F-15. The second role was derived from the need to replace the Vought A-7 Corsair II. For the US Navy and US Marine Corps, a mix of the F-14 and F/A-18 was determined, while the US Air Force adopted the combination of the F-15 and General Dynamics F-16 Fighting Falcon.

The Hornet was derived from the Northrop YF-17. In May 1975 it was announced that the new aircraft would be built by McDonnell Douglas as prime contractor with Northrop Corporation undertaking 30 per cent of airframe development and 40 per cent airframe production work. In developing it from the YF-17 its wing area was increased, and it was given a wing-fold

capability, a retractable inflight-refuelling probe, provision for AIM-7 Sparrow medium-range missiles, and increased fuel capacity.

Full-scale production of the **F/A-18A** began on 22 January 1976 and the maiden flight took place on 18 November 1978. Although the type was originally to have been produced in separate F-18 and A-18 forms suiting it to the two different roles, it was finalized in a single form and the process of conversion from one role to another is very simple and quick. In addition to those on order for the US Navy, delivery of 98 land-based **CF-18A** aircraft to the Canadian Armed Forces began in 1982, acceptance of 57 **AF-18A** aircraft for the Royal Australian Air Force is under way, and 60 **EF-18A** aircraft were produced for Spain.

After delivery of 371 F/A-18As, production switched in 1987 to the improved F/A-18C with databus-linked small computers rather than one large computer, a more modern ejector seat, provision for reconnaissance equipment as well as the AIM-120A AMRAAM and AGM-65F Maverick air-to-surface missile, and in current **F/A-18C Night Attack** aircraft the Hughes AAR-50 Thermal Imaging Navigation System. The F/A-18C has been bought by the US Navy and also by Finland, Kuwait and Switzerland.

## Specification: McDonnell Douglas F/A-18C Hornet
**Origin:** USA
**Type:** carrierborne fighter and attack aircraft
**Powerplant:** two 7257-kg (16,000-lb) afterburning thrust General Electric F404-GE-400 turbofans
**Performance:** maximum speed more than Mach 1.8 or 1,032 kt (1912 km/h; 1,183 mph) at 40,000ft (12190 m); combat ceiling about 50,000 ft (15240 m); combat radius 740 km (460 miles) in the fighter escort role or 1065 km (662 miles) in the attack role
**Weights:** empty 10455 kg (23,050 lb); maximum take-off 25401 kg (56,000 lb)
**Dimensions:** span 11.43 m (37 ft 6 in); length 17.07 m (56 ft 0 in); height 4.66 m (15 ft 3.5in); wing area 37.16 m² (400.0 sq ft)
**Armament:** one 20-mm M61A1 Vulcan six-barrel rotary cannon with 570 rounds; up to 7711 kg (17,000 lb) of disposable stores, including AAMs, ASMs, anti-ship missiles, free-fall or guided bombs, cluster bombs, dispenser weapons, napalm tanks, rocket launchers, drop tanks and ECM pods, carried on nine external hardpoints

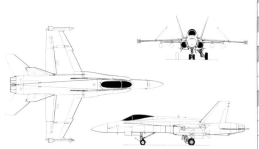

**McDonnell Douglas F/A-18A Hornet**

*Canada's Europe-based No.1 CAG replaced its ageing CF-104s with CF-18As, giving NATO a much-needed boost in capability. Three squadrons were based at Baden-Söllingen until the early 1990s.*

*An F/A-18A of the NAS Lemoore-based VFA-113 'Stingers' lands on USS Constellation. The F/A-18A has given the US Navy a versatile carrier-borne fighter and attack aircraft to replace its F-4s and A-7s.*

**Role**
Fighter
Close support
Counter-insurgency
Tactical strike
Strategic bomber
Tactical reconnaissance
Strategic reconnaissance
Maritime patrol
Anti-ship strike
Anti-submarine warfare
Search and rescue
Assault transport
Transport
Liaison
Trainer
Inflight-refuelling tanker
Specialized

**Performance**
All-weather capability
Rough field capability
STOL capability
VTOL capability
Airspeed 0-250 mph
Airspeed 250 mph-Mach 1
Airspeed Mach 1 plus
Ceiling 0-20,000 ft
Ceiling 20,000-40,000 ft
Ceiling 40,000ft plus
Ceiling 40,000 miles
Range 0-1,000 miles
Range 1,000-3,000 miles
Range 3,000 miles plus

**Weapons**
Air-to-air missiles
Air-to-surface missiles
Cruise missiles
Cannon
Trainable guns
Naval weapons
Nuclear-capable
Rockets
'Smart' weapon kit
Weapon load 0-4,000 lb
Weapon load 4,000-15,000 lb
Weapon load 15,000 lb plus

**Avionics**
Electronic Counter Measures
Electronic Support Measures
Search radar
Fire control radar
Look-down/shoot-down radar
Terrain-following radar
Forward-looking infra-red
Laser
Television

179

# McDonnell Douglas F/A-18B/D Hornet

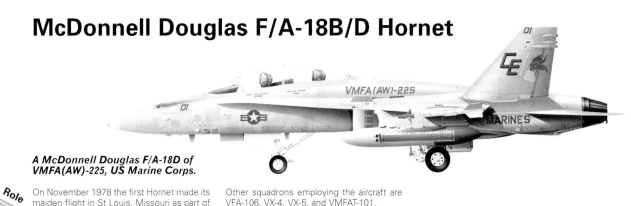

*A McDonnell Douglas F/A-18D of VMFA(AW)-225, US Marine Corps.*

On November 1978 the first Hornet made its maiden flight in St Louis, Missouri as part of a batch of 11 aircraft which included two combat-capable tandem-seat training versions, designated **McDonnell Douglas F/A-18B Hornet**. By March 1980 all 11 development aircraft had flown, including the two trainer aircraft. The F/A-18B is produced with the same nav/attack systems and ordnance capability as the single-seat Hornet, and is capable of the same performance with the exception of range, which is decreased marginally as a result of a 5 per cent reduction in fuel capacity entailed by the introduction of the second seat under a longer canopy.

The US Navy's first Hornet squadron, VFA-125, was commissioned at NAS Lemoore in November 1980, assigned the task of serving as the 'Combat Readiness Training Squadron for Pacific Fleet Units'. As a training unit, VFA-125 employed a 50/50 mix of single-seat and two-seat F/A-18s. The squadron operates under a dual service command structure with USN and US Marine Corps personnel represented in equal numbers. The first set of students began training in the summer of 1982, and VFA-125 now trains up to 70 new pilots per year. Each class lasts six months, during which each student receives over 100 hours flying time.

Other squadrons employing the aircraft are VFA-106, VX-4, VX-5, and VMFAT-101.

The US Navy currently plans to take a total of 1,157 Hornets including some 165 two-seaters. With the duplication of all instrumentation except the HUD in the rear cockpit, users no doubt see the advantage of the two-man crewing potential, especially in the attack role, and this has been fully exploited in the **F/A-18D Night Attack** current variant of the upgraded **F/A-18D** that is the two-seat counterpart of the F/A-18C discussed in the previous entry. Exports of the F/A-18B included 18 ATF-18A, 40 CF-18 and 12 EF-18B aircraft for Canada, Australia and Spain respectively, while exports of the F/A-18D stand at seven, eight and eight for Finland, Kuwait and Switzerland respectively.

The F/A-18D was also deemed ideal for development as a reconnaissance aircraft for the USMC. The resulting **F/A-18D(RC)** with a centreline pod carrying a Loral UPD-8 synthetic-aperture SLAR to supplement the optical and IR sensors located in the underside of the nose. Data are viewed in the rear cockpit and relayed to a ground station by a real-time data link. Further evolution of the Hornet is dedicated to an enlarged model that is being developed in **F/A-18E** single-seat and **F/A-18F** two-seat forms.

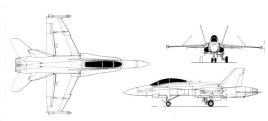

**McDonnell Douglas F/A-18B Hornet**

*This view of the first EF-18B Hornet after its roll-out ceremony shows to good effect the huge leading-edge strakes that give the Hornet its outstanding handling at high AOA.*

## Specification: McDonnell Douglas F/A-18D Hornet
**Origin:** USA
**Type:** combat-capable conversion trainer
**Powerplant:** two 7257-kg (16,000-lb) afterburning thrust General Electric F404-GE-400 turbofans
**Performance:** maximum speed more than Mach 1.8 or 1,032 kt (1912 km/h; 1,183 mph) at 40,000ft (12190 m); combat ceiling about 50,000 ft (15240 m); combat radius 1020 km (634 miles) in the attack role; ferry range 3520 km (2,187 miles) with external fuel
**Weights:** empty 10455 kg (23,050 lb); maximum take-off 25401 kg (56,000 lb)
**Dimensions:** span 11.43 m (37 ft 6 in); length 17.07 m (56 ft 0 in); height 4.66 m (15 ft 3.5in); wing area 37.16 m² (400.0 sq ft)
**Armament:** one 20-mm M61A1 Vulcan six-barrel rotary cannon with 570 rounds; up to 7711 kg (17,000 lb) of disposable stores, including AAMs, ASMs, anti-ship missiles, free-fall or guided bombs, cluster bombs, dispenser weapons, napalm tanks, rocket launchers, drop tanks and ECM pods, carried on nine external hardpoints

*The F/A-18Ds of the US Marine Corps played a vital role in the Gulf War, attacking a wide variety of targets with great precision. This aircraft wears the insignia of VMF(AW)-121.*

**Role**
Fighter
Close support
Counter-insurgency
Tactical strike
Strategic bomber
Tactical reconnaissance
Strategic reconnaissance
Maritime patrol
Anti-ship strike
Anti-submarine warfare
Search and rescue
Assault transport
Transport
Liaison
Trainer
Inflight-refuelling tanker
Specialized

**Performance**
All-weather capability
Rough field capability
STOL capability
VTOL capability
Airspeed 0-250 mph
Airspeed 250 mph-Mach 1
Airspeed Mach 1 plus
Ceiling 0-20,000 ft
Ceiling 20,000-40,000 ft
Ceiling 40,000ft plus
Range 0-1,000 miles
Range 1,000-3,000 miles
Range 3,000 miles plus

**Weapons**
Air-to-air missiles
Air-to-surface missiles
Cruise missiles
Cannon
Trainable guns
Naval weapons
Nuclear-capable
Rockets
'Smart' weapon kit
Weapon load 0-4,000 lb
Weapon load 4,000-15,000 lb
Weapon load 15,000 lb plus

**Avionics**
Electronic Counter Measures
Electronic Support Measures
Search radar
Fire control radar
Look-down/shoot-down
Terrain-following radar
Forward-looking infra-red
Laser
Television

# McDonnell Douglas/BAe AV-8B Harrier II

*McDonnell Douglas AV-8B Harrier II of the Spanish Navy.*

After both unsuccessfully pursuing their own lines of development to create a successor to the AV-8A and Harrier, McDonnell Douglas and British Aerospace decided to collaborate on the joint **McDonnell Douglas/BAe Harrier II** for the US Marine Corps (**AV-8B**) and the RAF (Harrier GR.Mk 5).

The AV-8B was designed specifically to meet the requirements of the USMC ground commander: an aircraft based as close as possible to the scene of action and with the ability to operate from a variety of assault ships or other bases. Although the AV-8A pioneered the idea of instant close support, the most significant advantage of the new model is that is it able to operate with the payload and range of most conventional attack aircraft, abilities beyond the AV-8A.

These improvements were made possible primarily by complete redesign of the wing, which is now constructed entirely of advanced carbonfibre epoxy composite material, which is not only particularly strong and light but also resists corrosion and fatigue better than metal. Other major improvements include improved engine air inlets, a revised cockpit with better fields of view, improved avionics, lift improvement devices, and modifications to the wing's leading edges for better manoeuvrability.

VMA-331, the first operational AV-8B squadron, was commissioned at MCAS Cherry Point, North Carolina in January 1985 and achieved initial operational capability in August of the same year.

Later-production aircraft are being completed to an improved **AV-8B Harrier II Night Attack** standard with a nose-mounted FLIR, and the latest variant is the **AV-8B Harrier II Plus** with APG-65 radar in a longer nose that increases length by 0.43 m (1 ft 5 in). Some 24 of this last are being delivered. The series has also been exported to Italy (16 Harrier II Plus aircraft with an option for a further eight) and Spain (12 **EAV-8B** aircraft together with a requirement for eight **EAV-8B Harrier II Plus** aircraft that would be supplemented by 11 EAV-8B conversions).

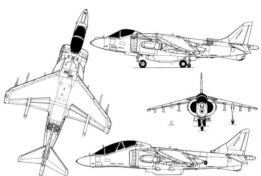

**McDonnell Douglas/BAe AV-8B Harrier II**

*An AV-8B Harrier II Plus of VMA-542, based at MCAS Cherry Point. The radar-equipped AV-8B is still something of a rarity in Marine Corps service.*

*The Italian Navy's AV-8Bs are radar-equipped aircraft broadly equivalent to the latest Marine Corps Harrier II Plus aircraft.*

**Specification:** McDonnell Douglas/BAe AV-8B Harrier II
**Origin:** USA and UK
**Type:** STOVL close-support aircraft
**Powerplant:** one 10796-kg (23,800-lb) dry thrust Rolls-Royce F402-RR-408 (Pegasus 11-61) vectored-thrust turbofan
**Performance:** maximum speed 575 kt (1065 km; 661 mph) at sea level; initial climb rate 14,715 ft (4485 m) per minute; service ceiling more than 50,000 ft (15240 m); combat radius 277 km (172 miles) with a 2722-kg (6,000-lb) bombload
**Weights:** empty 5936 kg (13,086 lb); maximum take-off 14061 kg (31,000 lb)
**Dimensions:** span 9.25 m (30 ft 4 in); length 14.12 m (46 ft 4 in); height 3.55 m (11 ft 7.75 in); wing area 21.37 m² (230.0 sq ft)
**Armament:** one 25-mm GAU-12/U cannon based with 300 rounds, plus provision for a STO total of 7711 kg (17,000 lb) or VTO total of 3175 kg (7,000 lb) of disposable stores, including AAMs, ASMs, free-fall or guided bombs, cluster bombs, dispenser weapons, napalm tanks, rocket launchers and ECM pods, carried on six external hardpoints

## Role

Fighter
Close support
Counter-insurgency
Tactical strike
Tactical bomber
Strategic bomber
Tactical reconnaissance
Strategic reconnaissance
Maritime patrol
Anti-ship strike
Anti-submarine warfare
Search and rescue
Assault transport
Transport
Liaison
Trainer
Inflight-refuelling tanker
Specialized

## Performance

All-weather capability
Rough field capability
STOL capability
VTOL capability
Airspeed 0-250 mph
Airspeed 250 mph-Mach 1
Airspeed Mach 1 plus
Airspeed 0-20,000 ft
Ceiling 0-20,000 ft
Ceiling 20,000-40,000 ft
Ceiling 40,000ft plus
Range 0-1,000 miles
Range 1,000-3,000 miles
Range 3,000 miles plus

## Weapons

Air-to-air missiles
Air-to-surface missiles
Cruise missiles
Cannon
Trainable guns
Naval weapons
Nuclear-capable
Rockets
'Smart' weapon kit
Weapon load 0-4,000 lb
Weapon load 4,000-15,000 lb
Weapon load 15,000 lb plus

## Avionics

Electronic Counter Measures
Electronic Support Measures
Search radar
Fire control radar
Look-down/shoot-down
Terrain-following radar
Forward-looking infra-red
Laser
Television

181

# McDonnell Douglas/BAe Harrier GR.Mk 5/7 and T.Mk 10

*McDonnell Douglas/BAe Harrier GR.Mk 7 of the Royal Air Force.*

Before the introduction into service of the original BAe Harrier, the manufacturer was testing ideas for a more potent successor. In a situation of high US commitment, British Aerospace decided therefore to collaborate with McDonnell Douglas on the Harrier II project. The result is designated AV-8B by the US Marine Corps and **McDonnell Douglas/BAe Harrier GR.Mk 5** by the RAF.

The major shortcoming of the original Harrier was its limited payload/radius capability, while the importance of maintaining the successful airframe/engine combination was also a primary consideration. The Harrier GR. Mk 5 differs in several ways from its predecessor, while the wings of far greater span and area which allow the aircraft to carry some 907 kg (2,000 lb) of additional fuel that provide greater radius. The new wings also have large, slotted flaps and ailerons (made of carbonfibre composite) which generate greater lift, in turn permitting operations at greater weights.

The improvements mentioned above apply both to the GR.Mk 5 and the AV-8B, but there are obviously differences too, inevitable given the divergent requirements of the two users. The RAF aircraft is equipped with certain additional features to meet the specific demands of operations in Europe. To make possible low-altitude missions at high speed in unpredictable weather conditions, the cockpit is fitted with a moving map display, and the aircraft is also provided with two additional underwing weapons stations which carry Sidewinder self-defence missiles. It has more extensive electronic warfare fit including an IR sensor and a strengthened cockpit canopy to reduce the risk of birdstrike damage. The new maximum payload possible is now about double that of the Harrier GR.Mk 3, at more than 4082 kg (9,000 lb), while the potential radius increases accordingly.

The Harrier GR.Mk 5 made its first flight in 30 April 1985 and entered service with No.1 Squadron in November 1988, and the RAF current's plans call for the delivery of 41 Harrier GR.Mk 5s, 19 **Harrier GR.Mk 5A** (partial Harrier GR.Mk 7) aircraft, 34 **Harrier GR.Mk 7** aircraft basically similar to the AV-8B Harrier Night Attack, and 13 **Harrier T.Mk 10** aircraft basically similar to the TAV-8B.

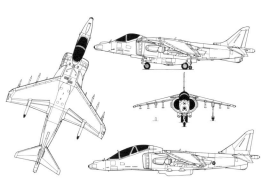

*McDonnell Douglas/BAe Harrier GR.Mk 7 and T.Mk10*

*This Harrier GR.Mk7 wears the overall grey colour scheme applied to aircraft participating in operations to protect the Kurds in Northern Iraq.*

*The Harrier T.Mk10 is basically equivalent to the latest USMC TAV-8Bs, but with the British equipment fitted to the GR.Mk7. It has the original 75% LERX*

**Specification:** McDonnell Douglas/BAe Harrier GR.Mk 7
**Origin:** USA and UK
**Type:** STOVL close-support aircraft
**Powerplant:** one 9866-kg (21,750-lb) dry thrust Rolls-Royce Pegasus Mk 105 vectored-thrust turbofan
**Performance:** maximum speed 575 kt (1065 km; 661 mph) at sea level; initial climb rate 14,715 ft (4485 m) per minute; service ceiling more than 50,000 ft (15240 m); combat radius 277 km (172 miles) with a 2722-kg (6,000-lb) bombload
**Weights:** empty 7050 kg (15,542 lb); maximum take-off 14061 kg (31,000 lb)
**Dimensions:** span 9.25 m (30 ft 4 in); length 14.36 m (47 ft 1.5 in); height 3.55 m (11 ft 7.75 in); wing area 21.37 m² (230.0 sq ft)
**Armament:** two 25-mm Aden 25 cannon based with 100 rounds per gun, plus provision for a STO total of more than 4082 kg (9,000 lb) or VTO total of 3175 kg (7,000 lb) of disposable stores, including AAMs, ASMs, free-fall or guided bombs, cluster bombs, dispenser weapons, napalm tanks, rocket launchers and ECM pods, carried on six external hardpoints

**Role**
Fighter
Close support
Counter-insurgency
Tactical strike
Strategic bomber
Tactical reconnaissance
Strategic reconnaissance
Maritime patrol
Anti-ship strike
Anti-submarine warfare
Search and rescue
Assault transport
Transport
Liaison
Trainer
Inflight-refuelling tanker
Specialized

**Performance**
All-weather capability
Rough field capability
STOL capability
VTOL capability
Airspeed 0-250 mph
Airspeed 250 mph-Mach 1
Airspeed Mach 1 plus
Ceiling 0-20,000 ft
Ceiling 20,000-40,000 ft
Ceiling 40,000ft plus
Range 0-1,000 miles
Range 1,000-3,000 miles
Range 3,000 miles plus

**Weapons**
Air-to-air missiles
Air-to-surface missiles
Cruise missiles
Cannon
Trainable guns
Naval weapons
Nuclear-capable
Rockets
'Smart' weapon kit
Weapon load 0-4,000 lb
Weapon load 4,000-15,000 lb
Weapon load 15,000 lb plus

**Avionics**
Electronic Counter Measures
Electronic Support Measures
Search radar
Fire control radar
Look-down/shoot-down
Terrain-following radar
Forward-looking infra-red
Laser
Television

# MBB/Kawasaki BK 117

Developed from the experience gained with the MBB BO 105 and in conjunction with Kawasaki Heavy Industries, the MBB/Kawasaki BK 117 was originally an 8/11-seat civil helicopter subsequently modified for the defence market. The first BK 117 flew on 13 June 1979, but its sales have been disappointing, due primarily to a downturn in the twin-turbine helicopter market. The initial production version was designated BK 117A-1, succeeded in 1985 by the BK 117A-3 for operation at a higher gross weight, early in 1987 by the BK 117A-4 with an uprated transmission and late in 1987 by the BK 117B-1 with LTS101-750-B-1 engines for improved hot-and-high performance.

For liaison tasks, the BK 177A-1 was delivered to the governments of Ciskei (VIP and border security), Spain (Gardia Civil) and Japan (Tokyo Fire Brigade), while the US Army has taken delivery of one for air combat testing at NAS Patuxent River, Maryland.

The **BK 117A-3M** is a military multi-role derivative of the civil machine, and was first shown at the 1985 Paris Air Show. So far only the development aircraft has been built, and no orders have been reported. The type combines good trooping capability with lat-

est-generation armament and support systems, and also possesses excellent performance which has resulted directly from the BO 105 pedigree. The BK 117A-3M is powered by two Avco Lycoming LTS101-650B-1 engines mounted above the fuselage, thus allowing the maximum usable floor area for seating 11 fully armed troops or (using the clamshell doors) taking 6-m (19.7-ft) long military freight. For assault operations, the helicopter's four main doors allow rapid egress in a 'hot' landing zone.

For anti-tank operations, the development BK 117A-3M has been fitted with eight Euromissile HOT missiles, using the roof-mounted SFIM APX M397 direct-view optical sight and digitized weapon electronics. In addition, provision has been made for the Lucas 12.7-mm (0.5-in) gun turret slaved to a helmet-mounted sighting system for close support, ground fire suppression and possible self-defence anti-helicopter operations. To facilitate this installation and to allow rough-terrain operations, the BK 117A-3M has been fitted with taller skid landing gear. The helicopter's self-defence package includes the installation of radar-warning receiver and countermeasures launcher equipment.

**Specification:** MBB/Kawasaki BK 117A-3
**Origin:** West Germany and Japan
**Type:** multi-role helicopter
**Powerplant:** two 410-kW (550-shp) Avco Lycoming LTS101-650B-1 turboshafts
**Performance:** maximum cruising speed 134 kt (243 km/h) 154 mph) at sea level; maximum operating altitude 10,000 ft (3050 m); operating range 493 km (306 miles) on standard fuel with no reserves; maximum endurance 2 hours 45 minutes
**Weights:** empty 1695 kg (3,737 lb); maximum take-off 3200 kg (7,055 lb) **Dimensions:** main rotor diameter 11.00 m (36 ft 1.1 in); length, rotors turning 13.00 m (42 ft 7.8 in); height 3.36 m (11 ft 0.3in); main rotor disc area 95.03 m² (1,022.93 sq ft)
**Armament:** none

*MBB/Kawasaki BK 117 of the Japanese government.*

*MBB/Kawasaki BK 117*

**BK 117s have only been ordered in small numbers by military customers, although some are in service with paramilitary police forces.**

**This BK 117 is seen wearing the markings of the Bophutatswana Defence Force. The aircraft were passed on to the South African Air Force when the nominally independent homelands were reabsorbed into South Africa.**

## Role

Fighter
Close support
Counter-insurgency
Tactical strike
Strategic bomber
Tactical reconnaissance
Strategic reconnaissance
Maritime patrol
Anti-ship strike
Anti-submarine warfare
Search and rescue
Assault transport
Transport
Liaison
Trainer
Inflight-refuelling tanker
Specialized

## Performance

All-weather capability
Rough field capability
STOL capability
VTOL capability
Airspeed 0-250 mph
Airspeed 250 mph-Mach 1
Airspeed Mach 1 plus
Ceiling 0-20,000 ft
Ceiling 20,000-40,000 ft
Ceiling 40,000ft plus
Range 0-1,000 miles
Range 1,000-3,000 miles
Range 3,000 miles plus

## Weapons

Air-to-air missiles
Air-to-surface missiles
Cruise missiles
Cannon
Trainable guns
Naval weapons
Nuclear-capable
Rockets
'Smart' weapon kit
Weapon load 0-4,000 lb
Weapon load 4,000-15,000 lb
Weapon load 15,000 lb plus

## Avionics

Electronic Counter Measures
Electronic Support Measures
Search radar
Fire control radar
Look-down/shoot-down
Terrain-following radar
Forward-looking infra-red
Laser
Television

# Mikoyan-Gurevich MiG-17 'Fresco'

*Mikoyan-Gurevich MiG-17 'Fresco' of the Bulgarian air force.*

**Role**
Fighter
Close support
Counter-insurgency
Tactical strike
Strategic bomber
Tactical reconnaissance
Strategic reconnaissance
Maritime patrol
Anti-ship strike
Anti-submarine warfare
Search and rescue
Assault transport
Transport
Liaison
Trainer
Inflight-refuelling tanker
Specialized

**Performance**
All-weather capability
Rough field capability
STOL capability
VTOL capability
Airspeed 0-250 mph
Airspeed 250 mph-Mach 1
Airspeed Mach 1 plus
Ceiling 0-20,000 ft
Ceiling 20,000-40,000 ft
Ceiling 40,000ft plus
Range 0-1,000 miles
Range 1,000-3,000 miles
Range 3,000 miles plus

**Weapons**
Air-to-air missiles
Air-to-surface missiles
Cruise missiles
Cannon
Trainable guns
Naval weapons
Nuclear-capable
Rockets
'Smart' weapon kit
Weapon load 0-4,000 lb
Weapon load 4,000-15,000 lb
Weapon load 15,000 lb plus

**Avionics**
Electronic Counter Measures
Electronic Support Measures
Search radar
Fire control radar
Look-down/shoot-down
Terrain-following radar
Forward-looking infra-red
Laser
Television

Early Korean encounters between the MiG-15 and fighters which Allied nations had regarded as superior caused a major shock to the West. The MiG-15 could show a 'clean pair of heels' to all but the North American F-86 Sabre, and even proved superior to the F-86 in rate of climb, operational ceiling and manoeuvrability at altitude. The following **Mikoyan-Gurevich MiG-17**, often regarded as merely an improved MiG-15, gained its place in aviation history from its extensive and effective use by the North Vietnamese air force during 1965-73, and went on to serve with some 30 air arms. Its development, starting at the beginning of 1949 as Aircraft SI or I-330, was intended to eliminate the shortcomings of the MiG-15, and when the type entered service in late 1952 it was given the designation MiG-17 and allocated the NATO reporting name **'Fresco'**.

Major revisions between the MiG-15 and the initial production MiG-17 included a new wing of thinner section with many aerodynamic changes, a slightly lengthened rear fuselage, tail surfaces of increased area, wider-track main landing gear units and, after initial tests, the addition of a ventral fin and

revised airbrakes. Internal changes provided a new ejector seat and better instrumentation, and the powerplant was the 2700-kg (5,952-lb) dry thrust Klimov VK-1A turbojet. Later variants were the **MiG-17P 'Fresco-B'** interceptor with Izumrud radar; the **MiG-17F 'Fresco-C'** major production type with the VK-1F afterburning turbojet and, later, AA-2 'Atoll' AAMs; the **MiG-17PF 'Fresco-D'** which introduced an improved Izumrud radar to the MiG-17F; and the generally similar **MiG-17PFU 'Fresco-E'** which replaced gun armament by four AA-1 'Alkali' beam-riding AAMs. Soviet production is estimated at 6,000, of which about 83 per cent were MiG-17Fs.

Licence production in Poland covered about 1,000 aircraft, mostly MiG-17Fs under the local designation **LiM-5P**, but the WSK PZL-Mielec works also developed a **LiM-5M** ground-attack version. This had extra bomb pylons forward of the wheel wells, provision for a braking parachute, and was equipped for the attachment of auxiliary take-off rockets to get the more-heavily laden aircraft airborne. The MiG-17 was also built in China (to the extent of some 2,000 aircraft) as the **Shenyang J-5** fighter and **JJ-5** trainer.

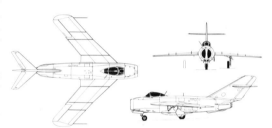

*Mikoyan-Gurevich MiG-17F 'Fresco-A'*

**Specification:** Mikoyan-Gurevich MiG-17F 'Fresco'
**Origin:** USSR (now CIS)
**Type:** fighter-bomber
**Powerplant:** one 3380-kg (7,452-lb) afterburning thrust Klimov VK-1F turbojet
**Performance:** maximum speed 617 kt (1144 km/h;711 mph) at 9,845ft (3000 m); afterburning climb to 16,405 ft (5000 m) in 1 minute 48 seconds; service ceiling 54,460 ft (16600 m); maximum range 1980 km (1,230 miles) with internal and external fuel
**Weights:** empty 3930 kg (8,664 lb); maximum take-off 6075 kg (13,393 lb)
**Dimensions:** span 9.63 m (31 ft 7.1 in); length 11.26 m (36 ft 11.3 in); height 3.80 m (12 ft 5.6 in); wing area 22.60 m² (243.27 sq ft)
**Armament:** one 37-mm N-37D cannon with 40 rounds and two 23-mm NR-23 cannon with 80 rounds per gun; four (later six) underwing hardpoints for bombs and/or rocket launchers and, later in the type's life, two AA-2 'Atoll' AAMs; the inboard hardpoints were usually reserved for drop tanks

*This is a LiM-5M (Polish licence-built MiG-17 ground-attack variant) of the Polish air force. The braking parachute and weapons pylons that distinguish this variant are clearly visible.*

*This row of battered-looking LiM-5M ground-attack fighters belonged to the Polish air force. The MiG-17 remains in service with several members of the old Soviet alliance and its client states.*

# Mikoyan-Gurevich MiG-19 'Farmer'

*Mikoyan-Gurevich MiG-19 'Farmer of the Cuban air force.*

There seems little agreement, beyond the year, for the first flight date of the **Mikoyan-Gurevich MiG-19**, and indeed this aeroplane was regarded as inferior both to the MiG-17 that preceded it and the MiG-21 which followed. The MiG-19's early claim to fame was as the USSR's first production fighter capable of sustained supersonic speed. The North American F-100 Super Sabre is regarded as the world s first production fighter to hold this achievement. But one of the MiG-19 prototypes might just as easily have been the world's first. In Soviet air force use, the new fighter entered service in late 1954 but production began to slow towards the end of 1957, apparently because more impressive aircraft were then entering service. One sure fact lies with the Chinese, who discovered the MiG-19's exceptional combat capability and continue to build it to this day as the **Shenyang J-6** fighter and **JJ-6** trainer, and also used it as basis for the Nanchang Q-5.

The MiG-19 took shape from experimental aircraft, a derivative of the MiG-17 providing the centre/rear fuselage, tail unit and twin Mikulin AM-5 axial turbojets. and another its forward fuselage and wing swept at 55°. When flown with 2000-kg (4,409-lb) dry thrust AM-5 turbojets, the resulting I-360

prototype failed to become supersonic, but in the late summer of 1953 AM-5F afterburning engines enabled the aircraft to attain Mach 1.12, and in early 1954 the type was ordered into production as the MiG-19, NATO reporting name **'Farmer-A'**. Early service use confirmed engine unreliability and a serious deficiency in elevator control at high speed, the ensuing **MiG-19S 'Farmer-C'** introducing slab-type all-moving horizontal tail surfaces, more powerful Tumanskii RD-9B turbojets and armament of three 30-mm NR-30 cannon. Later variants included the **MiG-19SF** with RD-9BF engines; the **MiG-19P 'Farmer-D'** introducing Izumrud radar and the reduced armament of two 23-mm NR-23 cannon; the **MiG-PF** with two 30-mm NR-30 cannon; the **MiG-19PFM** with radar and four AA-1 'Alkali' AAMs; the reconnaissance **MiG-19R** which replaced fuselage armament with a vertical/oblique camera outfit: and the **MiG-19UTI** tandem-seat trainer having reduced fuel but retaining armament. Soviet production of all versions is estimated at some 2,500 aircraft, and the type was used by the Warsaw Pact air forces (Czechoslovakia and Polish designations respectively **S-105** and **LiM-7**) and exported to many other nations.

**Specification:** Mikoyan-Gurevich MiG-19S 'Farmer-C'
**Origin:** USSR (now CIS)
**Type:** day/clear weather interceptor
**Powerplant:** two 3250-kg (7,165-lb) afterburning thrust Tumanskii RD-9B turbojets
**Performance:** maximum speed Mach 1.35 or 784 kt (1453 km/h; 903 mph) at 32,810 ft (10000 m); initial climb rate 22,640 ft (6900 m) per minute, service ceiling 58,725 ft (17900 m); combat radius 685 km (426 miles) with drop tanks
**Weights:** empty 5170 kg (11,397; maximum take-off 8900 kg (19,621 lb)
**Dimensions:** span 9.20 m (30 ft 2.2 in); length (excluding probe) 12.60 m (41 ft 4.1 in); height 3.90 m (12 ft 9.5 in); wing area 25.00 m² (269.11 sq ft)
**Armament:** three 30-mm NR-30 cannon with 55 and 75 rounds per gun for the one fuselage and two wing root-mounted guns respectively

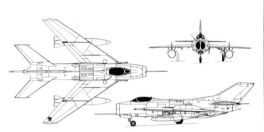

**Mikoyan-Gurevich MiG-19S 'Farmer-C'**

*The radar-equipped, missile-armed, all-weather MiG-19PFM is no longer in widespread service. This example is seen in East German markings. Eastern European MiG-19s are now used mainly for training.*

*These MiG-19 'Farmers' belong to the Czechoslovakian air force, which retained a small number of these aircraft into the later 1980s for support duties.*

### Role
Fighter
Close support
Counter-insurgency
Tactical strike
Tactical bomber
Strategic bomber
Strategic reconnaissance
Tactical reconnaissance
Maritime patrol
Anti-ship strike
Anti-submarine warfare
Search and rescue
Assault transport
Transport
Liaison
Trainer
Inflight-refuelling tanker
Specialized

### Performance
All-weather capability
Rough field capability
STOL capability
VTOL capability
Airspeed 0-250 mph
Airspeed 250 mph-Mach 1
Airspeed Mach 1 plus
Ceiling 0-20,000 ft
Ceiling 20,000-40,000 ft
Ceiling 40,000ft plus
Range 0-1,000 miles
Range 1,000-3,000 miles
Range 3,000 miles plus

### Weapons
Air-to-air missiles
Air-to-surface missiles
Cruise missiles
Cannon
Trainable guns
Naval weapons
Nuclear-capable
Rockets
'Smart' weapon kit
Weapon load 0-4,000 lb
Weapon load 4,000-15,000 lb
Weapon load 15,000 lb plus

### Avionics
Electronic Counter Measures
Electronic Support Measures
Search radar
Fire control radar
Look-down/shoot-down
Terrain-following radar
Forward-looking infra-red
Laser
Television

# Mikoyan-Gurevich MiG-21bis 'Fishbed-L' and 'Fishbed-N'

*Mikoyan-Gurevich MiG-21bis 'Fishbed' of the Soviet air force based in Afghanistan.*

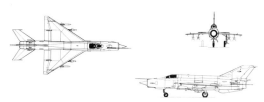

## Role
Fighter
Close support
Counter-insurgency
Tactical strike
Strategic bomber
Tactical reconnaissance
Strategic reconnaissance
Maritime patrol
Anti-ship strike
Anti-submarine warfare
Search and rescue
Assault transport
Transport
Liaison
Trainer
Inflight-refuelling tanker
Specialized

## Performance
All-weather capability
Rough field capability
STOL capability
VTOL capability
Airspeed 0-250 mph
Airspeed 250 mph-Mach 1
Airspeed Mach 1 plus
Ceiling 0-20,000 ft
Ceiling 20,000-40,000 ft
Ceiling 40,000ft plus
Range 0-1,000 miles
Range 1,000-3,000 miles
Range 3,000 miles plus

## Weapons
Air-to-air missiles
Air-to-surface missiles
Cruise missiles
Cannon
Trainable guns
Naval weapons
Nuclear-capable
Rockets
'Smart' weapon kit
Weapon load 0-4,000 lb
Weapon load 4,000-15,000 lb
Weapon load 15,000 lb plus

## Avionics
Electronic Counter Measures
Electronic Support Measures
Search radar
Fire control radar
Look-down/shoot-down
Terrain-following radar
Forward-looking infra-red
Laser
Television

The third and final Soviet generation of the **Mikoyan-Gurevich MiG-21 'Fishbed'** is represented by the **MiG-21bis**, which in its initial versions was reportedly flown during 1971 and allocated the NATO reporting name **'Fishbed-L'**. Outwardly similar to the preceding single-seat production variants, this was the first updated multi-role version of the earlier MiG-21PFMA/MF line with improved construction and updated avionics. Significant changes included the introduction of a wider and deeper dorsal fairing providing greater volume for installed equipment, and seven self-sealing tanks that, by comparison with the MiG-21MF, gave an increase of almost 12 per cent in internal fuel capacity.

Four years later a further refined version of the 'Fishbed-L' was introduced; this **'Fishbed-N'** benefited from additional improvements in construction which, collectively with those of the earlier 'Fishbed-L', were intended to provide a lighter-weight structure of increased service life. The opportunity was also taken for a further

update in avionics capability, noticeable externally by the provision of a so-called bow and arrow antenna at the aircraft's nose. However, the most important change in this variant relates to the introduction of new powerplant in the form of the Tumanskii R-25 two-spool turbojet. While this is installationally interchangeable with the earlier Tumanskii R-13, it represents a new design with a two-stage afterburner and a high pressure ratio compressor that gives a significant reduction in specific fuel consumption. The 'Fishbed-N' remains in current but limited and steadily declining service with the Russian air force.

Following the delivery of 75 Soviet-built aircraft, production of the 'Fishbed-N' was started by Hindustan Aeronautics Ltd in India (initially from Soviet-built components) where it superseded the MiG-21M on the line at Nasik in 1981. The R-25 engine has also been licence-built up to 1987, in this instance by HAL's Koraput division, where the final aircraft were completed during 1986-7.

***Mikoyan-Gurevich MiG-21bis 'Fishbed-N'***

**Specification:** Mikoyan-Gurevich MiG-21bis 'Fishbed-N'
**Origin:** USSR (now CIS)
**Type:** multi-role fighter
**Powerplant:** one 7500-kg (16,535-lb) afterburning thrust Tumanskii R-25 turbojet
**Performance:** maximum speed Mach 2.1 or 1,203 kt (2229 km/h; 1,385 mph) above 36,090 ft (11000 m); initial climb rate 58,000 ft (17680 m) per minute with 50 per cent fuel and two AA-2 'Atoll' AAMs; service ceiling 57,400 ft (17500 m); range 1160 km (721 miles) with maximum internal fuel
**Weights:** empty 5200 kg (11,464 lb); maximum take-off 22,925 lb (10400 kg)
**Dimensions:** span 7.15 m (23 ft 5.5 in); length (including probe) 15.76 m (51 ft 8.5 in); height 4.10 m (13 ft 5.4 in); wing area 23.00 m² (247.58 sq ft)
**Armament:** one 23-mm GSh-23 two-barrel cannon with 200 rounds, plus four underwing pylons suitable for AA-2 'Atoll' orAA-8 'Aphid' AAMs, UV-16-57 rocket launchers, 500- or 250-kg (1,102- or 551-lb) bombs, S-24 240-mm(9.45-in) air-to-surface rockets, or drop tanks

*Lieutenant Y. Cholokhyan is receiving last-minute instructions from Captain A. Fetisov before he boards his MiG-21bis somewhere in the Leningrad (now St Petersburg) military district.*

*The Finnish air force received the MiG-21bis from 1978 as a replacement for its ageing MiG-21F-12s. These aircraft serve with HavLv31 at Kuopio Rissala.*

# Mikoyan-Gurevich MiG-21U 'Mongol'

*Mikoyan-Gurevich MiG-21UM 'Mongol-B' of the Finnish air force.*

The desirability of developing a trainer version of the MiG-21 was recognized at an early date, and the Ye-6U prototype is reported to have flown for the first time in June 1960.

The initial production version, designated **Mikoyan-Gurevich MiG-21U** and allocated the NATO reporting name **'Mongol-A'**, was generally similar to the initial major production MiG-21F. The most obvious change, was, of course, the introduction of a second cockpit in tandem, both cockpits being enclosed by a sideways opening (to starboard) double canopy.

Other variations included the provision of a one-piece forward airbrake, deletion of the cannon armament, repositioning of the pitot boom above the engine inlet, and adoption of the larger mainwheels and tyres which had been first introduced on the MiG-21PF. Later in the production programme further revisions were adopted from subsequent single-seat models and were sufficiently distinctive to warrant the new NATO reporting name **'Mongol-B'**.

This included vertical tail surfaces of increased chord, a deeper dorsal spine, brake parachute housing repositioned beneath the rudder, and deletion of the dorsal fin fillet.

Towards the end of MiG-21U production the SPS flap-blowing system was introduced on the production line, together with a retractable periscope to enhance the instructor's forward field of view. This type, known as the **MiG-21US**, retained the NATO designation 'Mongol-B', as did the final two-seat trainer version, the **MiG-21UM**. This last, being based on the multi-role MiG-21MF, introduced that version's four underwing pylons and the Tumanskii R-13 turbojet.

In addition to production for the Soviet air force, the trainer variant was also built for other air arms. India initially procured small numbers of the MiG-21U 'Mongol-A' which were given the IAF designation **Type 66-400**, and larger quantities of the later MiG-21U 'Mongol-B', which were identified as the **Type 66-600**.

**Specification:** Mikoyan-Gurevich MiG-21US 'Mongol-B'
**Origin:** USSR (now CIS)
**Type:** two-seat trainer
**Powerplant:** one 5950-kg (13,118-lb) afterburning thrust Tumanskii R-11F2S-300 turbojet
**Performance:** maximum speed Mach 2.02 or 1,158 kt (2145 km/h; 1,333 mph) above 40,025 ft (12200 m); initial climb rate 20,995 ft (6400 m) per minute
**Weights:** not recorded
**Dimensions:** span 7.15 m (23 ft 5.5 in); length (including probe) 15.76 m (51 ft 8.5 in); height 4.10 m (13 ft 5.4 in); wing area 23.00 m² (247.58 sq ft)
**Armament:** none

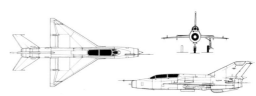

**Mikoyan-Gurevich MiG-21U 'Mongol-A'**

*This Czech trainer is an early-series MiG-21U 'Mongol-A', and lacks the retractable rear-seat periscope and repositioned brake chute housing of later versions.*

*India's large fleet of MiG-21 fighters is supported by numbers of two-seat 'Mongols', many of them licence-built at the Nasik plant of Hindustan Aeronautics.*

**Role**
Fighter
Close support
Counter-insurgency
Tactical strike
Strategic bomber
Tactical reconnaissance
Strategic reconnaissance
Maritime patrol
Anti-ship strike
Anti-submarine warfare
Search and rescue
Assault transport
Transport
Liaison
Trainer
Inflight-refuelling tanker
Specialized

**Performance**
All-weather capability
Rough field capability
STOL capability
VTOL capability
Airspeed 0-250 mph
Airspeed 250 mph-Mach 1
Airspeed Mach 1 plus
Ceiling 0-20,000 ft
Ceiling 20,000-40,000 ft
Ceiling 40,000ft plus
Range 0-1,000 miles
Range 1,000-3,000 miles
Range 3,000 miles plus

**Weapons**
Air-to-air missiles
Air-to-surface missiles
Cruise missiles
Cannon
Trainable guns
Naval weapons
Nuclear-capable
Rockets
'Smart' weapon kit
Weapon load 0-4,000 lb
Weapon load 4,000-15,000 lb
Weapon load 15,000 lb plus

**Avionics**
Electronic Counter Measures
Electronic Support Measures
Search radar
Fire control radar
Look-down/shoot-down
Terrain-following radar
Forward-looking infra-red
Laser
Television

# Mikoyan-Gurevich MiG-23 'Flogger-B', 'Flogger-E' and 'Flogger-G' and 'Flogger-J'

Quite early in its life it was realized that the MiG-21 had shortcomings in its payload/range performance, and in early 1965 a requirement was issued for a replacement to eliminate these problems. This resulted in two approaches by the Mikoyan-Gurevich bureau. One of these was basically an enlarged version of the MiG-21 with two lift-jet engines: identified by the NATO reporting name 'Faithless', it suffered the inherent weight/control problems associated with this type of powerplant and was soon abandoned.

The alternative Ye-23-11/1 prototype, with a variable-geometry wing to optimize low- and high-speed performance, was first seen during the Aviation Day flypast of 9 July 1967. Apart from its variable-geometry wing, the other notable feature was adoption of side inlets to allow incorporation of search radar in the nose and give greater fuselage volume for fuel. The Mikoyan-Gurevich MiG-23 prototype, powered by a 10000-kg (22,046-lb) afterburning thrust Lyul'ka AL-7F-1 turbojet, was followed by small batches of the similar pre-production MiG-23S, and MiG-23SM with four external pylons, all three being accorded the NATO reporting name 'Flogger-A'.

The MiG-23M 'Flogger-B' was the first series production version: entering service in 1972 it introduced the 10200-kg (22,487-lb) afterburning thrust Khachaturov R-29-300 turbojet. The use of this lighter engine dictated

that the wings be moved forward about 0.61 m (2 ft 0). Other changes included an increase of wing chord on the movable panels, a reduction in rear fuselage length, and adoption of a smaller dorsal fin. Introduced in about 1975, the MiG-23MF and MiG-23MS 'Flogger-E' are the export versions of the MiG-23M with the 10000-kg (22,046-lb) afterburning thrust Tumanskii R-27F2M-300 turbojet and the less capable 'Jay Bird' fire-control radar in place of the MiG-23M's Sapfir-23D-Sh 'High Lark' and no IR search/track system or Doppler navigation.

From 1978 the MiG-23M was complemented by the MiG-23ML 'Flogger-G' improved and lightened model with a smaller dorsal fin, new nose landing gear, Sapfir-23ML lightweight radar, a new undernose pod for the TP-23M IR search/tracker system, and the Khachaturov R-35F-300 turbojet. In 1985 more than 2,000 'Flogger-B' and 'Flogger-G' interceptors were estimated to be in Soviet air force use, and the variants are still the most important Russian interceptors in numerical terms.

The latest version of the MiG-23 to be identified is the MiG-23MLD 'Flogger-K', a variant of the MiG-23ML with new IFF, outboard underwing hardpoints, RWR and chaff/flare dispensers, and notches in the wing glove leading edges generate vortices which improve handling at high angles of attack .

**Specification:** Mikoyan-Gurevich MiG-23ML 'Flogger-G'
**Origin:** USSR (now CIS)
**Type:** air-combat fighter
**Powerplant:** one 13000-kg (28,660-lb) afterburning thrust Khachaturov R-35-300 turbojet
**Performance:** maximum speed Mach 2.35 or 1,350 kt (2500 km/h; 1,553 mph) at high altitude; initial climb rate 47,244 ft (14400 m) per minute; service ceiling 60,695 ft (18500 m); combat radius 1150 km (715 miles) with six AAMs; ferry range 2820 km (1,752 miles) with three drop tanks
**Weights:** empty 10200 kg (22,485 lb); maximum take-off 17800 kg (39,250 lb)
**Dimensions:** span 13.965 m (45 ft 10 in) spread and 7.779 m (25 ft 6.25 in); length (including probe) 16.71 m (54 ft 10 in); height 4.82 m (15 ft 9.75 in); wing area 37.25 m² (402.0 sq ft) spread
**Armament:** one 23-mm GSh-23L two-barrel cannon with 200 rounds; provision for up to 3000 kg (6,614 lb) of disposable stores, including AAMs, cannon pods, rocket-launcher pods, large-calibre rockets, and bombs, carried on six external hardpoints

*Mikoyan-Gurevich MiG-23MF 'Flogger-B' of the East German air force.*

*Mikoyan-Gurevich MiG-23M 'Flogger-B'*

*This MiG-23M 'Flogger-B' of Frontal Aviation carries R-23R (AA-7 'Apex') missiles underwing and R-60 (AA-8 'Aphid') missiles under the engine inlets.*

*Some Voyska PVO (Air-Defence Troops) 'Floggers' wore an over all air-superiority grey colour scheme. This aircraft wears a Distinguished Unit badge on the nose.*

**Role**
Fighter
Close support
Counter-insurgency
Tactical strike
Strategic bomber
Tactical reconnaissance
Strategic reconnaissance
Maritime patrol
Anti-ship strike
Anti-submarine warfare
Search and rescue
Assault transport
Transport
Liaison
Trainer
Inflight-refuelling tanker
Specialized

**Performance**
All-weather capability
Rough field capability
STOL capability
VTOL capability
Airspeed 0-250 mph
Airspeed 250 mph-Mach 1
Airspeed Mach 1 plus
Ceiling 0-20,000 ft
Ceiling 20,000-40,000 ft
Ceiling 40,000ft plus
Range 0-1,000 miles
Range 1,000-3,000 miles
Range 3,000 miles plus

**Weapons**
Air-to-air missiles
Air-to-surface missiles
Cruise missiles
Cannon
Trainable guns
Naval weapons
Nuclear-capable
Rockets
'Smart' weapon kit
Weapon load 0-4,000 lb
Weapon load 4,000-15,000 lb
Weapon load 15,000 lb plus

**Avionics**
Electronic Counter Measures
Electronic Support Measures
Search radar
Fire control radar
Look-down/shoot-down
Terrain-following radar
Forward-looking infra-red
Laser
Television

# Mikoyan-Gurevich MiG-23M 'Flogger-E' and MiG-23UB 'Flogger-C'

The MiG-23BN/BM 'Flogger-F' and MiG-23BK 'Flogger-H' are basically fighter-bomber versions of the MiG-23 air combat fighter that have been widely exported. However, before development of the first of them, the MiG-23BN, was complete, a version of the MiG-23M 'Flogger-B' air combat fighter was made available for export to nations other than those constituting the USSR's Warsaw Pact allies.

Identified as the **Mikoyan-Gurevich MiG-23MF 'Flogger-E'**, this is intentionally somewhat downgraded and has a lower standard of equipment than that installed in the MiG-23BNs equipping the Soviet air force and the WarPac nations. The 'Flogger-E' retains the same airframe as its predecessor but is powered by the 10000kg (22,046-lb) afterburning thrust Tumanskii R-27F2M-300 turbojet and is easily distinguishable by its shortened nose radome to house its earlier-generation 'Jay Bird' attack radar. 'Jay Bird' has reported search and tracking ranges of about 29 and 19 km (18 and 12 miles) respectively and no look-down capability, and coupled with the fact that it has no Doppler navigation or IR sensor pod, the MiG-23MF (or

**MiG-23MS** with slightly different equipment) is clearly far less capable than the MiG-23M. For inbuilt armament, the 'Flogger-E' carries the 23-mm GSh-23L two-barrel cannon, but instead of AA-7 'Apex' or AA-8 'Aphid' AAMs has the earlier-generation AA-2 'Atoll' AAM.

The versatile and capable MiG-23 family also includes a two-seat trainer for the conversion and proficiency roles although its retains full combat capability. Designated **MiG-23UB** and possessing the NATO reporting name **'Flogger-C'**, this is based on the MiG-23M but has the R-27F2M-300 turbojet. The second cockpit, for the instructor, is to the rear of the standard cockpit: it has the seat slightly raised and is provided with a retractable periscope sight to give a more comprehensive forward view. Each cockpit has an individual canopy, and because that at the rear is slightly higher to provide adequate headroom for the instructor, the dorsal fairing immediately to the rear of the aft canopy is of increased depth. In addition to serving with the Soviet air force and WarPac nations, the MiG-23UB has also been exported.

*Mikoyan-Gurevich MiG-23MF/MS 'Flogger-E' of the Libyan air force.*

*Mikoyan-Gurevich MiG-23MF/MS 'Flogger-E'*

*Two-seat 'Floggers' use the same 'Jay Bird' radar as export versions of the aircraft. This MiG-23UB 'Flogger-C' belonged to the East German air force and was used for conversion training.*

*This picture shows to advantage the small 'Jay Bird' radome fitted to the 'Flogger-E'. This aircraft was essentially for export, although this example carries Soviet insignia.*

## Specification: Mikoyan-Gurevich MiG-23MF/MS 'Flogger-E'
**Origin:** USSR (now CIS)
**Type:** air combat fighter
**Powerplant:** one 10000-kg (22,046-lb) afterburning thrust Tumanskii R-27F2M-300 turbojet
**Performance:** not disclosed but of a lower standard than that of the MiG-23ML
**Weights:** not disclosed
**Dimensions:** span 13.965 m (45 ft 10 in) spread and 7.779 m (25 ft 6.25 in); length (including probe) 16.71 m (54 ft 10 in); height 4.82 m (15 ft 9.75 in); wing area 37.25 m² (402.0 sq ft) spread
**Armament:** one 23-mm GSh-23L two-barrel cannon with 200 rounds; provision for up to 3000 kg (6,614 lb) of disposable stores, including AAMs, cannon pods, rocket-launcher pods, large-calibre rockets, and bombs, carried on six external hardpoints

| Role |
|---|
| Fighter |
| Close support |
| Counter-insurgency |
| Tactical strike |
| Strategic bomber |
| Tactical reconnaissance |
| Strategic reconnaissance |
| Maritime patrol |
| Anti-ship strike |
| Anti-submarine warfare |
| Search and rescue |
| Assault transport |
| Transport |
| Liaison |
| Trainer |
| Inflight-refuelling tanker |
| Specialized |

| Performance |
|---|
| All-weather capability |
| Rough field capability |
| STOL capability |
| VTOL capability |
| Airspeed 0-250 mph |
| Airspeed 250 mph-Mach 1 |
| Airspeed Mach 1 plus |
| Ceiling 0-20,000 ft |
| Ceiling 20,000-40,000 ft |
| Ceiling 40,000ft plus |
| Range 0-1,000 miles |
| Range 1,000-3,000 miles |
| Range 3,000 miles plus |

| Weapons |
|---|
| Air-to-air missiles |
| Air-to-surface missiles |
| Cruise missiles |
| Cannon |
| Trainable guns |
| Naval weapons |
| Nuclear-capable |
| Rockets |
| 'Smart' weapon kit |
| Weapon load 0-4,000 lb |
| Weapon load 4,000-15,000 lb |
| Weapon load 15,000 lb |

| Avionics |
|---|
| Electronic Counter Measures |
| Electronic Support Measures |
| Search radar |
| Fire control radar |
| Look-down/shoot-down |
| Terrain-following radar |
| Forward-looking infra-red |
| Laser |
| Television |

# Mikoyan-Gurevich MiG-23B/BK/BM/BN 'Flogger-F/-H'

*A Mikoyan-Gurevich MiG-23BM 'Flogger-F' of the the Algerian air force.*

## Role
Fighter
Close support
Counter-insurgency
Tactical strike
Strategic bomber
Tactical reconnaissance
Strategic reconnaissance
Maritime patrol
Anti-ship strike
Anti-submarine warfare
Search and rescue
Assault transport
Transport
Liaison
Trainer
Inflight-refuelling tanker
Specialized

## Performance
All-weather capability
Rough field capability
STOL capability
VTOL capability
Airspeed 0-250 mph
Airspeed 250 mph-Mach 1
Airspeed Mach 1 plus
Ceiling 0-20,000 ft
Ceiling 20,000-40,000 ft
Ceiling 40,000ft plus
Range 0-1,000 miles
Range 1,000-3,000 miles
Range 3,000 miles plus

## Weapons
Air-to-air missiles
Air-to-surface missiles
Cruise missiles
Cannon
Trainable guns
Naval weapons
Nuclear-capable
Rockets
'Smart' weapon kit
Weapon load 0-4,000 lb
Weapon load 4,000-15,000 lb
Weapon load 15,000 lb plus

## Avionics
Electronic Counter Measures
Electronic Support Measures
Search radar
Fire control radar
Look-down/shoot-down
Terrain-following radar
Forward-looking infra-red
Laser
Television

Mikoyan began studies of a 'jet *Shturmovik*' during 1969, to meet a Frontal Aviation requirement for a cheap, mass-produced attack aircraft offering the same level of capability as the SEPECAT Jaguar.

The original MiG-23's rugged airframe, strong undercarriage, powerful engine and variable geometry wing made it extremely suitable for conversion or adaptation to the fighter-bomber role. The use of a swing wing allowed high straight line performance, while also endowing excellent low-speed handling characteristics, turn performance and short take-off/landing distances.

The basic **MiG-23B (32-34)** was based on the airframe of the MiG-23S, but with a new nose giving an improved view forward and downward, and with a 112.78-kN (25,353-lb st) Lyul'ka AL-21F-300 powerplant in a shortened rear fuselage. Radar was not installed. Armour was scabbed on to the sides of the forward fuselage, and the fuel tanks were fitted with an inert gas fire protection system. A missile illuminator and a TV camera were housed in bullet-like fairings on the wingroot gloves. Piotr Ostapenko flew the first prototype on 20 August 1970. Production soon switched to the **MiG-23BN (32-23)**, an upgraded nav/attack system. The MiG-23B and MiG-23BN share the NATO reporting name '**Flogger-F**' but proved disappointing in service, and many were subsequently upgraded to **MiG-23BK (32-36)** or **MiG-23BM (32-25)** standards, or exported, mainly to Third World customers. Two new fighter-bombers were quickly developed, both sharing the same '**Flogger-H**' reporting name. They had new RWR fairings on the lower 'corners' of the fuselage. The MiG-23BK had the same nav/attack system and laser rangefinder as the MiG-27K. The MiG-23BM was similar, but with the same nav/attack system as the MiG-27D. Confusingly, the MiG-23BN designation seems to have been adopted as an overall service designation, sometimes being applied to aircraft designated BM or BK by the bureau. Many export 'Flogger-Hs' are described as MiG-23BNs, but are actually to MiG-23BK standards. East Germany's MiG-23BKs' documentation described them as MiG-24BNs.

**Specification:** Mikoyan-Gurevich MiG-23BN 'Flogger F'
**Origin:** USSR (now CIS)
**Type:** single-seat ground-attack aircraft
**Powerplant:** one Soyuz (Tumanski) R-29B-300 turbojet rated at 77 kN (17,310 lb) or 110kN (24,728 lb) with afterburner
**Weight:** maximum take-off 18850 kg (41,556 lb)
**Dimensions:** span (spread) 13.965 m (45.9 ft) and (swept) 7.779 m (25 ft 6.5 in); length 16.7 m (54.8 ft); height 4.82 m (14 ft 9.2 in); wing area (spread) 37.35 m² (402 sq ft)
**Armament:** one internal GSh-23L 23-mm twin-barrel cannon in semi-conformal fuselage gondola, plus up to 3000 kg of ordnance, including UV-32-57 (57 mm) and S-8 (80 mm) rocket pods, KMG-U bomblet dispensers, free-fall bombs up to 500 kg, UPK-23-250 cannon pods, AS-7 Kerry ASMs and podded reconnaissance sensors.

**Mikoyan-Gurevich MiG-23BN 'Flogger-H'**

**Two Frontal Aviation pilots walk away from their MiG-23BN 'Flogger-Hs' after a training sortie. Most MiG-23BMs and BNs have been for export customers.**

**The Indian Air Force is the largest operator of the MiG-23BM and BN, with some 80 in service with three squadrons. They are being augmented by locally-built MiG-27s.**

# Mikoyan-Gurevich MiG-25P 'Foxbat-A'

*Mikoyan-Gurevich MiG-25P 'Foxbat-A' of the Libyan air force.*

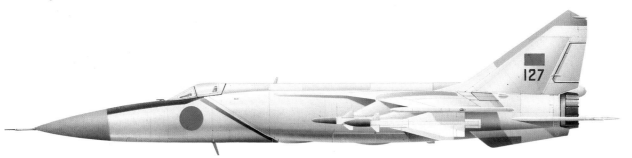

In December 1957 North American Aviation was contracted to begin development for the US Air Force of a replacement for the Boeing B-52 bomber. Few details were then published, but as the USAF had initiated development it was reasonable to assume that when it became hardware this strategic bomber would meet the specified requirement. This called for an out-and-back unrefuelled range of some 12230 km (7,600 miles) which, after the aircraft had gained cruising height, would be accomplished throughout at Mach 3.

Such capability posed serious defence problems for the USSR, and the utmost priority was given to design and development of an interceptor that could be operational in time to meet the planned 1964 in-service date for the USAF's North American B-70 Valkyrie bomber.

Even when in 1961 the B-70 was relegated to research status, after President John F. Kennedy stated that new US missiles made its development unjustifiable, work continued in the USSR to complete the development of the interceptor which became known as the **Mikoyan-Gurevich MiG-25** and was given the NATO reporting name **'Foxbat'**.

First seen by Western observers at the 1967 Soviet Aviation Day display held at Moscow's Domodedovo Airport, the distinctive shape of the MiG-25 embraces high-set wings incorporating 4° of anhedral, and compound wing sweep of 40° inboard and 38° outboard of the outer missile attachments. The slim fuselage is dominated by large rectangular inlets on each side that feed air to the two Tumanskii R-15 turbojets mounted side-by-side within the fuselage. The tail unit's twin outward-canted swept vertical surfaces, swept all-moving horizontal surfaces, and retractable single-wheel main/twin-wheel nose landing gear complete the outline of this formidable aircraft.

The initial version of the MiG-25 entered service in 1970 as the **MiG-25P**, and four of them were deployed to Egypt by the Soviet air force during the following year. Providing reconnaissance support for the Egyptian air force, these gave adequate proof over a four-year period of their invulnerability to interception by Sparrow-armed McDonnell Douglas F-4 Phantom IIs of the Israeli air force. Whether these were MiG-25P interceptors or the basic reconnaissance MiG-25R 'Foxbat-B' which followed is unsure; what is certain is that the introduction of the MiG-25R resulted in NATO redesignation of the MiG-25 as the **'Foxbat-A'**.

**Mikoyan-Gurevich MiG-25P 'Foxbat-A'**

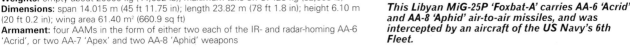

*Some MiG-25P 'Foxbat-A' interceptors are thought to remain in front-line service with the Voyska PVO, but large numbers have been converted to MiG-25 'Foxbat-E' configuration with new radar and avionics.*

**Specification:** Mikoyan-Gurevich MiG-25 'Foxbat-A'
**Origin:** USSR (now CIS)
**Type:** high-performance interceptor
**Powerplant:** two 10200-kg (22,487-lb) afterburning thrust Tumanskii R-15B-300 turbojets
**Performance:** maximum speed Mach 2.8 or 1,605 kt (2974 km/h; 1,848 mph) at high altitude with four AA-6 'Acrid' AAMs; initial climb rate 40,945 ft (12480 m) per minute; service ceiling 80,000 ft (24385 m); combat radius 1130 km (702 miles)
**Weights:** empty about 20000 kg (44,092 lb); maximum take-off 37425 kg (82,508 lb)
**Dimensions:** span 14.015 m (45 ft 11.75 in); length 23.82 m (78 ft 1.8 in); height 6.10 m (20 ft 0.2 in); wing area 61.40 m² (660.9 sq ft)
**Armament:** four AAMs in the form of either two each of the IR- and radar-homing AA-6 'Acrid', or two AA-7 'Apex' and two AA-8 'Aphid' weapons

*This Libyan MiG-25P 'Foxbat-A' carries AA-6 'Acrid' and AA-8 'Aphid' air-to-air missiles, and was intercepted by an aircraft of the US Navy's 6th Fleet.*

## Role

Fighter
Close support
Counter-insurgency
Tactical strike
Strategic bomber
Tactical reconnaissance
Strategic reconnaissance
Maritime patrol
Anti-ship strike
Anti-submarine warfare
Search and rescue
Assault transport
Transport
Liaison
Trainer
Inflight-refuelling tanker
Specialized

## Performance

All-weather capability
Rough field capability
STOL capability
VTOL capability
Airspeed 0-250 mph
Airspeed 250 mph-Mach 1
Airspeed Mach 1 plus
Ceiling 0-20,000 ft
Ceiling 20,000-40,000 ft
Ceiling 40,000ft plus
Range 0-1,000 miles
Range 1,000-3,000 miles
Range 3,000 miles plus

## Weapons

Air-to-air missiles
Air-to-surface missiles
Cruise missiles
Cannon
Trainable guns
Naval weapons
Nuclear-capable
Rockets
'Smart' weapon kit
Weapon load 0-4,000 lb
Weapon load 4,000-15,000 lb
Weapon load 15,000 lb plus

## Avionics

Electronic Counter Measures
Electronic Support Measures
Search radar
Fire control radar
Look-down/shoot-down
Terrain-following radar
Forward-looking infra-red
Laser
Television

191

# Mikoyan-Gurevich MiG-25R 'Foxbat-B' and 'Foxbat-D'

*Mikoyan-Gurevich MiG-25R 'Foxbat-D' of the Soviet air force.*

Almost certainly the success of four MiG-25P interceptors used in the reconnaissance role for Egypt from 1970 hastened final development of the dedicated reconnaissance version which entered service with the Soviet air force during 1971, about a year after the original MiG-25P interceptor. This, designated **Mikoyan- Gurevich MiG-25RB** and allocated the NATO reporting name **'Foxbat-B'**, differs in a number of details from its predecessor, the most noticeable externally being the new nose structure (of similar profile) housing the five optical cameras carried, and also incorporating a number of flush dielectric panels. Other structural changes involve the wing, which is of slightly reduced span and replaces the compound sweep of the MiG-25's leading edge with a planform that is constant from wing root to wingtip The five cameras of the 'Foxbat-B' are complemented by side-looking radar, and other equipment includes an Elint suite and an inertial navigation system with input from a Doppler navigation radar. Although its entered service as a pure reconnaissance type, the MiG-25RB can also be used at a precision bomber with 500-kg (1,102-lb) bombs released at high altitude against targets of exactly known geographical position.

The MiG-25RB was later supplemented by a number of slightly different models such as two 'Foxbat-B' subvariants (**MiG-25RBT** with different equipment and **MiG-25RBV** with the SRS-9 Elint suite) and three **'Foxbat-D'** subvariants (**MiG-25RBK** with different reconnaissance/Elint equipment, **MiG-25RBS** with different sensors, and **MiG-25RBSh** upgrade of the MiG-25RBS). The 'Foxbat-D' series is used for non-optical reconnaissance and retains a bombing capability. The variant has more flush dielectric panels, and on the starboard side has a much larger SLAR installation which, reportedly, can record surface detail up to a range of 200 km (124 miles).

It is estimated that a combined total of approximately 170 'Foxbat-B/D' aircraft entered service with the Soviet (now Russian) air force, and others were supplied to Soviet client states.

*Mikoyan-Gurevich MiG-25RBK 'Foxbat-D'*

**The MiG-25RB 'Foxbat-B' carries a small SLAR and a pack of one vertical and four oblique cameras in the nose. Large numbers are in service.**

**Two reconnaissance 'Foxbats' of the Soviet air force. Some MiG-25RBs carry no cameras, and are designated 'Foxbat-D' by NATO.**

**Specification:** Mikoyan-Gurevich MiG-25RB 'Foxbat-B'
**Origin:** USSR (now CIS)
**Type:** single-seat reconnaissance aircraft with limited precision bombing capability
**Powerplant:** two 11200-kg (24,691-lb) afterburning thrust Tumanskii R-15BD-300 turbojets
**Performance:** (estimated) maximum speed Mach 3.2 or 1,834 kt (3399 km/h; 2,112 mph) at high altitude; initial climb rate 41,995 ft (12800 m) per minute; service ceiling 88,585 ft (27000 m); operational radius 900 km (559 miles)
**Weights:** (estimated) empty 19600 kg (43,211 lb); maximum take-off 33400 kg (73,634 lb)
**Dimensions:** span 13.418 m (44 ft 0.25 in); length 23.82 m (78 ft 1.8 in); height 6.10 m (20 ft 0.2 in); wing area not disclosed
**Armament:** six 500-kg (1,102-lb) bombs carried as four under the wings and two under the fuselage

## Role
Fighter
Close support
Counter-insurgency
Tactical strike
Strategic bomber
Tactical reconnaissance
Strategic reconnaissance
Maritime patrol
Anti-ship strike
Anti-submarine warfare
Search and rescue
Assault transport
Transport
Liaison
Trainer
Inflight-refuelling tanker
Specialized

## Performance
All-weather capability
Rough field capability
STOL capability
VTOL capability
Airspeed 0-250 mph
Airspeed 250 mph-Mach 1
Airspeed Mach 1 plus
Ceiling 0-20,000 ft
Ceiling 20,000-40,000 ft
Ceiling 40,000ft plus
Range 0-1,000 miles
Range 1,000-3,000 miles
Range 3,000 miles plus

## Weapons
Air-to-air missiles
Air-to-surface missiles
Cruise missiles
Cannon
Trainable guns
Naval weapons
Nuclear-capable
Rockets
'Smart' weapon kit
Weapon load 0-4,000 lb
Weapon load 4,000-15,000 lb
Weapon load 15,000 lb plus

## Avionics
Electronic Counter Measures
Electronic Support Measures
Search radar
Fire control radar
Look-down/shoot-down
Terrain-following radar
Forward-looking infra-red
Laser
Television

# Mikoyan-Gurevich MiG-25E 'Foxbat-E' and MiG-25U 'Foxbat-C'

*Mikoyan-Gurevich MiG-25PU 'Foxbat-C' of No.106 Squadron, Indian Air Force.*

After a suitable space of time to allow for the record to be duly accredited, the Fédération Aéronautique Internationale announced that in the USSR on 31 August 1977 an aircraft identified as the E 266 M, flown by A. Fedotov, had established a new world absolute height record of 37650 m, the equivalent of 123,524 ft. More accurately known to the West as the Ye-266M, this specially prepared aircraft, powered by two turbojets of 14000-kg (30,865-lb) afterburning thrust, was used for the development of a more advanced version of the MiG-25 'Foxbat-A'. Basically the same in overall configuration and having a similar interceptor role, this new variant is identified as the **Mikoyan-Gurevich MiG-25PD** and was allocated the NATO reporting name **'Foxbat-E'**. Improved performance for this version comes from its uprated Tumanskii R-15BD-300 turbojets, and enhanced operational scope for this high-altitude interceptor is provided by the addition of an IR search/track sensor and the replacement of the original Smertch-A 'Fox Fire' radar by the new Sapfir-25 radar that provides a genuine look-down/ shoot-down capa-

bility. The type was built between 1978 and 1982, and all surviving 300 'Foxbat-A' interceptors surviving in Soviet service were rebuilt to the same standard from 1979 with the revised designation **MiG-25PDS**. Some of the aircraft were lengthened by 0.25 m (9.84 in) to accommodate inflight-refuelling equipment.

One other version of the MiG-25 is currently in service, namely the **MiG-25U 'Foxbat-C'** tandem two-seat trainer. This variant has a new forward fuselage which dispenses with nose radar and other sensors to accommodate instead a cockpit (with a separate canopy) for the pupil pilot, which is ahead of and below the level of the original cockpit. The type's subvariants are the **MiG-25PU** interceptor trainer based on the MiG-25P, and the **MiG-25RU** reconnaissance trainer based on the MiG-25RB. Neither type has armament.

In service with the Soviet (now Russian) air force, the MiG-25U is believed to have been supplied otherwise only to the Indian air force, which acquired two for training the crews of No.106 Squadron when they were converting from Canberras to the MiG-25RB 'Foxbat-B'.

**Specification:** Mikoyan-Gurevich MiG-25PU 'Foxbat-C'
**Origin:** USSR (now CIS)
**Type:** tandem two-seat trainer
**Powerplant:** two 10200-kg (22m487-lb) afterburning thrust Tumanskii R-15B-300 turbojets
**Performance:** (estimated) maximum speed Mach 2.5 or 1,433 kt (2655 km/h; 1,650 mph) at high altitude; service ceiling 65,615 ft (20000 m)
**Weights:** (estimated) maximum take-off 37425 kg (82,508 lb)
**Dimensions:** span 14.015 m (45 ft 11.75 in); length 23.82 m (78 ft 1.8 in); height 6. 10 m (20 ft 0.7 in); wing area 61.40 m (660.9 sq ft)
**Armament:** none

*Mikoyan-Gurevich MiG-25PD 'Foxbat-E' (lower side view: MiG-25PU 'Foxbat-C')*

*The MiG-25PD 'Foxbat-E' introduced a new pulse-Doppler radar with limited look-down/ shoot-down capability and a highly sensitive undernose IR detector.*

*A Soviet MiG-25PD 'Foxbat-E' with a full load of AA-6 'Acrid' air-to-air missiles. Two have IR homing and the other semi-active radar homing.*

## Role
Fighter
Close support
Counter-insurgency
Tactical strike
Strategic bomber
Strategic reconnaissance
Tactical reconnaissance
Maritime patrol
Anti-ship strike
Anti-submarine warfare
Search and rescue
Assault transport
Transport
Liaison
Trainer
Inflight-refuelling tanker
Specialized

## Performance
All-weather capability
Rough field capability
STOL capability
VTOL capability
Airspeed 0-250 mph
Airspeed 250 mph-Mach 1
Airspeed Mach 1 plus
Ceiling 0-20,000 ft
Ceiling 20,000-40,000 ft
Ceiling 40,000ft plus
Range 0-1,000 miles
Range 1,000-3,000 miles
Range 3,000 miles plus

## Weapons
Air-to-air missiles
Air-to-surface missiles
Cruise missiles
Cannon
Trainable guns
Naval weapons
Nuclear-capable
Rockets
'Smart' weapon kit
Weapon load 0-4,000 lb
Weapon load 4,000-15,000 lb
Weapon load 15,000 lb plus

## Avionics
Electronic Counter Measures
Electronic Support Measures
Search radar
Fire control radar
Look-down/shoot-down
Terrain-following radar
Forward-looking infra-red
Laser
Television

# Mikoyan-Gurevich MiG-27 'Flogger-D' and 'Flogger-J'

**Role**
Fighter
Close support
Counter-insurgency
Tactical strike
Strategic bomber
Tactical reconnaissance
Strategic reconnaissance
Maritime patrol
Anti-ship strike
Anti-submarine warfare
Search and rescue
Assault transport
Transport
Liaison
Trainer
Inflight-refuelling tanker
Specialized

**Performance**
All-weather capability
Rough field capability
STOL capability
VTOL capability
Airspeed 0-250 mph
Airspeed 250 mph-Mach 1
Airspeed Mach 1 plus
Ceiling 0-20,000 ft
Ceiling 20,000-40,000 ft
Ceiling 40,000ft plus
Range 0-1,000 miles
Range 1,000-3,000 miles
Range 3,000 miles plus

**Weapons**
Air-to-air missiles
Air-to-surface missiles
Cruise missiles
Cannon
Trainable guns
Naval weapons
Nuclear weapons
Rockets
'Smart' weapon kit
Weapon load 0-4,000 lb
Weapon load 4,000-15,000 lb
Weapon load 15,000 lb plus

**Avionics**
Electronic Counter Measures
Electronic Support Measures
Search radar
Fire control radar
Look-down/shoot-down
Terrain-following radar
Forward-looking infra-red
Laser
Television

Brief mention of the Mikoyan-Gurevich MiG-27 has already has already been made in connection with the MiG-23BN, as that 'Flogger-F' fighter-bomber variant incorporates some of the airframe features developed for this dedicated ground-attack aircraft. The most noticeable external difference from the MiG-23 family, apart from the MiG-23BN 'Flogger-F' and MiG-23BK 'Flogger-H', is the very different nose intended to give the pilot and enhanced view of the ground immediately ahead and below. However, this statement suggests only that the nose profile was changed whereas, in fact, the forward fuselage was completely redesigned. This and other revisions meant that the new ground-attack variant was different to warrant a changed designation for the aircraft that became known as the MiG-27 and which, in its initial version, was given the NATO reporting name **'Flogger-D'**.

The change in role meant that there were no conflicting requirements to demand any compromise in nose profile: with only a laser rangefinder and marked-target seeker to be housed, the nose tapers steeply down from the windscreen, optimizing a forward view which is further improved by the raising of the pilot's seat and the canopy. For operation in the hostile over-battlefield environment additional armour was added to the sides of the cockpit, and because maximum performance is needed at low altitude the powerplant's variable-geometry inlets and variable nozzle were replaced by lighter fixed inlets and nozzle, all set at an optimum position. The 'Flogger-D' has a 23-mm GSh-23L two-barrel cannon and, typically, can carry 16 250-kg (551-lb) bombs.

The 'Flogger-D' was introduced during the latter half of the 1970s, and was followed by the main 'Flogger-D' subvariant, the **MiG-27K** with a much improved PrNK-23 nav/attack system, 30-mm GSh-30-6 six-barrel cannon and a number of other important improvements, before the advent of the definitive **MiG-27D 'Flogger-J'** with an enhanced version of the nav/attack system allowing the use of a reconnaissance pod and 230mm cannon pods with angled-down barrels for strafing. First identified in 1981, the MiG-27D differs in having slight changes to the nose and has small wing root leading-edge extensions which are believed to house ECM equipment.

The export version of the MiG-27D is the **MiG-27L**, which is built under licence in India as the **MiG-27M** with the local name **Bahadur**.

**Specification:** Mikoyan-Gurevich MiG-27 'Flogger-D'
**Origin:** USSR (now CIS)
**Type:** ground-attack fighter
**Powerplant:** one 11500-kg (25,353-lb) afterburning thrust Tumanskii R-29B-300 turbojet
**Performance:** maximum speed Mach 1.7 or 1,017 kt (1885 km/h; 1,170 mph) at 26,250 ft (8000 m); initial climb rate 39,370 ft (12000 m) per minute; service ceiling 45,900 ft (14000 m); combat radius 540 km (335 miles) on a lo-lo-lo mission with two Kh-29 ASMs and three drop tanks
**Weights:** empty 11908 kg (26,252 lb); maximum take-off 20300 kg (44,750 lb)
**Dimensions:** span 13.965 m (45 ft 10in) spread and 7.779 m (25 ft 6.25 in) swept; length 17.076 m (56 ft 0.25 in); height 5.00 m (16 ft 5 in); wing area 37.35 m² (402.0 sq ft) spread
**Armament:** one 23-mm GSh-23L two-barrel cannon with 200 rounds; provision for 4000 kg (8,818 lb) of disposable stores, including nuclear weapons, AAMs, ASMs, free-fall and guided bombs, cluster bombs, dispenser weapons, rocket-launcher pods, large-calibre rockets, napalm tanks, drop tanks and ECM pods, carried on seven external hardpoints

*Mikoyan-Gurevich MiG-27 'Flogger-D' of the Soviet air force's Frontal Aviation.*

*Mikoyan-Gurevich MiG-27 'Flogger-D'*

*This MiG-27 'Flogger-D' is seen on approach. The 'Utkanos' duck nose is shown to advantage, as are the fixed inlet ramps and short afterburner nozzle.*

*Two MiG-27 'Flogger-Ds' of Frontal Aviation sit on the runway, ready for a paired take-off. These aircraft are 'clean', but the 'Flogger-D' can carry a wide range of missiles, bombs and other stores.*

# Mikoyan-Gurevich MiG-29 'Fulcrum-A', 'Fulcrum-B' and 'Fulcrum-C'

*Mikoyan-Gurevich MiG-29 'Fulcrum-A' of the Soviet air force based at Kubinka.*

The aircraft now identified as the **Mikoyan-Gurevich MiG-29** was initially spotted by an American reconnaissance satellite at the Ramenskoye test centre during 1977. First references to the new fighter, which was provisionally named **'Ram-L'**, appeared in the Western press during 1979, although rumours of a new Soviet equivalent to the F-16 and F/A-18 had been circulating for some years. The NATO reporting name **'Fulcrum'** was assigned when it became clear that 'Ram-L' was intended to be a production aircraft.

By January 1986 units in the Soviet Union, both in the Far East and west of the Urals, had been joined by at least one regiment assigned to the Group of Soviet Forces in Germany at Wittstock near Neubrandenburg. The West first saw the MiG-29 in July 1986 when six Kubinka-based aircraft made a four-day visit to Kuopio-Rissala, Finland. It had by then already attracted two important export orders, from India and Syria. The Syrian order for 80 aircraft, was originally though to be for a 'sanitized' variant known as the MiG-30, and followed the receipt of $330m of Saudi 'emergency aid'. The USSR originally wanted to delay delivery of the Syrian machines until mid-1987, but immediate delivery was then reluctantly agreed. The first aircraft were reportedly seen in Syria by diplomatic sources during August 1986. India refused to accept delivery of a downgraded export version of the 'Fulcrum', and this delayed delivery of her 40-aircraft order.

The visit to Rissala confirmed many of the provisional estimates as to size and configuration gleaned from US satellite photographs, although the aircraft was some 8 per cent larger than had been thought. The aircraft has enormous and widely-flared leading-edge root extensions (LERXes) similar to those found on the F/A-18 Hornet, and are very deep. A 30-mm single-barrel cannon is housed in the port LERX, behind a gridded flash suppressor. A set of five large 'venetian blind' auxiliary intake doors and three fore-and-aft slots are situated on the upper surface of each LERX above the main inlets, and are augmented by four smaller inlets and two more slots farther forward. These allow air to be ingested when the main inlets are closed: the doors in the main inlets are closed when the aircraft taxies, to prevent the ingestion of debris or slush and snow, and open only when the nose-wheel lifts off the ground.

The large nose radome contains the advanced RP-29 'Slot Dance' coherent pulse-Doppler look-down/shoot-down radar with formidable track-while-scan capability, and this is collimated with a laser rangefinder,. The advanced avionics also include an IR seeker/tracker system and a helmet-mounted target-designation system..

The initial version is the **'Fulcrum-A'**, and later developments are the **MiG-29UB 'Fulcrum-B'** trainer with a longer two-seat cockpit, and the **MiG-29S 'Fulcrum-C'** development of the 'Fulcrum-A' with a deeper dorsal fairing aft of the cockpit, probably containing avionics relocated from the lower fuselage to allow an increase in internal fuel capacity.

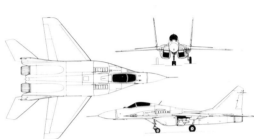

*Mikoyan-Gurevich MiG-29 'Fulcrum-A'*

*Four MiG-29s make a formation take-off during a visit to Finland. Deliveries of knocked-down MiG-29s to India began at the end of 1986.*

**Specification:** Mikoyan-Gurevich MiG-29 'Fulcrum-A'
**Origin:** USSR (now CIS)
**Type:** air-superiority fighter with secondary air-to-ground capability
**Powerplant:** two 8300-kg (18,298-lb) afterburning thrust Sarkisov RD-33 turbofans
**Performance:** maximum speed Mach 2.3 or 1,318 kt (2443 km/h; 1,518 mph) above 36,090 ft (11000 m); initial climb rate 64,960 ft (19800 m) per minute; service ceiling 55,775 ft (17000 m); range 1500 km (932 miles) with internal fuel
**Weights:** empty 10900 kg (24,030 lb); maximum take-off 18500 kg (40,785 lb)
**Dimensions:** span 11.36 m (37 ft 3.75 in); length (including probe) 17.32 m (56 ft 10 in); height 7.78 m (25 ft 6.25 in); wing area 38.00 m² (409.0 sq ft)
**Armament:** one 30-mm GSh-30-1 cannon with 150 rounds; provision for 3000 kg (6,614 lb) of disposable stores, including up to six AAMs, bombs, cluster bombs, rocket-launcher pods, large-calibre rockets, drop tanks and ECM pods, carried on six external hardpoints

*Major Chilin lands after his solo aerobatic display at Kuopio-Rissala. The cruciform braking parachute is usually streamed even before the nosewheel is lowered.*

Role
Fighter
Close support
Counter-insurgency
Tactical strike
Strategic bomber
Tactical reconnaissance
Strategic reconnaissance
Maritime patrol
Anti-ship strike
Anti-submarine warfare
Search and rescue
Assault transport
Transport
Liaison
Trainer
Inflight-refuelling tanker
Specialized

Performance
All-weather capability
Rough field capability
STOL capability
VTOL capability
Airspeed 0-250 mph
Airspeed 250 mph-Mach 1
Airspeed Mach 1 plus
Airspeed Mach 1 plus
Ceiling 0-20,000 ft
Ceiling 20,000-40,000 ft
Ceiling 40,000ft plus
Range 0-1,000 miles
Range 1,000-3,000 miles
Range 3,000 miles plus

Weapons
Air-to-air missiles
Air-to-surface missiles
Cruise missiles
Cannon
Trainable guns
Naval weapons
Nuclear-capable
Rockets
'Smart' weapon kit
Weapon load 0-4,000 lb
Weapon load 4,000-15,000 lb
Weapon load 15,000 lb plus

Avionics
Electronic Counter Measures
Electronic Support Measures
Search radar
Fire control radar
Look-down/shoot-down
Terrain-following radar
Forward-looking infra-red
Laser
Television

# Mikoyan-Gurevich MiG-29K and MiG-29M

*The sixth and final MiG-29M prototype.*

### Role
Fighter
Close support
Counter-insurgency
Tactical strike
Strategic bomber
Tactical reconnaissance
Strategic reconnaissance
Maritime patrol
Anti-ship strike
Anti-submarine warfare
Search and rescue
Assault transport
Transport
Liaison
Trainer
Inflight-refuelling tanker
Specialized

### Performance
All-weather capability
Rough field capability
STOL capability
VTOL capability
Airspeed 0-250 mph
Airspeed 250 mph-Mach 1
Airspeed Mach 1 plus
Ceiling 0-20,000 ft
Ceiling 20,000-40,000 ft
Ceiling 40,000ft plus
Range 0-1,000 miles
Range 1,000-3,000 miles
Range 3,000 miles plus

### Weapons
Air-to-air missiles
Air-to-surface missiles
Cruise missiles
Cannon
Trainable guns
Naval weapons
Nuclear-capable
Rockets
'Smart' weapon kit
Weapon load 0-4,000 lb
Weapon load 4,000-15,000 lb
Weapon load 15,000 lb plus

### Avionics
Electronic Counter Measures
Electronic Support Measures
Search radar
Fire control radar
Look-down/shoot-down
Terrain-following radar
Forward-looking infra-red
Laser
Television

Mikoyan began work on advanced MiG-29 variants during the late 1970s, concentrating on improving the range and the multi-role capability of their highly successful lightweight fighter. The **MiG-29M**, under test since 1986, has an analog fly-by-wire control system in place of the original electro-mechanical system, a semi-'glass' cockpit with a more advanced HUD and two multi-function digital HDDs, extended chord tailplane, and a recontoured dorsal fairing. It has no dorsal fin extensions of the type that in the land-based variant carry upward-firing chaff/flare dispensers, and the solid inlet doors and overwing auxiliary intakes are replaced by retractable grids and extra fuel in the LERXes. The more reliable and more fuel-efficient RD-33K engines developed for the naval version are incorporated. Other changes have extended the rear center of gravity limit to provide the relaxed stability associated with the fly-by-wire flight control system, and the result is a warplane that is more comfortable to fly as well as offering a greater angle of attack capability, enhanced agility, and improved cruise efficiency. The avionics have also been upgraded with a radar data-processor with four times greater capacity, and an improved IRSTS whose supercooled sensor offers much improved acquisition range in association with a collimated TV camera and a more powerful laser rangefinder. The MiG-29M also possesses two additional underwing hardpoints raising the maximum disposable war-

load to 4500 kg (9,921 lb) of weapons. Other notable features include the reduction of cannon ammunition capacity to 100 rounds. Despite the aircraft's potential and versatility it has not been ordered by the Russian air force, perhaps largely because the Sukhoi design bureau enjoys greater political clout.

Under the designation **MiG-33**, the MiG-29M has been offered for export, although a higher priority seems to be being accorded to the sale of the stockpile of unsold 'Fulcrum-As' which had been ordered by the Soviet air forces before the end of the Cold War. Another type was reported in 1992 as a development of the MiG-29M with two RD-37 turbofans, new aerodynamics, a full 'glass' cockpit and a digital fly-by-wire control system and vectoring engine nozzles.

From 1989 the USSR (later CIS) evaluated the **Mikoyan-Gurevich MiG-29K** as a possible part of the complement for its navy's new conventional aircraft carriers. Compared with the standard land-based 'Fulcrum-A', the naval version had the strengthened airframe, increased fuel capacity, new fly by wire control system and new avionics and weapons system of the MiG-29M together with a redesigned landing gear, uprated RD-33K turbofans, folding outer wing panels, an arrester hook, inflight-refuelling capability, provision for a 'buddy' refueling pack, a steerable IR seeker/tracker forward of the cockpit, and ESM bulges on the leading edges of the wing tips.

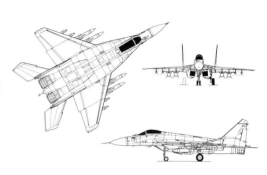

*Mikoyan MiG-29K (9-31)*

*Although the MiG-29M looks like a standard MiG-29, it is in many respects an entirely new aircraft, with a refined airframe, uprated engines, a new flight control system and new avionics and weapons systems.*

### Specification: Mikoyan-Gurevich MiG-29K
**Origin:** USSR (now CIS)
**Type:** carrierborne air-superiority fighter with secondary air-to-ground capability
**Powerplant:** two 92.22 kN (20,725-lb) afterburning thurst Sarkisov RD-33K turbofans
**Performance:** maximum speed about Mach 2.3 or 1,242 kt (2300 km/h; 1,430 mph) above 36,090 ft (11000 m)
**Weights:** normal take off 18480 kg (40,705 lb): maximum take off 22400 kg (49,340 lb)
**Dimensions:** span 12 m (39 ft 4 in); length (including probe) 17.37 m (57 ft 0 in); height 7.78 m (25 ft 6.25 in); wing area 41.60 m² (447.0 sq ft)
**Armament:** one 30-mm GSh-30-1 cannon with 100 rounds; provision for 4500 kg (9,921 lb) of disposable stores, including up to six AAMs, bombs, cluster bombs, rocket-launcher pods, large-calibre rockets, drop tanks and ECM pods, carried on eight external hardpoints

*The first prototype MiG-29K overshoots the deck of the carrier Kuznetsov. The MiG-29K has not been selected for production, despite its many attributes.*

# Mikoyan-Gurevich MiG-31 'Foxhound'

*Mikoyan-Gurevich MiG-31 'Foxhound-A' of the Soviet air force, based in the Arkhangel'sk district.*

Rumours of a new 'Super Foxbat' development of the MiG-25 had been circulating for Some time when Lieutenant Viktor Belenko defected to Hakodate airport, Japan, in his early model MiG-25P 'Foxbat-A'. His defection gave the West its first close-up look at the MiG-25, and allowed technical experts to examine the aircraft in the minutest detail. His debriefing revealed sketchy details of a new, improved two-seat variant said to be under development as the MiG-25MP, and thought to be armed with six M-X-9s AAMs and an internal gun. In 1978 a Soviet news release revealed that a 'modified MiG-25' flying at about 20,000 ft (6095 m) had successfully destroyed a small cruise missile type target flying at ultra-low level. In a later test-an aircraft flying at 55,000 ft (16765 m) was stated to have destroyed a target flying at 70,000 ft (21335 m). In retrospect it seems likely that these tests involved the **Mikoyan-Gurevich MiG-31** weapons system, including the new AA-9 missile and possibly a MiG-31 prototype or development aircraft.

Early reports suggested that the MiG-31, soon allocated the NATO reporting name **'Foxhound'**, was merely a new-generation 'Foxbat', but in fact the new type is very much more capable than its predecessor. Photographs of the new aircraft, taken in August 1985 by a Norwegian air force General Dynamics F-16, revealed many of the type's salient features. Solid cockpit hoods with small transparencies cover a new tan-

dem-seat cockpit, and an IR search and tracking sensor is located forward of the windscreen. The large radome covers a Zaslon 'Flash Dance' pulse-Doppler radar providing a true fire-and-forget engagement capability against multiple targets flying at considerably lower altitudes. The wingtips do not carry the distinctive anti-flutter and continuous-wave radar pods fitted to the MiG-25.

The variable afterburner nozzles are longer and of greater diameter than those fitted to the 'Foxbat', and this indicated a new and more potent powerplant.

The 'Foxhound' entered service with the Voyska PVO during 1983, slowly replacing ageing Tupolev Tu-28P 'Fiddlers' and early MiG-25 variants as well as the Mikoyan-Gurevich MiG-23 'Flogger' and Sukhoi Su-15 'Flagon'. Some 200 are currently in service with the Voyska PVO.

The initial model received the revised reporting name **'Foxhound-A'** after the advent of an improved model, the **MiG-31M 'Foxhound-B'** in the early 1990s. This model has a retractable inflight-refuelling probe on the starboard rather than port side of the fuselage, a wider dorsal spine, more rounded wing tips with front and rear dielectric panels, curved fin root extensions, and four underwing pylons for more advanced AAMs. This model was due to enter operational service in the mid-1990s, but may be delayed by the currently poor state of the CIS's finances.

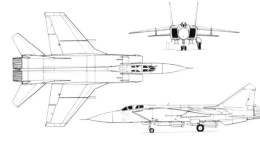

*Mikoyan-Gurevich MiG-31 'Foxhound-A'*

**Specification:** Mikoyan-Gurevich MiG-31 'Foxhound-A'
**Origin:** USSR (now CIS)
**Type:** all-weather interceptor and ECM aircraft
**Powerplant:** two 15500-kg (34,171-lb) afterburning thrust Soloviev D-30F6 turbofans
**Performance:** maximum speed Mach 2.83 or 1,620 kt (3000 km/h; 1,865 mph) at 57,400 ft (17500 m); climb to 32,810 ft (10000 m) 7 minutes 54 seconds; service ceiling 67,600 ft (20600 m); combat radius 1400 km (870 miles) with four AAMs and two drop tanks; ferry range 3300 km (2,050 miles) with internal and external fuel
**Weights:** empty 21825 kg (48,115 lb); maximum take-off 46200 kg (101,850 lb)
**Dimensions:** span 13.464 m (44 ft 2 in); length 22.688 m (74 ft 5.25 in); height 6.15 m (20 ft 2.25 in); wing area 61.6 m² (663.0 sq ft)
**Armament:** one 23-mm GSh-23-6 six-barrel cannon with 260 rounds; provision under the fuselage for four R-33 (AA-9 'Amos') AAMs and under the wings for two R-60T (AA-6 'Acrid') or four R-60 (AA-8 'Aphid') AAMs

*This AA-9 'Amos'-equipped MiG-31 was intercepted off eastern Finmark by an F-16 of the Royal Norwegian air force. This was the first time the MiG-31 had been seen in the West.*

*The MiG-31 'Foxhound' is deployed by the Russian air force primarily as a long-range interceptor, but some aircraft are used as long-range reconnaissance and ECM platforms.*

## Role

Fighter
Close support
Counter-insurgency
Tactical strike
Strategic bomber
Tactical reconnaissance
Strategic reconnaissance
Maritime patrol
Anti-ship strike
Anti-submarine warfare
Search and rescue
Assault transport
Transport
Liaison
Trainer
Inflight-refuelling tanker
Specialized

## Performance

All-weather capability
Rough field capability
STOL capability
VTOL capability
Airspeed 0-250 mph
Airspeed 250 mph-Mach 1
Airspeed Mach 1 plus
Ceiling 0-20,000 ft
Ceiling 20,000-40,000 ft
Ceiling 40,000ft plus
Range 0-1,000 miles
Range 1,000-3,000 miles
Range 3,000 miles plus

## Weapons

Air-to-air missiles
Air-to-surface missiles
Cruise missiles
Cannon
Trainable guns
Naval weapons
Nuclear-capable
Rockets
'Smart' weapon kit
Weapon load 0-4,000 lb
Weapon load 4,000-15,000 lb
Weapon load 15,000 lb plus

## Avionics

Electronic Counter Measures
Electronic Support Measures
Search radar
Fire control radar
Look-down/shoot-down
Terrain-following radar
Forward-looking infra-red
Laser
Television

# Mil Mi-6 'Hook'

*Mil Mi-6 'Hook' of the Algerian air force.*

## Role
Fighter
Close support
Counter-insurgency
Tactical strike
Strategic bomber
Tactical reconnaissance
Strategic reconnaissance
Maritime patrol
Anti-ship strike
Anti-submarine warfare
Search and rescue
Assault transport
Transport
Liaison
Trainer
Inflight-refuelling tanker
Specialized

## Performance
All-weather capability
Rough field capability
STOL capability
VTOL capability
Airspeed 0-250 mph
Airspeed 250 mph-Mach 1
Airspeed Mach 1 plus
Ceiling 0-20,000 ft
Ceiling 20,000-40,000 ft
Ceiling 40,000ft plus
Range 0-1,000 miles
Range 1,000-3,000 miles
Range 3,000 miles plus

## Weapons
Air-to-air missiles
Air-to-surface missiles
Cruise missiles
Cannon
Trainable guns
Naval weapons
Nuclear-capable
Rockets
'Smart' weapon kit
Weapon load 0-4,000 lb
Weapon load 4,000-15,000 lb
Weapon load 15,000 lb plus

## Avionics
Electronic Counter Measures
Electronic Support Measures
Search radar
Fire control radar
Look-down/shoot-down
Terrain-following radar
Forward-looking infra-red
Laser
Television

With development of the Mi-4 'Hound' completed and the helicopter in production, work began in 1954 on the design of a large helicopter that was intended to be suitable for use in several roles. When this **Mil Mi-6** was first flown in the autumn of 1957 it was the world's largest rotary-wing aircraft, but despite this size it retained the basic helicopter configuration. One unusual feature was the provision of stub wings of 15.30 m (50 ft 2.4 in) span which offloaded the main rotor to the extent of some 20 per cent in forward flight: these wings could be removed easily when the Mi-6 was being used in a flying-crane role. The other, and far more significant innovation, was the introduction of turboshaft powerplant in the form of two turboshafts mounted side-by-side above the cabin forward of the main rotor shaft. As a result the Mi-6 is large in capability as well as size, gaining the Sikorsky International Trophy in 1961 as the first helicopter to exceed a speed of 300 km/h (162 kt; 186 mph).

Before production ended more than 800 had been built for both civil and military use, the latter versions allocated the NATO reporting name **'Hook'**. Operated by a crew of five, the civil Mi-6 can seat as standard 65 passengers; accommodation in military use can include up to 70 fully equipped troops, or in an ambulance role up to 41 litters and two medical attendants. For cargo transport, hydraulically actuated rear clamshell doors and ramps give access to the hold, which is 12.0 m (39 ft 4.4 in) long and 2.65 m (8 ft 8.3 in) wide and has a floor stressed for loadings of 2000 kg/m² (410 lb/sq ft). Maximum internal payload amounts to 12000 kg (26,455 lb), and a pulley block system and 800-kg (1,764-lb) overhead winch are provided to simplify loading, A hatch in the cabin floor allows the attachment of a cargo sling system for bulky loads weighing up to 8000 kg (17,637 lb).

In both civil and military roles it is the heavy-lift capability of the Mi-6 that has been exploited most extensively, the Soviet air force using the type to transport cargo, men, tactical missiles and vehicles. The three variants are the 'Hook-A' described above, the **Mi-6 'Hook-B'** command support helicopters with external antennae, and the **Mi-22 'Hook-C'** improved command support helicopter.

## Specification: Mil Mi-6 'Hook-A'
**Origin:** USSR (now CIS)
**Type:** heavy transport helicopter
**Powerplant:** two 4101-kW (5,500-shp) Soloviev D-25V (TB-2BM) turboshafts
**Performance:** maximum speed 162 kt (300 km/h;186 mph); maximum cruising speed 135 kt (250 km/h;155 mph); service ceiling 14,765 ft (4500 m); range 620 km (365 miles) with a 6000-kg (17,637-lb) payload
**Weights:** empty 27240 kg (60,054 lb); maximum vertical take-off 42500 kg (93,696 lb)
**Dimensions:** main rotor diameter 35.00 m (114 ft 10 in); length, rotors turning 41.74 m (136 ft 11.5 in); height 9.86 m (32 ft 4.2 in); main rotor disc area 962.1 m² (110,356.5 sq ft)
**Armament:** normally none, but some have been seen with a 12.7-mm (0.5-in) trainable machine gun in the nose

*Mil Mi-6 'Hook-A'*

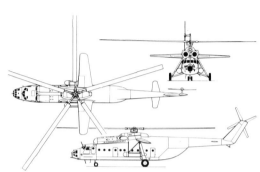

*An Egyptian air force 'Hook-A' displays its detachable stub wings. A machine gun is mounted in the nose, beneath the nosecone.*

*This photograph of a Peruvian air force Mi-6 'Hook' shows the huge size of this heavy transport helicopter. At least 17 were supplied to Peru, and at least two have been written off.*

# Mil Mi-8 'Hip'

*Mil Mi-8 'Hip-C' of the Peruvian air force.*

It is easy to oversimplify any preface to the **Mil Mi-8 'Hip'** by describing it as basically a turbine-powered version of the Mi-4. While in some respects this is true, a turboshaft powerplant gave it such improved performance that it was possible to design a new fuselage structure of almost 45 per cent greater volume and virtually double the passenger capacity. In any event, capability could be the Mi-8's middle name, and this factor accounts for production figures that exceed 10,000.

First seen at the 1961 Soviet Aviation Day display, the Mi-8 prototype (NATO reporting name 'Hip-A') had a single Soloviev turboshaft driving a four-blade rotor. When this was superseded by a five-blade rotor, subsequently standard, the NATO reporting name changed to 'Hip-B'. The second prototype, introduced in autumn 1962, was powered by the intended twin-turbine powerplant and resulted in the NATO reporting name **'Hip-C'** for the initial military and civil versions. The latter include the Mi-8 28/32-passenger transport, the utility Mi-8T intended primarily for internal or external freight but able to carry 24 passengers on tip-up seats; and the de luxe Mi-8 Salon furnished for nine or 11 passengers.

Military versions of the Mi-8 predominate and are identified by their NATO reporting names. They include the initial 'Hip-C', a basic assault transport with twin racks on each side of the cabin for rocket packs or other weapons; **'Hip-D'** and **'Hip-G'** for airborne communications relay, and differing by external antennae and avionics equipment; **'Hip-J'** which is an ECM variant; and **'Hip-K'** ECM version intended primarily for communications jamming and identified by a large antenna array on each side of the cabin. In addition there are the **Mi-9 'Hip-G'** special-duty airborne communications model and the **Mi-17** improved model combining the Mi-8 airframe with a powerplant of two 1454-kW (1,950-shp) TV3-117MT turboshafts and the tail rotor relocated from the starboard to the port side of the tail pylon.

The three variants of the last are the **Mi-17 'Hip-H'** transport, **Mi-17P 'Hip-K derivative'** communications jammer and **Mi-17I 'Hip-H'** upgraded transport with two 1566-kW (2,100-shp) TV3-117MV turboshafts. 'Hip-C' helicopters upgraded to Mi-17 standard are the **Mi-8T** and **Mi-8TB**.

## Specification: Mil Mi-8 'Hip-C'
**Origin:** USSR (now CIS)
**Type:** transport helicopter
**Powerplant:** two 1268-kW (1,700-shp) Isotov TV2-117A turboshafts
**Performance:** maximum speed 141 kt (260 km/h; 162 mph) at 3,280 ft (1000 m); service ceiling 14,765 ft (4500 m); range 500 km (311 miles0 with 28 passengers and 20-minute fuel reserve
**Weights:** empty 7260 kg (16,007 lb); maximum VTO 12000 kg (26,455 lb)
**Dimensions:** main rotor diameter 21.29 m (69 ft 10.2 in); length, rotors turning 25.24 m (82 ft 9.7 in); height 5.65 m (18 ft 6.4 in); main rotor disc area 356.0 m² (3,832.08 sq ft)
**Armament:** four packs for a total of 128 55-mm (2.17-in) rockets

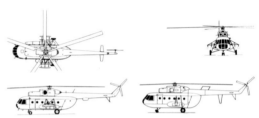

**Mil Mi-8 'Hip-C' (right-hand side view: 'Hip-D')**

*This Polish air force 'Hip-C' typifies the hundreds of Mi-8s serving as assault transport helicopters with the air forces of the Warsaw Pact. Many are armed with rocket pods.*

*No.4 Army Aviation Squadron, Pakistan Army Aviation Corps, operates the survivors of 12 Mi-8 'Hip-Cs' at Rawalpindi-Qasim, in the support and assault transport roles.*

## Role
Fighter
Close support
Counter-insurgency
Tactical strike
Strategic bomber
Tactical reconnaissance
Strategic reconnaissance
Maritime patrol
Anti-ship strike
Anti-submarine warfare
Search and rescue
Assault transport
Transport
Liaison
Trainer
Inflight-refuelling tanker
Specialized

## Performance
All-weather capability
Rough field capability
STOL capability
VTOL capability
Airspeed 0-250 mph
Airspeed 250 mph-Mach 1
Airspeed Mach 1 plus
Ceiling 0-20,000 ft
Ceiling 20,000-40,000 ft
Ceiling 40,000ft plus
Range 0-1,000 miles
Range 1,000-3,000 miles
Range 3,000 miles plus

## Weapons
Air-to-air missiles
Air-to-surface missiles
Cruise missiles
Cannon
Trainable guns
Naval weapons
Nuclear-capable
Rockets
'Smart' weapon kit
Weapon load 0-4,000 lb
Weapon load 4,000-15,000 lb
Weapon load 15,000 lb plus

## Avionics
Electronic Counter Measures
Electronic Support Measures
Search radar
Fire control radar
Look-down/shoot-down radar
Terrain-following radar
Forward-looking infra-red
Laser
Television

199

# Mil Mi-8 'Hip-E' and 'Hip-F'

*Mil Mi-8 'Hip-E' of the Soviet air force's Frontal Aviation.*

**Role**
Fighter
Close support
Counter-insurgency
Tactical strike
Strategic bomber
Tactical reconnaissance
Strategic reconnaissance
Maritime patrol
Anti-ship strike
Anti-submarine warfare
Search and rescue
Assault transport
Transport
Liaison
Trainer
Inflight-refuelling tanker
Specialized

**Performance**
All-weather capability
Rough field capability
STOL capability
VTOL capability
Airspeed 0-250 mph
Airspeed 250 mph-Mach 1
Airspeed Mach 1 plus
Ceiling 0-20,000 ft
Ceiling 20,000-40,000 ft
Ceiling 40,000ft plus
Range 0-1,000 miles
Range 1,000-3,000 miles
Range 3,000 miles plus

**Weapons**
Air-to-air missiles
Air-to-surface missiles
Cruise missiles
Cannon
Trainable guns
Naval weapons
Nuclear-capable
Rockets
'Smart' weapon kit
Weapon load 0-4,000 lb
Weapon load 4,000-15,000 lb
Weapon load 15,000 lb plus

**Avionics**
Electronic Counter Measures
Electronic Support Measures
Search radar
Fire control radar
Look-down/shoot-down
Terrain-following radar
Forward-looking infra-red
Laser
Television

The Korean War demonstrated the emancipation of the helicopter from its light transport and utility roles, and gave a first indication of its potential as a military weapon. From 1965 onward the Soviet military hierarchy monitored events in Vietnam very closely and soon appreciated that the growing capability of rotary-wing aircraft gave great potential for tasks such as airborne assault, with precision replacing the vagaries of parachuting. Introduction of the Mil Mi-8 'Hip-C' assault transport, carrying up to 24 troops and with sufficient weaponry to keep defenders' heads down as the troops were inserted, proved acceptance of these beliefs. The efficiency of 'Hip-C' was demonstrated during the 1967 Exercise Dniepr, when three battalions of heliborne troops were put down in a heavily defended area. There thus remained but a short step to evaluation of the gunship helicopter.

The **Mil Mi-8 'Hip-E'**, structurally similar to other versions of the Mi-8, introduced outriggers on each side of the fuselage to accommodate a combined total of six weapon pylons and four missile launch rails, the latter mounting four AT-2 'Swatter' anti-

tank missiles which, with a maximum range of 3500m (3,825 yards), are under command guidance of a weapons officer after launch to within proximity of the target, onto which the terminal approach is by IR homing. The weapon pylons normally mount six UV-32-57 rocket-launchers, with a combined total of 192 55-mm (2.17-in) unguided rockets, but alternatively each pylon can carry a 250-kg (551-lb) bomb. The armament of the 'Hip-E' is completed by a trainable 12.7-mm (0.5-in) gun mounted low in the fuselage nose and thus, collectively, the Mi-8 is formidably armed and even with a full weapon load can still airlift a dozen combat-equipped troops. The capability of the 'Hip-E' was confirmed in the 1970 Exercise Dvina, when it was first deployed against troop and armour concentrations. 'Hip-E' helicopters upgraded to Mil Mi-17 standard with a port-side tail rotor and two 1454-kW (1,950-shp) TV3-117MT turboshafts have the revised designation **Mi-8TBK**. The export version of the basic assault/gunship helicopter is identified by NATO as **'Hip-F'**, and this carries the less sophisticated wire-guided AT-3 'Sagger' shorter-range anti-tank missile.

**Specification:** Mil Mi-8 'Hip-E'
**Origin:** USSR (now CIS)
**Type:** assault gunship helicopter
**Powerplant:** two 1268-kW (1,700-shp) Isotov TV2-117A turboshafts
**Performance:** maximum speed 141 kt (260 km/h; 162 mph) at 3,280 ft (1000 m); service ceiling 14,765 ft (4500 m); range 500 km (311 miles0 with 28 passengers and 20-minute fuel reserve
**Weights:** empty 7260 kg (16,007 lb); maximum VTO 12000 kg (26,455 lb)
**Dimensions:** main rotor diameter 21.29 m (69 ft 10.2 in); length, rotors turning 25.24 m (82 ft 9.7 in); height 5.65 m (18 ft 6.4 in); main rotor disc area 35.60 m² (3,832.08 sq ft)
**Armament:** see text

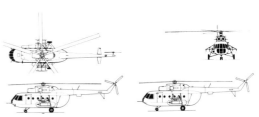

*Mil Mi-8 'Hip-E' (right-hand side view: Mi-8 'Hip-F')*

*The Mi-8 'Hip-E' is the world's most heavily armed helicopter, capable of carrying six UV-32-57 pods containing a total of 192 unguided rockets. These are augmented by four 'Swatter' anti-tank missiles and a chin-mounted gun.*

*The Mi-8 'Hip-E' forms the backbone of Frontal Aviation's assault helicopter force, and can augment the Mi-24 'Hind' in the anti-armour role*

# Mil Mi-10 'Harke'

*Mil Mi-10 'Harke' of the Soviet air force.*

The **Mil Mi-10**, NATO reporting name **'Harke-A'**, is a specialized flying crane development of the earlier Mi-6. Flown during 1960 and first appearing at the 1961 Aviation Day display at Tushino, it was seen to be similar except for the lower fuselage and landing gear. It retains the Mi-6's powerplant, rotors and transmission mounted on top of a fuselage which, above the cabin windows, is little changed. However, the lower fuselage has reduced depth, the undersurface running aft with only a slight upsweep to the rotor pylon, eliminating the pod-and-boom configuration, but the flight deck is also revised. The landing gear is not only changed from tricycle to quadricycle form, with twin wheels on each unit, but has tall long-stroke gear to give a clearance between the underside of the fuselage and the ground of 3.75 m (12 ft 3.6 in). Combined with nose and main unit wheel tracks of 6.01 m (19 ft 8.6 in) and 6.92 m (22 ft 8.4 in) respectively, this makes it possible for the Mi-10 to taxi over and position for transit almost any load it can carry. Another obvious external change is deletion of the Mi-6's stub wings, for with payload taking precedence over speed the weight saving is important.

Wheeled cargo platforms were designed to facilitate quick turn-round, the use of pre-packed platforms held by hydraulic clamps allowing the carriage of an external payload (including platform) of 15000 kg (33,069 lb). Large but less bulky loads, up to a maximum length of 20.0 m (65 ft 7.4 in) and width of 10.0 m (32 ft 9.7 in), can also be held by the clamps. The cabin can also carry freight, loaded via a door on the starboard side, or a maximum of 28 passengers .

The Mi-10 was complemented from 1966 by the more developed **Mi-10K 'Harke-B'**. This has landing gear of more normal height and introduces a pilot's gondola beneath the flight deck, which has full flying controls and a rear-facing seat. This makes if possible for the Mi-10K to be operated by a crew of only two pilots, the occupant of the gondola piloting the helicopter in hovering flight and having a clear view to control loading, unloading and hoisting. A total of about 60 of both versions was built, the majority of them Mi-10Ks, and many of them remain in service with Aeroflot and the Russian air force.

**Specification:** Mil Mi-10K 'Harke-B'
**Origin:** USSR (now CIS)
**Type:** heavy-duty flying crane helicopter
**Powerplant:** two 4101-kW (5,500-shp) Soloviev D-25V turboshafts
**Performance:** cruising speed, empty 135 kt (250 km/h;155 mph) and with sling load 109 kt (202 km/h; 125 mph); service ceiling 9,845 ft (3000 m); ferry range 795 km (494 miles) with internal auxiliary fuel
**Weights:** empty 24680 kg(54,410 lb); maximum take-off 38000 kg (83,776 lb) with slung cargo
**Dimensions:** main rotor diameter 35.00 m (114 ft 10 in); length, rotors turning 41.89 m (137 ft 5.2 in); height 7.80 m (25 ft 7.1 in); main rotor disc area 962.12 m² (10,356.46 sq ft)
**Armament:** none

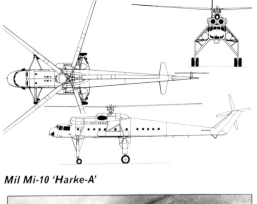

*Mil Mi-10 'Harke-A'*

**The Mi-10 'Harke-A' is essentially a development of the earlier Mi-6 'Hook', designed to carry outsized loads under its slender fuselage, between its stalky undercarriage legs.**

**Civilian Mi-10 'Harkes' would be requisitioned by the air force in time of crisis or war. The importance of the type has declined with the introduction of the 'Halo', however.**

**Role**
Fighter
Close support
Counter-insurgency
Tactical strike
Strategic bomber
Tactical reconnaissance
Strategic reconnaissance
Maritime patrol
Anti-ship strike
Anti-submarine warfare
Search and rescue
Assault transport
Transport
Liaison
Trainer
Inflight-refuelling tanker
Specialized

**Performance**
All-weather capability
Rough field capability
STOL capability
VTOL capability
Airspeed 0-250 mph
Airspeed 250 mph-Mach 1
Airspeed Mach 1 plus
Ceiling 0-20,000 ft
Ceiling 20,000-40,000 ft
Ceiling 40,000ft plus
Range 0-1,000 miles
Range 1,000-3,000 miles
Range 3,000 miles plus

**Weapons**
Air-to-air missiles
Air-to-surface missiles
Cruise missiles
Cannon
Trainable guns
Naval weapons
Nuclear-capable
Rockets
'Smart' weapon kit
Weapon load 0-4,000 lb
Weapon load 4,000-15,000 lb
Weapon load 15,000 lb plus

**Avionics**
Electronic Counter Measures
Electronic Support Measures
Search radar
Fire control radar
Look-down/shoot-down
Terrain-following radar
Forward-looking infra-red
Laser
Television

# Mil Mi-14 'Haze'

*Mil Mi-14PL 'Haze-A' of the Polish navy.*

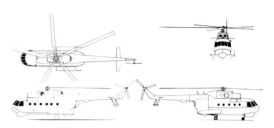

The provision of increased capability for helicopters of the Soviet air force was accepted as essential, the Mil Mi-8 'Hip' being introduced into service in the mid-1960s. The Soviet navy failed to gain similar priority and, during the approach to the 1970s, had nothing more modern to deploy in the coastal ASW role than the Mil Mi-4 'Hound-B', which was inadequate in performance and, moreover, unavailable in sufficient numbers. The more modern and more capable Kamov Ka-25 'Hormone-A' was entering service, but there were not enough to satisfy the demands for ship-based helicopters as well as those for coastal ASW. It was soon decided that the much larger and more capable Mi-8 'Hip' would be an ideal helicopter for conversion to this role, with work beginning about 1968, but as the resulting **Mil Mi-14** did not fly until 1973 it must be assumed that there were considerable development problems.

It must have been decided at an early stage that some amphibious capability was required, perhaps only for emergency, but this meant considerable revision to the fuselage which now incorporates a boat hull planing bottom, a sponson on each side at the rear, and a small strut-mounted float beneath

the tail boom. To ensure that the quadricycle landing gear does not hamper on-water operation this is now retractable and an enclosed weapons bay is incorporated in the bottom of the hull. The Mi-14 has shorter engine nacelles indicating its revision with a powerplant of two Isotov TV3-117 turboshafts, and the only other major change is a shift of the tail rotor from starboard to port side of the vertical stabilizer. A box projecting from the undersurface of the tail boom houses Doppler navigation radar, the undernose radome accommodates Type 12-M search radar, there are chutes for sonobuoys and/or flares, and a MAD (magnetic anomaly detection) 'bird' is stowed against the rear of the fuselage pod for deployment on a wire. This version, clearly for the ASW role, is the **Mi-14PL** that has the NATO reporting name **'Haze-A'**. The other two variants are the **Mi-14BT 'Haze-B'** mine countermeasures model with a starboard-side fuselage strake, and the **Mi-14PS 'Haze-C'** SAR model with 10 20-person liferafts, a rescue hoist and cabin accommodation for 10 survivors.

More than 150 of the type are in service with the Soviet navy, and modest numbers have been exported.

## Specification: Mil Mi-14PL 'Haze-A'
**Origin:** USSR (now CIS)
**Type:** coastal ASW helicopter
**Powerplant:** two 1454-kW (1,950-shp) Isotov TV3-117MT turboshafts
**Performance:** maximum speed 124 kt (230 km/h; 143 mph); service ceiling 11,500 ft (3500 m); range 1135 km (705 miles) with maximum fuel
**Weights:** empty 11750 kg (25,904 lb); maximum take-off 14000 kg (30,864 lb)
**Dimensions:** main rotor diameter 21.29 m (69 ft 10.25 in); length, rotors turning 25.30 m (83 ft 0 in); height 6.90 m (22 ft 7.7 in); main rotor disc area 35.60 m² (3,832.08 sq ft)
**Armament:** includes torpedoes and depth charges carried in a weapons bay

*Mil Mi-14PL 'Haze-A' (right-hand side view: Mi-14BT 'Haze-B')*

**The distinctive towed sonar/MAD bird and search radar of the 'Haze-A' are clearly visible on this Mi-14PW, as the Poles designate the Mi-14PL. A rescue hoist is fitted above the cabin door for SAR duties.**

*Looking somewhat sinister in its dark grey camouflage, a Mi-14PL 'Haze-A' of the Marineflieger unserer Nationalen Volksarmee (naval air arm of the former East Germany) flies over the Baltic coastline.*

# Mil Mi-24 'Hind-A, -B and -C'

*Mil Mi-24 'Hind-A' of the Libyan air force.*

Almost certainly work on the **Mil Mi-24** was initiated to combine the desirable features of the Mi-8 'Hip-C' assault and 'Hip-E' gunship helicopters in a purpose-designed airframe. Earlier emphasis of helicopter development had been first on troop transport with limited weaponry, while the 'Hip-E' provided far more potent weapons and reduced the troop-carrying capability. Deployment in either role made the helicopter highly vulnerable to enemy fire, and the Mil bureau had become convinced that higher speeds and increased armour were important for survival, with stub wings incorporated in the design not only for aerodynamic reasons, but also to make proper provision for the carriage of weapons: the 'Hip-E' was a typical case of weapons being 'strapped on' as an afterthought.

In original form the Mi-24 was of similar configuration to the Mi-8/14/17 family but smaller in size: the most conspicuous differences were the deeper tail boom faired into the fuselage; auxiliary wings of considerable anhedral with four weapon pylons and rails for four anti-tank missiles; and retractable tricycle landing gear. There was a roomy

cockpit for the crew of four, and a cabin seating up to eight combat-equipped troops. First seen on the East German airfields of Parchim and Stendal in early 1974, this version of the Mi-24 was allocated the NATO reporting name **'Hind-A'**, and it was discovered only later that there was a pre-production version, built in small numbers, which had flat wings and only four weapons pylons: this became known as **'Hind-B'**. Both versions had two 1268-kW (1,700-shp) Isotov TV2-117 turboshaft engines when first produced, with the tail rotor on the starboard side of the offset tail pylon. After a small batch of 'Hind-As' had been built the more powerful TV3-117 was introduced, the tail rotor then being repositioned on the port side and some early 'Hind-As' were retrospectively converted. In addition to the pylon-mounted weapons both the 'Hind-A' and 'Hind-B' have a 12.7-mm (0.5-in) machine gun in the nose slaved to an undernose sighting system. There is also a variant, known as **'Hind-C'**, which is similar to the late-production 'Hind-A' but without missile rails, nose gun and sighting system: this variant serves as the trainer with side-by-side dual controls.

**Specification:** Mil Mi-24 'Hind-A' (estimated)
**Origin:** USSR (now CIS)
**Type:** armed assault helicopter
**Powerplant:** two 1660-kW (2,225-shp) Isotov TV3-117 turboshafts
**Performance:** maximum speed 173 kt (320 km/h; 199 mph); cruising speed 159 kt (295 km/h; 183 mph); initial climb rate 2,955 ft (900 m) per minute; service ceiling 14,765 ft (4500 m); combat radius 160 km (99 miles) with maximum load
**Weights:** empty 8400 kg (18,519 lb); normal take-off 11000 kg (24,251 lb)
**Dimensions:** main rotor diameter 17.30 m (56 ft 9 in); stub wing span 6.536 m (21 ft 5.5 in); length rotors turning 21.35 m (70 ft 0.5 in); height 6.50 m (21 ft 3.9 in); main rotor disc area 235.06 m² (2,530.2 sq ft)
**Armament:** one remotely controlled 12.7-mm (0.5-in) machine gun in nose; provision for 1275 kg (2,811 lb) of disposable stores on four underwing pylons suitable for UV rocket pods, bombs or other stores and two wing tip pylons each carrying two rails for AT-2 'Swatter' anti-tank missiles

**Mil Mi-24 'Hind-A'**

*This late-model 'Hind-A' with its tail rotor to port and with uprated TV3-117 engines was retired to display duties at an aviation museum. Small numbers remain in Soviet service.*

*Early Mi-24 'Hind-As' had the tail rotor offset to starboard. Helicopters with this configuration were soon relegated to training duties.*

# Mil Mi-24D 'Hind-D' and Mi-25

*Mil Mi-24D 'Hind-D' of the Nicaraguan air force.*

### Role
Fighter
Close support
Counter-insurgency
Tactical strike
Strategic bomber
Tactical reconnaissance
Strategic reconnaissance
Maritime patrol
Anti-ship strike
Anti-submarine warfare
Search and rescue
Assault transport
Transport
Liaison
Trainer
Inflight-refuelling tanker
Specialized

### Performance
All-weather capability
Rough field capability
STOL capability
VTOL capability
Airspeed 0-250 mph
Airspeed 250 mph-Mach 1
Airspeed Mach 1 plus
Ceiling 0-20,000 ft
Ceiling 20,000-40,000 ft
Ceiling 40,000ft plus
Range 0-1,000 miles
Range 1,000-3,000 miles
Range 3,000 miles plus

### Weapons
Air-to-air missiles
Air-to-surface missiles
Cruise missiles
Cannon
Trainable guns
Naval weapons
Nuclear-capable
Rockets
'Smart' weapon kit
Weapon load 0-4,000 lb
Weapon load 4,000-15,000 lb
Weapon load 15,000 lb plus

### Avionics
Electronic Counter Measures
Electronic Support Measures
Search radar
Fire control radar
Look-down/shoot-down
Terrain-following radar
Forward-looking infra-red
Laser
Television

Early service use soon confirmed the 'Hind-A' as a reliable and capable helicopter and, furthermore, that its installed armament gave it a formidable attack capability. Soviet views on the deployment of helicopters was then in a transitional stage, with considerable interest in the potential of the helicopter as a more specialized anti-armour weapon, and as a result a new version of the 'Hind' was soon under development as the **Mil Mi-24D**, this being given the NATO reporting name **'Hind-D'** when it began to appear in service in 1975. In this case it was not a 'strap-on' modification of the existing airframe, but a complete redesign of the forward fuselage to optimize it for an anti-armour role. This change gave the variant what has become known as a 'typical gunship' layout. The four-crew flight deck introduced on 'Hind-B' disappeared in favour of a stepped tandem arrangement with the pilot in the elevated rear cockpit and the weapons operator forward under individual hinged canopies; the central and rear fuselage were unchanged.

To give the Mi-24D protection from ground weapons, titanium was introduced into the main rotor blades and the rotor head, providing the ability to withstand 20-mm cannon shells; windscreens of bulletproof material were provided for each cockpit, and the quantity and quality of structural armour was increased, and among the more advanced electronics introduced in this model are undernose sensor packs (one for optronic weapon guidance), and the warning systems include RWR and 'Odd Rods' IFF. Armament for the new role includes a 12.7-mm (0.5-in) JakB-12.7 four-barrel gun in an undernose turret plus weapons pylons on a stub wing similar that that of the 'Hind-A' but uprated to a maximum load. The 'Hind-D' superseded the 'Hind-A' from about 1975, and more than 2,300 have been built. This total includes the **Mi-24DU** training model with no undernose gun, Mi-24W 'Hind-E' and Mi-24P 'Hind-F' (see separate entry), **Mi-24RSh 'Hind-G1'** radiation sampler, **Mi-24K 'Hind-G2'** revised radiation sampler, and **Mi-25**, Mi-35 and Mi-35P export versions of the Mi-24D, Mi-24W and Mi-24P respectively.

**Specification:** Mil Mi-24D 'Hind-D'
**Origin:** USSR (now CIS)
**Type:** gunship helicopter, retaining assault transport capability
**Powerplant:** two 1660-kW (2,225-shp) Isotov TV3-117 turboshafts
**Performance:** maximum speed 180 kt (335 km/h; 208 mph); initial climb rate 2,461 ft (750 m) per minute; service ceiling 14,765 ft (4500 m); combat radius 160 km (99 miles) with maximum load
**Weights:** empty 8200 kg (18,078 lb); maximum take-off 12000 kg (26,455 lb)
**Dimensions:** main rotor diameter 17.30 m (56 ft 9 in); stub wing span 6.536 m (21 ft 5.5 in); length, rotors turning 21.35 m (70 ft 0.5 in); height 6.50 m (21 ft 4 in); rotor disc area 235.06 m² (2,530.2 sq ft)
**Armament:** one 12.7 mm (0.5-in) JakB-12.7 machine gun; provision for 2400 kg (5,291 lb) of disposable stores, including bombs, rocket-launcher pods, dispenser weapons, cannon pods, grenade launchers, anti-tank missile, drop tanks and ECM pods, carried on four underwing and two wing tip pylons

**Mil Mi-24D 'Hind-D'**

*An East German Mi-24D 'Hind-D' is seen with its gear down ready for landing. This helicopter carries UV-16-57 rocket pods on its outer pylons only.*

*IR jammers and suppressors are clearly visible clustered around the exhaust nozzles of this Polish air force Mi-24D 'Hind-D'. UV-32-57 rocket pods are carried under the wing.*

# Mil Mi-24 'Hind-E and -F' and Mi-35

Soon after its introduction into service, the Mi-24D 'Hind-D' was deployed in Soviet exercises to evaluate its potential not only to attack enemy armour, but also to provide close air support for its own tanks and infantry fighting vehicles. Furthermore, the growing capability of the helicopter as a weapons platform suggested to Soviet military leaders that gunship helicopters might be used in combat against an enemy's helicopters. For such a role an even wider range of weapons was desirable, and a new version of the Mi-24 was developed for evaluation of the more advanced deployment concepts.

A first stage in this development effort is represented by the version of the Mi-24 that was given the NATO reporting name **'Hind-E'** when it was first seen in service at the beginning of 1980 and later revealed as the **Mil Mi-24W**. This model retains basically the same airframe structure as the 'Hind-D' and differs primarily by having revised rails at the tips of the auxiliary wings to allow for the carriage of up to 12 examples of the longer-range anti-tank missile known as AT-6 'Spiral'. This is a far more significant weapon than the AT-2 'Swatter' that equips earlier versions of the

Mi-24, not least by having a maximum range said to be about 10 km (6.2 miles). More importantly, the AT-6 incorporates a laser seeker which enables it to home automatically on to a target which has been illuminated by a ground or airborne laser designator. The other visible change in the 'Hind-E' is its enlarged sensor pod beneath the nose on the port side, probably associated with the laser designation and homing of the AT-6 missile.

What must at present be regarded as the most advanced stage of this development is seen on a 'Hind-E' variant allocated the specific NATO reporting name **'Hind-F'** and now known to be the **Mi-24P**. This has the undernose gun turret deleted in favour of a pack mounted on the starboard side of the fuselage and carrying a 30-mm two-barrel cannon. While it is unlikely that either the 'Hind-E' or 'Hind-F' still has any transport function, it is believed that both helicopters carry reload missiles and a small support crew. Thus, having discharged the missiles on the launchers, the helicopter can be landed in a concealed position and rapidly reloaded.

The export versions of the Mi-24W and Mi-24P are the **Mi-35** and **Mi-35P** respectively.

*Mil Mi-24P 'Hind-F' of the Soviet air force's Frontal Aviation.*

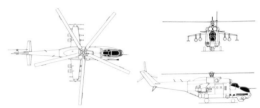

*Mil Mi-24P 'Hind-F'*

**Specification:** Mil Mi-24P 'Hind-F'
**Origin:** USSR (now CIS)
**Type:** gunship helicopter
**Powerplant:** two 1660-kW (2,225-shp) Isotov TV3-117 turboshafts
**Performance:** maximum speed 180 kt (335 km/h; 208 mph); initial climb rate 2,461 ft (750 m) per minute; service ceiling 14,765 ft (4500 m); combat radius 160 km (99 miles) with maximum load
**Weights:** empty 8200 kg (18,078 lb); maximum take-off 12000 kg (26,455 lb)
**Dimensions:** main rotor diameter 17.30 m (56 ft 9 in); stub wing span 6.536 m (21 ft 5.5 in); length, rotors turning 21.35 m (70 ft 0.5 in); height 6.50 m (21 ft 4 in); rotor disc area 235.06 m² (2,530.2 sq ft)
**Armament:** one 30-mm GSh-30-2 cannon with 750 rounds; provision for 2400 kg (5,291 lb) of disposable stores, including bombs, rocket-launcher pods, dispenser weapons, cannon pods, grenade launchers, anti-tank missile, drop tanks and ECM pods, carried on four underwing and two wing tip pylons

*The fearsome armament of the 'Hind-F' is clearly shown in this view, and comprises four UV-32-57 rocket pods and the huge 30-mm cannon. Four launcher rails are provided for AT-6 'Spiral' missiles.*

*Two Frontal Aviation Mi-24P 'Hind-Fs' on exercise in East Germany. The new gun is believed to offer longer range and greater firepower than the turret-mounted 12.7-mm gun.*

Role
Fighter
Close support
Counter-insurgency
Tactical strike
Strategic bomber
Tactical reconnaissance
Strategic reconnaissance
Maritime patrol
Anti-ship strike
Anti-submarine warfare
Search and rescue
Assault transport
Transport
Liaison
Trainer
Inflight-refuelling tanker
Specialized

Performance
All-weather capability
Rough field capability
STOL capability
VTOL capability
Airspeed 0-250 mph
Airspeed 250 mph-Mach 1
Airspeed Mach 1 plus
Ceiling 0-20,000 ft
Ceiling 20,000-40,000 ft
Ceiling 40,000ft plus
Range 0-1,000 miles
Range 1,000-3,000 miles
Range 3,000 miles plus

Weapons
Air-to-air missiles
Air-to-surface missiles
Cruise missiles
Cannon
Trainable guns
Naval weapons
Nuclear-capable
Rockets
'Smart' weapon kit
Weapon load 0-4,000 lb
Weapon load 4,000-15,000 lb
Weapon load 15,000 lb plus

Avionics
Electronic Counter Measures
Electronic Support Measures
Search radar
Fire control radar
Look-down/shoot-down radar
Terrain-following radar
Forward-looking infra-red
Laser
Television

# Mil Mi-26 'Halo'

*Mil Mi-26 'Halo' of the Soviet air force's Frontal Aviation used for firefighting in the aftermath of the Chernobyl nuclear disaster.*

**Role**

Fighter
Close support
Counter-insurgency
Tactical strike
Strategic bomber
Tactical reconnaissance
Strategic reconnaissance
Maritime patrol
Anti-ship strike
Anti-submarine warfare
Search and rescue
Assault transport
Transport
Liaison
Trainer
Inflight-refuelling tanker
Specialized

**Performance**

All-weather capability
Rough field capability
STOL capability
VTOL capability
Airspeed 0-250 mph
Airspeed 250 mph-Mach 1
Airspeed Mach 1 plus
Ceiling 0-20,000 ft
Ceiling 20,000-40,000 ft
Ceiling 40,000ft plus
Range 0-1,000 miles
Range 1,000-3,000 miles
Range 3,000 miles plus

**Weapons**

Air-to-air missiles
Air-to-surface missiles
Cruise missiles
Cannon
Trainable guns
Naval weapons
Nuclear-capable
Rockets
'Smart' weapon kit
Weapon load 0-4,000 lb
Weapon load 4,000-15,000 lb
Weapon load 15,000 lb plus

**Avionics**

Electronic Counter Measures
Electronic Support Measures
Search radar
Fire control radar
Look-down/shoot-down
Terrain-following radar
Forward-looking infra-red
Laser
Television

For just over a decade Mil's Mi-6 'Hook' held the title of 'world's largest helicopter'; it was overshadowed in 1969 by the Mi-12 with twin rotors each of Mi-6 diameter, spanning 67.00 m (219 ft 9.8 in) over the rotor tips, and with a maximum take-off weight of 105000 kg (231,4851b), but this was not developed beyond the prototype stage. The current **Mil Mi-26**, which has the NATO reporting name **'Halo'**, does not exceed the superlatives of the Mi-12, but is the world's heaviest production helicopter and also the first to be operating with an eight-blade main rotor.

The new type was intended for use as a heavy-duty transport by both the Soviet air force and Aeroflot, and the Mil bureau thus faced some difficult requirements, not least that of meeting the need for long-term reliability coupled with an empty weight approximating to 50 per cent of maximum take-off weight. This almost certainly prompted development, however difficult or protracted, of the eight-blade main rotor to limit structural size of the aircraft and yet provide adequate lift. The configuration of the Mi-26 is conventional. with a five-blade tail rotor mounted on the starboard side of the fin. The fuselage accommodates a flight crew of five, with up to 90 combat troops in the main hold, which is 3.25 m (10 ft 8 in) wide and 12.00 m (39 ft 4.4 in) in length excluding the ramp, a size very similar to that of the Lockheed C-130 Hercules. Freight loading is from the rear, the downward-hinged lower door incorporating a folding ramp, and rear fuselage height can be adjusted by hydraulically raising or lowering the main landing gear units. The landing gear itself is of non-retractable tricycle configuration with twin wheels on each unit. Attachments are provided for slung loads, and these can be monitored by closed-circuit TV.

Intended for operation by day or night, the 'Halo' is equipped with an automatic hover system, autopilot, autostabilization, Doppler navigation, horizontal situation indicator, moving map display and weather radar.

It is believed that initial examples of the Mi-26 entered service with the Soviet air force in 1983 to form a development squadron, but there are no accurate details available of the numbers built or in service, which are probably about 60. India ordered 10, the first examples being delivered in mid-1986.

**Mil Mi-26 'Halo'**

*The Mi-26 'Halo' is the world's heaviest helicopter and the first to operate successfully with an eight-blade main rotor. It has already shattered a number of payload to height records.*

*The only military customer for the Mi-26 'Halo' outside the USSR (now CIS) is India, which has already taken delivery of a small number of these impressive helicopters.*

**Specification:** Mil Mi-26 'Halo'
**Origin:** USSR (now CIS)
**Type:** heavy-duty transport helicopter
**Powerplant:** two 8380-kW (11,240-shp) Lotarev D-136 turboshafts
**Performance:** maximum speed 159 kt (295 km/h; 183 mph); cruising speed 137 kt (255 km/h; 158 mph); service ceiling 15,090 ft (4600 m); range 800 km (497 miles) with maximum payload
**Weights:** empty 28200 kg (62,170 lb); maximum take-off 56000 kg (123,459 lb)
**Dimensions:** main rotor diameter 32.00 m (104 ft 11.8 in); length, rotors turning 40.025 m (131 ft 3.75 in); height 8.145 m (26 ft 8.75 in); main rotor disc area 804.25 m² (8,657.16 sq ft)
**Armament:** none

# Mil Mi-28 'Havoc'

*The second prototype Mil Mi-28 'Havoc'with upgraded late-style nose sensor package but retaining original three-bladed tail rotor and early engine nacelles*

First flown in November 1982 for service from the early 1990s, the **Mil Mi-28 'Havoc-A'** seems to have confirmed Western doubts about the battlefield viability of the Mil Mi-24 'Hind' gunship models, for while this new new machine is clearly derived from earlier Mil helicopters (including the dynamic system of the Mi-24 driving a new five-blade articulated main rotor), it has adopted the US practice of a much slimmer and smaller fuselage for much increased manoeuvrability and reduced vulnerability over the modern high-technology battlefield.

The Mi-28 thus bears a passing resemblance to the McDonnell Douglas AH-64 Apache in US Army service, and among its operational features are IR suppression of the podded engines' exhausts, IR decoys, upgraded steel/titanium armour, optronic sighting and targeting systems for use in conjunction with the undernose 30-mm cannon and disposable weapons (including AAMs) carried on the stub wing hardpoints,

and millimetric-wavelength radar.

The type clearly possesses an air-combat capability against other battlefield helicopters, and other notable features are a far higher level of survivability and the provision of a small compartment on the left-hand side of the fuselage, probably for the rescue of downed aircrew.

In 1992 the Russians revealed that the type had been developed in competition with the Kamov V-80, and that the latter had been selected for Russian service as the Ka-50. Mil then offered the Mi-28 on the export market with a view to placing the type in production only should such an order materialize, but in 1993 it was announced that the type is in fact to be procured for Russian service alongside the Ka-50.

The **Mi-28N 'Havoc-B'**, which was due to fly in 1995 for a possible service debut in 1997, is a night/adverse-weather derivative of the Mi-28 with a specialized nav/attack system.

**Specification:** Mil Mi-28 'Havoc-A'
**Origin:** USSR (now CIS)
**Type:** air-combat and gunship helicopter
**Powerplant:** two 1640-kW (2,200-shp) Isotov TV3-117 turboshafts
**Performance:** maximum speed 162 kt (300 km/h; 186 mph) at sea level; maximum cruising speed 146 kt (270 km/h; 168 mph) at sea level; service ceiling 19,030 ft (5800 m); range 470 km (292 miles); endurance 2 hours 0 minutes
**Weights:** empty 7000 kg (15,432 lb); maximum take-off 10400 kg (22,928 lb)
**Dimensions:** main rotor diameter 17.20 m (56 ft 5 in); stub wing span 4.87 m (16 ft 0 in); length, fuselage 16.85 m (55 ft 3.5 in) excluding tail rotor; height 4.81 m (15 ft 9.4 in); main rotor disc area 232.35 m² (2,501.1 sq ft)
**Armament:** one 30-mm 2A42 cannon with 300 rounds; provision for an unrevealed weight of disposable stores, including 16 modified AT-6 'Spiral' anti-tank missiles in four four-tube boxes, or four UV-20-57 multiple launchers for 55-mm (2.17-in) rockets or UV-20-80 multiple launchers for 80-mm (3.15-in) rockets, or four AAMs in two twin launchers, or a combination of these weapon types, on four hardpoints under the stub wings

**Mil Mi-28 'Havoc'**

*The third prototype Mi-28, with definitive down-turned engine exhausts and close-set Delta H 'narrow X' tail rotor.*

*The fourth Mi-28 prototype in flight, showing the wingtip pods which will be featured by any production variant. A troop-carrying derivative has been designed as the Mi-40, but this remains unbuilt.*

**Role**
Fighter
Close support
Counter-insurgency
Tactical strike
Strategic bomber
Tactical reconnaissance
Strategic reconnaissance
Maritime patrol
Anti-ship strike
Anti-submarine warfare
Search and rescue
Assault transport
Transport
Liaison
Trainer
Inflight-refuelling tanker
Specialized

**Performance**
All-weather capability
Rough field capability
STOL capability
VTOL capability
Airspeed 0-250 mph
Airspeed 250 mph-Mach 1
Airspeed Mach 1 plus
Ceiling 0-20,000 ft
Ceiling 20,000-40,000 ft
Ceiling 40,000ft plus
Range 0-1,000 miles
Range 1,000-3,000 miles
Range 3,000 miles plus

**Weapons**
Air-to-air missiles
Air-to-surface missiles
Cruise missiles
Cannon
Trainable guns
Naval weapons
Nuclear-capable
Rockets
'Smart' weapon kit
Weapon load 0-4,000 lb
Weapon load 4,000-15,000 lb
Weapon load 15,000 lb plus

**Avionics**
Electronic Counter Measures
Electronic Support Measures
Search radar
Fire control radar
Look-down/shoot-down
Terrain-following radar
Forward-looking infra-red
Laser
Television

# Mitsubishi F-1

*Mitsubishi F-1 of the Japanese Air Self-Defence Force.*

**Role**
Fighter
Close support
Counter-insurgency
Tactical strike
Strategic bomber
Tactical reconnaissance
Strategic reconnaissance
Maritime patrol
Anti-ship strike
Anti-submarine warfare
Search and rescue
Assault transport
Transport
Liaison
Trainer
Inflight-refuelling tanker
Specialized

**Performance**
All-weather capability
Rough field capability
STOL capability
VTOL capability
Airspeed 0-250 mph
Airspeed 250 mph-Mach 1
Airspeed Mach 1 plus
Ceiling 0-20,000 ft
Ceiling 20,000-40,000 ft
Ceiling 40,000ft plus
Range 0-1,000 miles
Range 1,000-3,000 miles
Range 3,000 miles plus

**Weapons**
Air-to-air missiles
Air-to-surface missiles
Cruise missiles
Cannon
Trainable guns
Naval weapons
Nuclear weapons
Nuclear-capable
Rockets
'Smart' weapon kit
Weapon load 0-4,000 lb
Weapon load 4,000-15,000 lb
Weapon load 15,000 lb plus

**Avionics**
Electronic Counter Measures
Electronic Support Measures
Search radar
Fire control radar
Look-down/shoot-down
Terrain-following radar
Forward-looking infra-red
Laser
Television

Following the successful development of its T-2 supersonic twin-turbofan two-seat advanced trainer, the manufacturer proceeded with a close-support fighter version as the **Mitsubishi F-1**, converting the second and third T-2 prototypes to single-seat configuration. The first such conversion made its initial flight on 3 June 1975, and after a year's evaluation by the JASDF Air Proving Wing at Gifu, the F-1 was accepted for service and ordered into production as Japan's first indigenous supersonic fighter.

Dimensionally the single-seater is similar to the T-2, the space behind the pilot's (front) cockpit of the trainer now being occupied by a Mitsubishi Electric J/ASQ-1 fire-control system and bombing computer, Ferranti 6TNJ-F inertial navigation system and a radar warning and homing subsystem whose sensors are located at the top of the fin. One of the type's most important roles is anti-ship attack, in which the principal weapon is the ASM-1 (Type 80) missile with active radar seeker, of which two can be carried on the inboard wing pylons. The ASM-1 is compatible with the J/ASQ-1 fire-control system. A Mitsubishi J/AWG-12 air-to-air and air-to-ground radar replaces the J/AWG-11 search and ranging radar in the nose, operating with the retained Mitsubishi Electric (Thomson-CSF) head-up display. Also retained is the Lear Siegler 5010BL attitude and heading reference system. In the air combat role the principal weapon is the AIM-9L Sidewinder, produced under licence by Mitsubishi, four of which may be carried on the outboard wing pylons and on wing tip mountings. The single JM61 Vulcan rotary cannon is retained in the lower port side of the nose.

A total of 77 F-1s was ordered for the JASDF, and these aircraft entered service first with the 3rd Squadron of the 3rd Air Wing at Misawa and with the 8th Air Wing at Tsuiki, in each case replacing elderly North American F-86 Sabres. Original plans were for the production of about 160 aircraft, budgetary constraints then necessitating a reduction in this total.

**Specification:** Mitsubishi F-1
**Origin:** Japan
**Type:** close-support and anti-ship attack fighter
**Powerplant:** two 3315-kg (7,308-lb) afterburning thrust Ishikawajima-Harima TF40-IHI-801A (Rolls-Royce/Turbomeca Adour Mk 801A) turbofans
**Performance:** maximum speed Mach 1.6 or 921 kt (1708 km/h;1,061 mph) at 35,000 ft (10675 m); initial climb rate 35,000 ft (10675 m) per minute; service ceiling 50,000 ft (15240 m); combat radius 350 km (218 miles) on a hi-lo-hi mission with eight 227-kg (500-lb) bombs; ferry range 2600 km (1,616 miles)
**Weights:** empty 6358 kg (14,017 lb); maximum take-off 13700 kg (30,203 lb)
**Dimensions:** span 7.88 m (25 ft 10.2 in); length 17.86 m (58 ft 7.1 in); height 4.39 m (14 ft 4.8 in); wing area 21.17 m² (227.88 sq ft)
**Armament:** one 20-mm JM61 Vulcan six-barrel cannon with 750 rounds; provision for 2722 kg (6,000 lb) of disposable stores, including AAMs, ASMs, free-fall or guided bombs, rocket-launcher pods, drop tanks and ECM pods, carried on five external hardpoints and two wing tip positions

*Mitsubishi F-1*

*This F-1 serves in the anti-shipping, ground attack and fighter roles with the 3rd Hikotai of the 3rd Kokudan at Misawa, on the island of Honshu.*

*Japan's F-1s are concentrated at Misawa; this aircraft serves with the 8th Hikotai. The obvious similarity with the Anglo-French Jaguar extends to the Adour powerplant.*

# Mitsubishi T-2

*Mitsubishi T-2 of the 4th Kokudan, JASDF, based at Matsushita.*

In a fine exercise of farsighted ergonomics, Japan s first excursion into supersonic military aircraft design was of a two-seat combat trainer which would, it was argued, double as an aircraft in which JASDF pilots could be trained for the Lockheed F-104J and McDonnell Douglas F-4EJ combat aircraft, and which would provide design experience relevant to the subsequent creation of an indigenous supersonic fighter. In the event the **Mitsubishi T-2** itself proved readily adaptable to become that fighter, the F-1. First flown on 20 July 1971 as the XT-2, the trainer superficially resembles the American F-4 but features shoulder-mounted wings and fixed-geometry lateral air inlets (with blow-in doors) for the powerplant of two Rolls-Royce/Turbomeca Adour afterburning turbofans mounted side-by-side in the lower rear fuselage. All components of the tricycle landing gear retract into the fuselage. The instructor and pupil pilot are accommodated in tandem under separate canopy seats and are provided with Daiseru-built Weber ES-7J zero-zero ejector seats. The wing and tailplane incorporate marked anhedral, and roll control is effected by differential spoilers forward of the wide-span trailing-edge flaps. Total production orders amounted to 86 aircraft, of which 28 are T-2 advanced trainers and 58 are **T-2A** combat trainers, all

of which have been completed. The Adour engines are licence-built by Ishikawajima-Harima.

Military equipment includes an inbuilt 20-mm JM61 Vulcan six-barrel cannon in the lower port side of the nose, and external stores can be mounted on one centreline and four underwing hardpoints, while provision is made to mount AIM-9L Sidewinder AAMs on the wing tips. The electronics include the Mitsubishi Electric J/AWG-11 search and ranging radar in the nose, Mitsubishi Electric (Thomson-CSF) head-up display, Mitsubishi Electric J/ARC-51 UHF, Nippon Electric J/ARN-53 TACAN, Toyo Communication J/APX-101 SIF/IFF and Lear Siegler 5010BL AHRS.

The T-2 entered service in 1976, initially joining the 4th Air Wing at Mitsushima as replacement for the North American F-86, and has proved a popular and efficient aircraft, now obviously demonstrating the benefits of commonality with the F-1 fighter. One T-2 was extensively modified for the Technical R and D Institute of the Japan Defence Agency as a control-configured vehicle (CCV) with triplex digital fly-by-wire and computer control, and featured vertical and horizontal canard surfaces, plus test equipment in the rear cockpit. This T-2CCV was first flown on 9 August 1983.

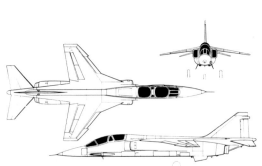

**Mitsubishi T-2**

*This T-2 was extensively modified to serve as an inherently unstable CCV (Control-Configured Vehicle) with canards and triplex digital fly-by-wire controls.*

*The T-2 is the mount of the 'Blue Impulse' aerobatic team of the JASDF, which previously used the F-86 Sabre. These aircraft are a component of the 4th Kokudan.*

**Specification:** Mitsubishi T-2
**Origin:** Japan
**Type:** supersonic advanced flying, weapon and combat trainer
**Powerplant:** two 3315-kg (7,308-lb) afterburning thrust Ishikawajima-Harima TF40-IHI-801A (Rolls-Royce/Turbomeca Adour Mk 801A) turbofans
**Performance:** maximum speed Mach 1.6 or 921 kt (1708 km/h;1,061 mph) at 35,000 ft (10675 m); initial climb rate 35,000 ft (10675 m) per minute; service ceiling 50,000 ft (15240 m); ferry range 2600 km (1,616 miles)
**Weights:** empty 6307 kg (13,904 lb); maximum take-off 12800 kg (28,219 lb)
**Dimensions:** span 7.88 m (25 ft 10.2 in); length 17.86 m (58 ft 7.1 in); height 4.39 m (14 ft 4.8 in); wing area 21.17 m² (227.88 sq ft)
**Armament:** one 20-mm JM61 Vulcan six-barrel cannon with 750 rounds; provision for 2722 kg (6,000 lb) of disposable stores, including AAMs, ASMs, free-fall or guided bombs, rocket-launcher pods, drop tanks and ECM pods, carried on five external hardpoints and two wing tip stations

## Role

Fighter
Close support
Counter-insurgency
Tactical strike
Strategic bomber
Tactical reconnaissance
Strategic reconnaissance
Maritime patrol
Anti-ship strike
Anti-submarine warfare
Search and rescue
Assault transport
Transport
Liaison
Trainer
Inflight-refuelling tanker
Specialized

## Performance

All-weather capability
Rough field capability
STOL capability
VTOL capability
Airspeed 0-250 mph
Airspeed 250 mph-Mach 1
Airspeed Mach 1 plus
Airspeed 0-20,000 ft
Ceiling 0-20,000 ft
Ceiling 20,000-40,000 ft
Ceiling 40,000ft plus
Range 0-1,000 miles
Range 1,000-3,000 miles
Range 3,000 miles plus

## Weapons

Air-to-air missiles
Air-to-surface missiles
Cruise missiles
Cannon
Trainable guns
Naval weapons
Nuclear-capable
Rockets
'Smart' weapon kit
Weapon load 0-4,000 lb
Weapon load 4,000-15,000 lb
Weapon load 15,000 lb plus

## Avionics

Electronic Counter Measures
Electronic Support Measures
Search radar
Fire control radar
Look-down/shoot-down radar
Terrain-following radar
Forward-looking infra-red
Laser
Television

# Morane-Saulnier MS.760 Paris

*Morane-Saulnier MS.760 Paris of the Armée de l'Air.*

Often regarded as the precursor of the light jet executive aircraft, the **Morane-Saulnier MS.760 Paris** was a four-seat development of the MS.755 Fleuret which had failed to beat the Fouga Magister in a competition held in the early 1950s for a French two-seat jet trainer. First flown as the **MS.760A Paris I** on 29 July 1954, the aircraft was a low-wing cabin monoplane powered by a pair of 400-kg (882-lb) dry thrust Marboré turbojets mounted side-by-side in the fuselage and exhausting under the tail: the air inlets were located in the wing roots and the tailplane was mounted at the top of the vertical fin. The tricycle landing gear employed relatively short components, thereby providing ease of access from the ground to the cabin door on the port side of the fuselage forward of the wing. Accommodation was for four occupants in two side-by-side pairs.

Orders for the Paris were received from the French Armée de l'Air and Aéronavale as well as a number of overseas air forces, including those of Brazil and Argentina (the latter acquiring 48 for assembly at the Cordoba state factory). In 1961 production switched to the **MS.760B Paris II**, powered by a pair of 480-kg (1,058-lb) dry thrust Marboré VI turbojets and introducing wing leading-edge fuel

tanks, improved cabin air-conditioning and enlarged baggage compartment. Production of the Paris II continued after the Morane-Saulnier company had been acquired by the Potez group in 1963, and on 24 February 1964 a six-seat version, the MS.760C Paris III, was first flown. However, production of the Paris II ended in that year and the enlarged version was abandoned.

A total of 165 Paris Is and IIs was completed, of which roughly half entered service with the French forces, being employed as trainers and liaison aircraft; by the mid-1980s a half-dozen were still being flown by Escadrille de Liaison Aérienne 41 at Metz, while 24 equipped the Escadron de Transport 2/65 at Villacoublay; in the Aéronavale nine Paris IIs flew communications duties with the Section Réacteur at Landivisiau: in the mid-1990s the air force and navy still operated 30 and eight aircraft respectively. Elsewhere the number of Paris Is still in service has dwindled to nought, for the handful of Brazilian aircraft handed over to Paraguay for training duties has been retired. Argentina's considerable fleet of Paris IIs, used mainly as weapons trainers and counter-insurgency aircraft, has been reduced to slightly more than 25 machines.

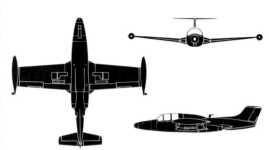

**Morane-Saulnier MS.760 Paris**

*This Paris is one of about 25 or slightly more in use with the Fuerza Aérea Argentina. Formerly used as COIN aircraft, these ageing French jets are now used as communications 'hacks'.*

*The Aéronavale retains a handful of Morane-Saulnier MS.760s for use in the communications role. They are based at Landivisiau with the Section Réacteur.*

## Specification: Morane-Saulnier MS.760B Paris II
**Origin:** France
**Type:** four/five-seat liaison and light transport aircraft
**Powerplant:** two 480-kg (1,058-lb) dry thrust Turbomeca Marboré VI turbojets
**Performance:** maximum speed 375 kt (695km/h; 432 mph) at 25,000 ft (7620 m); initial climb rate 2,460 ft (750 m) per minute; service ceiling 39,370 ft (12000 m); range 1740 km (1,081 miles)
**Weights:** empty 2067 kg (4,557 lb); maximum take-off 3920 kg (8,642 lb)
**Dimensions:** span 10.15 m (33 ft 3.6 in); length 10.24 m (33 ft 7.1 in); height 2.60m (8 ft 6.4 in); wing area 18.0 m2 (193.76 sq ft)
**Armament:** none normally, although in the COIN role the type can be fitted in the nose with two 7.62-mm (0.3-in) machine guns and under the wings with two 50-kg (110-lb) bombs or four 90-mm (3.54-in) rockets

# NAMC (Nihon) YS-11

*Much modified **NAMC (Nihon) YS-11E** of the JASDF.*

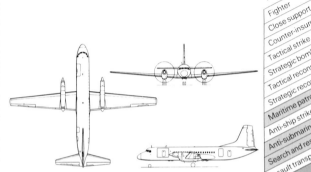

Following assurance of a subsidy from the Japanese government, design and development of an indigenous medium-range transport aircraft was started during 1957 as a major collaborative project involving six of the nation's aircraft manufacturers, namely Fuji, Kawasaki, Mitsubishi, Nippi, Shin Meiwa and Showa. Combined initially under the title Transport Aircraft Development Association, this grouping was later renamed the Nihon Aeroplane Manufacturing Company (NAMC). The resulting **NAMC (Nihon) YS-11** has, since the first of two prototypes was flown on 30 August 1962, found a ready if not very large commercial market and has thus undergone progressive increases in permitted take-off weight. Powered by two Rolls-Royce Dart turboprops, the aircraft is a low-wing monoplane with tricycle landing gear, its commercial passenger accommodation being varied according to model (YS-11-100 to -700) between 48 and 60. Production was halted by the Japanese government in 1972 after 182 examples had been built.

Of these, 23 were delivered to the armed forces: the JASDF and JMSDF received 13 and 10 aircraft respectively. The former included two **YS-11-103/105** VIP transports (delivered in the mid-1960s and later converted as flight check aircraft), two **YS-11A-218** all-troop transports, two **YS-11A-305** troop/cargo transports and seven **YS-11A-402** all-cargo transports: all served with the 503rd Squadron at Miho and Iruma. Those delivered to the JMSDF comprised two **YS-11-113** aircraft specially converted as all-cargo transports, six **YS-11T (YS-11A-206)** anti-submarine warfare trainers which equipped the 205th Squadron at Atsugi, and two **YS-11A-400** all-cargo transports flown by the 61st Squadron, also at Atsugi. The mixed-complement transports featured accommodation for 48 personnel and incorporated a cargo compartment at the rear of the fuselage with freight-loading door on the port side. Flight systems and avionics in the military transports remain virtually unchanged from the commercial versions, namely Toshiba weather radar, Bendix autopilot, Tokyo Keiba ILS, Mitsubishi HF communications, Collins VHF, ADF and ATC transponder, and Fairchild flight recorder.

During the 1970s several of the JASDF aircraft were withdrawn for modification as ECM trainers and were redelivered to the service under the designation **YS-11E**. More recently, in 1982 and as a direct consequence of increased Western interest in Soviet military activities in eastern Asia, the JASDF embarked on very limited Elint-gathering work, possibly to complement similar work by American agencies in the area. Another of the YS-11s (possibly a YS-11E) was withdrawn from service and underwent conversion by Nihon Hikoki (Nippi) to include Toshiba ALR-1 avionics and active jamming equipment. Externally this aircraft is distinguishable by three radomes which are assumed to enclose the Elint sensors.

**NAMC (Nihon) YS-11**

## Specification: NAMCYS 11A-200
**Origin:** Japan
**Type:** trainer for anti-submarine duties
**Powerplant:** two 2282-ekW (3,060-eshp) Rolls-Royce Dart Mk 542-10K turboprops
**Performance:** maximum cruising speed 253 kt (469 km/h; 291 mph) at 15,000 ft (4570 m); initial climb rate 1,220 ft (372 m) per minute; service ceiling 22,000 ft (6705 m); range 3215 km (1,998 miles) with maximum fuel
**Weights:** empty 15419 kg (33,993 lb); maximum take-off 24500 kg (54,013 lb)
**Dimensions:** span 32.00 m (104 ft 11.8 in); length 26.30 m (86 ft 3.4 in); height 8.98 m (29 ft 5.5 in); wing area 94.8 m² (1,020.5 sq ft)
**Armament:** none

*These are two of the six YS-11T anti-submarine warfare training platforms used by the Atsugi-based 205th Squadron, JMSDF. The Japanese Maritime Self Defence Force also operates four transports with No.61 Squadron.*

*This JASDF NAMC (Nihon) YS-11E is configured for ECM training duties. With the introduction of the Kawasaki C-1Kai, at least one of these aircraft has adopted an Elint role.*

## Role
Fighter
Close support
Counter-insurgency
Tactical strike
Strategic bomber
Tactical reconnaissance
Strategic reconnaissance
Maritime patrol
Anti-ship strike
Anti-submarine warfare
Search and rescue
Assault transport
Transport
Liaison
Trainer
Inflight-refuelling tanker
Specialized

## Performance
All-weather capability
Rough field capability
STOL capability
VTOL capability
Airspeed 0-250 mph
Airspeed 250 mph-Mach 1
Airspeed Mach 1 plus
Ceiling 0-20,000 ft
Ceiling 20,000-40,000 ft
Ceiling 40,000ft plus
Range 0-1,000 miles
Range 1,000-3,000 miles
Range 3,000 miles plus

## Weapons
Air-to-air missiles
Air-to-surface missiles
Cruise missiles
Cannon
Trainable guns
Naval weapons
Nuclear-capable
Rockets
'Smart' weapon kit
Weapon load 0-4,000 lb
Weapon load 4,000-15,000 lb
Weapon load 15,000 lb plus

## Avionics
Electronic Counter Measures
Electronic Support Measures
Search radar
Fire control radar
Look-down/shoot-down
Terrain-following radar
Forward-looking infra-red
Laser
Television

# Nanchang Q-5 'Fantan'

*Nanchang Q-5 'Fantan' of the Air Force of the Chinese People's Liberation Army.*

## Role
Fighter
Close support
Counter-insurgency
Tactical strike
Strategic bomber
Tactical reconnaissance
Strategic reconnaissance
Maritime patrol
Anti-ship strike
Anti-submarine warfare
Search and rescue
Assault transport
Transport
Liaison
Trainer
Inflight-refuelling tanker
Specialized

## Performance
All-weather capability
Rough field capability
STOL capability
VTOL capability
Airspeed 0-250 mph
Airspeed 250 mph-Mach 1
Airspeed Mach 1 plus
Ceiling 0-20,000 ft
Ceiling 20,000-40,000 ft
Ceiling 40,000ft plus
Range 0-1,000 miles
Range 1,000-3,000 miles
Range 3,000 miles plus

## Weapons
Air-to-air missiles
Air-to-surface missiles
Cruise missiles
Cannon
Trainable guns
Naval weapons
Nuclear-capable
Rockets
'Smart' weapon kit
Weapon load 0-4,000 lb
Weapon load 4,000-15,000 lb
Weapon load 15,000 lb plus

## Avionics
Electronic Counter Measures
Electronic Support Measures
Search radar
Fire control radar
Look-down/shoot-down
Terrain-following radar
Forward-looking infra-red
Laser
Television

Currently one of the most important combat aircraft in the air force inventory of the Chinese People's Republic, the **Nanchang Q-5 'Fantan'** close-support fighter was derived from a Soviet fighter, the Mikoyan-Gurevich MiG-19. Its true identity and significance went largely unrecognized by Western intelligence observers until 1980, by which time the Q-5 had been in service for 10 years. Its design had indeed started in 1958 and the prototype had flown in June 1965. Like the Shenyang J-6 (itself a direct copy of the MiG-19), the Q-5 is a mid-wing aircraft with a pair of Shenyang WP-6 afterburning turbojets mounted side-by-side in the fuselage. The type retains the multi-spar wing with quarter-chord sweepback of 57° 30' and deep semi-span fences, and the variable-incidence single-piece tailplane also remains unchanged. The original internal weapons bay has been altered to accommodate a large fuel tank in the **Q-5 I** version which also has four underfuselage pylons, uprated engines and an improved ejector seat. To make space available for an attack radar in the extreme nose the engine inlets have been shortened and are now of the lateral fixed-geometry type with splitter plates below the cockpit sills. By adopting a rear-hinged cockpit canopy in place of the original sliding type, the cross section of the dorsal spine has been reduced, permitting a tidier dorsal fin shape and a marginally larger main fin. Gun armament remains as two wing-root cannon, calibre 23 mm instead of 30 mm.

In 1980, when Western authorities became aware of the Q-5's true identity, not more than about 100 of the aircraft were in service, but at that time production at the Nanchang plant in Kiangsi Province was being stepped up to meet export orders as well as to increase deliveries to the PLA air force and navy. Some 52 **A-5C** aircraft (to a partially Westernized Q-5 I standard) were supplied to Pakistan. As well as about 800 Q-5s now thought to serve with the PLA air force and 100 with the PLA navy, 20 A-5Cs have been exported to Bangladesh and 40 examples of the **Q-5 IA** (Q-5 I with two additional underwing hardpoints) to North Korea. China also operates the Q-5 IA and its slightly upgraded version, the **Q-5 II** with a radar-warning receiver. Nanchang is also planning production of the **Q-5M** (export **A-5M**) modernized model developed with the aid of Alenia and including a large element of Western electronics, including FIAR Pointer 2500 ranging radar, in its nav/attack system.

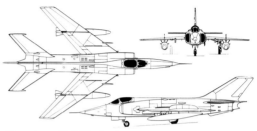

*Nanchang Q-5 'Fantan'*

*The Pakistan air force is a major operator of the Shenyang J-6 (Chinese-built MiG-19) and its derivative, the A-5 'Fantan'. This machine serves with the Peshawar-based No.26 Squadron.*

## Specification: Nanchang Q-5 IA
**Origin:** China
**Type:** close-support fighter with secondary air combat capability
**Powerplant:** two 3250-kg (7,165-lb) afterburning thrust Shenyang WP-6 (Tumanskii R-9BF 811) turbojets
**Performance:** maximum speed Mach1.12 or 642 kt (1190 km/h; 739 mph) at 36,090 ft (11000 m); climb rate at 16,405 ft (5000 m) 20,275 ft (6180 m) per minute; service ceiling 52,500 ft (16000 m); combat radius 400 km (249 miles) on a lo-lo-lo mission with maximum warload; range nearly 2000 km (1,243 miles) with maximum fuel
**Weights:** empty 6375 kg (14,054 lb); maximum take-off 11830 kg (26,080 lb)
**Dimensions:** span 9.68 m (31 ft 9 in); length (including probe) 15,65 m (51 ft 4.25 in); height 4.33 m (14 ft 2.75 in); wing area 27.95 m² (300.85 sq ft)
**Armament:** two 23-mm Type 23-2K cannon with 100 rounds per gun; provision for 2000 kg (4,409 lb) of disposable stores, including AAMs, free-fall bombs, cluster bombs, rocket-launcher pods, napalm tanks, drop tanks and ECMS pods, on 10 external hardpoints

*Q-5s and A-5s undergo final assembly at the Nanchang plant in Kiangsi province. More than 900 are now in Chinese service.*

# North American T-28 Trojan

*North American T-28 Trojan of the Chinese Nationalist air force.*

First flown on 24 September 1949, the **North American T-28** was conceived to fill the gap left by the T-6 Texan in the USAF's Air Training Command as a combined basic and primary trainer. Superficially, the new aircraft perpetuated the configuration of the Texan, being a low wing all-metal monoplane with tandem cockpits for pupil and instructor. New, however, was the was the tricycle landing gear with steerable nosewheel, while power was provided (in the **T-28A**) by a 597-kW (800-hp) Wright R-1300-1A radial driving a two-blade variable-pitch propeller A total of 1,194 T-28As was produced, and this version remained in USAF service until 1956. This initial type was followed by 489 **T-28B Trojan** aircraft powered by the 1063-kW (1,425-hp) Wright R-1820 engine driving a three-blade propeller, and by 299 **T-28C** aircraft with deck hook and strengthened airframe to withstand carrier landings, both these later versions serving with the US Navy and Marine Corps until the 1970s.

Many T-28As were, however, extensively re-engineered to become **T-28D** aircraft with the R-1820 engine driving a three-blade propeller, armour protection for the crew, and six underwing stores hardpoints. This updating programme was undertaken at the beginning of American involvement in Vietnam during the early 1960s to provide a light attack aircraft, and was effected by removal of aircraft from storage. In this role the T-28D served with US air commando squadrons, being fitted to carry podded 12.7-mm (0.5-in) guns, 227-kg (500-lb) bombs, rockets and napalm weapons. Their employment was not considered entirely satisfactory and about 100 aircraft were turned over to the air forces of South Vietnam and the Philippines; in the latter, two T-28D-equipped squadrons were still operational for COIN duties in the early 1980s.

France had acquired about 245 surplus T-28As during 1960-1 and these, under the name **Fennec**, saw widespread service in Algeria in the light attack role. Later, as the type was withdrawn from service, surplus Fennecs were sold to Morocco, Honduras and, modified with an arrester hook, to the Argentine navy. Ex-USAF T-28As were also sold to Mexico whose air force operated until the early 1980s four ground-attack/training squadrons equipped with the type. The T-28D remains the most widely used variant, and until recently served in training and counter-insurgency squadrons with the air forces of the Dominican Republic, Ethiopia, Nicaragua, the Philippines, Taiwan, Thailand and Zaïre.

**Specification:** North American T-28B Trojan
**Origin:** USA
**Type:** basic trainer (with COIN/battlefield support applications)
**Powerplant:** one 1063-kW (1,425-hp) Wright R-1820-86 Cyclone radial piston engine
**Performance:** maximum speed 298 kt (552 km/h; 343 mph); initial climb rate 3,540 ft (1079 m) per minute; service ceiling 35,500 ft (10820 m);range 1706 km (1,060 miles)
**Weights:** empty 2914 kg (6,424 lb); maximum take-off 3856 kg (8,500 lb)
**Dimensions:** span 12.22 m (40 ft 1 in); length 10.06 m (33ft 0 in); height 3.86 M (12 ft 8 in); wing area 24.90 m² (268.0 sq ft)
**Armament:** none; the T-28D features provision for up to 544 kg (1,200 lb) of disposable stores, including Minigun pods, rocket-launcher pods and light bombs, carried on six external hardpoints

*North American T-28A (lower side view: T-28D)*

*This ageing T-28D Trojan was one of about 30 survivors remaining in service with the Lao People's Liberation Army Air Force into the 1980s, serving in the close support role.*

*This is one of the eight ex-Moroccan air force T-28A Fennecs supplied to the Fuerza Aérea Hondurena. One was written off, but the other seven remained in use to the later 1980s.*

**Role**

Fighter
Close support
Counter-insurgency
Tactical strike
Strategic bomber
Tactical reconnaissance
Strategic reconnaissance
Maritime patrol
Anti-ship strike
Anti-submarine warfare
Search and rescue
Assault transport
Transport
Liaison
Trainer
Inflight-refuelling tanker
Specialized

**Performance**

All-weather capability
Rough field capability
STOL capability
VTOL capability
Airspeed 0-250 mph
Airspeed 250 mph-Mach 1
Airspeed Mach 1 plus
Airspeed 20,000 ft
Ceiling 0-20,000 ft
Ceiling 20,000-40,000 ft
Ceiling 40,000ft plus
Range 0-1,000 miles
Range 1,000-3,000 miles
Range 3,000 miles plus

**Weapons**

Air-to-air missiles
Air-to-surface missiles
Cruise missiles
Cannon
Trainable guns
Naval weapons
Nuclear-capable
Rockets
'Smart' weapon kit
Weapon load 0-4,000 lb
Weapon load 4,000-15,000 lb
Weapon load 15,000 lb plus

**Avionics**

Electronic Counter Measures
Electronic Support Measures
Search radar
Fire control radar
Look-down/shoot-down
Terrain-following radar
Forward-looking infra-red
Laser
Television

# Northrop F-5A and F-5B Freedom Fighter

*Northrop F-5A Freedom Fighter of the 341 Mira, Hellenic air force.*

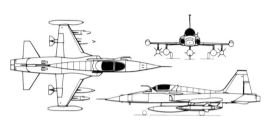

**Role**
Fighter
Close support
Counter-insurgency
Tactical strike
Strategic bomber
Tactical reconnaissance
Strategic reconnaissance
Maritime patrol
Anti-ship strike
Anti-submarine warfare
Search and rescue
Assault transport
Transport
Liaison
Trainer
Inflight-refuelling tanker
Specialized

**Performance**
All-weather capability
Rough field capability
STOL capability
VTOL capability
Airspeed 0-250 mph
Airspeed 250 mph-Mach 1
Airspeed Mach 1 plus
Ceiling 0-20,000 ft
Ceiling 20,000-40,000 ft
Ceiling 40,000ft plus
Range 0-1,000 miles
Range 1,000-3,000 miles
Range 3,000 miles plus

**Weapons**
Air-to-air missiles
Air-to-surface missiles
Cruise missiles
Cannon
Trainable guns
Naval weapons
Nuclear-capable
Rockets
'Smart' weapon kit
Weapon load 0-4,000 lb
Weapon load 4,000-15,000 lb
Weapon load 15,000 lb plus

**Avionics**
Electronic Counter Measures
Electronic Support Measures
Search radar
Fire control radar
Look-down/shoot-down
Terrain-following radar
Forward-looking infra-red
Laser
Television

In 1955 Northrop embarked on studies which led to the N-156 design, from which the T-38 Talon supersonic trainer was also subsequently developed. Based on the N-156F variant of the core design and ordered into production in 1962, the **Northrop F-5A Freedom Fighter** first flew in May 1963 and entered service in August 1964 with the 4441st Combat Crew Training School of the USAF's Tactical Air Command based at Williams AFB, Arizona. The F-5A was not adopted initially by the USAF, but established itself as a Military Assistance Program aircraft, supplementing the more complex Lockheed F-104 and replacing aircraft like the Republic F-84. Its success was attributable largely to its wide tactical capability coupled with relatively low cost of production and operation. Also developed was the two-seat **F-5B**, the second variant of the F-5 which first flew on 24 February 1964. While fully capable of combat duty, this was intended principally for the trainer role and lacks the internal cannon armament of the F-5A.

The Freedom Fighter is powered by two J85-GE-13 afterburning turbojets which have contributed to the type's outstanding safety record alongside the design's aerodynamic layout, which ensures good low-speed handling and safe landing behaviour. The first overseas orders came from the Imperial Iranian air force, which was sent a batch of 13 aircraft in January 1965, followed by the

South Korean air force, which received its order of 20 aircraft from April 1965.

During the mid 1960s another variant, the **RF-5A**, was developed specifically to the tactical reconnaissance role. This version is distinguishable from earlier F-5 models by its modified nose which houses four KS-92 cameras. Although, like the F-5A and F-5B, the type is lo longer in production, around 80 RF-5As were produced for delivery to Turkey, Greece, Iran, Thailand, South Korea and South Vietnam.

A full-scale US combat evaluation of the F-5 was completed in Vietnam. The 'Skoshi Tiger' programme began in October 1965 and involved 12 aircraft from the 4503d Tactical Fighter Squadron, based at Da Nang and Bien Hoa. The sortie rate was high and he experience led to the delivery of large numbers of F-5s to the South Vietnamese air force. Most of these were abandoned on the capitulation of 1975. Deliveries of the F-5A and F-5B were numerous, totalling 1,197. The largest orders came from Norway, Canada (the single-seat **CF-5A** and two-seat **CF-5D** with improvements such as upgraded navigation, two-position nosewheel leg and greater power in the form of two 1950-kg/4,300-lb afterburning thrust Orenda J85-CAN-15 turbojets), Spain (single-seat **SF-5A** and two-seat **SF-5B**), Netherlands (single-seat **NF-5A** and two-seat **NF-5B** built in Canada to an improved CF-5 standard with manoeuvring flaps), Iran, Greece, South Korea, Taiwan and Turkey.

**Northrop F-5A Freedom Fighter**

*This F-5B is one of six delivered to 1º Grupo de Aviação de Caca of the Força Aérea Brasileira during late 1975. They augment the survivors of 36 F-5Es also delivered.*

*This is one of the Canadian built CF-5As remaining in service with No.419 Squadron for conversion and tactical weapons training and in the 'aggressor' role.*

## Specification: Northrop F-5A Freedom Fighter

**Origin:** USA
**Type:** light tactical fighter
**Powerplant:** two 1850-kg (4,080-lb) afterburning thrust General Electric J85-GE 13 turbojets
**Performance:** maximum speed Mach 1.4 or 802 kt (1487 km/h; 924 mph) at 36,000 ft (10975 m); initial climb rate 28,700 ft (8750 m) per minute; service ceiling 50,500 ft (15390 m); combat radius 314 km (195 miles) with maximum warload; ferry range 2594 km (1,612 miles)
**Weights:** empty 3667 kg (8,085 lb); maximum take-off 9374 kg (20,667 lb)
**Dimensions:** span 7.70 m (25 ft 3 in); length 14.38 m ( 47 ft 2 in); height 4.01 m (13 ft 2 in); wing area 15.79 m² (170.0 sq ft)
**Armament:** two 20-mm M39 cannon with 280 rounds per gun; provision for 1996 kg (4,400 lb) of disposable stores, including AAMs, bombs, cluster bombs, rocket-launcher

# Northrop F-5E and F-5F Tiger II

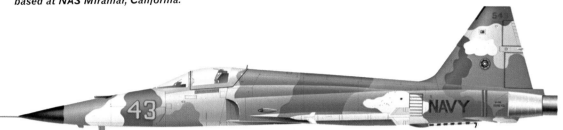

*Northrop F-5E Tiger II of the US Navy's Fighter Weapons School, based at NAS Miramar, California.*

In November 1970 the US government chose the **Northrop F-5E Tiger II** as winner of its International Fighter Aircraft competition to replace the obsolescent F-5A. Other contenders for the new type had included the Lockheed CL-1200 Lancer, Vought V-1000 and a stripped-down variant of the McDonnell Douglas F-4 Phantom II. A combination of increased engine power and a two-position extending nosewheel unit gave the F-5E an improvement of some 30 per cent in take-off performance over earlier versions, while the provision of arrester gear permitted operation from very short runways. The fuselage of the Tiger II is widened, which increases the wing span of the aircraft, and the wing loading on the F-5E is thus maintained at approximately the same value as that of the F-5A.

First flight of a production F-5E took place on 11 August 1972. and first deliveries were made on 4 April 1973 to the USAF's 425th Tactical Fighter Training Squadron. In the design and construction of the aircraft there was considerable emphasis on aerial agility rather than on high speed, particularly through the use of manoeuvring flaps. Powered by two General Electric J85 GE-21 turbojet engines, the Tiger II nonetheless has very

useful performance in terms of speed, climb rate and ceiling. As well as serving in the tactical fighter role with many countries in the US political orbit, the F-5E has also operated in the aggressor role at US combat training stations based in the USA, UK and Philippines. The 64th and 65th Aggressor Squadrons operate at Nellis AFB in the USA as part of the 57th Fighter Weapons Wing, and the 527th AS operated at RAF Alconbury in the UK, flying training missions for NATO. The Philippines-based unit, the 26th AS, was based at Clark AB and performed training missions for Far Eastern squadrons.

A two-seat trainer version of the F-5E was also produced with the designation F-5F, and this is also capable of carrying out combat duties. It has a fuselage lengthened by 1.02 m (3 ft 4 in), and its development was approved by the USAF in early 1974, the first flight taking place on 25 September 1974. Deliveries of 118 aircraft began In the summer of 1976. Export orders for the F-5E were numerous. The variant delivered to the Brazilian air force has a large dorsal fin to accommodate an ADF antenna. and those delivered to the Royal Saudi air force have a Litton LN-33 INS and inflight-refuelling capability.

### Specification: Northrop F-5E Tiger II
**Origin:** USA
**Type:** light tactical fighter
**Powerplant:** two 2268-kg (5,000-lb) afterburning thrust General Electric J85-GE-21B turbojets
**Performance:** maximum speed Mach 1.64 or 940 kt (1741 km/h; 1,082 mph) at 36,000 ft (10975 m); initial climb rate 34,500 ft (10516 m) per minute; service ceiling 51,800 ft (15790 m); combat radius 306 km (190 miles) with maximum warload; ferry range 3724 km (2,314 miles)
**Weights:** empty 4410 kg (9,723 lb); maximum take-off 11214 kg (24,722 lb)
**Dimensions:** span 8.13 m (26 ft 8 in); length 14.45 m (47 ft 4.7 in); height 4.07 m (13 ft 4.25 in); wing area 17.28 m² (186.0 sq ft)
**Armament:** two 20-mm M39 cannon with 280 rounds per gun; provision for 3175 kg (7,000 lb) of disposable stores, including AAMs, ASMs, bomber, cluster bombs, dispenser weapons, rocket-launcher pods, cannon pods, drop tanks and ECM pods, carried on five external hardpoints and two wing tip missile rails

*Northrop F-5E Tiger II*

*This Force Aérienne de la Republique de Tunisie Northrop F-5F Tiger II was seen on its delivery flight staging through RAF Alconbury, carrying a long-range ferry tank.*

*This F-5E of No.145 Sqwadron, 300 Wing, Tentara Nasional Indonesia-Angkatan Udara (Indonesian air force) is based at Meidun and operates primarily in the air defence role.*

## Role
Fighter
Close support
Counter-insurgency
Tactical strike
Strategic bomber
Tactical reconnaissance
Strategic reconnaissance
Maritime patrol
Anti-ship strike
Anti-submarine warfare
Search and rescue
Assault transport
Transport
Liaison
Trainer
Inflight-refuelling tanker
Specialized

## Performance
All-weather capability
Rough field capability
STOL capability
VTOL capability
Airspeed 0-250 mph
Airspeed 250 mph-Mach 1
Airspeed Mach 1 plus
Ceiling 0-20,000 ft
Ceiling 20,000-40,000 ft
Ceiling 40,000ft plus
Range 0-1,000 miles
Range 1,000-3,000 miles
Range 3,000 miles plus

## Weapons
Air-to-air missiles
Air-to-surface missiles
Cruise missiles
Cannon
Trainable guns
Naval weapons
Nuclear-capable
Rockets
'Smart' weapon kit
Weapon load 0-4,000 lb
Weapon load 4,000-15,000 lb
Weapon load 15,000 lb plus

## Avionics
Electronic Counter Measures
Electronic Support Measures
Search radar
Fire control radar
Look-down/shoot-down
Terrain-following radar
Forward-looking infra-red
Laser
Television

# Northrop RF-5E TigerEye

*Northrop RF-5E TigerEye of the Royal Saudi Air Force.*

## Role

Fighter
Close support
Counter-insurgency
Tactical strike
Strategic bomber
Tactical reconnaissance
Strategic reconnaissance
Maritime patrol
Anti-ship strike
Anti-submarine warfare
Search and rescue
Assault transport
Transport
Liaison
Trainer
Inflight-refuelling tanker
Specialized

## Performance

All-weather capability
Rough field capability
STOL capability
VTOL capability
Airspeed 0-250 mph
Airspeed 250 mph-Mach 1
Airspeed Mach 1 plus
Ceiling 0-20,000 ft
Ceiling 20,000-40,000 ft
Ceiling 40,000ft plus
Range 0-1,000 miles
Range 1,000-3,000 miles
Range 3,000 miles plus

## Weapons

Air-to-air missiles
Air-to-surface missiles
Cruise missiles
Cannon
Trainable guns
Naval weapons
Nuclear-capable
Rockets
'Smart' weapon kit
Weapon load 0-4,000 lb
Weapon load 4,000-15,000 lb
Weapon load 15,000 lb plus

## Avionics

Electronic Counter Measures
Electronic Support Measures
Search radar
Fire control radar
Look-down/shoot-down
Terrain-following radar
Forward-looking infra-red
Laser
Television

The F-5E, delivered from May 1973 to the extent of well over 1,000 aircraft to a wide assortment of nations, was a significant export success. As a result of its universal appeal, on 31 March 1978 the US government approved the production of a specialized tactical reconnaissance version of the Tiger II, designated as the **Northrop RF-5E** and later accorded the name **TigerEye**. The prototype made its international debut at the Paris Air Show of the same year following a flight from Edwards AFB in California. Aircraft performance is barely affected by the additional weight of the reconnaissance, navigation and communications equipment carried, and the TigerEye has essentially the same dimensions and characteristics as the F-5E except for its marginally increased weight.

The RF-5E is most readily distinguished from the conventional F-5E by its forward fuselage, which is modified to accommodate reconnaissance equipment: the nose is extended by 20.3 cm (8 in) and a KS-87D1 camera is fitted in a forward nose compartment. This camera is used in addition to either of three easily interchangeable pallets each with a different set of reconnaissance cameras/sensors permitting more diversity in the use of the aircraft. Pallet 1 consists of KA-95B and KA-56E panoramic cameras and an RS-710E infra-red linescanner, Pallet 2 has KA-56E and KA-93B6 panoramic cameras, and Pallet 3 carries one KS-147A camera for long-range oblique photography (LOROP) missions. Other pallet configurations were also studied.

The pilot of the RF-5E also has available a number of advanced navigation and communications systems and an ISCS (Integrated Sensor Control System) to lessen the workload and allow him more time to operate and monitor the reconnaissance and communications equipment. Otherwise the TigerEye has basically the same capabilities (including the external carriage of armament) as the F-5E.

Many of the nations currently employing the various versions of the F-5 expressed an interest in the aircraft after its debut, but only Malaysia and Saudi Arabia bought the type. The first production aircraft flew in December 1982, and was one of the two aircraft comprising the first export order, to the Royal Malaysian air force.

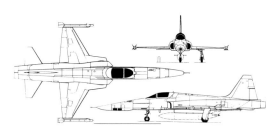

**Northrop F-5E TigerEye**

## Specification: Northrop RF-5E TigerEye

**Origin:** USA
**Type:** light tactical reconnaissance fighter
**Powerplant:** two 2268-kg (5,000-lb) afterburning thrust General Electric J85-GE-21B turbojets
**Performance:** maximum speed Mach 1.64 or 940 kt (1741 km/h; 1,082 mph) at 36,000 ft (10975 m); combat radius 760 km (472 miles) on a hi-lo-hi mission with two AIM-9 AAMs and one drop tank, or 463 km (288 miles) on a hi-hi-hi mission with internal fuel
**Weights:** empty 4423 kg (9,750 lb); maximum take-off 11192 kg (24,765 lb)
**Dimensions:** span 8.13 m (26 ft 8 in); length 14.65 m (48 ft 0.75 in); height 4.07 m (13 ft 4.25 in); wing area 17.28 m² (186.0 sq ft)
**Armament:** one 20-mm M39 cannon with 140 rounds; provision for 3175 kg (7,000 lb) of disposable stores, including AAMs, ASMs, bomber, cluster bombs, dispenser weapons, rocket-launcher pods, cannon pods, drop tanks and ECM pods, carried on five external hardpoints and two wing tip missile rails

*The fitting of an inflight-refuelling probe and the carriage of a long-range fuel tank endows the RF-5E with a phenomenal range in the tactical reconnaissance role.*

*At least one of Saudi Arabia's RF-5Es is finished in a sinister overall black colour scheme. A single cannon can be augmented by a full air-to-ground or air-to-air ordnance load.*

# Northrop-Grumman B-2 Spirit

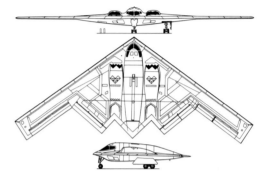

*A Northrop-Grumman B-2A Spirit of the US Air Force's 509th Bomb Wing, based at Whiteman AFB, Missourri.*

First revealed in November 1988 for an initial flight in July 1989, the **Northrop** (now **Northrop-Grumman**) **B-2 Spirit** was designed as successor to the Rockwell B-1B Lancer in the penetration bomber role. The new type was evolved for medium/high-altitude penetration at subsonic speed, relying on its stealth design and composite structure to evade detection by enemy air-defence systems until it has closed to within a few miles of its target. The main APQ-181 radar, which has features in common with the APG-70 used in the McDonnell Douglas F-15C/D/E Eagle, is a synthetic-aperture type and has 21 operational modes including coherent mapping.

The B-2 is a design of the relaxed-stability type, and is a flying wing with leading edges swept at 40 degrees and W-shaped trailing edges featuring simple flight-control surfaces operated by a digital fly-by-wire system. Design and manufacturing emphasis was placed on completely smooth surfaces with blended flight deck and nacelle bulges. As a result, the B-2's radar reflectivity is very low because of the use of radiation-absorbent materials and a carefully opti-

mized shape, including shielded upper-surface engine inlets. Additionally, the careful mixing of hot exhaust gases with cold freestream air before release through the engines' 2D nozzles reduces thermal and acoustic signatures to a very significant degree in this firmly subsonic design.

It was originally envisaged that Northrop would deliver 132 **B-2A** production aircraft as carriers for 2,000 of the 4,845 strategic nuclear weapons in the US Air Force's inventory. Further re-evaluation of the type, in the context of the USA's continued budget deficit and the reduction of the threat to the USA from a collapsing USSR (now CIS) resulted in a decision to trim production considerably more, perhaps to a total of just 20 bombers that entered service in 1994. In mid-1990 it was revealed that the USAF is to task its B-2s with a secondary maritime surveillance and attack role with weapons such as the AGM-84 Harpoon anti-ship missile. The advantage of the B-2 over the B-52 in this role is the ability of the 'stealth' bomber to fly higher while remaining undetected, thereby improving fuel economy (and thus range) and enlarging 'sensor grazing area'.

### Specification: Northrop-Grumman B-2A Spirit
**Origin:** USA
**Type:** two/three-seat strategic 'stealth' bomber and missile-launch platform
**Powerplant:** four 8618-kg (19,000-lb) dry thrust General Electric F118-GE-110 turbofans
**Performance:** maximum speed about 416 kt (764 km/h; 475 mph) at high altitude; service ceiling 50,000 ft (15240 m); range more 18532 km (11,515 miles) with one inflight refueling, 11675 km (7,255 miles) on a hi-hi-hi mission with a 16919-kg (37,300-lb) warload and standard fuel
**Weights:** empty between 45360 and 49900 kg (100,000 and 110,000 lb); maximum take-off 181437 kg (400,000 lb)
**Dimensions:** span 52.43 m (172 ft 0 in); length 21.03 m (69 ft 0 in); height 5.18 m (17 ft 0 in); wing area more than 464.50 m² (5,000.0 sq ft)
**Armament:** up to 22680 kg (50,000 lb) of disposable stores carried in two side-by-side lower-fuselage weapon bays; each bay can accommodate one eight-round Boeing Rotary Launcher for a total of 16 1.1 megaton B83 thermonuclear free-fall bombs; alternative loads are 20 megaton-range B61 thermonuclear free-fall bombs, or 22 680-kg (1,500-lb) or 80 227-kg (500-lb) free-fall bombs

*A B-2 on finals, with everything down. The B-2 is optimised for the deep penetration of hostile airspace, and is capable of finding and identifying mobile targets*

*The unique configuration of the B-2 is particularly evident from head-on. The smooth, flowing, blended body marks a different approach to stealth to the faceted angular body of the F-117.*

**Role**
Fighter
Close support
Counter-insurgency
Tactical strike
Strategic bomber
Tactical reconnaissance
Strategic reconnaissance
Maritime patrol
Anti-ship strike
Anti-submarine warfare
Search and rescue
Assault transport
Transport
Liaison
Trainer
Inflight-refuelling tanker
Specialized

**Performance**
All-weather capability
Rough field capability
STOL capability
VTOL capability
Airspeed 0-250 mph
Airspeed 250 mph-Mach 1
Airspeed Mach 1 plus
Ceiling 0-20,000 ft
Ceiling 20,000-40,000 ft
Ceiling 40,000ft plus
Range 0-1,000 miles
Range 1,000-3,000 miles
Range 3,000 miles plus

**Weapons**
Air-to-air missiles
Air-to-surface missiles
Cruise missiles
Cannon
Trainable guns
Naval weapons
Nuclear-capable
Rockets
'Smart' weapon kit
Weapon load 0-4,000 lb
Weapon load 4,000-15,000 lb
Weapon load 15,000 lb plus

**Avionics**
Electronic Counter Measures
Electronic Support Measures
Search radar
Fire control radar
Look-down/shoot-down
Terrain-following radar
Forward-looking infra-red
Laser
Television

# Northrop T-38 Talon

*Northrop T-38A Talon of the Força Aérea Portuguesa.*

**Role**
Fighter
Close support
Counter-insurgency
Tactical strike
Strategic bomber
Tactical reconnaissance
Strategic reconnaissance
Maritime patrol
Anti-ship strike
Anti-submarine warfare
Search and rescue
Assault transport
Transport
Liaison
Trainer
Inflight-refuelling tanker
Specialized

**Performance**
All-weather capability
Rough field capability
STOL capability
VTOL capability
Airspeed 0-250 mph
Airspeed 250 mph-Mach 1
Airspeed Mach 1 plus
Ceiling 0-20,000 ft
Ceiling 20,000-40,000 ft
Ceiling 40,000ft plus
Range 0-1,000 miles
Range 1,000-3,000 miles
Range 3,000 miles plus

**Weapons**
Air-to-air missiles
Air-to-surface missiles
Cruise missiles
Cannon
Trainable guns
Naval weapons
Nuclear-capable
Rockets
'Smart' weapon kit
Weapon load 0-4,000 lb
Weapon load 4,000-15,000 lb
Weapon load 15,000 lb plus

**Avionics**
Electronic Counter Measures
Electronic Support Measures
Search radar
Fire control radar
Look-down/shoot-down
Terrain-following radar
Forward-looking infra-red
Laser
Television

Initial development of the **Northrop T-38 Talon** resulted from studies carried out by the company which showed that the most significant cost factors in the life of an aircraft were those of maintenance and operation rather than those associated with research, development and production. The original outcome of these studies was the completion of designs, by Northrop, for a tactical fighter-bomber designated N-156F (developed as the F-5) and a two-seat trainer version designated N-156T. Development of these types was continued as a private venture until the USAF issued a General Operational Requirement for a supersonic basic trainer support system. Northrop met this requirement with a variant of the N-156T design, and was awarded a contract in 1956. During the next two years production of the trainer aircraft, designated **T-38A**, took precedence over that of the fighter.

The T-38 first flew on 10 April 1959, powered by two General Electric YJ85-GE-5 non-afterburning turbojets each rated at 953 kg (2,100 lb), and a second aircraft was flown on 12 June 1959. The first production aircraft was flown in January 1960, powered by two afterburning engines each giving a thrust of 1633 kg (3,600 lb); later production aircraft used the 1746-kg (3,850-lb) afterburning thrust J85-GE-5. The first supersonic aircraft designed from the outset specifically to fulfil the training role, the Talon entered service on 17 March 1961 with the USAF's Air Training Command Instructors School at Randolph AFB as a successor to the subsonic Lockheed T-33A; the first group of students began basic training in the aircraft in September 1961.

Excluding prototype and pre-production aircraft, 1,139 Talons were produced, and although the aircraft served primarily with the USAF, the type was also sold to West Germany among other countries. A number of performance records set by the T-38 reflect the high quality of its design, and the aircraft will remain operational for many years to come in its original form (now to be modernized) and **T-38B** 'Lead-In Fighter Trainer' form with provision for training weapons.

**Specification:** Northrop T-38A Talon
**Origin:** USA
**Type:** two-seat supersonic basic trainer
**Powerplant:** two 1746-kg (3,850-lb) dry thrust General Electric J85-GE-5 turbojets
**Performance:** maximum speed Mach 1.3 or 745 kt (1381 km/h; 858 mph) at 36,000 ft (10975 m); initial climb rate 33,600 ft (10241 m) per minute; service ceiling 53,600 ft (16340 m); range 1759 miles (1,093 miles) with maximum fuel
**Weights:** empty 3254 kg (7,174 lb); maximum take-off 5361 kg (11,820 lb)
**Dimensions:** span 7.70 m (25 ft 3 in); length 14.14 m (46 ft 4.5 in); height 3.92 m (12 ft 10.5 in); wing area 15.79 m² (170.0 sq ft)
**Armament:** none

*Northrop T-38A Talon*

*This Talon serves with the Air Force Flight Test Center for a variety of duties. The Talons sometimes act as chase aircraft, and are used by Shuttle pilots for training purposes.*

*In Turkish air force service the T-38 Talon serves with the Izmir-Cigli-based 121 Filo for advanced pilot training. About 30 were delivered, and most remain in use.*

# PZL Mielec TS-11 Iskra

*PZL Mielec TS-11 Iskra of the Polish air force.*

Like its contemporary, the Aero L-29 Delfin, the **PZL Mielec TS-11 Iskra** (spark) was designed to supersede a piston-engine trainer and was flown for the first time some 10 months after the L-29, on 5 February 1960. It was later evaluated against the L-29 for selection as a basic trainer for the Soviet air force, and possible supply to other WarPac nations, but came second best. The Polish air force nevertheless adopted the TS-11, the first examples being handed over in March 1963; quantity production was attained during the following year.

A mid-wing monoplane of all-metal construction, the TS-11 has a pod-and-boom type fuselage structure, adopted to raise the tail unit well clear of the efflux of the turbojet engine, which is mounted within the fuselage aft of the cockpit. The instructor and pupil are in tandem on lightweight ejector seats. the instructor's (rear) seat being slightly raised, and both positions are enclosed by a one-piece canopy which is hinged at its rear edge and is jettisonable. The retractable tricycle landing gear has a pneumatic emergency extension system, and underwing hardpoints allow for the carriage of training weapons. Fully aerobatic, the TS-11 is stressed to g limits of +8/-4.

**Specification:** PZL Mielec TS-11 Iskra-bis DF
**Origin:** Poland
**Type:** combat/reconnaissance trainer
**Powerplant:** one 1100-kg (2,425-lb) dry thrust IL SO-3W turbojet
**Performance:** maximum speed 415 kt (770 km/h; 478 mph); cruising speed 324 kt (600 km/h; 373 mph); initial climb rate 3,820 ft (1164 m) per minute; service ceiling 37,730 ft (11500 m); range 1260 km (783 miles) with maximum fuel
**Weights:** empty 2565 kg (5,655 lb); maximum take-off 3840 kg (8,466 lb) **Dimensions:** span 10.06 m (33 ft 0 in); length 11.15 m (36 ft 7 in); height 3.50 m (11 ft 5.8 in); wing area 17.50 m² (188.37 sq ft)
**Armament:** one 23-mm NR-23 cannon; provision for 400 kg (882 lb) of disposable stores, including bombs, rocket-launcher pods and gun pods, carried on four external hardpoints

The early production **Iskra-bis A** was powered initially by the Polish-designed H-10 turbojet of 780-kg (1,720-lb) dry thrust, pending availability of the intended 1000-kg (2,205-lb) dry thrust SO-1 turbojet designed by the Instytut Lotnictwa and manufactured by WSK-PZL Rzeszów; from the late 1960s the SO-1 was often replaced by the improved SO-3 of similar thrust rating.

Subsequent two-seat variants before production was suspended in mid-1979 included the similar **Iskra-bis B** with two additional underwing hardpoints and the **Iskra-bis D** which could carry an even wider range of external weapons; this last was also supplied to the Indian air force. Also built before mid-1979 was the single-seat reconnaissance **Iskra-bis C**, first flown in June 1972 and incorporating a camera mounting in the lower fuselage and increased fuel for extended range. Manufacture was resumed in 1982 with the **Iskra-bis DF**, a two-seat combat/reconnaissance trainer which was built into the later 1980s. This has an uprated engine, more comprehensive armament and three cameras, one in each inlet fairing and one beneath the fuselage. About 600 aircraft of all versions are reported to have been built.

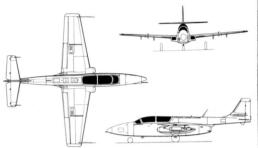

*PZL-Mielec TS-11 Iskra*

*India's TS-11 Iskras may soon be replaced, having been in service since 1968. Press reports have implied that the BAe Hawk has been virtually selected or that the Aero L-39 is in the running, but the IAF seems happy with the HAL HJT-16 Kiran.*

*The Iskra was not selected as the standard Warsaw Pact trainer, but was procured by Poland and India.*

## Role
Fighter
Close support
Counter-insurgency
Tactical strike
Tactical bomber
Strategic bomber
Tactical reconnaissance
Strategic reconnaissance
Maritime patrol
Anti-ship strike
Anti-submarine warfare
Search and rescue
Assault transport
Transport
Liaison
Trainer
Inflight-refuelling tanker
Specialized

## Performance
All-weather capability
Rough field capability
STOL capability
VTOL capability
Airspeed 0-250 mph
Airspeed 250 mph-Mach 1
Airspeed Mach 1 plus
Ceiling 0-20,000 ft
Ceiling 20,000-40,000 ft
Ceiling 40,000ft plus
Range 0-1,000 miles
Range 1,000-3,000 miles
Range 3,000 miles plus

## Weapons
Air-to-air missiles
Air-to-surface missiles
Cruise missiles
Cannon
Trainable guns
Naval weapons
Nuclear-capable
Rockets
'Smart' weapon kit
Weapon load 0-4,000 lb
Weapon load 4,000-15,000 lb
Weapon load 15,000 lb plus

## Avionics
Electronic Counter Measures
Electronic Support Measures
Search radar
Fire control radar
Look-down/shoot-down
Terrain-following radar
Forward-looking infra-red
Laser
Television

# PZL Swidnik Mi-2 'Hoplite'

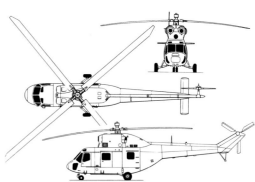

PZL Swidnik Mi-2 'Hoplite' of the Polish air force.

## Role
Fighter
Close support
Counter-insurgency
Tactical strike
Strategic bomber
Tactical reconnaissance
Strategic reconnaissance
Maritime patrol
Anti-ship strike
Anti-submarine warfare
Search and rescue
Assault transport
Transport
Liaison
Trainer
Inflight-refuelling tanker
Specialized

## Performance
All-weather capability
Rough field capability
STOL capability
VTOL capability
Airspeed 0-250 mph
Airspeed 250 mph-Mach 1
Airspeed Mach 1 plus
Ceiling 0-20,000 ft
Ceiling 20,000-40,000 ft
Ceiling 40,000ft plus
Range 0-1,000 miles
Range 1,000-3,000 miles
Range 3,000 miles plus

## Weapons
Air-to-air missiles
Air-to-surface missiles
Cruise missiles
Cannon
Trainable guns
Naval weapons
Nuclear-capable
Rockets
'Smart' weapon kit
Weapon load 0-4,000 lb
Weapon load 4,000-15,000 lb
Weapon load 15,000 lb plus

## Avionics
Electronic Counter Measures
Electronic Support Measures
Search radar
Fire control radar
Look-down/shoot-down
Terrain-following radar
Forward-looking infra-red
Laser
Television

The **PZL Swidnik Mi-2**, which has the NATO reporting name **'Hoplite'**, derives from the Soviet Mil design bureau as indicated by the Mi-2 in its designation. At first intended as a replacement for the mi-1 and flown initially during September 1961, two prototypes were completed and flying before, in January 1964, an agreement was concluded with the Polish government under which PZL at Swidnik was given full responsibility for development, manufacture and marketing of this helicopter. It was not until November 1965 that the first Polish-built Mi-2 was flown, and since that time PZL-Swidnik has built this utility light helicopter in many variants to a total that is now past the 5,250 mark.

Of conventional pod-and-boom configuration, with three-blade main and two-blade anti-torque rotors, the Mi-2 has a twin-turbine powerplant mounted above the cabin, non-retractable tricycle landing gear, and a cabin that seats a pilot and up to eight passengers in an air-conditioned environment. The seats are easily removable to permit the carriage of up to 700 kg (1,543lb) of cargo, and in an ambulance role the cabin can accommodate four litters and a medical attendant, or two stretchers and two seated casualties. For freight lifting, an external cargo hook of 800-kg (1,764-lb) capacity can be installed, and this weight represents the maximum payload which can be lifted by the Mi-2. Improved **Mi-2B** versions are also available, these having a revised electrical system and advanced navaids.

In addition to civil use (in tasks that include those above plus agricultural, photogrammetric, SAR, television relay and training), many of the helicopters are in military service for tasks such as SAR (with optional rescue hoists of up to 260-kg/573-lb capacity) and dual-control training. Other known military roles include casevac, naval support (**Mi-2RM**), armed reconnaissance (**Mi-2URN**), close support (**Mi-2US** with a 23-mm fixed cannon, two 7.62-mm/0.3-in machine gun pods and two 7.62-mm/0.3-in pintle-mounted machine guns) and anti-tank (**Mi-2URP** with four AT-3 'Sagger' anti-tank missiles carried on pylons on the cabin sides with four reload missiles in the cabin; later helicopters can also carry four examples of the SA-7 'Grail' SAM in the AAM role for the escort of other helicopters).

**Specification:** PZL Swidnik Mi-2 'Hoplite'
**Origin:** USSR (now CIS)/Poland
**Type:** general-purpose light helicopter
**Powerplant:** two 298-kW (400-shp) PZL-Rzeszów (Isotov) GTD-350 turboshafts
**Performance:** maximum cruising speed 108 kt (200 km/h 124 mph); long-range cruising 102 kt (190 km/h; 118 mph); initial climb rate 885 ft (270 m) per minute; service ceiling 13,125 ft (4000 m); range 170 km (106 miles) with maximum payload and 5 per cent fuel reserve
**Weights:** empty (dual-control version) 2424 kg (5,344 lb); maximum take-off 3700 kg (8,157 lb)
**Dimensions:** main rotor diameter 14.50 m (47 ft 6.9 in); length, rotors turning 17.42 m (57 ft 1.8 in); height 3.75 m (12 ft 3.6 in); main rotor disc area 165.13 m² (1,777.5 sq ft)
**Armament:** can include machine gun pods and AT-3 'Sagger' anti-tank missiles on fuselage-side pylons

More than 5,250 Mi-2s have been built by PZL-Swidnik, many of them for the Polish air force. The helicopter can carry rocket-launcher pods, AT-3 'Sagger' anti-tank missiles, or fuel tanks externally.

This Mi-2 'Hoplite' served as a liaison helicopter and general 'hack' with the Mi-24-equipped Kampfhübschraubergeschwader 'Adolf von Lützow' of the East German air force.

# PZL I-22 Iryda

*PZL I-22 Iryda prototype.*

Yet another training aircraft emanating from the Polish aircraft industry, the **PZL I-22 Iryda** (iridium) is in a very different category to the PZL-130 Iskierka. The I-22 is clearly intended to replace the TS-11 Iskra jet trainer which entered Polish service in 1964, but initial details became available in the West only in late 1986 despite the fact that the first of the type's two prototypes made its initial flight on 3 March 1985. Designed at the Instytut Lotnictwa in Warsaw under the supervision of Dr. Eng. Alfred Baron, the I-22 is a multi-role trainer suitable for advanced pilot training (by day or night and under all weather conditions) in roles that include air combat, ground attack and reconnaissance; with a maximum external stores load of 1200 kg (2,646 lb), the I-22 can also undertake the light attack role.

Very similar in configuration to the Dassault/Dornier Alpha Jet, the I-22 is a high-wing monoplane of typical light alloy construction. The wing, of laminar-flow aerofoil section, has some 20° sweepback on the leading edge and incorporates conventional ailerons and single-slotted flaps on its trailing edges. The fuselage, which is of semi-monocoque construction, includes a door-type airbrake in each side of the upper rear surface, and has pod-mounted on each lower side of its central structure one non-afterburning turbojet engine. The tail unit, which includes

a variable-incidence tailplane, has all swept surfaces. The retractable tricycle landing gear is designed for operation from unprepared strips, the single wheel on each unit having a low-pressure tyre. The tandem-seat accommodation is pressurized and air-conditioned, and the instructor's rear seat is elevated by 0.4 m (1 ft 3.75 in) to provide a good forward view. Both members of the crew have rocket-powered ejector seats that can be operated at zero altitude and speeds down to 81 kt (150 km/h; 93 mph). Full blind-flying instrumentation is standard, and the avionics can include VHF, UHF, ADF, marker beacon receiver, radar altimeter, radio compass and/or other equipment to meet individual customer requirements..

The capability of the I-22 in terms of light attack was evaluated in the second prototype, which was completed with a 23-mm two-barrel cannon on the centerline and four underwing hardpoints each stressed for a maximum load of 500 kg (1,102 lb), and the inboard pair are each 'plumbed' for drop tanks. The I-22 is fully aerobatic, the fuel system permitting inverted flight, and in aerobatic configuration the g limits are +8/-4.

The type has now entered low-volume production for the Polish air force, which received in first aircraft in 1993, and further development is centred on the **I-22MS** single-seat version optimized for the light attack role.

**PZL I-22 Iryda**

**Specification:** PZL I-22 Iryda
**Origin:** Poland
**Type:** multi-role trainer and light close-support aircraft
**Powerplant:** two 1100-kg (2,425-lb) dry thrust PZL-Rzeszów SO-3W22 turbojets
**Performance:** maximum speed 453 kt (840 km/h; 522 mph) at 16,405 ft (5000 m); initial climb rate 4,920 ft (1500 m) per minute; service ceiling 36,090 ft (11000 m); range 420 km (261 miles) with maximum warload
**Weights:** empty 10,361 lb (4700 kg); maximum take-off 15,211 lb (6900 lb)
**Dimensions:** span 9.60 m (31 ft 6 in); length 13.22 m (43 ft 4.5 in); height 4.30 M (14 ft 1.3 in); wing area 19.92 m² (214.42 sq ft)
**Armament:** one 23-mm GSh-23L two-barrel cannon with 200 rounds; provision for 1200 kg (2,645 lb) of disposable stores, including bombs, rocket-launcher pods and drop tanks, on four external hardpoints

*The new PZL I-22 Iryda trainer is similar in configuration and appearance to the FMA IA 63 Pampa and Dassault/Dornier Alpha Jet, and the overall performance is broadly similar.*

*The I-22 is scheduled to replace the PZL TS-11 Iskra in service with the Polish air force, but the Aero L-39 is probably to firmly established to permit widespread exports even to countries of the erstwhile Soviet bloc.*

Role
Fighter
Close support
Counter-insurgency
Tactical strike
Strategic bomber
Tactical reconnaissance
Strategic reconnaissance
Maritime patrol
Anti-ship strike
Anti-submarine warfare
Search and rescue
Assault transport
Transport
Liaison
Trainer
Inflight-refuelling tanker
Specialized

Performance
All-weather capability
Rough field capability
STOL capability
VTOL capability
Airspeed 0-250 mph
Airspeed 250 mph-Mach 1
Airspeed Mach 1 plus
Airspeed 40,000 ft
Ceiling 0-20,000 ft
Ceiling 20,000-40,000 ft
Ceiling 40,000ft plus
Range 0-1,000 miles
Range 1,000-3,000 miles
Range 1,000 miles plus
Range 3,000 miles plus

Weapons
Air-to-air missiles
Air-to-surface missiles
Cruise missiles
Cannon
Trainable guns
Naval weapons
Nuclear-capable
Rockets
'Smart' weapon kit
Weapon load 0-4,000 lb
Weapon load 4,000-15,000 lb
Weapon load 15,000 lb plus

Avionics
Electronic Counter Measures
Electronic Support Measures
Search radar
Fire control radar
Look-down/shoot-down
Terrain-following radar
Forward-looking infra-red
Laser
Television

# PZL Warszawa-Okecie PZL-130 Orlik

*PZL Warszawa-Okecie PZL-130 Orlik prototype.*

**Role**

Fighter
Close support
Counter-insurgency
Tactical strike
Strategic bomber
Tactical reconnaissance
Strategic reconnaissance
Maritime patrol
Anti-ship strike
Anti-submarine warfare
Search and rescue
Assault transport
Transport
Liaison
Trainer
Inflight-refuelling tanker
Specialized

**Performance**

All-weather capability
Rough field capability
STOL capability
VTOL capability
Airspeed 0-250 mph
Airspeed 250 mph-Mach 1
Airspeed Mach 1 plus
Ceiling 0-20,000 ft
Ceiling 20,000-40,000 ft
Ceiling 40,000ft plus
Range 0-1,000 miles
Range 1,000-3,000 miles
Range 3,000 miles plus

**Weapons**

Air-to-air missiles
Air-to-surface missiles
Cruise missiles
Cannon
Trainable guns
Naval weapons
Nuclear-capable
Rockets
'Smart' weapon kit
Weapon load 0-4,000 lb
Weapon load 4,000-15,000 lb
Weapon load 15,000 lb plus

**Avionics**

Electronic Counter Measures
Electronic Support Measures
Search radar
Fire control radar
Look-down/shoot-down
Terrain-following radar
Forward-looking infra-red
Laser
Television

In 1981 PZL started work on a multi-role trainer of all-metal construction with retractable tricycle landing gear, a low-set cantilever wing, and a comparatively long cockpit that seated the instructor behind and above his pupil. The resulting **PZL Warszawa-Okecie PZL-130 Orlik** (spotted eaglet) prototype flew on 12 October 1984 as an attractive type powered by one 246-kW (330-hp) VMKB (Vedeneyev) M-14Pm radial piston engine. The type offered just the capabilities that had been demanded of it, but plans to plan the Orlik into production were stymied by non-availability of the Soviet engine and the absence of any suitable Polish engine in this power bracket. In 1985, however, PZL had reached agreement with AirTech of Canada for the joint development of a turboprop-powered version, and the third of the six Orlik prototypes was revised as the **PZL-130T Turbo-Orlik** with the 410-kW (550-shp) Pratt & Whitney Canada PT6A-25A turboprop. The converted prototype first flew on 13 July 1986, and revealed much superior capability in terms of

greater performance and agility with an increased weapon load carried on two additional hardpoints. There followed two more prototypes in the forms of the **PZL-130TM** with the 560-kW (750-shp) Motorlet M 601 E turboprop and the **PZL-130TP** with the PT6A-25A. It was the PZL-130TM with the Czechoslovak turboprop that was adopted by the Polish air force, which has ordered 48 such aircraft with the designation **PZL-130TB** and longer-span wings.

PZL has also planned variants of the basic turbine-engined model with different engines and Western ejector seats such as the Martin-Baker Mk CH15A. The **PZL-130TC** is the most powerful of the currently planned developments, and differs from the PZL-130TB in details such as its powerplant of one 708-kW (950-shp) PT6A-62 turboprop and Bendix/King avionics. The **PZL-130TD** is an alternative export variant, and differs from the PZL-130TB in details such as its powerplant of one 559-kW (750-shp) PT6A-25C turboprop and Bendix/King avionics. The **PZL-130TE** is the economy variant for the export market.

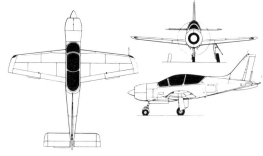

*PZL Warszawa-Okecie PZL-130 Orlik*

*The second flying prototype PZL-130 Orlik, seen at the 1985 Paris Air Show at Le Bourget. This piston-engined model has now been replaced by the turboprop-powered PZL-130T Turbo-Orlik.*

*The first prototype PZL-130 Orlik is seen during an early test flight. The turboprop-powered derivative is used for pilot training and can be fitted with weapons for the armament training role.*

**Specification:** PZL Warszawa-Okecie PZL-130TB Turbo-Orlik
**Origin:** Poland
**Type:** basic/advanced flying trainer with armament training and light attack capabilities
**Powerplant:** one 559-kW (750-shp) Motorlet (Walter) M 601E turboprop
**Performance:** maximum speed 270 kt (501 km/h; 311 mph) at 19,685 ft (6000 m) and 245 kt (282 mph; 454 km/h) at sea level; initial climb rate 2,620 ft (798 m) per minute; range 970 km (602 miles)
**Weights:** empty 1600 kg (3,527 lb); maximum take-off 2700 kg (5,952 lb)
**Dimensions:** span 9.00 m (29 ft 6.25 in; length 9.00 m (29 ft 6.25 in); height 3.53 m (11 ft 7 in); wing area 13.00 m² (139.93 sq ft)
**Armament:** provision for 800 kg (1,764 lb) of disposable stores, including 100-kg (220-lb) bombs, UV-8-57 multiple launchers each carrying eight 55-mm (2.17-in) unguided rockets, UV-4-80 multiple launchers carrying four 80-mm (3.15-in) unguided rockets and Zeus pods each containing two 7.62-mm (0.3-in) machine guns, carried on six external hardpoints

# Panavia Tornado IDS

*Panavia Tornado IDS of No.7 Squadron, Royal Saudi Air Force.*

Emanating from one of the most successful of all multi-national design, development and production programmes, the **Panavia Tornado** stems from the project originally identified as the Multi-Role Combat Aircraft. The partner nations were West Germany, Italy and the UK, and each had differing major requirements, covering air superiority, close air support/battlefield interdiction, interception/air defence, interdiction/counter air strike, naval strike, and reconnaissance, so the resolution of a design to meet the majority of these requirements in a single airframe represents a triumph for collaboration and common sense. Panavia Aircraft GmbH, the company to bring this programme to fruition, was formed on 26 March 1969 by BAC (later British Aerospace), MBB (later Deutsche Aerospace) and Fiat (later Aeritalia and now Alenia), the design being finalized in 1972 and the name Tornado adopted. Orders from the participating nations for the **Tornado IDS** version totalled 653 aircraft, comprising 212 for the Luftwaffe, 112 for the Marineflieger, 229 **Tornado GR.Mk 1** aircraft for the Royal Air Force, and 100 for the Aeronautica Militare Italiana. A further 173 examples of the Tornado ADV (Air Defence Variant) are being procured for the RAF, and this version is described separately.

The first of nine development prototypes was flown at Manching, West Germany on 14 August 1974, and initial deliveries to the Tri-National Tornado Training Establishment at RAF Cottesmore were made in early 1981, and to the two Weapon Conversion Units, WaKo (renamed JaboG 38 in August 1983) at Erding in West Germany and at RAF Honington in February 1982 and January 1984 respectively.

Each nation has communication and IFF equipment of its own choice installed, but all share the advanced and complex avionics that give the Tornado formidable all-weather, low-altitude terrain-following capability in a hostile environment, combined with superb navigation and weapon delivery accuracy. These features enabled the RAF to gain outstanding success in strategic/tactical bombing competitions in the USA, and in the 1991 UN-led campaign against Iraq. Tornados of all three European nations are armed with two 27-mm IWKA-Mauser cannon, and can carry up to 9000 kg (19,842 lb) of various weapons/stores on three underfuselage attachments and four swivelling hardpoints beneath the variable-geometry wings. Since the weapons stores carried can comprise almost the entire range deployed by the three nations, they are too extensive to list here.

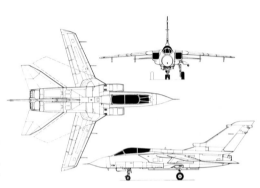

**Panavia Tornado IDS**

*The Tornado IDS replaced the Lockheed F-104G Starfighter as the German navy's main anti-ship attack and reconnaissance aircraft with Marinefliegergeschwadern 1 and 2. Some 112 aircraft were delivered.*

*No.14 Squadron was the last RAF Germany strike squadron to receive the Tornado, although the reconnaissance-dedicated No.2 Squadron later receive the type to replace its ageing Jaguars.*

**Specification:** Panavia Tornado GR.Mk 1
**Origin:** Germany, Italy and UK
**Type:** multi-role combat aircraft
**Powerplant:** two 7292-kg (16,075-lb) afterburning thrust Turbo-Union RB.199-34R Mk 103 turbofans
**Performance:** maximum speed Mach 2.2 or 1,261 kt (2337 km/h; 1,452 mph) above 36,090 ft (11000 m); climb to 30,000 ft (9145 m) under 2 minutes from brake release; service ceiling more than 50,000 ft (15240 m); combat radius 1390 km (864 miles) on a hi-lo-lo-hi mission with heavy weapon load
**Weights:** empty 14091 kg (31,065 lb); maximum take-off 27216 kg (60,000 lb)
**Dimensions:** span 13.91 m (45 ft 7.5 in) spread and 8.60 m (28 ft 2.5 in) swept; length 16.72 m (54 ft 10.25 in); height 5.95 m (19 ft 6.25 in); wing area 26.60 m² (286.3 sq ft)
**Armament:** two 27-mm IWKA-Mauser cannon with 180 rounds per gun; provision for 9000 kg (19,840 lb) of disposable stores, including a 500-kiloton nuclear weapon, Hunting JP233 weapon packs, ALARM anti-radar missiles, AAMs, ASMs, anti-ship missiles, free-fall and guided bombs, cluster bombs, drop tanks and ECM pods, carried on seven external hardpoints

**Role**

Fighter
Close support
Counter-insurgency
Tactical strike
Strategic bomber
Tactical reconnaissance
Strategic reconnaissance
Maritime patrol
Anti-ship strike
Anti-submarine warfare
Search and rescue
Assault transport
Transport
Liaison
Trainer
Inflight-refuelling tanker
Specialized

**Performance**

All-weather capability
Rough field capability
STOL capability
VTOL capability
Airspeed 0-250 mph
Airspeed 250 mph-Mach 1
Airspeed Mach 1 plus
Ceiling 0-20,000 ft
Ceiling 20,000-40,000 ft
Ceiling 40,000ft plus
Range 0-1,000 miles
Range 1,000-3,000 miles
Range 3,000 miles plus

**Weapons**

Air-to-air missiles
Air-to-surface missiles
Cruise missiles
Cannon
Trainable guns
Naval weapons
Nuclear-capable
Rockets
'Smart' weapon kit
Weapon load 0-4,000 lb
Weapon load 4,000-15,000 lb
Weapon load 15,000 lb plus

**Avionics**

Electronic Counter Measures
Electronic Support Measures
Search radar
Fire control radar
Look-down/shoot-down
Terrain-following radar
Forward-looking infra-red
Laser
Television

# Panavia Tornado ADV

*A Panavia Tornado ADV of No.29 Squadron, Royal Saudi Air Force*

**Role**
Fighter
Close support
Counter-insurgency
Tactical strike
Strategic bomber
Tactical reconnaissance
Strategic reconnaissance
Maritime patrol
Anti-ship strike
Anti-submarine warfare
Search and rescue
Assault transport
Transport
Liaison
Trainer
Inflight-refuelling tanker
Specialized

**Performance**
All-weather capability
Rough field capability
STOL capability
VTOL capability
Airspeed 0-250 mph
Airspeed 250 mph-Mach 1
Airspeed Mach 1 plus
Ceiling 0-20,000 ft
Ceiling 20,000-40,000 ft
Ceiling 40,000ft plus
Range 0-1,000 miles
Range 1,000-3,000 miles
Range 3,000 miles plus

**Weapons**
Air-to-air missiles
Air-to-surface missiles
Cruise missiles
Cannon
Trainable guns
Naval weapons
Nuclear-capable
Rockets
'Smart' weapon kit
Weapon load 0-4,000 lb
Weapon load 4,000-15,000 lb
Weapon load 15,000 lb plus

**Avionics**
Electronic Counter Measures
Electronic Support Measures
Search radar
Fire control radar
Look-down/shoot-down
Terrain-following radar
Forward-looking infra-red
Laser
Television

Planned procurement of the Tornado IDS for the RAF did not resolve the foreseen problem of providing a long-range interceptor for air defence of the British Isles and fulfilment of British commitments for protection of NATO's northern and western approaches. Clearly the RAF's BAe Lightnings and McDonnell Douglas Phantom IIs would need replacing in the future, and in 1969 work began to study adaptation of the Tornado IDS for an air-defence role. Air Staff Target 395, issued by the MoD in 1971, covered initial development of an interceptor with minimal changes to the Tornado IDS to carry advanced multi-mode radar and have, as primary armament, BAe Sky Flash medium-range AAMs. Early assessment showed that for adequate fighter performance the Sky Flashes would have to be semi-submerged in the underside of the fuselage. On 4 March 1976, development was authorized as the **Panavia Tornado ADV** (Air Defence Variant), identified as the **Tornado F.Mk 2** by the RAF, which had a requirement for 165. This designation now applies only to the first 18 built, subsequent aircraft with Mk 104 engines and automatic wing sweep being redesignated **Tornado F.Mk 3**, and F.Mk 2s upgraded to a virtual F.Mk 3 standard being redesignated as **Tornado F.Mk 2A** aircraft. Saudi Arabia later ordered 24 basically similar fighters.

The Tornado ADV has some 80 per cent commonality with its predecessor, and structural changes have been limited to the minimum. They include a lengthened nose for the radome of its Foxhunter radar, a small fuselage 'stretch' to allow two pairs of Sky Flash missiles to be carried in tandem, and a forward extension of the fixed inboard portion of the wings to compensate for changes in CG shift. Benefits gained from the lengthened fuselage are lowered transonic drag, a 10 per cent increase in internal fuel capacity, and more space for avionics.

A key element of the Tornado ADV is its AI-24 Foxhunter multi-mode track-while-scan pulse-Doppler radar, able to detect and track several targets simultaneously at a range in excess of 185 km (115 miles), and which in a ground-mapping mode can back-up the onboard navigation systems.

Other additions include a pilot's head-down display, radar homing and warning receiver, ESM and ECCM. Analog or digital electronic engine control units equip the Mk 103 and Mk 104 engines respectively. An internally mounted retractable inflight-refuelling probe is standard. The Tornado's Sky Flash missiles can engage targets from as low as 250 ft (76 m) up to high altitude at a range of some 48 km (30 miles), and are resistant to ECM.

Delivery to the RAF of Tornado F.Mk 2s has been completed, and the first F.Mk 3s were delivered in February 1986.

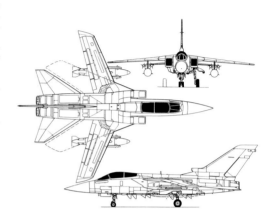

*Panavia Tornado F.Mk 3*

**Problems with the Foxhunter radar led to many early Tornado F.Mk2s being delivered with 'Blue Circle' - a block of concrete ballast - in the nose. F.Mk3s, like this No.229 OCU aircraft, all have a full standard working radar.**

**Saudi Arabia remains the only export customer for the Tornado F.Mk3, although the aircraft has now overcome its early problems and is an excellent long range air defence aircraft.**

## Specification: Panavia Tornado F.Mk 3
**Origin:** Germany, Italy and UK
**Type:** all-weather air-defence interceptor
**Powerplant:** two 7493-kg (16,520-lb) afterburning thrust Turbo-Union RB.199-34R Mk 104 turbofans
**Performance:** maximum speed Mach 2.2 or 1,261 kt (2337 km/h; 1,452 mph) above 36,090 ft (11000 m); operational ceiling about 70,000 ft (21335 m); intercept radius, supersonic more than 555 km (345 miles) and subsonic more than 1853 km (1,150 miles); endurance 2 hours on a CAP at 740 km (460 miles) from base including 10 minutes of combat
**Weights:** empty 14501 kg (31,970 lb); maximum take-off 27987 kg (61,700 lb)
**Dimensions:** span 13.91 m (45 ft 7.5 in) spread and 8.60 m (28 ft 2.5 in) swept; length 18.68 m (61 ft 3.5 in); height 5.95 m (19 ft 6.25 in); wing area 26.60 m² (286.3 sq ft)
**Armament:** one 27-mm IWKA-Mauser cannon with 180 rounds; provision for 5806 kg (12,800 lb) of disposable stores, including Sky Flash medium-range AAMs, AIM-9L Sidewinder short-range AAMs and drop tanks, carried on four underfuselage and two underwing hardpoints

# Panavia Tornado ECR

*An RAF Panavia Tornado GR.Mk 1A.*

The sixth, and initially least important, requirement for the Panavia Tornado IDS was a reconnaissance capability. This was almost certainly because it was realized that it would be comparatively simple at a later date for the aircraft to carry one or more of the specialized reconnaissance pods developed in recent years. German and Italian interest came first, and design and development of a multi-sensor reconnaissance pod for installation on the centreline fuselage attachment was undertaken by Messerschmitt-Bölkow-Blohm. The Royal Air Force was also looking for such capability, and it was reported in late 1985 that the first flight was imminent of a Tornado GR.Mk 1 with a reconnaissance pack installed in the ammunition bay for the 27-mm IWKA-Mauser cannon. This pack was believed to contain three BAe infra-red cameras and the Vinten Linescan 4000 IR surveillance system incorporating wide-angle linescan and two thermal imaging common modules. Computing Devices in East Sussex supplied the RMS 300 reconnaissance management system for the Tornado, which can record high-resolution video from all IR sensors as well as provide many other important facilities for this **Panavia Tornado GR.Mk 1A** version.

However, the most specific development in the reconnaissance role has been the **Tornado ECR** (Electronic Combat and Reconnaissance) version of the Tornado IDS to meet a Luftwaffe requirement for 40 (later reduced to 35) such aircraft, and supplemented by 16 conversions for Italy. The initial stage in the programme was the doubling of computing capacity of the central computer and the provision for capability for deployment of the AGM-88 HARM anti-radar missile. The Tornado ECR was then provided with a Texas Instruments emitter location system to pinpoint ground-based radar installations, and with advanced tactical displays for the pilot and systems operator, as well as a reconnaissance system comprising inbuilt infra-red sensors, plus the facilities to process and store reconnaissance data and/or transmit these data in real time to a ground station. Typically the Tornado ECR version uses the external attachments to carry two HARM anti-radar missiles and two self-defence AIM-9 Sidewinder AAMs, plus an active ECM pod, a chaff/flare dispenser pod and two drop tanks. Additional weapons can be carried on the underfuselage stations and, thus the Tornado ECR is deployable on missions other than pure ECR. As these are new-build Tornados they are powered by RB.199-34R Mk 105 turbofans offering some 10 per cent more power than the Mk 103.

**Specification:** Panavia Tornado ECR
**Origin:** Germany, Italy and UK
**Type:** electronic combat and reconnaissance aircraft
**Powerplant:** two 8021-kg (17,682-lb) afterburning thrust Turbo-Union RB.199-34R Mk 105 turbofans
**Performance:** maximum speed Mach 2,2 or 1,261 kt (2337 km/h; 1,452 mph) above 36,090 ft (11000 m); climb to 30,000 ft (9145 m) under 2 minutes from brake release; service ceiling more than 50,000 ft (15240m); unrefuelled operational endurance about 4 hours
**Weights:** (estimated) maximum take-off 27987 kg (61,700 lb)
**Dimensions:** span 13.91 m (45 ft 7.5 in) spread and 8.60 m (28 ft 2.5 in) swept; length 16.72 m (54 ft 10.25 in); height 5.95 m (19 ft 6.25 in); wing area 26.60 m² (286.3 sq ft)
**Armament:** see text

*Panavia Tornado ECR*

**The RAF's No.IX Squadron uses some ALARM capable Tornado IDSs in the SEAD role, but have a dedicated electronic reconnaissance version in the shape of the Tornado GR.Mk1A.**

**Wearing non-standard markings for participation in a NATO Tiger Meet, this Tornado ECR of JBG 32 also carries a pair of HARM anti-radiation missiles under the fuselage.**

**Role**
Fighter
Close support
Counter-insurgency
Tactical strike
Strategic bomber
Strategic reconnaissance
Tactical reconnaissance
Strategic reconnaissance
Maritime patrol
Anti-ship strike
Anti-submarine warfare
Search and rescue
Assault transport
Transport
Liaison
Trainer
Inflight-refuelling tanker
Specialized

**Performance**
All-weather capability
Rough field capability
STOL capability
VTOL capability
Airspeed 0-250 mph
Airspeed 250 mph-Mach 1
Airspeed Mach 1 plus
Ceiling 0-20,000 ft
Ceiling 20,000-40,000 ft
Ceiling 40,000ft plus
Range 0-1,000 miles
Range 1,000-3,000 miles
Range 3,000 miles plus

**Weapons**
Air-to-air missiles
Air-to-surface missiles
Cruise missiles
Cannon
Trainable guns
Naval weapons
Nuclear-capable
Rockets
'Smart' weapon kit
Weapon load 0-4,000 lb
Weapon load 4,000-15,000 lb
Weapon load 15,000 lb plus

**Avionics**
Electronic Counter Measures
Electronic Support Measures
Search radar
Fire control radar
Look-down/shoot-down
Terrain-following radar
Forward-looking infra-red
Laser
Television

# Pilatus PC-7 Turbo-Trainer and PC-9

*Pilatus PC-9 of the Royal Saudi Air Force.*

## Role
Fighter
Close support
Counter-insurgency
Tactical strike
Strategic bomber
Tactical reconnaissance
Strategic reconnaissance
Maritime patrol
Anti-ship strike
Anti-submarine warfare
Search and rescue
Assault transport
Transport
Liaison
Trainer
Inflight-refuelling tanker
Specialized

## Performance
All-weather capability
Rough field capability
STOL capability
VTOL capability
Airspeed 0-250 mph
Airspeed 250 mph-Mach 1
Airspeed Mach 1 plus
Ceiling 0-20,000 ft
Ceiling 20,000-40,000 ft
Ceiling 40,000ft plus
Range 0-1,000 miles
Range 1,000-3,000 miles
Range 3,000 miles plus

## Weapons
Air-to-air missiles
Air-to-surface missiles
Cruise missiles
Cannon
Trainable guns
Naval weapons
Nuclear-capable
Rockets
'Smart' weapon kit
Weapon load 0-4,000 lb
Weapon load 4,000-15,000 lb
Weapon load 15,000 lb plus

## Avionics
Electronic Counter Measures
Electronic Support Measures
Search radar
Fire control radar
Look-down/shoot-down
Terrain-following radar
Forward-looking infra-red
Laser
Television

First flown in P-3-06 (later P-3B) prototype form during April 1966 with a Pratt & Whitney Canada PT6A turboprop flat-rated at 410 kW (550 shp) for improved hot-and-high performance, this aircraft was schemed as a turbine-powered conceptual successor to the P-3 piston-engined trainer, and retains that type's basic layout as a cantilever low-wing monoplane with retractable tricycle landing gear and tandem accommodation. The all-metal airframe was thoroughly modernized however, and the cockpit is covered by a large and jettisonable clearview canopy rather than the P-3's framed unit. The type was soon renamed as the **Pilatus PC-7 Turbo-Trainer**, and after a very lengthy period of development entered production in the second half of the 1970s for use in the basic and intermediate training roles, with equipment options available for the instrument and armament/tactical training roles. What emerged, therefore, was a multi-role trainer with secondary light attack capability. The type entered service in 1978.

When rumours of a 'big brother' to the PC-7 began to circulate in 1983, this **PC-9** was thought to have a Garrett engine, but when the prototype made its first flight on 7 May 1984 it was powered by a Pratt & Whitney Canada PT6A-62. A family likeness

to the PC-7 was immediately evident, but was no more than skin deep, there being only some 10 per cent structural commonality between the two. The PC-9 is dimensionally similar, but recognizable easily by (among other things) its larger canopy, 'stepped' tandem cockpits with ejector seats, ventral airbrake and four-blade propeller.

By the time that the PC-9 was certificated on 19 September 1985, the RAF competition for which it had been planned had come and gone, the successful contender being the EMBRAER EMB-312 Tucano, but Pilatus retained its marketing link with British Aerospace that this was undoubtedly a major factor in clinching the initial PC-9 production order, announced only a week later, for 30 aircraft to be delivered to the Royal Saudi Air Force. Pilatus then switched its marketing effort to Australia, offering offset package deals on both the PC-7 and PC-9 to the Australian government as alternatives to the ailing Wamira programme for an RAAF trainer. This decision this time went in favour of the PC-9, which was co-produced with Australian industry. This opened the gates to a useful flow of additional orders, and both the PC-7 and PC-9 now have firm niches in the turboprop-powered trainer markets.

## Specification: Pilatus PC-9
**Origin:** Switzerland
**Type:** tandem-seat multi-stage trainer
**Powerplant:** one 857-kW (1,150-shp) Pratt & Whitney Canada PT6A-62 turboprop flat-rated at 708 kW (950 shp)
**Performance:** maximum speed 300 kt (556 km/h; 345 mph) at 20,000 ft (6095 m); initial climb rate 4,050 ft (1235 m) per minute; service ceiling 38,000 ft (11580 m); maximum range 1538 km (955 miles) at cruise power at 20,000 ft (6095 m) with 20-minute reserves
**Weights:** empty 1685 kg (3,715 lb); maximum take-off 3200 kg (7,055 lb)
**Dimensions:** span 10.12 m (33 ft 2.4 in); length 10.18 m (33 ft 4.8 in); height 3.26 m (10 ft 8.3 in); wing area 16.29 m² (175.3 sq ft)
**Armament:** as required and fitted by individual users, but not supplied by Pilatus; the aircraft can carry up to 1040 kg (2,293 lb) of disposable stores, including bombs, cluster bombs, rocket-launcher pods, cannon or machine gun pods and drop tanks, on six external hardpoints

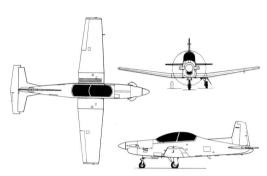

*Pilatus PC-9*

*The Pilatus PC-9 was an unsuccessful contender in the RAF's Jet Provost replacement competition, but the PC-9/BAe Hawk combination has been adopted by Saudi Arabia.*

*Saudi Arabia ordered the PC-9 as a replacement for its ageing BAe Strikemasters, to complement BAe Hawks in providing trained pilots for its Tornados and F-15s.*

# Pilatus Britten-Norman BN-2B Islander and Defender

*Pilatus Britten-Norman BN-2A-21 Defender of No.5 Squadron, Sultan of Oman's air force, based at Salalah.*

Design of the aircraft now known as the **Pilatus Britten-Norman BN-2 Islander** began in April 1964, when Desmond Norman and the late John Britten sought to enter the feederline transport market with a replacement for the de Havilland Dragon Rapide. The **BN-2** prototype was first flown on 13 July 1965. However, when the first production example flew, on 24 April 1967, the span had been increased and more powerful Avco Lycoming O-540-E engines had been installed; this is still the standard powerplant.

The original aim was to develop an easy-to-build aircraft, needing minimal maintenance to give trouble-free service, and this aim was met by adopting a simple, robust structure. Of high-wing configuration with wing-mounted engines, the Islander has a rectangular fuselage and fixed tricycle landing gear. Maximum use has been made of the cabin's 1.09 m (3 ft 7 in) width to accommodate a pilot and up to nine passengers by dispensing with an aisle and relying on three doors (two port and one starboard) to give access to all pairs of seats The BN-2 was followed by the improved **BN-2A** from July, and this was available optionally with alternative

powerplants, raked wing tips containing auxiliary fuel, and other modifications to enhance performance. The still current and improved **BN-2B** was introduced in 1979, becoming known as the Pilatus Britten-Norman BN-2B following acquisition of the company during that year Pilatus Flugzeugwerke of Switzerland.

Many small air arms adopted the BN-2 series for utility purposes, leading to a version known as the **BN-2 Defender** series which, with optional avionics/equipment, can be used for casevac, ECM/ESM, FAC, internal security, logistic support, long-range patrol, SAR and troop transport roles; an offensive capability can be provided by installation of four underwing pylons with a total capacity of 1043 kg (2,300 lb). Available for coastal patrol, oil rig/fishery protection and SAR is the **Maritime Defender** with Bendix RDR 1400 search radar. This variant can carry equipment to make it suitable for all-weather operation by day or night. Specialized equipment for this model can include a searchlight installation and the underwing pylons can be used to carry flares, a loudspeaker pods or dinghy packs as alternatives to weapons.

**Specification:** Pilatus Britten-Norman BN-2B Defender
**Origin:** UK
**Type:** multi-role military aircraft
**Powerplant:** two 224-kW (300-hp) Avco Lycoming IO-5400K1B5 flat-six piston engines
**Performance:** (pylons loaded) maximum speed 144 kt (267 km/h; 166 mph); initial climb rate 1,010 ft (308 m) per minute; service ceiling 18,900 ft (5760 m); maximum range 2773 km (1,723 miles) with auxiliary fuel
**Weights:** empty 1823 kg (4,020 lb); maximum take-off 2994 kg (6,600 lb)
**Dimensions:** span 16.15 m (53 ft 0 in) with extended wing tips; length 10.86 m (35 ft 7.75 in); height 4.18 m (13 ft 8.75 in); wing area 31.31 m² (337.0 sq ft)
**Armament:** provision for 907 kg (2,000 lb) of disposable stores, including 7.62-mm (0.3-in) machine gun pods, 113- and 227-kg (250- and 50-lb0 bombs, anti-personnel grenades, flares, rocket-launcher pods, wire-guided missiles and drop tanks, carried on four external hardpoints

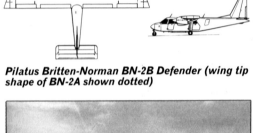

*Pilatus Britten-Norman BN-2B Defender (wing tip shape of BN-2A shown dotted)*

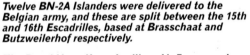

*Twelve BN-2A Islanders were delivered to the Belgian army, and these are split between the 15th and 16th Escadrilles, based at Brasschaat and Butzweilerhof respectively.*

*The Royal Hong Kong Auxiliary Air Force used a variety of aircraft. Its Islander was operated for transport and patrol duties, and is here seen in company with a Bulldog trainer.*

Role
Fighter
Close support
Counter-insurgency
Tactical strike
Strategic bomber
Tactical reconnaissance
Strategic reconnaissance
Maritime patrol
Anti-ship strike
Anti-submarine warfare
Search and rescue
Assault transport
Transport
Liaison
Trainer
Inflight-refuelling tanker
Specialized

Performance
All-weather capability
Rough field capability
STOL capability
VTOL capability
Airspeed 0-250 mph
Airspeed 250 mph-Mach 1
Airspeed Mach 1 plus
Ceiling 0-20,000 ft
Ceiling 20,000-40,000 ft
Ceiling 40,000ft plus
Range 0-1,000 miles
Range 1,000-3,000 miles
Range 3,000 miles plus

Weapons
Air-to-air missiles
Air-to-surface missiles
Cruise missiles
Cannon
Trainable guns
Naval weapons
Nuclear-capable
Rockets
'Smart' weapon kit
Weapon load 0-4,000 lb
Weapon load 4,000-15,000 lb
Weapon load 15,000 lb plus

Avionics
Electronic Counter Measures
Electronic Support Measures
Search radar
Fire control radar
Look-down/shoot-down
Terrain-following radar
Forward-looking infra-red
Laser
Television

# Pilatus Britten-Norman BN-2T Turbine Islander/Defender and ASTOR Islander

*Pilatus Britten-Norman Islander used to demonstrate the Ferranti CASTOR radar.*

## Role
Fighter
Close support
Counter-insurgency
Tactical strike
Strategic bomber
Tactical reconnaissance
Strategic reconnaissance
Maritime patrol
Anti-ship strike
Anti-submarine warfare
Search and rescue
Assault transport
Transport
Liaison
Trainer
Inflight-refuelling tanker
Specialized

## Performance
All-weather capability
Rough field capability
STOL capability
VTOL capability
Airspeed 0-250 mph
Airspeed 250 mph-Mach 1
Airspeed Mach 1 plus
Ceiling 0-20,000 ft
Ceiling 20,000-40,000 ft
Ceiling 40,000ft plus
Range 0-1,000 miles
Range 1,000-3,000 miles
Range 3,000 miles plus

## Weapons
Air-to-air missiles
Air-to-surface missiles
Cruise missiles
Cannon
Trainable guns
Naval weapons
Nuclear-capable
Rockets
'Smart' weapon kit
Weapon load 0-4,000 lb
Weapon load 4,000-15,000 lb
Weapon load 15,000 lb plus

## Avionics
Electronic Counter Measures
Electronic Support Measures
Search radar
Fire control radar
Look-down/shoot-down
Terrain-following radar
Forward-looking infra-red
Laser
Television

By 1986, some six years after Pilatus had taken control of Britten-Norman, almost 1,100 Islanders and Defenders had been delivered to civil and military operators in approximately 120 countries world-wide. There was little doubt that the basic design was right and the new company soon began development of a turboprop-powered version that would be quieter and more economical to operate. Selected powerplant was a pair of Allison 250-B17C turboprops, and the prototype of what is designated the **Pilatus Britten-Norman BN-2T Turbine Islander** was flown for the first time on 2 August 1980. Unfortunately, despite being available in both Islander and Defender versions, the BN-2T gained little commercial success and only a comparatively few sales have been finalized since the type's certification in 1981.

This may change in the future with growing interest in the ASTOR (Airborne STand-Off Radar) and allied systems developed by Ferranti to meet the UK GAS 3956 requirement for an airborne battlefield surveillance radar. Experience in the Falklands war of 1982 showed the need for such equipment, first envisaged for helicopter deployment, but it was decided in late 1983 to put in into the Turbine Islander. Modification of the BN-2T's nose for the radome to house the ASTOR's scanner has given this aircraft,

known as the **ASTOR Islander**, an unmistakable identification feature and which, according to flight tests, made little difference to normal handling characteristics. The only other significant change was adoption of modified BN-2A Trislander Mk III main landing gear units and a lengthened nose unit to give adequate ground clearance for the ASTOR scanner.

The programme's future is uncertain in the mid-1990s, for the RAF's desire is for a higher-performance platform in this role. Pilatus Britten-Norman has also developed a number of other special-mission derivatives of the BN-2 family, these including the **ASW/ASV Maritime Defender** with radar, FLIR and provision for four light anti-ship missiles; the ELINT Defender with the Racal Kestrel electronic intelligence system; the **Internal Security Defender** with optical, thermal and other imaging systems as well as provision for light armament; the **AEW Defender** with a Thorn EMI pulse-Doppler surveillance radar; the **AEW/MR Defender** version of the AEW Defender with two operator positions for improved capability; the **Defender 4000** multi-role type with the AEW Defender's larger wing and increased maximum weight; and the **Multi-Sensor Surveillance Aircraft** developed with Westinghouse for a variety of surveillance roles.

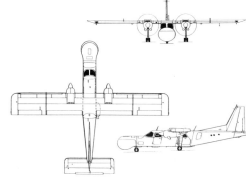

*Pilatus Britten-Norman BN-2T Turbine Islander*

*The Westinghouse-developed MSSA has been exported to Turkey, and an undisclosed Far Eastern nation.*

*Initially used as a demonstrator, this Turbine Islander has since been delivered to the RAF as an Islander CC.Mk2A. It is used for undisclosed duties by RAF Northolt's Station Flight.*

**Specification:** Pilatus Britten-Norman BN-2B AEW Defender
**Origin:** UK
**Type:** airborne early warning aircraft
**Powerplant:** two Allison 250-B17F turboprops each flat-rated at 280 kW (375 shp)
**Performance:** cruising speed 170 kt (315 km/h; 196 mph)
**Weights:** maximum take-off 3855 kg (8,500 lb)
**Dimensions:** span 16.15 m (53 ft 0 in); length 12.37 m (40 ft 7.25 in); height 4.18 m (13 ft 8.75 in); wing area 31.31 m²(337.0 sq ft)
**Armament:** none

# Piper PA-31 Navajo

*Piper PA-31 Navajo of the Aéronavale.*

On 17 April 1967 Piper made initial deliveries of a new six/nine-seat twin-engined light transport that was then the manufacturer's largest aircraft. Piper's intention to enter the commuter/corporate airline and executive market was announced in early 1965 after evaluation of the prototype's performance following a first flight on 30 September 1964. Powered by two 224-kW (300-hp) Avco Lycoming IO-540-M flat-six engines and designated **Piper PA-31-300 Navajo**, the type was marketed in eight-seat Commuter, six-seat Standard and six-seat Executive versions, with up to three extra seats optional for the six-seat models. Launched simultaneously was the six/eight-seat **PA-31-310 Turbo Navajo B** with 231-kW (310-hp) turbocharged engines.

Expansion of the Navajo family began in March 1970 with the **PA-31P Pressurized Navajo** powered by 317-kW (425-hp) turbocharged engines, its pressurization system giving a cabin altitude of 10,000 ft (3050 m) to the aircraft's certificated ceiling of 29,000 ft (8840 m). It was followed by the **PA-31-350 Navajo Chieftain** with 261-kW (350-hp) counter-rotating engines, a fuselage stretch of 0.61 m (2 ft 0 in) so that the Commuter version could seat a maximum of eight pas-

sengers, and a strengthened floor for the carriage of cargo. However, the most forward-looking member of the Navajo line was introduced in late 1973: this was the **PA-31T Cheyenne** which combined the pressurized fuselage of the PA-31P with turbine powerplant in the form of two 462-kW (620-shp) Pratt & Whitney Canada PT6A-28 turboprops. In 1974 the **PA-31-325 Turbo Navajo C/R** joined the family, this having a 242-kW (325-hp) version of the engines that powered the Navajo Chieftain. In 1977 the PA-31T was redesignated **PA-31T Cheyenne II** following introduction of the lower-powered **PA-31T1 Cheyenne I** with 373-kW (500-shp) PT6A-11 turboprops, and was followed in 1981 by the **PA-31T2 Cheyenne IIXL** which had the fuselage lengthened by 0.61 m (2 ft 0 in) and 559-kW (750-shp) PT6A-135 engines flat-rated at 462.5 kW (620 shp). In 1986 the PA-31-350, PA-31T1 and PA-31T2 remained in production and had been joined by the **PA-31-P350 Mojave**, basically a version of the Cheyenne II with counter-rotating engines of 261 kW (350 hp) Several nations selected versions of this popular family of aircraft off the shelf for use by their government or armed services.

**Specification:** Piper PA-31-350 Chieftain
**Origin:** USA
**Type:** six/ten-seat passenger transport
**Powerplant:** two 261-kW (350-hp) Avco Lycoming TIO/LTIO-540-J2BD flat-six counter-rotating piston engines
**Performance:** maximum speed 231 kt (428 km/h; 266 mph); economical cruising speed 173 kt (320 km/h; 199 mph) at 12,000 ft (3660m); initial climb rate 1,120 ft (341 m) per minute; maximum certificated altitude 24,000 ft (7315 m); maximum range 2388 km (1,484 miles) with maximum fuel, allowances and reserves
**Weights:** empty 1915 kg (4,221 lb); maximum take-off 3175 kg (7,000 lb)
**Dimensions:** span 12.40 m (40 ft 8 in); length 10.55 m (34 ft 7.5 in); height 3.96 m (13 ft 0 in); wing area 21.27 m² (229.0 sq ft)
**Armament:** none

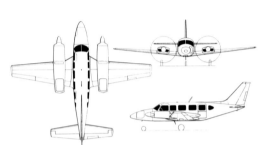

**Piper PA-31 Navajo**

*This Navajo carries the insignia of the para-military Indonesian police force, which uses it for transport, liaison and surveillance duties, including anti-piracy patrols.*

*The Finnish air forces operates five PA-31-350 Navajo Chieftains which were delivered between March 1983 and February 1984. A single Navajo had also been leased briefly during the 1970s.*

### Role
Fighter
Close support
Counter-insurgency
Tactical strike
Strategic bomber
Tactical reconnaissance
Strategic reconnaissance
Maritime patrol
Anti-ship strike
Anti-submarine warfare
Search and rescue
Assault transport
Transport
Liaison
Trainer
Inflight-refuelling tanker
Specialized

### Performance
All-weather capability
Rough field capability
STOL capability
VTOL capability
Airspeed 0-250 mph
Airspeed 250 mph-Mach 1
Airspeed Mach 1 plus
Ceiling 0-20,000 ft
Ceiling 20,000-40,000 ft
Ceiling 40,000ft plus
Range 0-1,000 miles
Range 1,000-3,000 miles
Range 3,000 miles plus

### Weapons
Air-to-air missiles
Air-to-surface missiles
Cruise missiles
Cannon
Trainable guns
Naval weapons
Nuclear-capable
Rockets
'Smart' weapon kit
Weapon load 0-4,000 lb
Weapon load 4,000-15,000 lb
Weapon load 15,000 lb plus

### Avionics
Electronic Counter Measures
Electronic Support Measures
Search radar
Fire control radar
Look-down/shoot-down
Terrain-following radar
Forward-looking infra-red
Laser
Television

# Piper PA-34 Seneca

*EMBRAER U-7A (licence-built PA-34 Seneca) of the Brazilian air force.*

## Role

Fighter
Close support
Counter-insurgency
Tactical strike
Strategic bomber
Tactical reconnaissance
Strategic reconnaissance
Maritime patrol
Anti-ship strike
Anti-submarine warfare
Search and rescue
Assault transport
Transport
Liaison
Trainer
Inflight-refuelling tanker
Specialized

## Performance

All-weather capability
Rough field capability
STOL capability
VTOL capability
Airspeed 0-250 mph
Airspeed 250 mph-Mach 1
Airspeed Mach 1 plus
Ceiling 0-20,000 ft
Ceiling 20,000-40,000 ft
Ceiling 40,000ft plus
Range 0-1,000 miles
Range 1,000-3,000 miles
Range 3,000 miles plus

## Weapons

Air-to-air missiles
Air-to-surface missiles
Cruise missiles
Cannon
Trainable guns
Naval weapons
Nuclear-capable
Rockets
'Smart' weapon kit
Weapon load 0-4,000 lb
Weapon load 4,000-15,000 lb
Weapon load 15,000 lb plus

## Avionics

Electronic Counter Measures
Electronic Support Measures
Search radar
Fire control radar
Look-down/shoot-down
Terrain-following radar
Forward-looking infra-red
Laser
Television

The **Piper PA-34 Seneca** six/seven-seat transport was announced by Piper in the autumn of 1971 and was in effect a twin-engined version of the company's successful PA-32 Cherokee SIX and its derivatives. However, when the Cherokee SIX was adopted for conversion to twin-engined configuration the structure was strengthened considerably and retractable tricycle landing gear (with an electro-hydraulic actuation system) was introduced. Selected powerplant was similar to that chosen for the PA-39 Twin Comanche C/R in early 1970, namely counter-rotating piston engines although the engine for the PA-34 was the Avco Lycoming IO-380 of 149-kW (200-hp) output. The PA-34 retained the same six/seven-seat accommodation (the seventh seat being optional), had dual controls as standard, and featured an interior arranged for easy conversion between all-passenger and partial or all cargo-carrying layout to give the Seneca maximum versatility in the utility role.

In 1975 Piper introduced the more capable **PA-34 Seneca II** with 200-hp Continental TSIO-360-E counter rotating turbocharged engines in new streamlined nacelles, and options available for this version included cabin air-conditioning and Bendix RDR

weather radar. The 2,602 Seneca IIs were superseded in early 1981 by the **PA-34-220T Seneca III** that introduced 164-kW (220-hp) turbocharged engines, and which remained the current product version until the suspension of the family's production in the early 1990s.

The market for the Seneca was expanded initially in August 1974 when EMBRAER (Empresa Brasileira de Aeronáutica S.A.) signed an agreement with Piper for the licensed assembly/manufacture of the Seneca II and Navajo Chieftain. The first was built as the **EMB-810C Seneca II**, and among the early output were 10 for the Brazilian air force, which designated the type U-7. A second agreement was finalized in 1976/77 between Piper and PZL Mielec of Poland for the assembly and distribution of the Seneca in Eastern Europe as the **M-20 Mewa** (gull). The initial aircraft assembled from US components were designated **M-20.00**, but later Polish-built aircraft with 153-kW (205-hp) PZL F engines have the designation **M-20.01**.

The six/seven-seat capacity of the Seneca tends to restrict its utility for military use, but some are in service with governments and air arms.

## Specification: Piper PA-34-220T Seneca III
**Origin:** USA
**Type:** six/seven-seat light transport
**Powerplant:** two 164-kW (220-hp) Continental TSIO/LTSIO-360-KB flat-six counter-rotating piston engines
**Performance:** maximum speed 196 kt (364 km/h; 226 mph) at optimum altitude; economical cruising speed 143 kt (266 km/h; 165 mph) at 10,000 ft (3050 m); initial climb rate 1,400 ft (427 m) per minute; maximum certificated ceiling 25,000 ft (7620 m); maximum range 1835 km (1,140 miles) with maximum fuel, allowances and reserves
**Weights:** empty 1294 kg (2852 lb); maximum take-off 2155 kg (4750 lb)
**Dimensions:** span 11.86 m (38 ft 10.75 in); length 8.72 m (28 ft 7.5 in); height 3.02 m (9 ft 10.75 in); wing area 19.39 m² (208.7 sq ft)
**Armament:** none

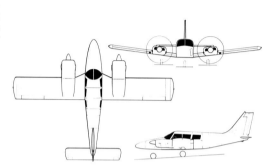

*Piper PA-34 Seneca II*

*The Seneca is licence-built by EMBRAER in Brazil, and is used by the Brazilian air force with the designation U-7. The Seneca is of limited military use, having only seven seats.*

*This aircraft is the first of 12 licence-built by EMBRAER in Brazil for the Força Aérea Brasileira. The aircraft later received weather radar.*

# Rockwell B-1 Lancer

*A Rockwell B-1B Lancer of the 77th Bomb Squadron, 28th Bomb Wing, based at Ellsworth AFB.*

To provide an important component of the United States' 'triad' defence system, studies initiated in 1962 led in 1965 to the USAF's Advanced Manned Strategic Aircraft (AMSA) requirement for a low-altitude penetration bomber. Following the usual USAF's procurement policy, the company then known as North American Rockwell was selected as prime contractor for a new bomber, to be designated **Rockwell B-1**, as was General Electric for the F101 turbofan engines to power it. Both companies were awarded contracts on 5 June 1970 for the prototypes of a planned 244 aircraft, all of them scheduled for delivery by 1981. The programme was duly initiated, the first B-1 prototype making its maiden flight on 23 December 1974, but was brought to a halt on 30 June 1977 when President 'Jimmy' Carter announced that the B-1 would be cancelled and financial priority given instead to cruise missiles .

USAF and DoD studies of a manned aircraft to serve as a cruise missile carrier led to selection of a derivative of the B-1 for this role, although the type was also to have a multi-mission capability. In October 1981 President Ronald Reagan announced that the USAF would receive 100 of the derived **B-1B** aircraft that later received the name **Lancer**. Contracts for prototype aircraft and engines were finalized on 20 January 1982.

The resulting B-1B has a low-set variable-geometry wing blended into the fuselage structure. Construction is largely of aluminium alloys and titanium, hardened to survive nuclear blast and overpressure, and the incorporation of 'low observability' technology features reduced the type's radar cross-section to only one per cent of that of the Boeing B-52. Its operational capability depends largely upon advanced avionics, including radar and navigation equipment developed for the latest-generation fighter aircraft, plus the offensive avionics developed for the origin B-1 and both the B-52G and B-52H. The B-1B's avionics fit includes an AFSATCOM communications link, Doppler radar altimeter, forward-looking and terrain-following radars, INS, and defensive avionics based on the ALQ-161 ECM system with wider frequency coverage, expendable decoys and tail-warning radar. The first production B-1B was flown on 18 October 1984, and the initial USAF delivery, to Dyess AFB, Texas, was made on 29 June 1985. And the type achieved initial operational capability in June 1986 with the 337th Bombardment Squadron of the 96th Bombardment Wing. The other B-1B bases are Ellsworth AFB, South Dakota; Grand Forks AFB, North Dakota; and McConnell AFB, Kansas, and all deliveries were completed in the late 1980s.

### Specification: Rockwell International B-1B Lancer
**Origin:** USA
**Type:** long-range multi-role strategic bomber
**Powerplant:** four 13962-kg (30,780-lb) afterburning thrust General Electric F101-GE-102 turbofans
**Performance:** maximum speed Mach 1.25 or 8716 kt (1328 km/h; 825 mph) at high altitude; penetration speed more than 521 kt (966 km/h; 600 mph) at about 200 ft (60 m); service ceiling more than 50,000 ft (15240 m); maximum unrefuelled range about 12000 km (7,455 miles)
**Weights:** empty 87090 kg (192,000 lb); maximum take-off 216364 kg (477,000 lb)
**Dimensions:** span 41.67 m (136 ft 8.5 in) spread and 23.84 m (78 ft 2.5in) swept; length 44.81 m (147 ft 0 in); height 10.36 m (34 ft 0 in); wing area 181.16 m² (1,950.0 sq ft)
**Armament:** three internal bays for up to 34019 kg (75,000 lb) of weapons, plus eight underfuselage stations with a capacity of 26762 kg (59,000 lb); weapons can include AGM-69 SRAMs, AGM-86B ALCMs, B-28, B-43, B-61 or B-83 nuclear bombs, and Mk 82 or Mk 84 conventional bombs

**Rockwell B-1B Lancer**

*This is a Rockwell B-1B of the 96th Bombardment Wing, first unit to receive this awesome new bomber to replace its lumbering B-52s. Serviceability problems and fuel leaks initially plagued the 96th.*

*A B-1B wearing the original disruptive camouflage applied to these highly effective bombers, now being replaced by an overall grey colour scheme. The aircraft has its wings swept fully forward.*

### Role
Fighter
Close support
Counter-insurgency
Tactical strike
Strategic bomber
Tactical reconnaissance
Strategic reconnaissance
Maritime patrol
Anti-ship strike
Anti-submarine warfare
Search and rescue
Assault transport
Transport
Liaison
Trainer
Inflight-refuelling tanker
Specialized

### Performance
All-weather capability
Rough field capability
STOL capability
VTOL capability
Airspeed 0-250 mph
Airspeed 250 mph-Mach 1
Airspeed Mach 1 plus
Ceiling 0-20,000 ft
Ceiling 20,000-40,000 ft
Ceiling 40,000ft plus
Range 0-1,000 miles
Range 1,000-3,000 miles
Range 3,000 miles plus

### Weapons
Air-to-air missiles
Air-to-surface missiles
Cruise missiles
Cannon
Trainable guns
Naval weapons
Nuclear-capable
Rockets
'Smart' weapon kit
Weapon load 0-4,000 lb
Weapon load 4,000-15,000 lb
Weapon load 15,000 lb plus

### Avionics
Electronic Counter Measures
Electronic Support Measures
Search radar
Fire control radar
Look-down/shoot-down
Terrain-following radar
Forward-looking infra-red
Laser
Television

# Rockwell OV-10 Bronco

*Rockwell OV-10E Bronco of the Fuerza Aérea Venezuela.*

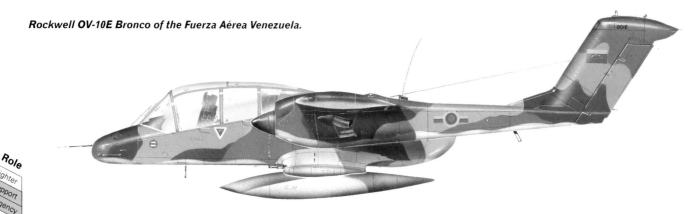

### Role
Fighter
Close support
Counter-insurgency
Tactical strike
Strategic bomber
Tactical reconnaissance
Strategic reconnaissance
Maritime patrol
Anti-ship strike
Anti-submarine warfare
Search and rescue
Assault transport
Transport
Liaison
Inflight-refuelling tanker
Trainer
Specialized

### Performance
All-weather capability
Rough field capability
STOL capability
VTOL capability
Airspeed 0-250 mph
Airspeed 250 mph-Mach 1
Airspeed Mach 1 plus
Ceiling 0-20,000 ft
Ceiling 20,000-40,000 ft
Ceiling 40,000ft plus
Range 0-1,000 miles
Range 1,000-3,000 miles
Range 3,000 miles plus

### Weapons
Air-to-air missiles
Air-to-surface missiles
Cruise missiles
Cannon
Trainable guns
Naval weapons
Nuclear-capable
Rockets
'Smart' weapon kit
Weapon load 0-4,000 lb
Weapon load 4,000-15,000 lb
Weapon load 15,000 lb plus

### Avionics
Electronic Counter Measures
Electronic Support Measures
Search radar
Fire control radar
Look-down/shoot-down
Terrain-following radar
Forward-looking infra-red
Laser
Television

In the early 1960s the US Marine Corps realized its need for a purpose-built counter-insurgency (COIN) aircraft and drew up the specification for what it identified as a LARA (Light Armed Reconnaissance Airplane). The procurement process was initiated by a design competition, with the North American NA-300 proposal chosen as the winner in August 1964. The initial contract covered seven YOV-10A prototypes, the first of them being flown on 16 July 1965 on the power of two 492-kW (660-shp) Garrett T76 turboprops, but development testing revealed some shortcomings. These were rectified by a 3.05-m (10-ft) increase in wing span and the introduction of an uprated version of the T76 engine in nacelles that were moved outboard slightly to reduce engine noise in the cockpit. The increased span was introduced on a prototype first flown on 15 August 1966, and the seventh prototype was given alternative Pratt & Whitney Canada T74 engines (military designation for PT6A turboprop) for comparative evaluation. The **Rockwell OV-10 Bronco** is of distinctive configuration with a shoulder-mounted, constant-chord wing and twin booms extending aft from the engine nacelles to terminate in vertical tail surfaces that are linked by a fixed-incidence tailplane with inset elevator. The landing gear is of the retractable tricycle type, and the slender pod-type fuselage accommodates the crew of two in tandem.

Procurement of the initial **OV-10A** covered 114 aircraft for the US Marine Corps, the first of them flown on 6 August 1967, and this service used the type for forward air control and helicopter escort in addition to the intended role of light armed reconnaissance The USAF acquired 157, primarily for forward air control but with a secondary limited ground-support role in the absence of tactical fighters. Six generally similar **OV-10B** aircraft were supplied to West Germany for use as target tugs, followed by 12 higher-performance **OV-10B(Z)** aircraft with a 1338-kg (2,950-lb) dry thrust General Electric J85-GE-4 turbojet pylon- mounted above the wing. Production of versions generally similar to the OV-10A also included the **OV-10C** (40 built) for the Royal Thai air force, the **OV-10E** (16) for the Venezuelan air force and the **OV-10F** (16) for the Indonesian air force. The remaining version, the OV-10D, is the subject of a separate entry.

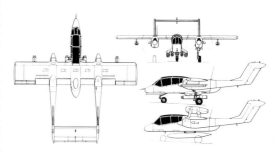

*Rockwell International OV-10A Bronco (lower side view: OV-10BZ)*

*This US Marine Corps OV-10A belongs to Marine Observation Squadron (VMO)-2, the Atlanta-based reserve squadron. The Bronco 's main roles are FAC and COIN.*

*This OV-10A Bronco is seen in the markings of the 601st Tactical Control Wing, based at Sembach in West Germany. The wing's Broncos were later passed to the George-based 27th TASS.*

**Specification:** Rockwell International OV-10A Bronco
**Origin:** USA
**Type:** multi-purpose counter-insurgency aircraft
**Powerplant:** two 533-ekW (715-eshp) Garrett T76-G-416/417 counter-rotating turboprops
**Performance:** maximum speed 244 kt (452 km/h; 281 mph) at sea level; initial climb rate 2,600 ft (792 m) per minute; service ceiling 24,000 ft (7315 m); combat radius 367 km (228 miles) with maximum weapon load and no loiter
**Weights:** empty 3127 kg (6,893 lb); maximum take-off 6552 kg (14,444 lb)
**Dimensions:** span 12.19 m (40 ft 0 in); length 12.67 m (41 ft 7 in); height 4.62 m (15 ft 2 in); wing area 27.03 m² (291.0sq ft)
**Armament:** four 7.62-mm (0.3-in) M60C machine guns with 500 rounds per gun; provision for 1633 kg (3,600 lb) of disposable stores, including bombs, rocket-launcher pods, machine gun and cannon pods, flares and smoke tanks, carried on five external hardpoints

# Rockwell OV-10D Bronco

*Rockwell OV-10D Bronco of the US Marine Corps.*

From early 1961 the US was busy advising the Republic of Vietnam how best to resist the incursions of communist guerrillas from North Vietnam. This became more urgent in late 1963 when infiltration into South Vietnam was stepped up. At this time the US Navy began procurement of the Light Armed Reconnaissance Airplane that led to the OV-10 designed for counter-insurgency operations. When the OV-10As began operating in South Vietnam, it was already clear that a prime task for aircraft in this theatre was to reduce the infiltration into South Vietnam of men and supplies moving down the Ho Chi Minh Trail. It was a difficult task at the best of times, and nearly impossible during the hours of darkness.

The OV-10, suitably equipped, seemed ideal to fulfil a night forward air control and strike designation role, and in the early 1970s 15 OV-10As were modified under the USAF's 'Pave Nail' programme. Specialized equipment given to these aircraft included a combined laser rangefinder/target illuminator, a Loran receiver and a Loran co-ordinate converter. After the US withdrawal from Vietnam these 'Pave Nail' OV-10s reverted to standard configuration. The US Navy had been slightly ahead of the USAF in considering the OV-10A for such a task, and in 1970 two US Navy OV-10As were converted as

YOV-10D Night Observation/Gunship System prototypes They were equipped with an undernose turret for installation of FLIR and a laser target designator, a rear underfuselage turret to mount a 20-mm cannon, and two underwing pylons carrying extra stores.

By the time that evaluation was complete the USA had withdrawn its forces from Vietnam, but in 1974 the US Navy contracted Rockwell to establish and test an OV-10D production configuration. This resulted in 17 of the US Marine Corps' OV-10As being converted to Rockwell OV-10D Bronco standard for the NOS (Night Observation Surveillance) role, all of the aircraft being redelivered to the USMC during 1979-80. They are equipped with an AAS-37 pod which incorporates a FLIR sensor, laser target designator and automatic video tracker, and can be armed with a 20-mm M197 three-barrel cannon with 1,500 rounds of ammunition (in place of the OV-10A's conventional armament) which can be directed by the AAS-37 system. These OV-10Ds also have uprated engines, and additional underwing pylons suitable for weapons or auxiliary fuel. It was at one time rumoured that Rockwell's production line might be reopened to build 24 OV-10D NOS aircraft for South Korea.

**Rockwell International OV-10D NOS Bronco**

**This OV-10D Bronco serves with VMO-1, based at MCAS New River, North Carolina, for night observation and surveillance duties with a useful light attack capability.**

**This is the Rockwell YOV-10D NOGS (Night Observation/Gunship System) prototype, complete with FLIR, laser designator and video tracker. A cannon turret could also be installed in the belly.**

## Specification: Rockwell International OV-10D Bronco

**Origin:** USA
**Type:** night surveillance aircraft
**Powerplant:** two 776-ekW (1,040-eshp) Garrett T76-G-420/421 counter-rotating turboprops
**Performance:** maximum speed 250 kt (463 km/h; 288 mph) at sea level; initial climb rate 3,020 ft (920 m) per minute; service ceiling 30,000 ft (9145 m); combat radius 367 km (228 miles) with maximum weapons load and no loiter
**Weights:** empty 3127 kg (6,893 lb); maximum take-off 6552 kg (14,444 lb)
**Dimensions:** span 12.19 m (40 ft 0 in); length 13.41 m (44 ft 0 in); height 4.62 m (15 ft 2 in); wing area 27.03m² (291.0 sq ft)
**Armament:** generally as for OV-10 Bronco, plus two underwing pylons with combined capacity of 544 kg (1,200 lb) and suitable for the carriage of cluster bombs, flares, laser-guided bombs and rocket-launcher pods; a 20-mm M197 cannon with 1,500 rounds can be installed on the centreline underfuselage station if no weapons are carried on the sponsons

# Rockwell T-2 Buckeye

*Rockwell T-2C Buckeye of VT-23, Training Wing 2, USA Navy.*

## Role
Fighter
Close support
Counter-insurgency
Tactical strike
Strategic bomber
Tactical reconnaissance
Strategic reconnaissance
Maritime patrol
Anti-ship strike
Anti-submarine warfare
Search and rescue
Assault transport
Transport
Liaison
Trainer
Inflight-refuelling tanker
Specialized

## Performance
All-weather capability
Rough field capability
STOL capability
VTOL capability
Airspeed 0-250 mph
Airspeed 250 mph-Mach 1
Airspeed Mach 1 plus
Ceiling 0-20,000 ft
Ceiling 20,000-40,000 ft
Ceiling 40,000 ft plus
Range 0-1,000 miles
Range 1,000-3,000 miles
Range 3,000 miles plus

## Weapons
Air-to-air missiles
Air-to-surface missiles
Cruise missiles
Cannon
Trainable guns
Naval weapons
Nuclear-capable
Rockets
'Smart' weapon kit
Weapon load 0-4,000 lb
Weapon load 4,000-15,000 lb
Weapon load 15,000 lb plus

## Avionics
Electronic Counter Measures
Electronic Support Measures
Search radar
Fire control radar
Look-down/shoot-down
Terrain-following radar
Forward-looking infra-red
Laser
Television

In 1956 the US Navy identified the requirement for a jet trainer that would be suitable to take the pupil, after his completion of the ab initio phase, through all the more advanced stages, including bombing, gunnery and fighter tactics, to the point of carrier qualification. Competitive procurement was contested by a number of US manufacturers but North American Aviation, which incorporated in its NA-249 design proposal proven features from in-production aircraft (the FJ-1 Fury and T-28 Trojan), was selected and contracted in late 1956 to build six YT2J-1 pre-production aircraft for evaluation; there was no prototype as such.

The first of the pre-production aircraft, flown initially on 31 January 1958, was a mid-wing monoplane with retractable tricycle landing gear and accommodation for the pupil and instructor in tandem on LS-1 ejector seats; the instructor's seat, at the rear, was raised to provide a good view forward. The design provided robust landing gear, powered controls, large trailing-edge flaps, an airbrake on each side of the fuselage and a retractable sting-type arrester hook, all of them hydraulically actuated. Power for the YT2J-1 and initial production **North American T2J-1** (**T-2A** from 1962) was one 1542-kg (3,400-lb) dry thrust Westinghouse J34-WE-48 turbojet within the fuselage.

Named **Buckeye** before entering service in July 1959, the T2J-1 initially equipped BTG-7, later renamed VT-7, based at NAS Meridian. T2J-1 production totalled 201 aircraft.

On 30 August 1962 the first of two YT2J-2 (converted T2J-1) test aircraft was flown with two 1361-kg (3,000-lb) dry thrust Pratt & Whitney J60-P-6 turbojets. This version was selected to supersede the T2J-1, the first of 97 **T-2B** production aircraft being flown on 21 May 1965 and entering service with Training Squadron VT-4 at NAS Pensacola in December 1965. Following evaluation of a T-2B converted to YT-2C configuration with two General Electric J85-GE-4 turbojets, 231 **T-2C** aircraft were built for the US Navy Air Training Command, the first production example being flown initially on 10 December 1968. At a later date, small numbers of T-2B and T-2C aircraft were converted as drone directors under the respective designations **DT-2B** and **DT-2C**. In 1982 17 US Navy T-2Bs were removed from storage and refurbished, 15 of them later entering service to supplement the T-2Cs which currently remain in service although being replaced by the BAe/McDonnell Douglas T-45 Goshawk. The US Navy also procured, on behalf of the Venezuelan and Greek air forces respectively, 24 **T-2D** and 40 **T-2E** aircraft basically similar to the T-2C.

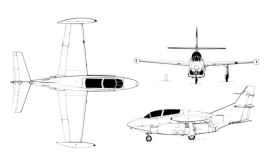

***Rockwell International T-2C Buckeye***

***This is a formation of Hellenic air force T-2E Buckeyes. Greece has two Buckeye squadrons, 362 and 363 Miras, both based at Kalamata with Air Training Command.***

*The Venezuelan air force operates the survivors of 24 T-2D Buckeyes for advanced training duties with Grupo de Entrenamiento Aéreo, Escuela de Aviacion Militar at Palo Negro, Maracay.*

**Specification:** Rockwell International T-2C Buckeye
**Origin:** USA
**Type:** general-purpose jet trainer
**Powerplant:** two 1338-kg (2,950-lb) dry thrust General Electric J85-GE-4 turbojets
**Performance:** maximum speed 460 kt (852 km/h; 530 mph) at 25,000 ft (7620 m); initial climb rate 5,900 ft (1798 m) per minute; service ceiling 45,500 ft (13870 m); maximum range 1722 km (1,070 miles)
**Weights:** empty 3681 kg (8,115 lb); maximum take-off 9133 kg (13,190 lb)
**Dimensions:** span 11.62 m (38 ft 1.5 in) over wing tip tanks; length 11.67 m (38 ft 3.5 in); height 4.51 m (14 ft 9.5 in); wing area 23.69 m² (255.0 sq ft)
**Armament:** provision for 1588 kg (3,500 lb) of disposable stores, including light bombs, rocket-launcher pods and gun pods, carried on four external hardpoints

# Rockwell Turbo Commander 690

*Rockwell Turbo Commander 681B of the Iranian air force.*

The aircraft which eventually became known as the **Rockwell Turbo Commander 690** series began life with a first flight on 31 December 1964 and was at that time designated **Aero Commander Turbo Commander**. The early success of the Aero Commander 500/560 line had indicated a worthwhile market for a derivative offering larger capacity and higher speed: in initial form this was the Grand Commander (first flown on 29 December 1962), with a fuselage lengthened by 1.88 m (6 ft 2 in) to seat the pilot and co-pilot or passenger on a separate flight deck, and between four and nine passengers in a cabin layout ranging from de luxe to austere high density. In other respects save for a slight reduction in wing span, the Grand Commander retained the configuration, layout and systems of its predecessors, as well as their piston-engined powerplant in the form of two 287-kW (380-hp) Lycoming IGSO-540s. In the summer of 1964 an optional and interim version became available with a pressurized and air-conditioned cabin pending the first flight, on 31 December 1964, of a turboprop-powered version that was introduced to maximize the benefits of the pressurized fuselage.

The Turbo Commander, as this last aircraft was known, was identical to the pressurized version except for the installation of two Garrett TPE331-43 turboprops. A higher cabin pressure differential was possible, the air-conditioning and pressurization systems being fed by bleed air from the turbine engines. Soon after deliveries began in May 1966 the name changed to **Turbo II Commander**, later became the **Hawk Commander**, and in 1971 changed again to **Turbo Commander 681B**. However, in 1971 North American Rockwell, as the company was then known, gained certification for an improved **Turbo Commander 690** with more powerful TPE331-5-251K turboprops driving larger-diameter propellers, and this later replaced the Turbo Commander 681B. The subsequent **Turbo Commander 690A** introduced an increased cabin pressure differential and a number of other improvements, and was certificated for operation at a higher gross weight. The final version, when production ended in 1979, was the basically similar **Turbo Commander 690B**. Popular as VIP transports of reasonable capacity and good performance, versions of the Turbo Commander have been procured off the shelf for this role by both armed forces and government agencies.

**Specification:** Rockwell International Turbo Commander 690B
**Origin:** USA
**Type:** 7/11-seat light transport
**Powerplant:** two 522-ekW (700-eshp) Garrett TPE331-5-251K turboprops
**Performance:** maximum cruising speed 287 kt (531 km/h; 330mph) at 17,500 ft (5335 m); economical cruising speed251 kt (465 km/h; 289 mph) at 31,000 ft (9450 m); initial climb rate 2,820 ft (860 m) per minute; service ceiling 32,800 ft (9995 m); range 1373 km (853 miles) with maximum payload and 45-minute reserves
**Weights:** empty 2810 kg (6,195 lb); maximum take-off 4683 kg (10,325 lb)
**Dimensions:** span 14.19 m (46 ft 6.5 in); length 13.52 m (44 ft 4.25 in); height 4.56 m (14 ft 11.5 in); wing area 24.71 m² (266.0 sq ft)
**Armament:** none

***Rockwell International Turbo Commander***

*This Commander Jetprop 1000 is equipped with an airborne search radar and underwing reconnaissance pods. Infra-red photographic equipment can also be carried.*

*The Turbo Commander offers a number of important advantages over the earlier members of the family, especially in being able to use common Avtur instead of Avgas, which is scarce in some areas.*

## Role
Fighter
Close support
Counter-insurgency
Tactical strike
Strategic bomber
Tactical reconnaissance
Strategic reconnaissance
Maritime patrol
Anti-ship strike
Anti-submarine warfare
Search and rescue
Assault transport
Transport
Liaison
Trainer
Inflight-refuelling tanker
Specialized

## Performance
All-weather capability
Rough field capability
STOL capability
VTOL capability
Airspeed 0-250 mph
Airspeed 250 mph-Mach 1
Airspeed Mach 1 plus
Ceiling 0-20,000 ft
Ceiling 20,000-40,000 ft
Ceiling 40,000ft plus
Range 0-1,000 miles
Range 1,000-3,000 miles
Range 3,000 miles plus

## Weapons
Air-to-air missiles
Air-to-surface missiles
Cruise missiles
Cannon
Trainable guns
Naval weapons
Nuclear-capable
Rockets
'Smart' weapon kit
Weapon load 0-4,000 lb
Weapon load 4,000-15,000 lb
Weapon load 15,000 lb plus

## Avionics
Electronic Counter Measures
Electronic Support Measures
Search radar
Fire control radar
Look-down/shoot-down
Terrain-following radar
Forward-looking infra-red
Laser
Television

# Saab 35 Draken

When the **Saab J 35A Draken** (dragon) entered service in March 1960, it was probably the finest all-weather interceptor in the world. This factor alone gives emphasis to the forward-looking design approach that provided such capability for an aircraft whose development had started a decade earlier. The challenge came from the Flygvapen which drew up a requirement in 1949 calling for performance 50 per cent better than that of fighters then entering service with other nations.

Initial design adopted a pure delta wing for low structural weight and low drag, combined with a robust structure giving ample space for fuel, equipment and the carriage of external armament. This proved impracticable, leading to the distinctive double-delta wing with a cranked leading edge, and this was extensively flight tested on the sevententh scale Saab 210. Three Saab 35 prototypes followed. Apart from wing configuration, with powered controls for each movable surface operated by two tandem hydraulic jacks fed by separate hydraulic systems, the rest of the structure was largely conventional. The prototypes were each powered by an imported Rolls-Royce Avon turbojet, but initial production J 35As had the licence-built Svenska Flygmotor (later Volvo Flygmotor) RM6B with a far more efficient afterburner developed by the Swedish company.

The J 35A had only a short tail cone, but the following air-defence **J 35B** had a lengthened rear fuselage and introduced retractable twin tailwheels intended, primarily, to permit more effective aerodynamic braking during the landing run: most J 35As were later modified to this configuration. The next air-defence version was the J 35D with the more powerful RM6C engine (needing larger inlets and greater fuel capacity) plus more advanced radar and equipment. The final new-build air-defence variant for the Flygvapen was the **J 35F**, developed from the J 35D with more capable radar and collision-course fire control, deleted one of the two 30-mm cannon, introduced a Hughes IR sensor and licence-built Hughes Falcon AAMs. Two other variants for the Swedish air force were the **Sk 35C** tandem two-seat operational conversion trainer and the **S 35E** reconnaissance derivative of the J 35D with the radar nose replaced by a pressurised section housing five cameras. About 140 J 35D and J 35F Drakens were in Flygvapen service in 1986, when three squadrons were scheduled to remain operational into the mid-1990s with the **J 35J**, which is the J 35F upgraded with improvements to the radar, IR sensor, IFF and navigation systems and well as a strengthened wing for heavier loads. Some 24 J 35Ds were sold to Austria with the designation **J 35Ö**, and others were exported to Denmark and Finland under the **J 35X** designation.

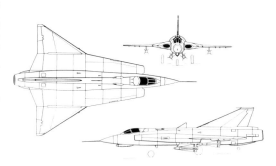

*Saab J 35J Draken of Flygflottilj 10 based at Angelholm-Barkakra.*

*Saab J 35F Draken*

*The J 35F served as the basis for the J 35J, of which 64 were produced as conversions with extra underwing pylons and modified radar, IR seeker and IFF systems.*

*A pair of Flygflottilj 16's J 35F Drakens lines up for take-off at Uppsala. The J 35J programme allowed the Draken to remain a credible interceptor well into the 1990s.*

**Specification:** Saab J 35F Draken
**Origin:** Sweden
**Type:** single-seat interceptor
**Powerplant:** one 7830-kg (17,262-lb) afterburning thrust Volvo Flygmotor RM6C turbojet
**Performance:** maximum speed Mach 2.0 or 1,146 kt (2124 km/h; 1,320 mph) at 36,090 ft (11000 m); initial climb rate 34,450 ft (10500 m) per minute; service ceiling more than 62,300 ft (19000 m); combat radius 560 km (348 miles) on a hi-lo-hi mission with internal fuel
**Weights:** empty 7425 kg (16,369 lb); maximum take-off 16000 kg (35,274 lb)
**Dimensions:** span 9.40 m (30 ft 10.1 in); length 15.35 m (50 ft 4.3 in); height 3.89 m (12 ft 9.1 in); wing area 49.20 m² (529.6 sq ft)
**Armament:** one 30-mm Aden M/55 cannon with 90 rounds, and two radar-homing Rb27 and two IR-homing Rb28 Falcon AAMs, or two or four Rb24 Sidewinder AAMs, or up to 4082 kg (9,000 lb) of bombs in an attack mission

# Saab 105

*Saab 105 of the Krigsflyskolan, Swedish air force.*

In the early 1960s the Saab aircraft company in Sweden began the private-venture design and development of a new twin-jet multi-role military aircraft under the company designation **Saab 105**. The first of two prototypes was flown on 29 June 1963, this being a shoulder-wing monoplane with the wing incorporating only moderate 12° 48' sweepback but with 6° anhedral. Of all-metal construction, the aircraft included hydraulic power to actuate the single-slotted flaps, air brakes, retractable tricycle landing gear and nosewheel steering, and to provide servo power to boost the ailerons and the elevators of the T-tail. The cockpit offered side by-side accommodation for two on ejector seats, but an optional arrangement allowed for four individual seats if the aircraft was to be used in the liaison or navigation trainer roles. The powerplant comprised two Turbomeca Aubisque turbofans.

Following satisfactory evaluation by the Swedish air force, orders were placed during 1964 for 150 production aircraft, the first of them being flown on 27 August 1965. The type began to enter service in the spring of 1966, initially with the flying training school at Ljungbyhed air base. Those used for training and liaison have the designation **Sk 60A**, the close-support attack version with a sta-

bilized gun sight, gun camera and ability to carry 700 kg (1,673 lb) of weapons is the **Sk 60B**, and a number of this latter with a permanent reconnaissance camera installation are identified as the **Sk 60C**. Most Sk 60As were later modified for quick conversion to Sk 60B close-support standard. Surviving aircraft were upgraded structurally in the late 1980s and are being improved in terms of powerplant and avionics in the mid-1990s.

On 29 April 1967 the Saab 105XT prototype was flown, this being developed from the Sk 60B with two 1293-kg (2,850-lb) dry thrust General Electric J85-GE-17B turbojets to give improved performance and the ability to carry a greater weapon load. The wing structure was beefed up to carry 2000 kg (4,409 lb) of weapons, and more internal fuel was provided for the thirstier engines. Forty of these aircraft were procured for the Austrian air force under the designation **Saab 105Ö**. Two experimental developments failed to win production orders, the first being the Saab 105XH for the Swiss air force with increased armament capability and fuel capacity, advanced avionics and better high-speed characteristics. The second was the Saab 105G, developed from the Saab 105Ö with improvements that included a weapon load increased to 2350 kg (5,180 lb).

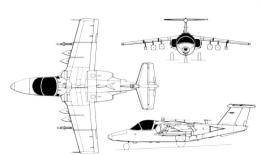

*Saab 105*

*Saab 105Ös serve with the surveillance wing, fighter-bomber wing and flying training school of the Austrian air force, the last including the Karo As national aerobatic team.*

*Four Saab 105s of the Ljungbyhed-based Krigsflyskolan. The Swedish air force designates the standard aircraft Sk 60A, the armed version Sk 60B and the reconnaissance-configured variant Sk 60C.*

## Specification: Saab 105 (Sk 60A)

**Origin:** Sweden

**Type:** training/liaison aircraft with secondary attack capability

**Powerplant:** two 744-kg (1,640-lb) dry thrust Turbomeca Aubisque turbofans

**Performance:** (trainer) maximum speed 415 kt (770 km/h; 478 mph) at 20,000 ft (6095 m); cruising speed 380 kt (705 km/h; 438 mph) at 30,000 ft (9145 m); initial climb rate 3,940 ft (1200 m) per minute; service ceiling 44,290 ft (13500 m ); range 1400 km (870 miles)

**Weights:** empty 2510 kg (5,534 lb); maximum take-off 4050 kg (8,929 lb) in the utility role

**Dimensions:** span 9.50 m (31 ft 2 in); length 10.50 m (34 ft 5.4 in); height 2.70 m (8 ft 10.3 in); wing area 16.30 m² (175.46 sq ft)

**Armament:** (in secondary attack role) provision for 700 kg (1,543 lb) of disposable stores, including two Saab Rb05 ASMs, or two 30-mm cannon pods, or 12 135-mm (5.31-in) rockets, or bombs, cluster bombs and rocket-launcher pods, on six external hardpoints

# Saab AJ 37 Viggen

*Saab AJ 37 Viggen of Flygflottilj 15, Swedish air force, based at Söderhamn.*

**Role**
Fighter
Close support
Counter-insurgency
Tactical strike
Strategic bomber
Tactical reconnaissance
Strategic reconnaissance
Maritime patrol
Anti-ship strike
Anti-submarine warfare
Search and rescue
Assault transport
Transport
Liaison
Trainer
Inflight-refuelling tanker
Specialized

**Performance**
All-weather capability
Rough field capability
STOL capability
VTOL capability
Airspeed 0-250 mph
Airspeed 250 mph-Mach 1
Airspeed Mach 1 plus
Ceiling 0-20,000 ft
Ceiling 20,000-40,000 ft
Ceiling 40,000ft plus
Range 0-1,000 miles
Range 1,000-3,000 miles
Range 3,000 miles plus

**Weapons**
Air-to-air missiles
Air-to-surface missiles
Cruise missiles
Cannon
Trainable guns
Naval weapons
Nuclear-capable
Rockets
'Smart' weapon kit
Weapon load 0-4,000 lb
Weapon load 4,000-15,000 lb
Weapon load 15,000 lb plus

**Avionics**
Electronic Counter Measures
Electronic Support Measures
Search radar
Fire control radar
Look-down/shoot-down
Terrain-following radar
Forward-looking infra-red
Laser
Television

When, in the late 1950s, the Swedish air force began to consider the successor that it would require for the Saab 35 Draken, which was then on the point of entering service, it studied with considerable care the overall weapon concept which had been adopted in the USA. The result of this was the evolution of the System 37 programme, involving not only the airframe of the aircraft, but also its powerplant, equipment and armament, and embracing as well the ground based back-up to optimize the aircraft's capability, namely service and test equipment, and special training facilities including the use of simulators. One important aspect of its airborne equipment was complete integration with the STRIL 60 electronic air-defence control system adopted by Sweden to protect the whole of the nation.

Saab was entrusted with the design of the aircraft which was the focal point of the system and, after extensive research, the company adopted a canard-delta configuration with a rear-mounted delta wing complemented by foreplanes that have the appearance of a second small delta wing The airframe therefore comprises mid-set foreplanes with trailing-edge flaps and, behind them, the main delta wing with trailing-edge elevons. This main wing has compound sweep on the leading edge and is mounted low on the fuselage, which is of similar construction to that of the Draken. Mounted above the rear fuselage is the vertical tail surfaces, and all control surfaces in the foreplanes, wing and tail unit are power operated. In all but the Sk 37 trainer version, accommodation is for a pilot only on a Saab zero-zero ejector seat in an air-conditioned and pressurized cockpit. The landing gear is of the retractable tricycle type. The powerplant breaks Saab's long association with Rolls-Royce as it is a Volvo Flygmotor RM8, which is a licence-built supersonic version of the Pratt & Whitney JT8D-22 turbofan that incorporates an afterburner and thrustreverser developed in Sweden.

The first of seven prototypes was flown initially on 8 February 1967, and the production **Saab AJ 37 Viggen** (thunderbolt) entered service with Flygflottilj 7 at Såtenäs on 21 June 1971. The equipment of this allweather attack version includes an air data unit, attitude instrumentation, automatic speed control system, Doppler navigation, head-up display, microwave landing guidance system, radar, radar altimeter and a tactical instrument landing system.

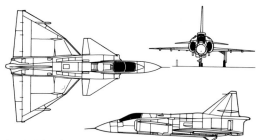

**Saab AJ 37 Viggen**

### Specification: Saab AJ 37 Viggen
**Origin:** Sweden
**Type:** all-weather attack aircraft
**Powerplant:** one 11800-kg (26,015-lb) afterburning thrust Volvo Flygmotor RM8 turbofan
**Performance:** maximum speed Mach 2.0 or 1,146 kt (2124 km/h; 1,320 mph) at high altitude; climb to 36,090 ft (11000 m) in less than 2 minutes from brake release; service ceiling 60,000 ft (18290 m); combat radius more than 1000 km (621 miles) on a hi-lo-hi mission with external armament
**Weights:** empty about 11800 kg (26,015 lb); maximum take-off 20500 kg (45,194 lb)
**Dimensions:** span 10.60 m (34 ft 9.3 in); length (including probe) 16.30 m (53 ft 5.7 in); height 5.60 m (18 ft 4.5 in); wing area 46.0 m² (495.16 sq ft)
**Armament:** provision for 6000 kg (13,228 lb) of disposable stores, including 30-mm Aden cannon pods, 135-mm (5.31-in) rocket pods, bombs, a variety of air-to-surface missiles and, as self-defence armament, Sidewinder or Falcon AAMs, carried on seven external hardpoints

*The AJ 37 Viggen provides the Swedish air force with its ground-attack capability, and is able to operate from dispersed sites to minimize its vulnerability to pre-emptive attack.*

*This AJ 37 Viggen carries the numerical markings of Flygflottilj 15 on its nose. The F15 wing is based at Söderhamn, and serves in the attack and training roles.*

# Saab JA 37 Viggen

*Saab JA 37 Viggen of Flygflottilj 13, Swedish air force, and the only JA 37 unit to carry a unit badge.*

The single-seat **Saab JA 37 Viggen**, interceptor element of the System 37 series, was the last of the variants to enter operational service, deliveries to a squadron of the F13 wing at Norrköping beginning in 1979. Externally the JA 37 is little different to the attack AJ 37, the most noticeable features being the taller fin adopted from the Sk 37 trainer and, to improve manoeuvrability, four elevon actuators under each wing rather than the three of other versions. However, the JA 37 involved considerably more development effort than the initial variant. Much of this work was involved with the engine which, in conjunction with Pratt & Whitney, was optimized for operation at high altitudes and during high-stress combat manoeuvres. Thus the JA 37's RM8B engine replaces the two-stage fan and four-stage low-pressure compressor of the RM8A by a three-stage fan and three-stage low-pressure compressor which gives more stable operation at all heights and attitudes, and introduces a new high-pressure turbine and a four-nozzle combustion burner system to provide more than eight per cent extra thrust.

As in most modern combat aircraft, however, it is the onboard avionics that have expanded the type's operational capability

and which have, of course, been responsible for the major portion of its development. This area of the programme was a task for modified AJ 37s and Saab 32 Lansens, especially for flight test and evaluation of the Ericsson UAP-1023 I/J-band long-range pulse-Doppler radar that provides target search and acquisition. This advanced system is resistant to ECM, suffers little from ground clutter, and is unaffected by changes in attitude and weather. It is complemented by aircraft attitude instrumentation, automatic speed control, central digital computer, digital air data computer, digital automatic flight control, Doppler navigation, ECM, head-up display, inertial DME, radar altimeter, radar display and radar warning systems, a microwave scanning beam landing guidance system, and a tactical instrument landing system together with state of the art communications.

Procurement of the JA 37 totalled 149 aircraft, of which the last was delivered in June 1990 to complete production of 329 System 37 aircraft also including 110 AJ 37, 26 SF 37, 26 SH 37 and 18 Sk 37 machines. JA 37s serve with the F4, F13, F17, and F21 wings at Östersund, Norrköping, Ronneby and Luleå respectively.

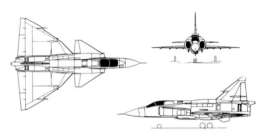

**Saab JA 37 Viggen**

## Specification: Saab JA 37 Viggen

**Origin:** Sweden
**Type:** single-seat interceptor with secondary attack capability
**Powerplant:** one 12750-kg (28,109-lb) afterburning thrust Volvo Flygmotor RM8B turbofan
**Performance:** maximum speed more than Mach 2.0 or1,146 kt (2124 km/h; 1,320 mph) above 36,090 ft (11000 m); climb to 32,800 ft (10000 m) in less than 1 minute 40 seconds from brake release; combat radius more than 500 km (311 miles) on a lo-lo-lo mission with external armament, or 1000 km (621 miles) on a hi-lo-hi mission with external armament
**Weights:** normal take-off 15000 kg (33,060 lb); maximum take-off 20500 kg (45,194 lb)
**Dimensions:** span 10.60 m (34 ft 9.3 in); length (including probe) 16.30 m (53 ft 7.75 in); height 5.90 m (19 ft 4.3 in); wing area 46.0 m² (495.16 sq ft)
**Armament:** one 30-mm Oerlikon KCA cannon with 150 rounds; provision for 6000 kg (13,228 lb) of disposable stores, including two Rb71 (BAe Sky Flash) and four Rb24 (Sidewinder) AAMs or bombs and/or 135-mm (5.31-in) rocket-launcher pods, carried on six external hardpoints

*Some JA37s are painted in an overall air superiority grey colour scheme, while others wear camouflage and a small number retain their natural metal delivery scheme.*

*This JA 37 Viggen is seen in service with Flygflottilj 4 based at Östersund/Froson. Most of the wing's aircraft have been repainted grey.*

**Role**
Fighter
Close support
Counter-insurgency
Tactical strike
Strategic bomber
Tactical reconnaissance
Strategic reconnaissance
Maritime patrol
Anti-ship strike
Anti-submarine warfare
Search and rescue
Assault transport
Transport
Liaison
Trainer
Inflight-refuelling tanker
Specialized

**Performance**
All-weather capability
Rough field capability
STOL capability
VTOL capability
Airspeed 0-250 mph
Airspeed 250 mph-Mach 1
Airspeed Mach 1 plus
Ceiling 0-20,000 ft
Ceiling 20,000-40,000 ft
Ceiling 40,000ft plus
Range 0-1,000 miles
Range 1,000-3,000 miles
Range 3,000 miles plus

**Weapons**
Air-to-air missiles
Air-to-surface missiles
Cruise missiles
Cannon
Trainable guns
Naval weapons
Nuclear-capable
Rockets
'Smart' weapon kit
Weapon load 0-4,000 lb
Weapon load 4,000-15,000 lb
Weapon load 15,000 lb plus

**Avionics**
Electronic Counter Measures
Electronic Support Measures
Search radar
Fire control radar
Look-down/shoot-down
Terrain-following radar
Forward-looking infra-red
Laser
Television

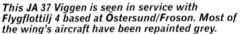

# Saab SF 37 and SH 37 and Sk 37 Viggen

*Saab Sk 37 Viggen of Flygflottilj 7, Swedish air force.*

## Role
Fighter
Close support
Counter-insurgency
Tactical strike
Strategic bomber
Tactical reconnaissance
Strategic reconnaissance
Maritime patrol
Anti-ship strike
Anti-submarine warfare
Search and rescue
Assault transport
Transport
Liaison
Trainer
Inflight-refuelling tanker
Specialized

## Performance
All-weather capability
Rough field capability
STOL capability
VTOL capability
Airspeed 0-250 mph
Airspeed 250 mph-Mach 1
Airspeed Mach 1 plus
Ceiling 0-20,000 ft
Ceiling 20,000-40,000 ft
Ceiling 40,000ft plus
Range 0-1,000 miles
Range 1,000-3,000 miles
Range 3,000 miles plus

## Weapons
Air-to-air missiles
Air-to-surface missiles
Cruise missiles
Cannon
Trainable guns
Naval weapons
Nuclear-capable
Rockets
'Smart' weapon kit
Weapon load 0-4,000 lb
Weapon load 4,000-15,000 lb
Weapon load 15,000 lb plus

## Avionics
Electronic Counter Measures
Electronic Support Measures
Search radar
Fire control radar
Look-down/shoot-down
Terrain-following radar
Forward-looking infra-red
Laser
Television

The first System 37 variant after the initial JA 37 was the **Saab Sk 37 Viggen** (thunderbolt) tandem two-seat trainer, whose prototype was initially flown on 2 July 1970. It has the attack capability of the JA 37 from which it was developed and, by revision of internal avionics and deletion of the forward fuselage fuel tank, the instructor's rear cockpit is provided without any increase in fuselage length. The loss of fuel capacity is not serious (the standard JA 37 fuel system including also a tank in each wing, one in each side of the fuselage, plus a saddle tank over the engine), but explains why the Sk 37 is always seen with a drop tank on the centreline pylon. The new raised cockpit is enclosed by a bulged canopy, and while the instructor has a good view it is restricted in the forward sector beneath the aircraft and, in consequence, he is provided with twin periscopes: resulting changes in directional stability are offset by incorporation of a taller fin. The first of 18 Sk 37s entered service in June 1972, and the type is operated by the conversion unit at Södehamn.

In early 1973 Saab received a production contract for all-weather day/night armed reconnaissance and maritime reconnaissance versions to replace respectively the S 35E Draken and S 32C Lansen: the armed reconnaissance **SF 37** was the first to fly, on 21 May 1973. Like the Sk 37, the SF 37 retains the full weapon capability of the JA 37 but is without attack radar. Instead its more tapered nose accommodates one infra-red, two high-altitude and four low-level cameras, plus a range of special sensors and data-recorders. In the reconnaissance configuration the external hardpoints normally carry ECM pods and/or drop tanks, plus self-defence Rb24 Sidewinder AAMs. Delivery of production SF37s began in April 1977, and 26 of the type were delivered to the F13, F17, F21 wings at Norrköping, Kallinge and Luleå. The maritime reconnaissance **SH 37**, developed simultaneously and flown on 10 December 1973, is somewhat less complex in terms of equipment and entered service earlier, the first of 26 joining the F13 wing on 19 June 1975, and later the F17 and F21 wings. Retaining the same dual attack capability as the Sk 37 and SF 37, it is equipped as standard with a surveillance radar in the nose and has a camera to record its display. In its intended role, the outer of the three under-fuselage pylons usually carry night reconnaissance and Red Baron multi-sensor pods, with a drop tank on the centreline and on the underwing pylons it has ECM pods and Rb24 AAMs.

In the mid-1990s 115 AJ 37, SF 37 and SH 37 aircraft are being converted to the **AJS 37** standard as interchangeable attack, defence and reconnaissance fighters.

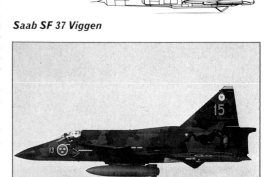

*Saab SF 37 Viggen*

## Specification: Saab SF 37 Viggen
**Origin:** Sweden
**Type:** all-weather armed photo-reconnaissance aircraft
**Powerplant:** 11800-kg (26,015-lb) afterburning thrust Volvo Flygmotor RM8 turbofan
**Performance:** maximum speed Mach 2 or 1,146 kt (2124 km/h; 1,320 mph) at high altitude; climb to 36,090 ft (11000 m) in less than 2 minutes from brake release; combat radius more than 1000 km (621 miles) on a hi-lo-hi mission with external armament
**Weights:** empty about 11800 kg (26,015 lb); maximum take-off about 17000 kg (37,479 lb)
**Dimensions:** span 10.60 m (34 ft 9.3 in); length (including probe) 16.30 m (53 ft 5.75 in ); height 5.60 m (18 ft 1.5 in); wing area 46.0 m² (495.16 sq ft)
**Armament:** (in secondary attack role) provision for 6000 kg (13,228 lb) of disposable stores, including 30-mm Aden cannon pods, 135-mm (5.31-in) rocket-launcher pods, bombs, a variety of air-to-surface missiles and, as self-defence armament, Sidewinder or Falcon AAMs, carried on seven external hardpoints

*The SH 37 can carry a Red Baron night reconnaissance pod, a long-range camera pod and ECM pods, and is fitted with a modified radar for maritime surveillance duties.*

*The SF 37 is a dedicated tactical reconnaissance aircraft, with one forward-looking and two vertical cameras backing up a fan of low-altitude cameras giving horizon-to-horizon coverage.*

# Saab JAS 39 Gripen

*The first Saab JAS 39A Gripen delivered to the Swedish air force.*

In the late 1970s the Swedish Air Matériel Department (FMV-F) was looking ahead to the procurement of an all-weather multi-role combat aircraft that would enter service in the early 1990s to replace, successively, the AJ, SH, SF and JA versions of the Saab 37 Viggen. In mid-1980 funding was approved by the Swedish government for project definition of such an aircraft: at the same time an industrial group was established by Saab-Scania, Volvo Flygmotor, Ericsson and Förenade Fabriksverken (now FFV Aerotech) as Industrigruppen JAS, to formulate its proposals for an aircraft to meet the requirement. Evaluation of the proposals by FMV-F led to an agreement between the two parties, approved by the Swedish government on 6 May 1982, covering the procurement of some 140 aircraft (including 20+ two-seaters) by the year 2000. On 30 June 1982 a contract was finalized for the first 30 aircraft, the construction of five prototypes was initiated during 1984, and the first **Saab JAS 39A Gripen** (griffin) flew on 9 December 1988.

The initials JAS in the designation indicate Jakt, Attack and Spaning (fighter, attack and reconnaissance), and the aircraft's configuration includes an aft-mounted cropped delta wing incorporating inboard and outboard trailing-edge elevons and leading-edge flaps, all-moving swept canard foreplanes,

and a swept vertical surface. All of these surfaces are operated by servo-actuators via a Lear Siegler triplex fly-by-wire control system. Landing gear is of the retractable tricycle type, and power is provided by a single General Electric F404J turbofan which, in collaboration with Volvo Flygmotor, was developed and is produced under the designation RM12. The JAS 39's pilot is seated on a Martin-Baker Mk S10LS zero-zero ejector seat in an air-conditioned and pressurized environment beneath a teardrop canopy.

Critical for the new aircraft's multi-role all-weather capability are advanced avionics, which include pulse-Doppler search and acquisition radar, pod-mounted FLIR, one head-up and three head-down displays (one replacing conventional flight instruments, one displaying terrain below and the other presenting data from radar and FLIR), an advanced digital computer, laser INS, and state-of-the-art ECM and nav/com systems.

To achieve weight savings of some 25 per cent, keeping normal take-off weight down to a figure of about 8000 kg (17,637 lb), extensive structural use is made of composite materials, but despite the complexity of the aircraft it is designed for easy maintenance by comparatively unskilled conscripts. The JAS 39A became operational in 1995, and the **JAS 39B** two-seater is under final development.

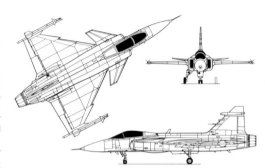

**Saab JAS 39A Gripen**

*The first prototype JAS 39 Gripen was subsequently destroyed in a spectacular landing accident. The blame was apportioned to the flight control system software.*

*The Gripen is an excellent lightweight fighter and attack aircraft, whose capabilities far exceed those of many larger fighters. The aircraft deserves export success.*

## Specification: Saab JAS 39A Gripen

**Origin:** Sweden
**Type:** single-seat all-weather fighter, attack and reconnaissance aircraft
**Powerplant:** one 8210-kg (18,100-lb) afterburning thrust Volvo Flygmotor RM12 turbofan
**Performance:** maximum speed supersonic at all altitudes
**Weights:** empty 6622 kg (14,600 lb); maximum take-off 12473 kg (27,500 lb)
**Dimensions:** span 8.00 m (26 ft 3 in); length 14.10 m (46 ft 3 in); height 4.70 m (15 ft 5 in)
**Armament:** one 27-mm Mauser BK27 cannon; provision for Sky Flash and Sidewinder AAMs, Maverick ASMs, Rb15F anti-ship missiles, bombs, cluster bombs, rocket-launcher pods, reconnaissance pods, drop tanks and ECM pods carried on six external hardpoints

# SEPECAT Jaguar A and E

*SEPECAT Jaguar A of Escadron de Chasse 4/11 'Jura', French air force, based at Bordeaux.*

## Role

Fighter
Close support
Counter-insurgency
Tactical strike
Strategic bomber
Tactical reconnaissance
Strategic reconnaissance
Maritime patrol
Anti-ship strike
Anti-submarine warfare
Search and rescue
Assault transport
Transport
Liaison
Trainer
Inflight-refuelling tanker
Specialized

## Performance

All-weather capability
Rough field capability
STOL capability
VTOL capability
Airspeed 0-250 mph
Airspeed 250 mph-Mach 1
Airspeed Mach 1 plus
Ceiling 0-20,000 ft
Ceiling 20,000-40,000 ft
Ceiling 40,000ft plus
Range 0-1,000 miles
Range 1,000-3,000 miles
Range 3,000 miles plus

## Weapons

Air-to-air missiles
Air-to-surface missiles
Cruise missiles
Cannon
Trainable guns
Naval weapons
Nuclear-capable
Rockets
'Smart' weapon kit
Weapon load 0-4,000 lb
Weapon load 4,000-15,000 lb
Weapon load 15,000 lb plus

## Avionics

Electronic Counter Measures
Electronic Support Measures
Search radar
Fire control radar
Look-down/shoot-down
Terrain-following radar
Forward-looking infra-red
Laser
Television

With a common Armée de l'Air and Royal Air Force requirement finalized for a dual-role training and tactical support aircraft, the defence ministries of the UK and France signed a memorandum of understanding on 17 May 1965. In May 1966 Breguet Aviation and the British Aircraft Corporation formed the joint production company Société Européenne de Production de l'Avion Ecole de Combat et Appui Tactique, a somewhat difficult mouthful of a name soon known universally by the acronym SEPECAT.

The aircraft was to be evolved from the Breguet Br.121 project, derived from the Breguet Br.1001 Taon light fighter prototype. The powerplant was also a collaborative effort, Rolls-Royce and Turbomeca being tasked to develop the Rolls-Royce RB.172 and Turbomeca Turmalet to provide an afterburning turbofan engine later named Adour. French versions among the five announced initially were the **SEPECAT Jaguar A**, **Jaguar E** and Jaguar M. The last, a carrier-based strike aircraft flown in prototype form on 14 November 1969, completed deck landing trials before falling victim to escalating costs. First to fly, however, were the two Jaguar E tandem-seat advanced trainer prototypes on 8 September 1968 and 11 February 1969 respectively. Early

achievement of a speed in excess of Mach 1 confirmed good design in a layout including a high-set monoplane wing of 3° anhedral and 40° sweepback, conventional tail unit with all-swept surfaces, retractable tricycle landing gear, and the two crew in air-conditioned and pressurized accommodation on tandem Martin-Baker Mk 4 ejector seats, the rear seat being raised by 0.38 m (15 in). Production totalled 40, initial deliveries to the Armée de l'Air being made in May 1972.

The two prototypes of the Jaguar A single-seat tactical support aircraft were flown respectively on 23 March and 27 May 1969, and this version began to equip the Armée de l'Air's EC1/7 'Provence' at St Dizier in 1973. The Jaguar A differs structurally by having a slightly shorter fuselage, but has the same powerplant of Adour Mk 102 turbofans. More comprehensive equipment for its tactical role includes an air data system, Doppler navigation, ECM, fire-control computer, IFF, inertial navigation, navigation computer, panoramic camera, weapon aiming computer, and provision for terrain-following radar and, in the last 30 aircraft, for the AS.30L laser-guided ASM. Production of the Jaguar A totalled 160, the aircraft equipping nine squadrons of the Armée de l'Air.

**SEPECAT Jaguar A**

## Specification: SEPECAT Jaguar A

**Origin:** France and UK
**Type:** single-seat tactical support and strike aircraft
**Powerplant:** two 3313-kg (7,305-lb) afterburning thrust Rolls-Royce/Turbomeca Adour Mk 102 turbofans
**Performance:** maximum speed Mach1.5 or 860 kt (1593 km/h; 990 mph) at 36,090 ft (11000 m); combat radius 575 km (357 miles) on a lo-lo-lo mission with internal fuel, or 1315 km (817 miles) on a hi-lo-hi mission with internal and external fuel
**Weights:** empty 7000 kg (15,432 lb); maximum take-off 15500 kg (34,172 lb)
**Dimensions:** span 8.69 m( 28ft 6.1 in); length 16.83 m (55 ft 2.6 in); height 4.89 m (16 ft 0.5 in); wing area 24.0 m² (258.34 sq ft)
**Armament:** two 30-mm DEFA cannon with 150 rounds per gun; provision for 4536 kg (10,000 lb) of disposable weapons, including one AN-52 tactical nuclear weapon or conventional loads such as one AS.37 Martel anti-radar missile and two drop tanks, or eight 454-kg (1,000-lb) bombs, or combinations of AAMs, bombs, drop tanks and rocket-launcher pods, and a reconnaissance pod, carried on five external hardpoints

*A desert-camouflaged Jaguar A of Escadron de Chasse 3/11 'Corse' which is tasked with the support of French forces deployed outside France. The unit has rapid-response capability.*

*Two Jaguar As of Escadron de Chasse 4/7 'Limousin', an Istres-based nuclear strike unit. The Jaguar A was the backbone of France's tactical nuclear air force alongside the Dassault Mirage IIIE.*

# SEPECAT Jaguar B and S

In reaching agreement with the Armée de l'Air on a dual-role aircraft suitable for training and tactical support, the Royal Air Force was influenced by its intention to use the aircraft almost exclusively for advanced flying training. French interest lay in a ground-attack aircraft with STOL performance. The design to meet these requirements resulted in a fairly large aircraft, and as its cost began to grow the British Air Staff had comprehensive second thoughts. Instead of procuring only advanced trainers, it finally decided to acquire 165 tactical support single-seaters and 35 two-seat operational trainers.

First British version to fly in prototype form on 12 October 1969 was the **SEPECAT Jaguar S**, the single-seat tactical support aircraft designated **Jaguar GR.Mk 1**. The airframe is similar to that of the French Jaguar A, but has rather more sophisticated installed equipment. With no radar, all-weather capability is restricted, and the heart of the Jaguar GR.Mk 1's system is its inertial navigation and weapon aiming subsystem, complete with digital computer, which projects on the pilot's head-up display all the essential data to navigate accurately to the target and attack it in a first pass. The Jaguar GR.Mk 1's equipment also includes an air data computer, IFF, laser rangefinder/marked-target seeker and TACAN. The introduction of a new Ferranti FIN 1064 inertial navigation system from 1983 brought redesignation as the **Jaguar GR.Mk 1A**. Reconnaissance capability is provided by a pod (mounted on the fuselage centreline) housing horizon-to-horizon optical cameras and an infra-red linescan to enhance poor-weather and night capability. The first production Jaguar GR.Mk 1 was flown on 11 October 1972, deliveries beginning in 1973. It later equipped eight first-line squadrons.

The **Jaguar B** two-seat trainer (service designation **Jaguar T.Mk 2**), was first flown on 30 August 1971. Basically similar to the French two-seat Jaguar E, it retains full operational capability and was equipped to the same standard as the Jaguar GR.Mk 1. From 1983 it too was revised with the Ferranti INS, converted aircraft being designated **Jaguar T.Mk 2A**. Deliveries of T.Mk 2s totalled 38, three more than originally planned.

The Jaguar GR.Mk 1A proved very useful in the 1991 UN-led campaign against Iraq, and some of the aircraft are being upgraded for continued viability with advanced equipment such as the TIALD (Thermal Imaging And Laser Designation) pod for use of laser-guided weapons.

**Specification:** SEPECAT Jaguar GR.Mk 1A
**Origin:** France and UK
**Type:** single-seat tactical support aircraft
**Powerplant:** two 3647-kg (8,040-lb) afterburning thrust Rolls-Royce/Turbomeca Adour Mk 104 turbofans
**Performance:** maximum speed Mach1.5 or 860 kt (1593 km/h; 990 mph) at 36,090 ft (11000 m); climb to 30,000 ft (9145 m) in 1 minute 30 seconds; service ceiling 46,000 ft (14020 m); combat radius 537 miles (334 miles) on a lo-lo-lo mission with internal fuel; ferry range 3525 km (2,190 miles) with internal and external fuel
**Weights:** empty 7700 kg (16,976 lb); maximum take-off 15700 kg (34,610 lb)
**Dimensions:** span 8.69 m (28 ft 6.1 in); length 16.83 m (55 ft 2.6 in); height 4.89 m (16 ft 0.5 in); wing area 24.0 m² (258.34 sq ft)
**Armament:** two 30-mm Aden Mk 4 cannon with 150 rounds per gun; provision for 4763 kg (10,500 lb) of disposable stores, including Sidewinder AAMs, AJ.168 Martel ASMs, laser-guided bombs, bombs, cluster bombs, anti-airfield bombs, rocket-launcher pods, napalm tanks, drop tanks and ECM pods, carried on five or optionally seven external hardpoints

*SEPECAT Jaguar T.Mk 2 of No.54 Squadron, RAF, based at Coltishall.*

*SEPECAT Jaguar GR.Mk 1*

*No.2 Squadron was the last RAF Germany Jaguar unit. Based at Laarbruch, the squadron's primary role was low-level tactical reconnaissance.*

*A Jaguar GR.Mk 1 of No.6 Squadron on final approach displays the distinctive chisel nose with glazed panels which houses the Laser Ranger and Marked-Target Seeker (LRMTS). The long fin-tip fairing contains ECM equipment.*

**Role**

Fighter
Close support
Counter-insurgency
Tactical strike
Strategic bomber
Tactical reconnaissance
Strategic reconnaissance
Maritime patrol
Anti-ship strike
Anti-submarine warfare
Search and rescue
Assault transport
Transport
Liaison
Trainer
Inflight-refuelling tanker
Specialized

**Performance**

All-weather capability
Rough field capability
STOL capability
VTOL capability
Airspeed 0-250 mph
Airspeed 250 mph-Mach 1
Airspeed Mach 1 plus
Ceiling 0-20,000 ft
Ceiling 20,000-40,000 ft
Ceiling 40,000ft plus
Range 0-1,000 miles
Range 1,000-3,000 miles
Range 3,000 miles plus

**Weapons**

Air-to-air missiles
Air-to-surface missiles
Cruise missiles
Cannon
Trainable guns
Naval weapons
Nuclear-capable
Rockets
'Smart' weapon kit
Weapon load 0-4,000 lb
Weapon load 4,000-15,000 lb
Weapon load 15,000 lb plus

**Avionics**

Electronic Counter Measures
Electronic Support Measures
Search radar
Fire control radar
Look-down/shoot-down
Terrain-following radar
Forward-looking infra-red
Laser
Television

# SEPECAT Jaguar International

*SEPECAT Jaguar International of No.20 Squadron, Sultan of Oman's air force.*

Long before production of the Jaguar A and E for France and of the Jaguar S and B for the UK had been completed, the manufacturers had begun development of an export version to which they gave the name **SEPECAT Jaguar International**. Large export orders were predicted, but such hopes have failed to materialize for, since the first Jaguar International development aircraft (G27-266) made its first flight on 19 August 1976, a total of only 169 had been ordered by four nations up to the mid-1990s. This does not reflect upon the capability of the Jaguar, but rather highlights the aggressive marketing of other manufacturers.

In structural terms the Jaguar International differs little from the basic single- or two-seat versions serving in France and the UK, but options available to potential customers include provision for anti-shipping and air-defence dogfight missiles (the latter carried on overwing pylons), multi-purpose radar, and night sensors such as low-light-level television. Performance comparable to that of the RAF's Jaguar GR.Mk 1 was provided by the installation of the Rolls-Royce/Turbomeca Adour Mk 804 turbofan, the export version of the Jaguar GR.Mk 1's Adour Mk 104, and having the same after-

burning thrust of 3647 kg (8,040 lb). Late-production aircraft introduced the more developed Adour Mk 811 which has some five per cent increase in maximum output.

As might be expected, the biggest changes in these export versions are to be found in armament and installed equipment. The former includes 30-mm Aden or DEFA 553 cannon, Belouga or Hunting BL755 cluster bombs, Durandal penetration bombs, rockets, and R.550 Magic or AIM-9 Sidewinder AAMs. In India, where Hindustan Aeronautics Ltd. assembled 45 Jaguars from British-supplied kits before moving to local manufacture, the more recent aircraft have an avionics system which is somewhat more advanced than that in RAF service. Known as the DARIN system, this includes Ferranti COMED 2045 combined map and electronic display, a Sagem inertial navigation system and a Smiths head-up display and weapon aiming system; this version also retains the Ferranti laser rangefinder and marked-target seeker. Some 17 of the Indian aircraft are tasked with maritime attack, and have the Agave radar and provision for anti-ship missiles. Each of the four export customers (Ecuador, India, Nigeria and Oman) has a handful of two-seat trainers.

**SEPECAT Jaguar International**

*A pair of Omani Jaguar Internationals, the nearer a two-seater, lands at Masirah, the former RAF base which is now home to Nos 8 and 20 Squadrons of the Omani air force.*

*Nigeria's Jaguar Internationals wear an interesting and attractive three-tone green colour scheme, and equip a Makurdi-based attack squadron.*

## Specification: SEPECAT Jaguar International
**Origin:** France and UK
**Type:** single-seat tactical support aircraft
**Powerplant:** two 3810-kg (8,400-lb) afterburning thrust Rolls-Royce/Turbomeca Adour Mk 811 turbofans
**Performance:** maximum speed Mach 1.6 or 917 kt (1699 km/h; 1,056 mph) at 36,000 ft (10970 m); combat radius 537 km (334 miles) on a lo-lo-lo mission with internal fuel, or 1408 km (875 miles) on a hi-lo-hi mission with internal and external fuel
**Weights:** empty 7700 kg (16,976 lb); maximum take-off 15700 kg (34,613 lb)
**Dimensions:** span 8.69 m (28 ft 6.1 in); length 16.83 m (55 ft 2.6 in); height 4.89 m (16 ft 0.5 in); wing area 24.18 m² (260.28 sq ft)
**Armament:** two 30-mm Aden Mk 4 cannon with 150 rounds per gun; provision for 4763 kg (10,500 lb) of disposable stores, including Sidewinder or Magic AAMs, Exocet or Sea Eagle anti-ship missiles, laser-guided bombs, bombs, cluster bombs, anti-airfield bombs, rocket-launcher pods, napalm tanks, drop tanks and ECM pods, carried on seven external hardpoints

**Role**
Fighter
Close support
Counter-insurgency
Tactical strike
Strategic bomber
Tactical reconnaissance
Strategic reconnaissance
Maritime patrol
Anti-ship strike
Anti-submarine warfare
Search and rescue
Assault transport
Transport
Liaison
Trainer
Inflight-refuelling tanker
Specialized

**Performance**
All-weather capability
Rough field capability
STOL capability
VTOL capability
Airspeed 0-250 mph
Airspeed 250 mph-Mach 1
Airspeed Mach 1 plus
Ceiling 0-20,000 ft
Ceiling 20,000-40,000 ft
Ceiling 40,000 ft plus
Range 0-1,000 miles
Range 1,000-3,000 miles
Range 3,000 miles plus

**Weapons**
Air-to-air missiles
Air-to-surface missiles
Cruise missiles
Cannon
Trainable guns
Naval weapons
Nuclear-capable
Rockets
'Smart' weapon kit
Weapon load 0-4,000 lb
Weapon load 4,000-15,000 lb
Weapon load 15,000 lb plus

**Avionics**
Electronic Counter Measures
Electronic Support Measures
Search radar
Fire control radar
Look-down/shoot-down
Terrain-following radar
Forward-looking infra-red
Laser
Television

# Shenyang JJ-5

*Shenyang J-2 (Chinese-built Mikoyan-Gurevich MiG-15) of the Chinese People's Liberation Army Air Force.*

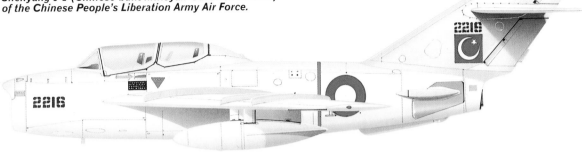

Aircraft built in the People's Republic of China are designated according to their source of manufacture and purpose. The **Shenyang JJ-5** was so name as it was though to be built at Shenyang, although it is now known that the type was in fact built in Chengdu as should therefore be known as the **Chengdu JJ-5**. JJ stands for Jianjiji Jiaolianji (fighter training aircraft), sometimes shortened to Jianjiao, and the numeral indicates that this was the fifth aircraft of that type in inventory. After the end of World war II the factory at Shenyang, which had initially been established by the Japanese as the Mansyu Aeroplane Manufacturing Company, was refurbished with Soviet assistance and turned once again to the construction of aircraft, initially machines of Soviet design that were then further developed by the Chinese.

The first turbojet-powered aircraft to be built in China were single-seat and two-seat versions of the Mikoyan-Gurevich MiG-15, followed by the basic MiG-17F. From experience gained in their manufacture, designers and engineers at Chengdu evolved what is in effect an indigenous two-seat advanced train-er by incorporating features of these two aircraft to form one that is unique. In effect, it adopts the forward fuselage and tandem cockpits of the MiG-15UTI and completes the airframe by utilizing the remaining structure from the MiG-17PF. The powerplant comprises a single WP-5D non- afterburning turbojet engine, originally a licence-built version of the Soviet Klimov VK-1A, mounted within the central fuselage and aspirated via a nose inlet. The tandem accommodation, with dual controls and Chinese-developed semi-automatic ejector seats as standard, provides a raised rear seat for the instructor and is enclosed beneath a rearward- sliding canopy. The landing gear is of retractable tricycle type, but the wheel brakes are limited to pneumatic operation .

In this configuration the JJ-5 first flew on 8 May 1966 and currently serves in the Air Force of the People's Liberation Army as its standard advanced trainer, following the pupil's completion of the basic training phase. In addition to this use a number have been exported, known users including the Pakistan air force with the designation **FT-5** and the Sudanese air force with the designation **F-5T**.

*Chengdu JJ-5 (FT-5)*

**The Chengdu JJ-5 is used by the Pakistan air force as the FT-5 for advanced pilot training and basic weapons training before type conversion and advanced weapons training.**

**One Pakistani Chengdu JJ-5 wears an overall pale grey colour scheme, but others are in polished natural metal. The aircraft serve with the Mianwali-based No.1 (Fighter) Conversion Unit.**

## Specification: Chengdu JJ-5

**Origin:** China (from original Soviet design)
**Type:** two-seat advanced trainer
**Powerplant:** one 2700-kg (5,952-lb) dry thrust Xian WP-5D turbojet
**Performance:** normal operating speed 418 kt (775 km/h; 482 mph); initial climb rate 5,315 ft (1620 m) per minute; service ceiling 46,915 ft (14300 m); range 1230 km (764 miles) with maximum fuel
**Weights:** empty 4080 kg (8,995 lb); maximum take-off 6215 kg (13,702 lb)
**Dimensions:** span 9.63 m (31 ft 7.1 in); length 11.50 m (37 ft 8.8 in); height 3.80 m (12 ft 5.6 in)
**Armament:** one 23-mm Type 23-1 cannon in a removable underfuselage pack

**Role**
Fighter
Close support
Counter-insurgency
Tactical strike
Strategic bomber
Tactical reconnaissance
Strategic reconnaissance
Maritime patrol
Anti-ship strike
Anti-submarine warfare
Search and rescue
Assault transport
Transport
Liaison
Trainer
Inflight-refuelling tanker
Specialized

**Performance**
All-weather capability
Rough field capability
STOL capability
VTOL capability
Airspeed 0-250 mph
Airspeed 250 mph-Mach 1
Airspeed Mach 1 plus
Ceiling 0-20,000 ft
Ceiling 20,000-40,000 ft
Ceiling 40,000ft plus
Range 0-1,000 miles
Range 1,000-3,000 miles
Range 3,000 miles plus

**Weapons**
Air-to-air missiles
Air-to-surface missiles
Cruise missiles
Cannon
Trainable guns
Naval weapons
Nuclear-capable
Rockets
'Smart' weapon kit
Weapon load 0-4,000 lb
Weapon load 4,000-15,000 lb
Weapon load 15,000 lb plus

**Avionics**
Electronic Counter Measures
Electronic Support Measures
Search radar
Fire control radar
Look-down/shoot-down
Terrain-following radar
Forward-looking infra-red
Laser
Television

# Shenyang J-6 and JJ-6

*Shenyang F-6 of the Pakistan air force.*

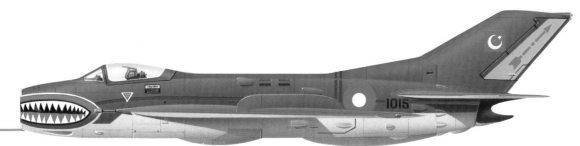

**Role**
Fighter
Close support
Counter-insurgency
Tactical strike
Strategic bomber
Tactical reconnaissance
Strategic reconnaissance
Maritime patrol
Anti-ship strike
Anti-submarine warfare
Search and rescue
Assault transport
Transport
Liaison
Trainer
Inflight-refuelling tanker
Specialized

**Performance**
All-weather capability
Rough field capability
STOL capability
VTOL capability
Airspeed 0-250 mph
Airspeed 250 mph-Mach 1
Airspeed Mach 1 plus
Ceiling 0-20,000 ft
Ceiling 20,000-40,000 ft
Ceiling 40,000ft plus
Range 0-1,000 miles
Range 1,000-3,000 miles
Range 3,000 miles plus

**Weapons**
Air-to-air missiles
Air-to-surface missiles
Cruise missiles
Cannon
Trainable guns
Naval weapons
Nuclear-capable
Rockets
'Smart' weapon kit
Weapon load 0-4,000 lb
Weapon load 4,000-15,000 lb
Weapon load 15,000 lb plus

**Avionics**
Electronic Counter Measures
Electronic Support Measures
Search radar
Fire control radar
Look-down/shoot-down
Terrain-following radar
Forward-looking infra-red
Laser
Television

The national aircraft factory of the Chinese People's Republic at Shenyang built versions of the Mikoyan-Gurevich MiG-19 fighter since the early 1960s under the designation **Shenyang J-6**. Before that time, when ideological friction destroyed the close relationship between China and the USSR, a licence agreement of January 1958 had seen the MiG-19 being assembled in China from knocked-down kits. Thus a great deal of valuable knowledge was gained by Chinese designers and engineers before the split came in 1960, and by December 1961 the first MiG-19S of Chinese manufacture was flown under the designation J-6 (Jianjiji-6 or Fighter Aircraft type 6). This entered service with the Air Force of the People's Liberation Army from mid-1962, soon becoming its standard day fighter. More recently, versions of the J-6 have also been produced by the national aircraft factory at Tianjin (formerly known as Tientsin).

Since production started at the beginning of the 1960s, seven different versions of Chinese manufacture have been identified. They include the J-6 mentioned above, which was a direct equivalent of the MiG-19S/SF day fighter and has the same NATO reporting name of 'Farmer-C'. It was superseded in production by the generally similar **J-6C**, which varies primarily by having the

braking parachute relocated in a fairing at the base of the rudder. The J-6 was at first complemented by the **J-6A**, a limited all-weather fighter (with gun and rocket armament) similar to the MiG-19PF and with the same NATO reporting name 'Farmer-D'. Other 'Farmer-D' variants are the **J-6B** armed with a semi-active radar homing AAM derived from the Soviet AA-1 'Alkali', and the final **J-6Xin** (Xin = new) with a Chinese developed AI radar characterized by a 'sting' type radome mounted on the inlet splitter plate. The remaining two versions are the single-seat **JZ-6** (Jianjiji Zhenchaji 6) reconnaissance fighter similar to the MiG-19R, with cameras installed in the lower forward fuselage, and the **JJ-6** (Jianjiji Jiaolianji-6) tandem two-seat trainer. The JJ-6 has a fuselage lengthened by 0.84 m (2 ft 9 in) forward of the wing to accommodate the additional cockpit, braking parachute stowage as introduced on the J-6C, and two ventral strakes added beneath the rear fuselage to maintain directional stability.

Chinese production was numbered in thousands, J-6 versions equipping some 40 air regiments of the Air Force of the PLA. The type has also been exported in some numbers, the Pakistan air force being a major operator of both the J-6 and JJ-6 in its **F-6** and **FT-6** export versions.

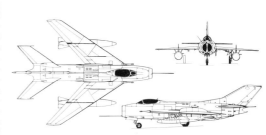

*Shenyang J-6*

*This FT-6 two-seat trainer serves in the conversion and continuation training role. The Pakistan air force is a major user of the F-6 and FT-6, and many aircraft received Western avionics and armament.*

*The 'Black Spiders' have now re-equipped with the Nanchang A-5, but their aircraft were passed on to other units for continued front-line service.*

## Specification: Shenyang J-6

**Origin:** China and USSR
**Type:** single-seat day fighter
**Powerplant:** two 3250-kg (7,165-lb) afterburning thrust Shenyang WP-6 turbojets
**Performance:** maximum speed Mach 1.45 or 831 kt (1540 km/h; 957 mph) at 36,090 ft (11000 m); cruising speed 512 kt (950km/h; 590mph); initial climb rate more than 30,000 ft (9145m) per minute; serviceceiling58,725 ft (17900 m); normal range1390 km (864 miles) with internal fuel
**Weights:** empty 5760 kg (12,699 lb); maximum take-off about 10000 kg (22,046 lb0
**Dimensions:** span 9.20 m (30 ft 2.2 in); length (including probe) 14.90 m (48 ft 10.6 in); height 3.88 m (12 ft 8.8 in); wing area 25.0 m² (269.11sq ft)
**Armament:** three 30-mm NR-30 cannon; provision for 50 kg (1102 lb) of disposable stores, including AAMs, 250-kg (551-lb) bombs, 55-mm (2.17-in) rocket-launcher pods, 212-mm (8.35-in) rockets or drop tanks, carried on four external hardpoints

# Shin Meiwa SS-2A (US-1)

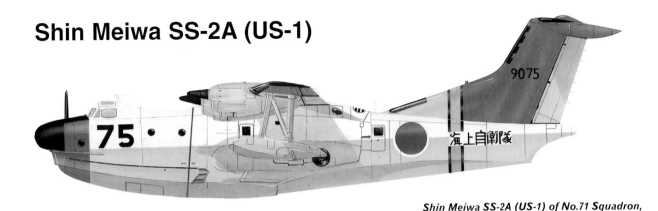

When the design and development of the Shin Meiwa SS-2 anti-submarine flying boat was under way, the Japan Maritime Self-Defence Force also had a requirement for a search-and-rescue aircraft. It was decided that subject to acceptance of the SS-2 for service, an amphibious variant would be developed for the role and design of this version was started in June 1970 under the designation **Shin Meiwa SS-2A**. Basically the airframe differs little from that of the SS-2 except that the flying-boat hull is modified to incorporate tricycle landing gear: each unit of this gear has twin wheels, the nose unit being steerable and the main gears retracting rearward into a fairing on each side of the hull. The first SS-2A was flown initially on 16 October 1974 following a water take-off, with the first land take-off accomplished on 3 December 1974. Following manufacturer's tests the JMSDF received its first SS-2A on 5 March 1975, the type being given the service designation **US-1**; all six aircraft had been delivered by the end of February 1982 with a powerplant of four 2285-kW (3,064-shp) Ishikawajima-Harima (General Electric) T64-IHI-10 turboprops and further construction was centred on the **US-1A** variant.

While the US-1 is very similar to the PS-1 with the exception of its amphibian landing gear, it benefits from having more powerful T64-IHI-10J engines installed from the start in the US-1A model and then retrofitted in the first six. The very different task of the US-1/1A means, of course, that the interior layout and equipment differ considerably. Basic accommodation is for a crew of nine and up to 20 seated survivors or, alternatively, 12 injured survivors on litters. A sliding rescue door is incorporated in the port side of the fuselage, just aft of the port main landing gear housing, and comprehensive rescue equipment includes the essential flares, float lights and marine markers, plus items such as droppable life raft containers, a lifeboats with outboard motor, and lifebuoys. Sea search and navigation equipment is very similar to that of the PS-1, but in place of the earlier type's sonobuoy equipment the US-1/1A has more comprehensive communications equipment, including a loudspeaker to direct rescue activities. To allow for extensive search operations, the US-1/1A can be refuelled on the open sea, either from a surface vessel or from a second US-1/1A equipped with at-sea refuelling gear to serve as a tanker. Under a five-year defence build-up programme authorized by the Japanese government in April 1986, three more US-1As were procured for service with the JMSDF.

**Specification:** Shin Meiwa SS-2A (US-1A)
**Origin:** Japan
**Type:** search-and-rescue amphibian
**Powerplant:** four 2602-ekW (3,490-eshp) Ishikawajima-Harima (General Electric) T64-IHI-10J turboprops
**Performance:** maximum speed 276 kt (511 km/h; 318 mph); cruising speed 230 kt (426 km/h; 265 mph) at 10,000 ft (3050 m); initial climb rate 2,340 ft (713 m) per minute; service ceiling 23,600 ft (7195 m); maximum range 3817 km (2,371 miles)
**Weights:** empty 25500 kg (56,218 lb); maximum take-off 43000 kg (94,799 lb) from water or 45000 kg (99,208 lb) from land
**Dimensions:** span 33.15 m (108 ft 9.1 in); length 33.46 m (109 ft 9.3 in); height 9.95 m (32 ft 7.7 in); wing area 135.8 m² (1,461.79 sq ft)
**Armament:** none

*Shin Meiwa SS-2A (US-1) of No.71 Squadron, Japan Maritime Self-Defence Force.*

*Shin Meiwa SS-2A (US-1A)*

*The US-1 and US-1A amphibians serve with the Iwakuni-based 71st Kokutai of the 31st Kokugun, initially alongside the now-retired PS-1s of the 31st Kokutai.*

*The US-1A was fitted from the start with more powerful T64-IHI-10J turboprops, and the earlier US-1s were later revised with these engines.*

## Role

- Fighter
- Close support
- Counter-insurgency
- Tactical strike
- Strategic bomber
- Tactical reconnaissance
- Strategic reconnaissance
- **Maritime patrol**
- Anti-ship strike
- Anti-submarine warfare
- **Search and rescue**
- Assault transport
- Transport
- Liaison
- Trainer
- Inflight-refuelling tanker
- Specialized

## Performance

- All-weather capability
- Rough field capability
- STOL capability
- VTOL capability
- Airspeed 0-250 mph
- Airspeed 250 mph-Mach 1
- Airspeed Mach 1 plus
- Ceiling 0-20,000 ft
- Ceiling 20,000-40,000 ft
- Ceiling 40,000ft plus
- Range 0-1,000 miles
- Range 1,000-3,000 miles
- Range 3,000 miles plus

## Weapons

- Air-to-air missiles
- Air-to-surface missiles
- Cruise missiles
- Cannon
- Trainable guns
- Naval weapons
- Nuclear-capable
- Rockets
- 'Smart' weapon kit
- Weapon load 0-4,000 lb
- Weapon load 4,000-15,000 lb
- Weapon load 15,000 lb plus

## Avionics

- Electronic Counter Measures
- Electronic Support Measures
- Search radar
- Fire control radar
- Look-down/shoot-down
- Terrain-following radar
- Forward-looking infra-red
- Laser
- Television

247

# Shorts 330/C-23 Sherpa

### Role
Fighter
Close support
Counter-insurgency
Tactical strike
Strategic bomber
Tactical reconnaissance
Strategic reconnaissance
Maritime patrol
Anti-ship strike
Anti-submarine warfare
Search and rescue
Assault transport
Transport
Liaison
Trainer
Inflight-refuelling tanker
Specialized

### Performance
All-weather capability
Rough field capability
STOL capability
VTOL capability
Airspeed 0-250 mph
Airspeed 250 mph-Mach 1
Airspeed Mach 1 plus
Ceiling 0-20,000 ft
Ceiling 20,000-40,000 ft
Ceiling 40,000ft plus
Range 0-1,000 miles
Range 1,000-3,000 miles
Range 3,000 miles plus

### Weapons
Air-to-air missiles
Air-to-surface missiles
Cruise missiles
Cannon
Trainable guns
Naval weapons
Nuclear-capable
Rockets
'Smart' weapon kit
Weapon load 0-4,000 lb
Weapon load 4,000-15,000 lb
Weapon load 15,000 lb plus

### Avionics
Electronic Counter Measures
Electronic Support Measures
Search radar
Fire control radar
Look-down/shoot-down
Terrain-following radar
Forward-looking infra-red
Laser
Television

Market research having confirmed to Short Brothers & Harland that many air service and commuter operators had a requirement for a small transport that was larger than the 18/20-seaters then available, the company initiated design of the **Shorts SD.3-30**. The last two figures indicated its passenger seating capacity, but this designation was soon changed to **Shorts 330**. Basically an extension of the SC.7 Skyvan design, the later aircraft retains many features of its predecessor including a braced high aspect ratio wing (its centre section integral with the upper centre fuselage structure) which also provides the mounting for the turboprop engines. The lengthened fuselage is of similar rectangular cross-section, and carries at its rear a tail unit with twin endplate vertical surfaces. The tricycle landing gear differs by being retractable, the main units lifting upward into small sponsons. Construction began with two prototypes, the first of them making the type's initial flight on 22 August 1974. Early production aircraft were also used in the development programme leading to certification on 18 February 1976.

Three versions of the Shorts 330 were built, the standard civil aircraft being the **Shorts 330-200** of which the first 26 were powered by the 875-kW (1,173-shp) Pratt & Whitney Canada PT6A-45A, the next 60 by the PT6A-45B of similar output and, from that production point, by the PT6A-45R which is the current engine variant.

The freighter version is the **Sherpa**, which retains the forward freight door of the Shorts 330-200 and introduces a hydraulically actuated full-width rear ramp/door to facilitate the loading of freight or vehicles The Sherpa prototype was flown first on 23 December 1982 and an early customer was the US Air Force which procured 18 in March 1984 (under the designation **C-23A**) the contract including 10 years of logistic support and servicing. All have been delivered and these were operated in a European Distribution System Aircraft role by the 10th Military Airlift Squadron for the movement of high-priority spares between European bases. In the late 1980s the aircraft were pulled back to the USA, where two remain on USAF charge and the other 16 have been reallocated to the US Forestry Service and the US Army, which also procured 10 C-23B aircraft to replace its de Havilland Canada CV-2 Caribou transports. The third variant is the Shorts 330-UTT utility tactical transport, which is basically similar to the Shorts 330-200 except for its strengthened floor and equipment to carry up to 33 troops, or 30 paratroops and a despatcher, or 15 litters plus four seated casualties or other personnel.

Orders for all versions of the Short 330 now total about 200, of which many serve with armed forces and government agencies.

## Specification: Shorts Sherpa
**Origin:** UK
**Type:** freight/utility transport
**Powerplant:** two 893-kW (1,198-shp) Pratt & Whitney Canada PT6A-45R turboprops
**Performance:** maximum cruising speed 190 kt (352 km/h; 218 mph) at 10,000 ft (3050 m); economical cruising speed 157 kt (291 km/h; 181 mph); initial climb rate 1,180 ft (360 m) per minute; range 363 km (225 miles) with a 3175-kg (7,000-lb) payload and reserves
**Weights:** empty 6680 kg (14,727 lb); maximum take-off 10387 kg (22,900 lb)
**Dimensions:** span 22.76 m (74 ft 8 in); length 17.69 m (58 ft 0.5 in); height 4.95 m (16 ft 3 in); wing area 42.08 m² (453.0 sq ft)
**Armament:** none

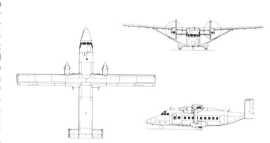

*Shorts 330-UTT of the Royal Thai air force.*

*Shorts Sherpa*

*This is a C-23A Sherpa of the USAF, looking purposeful in its 'European One' colour scheme. The C-23A proved disappointing in service, through no fault of its own.*

*A C-23A of the 10th MAS, based at Zweibrücken as part of the European Distribution System. The requirement did not take account of the equipment the C-23 was to carry.*

# SIAI-Marchetti SF.260

*SIAI-Marchetti SF.260W Warrior of the Tunisian air force.*

On 15 July 1964 the Italian company Aviamilano Costruzioni Aeronautiche flew the prototype of a new three-seat monoplane, designed by Ing. Stelio Frati and designated Aviamilano F.250. Of all-metal construction, it had a low-set wing incorporating Frise-type ailerons and electrically operated slotted flaps, and carried auxiliary tanks at the wing tips. The fuselage mounted its 186-kW (250-hp) Avco Lycoming O-540-AID5 flat-six engine in the nose and a conventional tail unit at the rear, and provided an enclosed cockpit seating two forward side-by-side and with a single seat aft The landing gear was of electrically retractable tricycle type with a steerable nosewheel.

From the outset it was arranged that the F.250 would be manufactured under licence by SIAI-Marchetti. which designated it the **SIAI-Marchetti SF.260** and installed a more powerful version of the O-540 engine. Subsequently SIAI-Marchetti acquired the type certificate and all production rights, marketing the aircraft originally as the SF.260A (and in the USA as the Waco Meteor) but soon discovering that its comparatively high cost resulted in disappointing civil sales. The company then concentrated on the development of a military primary/basic trainer, the **SF.260M**, flown in prototype form on 19 October 1970. This

introduced structural strengthening and was equipped with instrumentation to make it suitable for a variety of training roles. With the SF.260M selling well, SIAI developed a tactical support version retaining the same training capability, designating it the **SF.260W Warrior** with two or four underwing hardpoints to accept NATO standard pylons with a combined capacity of 300 kg (661 lb) to make it suitable for air support, armed reconnaissance, forward air control, liaison and low-level attack roles. This version also serves with several air arms, but the SAR/supply/surveillance variant known as the SF.260SW Sea Warrior, which adds to the Warrior's equipment enlarged auxiliary tanks incorporating lightweight radar (port) and photo-reconnaissance equipment (starboard), failed to gain an order.

Other variants include the civil SF.260B, incorporating the structural improvements of the SF.260M, the similar but later SF.260C, and an improved SF.260D. In July 1980 SIAI-Marchetti flew the prototype **SF.260TP**, which combines the airframe of the SF.260M/W with an Allison 250-B17C turboprop engine flat-rated at 261 kW (350 shp). This has proved of interest to several air arms with more than 70 ordered, a figure included in the total of some 900 SF.260s of all variants ordered by the mid-1990s.

**SIAI-Marchetti SF.260W Warrior**

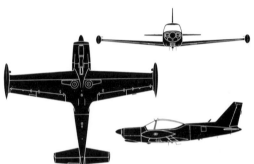

*This SF.260 serves with the Fuerza Aérea Hondurena in the COIN, light attack and advanced training roles. The aircraft is fast and manoeuvrable compared with similar trainers.*

*Belgium uses the SF.260M as its standard primary trainer. This aircraft serves with the Ecole de Pilotage Elementaire at Goetshoven.*

**Specification:** SIAI-Marchetti SF.260 Warrior
**Origin:** Italy
**Type:** light trainer/tactical support aircraft
**Powerplant:** one194-kW (260-hp) Avco Lycoming O-540-F4A5 flat-six piston engine
**Performance:** maximum speed 165 kt (305 km/h; 190 mph) at sea level; maximum cruising speed 152 kt (281 km/h; 175 mph) at 4,920 ft (1500 m); initial climb rate 1,250 ft (381 m) per minute; service ceiling 14,700 ft (4480 m); combat radius 92 km (57 miles) on a single-seat armed patrol mission with 5 hours 35 minutes in operating area, or 278 km (173 miles) on a single-seat photo-reconnaissance mission with three 1-hour loiters over separate operating areas
**Weights:** empty 770 kg (1,698 lb); maximum take-off 1300 kg (2,866 lb)
**Dimensions:** span over tip tanks 8.35 m (27 ft 4.7 in); length 7.10 m (23 ft 3.5 in); height 2.41 m (7 ft 10.9 in); wing area 10.1 m² (108.72 sq ft)
**Armament:** can include gun pods to provide two or four 7.62-mm (0.3-in) machine guns, fragmentation, general-purpose and practice bombs, flares, and one or two photo-reconnaissance pods or auxiliary drop tanks

**Role**
Fighter
Close support
Counter-insurgency
Tactical strike
Strategic bomber
Tactical reconnaissance
Strategic reconnaissance
Maritime patrol
Anti-ship strike
Anti-submarine warfare
Search and rescue
Assault transport
Transport
Liaison
Trainer
Inflight-refuelling tanker
Specialized

**Performance**
All-weather capability
Rough field capability
STOL capability
VTOL capability
Airspeed 0-250 mph
Airspeed 250 mph-Mach 1
Airspeed Mach 1 plus
Ceiling 0-20,000 ft
Ceiling 20,000-40,000 ft
Ceiling 40,000ft plus
Range 0-1,000 miles
Range 1,000-3,000 miles
Range 3,000 miles plus

**Weapons**
Air-to-air missiles
Air-to-surface missiles
Cruise missiles
Cannon
Trainable guns
Naval weapons
Nuclear-capable
Rockets
'Smart' weapon kit
Weapon load 0-4,000 lb
Weapon load 4,000-15,000 lb
Weapon load 15,000 lb plus

**Avionics**
Electronic Counter Measures
Electronic Support Measures
Search radar
Fire control radar
Look-down/shoot-down
Terrain-following radar
Forward-looking infra-red
Laser
Television

# Sikorsky S-58 (H-34 Choctaw/Seabat and Seahorse)

Developed to meet a US Navy requirement for an ASW helicopter, the **Sikorsky S-58** was slightly larger than the S-55 which, operated by the US Navy under the designation HO4S (later H-19) had proved to have inadequate payload/range for the taxing ASW role. The S-58 differed primarily in having a Wright R-1820-84 radial engine with virtually double the power output of the HO4S's powerplant, but installed in a similar angular mounting in the nose. Other changes saw the introduction of four-blade main and tail rotors, and a now-conventional type of fuselage structure (with considerably more capacity than that of the S-55) carried on non-retractable tailwheel landing gear. For shipboard stowage the main rotor blades and the rear section of the fuselage could be folded.

The S-58 prototype, US Navy designation XHSS-1, flew for the first time on 8 March 1954, with the first production **HSS-1 Seabat** (from 1962 **SH-34G**) following on 20 September 1954. Deliveries of production aircraft to anti-submarine squadron HS-3, began in August 1955. The HSS-1 was followed by the **HSS-1N** (**SH-34J**) which, intended for night operations, introduced APN-97 Doppler navigation, a stabilization system and an automatic hover coupler. In service both of these SH-34s had inadequate payload capability for the ASW role and had to be employed either as hunters or, with homing torpedoes, as killers often operating in pairs. When replaced in service by the SH-3A, many SH-34G/SH-34Js were stripped of their ASW equipment to serve in the utility role as the **UH-34G** and **UH-34J** respectively. US Marine Corps procurement of the S-58 saw initial deliveries of the **HUS-1** (**UH-34D**) **Seahorse** 12-passenger utility transport to the HMRL-363 squadron in February 1957. Forty UH-34Ds were later given amphibious pontoons, then being redesignated **HUS-1A** (**UH-34E**), four modified for Arctic operation were designated **HUS-1L** (**LH-34D**), six were transferred to the US Coast Guard for SAR duties as **HUS-1G** (**HH-34F**) and seven **HUS-1Z** (**VH-34D**) VIP transports were used by the joint US Army/Marine Corps Executive Flight Detachment at Andrews AFB, Washington.

The US Army also acquired a transport version of the US Navy's HSS-1 as the **H-34A Choctaw**, the 506th Helicopter Company at Fort Benning being the first unit to equip with the type in September 1955. These were equipped for a crew of two and up to 16 troops or, alternatively, could carry eight litters. The H-34A was followed by the **H-34B** and **H-34C** which differed only in equipment changes and detail modifications. Sikorsky also built military versions for export plus the S-58B and S-58D civil helicopters, with total construction of all versions exceeding 1,800 when production ended in 1970. The S-58 was also licence built in France and the UK.

*Sikorsky S-58 of the Haitian air force.*

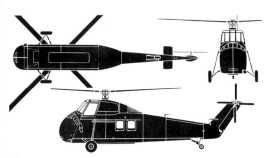

*Sikorsky S-58 (H-34)*

## Specification: UH-34D Seahorse

**Origin:** USA
**Type:** utility transport helicopter
**Powerplant:** one 1151-kW (1,525-hp) Wright R-1820-84 radial piston engine
**Performance:** maximum speed 107 kt (198 km/h; 123 mph) at sea level; cruising speed 85 kt (158 km/h; 98 mph); initial climb rate 1,100 ft (335m) per minute; service ceiling 9,500 ft (2895 m); range 293 km (182 miles)
**Weights:** empty 3583 kg (7,900 lb); maximum take-off 6350 kg(14,000 lb)
**Dimensions:** main rotor diameter 17.07 m (56 ft 0 in); length, rotors turning 17.28 m (56 ft 8.5 in); height 4.85 m (15 ft 11 in); main rotor disc area 228.81 m$^2$ (2,463.0sq ft)
**Armament:** none

*This Sikorsky S-58T is in service with the 201st Squadron, Royal Thai Air Force, based at Lop Buri as part of the 2nd Wing. The helicopters were active in COIN operations.*

*Thailand's 18 Sikorsky S-58Ts are actually CH34Cs converted to turbine power by Thai-Am Inc. in 1977. They are powered by a pair of Pratt & Whitney Canada PT6T turboshafts.*

# Sikorsky S-65 (CH-53 Sea Stallion)

*Sikorsky CH-53G of the Heeresflieger (West Germany army aviation).*

Sikorsky started design and development of large transport helicopters at the beginning of the 1950s, and its S-56 which saw service with the US Army, Navy and Marine Corps from 1955 was, for almost a decade, the largest helicopter flying outside the USSR. In the late 1950s the company began work on large flying-crane helicopters and then drew up its proposals to meet a US Marine Corps' requirement for a ship-based heavy assault transport. Identified as the **Sikorsky S-65A**, this was selected by the USMC in August 1962 to fill this role, being allocated the service designation **CH-53A** and named **Sea Stallion**.

The S-65A was something of a hybrid, with features of the S-64 Skycrane developed at about the same time and a watertight hull that benefited from experience with the S-61 family. The S-65 was much larger than the latter, however, with sufficient volume in a fuselage structure which equated with that of a conventional fixed-wing aircraft to accommodate a crew of three and up to 38 equipped troops. Alternative loads included 24 litters, or some 3629 kg (8,000 lb) of cargo or, via a rear door/ramp, such military loads as a 1.5-ton truck and its trailer, a 105-mm (4.13-in) howitzer, a HAWK SAM system or an Honest John SSM on its trailer. Alternatively, an external slung load of 5897 kg (13,000 lb)

could be carried. The configuration includes six-blade main and four-blade tail rotors, stabilizing sponsons on each side of the fuselage for on-water operations and into which the main units of the tricycle landing gear retract, and twin-turbine powerplant mounted above the cabin. In the initial CH-53A, first flown on 14 October 1964 and entering service in mid-1966, the powerplant consisted of two 2125-kW (2,850-shp) General Electric T64-GE-6 turboshafts, but the alternative T64-GE-1 of 2297 kW (3,080 shp) or T64-GE-16 (mod) of 2561 kW (3,485 shp) could be installed without modification.

An improved **CH-53D** version was introduced on the production line late in 1968, with initial deliveries made on 3 March 1969. The major changes involved were internal revisions to make it possible to seat up to 55 troops, the installation of either 2755-kW (3,695-shp) T64-GE-412 or 2927-kW (3,925-shp) T64-GE-413 turboshafts, and the incorporation of automatic folding of the main and tail rotors to simplify stowage on board aircraft-carriers. Production for the USMC ended in January 1972 after 139 CH-53A and 126 CH-53D Sea Stallions had been completed. Two CH-53G helicopters, of a type basically similar to the CH-53D, were built as sample aircraft for West Germany, where VFW-Fokker assembled under licence an additional 110 helicopters.

*Sikorsky CH-53 Sea Stallion*

**Specification:** Sikorsky CH-53D Sea Stallion
**Origin:** USA
**Type:** assault transport helicopter
**Powerplant:** two 2927-kW (3,925-shp) General Electric T64-GE-413 turboshafts
**Performance:** maximum speed 170 kt (315 km/h;196 mph) at sea level; cruising speed 150 kt (278 km/h; 173 mph); initial climb rate 2,180 ft (664 m) per minute; service ceiling 21,000 ft (6400 m)l range 414 km (257 miles) with maximum standard fuel and 10 per cent reserves
**Weights:** empty 10653 kg (23,485 lb), mission take-off 16511 kg (36,400 lb); maximum take-off 19051 kg (42,000 lb)
**Dimensions:** main rotor diameter 22.02 m (72 ft 3 in); length, rotors turning 26.90 m (88 ft 3 in); height 7.59 m (24 ft 11 in); main rotor disc area 380.87 m² (4,099.8 sq ft)
**Armament:** none

*This elderly CH-53A served with the shore-based heavy transport squadron HMT-301 at MCAS Tustin, California, a composite unit which also operated the CH-46E and the CH-53E.*

*Over 100 CH-53Gs were delivered to the Heeresflieger, and most remain in front-line service. The CH-53G is essentially similar to the CH-53D.*

### Role
Fighter
Close support
Counter-insurgency
Tactical strike
Strategic bomber
Tactical reconnaissance
Strategic reconnaissance
Maritime patrol
Anti-ship strike
Anti-submarine warfare
Search and rescue
Assault transport
Transport
Liaison
Trainer
Inflight-refuelling tanker
Specialized

### Performance
All-weather capability
Rough field capability
STOL capability
VTOL capability
Airspeed 0-250 mph
Airspeed 250 mph-Mach 1
Airspeed Mach 1 plus
Ceiling 0-20,000 ft
Ceiling 20,000-40,000 ft
Ceiling 40,000ft plus
Range 0-1,000 miles
Range 1,000-3,000 miles
Range 3,000 miles plus

### Weapons
Air-to-air missiles
Air-to-surface missiles
Cruise missiles
Cannon
Trainable guns
Naval weapons
Nuclear-capable
Rockets
'Smart' weapon kit
Weapon load 0-4,000 lb
Weapon load 4,000-15,000 lb
Weapon load 15,000 lb plus

### Avionics
Electronic Counter Measures
Electronic Support Measures
Search radar
Fire control radar
Look-down/shoot-down radar
Terrain-following radar
Forward-looking infra-red
Laser
Television

# Sikorsky S-80 (CH-53E Super Stallion and MH-65E Sea Dragon)

## Role

Fighter
Close support
Counter-insurgency
Tactical strike
Strategic bomber
Tactical reconnaissance
Strategic reconnaissance
Maritime patrol
Anti-ship strike
Anti-submarine warfare
Search and rescue
Assault transport
Transport
Liaison
Trainer
Inflight-refuelling tanker
Specialized

## Performance

All-weather capability
Rough field capability
STOL capability
VTOL capability
Airspeed 0-250 mph
Airspeed 250 mph-Mach 1
Airspeed Mach 1 plus
Ceiling 0-20,000 ft
Ceiling 20,000-40,000 ft
Ceiling 40,000ft plus
Range 0-1,000 miles
Range 1,000-3,000 miles
Range 3,000 miles plus

## Weapons

Air-to-air missiles
Air-to-surface missiles
Cruise missiles
Cannon
Trainable guns
Naval weapons
Nuclear-capable
Rockets
'Smart' weapon kit
Weapon load 0-4,000 lb
Weapon load 4,000-15,000 lb
Weapon load 15,000 lb plus

## Avionics

Electronic Counter Measures
Electronic Support Measures
Search radar
Fire control radar
Look-down/shoot-down
Terrain-following radar
Forward-looking infra-red
Laser
Television

Although both the US Marine Corps and US Navy had gained good service in the heavy transport and minesweeping roles from the Sikorsky CH-43D and RH-53D respectively, it was clear by the early 1970s that an even more capable helicopter could be built to fulfil such tasks. In 1973 the Sikorsky S-65 was selected for further development as the S-80, and in May of that year the construction of two YCH-53E prototypes was initiated, the first of them flying on 1 March 1974. The first of two pre-production helicopters flew on 13 December 1980, and production deliveries of the **CH-53E Super Stallion** to USMC squadron HMH-464, at MCAS New River, North Carolina, began on 16 June 1981. The US Navy planned to procure ultimately at least 300 of these helicopters, although the total was later reduced to 177. Compared with the CH-53D, the new helicopter has a lengthened fuselage, three turboshaft engines, a seven-blade main rotor of increased diameter and an uprated transmission, giving double the lift capability of the twin-turbine H-53s with only 50 per cent more engine power. With a single-point cargo hook rated at 16329 kg (36,000 lb), the CH-53E is suitable for combat tasks such as lifting battle-damaged aircraft from carrier decks or the support of mobile construction battal-

ions, and for vertical onboard delivery has an internal cargo load of 13608 kg (30,000 lb).

Further capability enhancement for the mine countermeasures helicopter was explored first with a prototype, initially designated **CH/MH-53E**, which was a conversion from a pre-production CH-53E and first flown on 23 December 1981. Early evaluation by the US Navy resulted in the construction of a pre-production helicopter, then designated **MH-53E** and named **Sea Dragon**, which was flown on 1 September 1983. Since then the Navy has stated its requirement for at least 57 (later reduced to 46) of these helicopters, and the first production example was scheduled for delivery during 1986. The MH-53E is easily identified externally by its enlarged sponsons containing additional fuel and allowing the helicopter to operate for up to six hours on station; it is also equipped with an inflight-refuelling probe and, at the hover, can refuel by hose from a surface vessel. Extended capability is provided by duplicated digital automatic flight-control systems and automatic tow couplers which allow automatic approach to and departure from the hover.

Export versions of the CH-53E and MH-53E are offered by Sikorsky under the respective designations **S-80E** and **S-80M**, of which Japan has ordered the latter.

## Specification: Sikorsky CH-53E Super Stallion

**Origin:** USA
**Type:** heavy-duty multi-role helicopter
**Powerplant:** three 3266-kW (4,380-shp) General Electric T64-GE-416 turboshafts
**Performance:** maximum speed 170 kt (315 km/h; 196 mph) at sea level; cruising speed 150 kt (278 km/h; 173 mph) at sea level; initial climb rate 2,500 ft (762 m) per minute; service ceiling 18,500 ft (5640 m); unrefuelled self-ferry range 2076 km (1,290 miles)
**Weights:** empty 15071 kg (33,226 lb); maximum take-off 31638 kg (69,750 lb) with an internal payload or 33339 kg (73,500 lb) with an external payload
**Dimensions:** main rotor diameter 24.08 m (79 ft 0 in); length, rotors turning 30.19 m (99 ft 0.5 in); height, tail rotor turning 8.66 m (28 ft 5 in); main rotor disc area 455.37 m² (4,901.68 sq ft)
**Armament:** none, but there are suggestions that AIM-9 Sidewinders might be provided to give a self-defence capability

*Sikorsky MH-53E Sea Dragon of the US Navy.*

*Sikorsky CH-53E Super Stallion*

**Two CH-53E Super Stallions of the US Marine Corps refuel from a KC-130T Hercules. The CH-53E differs from earlier variants in having three engines and an uprated transmission.**

**This CH-53E Super Stallion served with the US Navy's VC-5 'Workhorse of the Fleet', a composite evaluation and general duties squadron which operated from Cubi Point, Philippines.**

# Sikorsky S-65 (RH-53)

Sikorsky RH-53D of Helicopter Mine Countermeasures Squadron 12 (HM-12), US Navy.

The growing range and heavy-lift capability of helicopters led to their evaluation for one of the most difficult naval operations, the sweeping of enemy mines. It was realized that with an aircraft operating at a height well above the surface to tow sweep gear or mine detectors, there was little chance of the helicopter being endangered by the detonation of a mine, making it a most attractive towing vehicle for use in this role.

Bearing in mind such a potential use for its CH-53As, the US Marine Corps ensured that of the 139 of this version procured, all but the first 32 were equipped with hardpoints allowing the helicopters to tow minesweeping gear. Evaluation by the US Navy of the capability of the CH-53A when deployed for minesweeping led in 1971 to the transfer from the USMC to the USN of 15 CH-53As with hardpoints. Since these were intended specifically for a minesweeping role, a task requiring good heavy-lift capability, they were first re-engined with 2927-kW (3,925-shp) T64-GE-413 turboshafts, then being redesignated **RH-53A**, and were used to equip the USN's first helicopter mine countermeasures squadron, HM-12.

US Navy experience with the RH-53A resulted in the procurement of a version of the S-65 optimized for the minesweeping

task, Sikorsky receiving a contract for 30 under the service designation **RH-53D**. Based upon the improved CH-53D, they were given structural strengthening for the towing task and reinforced landing gear for operation at a higher gross weight. Powered initially by T64-GE-413 turboshafts, they were later retrofitted with T64-GE-415s, each developing a maximum 3266kW (4,380 shp). To provide worthwhile mission endurance, a 1893-litre (500-US gal) fuel tank was mounted under each sponson, and a nose-mounted inflight-refuelling probe was installed. Special equipment included interconnection to the AFCS to provide automatic tow cable yaw angle retention, with an automatic cable release should preset limits of tow cable tension and yaw angle be exceeded. First flown on 27 October 1972, and entering service with US Navy squadron HM-12 in September 1973, the RH-53D is suitable for sweeping acoustic, magnetic and mechanical mines. When required to deploy sweep gear too large to be carried internally, it uses its tow hook to pick up equipment first streamed behind a surface vessel. In addition to the contract for 30 RH-53Ds for its own use, the US Navy also procured six additional examples which were supplied for service with Iran's naval air arm.

**Specification:** Sikorsky RH-53D
**Origin:** USA
**Type:** minesweeping and multi-role helicopter
**Powerplant:** two 3266-kW (4,380-shp) General Electric T64-GE-415 turboshafts
**Performance:** unrefuelled endurance over 4 hours
**Weights:** normal take-off 19051 kg (42,000 lb); maximum take-off 22680 kg (50,000 lb)
**Dimensions:** main rotor diameter 22.02 m (72 ft 3 in); length, rotors turning 26.90 m (88 ft 3 in); height 7.59 m (24 ft 11 in); main rotor disc area 380.87 m² (4,099.8 sq ft)
**Armament:** provision for two 12.7-mm (0.5-in) machine guns for use in the detonation of surfaced mines

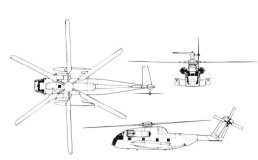

Sikorsky S-65 (RH-53)

The RH-53D was the helicopter used in the abortive Operation 'Eagle Claw', the ill-fated and ultimately disastrous mission to rescue the American hostages held in Tehran during April 1980.

This RH-53D wears an orthodox sea grey colour scheme and serves with the US Navy's HM-12 'Sea Dragons', the mine countermeasures unit based at Norfolk, Virginia.

**Role**
Fighter
Close support
Counter-insurgency
Tactical strike
Strategic bomber
Tactical reconnaissance
Strategic reconnaissance
Maritime patrol
Anti-ship strike
Anti-submarine warfare
Search and rescue
Assault transport
Transport
Liaison
Trainer
Inflight-refuelling tanker
Specialized

**Performance**
All-weather capability
Rough field capability
STOL capability
VTOL capability
Airspeed 0-250 mph
Airspeed 250 mph-Mach 1
Airspeed Mach 1 plus
Ceiling 0-20,000 ft
Ceiling 20,000-40,000 ft
Ceiling 40,000ft plus
Range 0-1,000 miles
Range 1,000-3,000 miles
Range 3,000 miles plus

**Weapons**
Air-to-air missiles
Air-to-surface missiles
Cruise missiles
Cannon
Trainable guns
Naval weapons
Nuclear-capable
Rockets
'Smart' weapon kit
Weapon load 0-4,000 lb
Weapon load 4,000-15,000 lb
Weapon load 15,000 lb plus

**Avionics**
Electronic Counter Measures
Electronic Support Measures
Search radar
Fire control radar
Look-down/shoot-down
Terrain-following radar
Forward-looking infra-red
Laser
Television

# Sikorsky S-70 (EH-60, HH-60 and UH-60 Black Hawk)

**Role**
Fighter
Close support
Counter-insurgency
Tactical strike
Strategic bomber
Tactical reconnaissance
Strategic reconnaissance
Maritime patrol
Anti-ship strike
Anti-submarine warfare
Search and rescue
Assault transport
Transport
Liaison
Trainer
Inflight-refuelling tanker
Specialized

**Performance**
All-weather capability
Rough field capability
STOL capability
VTOL capability
Airspeed 0-250 mph
Airspeed 250 mph-Mach 1
Airspeed Mach 1 plus
Ceiling 0-20,000 ft
Ceiling 20,000-40,000 ft
Ceiling 40,000ft plus
Range 0-1,000 miles
Range 1,000-3,000 miles
Range 3,000 miles plus

**Weapons**
Air-to-air missiles
Air-to-surface missiles
Cruise missiles
Cannon
Trainable guns
Naval weapons
Nuclear-capable
Rockets
'Smart' weapon kit
Weapon load 0-4,000 lb
Weapon load 4,000-15,000 lb
Weapon load 15,000 lb plus

**Avionics**
Electronic Counter Measures
Electronic Support Measures
Search radar
Fire control radar
Look-down/shoot-down
Terrain-following radar
Forward-looking infra-red
Laser
Television

The US Army's need for a Utility Tactical Transport Aircraft System (UTTAS) led, in late August 1972, to the selection of Boeing Vertol and Sikorsky to build competing prototypes of their design proposals. The first of three **Sikorsky S-70** flying prototypes was flown on 17 October 1974, these having the service designation YUH-60A. Technical evaluation and seven months of competitive flight test against Boeing Vertol's YUH-61A saw Sikorsky's design selected for production as the **UH-60A** with the name **Black Hawk**. The Army planned to procure a total of 2,262 helicopters although this has since been trimmed to some 1,400, and following the first flight of a production aircraft during October 1978 some 1,050 were in service by 1995.

Intended as the US Army's primary combat assault helicopter, carrying 11 equipped troops and a crew of three, the UH-60A has a cabin which is suitable also for the medevac, reconnaissance or troop resupply missions, and is fitted with an external cargo hook rated at 3629 kg (8,000 lb). One UTTAS requirement was that it could be easily airlifted: with the use of kits designed by Sikorsky, the USAF's Lockheed C-130, C-141 and C-5 can carry respectively one, two and six. Battlefield survivability features of the UH-60A include main rotor blades tolerant to 23-mm cannon fire, transmission system operable for up to 30 minutes following total oil loss, twin turbines, crashworthy bullet-proof fuel cells, and armour-protected seats for pilot and co-pilot. An External Stores Support System, with con-version kits delivered from early 1986, allows the carriage on four pylons of auxiliary fuel stores or weapons. The latest variant is the **UH-60L** with T700-GE-7-1 turboshafts and a transmission uprated to 2535 kW (3,400 shp).

Following 1981 preparation of a YEH-60C prototype, flown for the first time on 24 September 1981 and equipped with 'Quick Fix IIB' ECM to intercept, monitor and jam enemy communications, the conversion of an initial 40 UH-60As to **EH-60C** ECM/ESM configuration began following the award of a contract to Tracor Aerospace Group, which was responsible for production and installation of the ECM/ESM equipment. US Army plans to procure up to 132 EH-60Cs under its Special Electronic Mission Aircraft programme were eventually curtailed to 66 helicopters.

The US Air Force's HH-60D Night Hawk day/night combat rescue and special operations version, was cancelled after the completion of one prototype, and the role was then assumed by the **MH-60G 'Pave Hawk'**, of which 98 were delivered as UH-60A/L conversions with a crew of two and 10 passengers, or four litters and three seated casualties, plus equipment that includes a rescue hoist, external auxiliary fuel and inflight-refuelling capability for adequate mission radius, advanced avionics for accurate navigation, and defensive equipment. In January 1992, it was decided to retain 16 solely for the special operations role and use the other 82 for the combat SAR role with the designation **HH-60G**.

*Sikorsky UH-60A Black Hawk of the 101st Airborne Division, US Army, based at Fort Campbell.*

*Sikorsky S-70 (UH-60 Black Hawk)*

*This UH-60 serves with the 377th Medical Detachment at Camp Humphreys, Korea, and wears high-conspicuity yellow stripes to enable it to fly in the DMZ (De-Militarized Zone).*

*A Sikorsky UH-60A Black Hawk of the 17th Army Helicopter Company, 25th Aviation Brigade. The UH-60 is a superb support helicopter, but was initially plagued by unreliability.*

**Specification:** Sikorsky UH-60A Black Hawk
**Origin:** USA
**Type:** combat assault transport helicopter
**Powerplant:** two 1163-kW (1,560-shp) General Electric T700-GE-700 turboshafts
**Performance:** maximum speed 160 kt (296 km/h; 184 mph) at sea level; initial vertical climb rate more than 450 ft (137 m) per minute; service ceiling 19,000 ft (5790 m); range 2221 km (1.380 miles) with maximum internal and external fuel
**Weights:** empty 4819 kg (10,624 lb); mission take-off 7375 kg (16,260 lb); maximum take-off 9185 kg (20,250 lb)
**Dimensions:** main rotor diameter 16.36 m (53 ft 8 in); length, rotors turning 19.76 m (64 ft 10 in); height 5.13 m (16 ft 10 in); main rotor disc area 210.14 m² (2,262.04 sq ft)
**Armament:** one or two side-firing 7.62-mm (0 3-in) M60 machine-guns in cabin, plus Hellfire ASMs, rocket-launcher pods, mine dispensers, jamming flares and chaff dispensers on pylons

# Sikorsky S-70B (SH-60 Seahawk and Ocean Hawk)

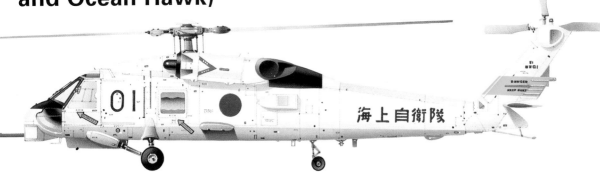

The undoubted success of the US Navy's LAMPS (Light Airborne Multi-Purpose System) helicopter in the ASW/ASST/SAR roles spurred the development of more capable systems. However, the Kaman SH-2F LAMPS Mk I helicopter was considered to be unsuitable to carry more advanced equipment and a LAMPS Mk II system was abandoned pending the availability of a more suitable carrier. In 1977, about a year after the Sikorsky S-70A had been selected by the US Army to meet its UTTAS requirement, the US Navy conducted a similar fly-off and technical evaluation of a developed version of the Boeing Vertol YUH-61A and Sikorsky YUH-60A, selecting the Sikorsky airframe for integration of the LAMPS Mk III system. This last had been under development by IBM Federal Systems Division since 1974, a three-year period which highlights the complexity and, consequently, the cost and capability of this advanced system.

US Navy adoption of the **Sikorsky S-70B** airframe as the **SH-60B Seahawk** LAMPS Mk III carrier resulted in the construction of five YSH-60B prototypes, the first flying initially on 12 December 1979. Over two years of development and operational tests followed before the initial production contract was authorized, the first production helicopter flying on 11 February 1983. HSL-41, based al North Island, San Diego, was the first USN squadron to be equipped, gaining initial operational capability in 1984.

The SH-60B differs in several ways from the US Army's UH-60A, including the introduction of more powerful and navalized engines, automatic main rotor folding, a rotor brake, tail pylon folding, buoyancy features incorporated in the airframe structure, simplified landing gear, a sliding cabin door, rescue hoist and unarmoured pilot/co-pilot seats. Optimum mission capability is provided by increased fuel and hovering inflight-refuelling capability, cargo hook, Recovery, Assist, Secure and Traversing gear to help land and hangar the helicopter in rough seas, search radar, a pylon for MAD gear, a pylon on each side for torpedoes or auxiliary fuel tanks, a sonobuoy launcher, and chin-mounted pods for ESM equipment. Secure communications are provided, plus a data-link between the helicopter and its mother ship, and the LAMPS Mk III system provides comprehensive avionics for the expected roles.

The US Navy hopes to procure a total of 260 SH-60Bs, plus 150 of the **SH-60F Ocean Hawk** inner-zone carrier battle group protection type with the LAMPS Mk III equipment replaced by anti-submarine mission equipment including the Bendix ASQ-13F dunking sonar. There are also the **HH-60H** special warfare support and **HH-60J Jayhawk** SAR types, and S-70B and **S-70C** export versions.

**Sikorsky XSH-60J** Seahawk of the Japanese Maritime Self-Defence Force.

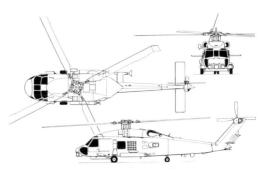

**Sikorsky S-70B (SH-60B Seahawk)**

**Specification:** Sikorsky SH-60B Seahawk
**Origin:** USA
**Type:** ASW/ASST/SAR helicopter
**Powerplant:** two 1260-kW (1,690-shp) General Electric T700-GE-401 turboshafts
**Performance:** maximum speed 126 kt (233 km/h; 145 mph) at 5,000 ft (1525 m); initial vertical climb rate 700 ft (213 m) per minute; combat radius 92.5 km (57.5 miles) with a 3-hour loiter in the patrol area
**Weights:** empty 6191 kg (13,648 lb); maximum take-off 9926 kg (21,884 lb)
**Dimensions:** main rotor diameter 16.36 m (53 ft 8 in); length, rotors turning 19.76 m (64 ft 10 in); height 5.18 m (17 ft 0 in); main rotor disc area 210.14 m² (2,262.04 sq ft)
**Armament:** can include two Mk 46 or Mk 50 Barracuda torpedoes

*This is a SH-60B Seahawk of VX-1, a Patuxent River-based evaluation and experimental unit. The Seahawk is replacing the Kaman SH-2F Seasprite as the US Navy's LAMPS platform.*

*NAS North Island is a major US Navy air base in California, with a large number of resident units, including two SH-60B squadrons, HSL-43 'Battle Cats' and HSL-41.*

# Sikorsky S-76 (H-76 Eagle)

**Role**
Fighter
Close support
Counter-insurgency
Tactical strike
Strategic bomber
Tactical reconnaissance
Strategic reconnaissance
Maritime patrol
Anti-ship strike
Anti-submarine warfare
Search and rescue
Assault transport
Transport
Liaison
Trainer
Inflight-refuelling tanker
Specialized

**Performance**
All-weather capability
Rough field capability
STOL capability
VTOL capability
Airspeed 0-250 mph
Airspeed 250 mph-Mach 1
Airspeed Mach 1 plus
Ceiling 0-20,000 ft
Ceiling 20,000-40,000 ft
Ceiling 40,000ft plus
Range 0-1,000 miles
Range 1,000-3,000 miles
Range 3,000 miles plus

**Weapons**
Air-to-air missiles
Air-to-surface missiles
Cruise missiles
Cannon
Trainable guns
Naval weapons
Nuclear-capable
Rockets
'Smart' weapon kit
Weapon load 0-4,000 lb
Weapon load 4,000-15,000 lb
Weapon load 15,000 lb plus

**Avionics**
Electronic Counter Measures
Electronic Support Measures
Search radar
Fire control radar
Look-down/shoot-down
Terrain-following radar
Forward-looking infra-red
Laser
Television

Seeking to gain a larger share of the growing market for civil helicopters, Sikorsky Aircraft announced in January 1975 the company's intention to develop a new 12-passenger twin-turbine helicopter suitable for a variety of air transport operations. Several months of market research, during which period a number of firm orders were finalized, led to the initiation of construction in May 1976, the second of four prototypes recording the type's maiden flight on 13 March 1977. The helicopter was allocated the designation **Sikorsky S-76**, and though the name Spirit was also used in early promotional stages it was then dropped. The first delivery of a production S-76 was made on 27 February 1979.

The S-76 benefits from the company's research and development activities to evolve an advanced and efficient dynamic system for the Sikorsky UH-60 Black Hawk military helicopter. In addition, design and certification to the requirements of US FAR Pt 29 Category A IFR has ensured that the S-76 is a rugged all-weather helicopter. As flown initially, the S-76 had a powerplant comprising two 485-kW (650-shp) Allison 250-C30 turboshafts mounted above the cabin and driving four-blade main and tail rotors, the latter mounted on the port side of the tail pylon; the tail unit also incorporates an all-moving tailplane. Retractable tricycle landing gear is standard. The cabin has accommodation for a pilot, co-pilot and up to

12 passengers, but there are optional VIP layouts and three 'quick change' kits for conversion to differing air ambulance roles.

The current production version are the **S-76 Mk II**, **S-76B** and **S-76C**, the first an improved version delivered from 1 March 1982, and the latter two version of the S-76 Mk II with two 732-kW (981-shp) Pratt & Whitney Canada PT6B-36A or 539-kW (723-shp) Turbomeca Arriel 1S1 turboshafts respectively. A variant known as the **S-76 Utility** is also available. This last has a more basic interior for utility roles, a strengthened floor and a number of options including non-retractable landing gear with low-pressure tyres for operation in rough terrain. The most important military variants are the **H-76 Eagle** and **H-76N**. The former has armoured crew seats, sliding cabin doors and strengthened floors, and was designed for the airborne assault, air observation, ambulance, evacuation, combat or conventional SAR, gunship, and troop transport/logistic support roles: the major operator is to by South Korea, which plans to acquire 175 such helicopters. The latter, which has secured no orders, is intended for the naval ASV, ASW, SAR and utility roles. For ASV the H-76N would be equipped with Ferranti Seaspray 3 or MEL Super Searcher radar, and would be armed with BAe Sea Skua ASMs. The ASW version would be equipped with dunking sonar and be armed with Gould Mk 46 or Marconi Stingray torpedoes.

*Sikorsky S-76 of the Royal Jordanian air force.*

**Sikorsky S-76**

**The Sikorsky H-76 Eagle** is a dedicated military derivative of the S-76B with mast- or roof-mounted sight, armour, weapons pylons and sophisticated attack avionics.

*This white-painted Sikorsky S-76 Mark II is in service with the Royal Jordanian air force as an air ambulance. The original two S-76s have been sold back to Sikorsky and replaced by newer models.*

## Specification: Sikorsky S-76 Mk II
**Origin:** USA
**Type:** general-purpose all-weather helicopter
**Powerplant:** two 485-kW (650-shp) Allison 250-C30S turboshafts
**Performance:** maximum cruising speed 145 kt (269 km/h; 167 mph); initial climb rate 1,350 ft (411 m) per minute; range 748 km (465 miles) with 12 passengers, standard fuel and 30-minute reserves, or 1112 km (691 miles) with 8 passengers, offshore equipment and auxiliary fuel
**Weights:** empty 2540 kg (5,600 lb); maximum take-off 4672 kg (10,300 lb)
**Dimensions:** main rotor diameter 13.41 m (44 ft 0 in); length, rotors turning 16.00 m (52 ft 6 in); height 4.41 m (14 ft 5.75 in); main rotor disc area 141.26 m² (1,520.53 sq ft)
**Armament:** none

# SOKO G-2A Galeb

*SOKO G-2A Galeb of the Yugoslav air force.*

The Yugoslav aircraft manufacturer SOKO was established in 1951, and in 1957 began the design of an armed jet basic trainer for service with the Jugoslovensko Ratno Vazduhoplovstvo (Yugoslav air force). Of low-wing monoplane configuration and of all-metal construction, the design incorporated an entirely conventional tail unit with a fixed-incidence tailplane, retractable tricycle landing gear, underfuselage door-type airbrakes, and a powerplant comprising one Bristol Siddeley (now Rolls-Royce) Viper turbojet engine. This last was mounted in the rear fuselage and aspirated via an inlet on each side of the fuselage; its fuel was contained in two flexible tanks immediately aft of the cockpits and supplemented by two jettisonable wing tip tanks. The crew of two was seated in tandem on Folland Type 1-B lightweight ejector seats, and the two men were enclosed by separate sideways-opening and jettisonable canopies. The accommodation was heated and ventilated as standard, but an optional air-conditioning system was also available. Avionics were limited to a radio compass and communications transceiver, and full blind-flying instrumentation was also standard. With aerobatics included among

its training roles, the aircraft was stressed to +8/-4 g, and the fuel system was designed to permit 15 seconds of inverted flight. To optimize the aircraft's multi-role capability to the full, there was provision for the installation of a small reconnaissance camera beneath the rear cockpit floor (night photography being made possible by flares carried on the underwing racks), and the type was also equipped to tow air-firing targets.

The first of two prototypes was flown during May 1961, with production for the Yugoslav air force under the designation **SOKO G-2A Galeb** (seagull) starting in 1963. Subsequent foreign interest in the Galeb resulted in the development of an export variant as the **G-2A-E**, first flown in late 1964 and entering production during the following year. This is of the same basic configuration as the G-2A for the Yugoslav air force, but has a more comprehensive UHF/VHF radio transceiver, Marconi AD370B radio compass, an instrument landing system, and for navigational assistance a VOR/LOC installation and marker beacon receiver. In this export version, the Galeb proved popular with several air arms and production continued until 1983.

**Specification:** SOKO G-2A Galeb
**Origin:** Yugoslavia
**Type:** basic trainer
**Powerplant:** one 1134-kg (2,500-lb) dry thrust Rolls Royce Viper 11 Mk 226 turbojet
**Performance:** maximum speed 439 kt (812 km/h; 505 mph) at 20,340 ft (6200 m); maximum cruising speed 394 kt (730 km/h; 454 mph) at 19,685 ft (6000 m); initial climb rate 4,495 ft (1370 m) per minute; service ceiling 39,370 ft (12000 m); range 1240 km (771 miles) with maximum standard fuel
**Weights:** empty 2620 kg (5,776 lb); normal take-off 3374 kg (7,438 lb) for aerobatics; maximum take-off 4300 kg (9,480 lb)
**Dimensions:** span 9.73 m (31 ft 11.1 in); length 10.34 m (33 ft 11.1 in); height 3.28 m (10 ft 9.1 in); wing area 19.43 m² (209.15 sq ft)
**Armament:** two 12.7-mm (0.5-in) machine gun with 80 rounds per gun; provision for 150-kg (331-lb) bomblet containers, 100-kg (220-lb) bombs, 127-mm 5-in) rockets, and 55-mm (2.17-in) rocket-launcher pods carried on underwing racks

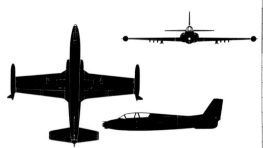

**SOKO G-2A Galeb**

*Flaps and airbrakes extended, this G-2A Galeb is pictured landing at a remote airfield somewhere in Yugoslavia. The Galeb has proved to be a successful and popular trainer.*

*A SOKO Galeb (nearer the camera) takes off in company with a single-seat Jastreb light attack aircraft. The close family resemblance between the two aircraft is immediately apparent.*

**Role**
Fighter
Close support
Counter-insurgency
Tactical strike
Strategic bomber
Tactical reconnaissance
Strategic reconnaissance
Maritime patrol
Anti-ship strike
Anti-submarine warfare
Search and rescue
Assault transport
Transport
Liaison
Trainer
Inflight-refuelling tanker
Specialized

**Performance**
All-weather capability
Rough field capability
STOL capability
VTOL capability
Airspeed 0-250 mph
Airspeed 250 mph-Mach 1
Airspeed Mach 1 plus
Ceiling 0-20,000 ft
Ceiling 20,000-40,000 ft
Ceiling 40,000ft plus
Range 0-1,000 miles
Range 1,000-3,000 miles
Range 3,000 miles plus

**Weapons**
Air-to-air missiles
Air-to-surface missiles
Cruise missiles
Cannon
Trainable guns
Naval weapons
Nuclear-capable
Rockets
'Smart' weapon kit
Weapon load 0-4,000 lb
Weapon load 4,000-15,000 lb
Weapon load 15,000 lb plus

**Avionics**
Electronic Counter Measures
Electronic Support Measures
Search radar
Fire control radar
Look-down/shoot-down
Terrain-following radar
Forward-looking infra-red
Laser
Television

# SOKO G-4 Super Galeb

*SOKO G-4 Super Galeb of the Yugoslav air force.*

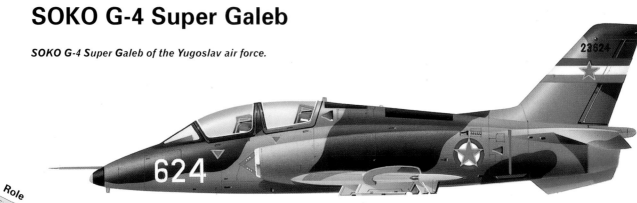

## Role

Fighter
Close support
Counter-insurgency
Tactical strike
Strategic bomber
Tactical reconnaissance
Strategic reconnaissance
Maritime patrol
Anti-ship strike
Anti-submarine warfare
Search and rescue
Assault transport
Transport
Liaison
Trainer
Inflight-refuelling tanker
Specialized

## Performance

All-weather capability
Rough field capability
STOL capability
VTOL capability
Airspeed 0-250 mph
Airspeed 250 mph-Mach 1
Airspeed Mach 1 plus
Ceiling 0-20,000 ft
Ceiling 20,000-40,000 ft
Ceiling 40,000ft plus
Range 0-1,000 miles
Range 1,000-3,000 miles
Range 3,000 miles plus

## Weapons

Air-to-air missiles
Air-to-surface missiles
Cruise missiles
Cannon
Trainable guns
Naval weapons
Nuclear-capable
Rockets
'Smart' weapon kit
Weapon load 0-4,000 lb
Weapon load 4,000-15,000 lb
Weapon load 15,000 lb plus

## Avionics

Electronic Counter Measures
Electronic Support Measures
Search radar
Fire control radar
Look-down/shoot-down
Terrain-following radar
Forward-looking infra-red
Laser
Television

Long before production of the G-2A/G-2A-E Galeb ended, SOKO began the design of an improved trainer/light attack aircraft which was intended to replace the G-2A (as well as the Lockheed T-33) in basic and advanced training units of the Yugoslav air force. The new aircraft was designated **SOKO G-4 Super Galeb** (gull), retention of the name Galeb giving the impression that this new aircraft is a derivative of the G-2 despite the fact that it is of wholly different design. While the low-wing monoplane configuration is retained, the wing is entirely new, incorporating 22° of sweepback at quarter chord; the tail unit also has all-swept surfaces, introduces an all-moving tailplane and houses a raking parachute at the base of the rudder; both the ailerons and anhedralled tailplane halves are hydraulically powered and incorporate artificial feel. Retractable tricycle landing gear is retained but, in addition to being suitable for operation at a gross weight some 50 per cent higher than that of the G-2A, it also has powered steering for the nosewheel. The fuselage, still housing a Rolls-Royce Viper turbojet at the rear and with its inlets on each side, is very different forward to provide a tandem cockpit of far more modern concept, which has full blind-flying instrumentation in each cockpit, and is pressurized and air-conditioned as standard. Pupil (forward) and instructor are seated on Martin-Baker ejector seats which can be either Mk J8 (zero height/90 kt) or Mk

J10 (zero-zero), and enclosed by individual side-opening transparencies. The rear seat in raised (in this instance by 0.25 m/10 in) above that of the pupil to provide the instructor with a better field of vision.

The G-4's standard avionics fit is far more comprehensive than that of the G-2A, comprising DME, radio altimeter, radio compass, VHF communications transceiver, VOR/ILS and VOR marker beacon, but there is ample room for variations and additions to suit individual customer requirements. Structural changes and strengthening mean that, by comparison with the G-2A, the empty equipped weight of the G-4 has risen by some 25 per cent. However, maximum take-off weight is approaching 50 per cent higher, and this has given scope for heavier and significantly more comprehensive armament.

The prototype flew initially on 17 July 1978 and was followed on 17 December 1980 by the first of six generally similar G-4PPP pre-production aircraft. All of these early aircraft had conventional tailplanes and elevators, but the production aircraft introduced all-moving horizontal tail surfaces as described above. The first G-4 production aircraft flew in 1983, and numbers had been delivered before the break-up of Yugoslavia and the effective end of the Super Galeb programme that was also to have included a G-4M variant with a more capable nav/attack system and provision for more externally carried weapons.

**SOKO G-4 Super Galeb**

*From some angles the SOKO G-4 Super Galeb resembles the British Aerospace Hawk, although the British aircraft has a more distinctively stepped rear cockpit.*

*The SOKO G-4 Super Galeb inherited little from the earlier Galeb which it was designed to replace in the advanced training role. Substantial numbers were ordered by the Yugoslav air force before the country's dissolution.*

## Specification: SOKO G-4 Super Galeb .
**Origin:** Yugoslavia
**Type:** basic trainer/light attack aircraft
**Powerplant:** one 1814-kg (4,000-lb) dry thrust Rolls Royce Viper Mk 632 turbojet
**Performance:** maximum speed 491 kt (910 km/h; 665 mph) at 13,125 ft (4000 m); initial climb rate 5,905 ft (1800m) per minute; service ceiling 42,160 ft (12850 m); range 1900 km (1,180 miles) with internal fuel
**Weights:** empty 3172 kg (6,993 lb); maximum take-off 6300 kg (13,889 lb)
**Dimensions:** span 9.88 m (32 ft 5 in); length including probe 12.25 m (40 ft 2.25 in); height 4.30 m (14 ft 1.25 in); wing area 19.50 m² (209.9 sq ft)
**Armament:** provision for one 23-mm GSh-23L two-barrel cannon with 200 rounds; provision for 2053 kg (4,526 lb) of disposable stores, including AAMs, bombs, cluster bombs, dispenser weapons, napalm tanks, large-calibre rockets, rocket-launcher pods, drop tanks and ECM pods, carried on four external hardpoints

# SOKO J-1, RJ-1 and TJ-1 Jastreb

*SOKO J-1 Jastreb of the Yugoslav air force.*

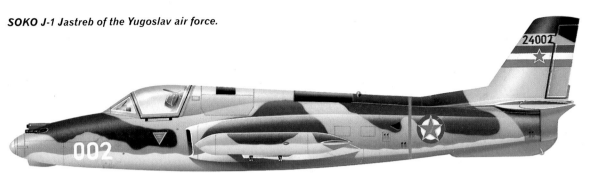

In service with the Yugoslav air force, the G-2A Galeb soon proved its reliability, and thought was therefore given to the development of a single-seat version optimized for light attack or reconnaissance. Thus the airframe of the Galeb was adopted as the basis for this new version with suitable modification to equip it for the new roles. The simplest part of the conversion was the change that from two- to single-seat accommodation, the forward cockpit of the Galeb being retained and the rear cockpit merely faired over by sheet metal. Little change was made to the front cockpit, the pilot still being seated on a Folland Type 1-B ejector seat, but there were detail revisions to cater for alternative equipment and the changed roles.

For use as a light attack aircraft it was necessary to make provision for increased and more varied armament, which meant operation at a higher gross weight. In consequence an uprated version of the standard Rolls-Royce Viper turbojet was introduced, giving 20 per cent more thrust than the Viper 11 Mk 22-6, and at the same time provision was made for two 454-kg (1,000-lb) thrust JATO rockets to be mounted beneath the fuselage to give more thrust, if needed, at take-off or during flight. Apart from local airframe strengthening, installation of a braking parachute and the introduction of uprated wing hardpoints for heavier weapon loads,

there was little other change but for a revised electrical system to give the Viper self-start capability.

Five versions entered production, the first two (for the Yugoslav air force) being the **SOKO J-1 Jastreb** (hawk) attack and **RJ-1** tactical reconnaissance aircraft, with export equivalents designated **J-1-E** and **RJ-1-E** respectively, plus a **TJ-1** trainer for the Yugoslav air force. The J-1 and RJ-1 both had a VHF transceiver, radio compass and full IFR instrumentation, and the RJ-1 differed by having a reconnaissance installation comprising one camera in the lower fuselage and one camera in the nose of each tip tank, the latter also being available for the domestic and export attack variants. The RJ-1 and RJ-1-E also differed from the attack versions by having only four underwing hardpoints, primarily for flash bombs, but alternatively could carry HE bombs in the form of two 250-kg (551-lb) weapons inboard and two 150-kg (331-lb) weapons outboard. The J-1-E and RJ-1-E had similar nav/com equipment to the export G-2A-E Galeb, but night reconnaissance capability for the RJ-1-E was provided by a fourth camera (Vinten 1025/527) in the fuselage. Both J-1 and J-1-E carry the same armament, as detailed in the specification below. The TJ-1 differed from the J-1 only by having a second cockpit and the installation of a marker beacon receiver and an intercom system.

## Specification: SOKO J-1 Jastreb

**Origin:** Yugoslavia
**Type:** light attack aircraft
**Powerplant:** one 1361-kg (3,000-lb) dry thrust Rolls-Royce Viper Mk 531 turbojet
**Performance:** maximum speed 443 kt (820 km/h; 510 mph) at 19,685 ft (6000 m); cruising speed 399 kt (740 km/h; 460 mph) at 16,405 ft (5000 m); initial climb rate 4,135 ft (1260 m) per minute; service ceiling 39,370 ft (12000 m); range 1520 km (944 miles) with maximum standard fuel
**Weights:** empty 2820 kg (6,217 lb); maximum take-off 5100 kg( 11,244 lb)
**Dimensions:** span over tip tanks 11.68 m (38 ft 3.8 in); length 10.88 m (35 ft 8.3 in); height 3.64 m (11 ft 11.3in); wing area 19.43 m² (209. 15 sq ft)
**Armament:** three 12.7-mm (0.5-in) machine guns with 135 rounds per guns; provision for 500 kg (1,102 lb) of disposable stores, including bombs, bomblet containers, flares, rocket-launcher pods and gun pods carried on two inboard hardpoints, and for six 127-mm (5-in) air-to-surface rockets on outboard attachments

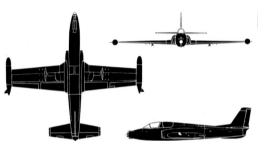

**SOKO J- 1 Jastreb**

*A Yugoslav Jastreb shows off its planform for the camera. From this angle the aircraft could easily be mistaken for a Lockheed T-33 Shooting Star.*

*The Jastreb can carry a wide range of external ordnance on its eight underwing hardpoints, some of it locally produced. Three 12.7-mm (0.5-in) machine guns are carried in the nose.*

## Role

Fighter
Close support
Counter-insurgency
Tactical strike
Strategic bomber
Strategic reconnaissance
Tactical reconnaissance
Strategic reconnaissance
Maritime patrol
Anti-ship strike
Anti-submarine warfare
Search and rescue
Assault transport
Transport
Liaison
Trainer
Inflight-refuelling tanker
Specialized

## Performance

All-weather capability
Rough field capability
STOL capability
VTOL capability
Airspeed 0-250 mph
Airspeed 250 mph-Mach 1
Airspeed Mach 1 plus
Ceiling 0-20,000 ft
Ceiling 20,000-40,000 ft
Ceiling 40,000ft plus
Range 0-1,000 miles
Range 1,000-3,000 miles
Range 3,000 miles plus

## Weapons

Air-to-air missiles
Air-to-surface missiles
Cruise missiles
Cannon
Trainable guns
Naval weapons
Nuclear-capable
Rockets
'Smart' weapon kit
Weapon load 0-4,000 lb
Weapon load 4,000-15,000 lb
Weapon load 15,000 lb plus

## Avionics

Electronic Counter Measures
Electronic Support Measures
Search radar
Fire control radar
Look-down/shoot-down
Terrain-following radar
Forward-looking infra-red
Laser
Television

# SOKO J-20 Kraguj

**SOKO J-20 Kraguj of the Yugoslav air force.**

## Role
Fighter
Close support
Counter-insurgency
Tactical strike
Strategic bomber
Tactical reconnaissance
Strategic reconnaissance
Maritime patrol
Anti-ship strike
Anti-submarine warfare
Search and rescue
Assault transport
Transport
Liaison
Trainer
Inflight-refuelling tanker
Specialized

## Performance
All-weather capability
Rough field capability
STOL capability
VTOL capability
Airspeed 0-250 mph
Airspeed 250 mph-Mach 1
Airspeed Mach 1 plus
Ceiling 0-20,000 ft
Ceiling 20,000-40,000 ft
Ceiling 40,000ft plus
Range 0-1,000 miles
Range 1,000-3,000 miles
Range 3,000 miles plus

## Weapons
Air-to-air missiles
Air-to-surface missiles
Cruise missiles
Cannon
Trainable guns
Naval weapons
Nuclear-capable
Rockets
'Smart' weapon kit
Weapon load 0-4,000 lb
Weapon load 4,000-15,000 lb
Weapon load 15,000 lb plus

## Avionics
Electronic Counter Measures
Electronic Support Measures
Search radar
Fire control radar
Look-down/shoot-down
Terrain-following radar
Forward-looking infra-red
Laser
Television

In the early 1950s the Fletcher Aviation Corporation in the USA designed and developed a lightweight single-seat monoplane which was purpose-built for small air arms to deploy in the counter-insurgency role. Designated as the FD-25 Defender it pioneered a new role for lightplanes, its armament comprising two wing-mounted 7.62-mm (0.3-in) machine guns and two underwing racks for bombs of up to 113 kg (250 lb) in weight, or two napalm tanks, or two rocket-launcher pods.

Although the concept was valid, few air arms with such a requirement had the capital for new-build aircraft, and many early COIN aircraft were conversions of single-seat fighters that might, otherwise, have found their way to the scrap heap.

In the mid-1960s the Yugoslav air force expressed interest in an aircraft suitable for the COIN role, and SOKO began the design of such an aircraft, the prototype reportedly flying for the first time during 1966. Considerable effort had been expended at the design stage to ensure that the structure and systems would be uncomplicated, and thus cheaper to build and, perhaps even more important, easy to maintain. The aircraft was of low-wing monoplane configuration and of all-metal construction, the wing incorporating fixed leading-edge slots and manually operated trailing-edge flaps. The fuselage was a stressed-skin metal structure, mounting at the rear a conventional tail unit, and was carried on simple non-retractable tailwheel landing gear. The accommodation was also somewhat austere, the pilot being seated beneath a rearward-sliding bubble canopy and having little more in the way of comprehensive equipment than full blind-flying instrumentation and a VHF transceiver: creature comforts were provided by a heating and ventilation system.

Most important for the COIN role was the provision of adequate armament, in this instance comprising a 7.62-mm (0.3-in) machine gun with 650 rounds mounted in each wing outboard of the propeller disc, and six underwing hardpoints. Under wing the inboard point was stressed to carry a bomb of up to 100-kg (220-lb) weight, or a 150-litre (33-Imp gal) napalm tank, or a cluster of small bombs, or launcher for 12 rockets. The two remaining hardpoints under each wing were each able to carry 127-mm (5-in) or 55-mm (2.17-in) air-to-surface rockets.

Production aircraft, designated **SOKO J-20 Kraguj**, are reported to have entered service with the Yugoslav air force during 1968, but were soon seen by this air arm to be of limited capability. This realization restricted production to about 30 aircraft.

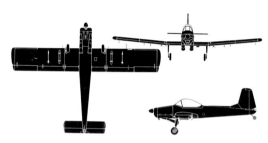

**SOKO J-20 Kraguj**

**The piston-engined, single-seat Kraguj was designed from the start as a COIN aircraft, and is thus cleared to carry a variety of underwing weapon loads, albeit of the lighter types.**

*A Yugoslav SOKO J-20 Kraguj shares the apron with a pair of Galeb jet trainers. Production of the Kraguj was limited to about 30 aircraft when it was realized that jets were more versatile.*

## Specification: SOKO J-20 Kraguj
**Origin:** Yugoslavia
**Type:** single-seat COIN aircraft
**Powerplant:** one 254-kW (340-hp) Avco Lycoming GSO-480-B1A6 flat-six piston engine
**Performance:** maximum speed 159 kt (295 km/h; 183 mph) at 4,920 ft (1500 m); initial climb rate 1,575 ft (480 m) per minute; range 800 km (497 miles) with maximum standard fuel
**Weights:** empty 1130 kg (2,491 lb); maximum take-off 1624 kg (3,580 lb)
**Dimensions:** span 10.64 m (34 ft 10.9 in); length 7.93 m (26 ft 0.2 in); height 3.00 m (9 ft 10.1 in); wing area 17.0 m² (182.99 sq ft)
**Armament:** see text

# SOKO J-22 Orao and Avioane IAR-93

*Avioane IAR-93 of the Romanian air force.*

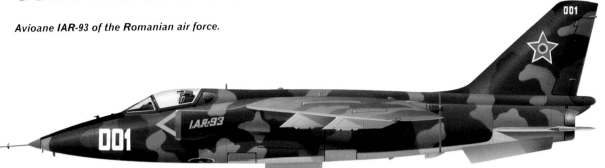

With a joint requirement for a twin-jet close-support and ground-attack aircraft for service with their air forces, Romania and Yugoslavia decided (however unlikely this union may seem) to collaborate in the design and development of such an aircraft. The national companies selected for its construction were the IAv at Craiova (later Avioane) in Romania and SOKO in Yugoslavia. Unusually, responsibility for the initial design, which began in 1970, was not that of the manufacturers, but of teams at the Institual de Aviatie in Romania and the Vazduhoplovno Tehnicki Institut in Yugoslavia.

The aircraft is a shoulder-wing monoplane whose wing design includes 35° sweepback at quarter chord, hydraulically actuated leading- edge slats and trailing-edge flaps, two boundary-layer fences on the upper surface of each wing, and powered ailerons. The fuselage incorporates hydraulically actuated door-type airbrakes, is carried on retractable tricycle landing gear, and has a tail unit with swept surfaces, the low-set all-moving tailplane and rudder being actuated hydraulically. An inlet on each side of the fuselage feeds air to the two licence-built Rolls-Royce Viper turbojets in the rear fuselage: built by Turbomecanica/Orao, these can be non-afterburning Viper Mk 632 41Rs each of

1814-kg (4,000-lb) thrust, or afterburning Viper Mk 633-41s each of 2268-kg (5,000-lb) thrust. According to version, there are single-seat or tandem two-seat cockpits, in both cases with ejector seat(s), in pressurized and air-conditioned accommodation.

Early events in each country took place simultaneously: these included initiation of the manufacture of two single-seat prototypes in 1972; the first flights of these two aircraft on 31 October 1974; and the first flights of the two-seat prototypes on 29 January 1977. Manufacture of initial batches of 15 pre-production aircraft began in 1977, first flights being made in 1978. Romanian production is of the **Avioane IAR-93A** with the Viper Mk 632 as 26 single- and 10 two-seat aircraft, and of the **IAR-93B** with the Viper Mk 633 to the extent of 165 single- and two-seat aircraft. Yugoslav production has been more complex, resulting the ordering of the following: 15 **SOKO IJ-22 Orao 1** (eagle) single- and **INJ-22 Orao 1** two-seat pre-production tactical reconnaissance and training aircraft with the Viper Mk 632, 35 **NJ-22 Orao 2** production two-seat tactical reconnaissance aircraft with the Viper Mk 632 or Mk 633 turbojet, and 165 **J-22 Orao 2** production single-seat attack aircraft, of which perhaps 80 were delivered, with the Viper Mk 632 or Mk 633 turbojet.

## Specification: SOKO J-22 Orao
**Origin:** Romania and Yugoslavia
**Type:** single-seat attack aircraft
**Powerplant:** two 2268-kg (5,000-lb) afterburning thrust Turbomecanica/Orao Viper Mk 633-41 turbojets
**Performance:** maximum speed 610 kt (1130 km/h; 702 mph) at high altitude; initial climb rate 17,520 ft (5340 m) per minute; service ceiling 49,210 ft (15000 m); tactical radius 460 km (286 miles) on a hi-lo-hi mission with four cluster bombs and one drop tank
**Weights:** empty 5500 kg (12,125 lb); maximum take-off 11080 kg (24,427 lb)
**Dimensions:** span 9.30 m (30 ft 6.25 in); length including probe 14.90 m (48 ft 10.625 in); height 4.52 m (14 ft 10 in); wing area 26.0 m² (279.86 sq ft)
**Armament:** two 23-mm GSh-23L two-barrel with 200 rounds per gun; provision for 2800 kg (6,173 lb) of disposable stores, including AAMs, ASMs, bombs, cluster bombs, weapon dispensers, napalm tanks, rocket-launcher pods and drop tanks, carried on five external hardpoints

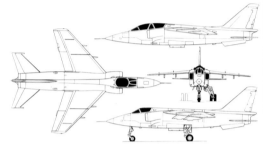

**SOKO J-22 Orao**

*This is a single-seat Avioane IAR-93A of the Romanian air force. Twenty of these non-afterburning aircraft were followed by 165 examples of the IAR-93B afterburning type.*

*Yugoslavia ordered the pre-production Orao 1 in single/two-seat non-afterburning versions, and the Orao 2 in single/two-seat training/operational versions with non-afterburning/ afterburning engines.*

### Role
Fighter
Close support
Counter-insurgency
Tactical strike
Strategic bomber
Tactical reconnaissance
Strategic reconnaissance
Maritime patrol
Anti-ship strike
Anti-submarine warfare
Search and rescue
Assault transport
Transport
Liaison
Trainer
Inflight-refuelling tanker
Specialized

### Performance
All-weather capability
Rough field capability
STOL capability
VTOL capability
Airspeed 0-250 mph
Airspeed 250 mph-Mach 1
Airspeed Mach 1 plus
Airspeed 0-20,000 ft
Ceiling 0-20,000 ft
Ceiling 20,000-40,000 ft
Ceiling 40,000ft plus
Range 0-1,000 miles
Range 1,000-3,000 miles
Range 3,000 miles plus

### Weapons
Air-to-air missiles
Air-to-surface missiles
Cruise missiles
Cannon
Trainable guns
Naval weapons
Nuclear-capable
Rockets
'Smart' weapon kit
Weapon load 0-4,000 lb
Weapon load 4,000-15,000 lb
Weapon load 15,000 lb plus

### Avionics
Electronic Counter Measures
Electronic Support Measures
Search radar
Fire control radar
Look-down/shoot-down
Terrain-following radar
Forward-looking infra-red
Laser
Television

# Sukhoi Su-15 and Su-21 'Flagon'

*Sukhoi Su-15 'Flagon-F' of the Soviet air force.*

## Role
Fighter
Close support
Counter-insurgency
Tactical strike
Strategic bomber
Tactical reconnaissance
Strategic reconnaissance
Maritime patrol
Anti-ship strike
Anti-submarine warfare
Search and rescue
Assault transport
Transport
Liaison
Trainer
Inflight-refuelling tanker
Specialized

## Performance
All-weather capability
Rough field capability
STOL capability
VTOL capability
Airspeed 0-250 mph
Airspeed 250 mph-Mach 1
Airspeed Mach 1 plus
Ceiling 0-20,000 ft
Ceiling 20,000-40,000 ft
Ceiling 40,000ft plus
Range 0-1,000 miles
Range 1,000-3,000 miles
Range 3,000 miles plus

## Weapons
Air-to-air missiles
Air-to-surface missiles
Cruise missiles
Cannon
Trainable guns
Naval weapons
Nuclear-capable
Rockets
'Smart' weapon kit
Weapon load 0-4,000 lb
Weapon load 4,000-15,000 lb
Weapon load 15,000 lb plus

## Avionics
Electronic Counter Measures
Electronic Support Measures
Search radar
Fire control radar
Look-down/shoot-down
Terrain-following radar
Forward-looking infra-red
Laser
Television

Western observers of the Soviet Aviation Day display in July 1967 were intrigued by 10 delta-winged pre-production aircraft of an unidentified type. The wing and tail unit of this type suggested a relationship to the earlier Sukhoi Su-9 and Su-11, and it was therefore assumed that they had a common ancestry with that bureau's T-series delta-winged prototypes. This was confirmed when the **Sukhoi Su-15** entered service later in 1967 in the form of a small batch of pilot production interceptors with a powerplant of two 6200-kg (13,668-lb) afterburning thrust Tumanskii R-11F2S turbojets, Uragan 5B radar with its antenna in a conical rather than the more standard ogival nosecone, AA-3 'Anab' AAMs, and apparently the wings of the Su-11 with straight leading edges for a span of 9.30 m (30 ft 6.15 in). NATO accorded the reporting name **'Flagon-A'** to this type, and 'Flagon-B' to the Su-15VD (otherwise Su-15DPD) experimental STOVL development with a double-delta wing and part of the fuselage fuel tankage replaced by a battery of three Koliesov vertical-lift turbojets.

The **Su-15U 'Flagon-C'** was the combat-capable conversion trainer derived from the 'Flagon-D' initial-production single-seater but fitted with two separate cockpits, though these were not staggered vertically and required that the instructor be provided with a periscope for forward vision. The **Su-15F** or **Su-15MF 'Flagon-D'** was first true production model, based on the 'Flagon-A' but having deeper inlets, probably signifying the adoption of a revised powerplant in the form of two R-13F2-300 turbojets. The **Su-15TM 'Flagon-E'** improved version of the 'Flagon-D' was introduced in 1973 with compound-sweep wings of greater span carrying two additional hardpoints, internal fuel tankage increased by the adoption of an integral tank in the vertical tail surface, provision for larger ventral drop tanks, upgraded avionics, twin nosewheels, and the Tyfon ('Twin Scan') interception radar.

The **Su-21bis 'Flagon-F'** was the definitive single-seat model introduced from 1975 with a low-drag ogival rather than conical radome for a larger radar providing limited look-down/shoot-down capability. Finally, the **Su-21Ubis 'Flagon-G'** was the two-seat conversion trainer based on the 'Flagon-F' with a periscope-fitted rear cockpit behind the standard cockpit. The type had been completely retired by the beginning of the 1990s.

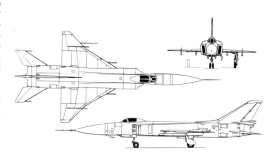

**Sukhoi Su-21bis 'Flagon-F'**

*An unusual dark camouflage colour scheme is worn by this Su-21bis 'Flagon-F', seen taking off from an airfield in the western USSR. The aircraft is unarmed, although pylons are fitted.*

*This 'Flagon-F', intercepted over the Baltic by the Swedish Coast Guard, carries AA-3 'Anabs' under the outer wings and twin cannon pods under the fuselage.*

## Specification: Sukhoi Su-21bis 'Flagon-F' (estimated)
**Origin:** USSR (now CIS)
**Type:** single-seat all-weather interceptor
**Powerplant:** two 7200-kg (15,873-lb) afterburning thrust Tumanskii R-13F2-300 turbojets
**Performance:** maximum speed Mach 2.1 or 1204 kt (2230 km/h; 1,386 mph) above 36,090 ft (11000 m); climb to 36,090 ft (11000 m) in 2 minutes 30 seconds; service ceiling 65,615 ft (20000 m); combat radius 725 km (450 miles)
**Weights:** maximum take-off 16000 kg (35,274 lb)
**Dimensions:** span 10.53 m (34 ft 6.6 in); length 20.50 m (67 ft 3.l in); wing area about 36.0 m² (387.5 sq ft)
**Armament:** four underwing pylons carrying two AA-3 'Anab' medium-range AAMs outboard and two AA-8 'Aphid' short-range AAMs inboard, plus two underfuselage pylons for 23-mm GSh-23L two-barrel cannon pods or auxiliary fuel tanks

# Sukhoi Su-17 'Fitter'

*Sukhoi Su-17M-4 'Fitter-K' of the Soviet air force.*

In the early 1960s the USSR learned that the UK and USA had solved the early problems relating to variable-geometry aircraft and began development in this field. The Sukhoi Su-7 was a prime candidate for VG, but conversion of the existing wing was seen as a major problem, leading to the adoption of a new wing centre section with pivoting outer panels at about half-span. Tested on the S-221 or Su-7IG (Izmenyaemaya Geometriya or VG) R&D prototype, which was first flown on 2 August 1966, these wings gave improved take-off and landing performance plus an increase in range. NATO allocated the reporting name **'Fitter-B'** to this version of the Sukhoi Su-7, but did not expect the type would enter service. This conclusion proved wrong, the West discovering some five years later that this initial **Sukhoi Su-17** (retaining the Su-7's Lyul'ka AL-7F engine) was in Soviet service in small numbers. But before that, the first true production version had entered service as the **Su-17M** with the more efficient AL-21F-3 engine.

The Su-17M was duly allocated the NATO reporting name 'Fitter-C' and served with the Soviet air force and navy. This model was followed by the similar **Su-17M-2 'Fitter-D'** with a slightly lengthened and drooped nose,

terrain-avoidance radar in an undernose pod and a laser rangefinder within the inlet centrebody. The name **'Fitter-E'** identifies the **Su-17UM-2** tandem two-seat trainer, similar to the 'Fitter-D' but without the undernose pod and with a wider and deeper dorsal fairing to contain extra fuel. The reporting name **'Fitter-G'** identifies the **Su-17UM-3** trainer version of the **Su-17M-3 'Fitter-H'** improved single-seater with internal Doppler navigation, taller vertical tail surface and provision for two AA-8 'Aphid' AAMs. First identified in 1984, the final development of the Su-17 was the **Su-17M-4** that has the reporting name **'Fitter-K'**. This remained in production to the late 1980s as a development of the Su-17M-3 with a small cooling air inlet at the base of the fin and armament capability including launchers for four 325-mm (12.8-in) S-25 rockets or four SPPU-22 23-mm ground-attack cannon pods, two of them installed to fire rearward. All the foregoing Su-17 versions serve, or have served, with the Soviet air arms; some 1,060 were delivered for Soviet service, but many of these are now thought to have been put in store by the CIS air force. About 165 Su-17M-3 and Su-17M-4 aircraft are equipped for carriage of a centreline tactical reconnaissance pod.

## Specification: Sukhoi Su-17 'Fitter-C'

**Origin:** USSR (now CIS)
**Type:** single-seat ground-attack fighter
**Powerplant:** one 11250-kg (24,802-lb) afterburning thrust Lyul'ka AL-21F-3 turbojet
**Performance:** maximum speed Mach 2.09 or 1,198 kt (2220 km/h; 1,380 mph) at high altitude; initial climb rate 45,275 ft (13800 m) per minute; service ceiling 49,865 ft (15200 m) combat radius 675 km (419 miles) on a hi-lo-hi mission with 2000 kg (4,409 lb) of bombs and two auxiliary fuel tanks
**Weights:** empty 9500kg (20,944 lb); maximum take-off 19500 kg (42,990 lb)
**Dimensions:** span 13.80 m (45 ft 3 in) spread and 10.00 m (32 ft 10 in) swept; length including probes 18.75 m(61 ft 6.2 in); height 5.00 m (16 ft 5 in); wing area 40.0 m² (430.0 sq ft) spread
**Armament:** two 30-mm NR-30 with 80 rounds per gun; provision for 4250 kg (9,370 lb) of disposable stores, including tactical nuclear weapons, AAMs, ASMs, guided bombs, bombs, cluster bombs, dispenser weapons, napalm tanks, large-calibre rockets, rocket-launcher pods, cannon pods, drop tanks and ECM pods, carried on nine external hardpoints

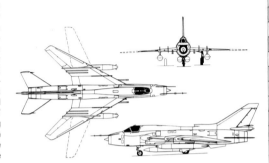

**Sukhoi Su- 17M-4 'Fitter-K'**

*Poland and East Germany were early recipients of the full-standard 'Fitter-K', having previously operated only simplified export versions of this powerful strike fighter.*

*Four large underwing fuel tanks usefully extend the range of the 'Fitter'. Some export variants of the 'Fitter' have the Tumanskii R-29B in place of the Lyul'ka AL-21 engine.*

## Role

- Fighter
- Close support
- Counter-insurgency
- Tactical strike
- Strategic bomber
- Tactical reconnaissance
- Strategic reconnaissance
- Maritime patrol
- Anti-ship strike
- Anti-submarine warfare
- Search and rescue
- Assault transport
- Transport
- Liaison
- Trainer
- Inflight-refuelling tanker
- Specialized

## Performance

- All-weather capability
- Rough field capability
- STOL capability
- VTOL capability
- Airspeed 0-250 mph
- Airspeed 250 mph-Mach 1
- Airspeed Mach 1 plus
- Ceiling 0-20,000 ft
- Ceiling 20,000-40,000 ft
- Ceiling 40,000ft plus
- Range 0-1,000 miles
- Range 1,000-3,000 miles
- Range 3,000 miles plus

## Weapons

- Air-to-air missiles
- Air-to-surface missiles
- Cruise missiles
- Cannon
- Trainable guns
- Naval weapons
- Nuclear-capable
- Rockets
- 'Smart' weapon kit
- Weapon load 0-4,000 lb
- Weapon load 4,000-15,000 lb
- Weapon load 15,000 lb plus

## Avionics

- Electronic Counter Measures
- Electronic Support Measures
- Search radar
- Fire control radar
- Look-down/shoot-down
- Terrain-following radar
- Forward-looking infra-red
- Laser
- Television

263

# Sukhoi Su-20 and Su-22 'Fitter'

*Sukhoi Su-22 'Fitter-F' of the Force Aérea Populaire de Angola.*

## Role

Fighter
Close support
Counter-insurgency
Tactical strike
Strategic bomber
Tactical reconnaissance
Strategic reconnaissance
Maritime patrol
Anti-ship strike
Anti-submarine warfare
Search and rescue
Assault transport
Transport
Liaison
Trainer
Inflight-refuelling tanker
Specialized

## Performance

All-weather capability
Rough field capability
STOL capability
VTOL capability
Airspeed 0-250 mph
Airspeed 250 mph-Mach 1
Airspeed Mach 1 plus
Ceiling 0-20,000 ft
Ceiling 20,000-40,000 ft
Ceiling 40,000ft plus
Range 0-1,000 miles
Range 1,000-3,000 miles
Range 3,000 miles plus

## Weapons

Air-to-air missiles
Air-to-surface missiles
Cruise missiles
Cannon
Trainable guns
Naval weapons
Nuclear-capable
Rockets
'Smart' weapon kit
Weapon load 0-4,000 lb
Weapon load 4,000-15,000 lb
Weapon load 15,000 lb plus

## Avionics

Electronic Counter Measures
Electronic Support Measures
Search radar
Fire control radar
Look-down/shoot-down
Terrain-following radar
Forward-looking infra-red
Laser
Television

The Su-17 was an aircraft type likely to appeal also to those nations that relied upon the USSR for military equipment and, at quite an early date, the Su-17M 'Fitter-C' was made available for export under the designation **Sukhoi Su-20**. This differed little from the Su-17M of the Soviet air force and had the same powerplant but, as with most export variants of Soviet aircraft, a reduced standard of equipment. There was also an **Su-20R** reconnaissance version.

The next version made available for export was generally similar to the Su-17M-2 'Fitter-D' but, instead of being designated Su-20 like the Su-17M export variant, was found to be designated **Su-22**. It had a modified undernose pod for electronics, retained a gun in each wing root and could be armed with AA-2 'Atoll' air-to-air missiles: sharp-eyed observers also noted that whereas the Su-17s of the Soviet air force had a rear fuselage of basically constant diameter, the Su-22 had a bulged section which suggested that an engine of larger diameter might have been installed. It was learned later that the deduction had been correct, the Lyul'ka turbojet being replaced by a Khachaturov R-

29BS-300 similar to that which powers the Mikoyan-Gurevich MiG-27; this first Su-22 was thus allocated the separate NATO reporting name **'Fitter-F'**. The need for an export version of the two-seat Su-17UM-2 resulted in production of the **Su-22U** that shares the 'Fitter-E' designation, and apart from having the R-29B installed it differed very little from the original model. The improved Su-17M-3 also became a candidate for production in an export version with the R-29B engine, resulting in the **Su-22M-3 'Fitter-J'**. This also has increased fuel capacity and a revised dorsal fin, but whereas the Su-17M-3 can be armed with an air-to-surface missile, the Su-22M-3 is equipped to carry the AA-2 'Atoll' air-to-air missile. The two-seat counterpart to the Su-22M-3 was the **Su-22UM-3K 'Fitter-G'** based on the Su-17UM-3 and delivered with either the AL-21F-3 or R-29B engine. The final version of the Su-22 family was the Su-22M-4 version of the Su-17M-4, which shares the 'Fitter-K' reporting name and retains the AL-21F-3 engine of the original Soviet model. These export versions arc in service with several air arms, but production figures are not known.

## Specification: Sukhoi Su-20 'Fitter-C'
**Origin:** USSR (now CIS)
**Type:** single-seat ground-attack fighter
**Powerplant:** one 11250-kg (24,802-lb) afterburning thrust Lyul'ka AL-21F-3 turbojet
**Performance:** maximum speed Mach 2.09 or 1,198 kt (2220 km/h; 1,380 mph) at high altitude; initial climb rate 45,275 ft (13800 m) per minute; service ceiling 49,865 ft (15200 m) combat radius 675 km (419 miles) on a hi-lo-hi mission with 2000 kg (4,409 lb) of bombs and two auxiliary fuel tanks
**Weights:** empty 9500kg (20,944 lb); maximum take-off 19500 kg (42,990 lb)
**Dimensions:** span 13.80 m (45 ft 3 in) spread and 10.00 m (32 ft 10 in) swept; length including probes 18.75 m(61 ft 6.2 in); height 5.00 m (16 ft 5 in); wing area 40.0 m² (430.0 sq ft) spread
**Armament:** two 30-mm NR-30 with 80 rounds per gun; provision for 4250 kg (9,370 lb) of disposable stores, including tactical nuclear weapons, AAMs, ASMs, guided bombs, bombs, cluster bombs, dispenser weapons, napalm tanks, large-calibre rockets, rocket-launcher pods, cannon pods, drop tanks and ECM pods, carried on nine external hardpoints

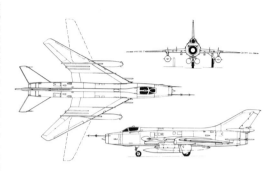

*Sukhoi Su-20 'Fitter-C'*

*Armed Su-22 'Fitter-Fs' await their pilots at Lima. The aircraft have proved unreliable and maintenance-heavy in Peruvian service.*

*This Su-22 'Fitter-F' of the Libyan air force was intercepted over the Mediterranean by a Grumman F-14A Tomcat from the USS Saratoga during the build-up for Operation 'El Dorado Canyon'.*

# Sukhoi Su-24 'Fencer'

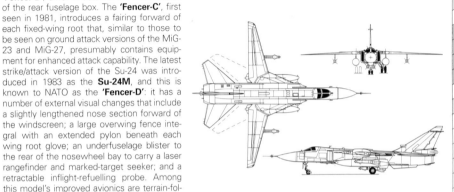

The variable-geometry **Sukhoi Su-24**, which was flown for the first time during January 1970 and subsequently received the NATO reporting namo **'Fencer'**, entered service with the Soviet air force in December 1974 with the initial designation **Su-19** that was later changed to Su-24. So advanced, and regarded as being far too important to risk any details of its detail design, equipment and capability being ascertained by Western sources, it was not until some eight years later that the first fully operational unit was based outside the USSR, when a unit was deployed to East Germany.

Of shoulder-wing configuration, the Su-24 has variable-geometry wings each consisting of a fixed glove box and a pivoted outer panel with three-position sweep settings of 16° when fully forward, an intermediate 45°, and fully swept 68°. The wings also incorporate full-span leading-edge slats, wide-span double-slotted flaps that occupy almost the entire trailing edge, and spoilers forward of the flaps used differentially to provide roll control at low speeds and collectively as lift dumpers during the landing run. In high-speed flight, when the wings are fully swept, roll control relies entirely upon differential use of the all-moving horizontal tail surfaces, which are also used collectively for control in pitch. Side-by-side ejector seats are provided for the crew of two, the Su-24 being the first modern Soviet aircraft to carry a weapons systems officer. The retractable tricycle type landing gear has twin wheels on each unit, and there are a total of nine weapon pylons (five beneath the fuselage, one under each fixed wing glove, and

one swivelling unit under each outer panel).

The initial Su-19 and Su-24 production versions (identified in the West as **'Fencer-A'** and **'Fencer-B'**) differ in detail in the construction of the rear fuselage box. The **'Fencer-C'**, first seen in 1981, introduces a fairing forward of each fixed-wing root that, similar to those to be seen on ground attack versions of the MiG-23 and MiG-27, presumably contains equipment for enhanced attack capability. The latest strike/attack version of the Su-24 was introduced in 1983 as the **Su-24M**, and this is known to NATO as the **'Fencer-D'**: it has a number of external visual changes that include a slightly lengthened nose section forward of the windscreen; a large overwing fence integral with an extended pylon beneath each wing root glove; an underfuselage blister to the rear of the nosewheel bay to carry a laser rangefinder and marked-target seeker; and a retractable inflight-refuelling probe. Among this model's improved avionics are terrain-following rather than terrain-avoidance radar. Variants related to the strike/attack Su-24M, which was exported as the **Su-24MK** with downgraded avionics, include the **Su-24MR 'Fender-E'** reconnaissance variant that entered service in 1985 as replacement for the Tupolev Tu-16 with a selection of underfuselage and underwing sensor pods, and the **Su-24MP 'Fencer-F'** jamming and Sigint variant that entered service in the late 1980s as replacement for the Yakovlev Yak-28 'Brewer-E' as a derivative of the Su-24MR with a different arrangement of dielectric panels and pods. Deliveries of some 900 aircraft were completed in the early 1990s.

### Specification: Sukhoi Su-24M 'Fencer-D'

**Origin:** USSR (now CIS)
**Type:** strike and attack aircraft
**Powerplant:** two 11250-kg (24,802-lb) afterburning thrust Lyul'ka AL-21F-3A turbojets
**Performance:** maximum speed Mach 2.18 or 1,250 kt (2316 km/h; 1,439 mph) at high altitude; or Mach 1.2 or 793 kt (1469 km/h; 913 mph) at sea level; service ceiling 57,415 ft (17500 m); combat radius 1050 km (650 miles) on a hi-lo-hi mission with a 3000-kg (6,614-lb) weapon load and two external tanks
**Weights:** empty 19000 kg (41,888 lb); maximum take-off 39700 kg (87,520 lb)
**Dimensions:** span 17.63 m (57 ft 10 in) spread and 10.36 m (34 ft 0 in) swept; length including probe 24.53 m (80 ft 5.75 in); height 4.97 m (16 ft 3.75 in); wing area 42.0 m² (452.1 sq ft)
**Armament:** one 23-mm GSh-23-6 six-barrel cannon; provision for 8000 kg (17,635 lb) of disposable stores, including nuclear weapons, AAMs, ASMs, guided bombs, bombs, cluster bombs, dispenser weapons, large-calibre rockets, rocket-launcher pods, drop tanks and ECM pods, carried on nine external hardpoints

*An Sukhoi Su-24MR 'Fencer-E' of the 11th Independent Reconnaissance Regiment.*

*Sukhoi Su-24M 'Fencer-D'*

*The Su-24MP 'Fencer-F' is a dedicated ECM jamming platform designed to replace the Yak-28PP 'Brewer-E'. Only a handful were built and these served with the Western Group of Forces before going to the Ukrainian air force. .*

*The 'Fencer-B' and 'Fencer-C' differ from one another only in their RWR and ECM fit, the 'Fencer-C' having prominent antennas on the intakes and on the sides of the tailfin. The later Su-24M 'Fencer-D' introduced a new attack radar and inflight refuelling capability.*

## Role

Fighter
Close support
Counter-insurgency
Tactical strike
Tactical bomber
Strategic bomber
Tactical reconnaissance
Strategic reconnaissance
Maritime patrol
Anti-ship strike
Anti-submarine warfare
Search and rescue
Assault transport
Transport
Liaison
Trainer
Inflight-refuelling tanker
Specialized

## Performance

All-weather capability
Rough field capability
STOL capability
VTOL capability
Airspeed 0-250 mph
Airspeed 250 mph-Mach 1
Airspeed Mach 1 plus
Ceiling 0-20,000ft
Ceiling 20,000ft-40,000 ft
Ceiling 40,000ft plus
Range 0-1,000 miles
Range 1,000-3,000 miles
Range 3,000 miles plus

## Weapons

Air-to-air missiles
Air-to-surface missiles
Cruise missiles
Cannon
Trainable guns
Naval weapons
Nuclear-capable
Rockets
'Smart' weapon kit
Weapon load 0-4,000 lb
Weapon load 4,000-15,000 lb
Weapon load 15,000 lb plus

## Avionics

Electronic Counter Measures
Electronic Support Measures
Search radar
Fire control radar
Look-down/shoot-down
Terrain-following radar
Forward-looking infra-red
Laser
Television

# Sukhoi Su-25 'Frogfoot'

*A Sukhoi Su-25 'Frogfoot-A' of the Czechoslovakian air force.*

## Role

Fighter
Close support
Counter-insurgency
Tactical strike
Strategic bomber
Tactical reconnaissance
Strategic reconnaissance
Maritime patrol
Anti-ship strike
Anti-submarine warfare
Search and rescue
Assault transport
Transport
Liaison
Trainer
Inflight-refuelling tanker
Specialized

## Performance

All-weather capability
Rough field capability
STOL capability
VTOL capability
Airspeed 0-250 mph
Airspeed 250 mph-Mach 1
Airspeed Mach 1 plus
Ceiling 0-20,000 ft
Ceiling 20,000-40,000 ft
Ceiling 40,000ft plus
Range 0-1,000 miles
Range 1,000-3,000 miles
Range 3,000 miles plus

## Weapons

Air-to-air missiles
Air-to-surface missiles
Cruise missiles
Cannon
Trainable guns
Naval weapons
Nuclear-capable
Rockets
'Smart' weapon kit
Weapon load 0-4,000 lb
Weapon load 4,000-15,000 lb
Weapon load 15,000 lb plus

## Avionics

Electronic Counter Measures
Electronic Support Measures
Search radar
Fire control radar
Look-down/shoot-down
Terrain-following radar
Forward-looking infra-red
Laser
Television

First identified by the USA in the late 1970s, when recorded by orbiting satellites while undergoing early flight test, after an initial flight on 22 February 1975, at the USSR's Ramenskoye test centre, this aircraft was given the provisional designation 'Ram-J' by the US Department of Defense. When deliveries to the Soviet air force began in late 1980 it was learned that this new aircraft was the **Sukhoi Su-25**, and in 1982 NATO allocated to it the reporting name **'Frogfoot'**.

The **'Frogfoot-A'** initial model may be regarded as a Soviet equivalent of the US Air Force's Fairchild A-10A Thunderbolt II, and as such it is intended for deployment in a similar battlefield close-support role, but performance figures show that the Su-25's higher maximum speed was gained at the cost of reduced weapons load and also of lesser range and/or endurance. In configuration the Su-25 is a shoulder-wing monoplane, the wing incorporating considerable anhedral and about 20° of sweepback. The leading edge of the wing has full-span slats, and a dogtooth at 50 per cent span with extended chord outboard to the wing tip; the entire trailing edge is occupied by ailerons and double-slotted flaps. At each wing tip is a fairing of flattened ovoid cross-section that houses (in the lower forward end) a retractable landing light, and which is formed

at the rear by upper and lower split spoilers that can be extended collectively to serve as air brakes or operated differentially to improve manoeuvrability in low-level flight. The tail unit is conventional, the landing gear is of retractable tricycle type with low-pressure tyres and designed specifically for operation from rough surfaces, and power is provided by two turbojets mounted in long nacelles at each wing root. The single-seat accommodation for the pilot is protected by armour which is incorporated in the fuselage side structure and by a flat bullet-proof windscreen. External antennae indicate that avionics include 'Odd Rods' IFF and a Sirena-3 radar-warning system, and the tailcone serves to house a chaff/decoy flare dispenser. A laser rangefinder and marked-target seeker is mounted within the nose.

The Su-25 was deployed for experimental operational use in Afghanistan, where the Soviet air force placed early emphasis on the development of co-ordination techniques to maximize the efficiency of close-support operations in which Su-25s and Mil Mi-24 'Hind' helicopter gunships were collaborating. Attaining full operational capability in 1984, the Su-25 force in CIS service now totals some 700 aircraft, and the type has also been exported to a number of favoured customers in its **Su-25K** version.

### Specification: Sukhoi Su-25K 'Frogfoot-A'
**Origin:** USSR (now CIS)
**Type:** single-seat close-support aircraft
**Powerplant:** two 4500-kg (9,921-lb) dry thrust Tumanskii R-195 turbojets
**Performance:** maximum speed 526 kt (975 km/h; 606 mph) at sea level; service ceiling 22,965 ft (7000 m); range 750 km (466 miles) at sea level with a 4400-kg (9,700-lb) warload and two drop tanks
**Weights:** empty 9500 kg (20,944 lb); maximum take-off 17600 kg (38,801 lb)
**Dimensions:** span 14.36 m (47 ft 1.5 in); length 15.53 m (50 ft 11.5 in); height 4.80 m (15 ft 9 in); wing area 33.7 m² (362.75 sq ft)
**Armament:** one 30-mm GSh-30-2 two-barrel cannon with 250 rounds; provision for 4400 kg (9,700 lb) of disposable stores, including AAMs, guided bombs, bombs, cluster bombs, dispenser weapons, napalm tanks, 23-mm cannon pods, large-calibre rockets, rocket-launcher pods and drop tanks, carried on eight external hardpoints

**Sukhoi Su-25 'Frogfoot-A'**

*These are Su-25s of the Czechoslovak air force, which was the first export customer for this interesting Soviet ground-attack aircraft. The eight hardpoints are clearly visible.*

*Wearing a non-standard camouflage scheme, this Su-25 served with one of the two Independent Shturmovik Aviation Regiments that served with the Group of Soviet Forces in Germany.*

# Sukhoi Su-25T, Su-25TK, Su-25UB, Su-25UT and Su-25UTB 'Frogfoot'

The importance placed by the USSR on the Su-25 is attested by the number of variants that have evolved during the aircraft's still comparatively short life. The **Sukhoi Su-25UB 'Frogfoot-B'** is the two-seat trainer derivative of the Su-25 with a longer forward fuselage to allow the insertion of a second cockpit behind and considerably above the original enclosure. The Su-25UB is exported as the **Su-25UBK**. Fitted with an arrester hook, the **Su-25UTG** is the navalized two-seat 'Frogfoot-B' model evaluated from November 1989 as a possible part of the warplane complement for the CIS navy's new conventional aircraft carriers. First flown in August 1985 as the **Su-25UT**, the **Su-28** is a 'Frogfoot-B' flying trainer derivative powered by two 4100-kg (9,039-lb) dry thrust R-95Sh turbojets and lacking the nose cannon, armoured cockpit and (normally) the underwing hardpoints of the operational models. The type is 15.36 m (50 ft 4.75 in) long, and has empty and normal take-off weights of 9500 and about 15000 kg (20,944 and about 33,069 lb) respectively. The Su-28 was considered as a replacement for older basic and advanced flying trainers in Soviet service, notably the Aero L-29, but only a few have been built.

First flown in August 1984 as the **Su-25T** and briefly known as the **Su-34**, the **T-8M** is a considerably upgraded development of the basic Su-25 for the anti-tank role. The erstwhile rear cockpit is plated over and its volume used for extra mission electronics including automatically operated defensive systems including chaff/flare launchers (in the top of the tailcone and in the cylindrical fairing at the base of the rudder) and a tail-mounted IR jammer. There is also a threat-evaluating RWR capable of priming two underwing Kh-58 (AS-11 'Kilter') anti-radar missiles with target data. The new variant is fitted with an automatic stability system, a powerplant of lower IR signature despite the use of engines developing 10% greater thrust, and a central fuselage structure with improved resistance to fire damage.

The Su-34 is fully optimized for its anti-tank role with the Voshkod nav/attack system with its two digital computers, INS, and Schkval optronic system: this last is located behind a nose window, and uses a high-magnification TV camera and LRMTS to acquire targets at a range of some 10 km (6.1 miles), whereupon the optronic image is displayed on a CRT for identification by the pilot, who then designates the target in his HUD for the Vikhr laser-guided missile, of which 16 can be carried; target tracking, weapon selection and weapon release are fully automatic after target designation.

The Su-34 can also carry the Mercuri night navigation system whose FLIR sensor can detect a tank at a range of 3 km (1.8 miles) under night/adverse-weather conditions. In 1991 the CIS revealed a **Su-25TK** export variant.

### Specification: Sukhoi Su-25T 'Frogfoot'
**Origin:** USSR (now CIS)
**Type:** single-seat close-support and anti-tank aircraft
**Powerplant:** two 4500-kg (9,921-lb) dry thrust Tumanskii R-195 turbojets
**Performance:** maximum speed 512 kt (950 km/h; 590 mph) at sea level; service ceiling 32,810 ft (10000 m); combat radius 400 km (248 miles) on a lo-lo-lo mission with a 4400-kg (9,700-lb) warload
**Weights:** maximum take-off 19500 kg (42,989 lb)
**Dimensions:** span 14.36 m (47 ft 1.5 in); length 15.53 m (50 ft 11.5 in); height 5.20 m (17 ft 0.75 in); wing area 33.7 m² (362.75 sq ft)
**Armament:** one 30-mm GSh-30-2 two-barrel cannon with 250 rounds; provision for 4400 kg (9,700 lb) of disposable stores, including AAMs, ASMs, ARMs, anti-tank missiles, guided bombs, bombs, cluster bombs, dispenser weapons, napalm tanks, 23-mm cannon pods, large-calibre rockets, rocket-launcher pods and drop tanks, carried on eight external hardpoints

*One of the Su-25UTGs taken over by the Ukrainian air force after the break-up of the USSR.*

*Sukhoi Su-25UB*

*The Su-25TK is a single-seat attack aircraft based on the airframe of the two seat Su-25UB. It features an advanced new all-weather attack avionics suite, and is compatible with the latest guided air-to-surface weapons.*

*This Su-25UB wears the markings of the Czechoslovakian air force. The Su-25UB is fully operationally capable.*

**Role**
Fighter
Close support
Counter-insurgency
Tactical strike
Strategic bomber
Tactical reconnaissance
Strategic reconnaissance
Maritime patrol
Anti-ship strike
Anti-submarine warfare
Search and rescue
Assault transport
Transport
Liaison
Trainer
Inflight-refuelling tanker
Specialized

**Performance**
All-weather capability
Rough field capability
STOL capability
VTOL capability
Airspeed 0-250 mph
Airspeed 250 mph-Mach 1
Airspeed Mach 1 plus
Ceiling 0-20,000 ft
Ceiling 20,000-40,000 ft
Ceiling 40,000ft plus
Range 0-1,000 miles
Range 1,000-3,000 miles
Range 3,000 miles plus

**Weapons**
Air-to-air missiles
Air-to-surface missiles
Cruise missiles
Cannon
Trainable guns
Naval weapons
Nuclear-capable
Rockets
'Smart' weapon kit
Weapon load 0-4,000 lb
Weapon load 4,000-15,000 lb
Weapon load 15,000 lb plus

**Avionics**
Electronic Counter Measures
Electronic Support Measures
Search radar
Fire control radar
Look-down/shoot-down
Terrain-following radar
Forward-looking infra-red
Laser
Television

# Sukhoi Su-27 'Flanker'

### Role
Fighter
Close support
Counter-insurgency
Tactical strike
Strategic bomber
Tactical reconnaissance
Strategic reconnaissance
Maritime patrol
Anti-ship strike
Anti-submarine warfare
Search and rescue
Assault transport
Transport
Liaison
Trainer
Inflight-refuelling tanker
Specialized

### Performance
All-weather capability
Rough field capability
STOL capability
VTOL capability
Airspeed 0-250 mph
Airspeed 250 mph-Mach 1
Airspeed Mach 1 plus
Ceiling 0-20,000 ft
Ceiling 20,000-40,000 ft
Ceiling 40,000ft plus
Range 0-1,000 miles
Range 1,000-3,000 miles
Range 3,000 miles plus

### Weapons
Air-to-air missiles
Air-to-surface missiles
Cruise missiles
Cannon
Trainable guns
Naval weapons
Nuclear-capable
Rockets
'Smart' weapon kit
Weapon load 0-4,000 lb
Weapon load 4,000-15,000 lb
Weapon load 15,000 lb plus

### Avionics
Electronic Counter Measures
Electronic Support Measures
Search radar
Fire control radar
Look-down/shoot-down
Terrain-following radar
Forward-looking infra-red
Laser
Television

With the Soviet air force requiring a new combat aircraft in the mould of the US Air Force's McDonnell Douglas F-15 Eagle, in the mid-1970s the Sukhoi bureau was given responsibility for the design and development of such an aircraft. First flown on 20 May 1977, The Su-27 was first observed by US reconnaissance satellites at the Ramenskoye test centre and duly received the temporary reporting name 'Ram-K' when first observed in 1977. Development was somewhat protracted and the type underwent a number of significant changes. The type entered production at Komsomolsk in 1980-1 and entered service in 1984 as the **Sukhoi Su-27** that received the NATO reporting name **'Flanker-B'**. The prototype and pre-production type had been of the **'Flanker-A'** type with curved wing tips, fins mounted centrally above the engines, and a rearward-retracting nosewheel unit rather than the definitive forward-retracting unit.

The Su-27's mid-set wing has basic sweepback of 40°, but it also has long leading-edge root extensions that blend into the fuselage at approximately the pilot's position, and these have 77° sweepback. The wing leading edge at 40° sweepback incorporates manoeuvring flaps, and the trailing edge carries ailerons and flaps. The tail unit consists of twin vertical surfaces and sharply swept all-moving horizontal surfaces, and the powerplant comprises two Lyul'ka AL-31F turbofans.

Like most new-generation aircraft in this category, the Su-27 rrelies heavily upon advanced avionics for its combat capability, and such equipment includes a digital data-link, an IR search and track system, and a powerful track-while-scan radar of the pulse-Doppler type with a search range in the order of 240 km (150 miles). Combined with the basic armament of six AA-10 'Alamo' medium-range AAMs, this gives the Su-27 great capability for the interception and destruction of low-flying aircraft and/or cruise missiles.

The two developments of the basic type are the **Su-27UB 'Flanker-C'** tandem two-seat trainer, and the derived two-seat multi-role Su-27PU (now Su-30) with full combat capability, and the **Su-27K** (now **Su-33**) navalized model with moving foreplanes and a number of other modifications for embarkation on the CIS's new aircraft carriers. Other developments include the Su-27IB (now Su-34) fighter-bomber prototype with side-by-side seating in a revised forward fuselage, and an improved Su-27M (now Su-35) multi-role fighter with moving canard foreplanes as a digital rather than analog fly-by-wire control system.

### Specification: Sukhoi Su-27 'Flanker-C'
**Origin:** USSR (now CIS)
**Type:** single-seat all-weather counter-air fighter
**Powerplant:** two 12500-kg (27,557-lb) afterburning thrust Lyul'ka AL-31F turbofans
**Performance:** maximum speed Mach 2.35 or 1,345 kt (2500 km/h; 1550 mph) at high altitude; service ceiling 59,055 ft (18000 m); combat radius 1500 km (930 miles)
**Weights:** maximum take-off 30000 kg (66,138 lb)
**Dimensions:** span 14.70 m (48 ft 2.75 in); length excluding probe 21.935 m (71 ft 11.5 in); height 5.932 m (19 ft 5.5 in); wing area 46.5 m² (500.5 sq ft)
**Armament:** one 30-mm GSh-30-1 cannon with 149 rounds; provision for about 6000 kg (13,228 lb) of disposable stores, including AAMs, bombs and rocket-launcher pods, carried on 10 external hardpoints

*A Sukhoi Su-27UB 'Flanker-C' of the 234th 'Proskurovskii' Guards Fighter Regiment's 'Russian Knights' aerobatic team.*

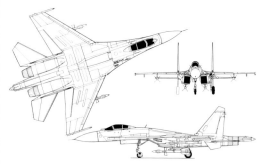

*Sukhoi Su-27 'Flanker-B'*

*An Su-27UB of a frontline Frontal Aviation fighter regiment formerly based in Poland. Most Su-27s serve with the IA-PVO and are charged with the air defence of the Russian homeland.*

*The basic Su-27 has only a limited and very secondary ground attack capability, and the aircraft assigned to Frontal Aviation units are charged with battlefield air superiority roles.*

# Transall C-160

*Transall C-160NG of the Armée de l'Air.*

From the mid-1950s France and West Germany were interested in procuring a medium-range transport aircraft suitable for the usual spectrum of military roles, leading in January 1959 to formation of Transporter Allianz. From this title the word Transall was adopted for the group formed to develop and produce this aircraft for both nations, and combining the French company Aérospatiale with two German companies, Messerschmitt-Bölkow-Blohm and VFW-Fokker.

The resulting **Transall C-160** was of typical transport aircraft configuration with a high-set wing to maximize cabin volume and give adequate ground clearance for the propellers of the two wing-mounted Rolls-Royce Tyne turboprops. The fuselage was upswept at the rear to incorporate a hydraulically actuated door/loading ramp, had a large fairing on each side into which the main units of the tricycle landing gear retracted, and provided pressurized accommodation for a crew of four and up to 93 troops, or a maximum 81 fully equipped paratroops, or 62 litters and four attendants, or a wide range of vehicles or cargo up to a maximum weight of 16000 kg (35,274 lb). The landing gear was designed for operation from and to semi-prepared surfaces, and STOL operation was provided by airbrakes and spoilers mounted in the wing upper surface forward of double-slotted flaps and reversible propellers. There was also provision for underwing installation of auxiliary turbojet engines with thrust reversers.

The first C-160 prototype was flown on 25 February 1963, followed by two more prototypes before the first of six pre-production C-160A aircraft, which differed in having the fuselage lengthened by 0.51 m (1 ft 8 in). Later production comprised 90 for West Germany (**C-160D**), 50 for France (**C-160F**), 20 for Turkey (**C-160T**) and nine for South Africa (**C-160Z**). Under the designation C-160P four of the C-160Fs were later converted for use by Air France in night postal operations. All C-160 orders had been completed by the end of 1972, but in 1977 the programme was reinstated for the building of a second series of 25 (later 29) aircraft for France. Manufactured by Aérospatiale and MBB, the first of these **C-160 Nouvelle Génération** (new generation) aircraft was flown on 9 April 1981. They have more advanced avionics, an inflight-refuelling boom and provision for a range-extending fuel tank in the wing centre-section. Additionally, 10 of the aircraft are equipped to serve as inflight-refuelling tankers with hose-and-drogue gear, and five have provision for such equipment to be installed. The four additional French aircraft, designated **C-160 Astarté** and equipped as communications relay aircraft, entered service in 1987. Two other aircraft were adapted to the **C-160 GABRIEL** Sigint role.

Transall designed conversion kits to allow use of the C-160 in other roles, such as a maritime surveillance C-160S, electronic surveillance C-160SE and airborne early warning C-160AAA, but these won no orders.

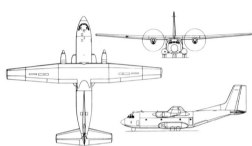

**Transall C-160**

**This Luftwaffe Transall of LTG61 is seen shortly after its return from Ethiopia, where it had been operating on famine relief sorties with loads of grain and medical supplies.**

**The replacement for Turkey's ageing but still capable C-160s is the Airtech CN-235, although the completion of this process is still far from full attainment.**

## Specification: Transall C-160NG
**Origin:** France and West Germany
**Type:** transport aircraft
**Powerplant:** two 4549-ekW (6,100-ehp) Rolls-Royce Tyne Mk 22 turboprops
**Performance:** maximum speed 277 kt (513 km/h; 319 mph) at 16,000 ft (4875 m); initial climb rate 1,300 ft (396 m) per minute; service ceiling 27,000 ft (8230 m); range 1853 km (1,151 miles) with maximum payload, 5 per cent fuel reserve and allowance for 30-minute hold
**Weights:** empty 29000 kg (63,934 lb); maximum take-off 51000 kg (112,436 lb)
**Dimensions:** span 40.00 m (131 ft 2.8 in); length 32.40 m (106 ft 3.6 in); height 11.65 m (38 ft 2.7 in); wing area 160.0 m² (1,722.28sq ft)
**Armament:** none

**Role**
Fighter
Close support
Counter-insurgency
Tactical strike
Strategic bomber
Tactical reconnaissance
Strategic reconnaissance
Maritime patrol
Anti-ship strike
Anti-submarine warfare
Search and rescue
Assault transport
Transport
Liaison
Trainer
Inflight-refuelling tanker
Specialized

**Performance**
All-weather capability
Rough field capability
STOL capability
VTOL capability
Airspeed 0-250 mph
Airspeed 250 mph-Mach 1
Airspeed Mach 1 plus
Ceiling 0-20,000 ft
Ceiling 20,000-40,000 ft
Ceiling 40,000ft plus
Range 0-1,000 miles
Range 1,000-3,000 miles
Range 3,000 miles plus

**Weapons**
Air-to-air missiles
Air-to-surface missiles
Cruise missiles
Cannon
Trainable guns
Naval weapons
Nuclear-capable
Rockets
'Smart' weapon kit
Weapon load 0-4,000 lb
Weapon load 4,000-15,000 lb
Weapon load 15,000 lb plus

**Avionics**
Electronic Counter Measures
Electronic Support Measures
Search radar
Fire control radar
Look-down/shoot-down
Terrain-following radar
Forward-looking infra-red
Laser
Television

269

# Tupolev Tu-16 'Badger' (bombers, missile carriers and tankers)

*Tupolev Tu-16 'Badger-A' of the Soviet air force.*

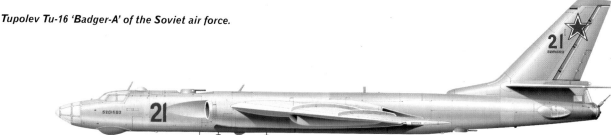

More than 40 years ago, on May Day 1954, Western observers of the fly-past over Moscow's Red Square gained their first sight of a new and very large-swept-wing aircraft to which the NATO reporting name **'Badger'** was later allocated. Nine aircraft took part in that May Day fly-past, one being the Tu-88 prototype that had first flown on 27 April 1952, and the other eight were pre-production **Tupolev Tu-16** bombers. The design of this type had been made possible through the development by Mikulin of a new and powerful turbojet, the AM-3 (later RD-3) axial-flow unit that ended the USSR's reliance upon Western aircraft technology.

The Tu-16 entered service with the Soviet air force in 1955, equipping what was then known as the DA (long-range aviation) force. The design was a blend of old and new, the fuselage structure being derived from that of the Tu-4 but in combination with a completely new swept wing, all-swept trail surfaces and tricycle landing gear including main units that retracted into wing trailing-edge pods. Power was provided by two 8750-kg (19,290-lb) dry thrust AM-3A turbojets but, after about 50 of the original version had been completed, the more powerful AM-3M engine was introduced. Production continued to 1959-60 and amounted to a total of 2,000 Tu-16s of which the vast majority were of the **'Badger-A'** bomber version. More of the later variants were conversions of these original aircraft.

The 'Badger-A' is the original strategic bomber version, carrying nuclear or conventional free-fall weapons in an underfuselage weapons bay which has a maximum capacity of 9000 kg (19,842 lb). Most of the aircraft were later equipped for inflight-refuelling, with a receptacle at the port wing tip, and a number were converted as **Tu-16N** inflight-refuelling tankers with fuel tanks in the erstwhile weapons bay and with the refuelling hose streamed from the starboard wing tip. The **'Badger-B'** is similar to the 'Badger-A' and is now used for free-fall weapons delivery it was originally equipped for the anti-ship role carrying the AS-1 'Kennel' anti-ship missile beneath each wing. The following **Tu-16K-10 'Badger-C'** has no free-fall weapons capability and carries a large K-10 (AS-2 ''Kipper') anti-ship missile recessed into the lower fuselage, or in its **'Badger-C Mod'** form one smaller AS-6 'Kingfish' missile beneath each wing, and also differs from the 'Badger-A' by having a wide radome in place of the nose gun and glazing. The final anti-shipping versions are the **'Badger-G'** and **'Badger-G Mod'**, the first with free-fall weapon capability and carrying two AS-5 'Kelt' missiles, and the second with two AS-6 'Kingfish' missiles and a large radome under the central fuselage. Small numbers of the 'Badger-B' remain in service with Long-Range Aviation, and an estimated 240 'Badger-C' and 'Badger-G' aircraft of both variants service with Naval Aviation.

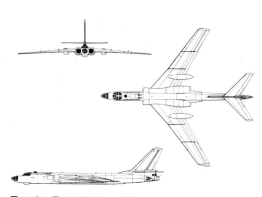

*Tupolev Tu-16 'Badger-A'*

*Intercepted over the Baltic by a Swedish air force fighter, this Tu-16 'Badger' carries an AS-6 'Kingfish' missile under its starboard wing.*

*This 'Badger-G' of the Egyptian air force carries a pair of AS-5 'Kelt' ASMs under its wings. Some Egyptian 'Badgers' were also supplied to Iraq for use in the Gulf War.*

**Specification:** Tupolev Tu-16 'Badger-G'
**Origin:** USSR (now CIS)
**Type:** missile launch platform
**Powerplant:** two 9500-kg (20,944-lb) dry thrust Mikulin RD-3M turbojets
**Performance:** maximum speed 566 kt (1050 km/h; 652 mph) at 19,685 ft (6000 m); service ceiling 49,215 ft (15000 m); range 7200 km (4,475 miles) with a 3000-kg (6,614-lb) warload
**Weights:** empty 37200 kg (82,011 lb); maximum take-off 75800 kg (167,110 lb)
**Dimensions:** span 32.99 m (108 ft 3 in); length 34.80 m (114 ft 2.1 in); height 10.36 m (34 ft 0 in); wing area 164.65 m² (1,772.34 sq ft)
**Armament:** seven 23-mm NR-23 cannon (two each in forward dorsal, rear ventral and tail position plus one fixed forward-firing weapon); provision for two AS-6 'Kingfish' air-to-surface/anti-ship missiles

**Role**

Fighter
Close support
Counter-insurgency
Tactical strike
Strategic bomber
Tactical reconnaissance
Strategic reconnaissance
Maritime patrol
Anti-ship strike
Anti-submarine warfare
Search and rescue
Assault transport
Transport
Liaison
Trainer
Inflight-refuelling tanker
Specialized

**Performance**

All-weather capability
Rough field capability
STOL capability
VTOL capability
Airspeed 0-250 mph
Airspeed 250 mph-Mach 1
Airspeed Mach 1 plus
Ceiling 0-20,000 ft
Ceiling 20,000-40,000 ft
Ceiling 40,000ft plus
Range 0-1,000 miles
Range 1,000-3,000 miles
Range 3,000 miles plus

**Weapons**

Air-to-air missiles
Air-to-surface missiles
Cruise missiles
Cannon
Trainable guns
Naval weapons
Nuclear-capable
Rockets
'Smart' weapon kit
Weapon load 0-4,000 lb
Weapon load 4,000-15,000 lb
Weapon load 15,000 lb plus

**Avionics**

Electronic Counter Measures
Electronic Support Measures
Search radar
Fire control radar
Look-down/shoot-down
Terrain-following radar
Forward-looking infra-red
Laser
Television

# Tupolev Tu-22 'Blinder'

*Tu-22 'Blinder' of the Iraqi air force.*

In the early 1950s the growing capability of Western manned interceptors and surface-to-air missile systems made it clear to Soviet planners that the days of the Tupolev Tu-16 as a viable strategic weapon were numbered. To remedy this, in 1955-6 the Tupolev bureau began the design of a successor and the resulting Tu-105 prototype is thought to have flown in 1959. Western sources were unaware of this aircraft until a formation of 10 took part in the 1961 Aviation Day fly-past at Tushino. Nine of them were similar, and these were allocated the NATO reporting name **'Blinder-A'**; the tenth carried an AS-4 'Kitchen' air-to-surface strategic missile recessed into the weapon bay and was identified as the **'Blinder-B'**. When the 'Blinder-A' entered service with the DA (long-range aviation) in the early 1960s the type was designated **Tupolev Tu-22**.

Apart from its engine installation, the Tu-22 appears at first glance to be of similar basic configuration to the Tu-16 with a mid-set swept wing, all-swept tail surfaces and the main units of its tricycle landing gear retracting into wing pods. However, the wing differs considerably from that of the Tu-16 in having compound sweep on the leading edge and less anhedral. The fuselage is waisted to conform to area-rule principles, has at the nose an ogival radome and a semi-retractable inflight-refuelling probe, and at the tail sports a radar-controlled turret for one 23-mm cannon. Nevertheless, the Tu-22 can be recognized

easily by the powerplant installation, comprising two afterburning turbojets mounted in pods, one on each side of the rear fuselage adjacent to the fin, a configuration obviously used to eliminate the drag and weight penalties of long inlet ducts.

Production of the Tu-22 is believed to have totalled about 250 aircraft, a number foreshortened by the growing interest in strategic missiles and the rapid development of more capable aircraft. The 'Blinder-A' was a basic bomber version carrying conventional or nuclear free-fall bombs; it entered service in only small numbers and was probably intended purely as a pre-production type for familiarization and evaluation. The major production version was the nuclear missile-carrying 'Blinder-B' (about 150 built), followed by the maritime reconnaissance **Tu-22R 'Blinder-C'** (about 60 built) with an inflight-refuelling capability and six camera windows in the weapon bay doors; there is evidence to suggest that this variant is equipped, or can easily be equipped, for the Elint and/or ECM roles. The final version is the **Tu-22U 'Blinder-D'** trainer with a raised instructor's cockpit to the rear of the standard flight deck. It was estimated in 1986 that about 140 'Blinder-B' and 'Blinder-D' plus 40 'Blinder-C' and 'Blinder-D' aircraft remained in service with Soviet Long-Range Aviation and naval aviation respectively, but by the mid-1990s this had fallen to 20 naval 'Blinder-Cs'.

**Specification:** Tupolev Tu-22 'Blinder-B'
**Origin:** USSR (now CIS)
**Type:** supersonic stand-off missile carrier
**Powerplant:** two 16000-kg (35,273-lb) afterburning thrust Koliesov VD-7M turbojets
**Performance:** maximum speed Mach 1.4 or 802 kt (1487 km/h; 924 mph) at 40,025 ft (12200 m); service ceiling 60,040 ft (18300 m); combat radius 3100 km (1,926 miles) with maximum internal fuel
**Weights:** empty 40000 kg (88,185 lb); maximum take-off 84000 kg (185,188 lb)
**Dimensions:** span 23.75 m (77 ft 11 in); length 40.53 m (132 ft 11.7 in); height 10.67 m (35 ft 0 in)
**Armament:** one 23-mm NR-23 cannon in radar-controlled tail turret, plus one AS-4 'Kitchen' stand-off missile recessed into the weapons bay

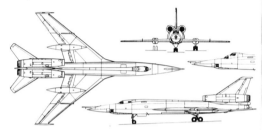

*Tupolev Tu-22 'Blinder-A' (scrap view: nose of Tu-22U 'Blinder-D')*

*This is a Tu-22 'Blinder' of the Libyan air force, which used one of its aircraft to bomb N'Djamena airport in Chad in response to the French attack on Quadi Doum.*

*This Tu-22 'Blinder' was intercepted over the Baltic by a Swedish Viggen. The 'Blinder' has been largely replaced by the Tu-22M 'Backfire'.*

## Role

- Fighter
- Close support
- Counter-insurgency
- Tactical strike
- Strategic bomber
- Tactical reconnaissance
- Strategic reconnaissance
- Maritime patrol
- Anti-ship strike
- Anti-submarine warfare
- Search and rescue
- Assault transport
- Transport
- Liaison
- Trainer
- Inflight-refuelling tanker
- Specialized

## Performance

- All-weather capability
- Rough field capability
- STOL capability
- VTOL capability
- Airspeed 0-250 mph
- Airspeed 250 mph-Mach 1
- Airspeed Mach 1 plus
- Ceiling 0-20,000 ft
- Ceiling 20,000-40,000 ft
- Ceiling 40,000ft plus
- Range 0-1,000 miles
- Range 1,000-3,000 miles
- Range 3,000 miles plus

## Weapons

- Air-to-air missiles
- Air-to-surface missiles
- Cruise missiles
- Cannon
- Trainable guns
- Naval weapons
- Nuclear-capable
- Rockets
- 'Smart' weapon kit
- Weapon load 0-4,000 lb
- Weapon load 4,000-15,000 lb
- Weapon load 15,000 lb plus

## Avionics

- Electronic Counter Measures
- Electronic Support Measures
- Search radar
- Fire control radar
- Look-down/shoot-down
- Terrain-following radar
- Forward-looking infra-red
- Laser
- Television

# Tupolev Tu-22M 'Backfire'

*Tupolev Tu-22M-2 'Backfire' of the Soviet air force.*

While the Tupolev Tu-22 had given the Soviet air force a bomber aircraft of supersonic capability, its combat radius, estimated in the West as 3100 km (1,926 miles) was inadequate for a true strategic bombing role. An ability to reach major targets in the USA was regarded as essential for maintenance of the deterrent policy. The Tupolev bureau began work in 1964-5 on the design of a successor to the Tu-22, taking as a basis the Tu-22 airframe which it adapted to incorporate a variable-geometry wing and powerplant mounted within the fuselage The task was complicated by the decision to retain the tricycle landing gear of the Tu-22 with the main units retracting into wing trailing-edge fairings, which meant that only the outer third of the wing could pivot. The powerplant adopted for this new aircraft was the Kuznetsov NK-144 afterburning turbofan under development for the Tu-144 supersonic airliner.

First spotted by reconnaissance satellites in late 1969, and subsequently photographed in more detail in mid-1970, the new Tupolev bomber was allocated the NATO reporting name 'Backfire'. This became 'Backfire-A' when the type entered service, reportedly with only one squadron, but its true Soviet designation at first remained uncertain. During the SALT 2 treaty talks Soviet sources referred to it as **Tupolev Tu-22M**, and it has since become clear that the 'Backfire-A' was indeed the **Tu-22M-1**.

During the test and evaluation programme, the range of the Tu-22M-1 was found to be far short of expectations, and it seems likely that low-level performance was also inadequate, leading to major design changes. This involved the virtual elimination of the fairings into which the main landing gear units had retracted, redesign of the main gear units to retract inwards into the fuselage structure, and the introduction of new pivoting outer wings of increased span. This version, which was at first thought to have the designation Tu-26 but is now known to be the **Tu-22M-2**, entered service in 1975 and has the NATO reporting name **'Backfire-B'**.

A version with wedge-type inlets similar to those of the Mikoyan-Gurevich MiG-25 has been reported, these presumably giving enhanced performance, and this variant is the **Tu-22M-3** or **'Backfire-C'**.

It is estimated that some 360 Tu-22M-2 and Tu-22M-3 bombers and missile launch platforms, with perhaps 200 equipping Long-Range Aviation and 160 serving with Naval Aviation, and the capability of these aircraft is such that they are expected to remain in use for some years.

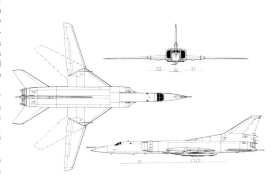

*Tupolev Tu-22M-2 'Backfire-B'*

*This is a stern view of a Tu-22m-2 'Backfire-B' with its wings at minimum sweep. The Tu-22M's range and speed make it a potent strategic weapon.*

*This Tu-22M-2 'Backfire-B' carries one **AS-4** 'Kitchen' anti-ship missile semi-recessed into the lower fuselage. The AS-4 can be fitted with either a conventional or nuclear warhead.*

## Specification: Tupolev Tu-22M-2 'Backfire-B'

**Origin:** USSR (now CIS)

**Type:** medium strategic bomber and maritime reconnaissance/attack aircraft

**Powerplant:** two 20000-kg (44,092-lb) afterburning thrust turbofans of unknown designation

**Performance:** maximum speed Mach 2.0 or 1,147 kt (2125 km/h; 1,321 mph) at high altitude; service ceiling 59,055 ft (18000 m); combat radius 4000 km (2,485 miles) with internal fuel

**Weights:** maximum take-off 130000 kg (286,596 lb)

**Dimensions:** span 34.30 m (112 ft 6.5 in) spread and 23.40 m (76 ft 9.25 in) swept; length 39.60 m (129 ft 11 in); height 10.80 m (35 ft 5.25 in)

**Armament:** two 23-mm GSh-23 two-barrel cannon in a radar-controlled tail barbette; provision for 12000 kg (26,455 lb) of disposable stores, including nuclear weapons and free-fall bombs carried internally, or two AS-4 'Kitchen' missiles carried under the wings, or one AS-4 'Kitchen' missile carried semi-recessed into the lower fuselage, or up to three AS-6

### Role
Fighter
Close support
Counter-insurgency
Tactical strike
Strategic bomber
Tactical reconnaissance
Strategic reconnaissance
Maritime patrol
Anti-ship strike
Anti-submarine warfare
Search and rescue
Assault transport
Transport
Liaison
Trainer
Inflight-refuelling tanker
Specialized

### Performance
All-weather capability
Rough field capability
STOL capability
VTOL capability
Airspeed 0-250 mph
Airspeed 250 mph-Mach 1
Airspeed Mach 1 plus
Ceiling 0-20,000 ft
Ceiling 20,000-40,000 ft
Ceiling 40,000ft plus
Range 0-1,000 miles
Range 1,000-3,000 miles
Range 3,000 miles plus

### Weapons
Air-to-air missiles
Air-to-surface missiles
Cruise missiles
Cannon
Trainable guns
Naval weapons
Nuclear-capable
Rockets
'Smart' weapon kit
Weapon load 0-4,000 lb
Weapon load 4,000-15,000 lb
Weapon load 15,000 lb plus

### Avionics
Electronic Counter Measures
Electronic Support Measures
Search radar
Fire control radar
Look-down/shoot-down
Terrain-following radar
Forward-looking infra-red
Laser
Television

# Tupolev Tu-95 'Bear'

*Tupolev Tu-95 'Bear-C' of the Soviet air force.*

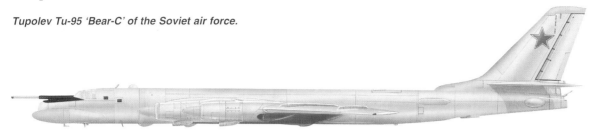

Another of the long-lived aircraft designed by the Tupolev bureau, the **Tupolev Tu-95** was first flown in prototype form during the autumn of 1954. When seen during the Aviation Day fly-past at Tushino in July 1955, this giant swept-wing heavy bomber demonstrated remarkable performance under the power of its four turboprop engines. US defence planners were aware that fighter aircraft then in US service would probably be unable to intercept these mighty bombers.

Of mid-wing configuration, the Tu-95 has a swept wing incorporating powered ailerons, large trailing-edge flaps, upper-surface spoilers and boundary-layer fences. The wing also carried the four turboprop engines in leading-edge nacelles; it also retains the typical Tupolev feature of trailing-edge nacelles into which the main units of the tricycle landing gear retract. The circular-section fuselage has three pressurized crew compartments, incorporates a bomb bay to contain up to 20000 kg (44,092 lb) of free-fall weapons, and mounts a tail unit with all-swept surfaces.

The first version to enter service with the Soviet air force was the basic strategic bomber to which NATO allocated the reporting name **'Bear-A'**. The following **'Bear-B'**, first seen in 1961, showed that Soviet sources were fully aware of growing USAF interception capability, for it was equipped to carry the AS-3 'Kangaroo' strategic missile

clamped under the cutaway bomb bay, thus giving the aircraft a stand-off weapon with a range of some 650 km (404 miles). The **'Bear-B'** also differs by having a wide under-nose radome for the 'Crown Drum' radar associated with the AS-3. A few examples have also been seen in the maritime reconnaissance role, and these have an inflight-refuelling probe for significantly enhanced range. There was also another 'Kangaroo'-carrying version known as the **'Bear-C'**, generally similar to the 'Bear-B' but distinguishable by a blister fairing on each side of the rear fuselage. The remaining strike version is the 'Bear-G' similar to the 'Bear-B' and 'Bear-C': this has 'Down Beat' radar and replaces the 'Kangaroo' subsonic missile by two examples of the AS-4 'Kitchen' strategic missile on single pylons beneath each wing root. Although a shorter-range weapon (about 300km/186 miles) its speed of more Mach 3.5 confers far increased capability

When the 'Bear-A' initially entered service, the designation **Tu-20** was allocated But it was reported subsequently that the bureau designation Tu-95 had been adopted for the bomber and missile launch variants which, with only a few exceptions, are operated by the Soviet air force. It is believed that about 115, comprising examples of the four variants mentioned in this entry, remained in service in 1986 and that many of these were still operational in the mid-1990s.

**Specification:** Tupolev Tu-95 'Bear-C'
**Origin:** USSR (now CIS)
**Type:** long-range strategic missile carrier
**Powerplant:** four 11186-ekW (15,000-eshp) Kuznetsov NK-12MV turboprops
**Performance:** maximum speed 470 kt (870 km/h; 541 mph) at 29,530 ft (9000 m); economical cruising speed 405 kt (750 km/h; 466 mph) at 35,105 ft (10700 m); service ceiling 41,010 ft (12500 m); maximum range 12550 km (7,798 miles) with two AS-4 'Kitchen' missiles
**Weights:** empty 80000 kg (176,370 lb); maximum take-off 188000 kg (414,469 lb)
**Dimensions:** span 51.10 m (167 ft 7.8 in); length 49.50 m (162 ft 4.8 in); height 12.12 m (39 ft 9.2 in); wing area 297.0 m² (3,196.9 sq ft)
**Armament:** six 23-mm NR-23 cannon in pairs in two remotely controlled barbettes and manned tail turret, plus one AS-3 'Kangaroo' strategic missile

*Tupolev Tu-95 'Bear-C'*

*This 'Bear-C' carries unidentified pods under its outer wings. These may be associated with the 'Kangaroo' missiles sometimes carried by this variant, or may have an Elint function.*

*A Soviet air force 'Bear-C' is intercepted at high level by a US Navy fighter during a long-range reconnaissance mission. The 'Bear-C' is usually equipped with an inflight-refuelling probe.*

## Role

Fighter
Close support
Counter-insurgency
Tactical strike
Strategic bomber
Tactical reconnaissance
Strategic reconnaissance
Maritime patrol
Anti-ship strike
Anti-submarine warfare
Search and rescue
Assault transport
Transport
Liaison
Trainer
Inflight-refuelling tanker
Specialized

## Performance

All-weather capability
Rough field capability
STOL capability
VTOL capability
Airspeed 0-250 mph
Airspeed 250 mph-Mach 1
Airspeed Mach 1 plus
Ceiling 0-20,000 ft
Ceiling 20,000-40,000 ft
Ceiling 40,000ft plus
Range 0-1,000 miles
Range 1,000-3,000 miles
Range 3,000 miles plus

## Weapons

Air-to-air missiles
Air-to-surface missiles
Cruise missiles
Cannon
Trainable guns
Naval weapons
Nuclear-capable
Rockets
'Smart' weapon kit
Weapon load 0-4,000 lb
Weapon load 4,000-15,000 lb
Weapon load 15,000 lb plus

## Avionics

Electronic Counter Measures
Electronic Support Measures
Search radar
Fire control radar
Look-down/shoot-down
Terrain-following radar
Forward-looking infra-red
Laser
Television

# Tupolev Tu-95MS 'Bear'

*Tupolev Tu-95MS 'Bear-H' of the Soviet air force.*

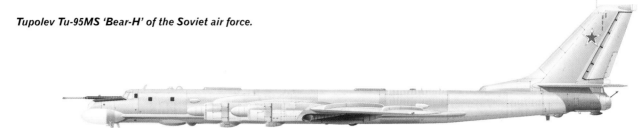

**Role**
Fighter
Close support
Counter-insurgency
Tactical strike
Strategic bomber
Tactical reconnaissance
Strategic reconnaissance
Maritime patrol
Anti-ship strike
Anti-submarine warfare
Search and rescue
Assault transport
Transport
Liaison
Trainer
Inflight-refuelling tanker
Specialized

**Performance**
All-weather capability
Rough field capability
STOL capability
VTOL capability
Airspeed 0-250 mph
Airspeed 250 mph-Mach 1
Airspeed Mach 1 plus
Ceiling 0-20,000 ft
Ceiling 20,000-40,000 ft
Ceiling 40,000ft plus
Range 0-1,000 miles
Range 1,000-3,000 miles
Range 3,000 miles plus

**Weapons**
Air-to-air missiles
Air-to-surface missiles
Cruise missiles
Cannon
Trainable guns
Naval weapons
Nuclear-capable
Rockets
'Smart' weapon kit
Weapon load 0-4,000 lb
Weapon load 4,000-15,000 lb
Weapon load 15,000 lb plus

**Avionics**
Electronic Counter Measures
Electronic Support Measures
Search radar
Fire control radar
Look-down/shoot-down
Terrain-following radar
Forward-looking infra-red
Laser
Television

The Tupolev Tu-95MS that is known to NATO as the 'Bear-H' achieved initial operational capability in 1984. The aircraft is based on an airframe possessing several Tu-142 features but carrying the large internal weapons bay of the Tu-95. The fuselage of the new variant was extensively 'cleaned up' in aerodynamic terms by the elimination of the underfuselage cannon barbette, rear-fuselage observation blisters, and plethora of ECM and ESM radomes that are so common in other 'Bears'. A new internal ECM/ESM suite is almost certainly installed, evidenced externally by a new and slightly bulged fin top possibly containing the receivers.

The Tu-95MS has an enlarged nose-mounted search and surveillance radar which is undoubtedly associated with the RK-55 'AS-15 'Kent') long-range cruise missile that forms the variant's primary armament. Searching ahead of the aircraft through 180° in azimuth, the scanner of this radar is only marginally smaller than that of the 'Short Horn' radar installed in the 'Bear-D'. The RK-55 is similar in configuration to the American BGM-109 Tomahawk cruise missile but in a much larger weapon. It carries a nuclear warhead, and probably employs a sophisticated guidance package using terrain profile matching to give a high level of accuracy over a

range of some 3000 km (1,864 miles). The RK-55 is also carried by the Tupolev Tu-160 'Blackjack' supersonic bomber, and the Tu-95MS/RK-55 combination was probably an interim method of boosting Soviet intercontinental strategic strike capabilities pending the arrival of the Tu-160.

Entering service in the mid-1980s, and being built to the extent of some 80 aircraft by the autumn of 1991 just before the end of production, the Tu-95MS has a number of advanced avionics items including radar and missile warning systems, an active ECM system, and a combination of chaff and flare dispensers. The West was vouchsafed its first glimpse of the new aircraft in May 1985, when a Tu-95MS was intercepted and photographed over the Barents Sea by a General Dynamics F-16 Fighting Falcon of No.331 Squadron of the Royal Norwegian air force. The Tu-95MS retains the inflight-refuelling probe of earlier variants, giving this formidable type excellent range and endurance.

The 'Bear' series is now long in the tooth in technical terms, but remains an effective reconnaissance and patrol platform, and in its much modernized Tu-95MS continues to form an important element of the Russian strategic air capability in the mid-1990s.

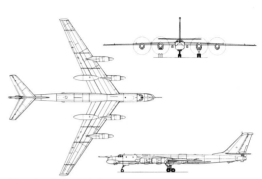

*Tupolev Tu-95MS 'Bear-H'*

*This Tu-95MS 'Bear-H' was intercepted by a McDonnell Douglas CF-18 Hornet of the Canadian Armed Forces off the Canadian coast as the soviet aircraft undertook a simulated strike mission.*

*The airframe of the Tu-95MS 'Bear-H' has much in common with that of the Tu-142 'Bear-F', but the armament comprises 16 subsonic cruise missiles and the type also has new primary radar under the nose.*

## Specification: Tupolev Tu-95MS 'Bear-H'
**Origin:** USSR (now CIS)
**Type:** long-range strategic bomber and cruise missile platform
**Powerplant:** four 11186-ekW (15,000-eshp) Kuznetsov NK-12MV turboprops
**Performance:** maximum speed 440 kt (815 km/h; 506 mph) at 25,000 ft (7620 m); economical cruising speed 384 kt (711 km/h; 442 mph); service ceiling 39,370 ft (12000 m); combat radius 6400 km (3,975 miles) with a 11340-kg (25,000-lb) warload
**Weights:** empty 120000 kg (264,550 lb); maximum take-off 188000 kg (414,469 lb)
**Dimensions:** span 51.10 m (167 ft 7.8 in); length 49.50 m (162 ft 4.8 in); height 12.12 m (39 ft 9.2 in); wing area 297.0 m² (3,196.9 sq ft)
**Armament:** two 23-mm NR-23 cannon in a manned tail turret, plus 16 RK-55 (AS-15 'Kent') cruise missiles carried in the weapons bay (six on a rotary launcher), under the wing roots (two on each side) and between the engine pairs (three on each side)

# Tupolev Tu-95 and Tu-142 'Bear-D/E/F/J'

*Tupolev Tu-92 'Bear-D' of the Soviet navy.*

As mentioned in the entry for the Tu-95 strike variants, a small number of the 'Bear-B' model that entered service in 1961 were modified for use in the maritime reconnaissance role. However, it was not until August 1967 that a specifically naval version of thus Tupolev giant was identified by US Coast Guard icebreakers operating in Arctic seas.

These aircraft, not all identical, had sufficient common detail for NATO to allocate them the reporting name **'Bear-D'**. Conversions from 'Bear-A' aircraft, they had features such as a glazed nose, an inflight-refuelling probe mounted over the nose, an undernose navigation and weapons delivery radar known to NATO as 'Short Horn' and, beneath was in the 'Bear-A' had been the weapons bay, a large radome for the 'Big Bulge' surface-search radar. Streamlined pods at the tips of the tailplane are assumed to house antennae, and there is a blister fairing on each side of the rear fuselage. It is in variation of their antennae that the 'Bear-D' aircraft differ, and some have also been seen with their tail turret and associated radome deleted in favour of a long radome similar to that of the Tupolev Tu-126 AEW platform, and clearly housing specialized equipment. The primary task of the 'Bear-D' is to locate targets, transmit the data to distant missile-carrying ships and, if required, provide mid-course target correction data to the in-flight missile.

The **'Bear-E'** is a true maritime reconnaissance variant. It is similar to the 'Bear-A' and uses the weapons bay to house six or seven optical cameras and possibly other sensors plus additional fuel. Hover, it differs from the 'Bear-A' in adopting the refuelling probe and rear-fuselage blister fairings to be seen on both the 'Bear-C' and 'Bear-D'.

Neither the 'Bear-C' nor the 'Bear-D' can carry offensive weapons, but this is not the case with the **Tupolev Tu-142 'Bear-F'**, which is a dedicated anti-submarine variant first seen in 1970 and based on a considerably revised airframe characterized by a more cambered wing with double-slotted flaps, a broader-chord rudder, a longer forward fuselage and a lengthened pressure cabin for the accommodation of the relief crew and improved galley facilities required for long-endurance missions. Since its debut the variant has been updated through four subvariants with a refuelling probe, increased head room on the flight deck, bulged nosewheel doors that suggest a change to larger low-pressure tyres, and the deletion of all defensive armament except the tail turret. Some of the aircraft lack the undernose radar and others have a different radome, but all have the underfuselage radar moved farther forward. Some of the aircraft have a MAD 'sting' extending aft from the top of the fin, but the tailplane tip pods of the 'Bear-D' are missing.

Identified in 1986, the **'Bear-J'** variant of the Tu-142 is used to provide a VLF radio relay link between the national command authorities and submerged submarines.

**Tupolev Tu-142 'Bear-F'**

### Specification: Tupolev Tu-142 'Bear-F Mod 3'
**Origin:** USSR (now CIS)
**Type:** long-range anti-submarine aircraft
**Powerplant:** four 11186-ekW (15,000-eshp) Kuznetsov NK-12MV turboprops
**Performance:** over-target speed 499 kt (925 km/h; 575 ft) at 41,010 ft (12500 m); combat radius 8285 km (5,148 miles) with a 5000-kg (11,023-lb) warload; range 12550 km (7,798 miles) with maximum weapons load
**Weights:** maximum take-off 185000 kg (407,848 lb)
**Dimensions:** span 51.10 m (167 ft 7.8 in); length 49.50 m (162 ft 4.8 in); height 12.12 m (39 ft 9.2 in); wing area 297.0 m² (3,196.9 sq ft)
**Armament:** two 23-mm NR-23 cannon in a manned tail turret, plus 11340 kg (25,000 lb) of disposable stores, including torpedoes and nuclear depth charges, carried in the weapons bay

*The 'Bear-E' is a dedicated reconnaissance platform, probably converted from the 'Bear-A', with seven optical camera ports in its weapon-bay doors. An inflight-refuelling probe is fitted.*

*The 'Bear-D' is a multi-role maritime variant used for a variety of intelligence gathering, maritime reconnaissance and patrol, and missile mid-course guidance duties*

# Tupolev Tu-160 'Blackjack'

*Tupolev Tu-160 'Blackjack' of the Soviet air force.*

## Role

Fighter
Close support
Counter-insurgency
Tactical strike
Strategic bomber
Tactical reconnaissance
Strategic reconnaissance
Maritime patrol
Anti-ship strike
Anti-submarine warfare
Search and rescue
Assault transport
Transport
Liaison
Trainer
Inflight-refuelling tanker
Specialized

## Performance

All-weather capability
Rough field capability
STOL capability
VTOL capability
Airspeed 0-250 mph
Airspeed 250 mph-Mach 1
Airspeed Mach 1 plus
Ceiling 0-20,000 ft
Ceiling 20,000-40,000 ft
Ceiling 40,000ft plus
Range 0-1,000 miles
Range 1,000-3,000 miles
Range 3,000 miles plus

## Weapons

Air-to-air missiles
Air-to-surface missiles
Cruise missiles
Cannon
Trainable guns
Naval weapons
Nuclear-capable
Rockets
'Smart' weapon kit
Weapon load 0-4,000 lb
Weapon load 4,000-15,000 lb
Weapon load 15,000 lb plus

## Avionics

Electronic Counter Measures
Electronic Support Measures
Search radar
Fire control radar
Look-down/shoot-down
Terrain-following radar
Forward-looking infra-red
Laser
Television

The latest military product of the Tupolev Design Bureau is a large variable-geometry strategic bomber. When this aircraft was first spotted by US reconnaissance satellites during 1979, its size was at first very difficult to determine. At a later date, 25 November 1981, one of the aircraft was photographed at the Ramenskoye flight test centre, and on this occasion it was parked in fairly close proximity to a couple of Tupolev Tu-144 supersonic transports. This allowed a rough estimate of its dimensions to be made.

The aircraft therefore has a blended fuselage/wing design in which the fixed inner portions of the wing merge gradually into the fuselage. The fixed inner portions of the wing have curved compound sweep on the leading edges, carry two pairs of afterburning turbofans in long undersurface nacelles, and carry the pivoted outer wing panels, which can be selected for movement between minimum and maximum sweep angles of 20° and 68° respectively. The airframe is completed by the conventional all-swept tail unit with the all-moving horizontal surface located about one-third of the way up the vertical surfaces. The crew of four is carried on individual ejector seats located in tandem pairs on the flight deck.

Later information confirmed the identity of the new aircraft as the **Tupolev Tu-160**, which entered service in 1988 and then received the NATO reporting name **'Blackjack-A'** after development from a first flight on 21 December 1981. The aircraft is some 20% longer than the B-1B and offers both a higher maximum speed and a considerably greater unrefuelled combat radius on a mission using high-level subsonic cruise, low-level transonic penetration and high-level supersonic attack. The warload is carried in two lower-fuselage weapon bays, each 10.00 m (32 ft 9.75 in) long and able to carry a rotary launcher.

The Tu-160 has suffered considerably in its early career from a number of flight-control difficulties, poor serviceability, and a shift in strategic emphasis since the dissolution of the USSR in the late 1990s and the emergence of the CIS as a country no longer in direct confrontation with the USA. Production of the Tu-160 has been ended, and perhaps no more than 60 aircraft were built in all, and it is possible that the service lives of the comparatively small number of aircraft that entered service may be short.

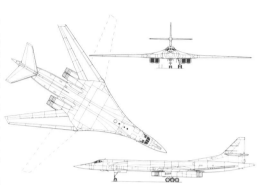

*Tupolev Tu-160 'Blackjack-A'*

*An unpainted Tu-160 retracts its gear and flaps during an airshow flyby. The Tu-160 is appreciably bigger than the American B-1B and is optimised for high level penetration.*

*A Tu-160 under escort by a pair of 'Flankers'. The standard Tu-160 colour scheme is an overall white finish reminiscent of the anti-flash paint once applied to Britain's V-bombers.*

## Specification: Tupolev Tu-160 'Blackjack-A'
**Origin:** USSR (now CIS)
**Type:** long-range strategic penetration bomber and missile platform
**Powerplant:** four 25000-kg (55,115-lb) afterburning thrust Kuznetsov NK-321 turbofans
**Performance:** maximum speed Mach 1.88 or 1,079 kt (2000 km/h; 1,243 mph; 2000 km/h) at 36,090 ft (11000 m); economical cruising speed 460 kt (850 km/h; 528 mph); service ceiling 60,040 ft (18300 m); range 14000 km (8,699 miles) with standard fuel
**Weights:** empty 118000 kg (260,140 lb); maximum take-off 275000 kg (606,261 lb)
**Dimensions:** span 55.70 m (182 ft 9 in) spread and 35.60 m (116 ft 9.75 in) swept; length 54.10 m (177 ft 6 in); height 13.10 m (43 ft 0 in); wing area 360.0 m² (3,875.13 sq ft) spread
**Armament:** provision for 16500 kg (36,376 lb) of disposable stores carried in two lower-fuselage weapon bays and on hardpoints under the wing gloves; typical weapons are free-fall nuclear and/or HE bombs, and/or missiles including up to 12 RK-55 (AS-15 'Kent') cruise missiles or 24 RKV-500B (AS-16 'Kickback') short-range attack missiles

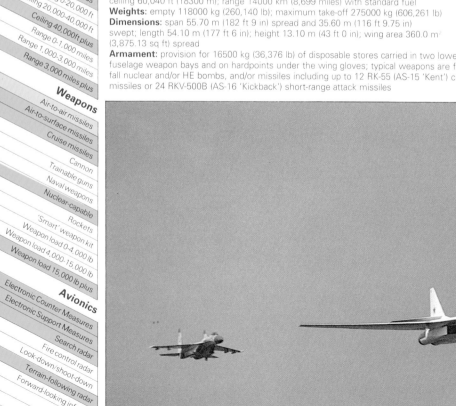

# Vought A-7 Corsair II (export versions)

*Vought A-7H of the Hellenic air force.*

Interest was shown in the **Vought A-7 Corsair II** by a number of foreign nations from a relatively early stage in the programme. A Swiss requirement for a de Havilland Venom/Hawker Hunter replacement in the ground attack role led to the modification of two USAF A-7Ds to A-7G standard for evaluation by the Flugwaffe at Emmen during April 1972. The Swiss air force was not impressed, however, and instead ordered more Hunters.

A second prospective customer for the A-7D was Pakistan, which would have used the aircraft to replace its elderly Martin B-57s. The suspension of US military aid had forced Pakistan to use its Shenyang J-6s (Chinese-built MiG-19s) in the ground-attack role for which they were not ideally suited. By the 1970s relations had improved, but Pakistan's purchase of a nuclear reprocessing plant from France in 1976 prompted President 'Jimmy' Carter to veto the sale of 110 Corsairs.

The first foreign nation actually to receive the A-7 was Greece, which was offered 60 Corsair IIs in 1972 as part of a wider US military aid package. Military aid to Greece had been suspended in 1967, when the military seized power, but was resumed after some liberal reforms and in response to a growing Soviet presence in the Mediterranean. Greece eventually received 60 examples of the single-seat Vought A-7H, basically a land-based version of the US Navy's A-7E with a

6804-kg (15,000-lb) dry thrust Allison TF41-A-400 turbofan. The first made its maiden flight on 6 May 1975, and deliveries were completed by 1977. Six two-seaters were ordered in 1978, and all of these **TA-7H** aircraft were delivered in 1980. All of the Greek aircraft, with the exception of one two-seater, were new production aircraft.

The Greek air force has three A-7 squadrons, serving with two wings. The 115 Pterix Mahis is based at Souda Bay in Crete with two squadrons, 340 and 345 Mire Dioseos. These aircraft have an important secondary air-defence responsibility using 300 AIM-9L Sidewinders ordered in mid-1980. The remaining squadron, the 347 Mira Dioseos, is based at Larissa as an element of the 110 Pterix. Its aircraft are used for the tactical air support of maritime operations.

The final foreign operator of the Corsair II is Portugal, which eventually took delivery of 50 single-seaters and six two-seaters under the designations **A-7P** and **TA-7P** respectively. All of Portugal's Corsair IIs were converted from redundant US Navy A-7As and A-7Bs, with the inbuilt armament of two 20-mm Mk 12 cannon and the Pratt & Whitney TF30 turbofan of these early aircraft but with the avionics suite and HUD of the A-7D and A-7E. The aircraft serve with Escuadra 302 and Escuadra 304 of Grupo Operacional 521 at Monte Real.

## Specification: Vought A-7P

**Origin:** USA
**Type:** single-seat tactical fighter
**Powerplant:** one 6078-kg (13,400-lb) dry thrust Pratt & Whitney TF30-P-408 turbofan
**Performance:** maximum speed 600 kt (1112 km/h; 691 mph) at sea level, or 561 kt (1040 km/h; 646 mph) t 5,000 ft (1525 m) with a 2722-kg (6,000-lb) bombload; service ceiling 51,000 ft (15545 m); ferry range 3669 km (2,280 miles) with internal fuel
**Weights:** empty 8676 kg (19,127 lb); maximum take-off 19051 kg (42,000 lb)
**Dimensions:** span 11.81 m (38 ft 9 in); length 14.06 m (46 ft 1.5 in); height 4.90 m (16 ft 0.75 in); wing area 34.84 m² (375.0 sq ft)
**Armament:** two 20-mm Mk 12 cannon with 340 rounds per gun; provision for more than 6804 kg (15,000 lb) of disposable stores on eight external hardpoints

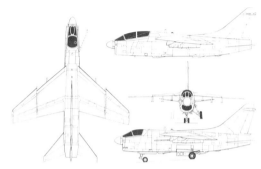

*Vought A-7P Corsair II (additional side view, top: TA-7P)*

*This is one of five new-build **TA-7Hs** delivered to the Hellenic air force. One more **TA-7H**, converted from a surplus US Navy Corsair, was also delivered. Each squadron has two two-seaters.*

*All of Portugal's **A-7Ps** are conversions from surplus US Navy A-7As and A-7Bs. Large quantities of spares were delivered with the 50 single-seat and six two-seat Corsair IIs.*

## Role
Fighter
Close support
Counter-insurgency
Tactical strike
Strategic bomber
Tactical reconnaissance
Strategic reconnaissance
Maritime patrol
Anti-ship strike
Anti-submarine warfare
Search and rescue
Assault transport
Transport
Liaison
Trainer
Inflight-refuelling tanker
Specialized

## Performance
All-weather capability
Rough field capability
STOL capability
VTOL capability
Airspeed 0-250 mph
Airspeed 250 mph-Mach 1
Airspeed Mach 1 plus
Ceiling 0-20,000 ft
Ceiling 20,000-40,000 ft
Ceiling 40,000ft plus
Range 0-1,000 miles
Range 1,000-3,000 miles
Range 3,000 miles plus

## Weapons
Air-to-air missiles
Air-to-surface missiles
Cruise missiles
Cannon
Trainable guns
Naval weapons
Nuclear-capable
Rockets
'Smart' weapon kit
Weapon load 0-4,000 lb
Weapon load 4,000-15,000 lb
Weapon load 15,000 lb plus

## Avionics
Electronic Counter Measures
Electronic Support Measures
Search radar
Fire control radar
Look-down/shoot-down
Terrain-following radar
Forward-looking infra-red
Laser
Television

# Vought F-8E(FN) Crusader

*Vought F-8E(FN) Crusader of Flottille 12F, Aéronavale.*

To meet a US Navy requirement of 1952 for an air superiority fighter with supersonic capability in level flight, no fewer than eight US manufacturers made a total of 22 design proposals. Vought was selected in May 1953 as winner of the design competition and was awarded a contract for three (subsequently reduced to two) XF8U-1 (later XF-8A) prototypes. The first of these made its initial flight on 25 March 1955. The **Vought F-8U** (later **F-8) Crusader** was the first aircraft designed from the start with a fuselage structure incorporating area rule, and was thus optimized for high performance from the very beginning. Its high-mounted swept wing had variable incidence capability to give an increased angle of attack during low-speed operations, keeping the fuselage more nearly level to enhance the pilot's view during take-off and landing, and also making it possible to have retractable tricycle landing gear with short shock struts. Power for the prototypes was provided by the 6713-kg (16,200-lb) afterburning thrust Pratt & Whitney J57-P-11 turbojet, changed to the 7348-kg (16,200-lb) afterburning thrust J57-P-41 in the initial production model that was delivered to the US Navy from March 1957.

The Crusader provided the US Navy and US Marine Corps with a valuable aircraft that saw effective service through most of the Vietnam War, and in consequence the type appeared in many variants for the fighter,

fighter-bomber, reconnaissance and training roles. The only variant now left in service is the **F-8E(FN)**, of which 42 were built to an improved F-8E standard with blown flaps and other high-lift devices for service on the comparatively short flightdecks of the French navy's two aircraft carriers.

The aircraft were ordered in 1963, and the prototype was a converted F-8D that first flew in February 1964. The first production warplane flew in June 1964 and all the aircraft had been delivered by January 1965. The type is a derivative of the F-8E with larger depression angles for the drooping ailerons and trailing-edge flaps, of which the latter were now of the blown type, and two-stage leading-edge flaps (with a 55° angle added to the original 27° angle), and its armament includes French short-range AAMs in place of the Sidewinders. As the F-8E(FN)'s successor, the Dassault Rafale-M, will not enter service until 1998 at the earliest, France planned to modernize 23 of its surviving F-8E(FN)s with the nav/attack system of the Dassault Mirage F1C (including the Thomson-CSF Cyrano IV radar to allow use of the Super 530 AAM), but in mid-1990 it was decided that the upgrade was not cost-effective (the price too great for the benefits offered) and the plan was therefore cancelled. Some 12 of the aircraft are instead being modernized very slightly with equipment such as the Thomson-CSF Sherloc RWR.

**Specification:** Vought F-8E(FN) Crusader
**Origin:** USA
**Type:** single-seat carrierborne interceptor and attack warplane
**Powerplant:** one 8165-kg (18,000-lb) afterburning thrust Pratt & Whitney J57-P-20A turbojet
**Performance:** maximum speed Mach 1.72 or 986 kt (1827 km/h; 1,135 mph) at 36,000 ft (10975 m); cruising speed 486 kt (901 km/h; 560 mph) at 40,000 ft (12190 m); initial climb rate about 21,000 ft (6400 m) per minute; service ceiling 58,000 ft (17680 m); combat radius 966 km (600 miles)
**Weights:** empty 9038 kg (19,925 lb); maximum take-off 15420 kg (34,000 lb)
**Dimensions:** span 10.87 m (35 ft 8 in); length 16.61 m (54 ft 6 in); height 4.80 m (15 ft 9 in); wing area 32.515 m² (350.0 sq ft)
**Armament:** four 20-mm M39 cannon with 144 rounds per gun; provision for 2268 kg (5,000 lb) of disposable stores, including two Matra R530 AAMs or eight 5-in (127-mm)

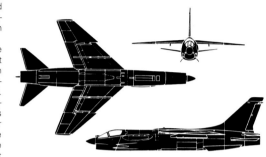

*Vought F-8E(FN) Crusader*

*Aéronavale F-8E(FN) Crusaders will continue to serve until the turn of the century, when they will be replaced by a navalized version of the Dassault Rafale multi-role fighter.*

*France's two aircraft-carriers, Foch and Clemenceau, will be replaced by Richelieu and Charles de Gaulle in the early 2000. Clemenceau's Crusaders have been involved in the Gulf War.*

# Westland Lynx (naval versions)

The original intention of the Anglo-French partners had been to adopt Westland's WG.13 design for shipboard use. However, the Lynx AH.Mk 1 for the UK's Army Air Corps was the first variant to enter service, a fact which helps to stress the difficulty of developing this helicopter to have the minimum of restrictions when operating from small ships. From the outset the design was optimized for shipboard use, and the military version was therefore an adaptation retaining features that had been intended for the naval Lynx, such as its foldable main rotor with a negative-pitch blade setting, but differing most noticeably by having skid rather than wheeled landing gear.

Royal Navy versions vary from the Lynx AH.Mk 1 by having a manually foldable rotor pylon and fixed tricycle landing gear with a twin-wheel nose unit and single-wheel main units. Each of the wheels has sprag-type brakes, providing a positive mechanical lock to prevent movement on a pitching/rolling deck, and these combine with a 6° negative pitch setting of the main rotor blades to give new operational capability, especially when combined with optional flotation gear and a harpoon deck-lock system. The Royal Navy's initial **Lynx HAS.Mk 2** is, like the Lynx AH.Mk 1, powered by two Rolls-Royce Gem 2 turboshafts, and entered service with No.702 Squadron in December 1977 after the completion of intensive trials. No.815 Squadron, the HQ unit for Lynx ship's flights, was com-

missioned at RNAS Yeovilton on 27 January 1981. In RN service, the Lynx's primary roles are ASW and ASV, but the type is also suitable for communications, fire support, liaison, reconnaissance, troop transport and vertical replenishment. The RN's 60 Lynx HAS.Mk 2s have since been complemented by 31 examples of the **Lynx HAS.Mk 3** with 835-kW (1,135-shp) Gem 41-1 turboshafts and an uprated transmission.

Versions for the French Aéronavale comprise the **Lynx Mk 2**, basically as the Lynx HAS.Mk 2 except for installed equipment and replacement of sprag brakes by conventional wheel brakes, followed by the **Lynx Mk 4** which has the uprated powerplant and transmission of the Lynx HAS.Mk 3. Comparable versions based on the Lynx HAS.Mk 2 have been ordered by countries such as Argentina (**Lynx Mk 23**), the Netherlands (**Lynx Mk 25**), Denmark (**Lynx Mk 80**) and Brazil (**Lynx Mk 89**), while those based on the Lynx HAS.Mk 3 have been ordered by the Netherlands (**Lynx Mk 27**), Norway (**Lynx Mk 86**) and Germany (**Lynx Mk 88**).

The latest standard is the Super Lynx naval counterpart of the Battlefield Lynx (see army Lynx entry), and to date the three most important customers for this type are the Royal Navy, the Portuguese navy and the South Korean navy, which have ordered the **Lynx HAS.Mk 8** conversion of the Lynx HAS.Mk 3, **Lynx Mk 95** (five) and **Lynx Mk 99** (12) versions respectively.

### Specification: Westland Lynx HAS.Mk 2
**Origin:** UK
**Type:** multi-role naval helicopter
**Powerplant:** two 671-kW (900-shp) Rolls-Royce Gem 2 turboshafts
**Performance:** maximum cruising speed 125 kt (232 km/h; 144 mph); best-endurance speed 70 kt (130 km/h; 81 mph); initial climb rate 2,170 ft (661 m) per minute; combat radius 93 km (58 miles) for a 2-hour patrol with two torpedoes and 10 per cent reserve
**Weights:** empty 3343 kg (7,370 lb) equipped for the ASW role; maximum take-off 4763 kg (10,500 lb)
**Dimensions:** main rotor diameter 12.80 m (42 ft 0 in); length, rotors turning 15.16 m (49 ft 9 in); height 3.60 m (11 ft 9.75 in); main rotor disc area 128.71 m² (1,385.45 sq ft)
**Armament:** two Mk 46 or Stingray torpedoes or Mk 11 depth charges in the ASW role, of four Sea Skua missiles in the anti-ship role

*Westland Lynx HAS.Mk 2(FN) of Flottille 31, Aéronavale, based at Lanvéoc-Poulmic.*

*Westland Lynx HAS.Mk 2*

*This Portland-based Lynx HAS.Mk 3 carries no squadron markings, but a heli-tele is mounted on the port fuselage side, with an unidentified pod to starboard and possibly housing a data-link system.*

*Three Lynx Mk 89s equip nO.101 Squadron, Nigerian navy, for use on the frigate NNS Aradu. They are shore-based at Ojo Navytown.*

**Role**

Fighter
Close support
Counter-insurgency
Tactical strike
Strategic bomber
Tactical reconnaissance
Strategic reconnaissance
Maritime patrol
Anti-ship strike
Anti-submarine warfare
Search and rescue
Assault transport
Transport
Liaison
Trainer
Inflight-refuelling tanker
Specialized

**Performance**

All-weather capability
Rough field capability
STOL capability
VTOL capability
Airspeed 0-250 mph
Airspeed 250 mph-Mach 1
Airspeed Mach 1 plus
Ceiling 0-20,000 ft
Ceiling 20,000-40,000 ft
Ceiling 40,000ft plus
Range 0-1,000 miles
Range 1,000-3,000 miles
Range 3,000 miles plus

**Weapons**

Air-to-air missiles
Air-to-surface missiles
Cruise missiles
Cannon
Trainable guns
Naval weapons
Nuclear-capable
Rockets
'Smart' weapon kit
Weapon load 0-4,000 lb
Weapon load 4,000-15,000 lb
Weapon load 15,000 lb plus

**Avionics**

Electronic Counter Measures
Electronic Support Measures
Search radar
Fire control radar
Look-down/shoot-down
Terrain-following radar
Forward-looking infra-red
Laser
Television

# Westland Lynx (army versions)

*Westland Lynx HC.Mk 28 of the Qatari police, sole export customer for the type.*

**Role**
Fighter
Close support
Counter-insurgency
Tactical strike
Strategic bomber
Tactical reconnaissance
Strategic reconnaissance
Maritime patrol
Anti-ship strike
Anti-submarine warfare
Search and rescue
Assault transport
Transport
Liaison
Trainer
Inflight-refuelling tanker
Specialized

**Performance**
All-weather capability
Rough field capability
STOL capability
VTOL capability
Airspeed 0-250 mph
Airspeed 250 mph-Mach 1
Airspeed Mach 1 plus
Ceiling 0-20,000 ft
Ceiling 20,000-40,000 ft
Ceiling 40,000ft plus
Range 0-1,000 miles
Range 1,000-3,000 miles
Range 3,000 miles plus

**Weapons**
Air-to-air missiles
Air-to-surface missiles
Cruise missiles
Cannon
Trainable guns
Naval weapons
Nuclear-capable
Rockets
'Smart' weapon kit
Weapon load 0-4,000 lb
Weapon load 4,000-15,000 lb
Weapon load 15,000 lb plus

**Avionics**
Electronic Counter Measures
Electronic Support Measures
Search radar
Fire control radar
Look-down/shoot-down
Terrain-following radar
Forward-looking infra-red
Laser
Television

Mutual French and UK interest in helicopters for their armed forces led to proposals made officially in February 1967 for collaboration between Aérospatiale in France and Westland in the UK: three helicopters were covered by an agreement finalized on 2 April 1968. The most important for Westland was that identified as the WG.13 for which the UK company had design leadership.

Although it was intended that the WG.13 would be developed for naval and civil use, was soon realized that there could also be a worthwhile military market and the programme was expanded to cater for this. The WG.13 designation was soon changed to the name **Westland Lynx**, and such was the emphasis placed on this helicopter by the Anglo-French partners that the first prototype was flown on 21 March 1971. Its configuration included a pod and boom fuselage structure accommodating an pilot and co-pilot plus a maximum of 12 lightly armed troops. Power for the four-blade semi-rigid main rotor and four-blade tail rotor was provided by two Rolls-Royce Gem 2 turboshafts mounted above the fuselage.

The team of prototypes used to speed the development programme had accumulated more than 2,000 flight hours by April 1975; soon after that date the first two production Lynx AH.Mk 1 helicopters for the British army began final testing at the A&AEE Boscombe Down. In mid-1977 an Army Aviation unit was formed at Middle Wallop,

Hampshire, and following completion of intensive trials delivery of production Lynx AH.Mk 1 helicopters began. Suitable for anti-tank attack, armed escort, casevac, command post, logistic support, reconnaissance, SAR and tactical transport roles, the army's Lynx AH.Mk 1 was the first version to be see active service when deployed to squadrons in West Germany. The British army ordered a total of 113 for the Army Air Corps, 60 of them equipped to carry TOW anti-tank missiles, and all had been delivered by February 1984. The army later ordered four similar **Lynx AH.Mk 5** helicopters that differed primarily by introducing Gem 41-1 turboshafts with a maximum rating of 835 kW (1,120 shp), two of them for the RAE and two for the MoD(PE) for continuing R&D. Thirteen **Lynx AH.Mk 7** helicopters ordered from 1985 are based on the Lynx AH.Mk 5 but have an opposite-rotation tail rotor and improved systems.

On 29 November 1989 Westland flew a Lynx Mk 7 converted as prototype of the Battlefield Lynx improved version intended for the export market with an advanced-technology four-blade main rotor powered by two 835-kW (1,120-shp) Gem 42-1 turboshafts. This type introduced a number of other important improvements, most notably to its systems, and the army ordered 16 such **Lynx AH.Mk 9** helicopters that were supplemented by eight Lynx AH.Mk 7 conversions, all with fixed tricycle landing gear.

## Specification: Westland Lynx AH.Mk 1
**Origin:** UK
**Type:** multi-role battlefield helicopter
**Powerplant:** two 671-kW (900-shp) Rolls-Royce Gem 2 turboshafts
**Performance:** maximum cruising speed 140 kt (249 km/h; 161 mph; best-endurance speed 70 kt (130 km/h; 81 mph); initial climb rate 2,480 ft (756 m) per minute; range 541 km (336 miles) as a troop transport with reserves
**Weights:** empty 2787 kg (6,144 lb); maximum take-off 4536 kg (10,000 lb)
**Dimensions:** main rotor diameter 12.80 m (42 ft 0 in); length, rotors turning 15.16 m (49 ft 9 in); height 3.66 m (12 ft 0 in); main rotor disc area 128.71 m² (1,385.45 sq ft)
**Armament:** can include 20- or 25-mm cannon, 7.62-mm (0.3-in) machine guns, rocket-launcher pods, or a variety of air-to-surface missiles

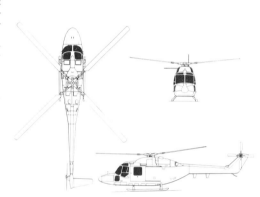

*Westland Lynx AH.Mk 1*

*The Lynx AH.Mk 1 forms the backbone of the Army Air Corps anti-tank squadrons supporting the British Army of the Rhine. This example carries TOW anti-tank missiles.*

*The Lynx AH.Mk 1 has now been complemented by the Lynx AH.Mk 7, which features more powerful engines and an opposite-rotating tail rotor as well as improved systems.*

# Westland Sea King (HAR and HAS)

*Westland Sea King Mk 45 of the Pakistan navy.*

However successful the Westland Wessex had proved, it failed to meet Westland's hopes for a combined hunter/killer helicopter for the Royal Navy's ASW requirement. Thus the company began licence negotiations for the twin-turbine Sikorsky S-61, of which the first prototype had flown on 11 March 1959. Procured by the US Navy as the HSS-2 Sea King, this was redesignated SH-3 Sea King in 1962.

Westland's licence agreement with Sikorsky covered the basic airframe, its dynamic system and the supply of four sample SH-3s. These reached the UK in the summer of 1967, complete with General Electric T58 turboshafts, and following its assembly the first of these helicopters was flown on 8 September 1967. Westland adopted with minimal change the airframe and rotor system of the SH-3 for the initial **Westland Sea King HAS.Mk 1**, which thus had five-blade main and tail rotors, and a fuselage structure that was basically an amphibious boat hull with, on each side, a stabilizing float into which the main units of the tailwheel landing gear retracted. However, the British helicopter introduced 1119-kW (1,500-shp) Rolls-Royce Gnome H.1400 turboshafts, advanced Newmark AFCS, Marconi Doppler, and for the 'hunter' side of its role Ecko search radar and Plessey sonar, the 'killer' aspect relying on a maximum of four homing torpedoes or depth charges. The first production Sea King HAS.Mk 1 was flown on 7 May 1969, and deliveries of six production helicopters to the Royal Navy allowed No.700S Squadron to be commissioned on

19 August 1969 for intensive flying trials.

This first British version of the S-61 led to the belief that all Westland Sea Kings were merely copies of the US design, but over the years Westland has introduced many improvements. The Sea King HAS.Mk 1 was followed by the upgraded **Sea King HAS.Mk 2** with uprated Gnome H.1400-1 engines and a six-blade tail rotor; the RN later modified its Sea King HAS.Mk 1s to this standard. Ten of the helicopters were later converted to **Sea King AEW.Mk 2A** standard with Thorn EMI Searchwater radar with its antenna in a large side-mounted radome projecting below the hull.

A similarly powered **Sea King HAR.Mk 3** for the RAF carries a crew of four and up to 19 survivors, or 11 survivors and two litters, or six litters. The RN's **Sea King HAS.Mk 5**, identifiable by the larger dorsal radome for its search radar, has GEC Avionics LAPADS acoustic processing/display for better ASW capability; space for the equipment and its operator was gained by moving the rear bulkhead farther to the rear. Export equivalents of these RN and RAF versions include the **Sea Kings Mk 41, 42, 42A, 43, 43A, 45, 47, 48** and **50**. Potentially the most important is the **Sea King Mk 42B** ordered by the Indian navy in the ASW role, for this is based on Westland's Advanced Sea King concept with composite main rotor blades, uprated transmission, strengthened airframe, GEC Avionics ASQ-902 sonobuoy/tactical processor, and provision for Sea Eagle anti-ship missiles. The RN has ordered a basically similar type as the **Sea King HAS.Mk 6**.

*Westland Sea King HAS.Mk 5*

*These are Sea King HAS.Mk 5s of the Culdrose-based No.820 Squadron. The Sea King HAS.Mk 5 is equipped with Sea Searcher radar and advanced avionics for its primary ASW role.*

*A Sea King HAR.Mk 3 of No.202 Squadron, RAF, hovers over an RNLI lifeboat during a search-and-rescue co-operation exercise. Rescue Sea Kings in the Falklands wear a grey colour scheme.*

**Specification:** Sea King HAS Mk 5
**Origin:** UK
**Type:** ASW and SAR naval helicopter
**Powerplant:** two 1238-kW (1,660-shp) Rolls-Royce Gnome H.1400-1 turboshafts
**Performance:** cruising speed 112 kt (108 km/h; 129 mph) at sea level; initial climb rate 2,020 ft (616 m) per minute; range 1230 km (764 miles) with standard fuel
**Weights:** empty 6202 kg (13,672 lb); maximum take-off 9525 kg (21,000 lb)
**Dimensions:** main rotor diameter 18.90 m (61 ft 0 in); length, rotors turning 22.15 m (72 ft 8 in); height 5.13 m (16 ft 10 in); main rotor disc area 280.47 m² (3,019.08 sq ft)
**Armament:** four Mk 11 depth charges, or Mk 46 or Stingray torpedoes

**Role**
Fighter
Close support
Counter-insurgency
Tactical strike
Strategic bomber
Tactical reconnaissance
Strategic reconnaissance
Maritime patrol
Anti-ship strike
Anti-submarine warfare
Search and rescue
Assault transport
Transport
Liaison
Trainer
Inflight-refuelling tanker
Specialized

**Performance**
All-weather capability
Rough field capability
STOL capability
VTOL capability
Airspeed 0-250 mph
Airspeed 250 mph-Mach 1
Airspeed Mach 1 plus
Ceiling 0-20,000 ft
Ceiling 20,000-40,000 ft
Ceiling 40,000ft plus
Range 0-1,000 miles
Range 1,000-3,000 miles
Range 3,000 miles plus

**Weapons**
Air-to-air missiles
Air-to-surface missiles
Cruise missiles
Cannon
Trainable guns
Naval weapons
Nuclear-capable
Rockets
'Smart' weapon kit
Weapon load 0-4,000 lb
Weapon load 4,000-15,000 lb
Weapon load 15,000 lb

**Avionics**
Electronic Counter Measures
Electronic Support Measures
Search radar
Fire control radar
Look-down/shoot-down
Terrain-following radar
Forward-looking infra-red
Laser
Television

# Westland Sea King (HC and Commando)

**Role**
Fighter
Close support
Counter-insurgency
Tactical strike
Strategic bomber
Tactical reconnaissance
Strategic reconnaissance
Maritime patrol
Anti-ship strike
Anti-submarine warfare
Search and rescue
Assault transport
Transport
Liaison
Inflight-refuelling tanker
Trainer
Specialized

**Performance**
All-weather capability
Rough field capability
STOL capability
VTOL capability
Airspeed 0-250 mph
Airspeed 250 mph-Mach 1
Airspeed Mach 1 plus
Ceiling 0-20,000 ft
Ceiling 20,000-40,000 ft
Ceiling 40,000ft plus
Range 0-1,000 miles
Range 1,000-3,000 miles
Range 3,000 miles plus

**Weapons**
Air-to-air missiles
Air-to-surface missiles
Cruise missiles
Cannon
Trainable guns
Naval weapons
Nuclear-capable
Rockets
'Smart' weapon kit
Weapon load 0-4,000 lb
Weapon load 4,000-15,000 lb
Weapon load 15,000 lb plus

**Avionics**
Electronic Counter Measures
Electronic Support Measures
Search radar
Fire control radar
Look-down/shoot-down
Terrain-following radar
Forward-looking infra-red
Laser
Television

Evaluation by Westland of the lifting capacity of the Sea King brought the realization that a specialized land-based helicopter derived from the Sea King could generate additional sales. Work therefore began on a tactical military helicopter, later named **Westland Commando**, and the first **Commando Mk 1** made its maiden flight on 12 September 1973. This was developed as a multi-role helicopter for primary roles that include cargo transport, casualty evacuation, logistic support and tactical troop transport as well, but is also suitable for secondary tasks such as SAR and air-to-surface attack.

In its original Commando Mk 1 form, this helicopter was basically a minimum-change version of the Sea King Mk 41 which had been supplied to the West German navy, retaining its Gnome H.1400 engines but stripped of the avionics required for the ASW/SAR role to provide internal volume for a maximum of 21 seated troops. The initial order for the Commando was placed by Saudi Arabia, which procured a total of 24 for the Egyptian air force. The first of these helicopters was delivered in January 1974 and was one of five interim Commando Mk 1s, the other 19 being completed to full **Commando Mk 2** standard that that first taken to the air on 16 January 1975. Changes in the Mk 2 version were a non-folding main rotor and a six-blade tail rotor, but the folding tail section was retained to facilitate storage. The uprated Gnome

H.1400-1 powerplant was installed, non-retractable landing gear was adopted, and the stabilizing floats of the Sea King were replaced by short stub wings. Internal accommodation was provided for a crew of two and up to 28 troops, although the cabin can also be laid out for 2722 kg (6,000 lb) of freight. In addition to the standard Commando Mk 2s for the Egyptian air force, Westland supplied two **Commando Mk 2B** VIP transports to Egypt, and also the **Commando Mk 2A** and **Commando Mk 2C** to the Qatari air force for transport and VIP use respectively.

The Royal Navy also became interested in the commando, and began procurement of a revised utility version as the **Sea King HC.Mk 4**. In services with Nos 707, 845 and 846 Squadrons for the naval air commando role, the helicopter retains many features of the Commando Mk 2 but differs primarily in having folding main rotor blades. It can accommodate the same internal load of up to 28 fully equipped troops or 2722 kg (6,000 lb) of cargo, and carry an external slung load of up to 3629 kg (8,000 lb). The RN's Sea King HC.Mk 4 carry a door-mounted 7.62-mm (0.3-in) machine gun as standard, but all Commandos have provision for a range of alternative guns, rockets and missiles. Included in the RN orders were two helicopters for development purposes at the RAE Farnborough, and these have the designation **Sea King Mk 4X**.

## Specification: Sea King HC Mk.4
**Origin:** UK
**Type:** tactical transport helicopter
**Powerplant:** two 1238-kW (1,660-shp) Rolls-Royce Gnome H.1400-1 turboshafts
**Performance:** cruising speed 112 kt (108 km/h; 129 mph) at sea level; initial climb rate 2,020 ft (616 m) per minute; range 444 km (276 miles) with 28 troops and fuel for a 30-minute stand-off
**Weights:** empty 5700 kg (12,566 lb); maximum take-off 9525 kg (21,000 lb)
**Dimensions:** main rotor diameter 18.90 m (61 ft 0 in); length, rotors turning 22.15 m (72 ft 8 in); height 5.13 m (16 ft 10 in); main rotor disc area 280.47 m² (3,019.08 sq ft)
**Armament:** see text

*Westland Commando of the Egyptian air force.*

*Westland Commando*

*These are Sea King HC.Mk 4s of No.846 Squadron, Royal Navy, a Yeovilton-based support helicopter unit. The fixed landing gear of this variant is immediately apparent.*

*The Qatari air force operates 12 Commandos on general, VIP and assault transport duties. Four of the helicopters have been converted to carry Exocet anti-ship missiles.*

# Westland Wasp

Simultaneously with its development of the Scout for service with the UK Army Air Corps, Westland began work to provide from the same source (the Saunders-Roe P.531) a five-seat general-purpose helicopter optimized for operation from and to ships at sea. After first being evaluated at the A&AEE Boscombe Down, the second of the P.531 prototypes was used by the Royal Navy from November 1959 in an extended period of testing before the procurement and supply of three additional P.531-O/N prototypes for continuation and expansion of the test programme.

The task was not merely test and evaluation of the P.531 but, in conjunction with the RN, Westland decided to investigate problems relating to operation of helicopters from and to small ships and, if possible, to find solutions that would allow ships such as frigates to carry and use a helicopter in most sea states. Thus this type of vessel was involved primarily in the investigation, during which literally hundreds of take-offs and landings were made to establish the most effective combination of landing gear/deck securing system. At the same time, a Saro Skeeter was being used by Westland and Louis Newmark to develop a suitable autopilot/autostabilization system to widen the operational envelope.

By the end of the tests, the RN had sufficient confidence in the capability of the P.531 to order the type into production as the Sea Scout HAS.Mk 1, with two pre-production helicopters for familiarization. The first of these was flown initially on 28 October 1962, by which time the designation had been changed to **Wasp HAS. Mk 1**, and deliveries of production helicopters began in mid-1963; these differed by having a more powerful engine, plus foldable main rotor blades and tail rotor pylon, and were easily distinguishable from the Scout by their quadricycle landing gear. The production Wasps equipped first an Initial Flying Trials Unit which formed as RNAS Culdrose on 4 June 1963. It is worth recording that during February 1963 pre-production helicopters, used in tests on board the frigate HMS Nubian, made more than 200 take-offs and landing by day and night and in all conditions of wind and sea.

Production of the Wasp HAS.Mk 1 for the Royal Navy totalled 98, of which about 40 remained in use in the mid-1980s. Most of these were phased out of service during 1988, but a few operating from survey and hospital ships continued in use for two or three more years. As well as those Wasps built for the Royal Navy, 35 were exported for use by the naval air arms of four countries.

**Westland Wasp HAS.Mk 1 of No.829 Squadron, Royal Navy.**

**Westland Wasp HAS.Mk 1**

**This ex-Dutch Wasp serves with No.400 Skwadron, Indonesian navy. Ten Wasps were delivered and nine remain in service, mainly for advanced and weapon training duties.**

**Three Wasps are attached to No.3 Squadron, Royal New Zealand Air Force, for use on board the Royal New Zealand Navy frigates HMNZS Waikato and Canterbury.**

**Specification:** Westland Wasp HAS.Mk 1
**Origin:** UK
**Type:** shipboard multi-role helicopter
**Powerplant:** one 783-kW (1,050-shp) Rolls Royce (Bristol) Nimbus Mk 103 or Mk 104 turboshaft de-rated to 529 kW (710 shp)
**Performance:** maximum speed 104 kt (193 km/h; 120 mph) at sea level; maximum cruising speed 96 kt (179 km/h: 111 mph); initial climb rate 1,440 ft (439 m) per minute; service ceiling 12,200 ft (3720 m); maximum range 488 km (303 miles) with standard fuel
**Weights:** empty 1566 kg (3,452 lb); maximum take-off 2495 kg (5,500 lb)
**Dimensions:** main rotor diameter 9.83 m (32 ft 3 in); length, rotors turning 12.29 m (40 ft 4 in); height 2.72 m (8 ft 11 in); main rotor disc area 75.89 m² (816.87sq ft)
**Armament:** an underfuselage weapons load of some 245 kg (540 lb) can include two Mk 44 or Mk 46 homing torpedoes, or bombs or depth charges; some helicopters were equipped to carry Nord AS.11 or AS.12 missiles

### Role
Fighter
Close support
Counter-insurgency
Tactical strike
Strategic bomber
Tactical reconnaissance
Strategic reconnaissance
Maritime patrol
Anti-ship strike
Anti-submarine warfare
Search and rescue
Assault transport
Transport
Liaison
Trainer
Inflight-refuelling tanker
Specialized

### Performance
All-weather capability
Rough field capability
STOL capability
VTOL capability
Airspeed 0-250 mph
Airspeed 250 mph-Mach 1
Airspeed Mach 1 plus
Ceiling 0-20,000 ft
Ceiling 20,000-40,000 ft
Ceiling 40,000ft plus
Range 0-1,000 miles
Range 1,000-3,000 miles
Range 3,000 miles plus

### Weapons
Air-to-air missiles
Air-to-surface missiles
Cruise missiles
Cannon
Trainable guns
Naval weapons
Nuclear-capable
Rockets
'Smart' weapon kit
Weapon load 0-4,000 lb
Weapon load 4,000-15,000 lb
Weapon load 15,000 lb plus

### Avionics
Electronic Counter Measures
Electronic Support Measures
Search radar
Fire control radar
Look-down/shoot-down
Terrain-following radar
Forward-looking infra-red
Laser
Television

# Yakovlev Yak-38 'Forger'

*Yakovlev Yak-38 'Forger-A' of the Soviet navy.*

**Role**
Fighter
Close support
Counter-insurgency
Tactical strike
Strategic bomber
Tactical reconnaissance
Strategic reconnaissance
Maritime patrol
Anti-ship strike
Anti-submarine warfare
Search and rescue
Assault transport
Transport
Liaison
Trainer
Inflight-refuelling tanker
Specialized

**Performance**
All-weather capability
Rough field capability
STOL capability
VTOL capability
Airspeed 0-250 mph
Airspeed 250 mph-Mach 1
Airspeed Mach 1 plus
Ceiling 0-20,000 ft
Ceiling 20,000-40,000 ft
Ceiling 40,000ft plus
Range 0-1,000 miles
Range 1,000-3,000 miles
Range 3,000 miles plus

**Weapons**
Air-to-air missiles
Air-to-surface missiles
Cruise missiles
Cannon
Trainable guns
Naval weapons
Nuclear-capable
Rockets
'Smart' weapon kit
Weapon load 0-4,000 lb
Weapon load 4,000-15,000 lb
Weapon load 15,000 lb plus

**Avionics**
Electronic Counter Measures
Electronic Support Measures
Search radar
Fire control radar
Look-down/shoot-down
Terrain-following radar
Forward-looking infra-red
Laser
Television

Although a completely new design, the aircraft now known as the **Yakovlev Yak-38** was derived from the Yak-36MP prototype that first flew in 1971,using the jet-powered VTOL system first developed in the Yak-36 VTOL research aircraft. Production began in 1975 and it entered service in 1976, first with a development squadron operating aboard the name ship of the 'Kiev' class aircraft carriers and then on her three sister ships.

In configuration the Yak-38, which has the NATO reporting name **'Forger-A'**, has a mid-set wing which is of small area and has some 45° of sweep on the leading edge The wing folds at approximately mid-span for carrier stowage: the trailing edges of the inner panels have Fowler-type flaps, and those of the outer panels carry the ailerons. At each wing tip there are jet reaction control valves. The landing gear is of retractable tricycle type and the conventional tail unit has sweepback on all surfaces. The fuselage provides single-seat accommodation for a pilot on a zero-zero ejector seat, houses the mixed powerplant, and at the extreme rear has a small tailcone incorporating a reaction control nozzle in each side. Power is provided by two Rybinsk lift-jets mounted in tandem behind the cockpit and a Tumanskii turbojet in the central fuselage. The latter is the main engine and exhausts via twin nozzles, one on each side of the fuselage, that can be vectored through about 100°. Combined use of the lift-jets and the vectored thrust make VTOL operations possible but, as was the case with the BAe Harrier, a short take-off run with lift-jets operative is essential for the carriage of a tactically useful quantity of fuel and weapons.

In addition to the single-seat 'Forger-A' there is a two-seat **'Forger-B'** with a lengthened nose to provide a second (pupil's) cockpit forward of the standard pilot's (instructor's) cockpit. This displaces the ranging radar of the 'Forger-A' and the longer nose is balanced by a fuselage 'plug' aft of the wing. Deletion of the underwing pylons leaves little doubt that the 'Forger-B' is used solely for conversion training.

First deployed by a development squadron on board the carrier *Kiev* on her shakedown cruise in 1976, the Yak-38 was later allocated to squadrons on board her sister ships *Minsk*, *Novorossiysk* and *Admiral of the Fleet Gorshkov* (later *Baku*) with a strength of 12 'Forger-A' and one 'Forger-B' aircraft per squadron. The primary task of the 'Forger-A' is assumed to be fleet defence, reconnaissance and, to a more limited extent, attack against small surface vessels.

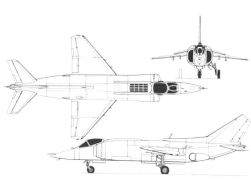

**Yakovlev Yak-38 'Forger-A'**

**Specification:** Yakovlev Yak-38 'Forger-A'
**Origin:** USSR (now CIS)
**Type:** carrierborne V/STOL combat aircraft
**Powerplant:** one 6950-kg (15,322-lb) dry thrust Tumanskii R-27V-300 vectored-thrust turbojet, and two 3050-kg (6,724-lb) dry thrust Rybinsk RD-36-35VFR lift turbojets
**Performance:** maximum speed 545 kt (1009 km/h; 627 mph) at high altitude; initial climb rate 14,765 ft (4500 m) per minute; service ceiling 39,370 ft (12000 m); combat radius 370 km (230 miles) on a hi-lo-hi mission with maximum warload, or 240 km (150 miles) on a lo-lo-lo mission with maximum warload
**Weights:** empty 7485 kg (16,502 lb); maximum take-off 11700 kg (25,795 lb0
**Dimensions:** span 7.32 m (24 ft 0.2 in); length 15.50 m (50 ft 10.2 in); height 4.37 m (14 ft 4 in); wing area18.5 m² (199.14 sq ft)
**Armament:** provision for 2000 kg (4,409 lb) of disposable stores, including AAMs, ASMs, bombs, rocket-launcher pods, cannon pods and drop tanks, carried on four external hardpoints

*The Yak-38 'Forger-B' is a two-seat trainer variant of this versatile but limited V/STOL attack fighter, and one or two are generally deployed on each of the 'Kiev' class aircraft carriers.*

*Until the Russian navy deploys its new full-scale aircraft carrier, the Yak-38 will remain its primary air superiority and close air support tool.*

# INDEX

20H Gardian, see Dassault-Breguet Falcon
35 Draken, see Saab
105, see Saab
146, see British Aerospace (HS)
206, see Bell
212 Aviocar, see CASA
330/C-23 Sherpa, see Shorts
406, see Bell
690B, see Rockwell International Turbo
    Commander
748, see British Aerospace (Avro/HS)

## A

A-4 Skyhawk, see McDonnell Douglas
A-6 Intruder, see Grumman
A-7 Corsair II, see Vought
A-10A Thunderbolt II, see Fairchild Republic
A-37 Dragonfly, see Cessna
A-50 'Mainstay', see Ilyushin
A 129 Mangusta, see Agusta
AB 205, see Agusta-Bell
AB 206, see Agusta-Bell
AB 212ASW, see Agusta-Bell
AB 412 Grifone, see Agusta-Bell
AC-130 Hercules, see Lockheed
ADV, see Panavia Tornado
Aeritalia G222: 14
Aeritalia (Lockheed) F-104S Starfighter: 13
Aeritalia (Lockheed) F-104S ASA Starfighter: 12
Aeritalia/Aermacchi/EMBRAER AMX: 15
Aermacchi Atlas Impala: 16
Aermacchi M.B.326: 17
Aermacchi M.B.326K: 16
Aermacchi M.B.339: 18
Aermacchi M.B.339K Veltro 2: 19
Aero L-29 Delfin: 20
Aero L-39 Albatros: 21
Aerospatiale AS.332 Super Puma: 23
Aerospatiale AS.350 Asta: 22
Aerospatiale AS.350 Ecureuil: 22
Aerospatiale AS.355 Ecureuil 2: 22
Aerospatiale AS.355 Twin Star: 22
Aerospatiale HH-65A Dolphin: 28
Aerospatiale SA.316B Alouette III: 29
Aerospatiale SA.319B Alouette III: 29
Aerospatiale SA.321 Super Frelon: 30
Aerospatiale SA.341 Gazelle: 25
Aerospatiale SA.342 Gazelle: 26
Aerospatiale SA.360 Dauphin: 27
Aerospatiale SA.365 Dauphin 2: 27
Aerospatiale/Westland SA.330 Puma: 24
Agusta A 129 Mangusta: 31
Agusta-Bell AB 205: 32
Agusta-Bell AB 206: 53
Agusta-Bell AB 212ASW: 33
Agusta-Bell AB 412 Griffon: 34
Agusta-Sikorsky AS-61: 35
AH-1 Huey Cobra, see Bell
AH-1J/T Sea Cobra, see Bell
AH-64 Apache, see McDonnell Douglas
AIDC AT-TC-3: 36
AIDC Ching Kuo: 37
Airtech CN-235: 38
AJ37 Viggen, see Saab
Albatros, see Aero L-39
Albatross, see Grumman U-16
Alenia, see Aeritalia
Alouette III, see Aeropatiale SA.316B, 319B
Alpha Jet, see Dassault-Breguet/Dornier
AMX, see Aeritalia/Aermacchi/EMBRAER
An-2, see Antonov
An-12 'Cub', see Antonov
An-14, see Antonov
An-22, see Antonov
An-24, see Antonov
An-26, see Antonov

An-30, see Antonov
An-32, see Antonov
An-72, see Antonov
An-74, see Antonov
An-124 Ruslan, see Antonov
Andover, see British Aerospace (Avro/HS)
Antonov An-2: 39
Antonov An-12 'Cub-A': 40
Antonov An-12 'Cub-B/C/D': 41
Antonov An-14: 42
Antonov An-22: 43
Antonov An-24: 44
Antonov An-26: 45
Antonov An-30: 46
Antonov An-32: 47
Antonov An-72: 48
Antonov An-74: 48
Antonov An-124 Ruslan: 49
Apache, see McDonnell Douglas AH-64
AS-61, see Agusta-Sikorsky
AS.332 Super Puma, see Aerospatiale
AS.350 Asta, see Aerospatiale
AS.350 Ecureuil, see Aerospatiale
AS.355 Ecureuil 2, see Aerospatiale
AS.355 Twin Star, see Aerospatiale
Asta, see Aerospatiale AS.350
ASTA, see GAF
AT-TC-3, see AIDC
Atlantic, see Dassault-Breguet Br.1150
Atlantique 2, see Dassault-Breguet
Atlas Cheetah: 50
Atlas Impala, see Aermacchi
AV-8A/C Harrier, see British
    Aerospace/McDonnell Douglas
AV-8B Harrier II, see McDonnell Douglas/BAe
AV-8S Matador, see British Aerospace/McDonnell
    Douglas
Aviocar, see CASA 212
Aviojet, see CASA C-101

## B

B-1B Lancer, see Rockwell
B-2, see Northrop/Grumman
B-52H Stratofortress, see Boeing
'Backfire', see Tupolev Tu-22M
BAe (Hawker/HS) Hunter (fighter/bombers): 73
Bandeirante, see EMBRAER EMB-110, EMB-111
'Beagle', see Ilyushin Il-28
'Bear', see Tupolev Tu-95, Tu-142
Bell 206 (OH-58A Kiowa): 58
Bell 406 (OH-58D Kiowa): 58
Bell AH-1 Huey Cobra: 54
Bell AH-1J/T Sea Cobra: 55
Bell Model 204: 51
Bell Model 205: 52
Bell Model 206: 53
Bell Model 206L Texas Ranger: 53
Bell Model 209 (single-engine): 54
Bell Model 209 (twin-engine): 55
Bell Model 212 Twin Two-Twelve: 56
Bell Model 214: 57
Bell Model TH57 Sea Ranger: 53
Bell Model UH-1 Iroquois: 51
Bell Model UH-1D Iroquois: 52
Bell Model UH-1H Iroquois: 52
Bell Model UH-1N: 56
Bell OH-58 Kiowa: 58
Bell/Boeing Vertol V-22 Osprey: 59
BK 117, see MBB/Kawasaki
'Blackjack', see Tupolev Tu-160
'Blinder', see Tupolev Tu-22
BN-2B Islander/Defender, see Pilatus/Britten-
    Norman
BN-2T Turbine Islander/Defender, see
    Pilatus/Britten-Norman
Boeing B-52H Stratofortress: 60

Boeing C-137: 64
Boeing EC-135: 61
Boeing KC-135E and KC-135R: 62
Boeing RC-135: 63
Boeing Vertol CH-46 Sea Knight: 65
Boeing Vertol CH-47 Chinook: 66
Boeing Vertol Model 107: 65
Boeing Vertol Model 114: 66
Br.1150 Atlantic, see Dassault-Breguet
British Aerospace (Avro/HS) 748: 68
British Aerospace (Avro/HS) Andover: 68
British Aerospace (BAC) One-Eleven: 76
British Aerospace (BAC) Strikemaster: 79
British Aerospace (EECo/BAC) Canberra
    (bomber versions): 69
British Aerospace (EECo/BAC) Canberra
    (reconnaissance versions): 70
British Aerospace (HS) 146: 67
British Aerospace (HS) Harrier T.Mk 4: 71
British Aerospace (HS) Hawk: 72
British Aerospace (HS) Nimrod MR.Mk 1: 75
British Aerospace (HS) Nimrod MR.Mk 2: 74
British Aerospace (Vickers-Armstrongs/BAC)
    VC10: 80
British Aerospace Sea Harrier FRS.Mk1: 77
British Aerospace Sea Harrier FRS.Mk2: 78
British Aerospace/McDonnell Douglas AV-8A/C
    Harrier: 81
British Aerospace/McDonnell Douglas AV-8S
    Matador: 81
British Aerospace/McDonnell Douglas T-45
    Goshawk: 82
Bronco, see Rockwell OV-10
Buckeye, see Rockwell T-2

## C

C-1, see Kawasaki
C-5 Galaxy, see Lockheed
C-17, see McDonnell Douglas
C-47 Skytrain/Dakota, see Douglas
C-101 Aviojet, see CASA
C-130A/G Hercules, see Lockheed
C-130H/K Hercules, see Lockheed
C-137, see Boeing
C-141 StarLifter, see Lockheed
C-160, see Transall
Canadair CF-5 Freedom Fighter: 83
Canadair CL-41 Tutor: 84
Canberra (bomber versions), see British
    Aerospace (EECo/BAC)
Canberra (reconnaissance versions), see British
    Aerospace (EECo/BAC)
'Candid', see Ilyushin Il-76
CASA 212 Aviocar: 85
CASA C-101 Aviojet: 86
Cessna A-37 Dragonfly: 87
Cessna Model 318E: 87
Cessna Model 337 Skymaster: 88
Cessna O-2: 88
CF-5 Freedom Fighter, see Canadair
CH-34 Choctaw, see Sikorsky
CH-46 Sea Knight, see Boeing Vertol
CH-47 Chinook, see Boeing Vertol
CH-53, see Sikorsky
Cheetah, see Atlas
Ching Kuo, see AIDC
Chinook. see Boeing Vertol CH-47 :
Choctaw, see Sikorsky CH-34
CL-41 Tutor, see Canadair
CN-235, see Airtech
Convair F-106 Delta Dart: 89
'Coot', see Ilyushin Il-18
'Coot-A', see Ilyushin Il-20
Corsair II, see Vought A-7
Crusader, see Vought F-8E (FN)
'Cub', see Antonov An-12

## D

D.140 Mousquetaire, see Jodel
Dakota, see Douglas C-47
Dassault-Breguet Atlantique 2: 91
Dassault-Breguet Br.1150 Atlantic: 90
Dassault-Breguet Etendard: 92
Dassault-Breguet Falcon 20: 93
Dassault-Breguet Falcon 20H Gardian: 93
Dassault-Breguet Falcon 200: 93
Dassault-Breguet III/V upgrades: 96
Dassault-Breguet Mirage III trainers: 95
Dassault-Breguet Mirage IIIR: 94
Dassault-Breguet Mirage IV: 97
Dassault-Breguet Mirage 5: 98
Dassault-Breguet Mirage 5R: 94
Dassault-Breguet Mirage 50: 99
Dassault-Breguet Mirage 2000B: 103
Dassault-Breguet Mirage 2000C: 104
Dassault-Breguet Mirage 2000N: 104
Dassault-Breguet Mirage F1A: 100
Dassault-Breguet Mirage F1C: 101
Dassault-Breguet Mirage F1E: 100
Dassault-Breguet Mirage F1R: 102
Dassault-Breguet Rafale A/B/C/M: 105
Dassault-Breguet Super Etendard: 106
Dassault-Breguet/Dornier Alpha Jet Close
    Support Version): 107
Dauphin, see Aerospatiale SA.360
de Havilland Canada DHC-6 Twin Otter: 108
Delfin, see Aero L-29
Delta Dart, see Convair F-106
DHC-6 Twin Otter, see de Havilland Canada
Do-28, see Dornier
Do-228, see Dornier
Dolphin, see Aerospatiale HH-65A
Dornier Do-28: 109
Dornier Do-228: 110
Dornier Model 128: 109
Douglas C-47 Skytrain/Dakota: 111
Dragonfly, see Cessna A-37
Draken, see Saab 35

## E

E-2 Hawkeye, see Grumman
EA-6B Prowler, see Grumman
Eagle, see McDonnell Douglas F-15
EC-135, see Boeing
Ecureuil, see Aerospatiale AS.350
Ecureuil 2, see Aerospatiale AS.355
EF-111A Raven, see Grumman/General
    Dynamics
EF-2000, see Eurofighter
EH-60, see Sikorsky
EH.101, see EH Industries
EH Industries EH.101: 112
EMB-110 Bandeirante, see EMBRAER
EMB-111 Bandeirante, see EMBRAER
EMB-312 Tucano, see EMBRAER
EMBRAER EMB-110 Bandeirante: 113
EMBRAER EMB-111 Bandeirante: 114
EMBRAER EMB-312 Tucano: 115
EP-3 Orion, see Lockheed
Eurocopter, see Aerospatiale
Etendard, see Dassault-Breguet
Eurofighter EF-2000: 116

## F

F-1, see Mitsubishi
F-4C/D Phantom II, see McDonnell Douglas
F-4E/F Phantom II, see McDonnell Douglas
F-4G 'Wild Weasel V', see McDonnell Douglas
F-5A /B Freedom Fighter, see Northrop
F-5E, see Northrop
F-8E (FN) Crusader, see Vought
F-14A Tomcat, see Grumman

F-14B/D Tomcat, see Grumman
F-15A/C Eagle, see McDonnell Douglas
F-15B/D Eagle, see McDonnell Douglas
F-15E Eagle, see McDonnell Douglas
F-16A/C/N Fighting Falcon, see General
    Dynamics
F-16B/D Fighting Falcon, see General Dynamics
F-22, see Lockheed/Boeing
F.27 (surveillance versions), see Fokker
F-104S ASA Starfighter, see Aeritalia (Lockheed)
F-104S Starfighter, see Aeritalia (Lockheed)
F-106 Delta Dart, see Convair
F-111, see General Dynamics
F-117 Night Hawk, see Lockheed
F/A-18A/C Hornet, see McDonnell Douglas
F/A-18B/D Hornet, see McDonnell Douglas
Fairchild Republic A-10A Thunderbolt II: 119
Falcon 20, see Dassault-Breguet
Falcon 200, see Dassault-Breguet
'Farmer', see Mikoyan-Gurevich MiG-19 and
    Shenyang J-6
'Fencer', see Sukhoi Su-24
Fighting Falcon, see General Dynamics F-16
'Fitter', see Sukhoi Su-17, Su-20 and Su-22
'Flagon', see Sukhoi Su-15 and Su-21
'Flanker', see Sukhoi Su-27
'Flogger', see Mikoyan-Gurevich MiG-23,
    Mikoyan MiG-27
'Frogfoot', see Sukhoi Su-25
FMA IA 58A Pucará: 117
FMA IA 63 Pampa: 118
Fokker F.27 (surveillance versions): 120
'Forger', see Yakovlev Yak-38
'Foxbat-A', see Mikoyan MiG-25
'Foxhound', see Mikoyan MiG-31
Freedom Fighter CF-5, see Canadair
Freedom Fighter F-5A /B, see Northrop
'Fresco', see Mikoyan-Gurevich MiG-17
FRS.Mk1, see British Aerospace Sea Harrier
FRS.Mk2, see British Aerospace Sea Harrier
Fuji T-1: 121
'Fulcrum', see Mikoyan MiG-29

## G

G-2A Galeb, see SOKO
G-4 Super Galeb, see SOKO
G222, see Aeritalia
GAF Nomad: 122
Galaxy, see Lockheed C-5
Galeb, see SOKO G-2A
Gazelle SA.341/342,, see Aerospatiale
General Dynamics F-16A/C/N Fighting Falcon:
    123
General Dynamics F-16B/D Fighting Falcon: 124
General Dynamics F-111: 125
Goshawk, see British Aerospace/McDonnell
    Douglas T-45
GR.Mk 5, see McDonnell Douglas/BAe Harrier II
GR.Mk 7, see McDonnell Douglas/BAe Harrier II
Griffon, see Bell CH146
Grifone, see Agusta-Bell AB 412
Gripen, see Saab JAS39
Grumman/General Dynamics EF-111A Raven:
    129
Grumman A-6 Intruder: 126
Grumman E-2 Hawkeye: 128
Grumman EA-6B Prowler: 127
Grumman F-14A Tomcat: 130
Grumman F-14B/D Tomcat: 131
Grumman OV-1 Mohawk: 132
Grumman S-2 Tracker: 133
Grumman U-16 Albatross: 134

## H

H-2 Seasprite, see Kaman
H-34 Choctaw, see Sikorsky

Halo', see Mil Mi-26
HAR/HAS, see Westland Sea King
Harbin Y-8: 135
Harbin Y-11: 136
Harbin Y-12: 136
'Harke', see Mil Mi-10
Harrier, see British Aerospace (HS)
Harrier II, see McDonnell Douglas/BAe
Harrier AV-8A/C, see British
    Aerospace/McDonnell Douglas
'Havoc', see Mil Mi-28
Hawk, see British Aerospace (HS)
Hawkeye, see Grumman E-2
'Haze', see Mil Mi-14
HC-130 Hercules, see Lockheed
HC/Commando, see Westland Sea King
'Helix', see Kamov Ka-27
Hercules, see Lockheed C-130
HH60, see Sikorsky
HH-65A Dolphin, see Aerospatiale
'Hind', see Mil Mi-24
'Hip', see Mil Mi-8
'Hokum', see Kamov
'Hoodlum', see Kamove Ka-26
'Hook', see Mil Mi-6
'Hormone', see Kamov Ka-25
'Hornet, see McDonnell Douglas F/A-18
Huey Cobra, see Bell AH-1
Hunter (fighter/bombers), see BAe (Hawker/HS)

## I

I-22, see PZL Iryda
IA 58A Pucará, see FMA
IA 63 Pampa, see FMA
IDS, see Panavia Tornado
Il-18 'Coot', see Ilyushin
Il-20 'Coot-A', see Ilyushin
Il-28 'Beagle', see Ilyushin
Il-38 'May', see Ilyushin
Il-76 'Candid', see Ilyushin
Il-78 'Midas', see Ilyushin
Ilyushin A-50 'Mainstay': 141
Ilyushin Il-18 'Coot': 137
Ilyushin Il-20 'Coot-A': 138
Ilyushin Il-28 'Beagle': 139
Ilyushin Il-38 'May': 140
Ilyushin Il-76 'Candid': 141
Ilyushin Il-78 'Midas': 141
Impala, see Aermacchi Atlas
Intruder, see Grumman A-6
Iroquois, see Bell Model UH-1
Iskra, see PZL Mielec TS-11
Islander/Defender, see Pilatus/Britten-Norman
    BN-2B

## J

J-1/RJ-1/JT-1 Jastreb, see SOKO
J-6 'Farmer', see Shenyang
J-22 Orao/IAR-93, see SOKO/IAv Craiova
JA37 Viggen, see Saab
Jaguar A/E, see SEPECAT
Jaguar B/S, see SEPECAT
Jaguar International, see SEPECAT
JAS39 Gripen, see Saab
Jastreb, see SOKO J-1/RJ-1/JT-1
JJ-5, see Shenyang
Jodel D.140 Mousquetaire: 142

## K

K-MAX, see Kaman
Ka-25 'Hormone', see Kamov
Ka-26 'Hoodlum', see Kamov
Ka-27 'Helix', see Kamov
Ka-50 Werewolf 'Hokum', see Kamov
Kaman H-2 Seasprite: 143

Kaman K-MAX: 144
Kamov Ka-25 'Hormone': 145
Kamov Ka-26 'Hoodlum': 146
Kamov Ka-27 Helix: 147
Kamov Ka-50 Werewolf 'Hokum': 148
Kawasaki (Boeing Vertol) KV-107: 150
Kawasaki C-1: 149
KC-130 Hercules, see Lockheed
KC-135E and KC-135R, see Boeing
Kraguj, see SOKO P-2
KV-107, see Kawasaki (Boeing Vertol)

**L**

L-29 Delfin, see Aero
L-39 Albatros, see Aero
L-1011 TriStar, see Lockheed
Lancer, see Rockwell B-1B
Lockheed AC-130 Hercules: 154
Lockheed C-130A/G Hercules: 152
Lockheed C-130H/K Hercules: 153
Lockheed C-141 StarLifter: 158
Lockheed C-5 Galaxy: 151
Lockheed EP-3 Orion: 163
Lockheed F-117 Night Hawk: 159
Lockheed HC-130 Hercules: 155
Lockheed KC-130 Hercules: 156
Lockheed L-1011 TriStar: 160
Lockheed MC-130 Hercules: 157
Lockheed Orion AEW & C: 164
Lockheed P-3A/B Orion: 161
Lockheed P-3C Orion: 162
Lockheed S-3 Viking: 165
Lockheed SR-71: 166
Lockheed T-33: 168
Lockheed TR-1 and U-2R: 169
Lockheed/Boeing F-22: 167

**M**

M.B.326/326K, see Aermacchi
M.B.339/339K Veltro 2, see Aermacchi
'Mainstay', see Ilyushin A-50
Mangusta, see Agusta A 129
Matador, see British Aerospace/McDonnell
    Douglas AV-8S
'May', see Ilyushin Il-38
MBB/Kawasaki BK 117: 183
MC-130 Hercules, see Lockheed
McDonnell Douglas A-4 Skyhawk: 170
McDonnell Douglas AH-64 Apache: 171
McDonnell Douglas C-17: 172
McDonnell Douglas F-4C/D Phantom II: 173
McDonnell Douglas F-4E/F Phantom II: 174
McDonnell Douglas F-4G 'Wild Weasel V': 175
McDonnell Douglas F-15A/C Eagle: 176
McDonnell Douglas F-15B/D Eagle: 177
McDonnell Douglas F-15E Eagle: 178
McDonnell Douglas F/A-18A/C Hornet: 179
McDonnell Douglas F/A-18B/D Hornet: 180
McDonnell Douglas/BAe AV-8B Harrier II: 181
McDonnell Douglas/BAe Harrier II GR.Mk 5: 182
McDonnell Douglas/BAe Harrier II GR.Mk 7: 182
McDonnell Douglas/BAe TAV-8B Harrier II: 181
Mi-2 'Hoplite', see PZL Swidnik Mi-2
Mi-6 'Hook', see Mil
Mi-8 'Hip', see Mil
Mi-10 'Harke', see Mil
Mi-14 'Haze', see Mil
Mi-24 'Hind', see Mil
Mi-24 'Hind-A,/B/C', see Mil
Mi-24P 'Hind-F', see Mil
Mi-24V 'Hind-E', see Mil
Mi-25, see Mil
Mi-26 'Halo', see Mil
Mi-28 'Havoc', see Mil
'Midas', see Ilyushin Il-78
MiG-17 'Fresco', see Mikoyan-Gurevich

MiG-19 'Farmer', see Mikoyan-Gurevich
MiG-21, see Mikoyan-Gurevich
MiG-23 'Flogger', see Mikoyan-Gurevich
MiG-25 'Foxbat', see Mikoyan-Gurevich
MiG-27 'Flogger', see Mikoyan
MiG-29 'Fulcrum', see Mikoyan
MiG-31 'Foxhound', see Mikoyan
Mikoyan MiG-27 'Flogger-D': 194
Mikoyan MiG-27 'Flogger-J': 194
Mikoyan MiG-29 'Fulcrum-A': 195
Mikoyan MiG-29 'Fulcrum-B': 195
Mikoyan MiG-29 'Fulcrum-C': 195
Mikoyan MiG-29K: 196
Mikoyan MiG-29M: 196
Mikoyan MiG-31 'Foxhound': 197
Mikoyan-Gurevich MiG-17 'Fresco': 184
Mikoyan-Gurevich MiG-19 'Farmer': 185
Mikoyan-Gurevich MiG-21: 186
Mikoyan-Gurevich MiG-21U: 187
Mikoyan-Gurevich MiG-23 'Flogger-B': 188
Mikoyan-Gurevich MiG-23 'Flogger-E': 189
Mikoyan-Gurevich MiG-23 'Flogger-G': 188
Mikoyan-Gurevich MiG-23 'Flogger-J': 188
Mikoyan-Gurevich MiG-23B/BK/BM/BN 'Flogger-
    F/-H': 190
Mikoyan-Gurevich MiG-23BN 'Flogger-H': 190
Mikoyan-Gurevich MiG-23U 'Flogger-C': 189
Mikoyan-Gurevich MiG-25 'Foxbat-A': 191
Mikoyan-Gurevich MiG-25M 'Foxbat-E': 193
Mikoyan-Gurevich MiG-25R 'Foxbat-B': 192
Mikoyan-Gurevich MiG-25R 'Foxbat-D': 192
Mikoyan-Gurevich MiG-25U 'Foxbat-C': 193
Mil Mi-6 'Hook': 198
Mil Mi-8 'Hip': 199
Mil Mi-8 'Hip-E': 200
Mil Mi-8 'Hip-F': 200
Mil Mi-10 'Harke': 201
Mil Mi-14 'Haze': 202
Mil Mi-24 'Hind': 204
Mil Mi-24 'Hind-A,/B/C'": 203
Mil Mi-24P 'Hind-F': 205
Mil Mi-24V 'Hind-E': 205
Mil Mi-25: 204
Mil Mi-26 'Halo': 206
Mil Mi-28 'Havoc': 207
Mirage III trainers, see Dassault-Breguet
Mirage IIIR, Dassualt-Breguet
Mirage IV, see Dassault-Breguet
Mirage 5, see Dassault-Breguet
Mirage 5R, see Dassault-Breguet
Mirage 50, see Dassault-Bregeut
Mirage 2000B, see Dassault-Breguet
Mirage 2000C, see Dassault-Breguet
Mirage 2000N, see Dassault-Breguet
Mirage F1A, see Dassault-Breguet
Mirage F1C, see Dassault-Breguet
Mirage F1E, see Dassault-Breguet
Mirage F1R, see Dassault-Breguet
Mitsubishi F-1: 208
Mitsubishi T-2: 209
Model 107, see Boeing Vertol
Model 114, see Boeing Vertol
Model 128, see Dornier
Model 204, see Bell
Model 205, see Bell
Model 206, see Bell
Model 206L Texas Ranger, see Bell
Model 209 (single-engine), see Bell
Model 209 (twin-engine), see Bell
Model 212 Twin Two-Twelve, see Bell
Model 214, see Bell
Model 318E, see Cessna
Model 337 Skymaster, see Cessna
Model TH57 Sea Ranger, see Bell
Model UH-1 Iroquois, see Bell
Model UH-1D Iroquois, see Bell
Model UH-1H Iroquois, see Bell
Model UH-1N, see Bell

Mohawk, see Grumman OV-1
Morane Saulnier MS.760 Paris: 210
Mousquetaire, see Jodel D.140
MS.760 Paris, see Morane Saulnier
MR.Mk 1, see British Aerospace (HS) Nimrod
MR.Mk 2, see British Aerospace (HS) Nimrod

**N**

NAMC (Nihon) YS-11: 211
Nanchang Q-5 'Fantan': 212
Navajo, see Piper PA-31
Night Hawk, see Lockheed F-117
Nimrod, see British Aerospace (HS)
Nomad, see GAF
North American T-28 Trojan: 213
Northrop F-5A /B Freedom Fighter: 214
Northrop F-5E: 215
Northrop RF-5E Tigereye: 216
Northrop T-38 Talon: 218
Northrop Grumman B-2: 217

**O**

O-2, see Cessna
OH-58 Kiowa, see Bell
One-Eleven, see British Aerospace (BAC)
Orao, see SOKO/IAv Craiova J-22
Orion, see Lockheed
Orlik, see PZL Warszawa-Okecie PZL-130
Osprey, see Bell/Boeing Vertol V-22
OV-1 Mohawk, see Grumman
OV-10 Bronco, see Rockwell

**P**

P-2 Kraguj, see SOKO
P-3A/B/C Orion, see Lockheed
PA-31 Navajo, see Piper
PA-34 Seneca, see Piper
Pampa, see FMA 1A 63
Panavia Tornado ADV: 224
Panavia Tornado IDS: 223
Panavia Tornado reconnaissance/ECR versions:
    225
Paris, see Morane Saulnier MS.760
PC-7, see Pilatus
PC-9, see Pilatus
Phantom II, see McDonnell Douglas F-4
Pilatus PC-7: 226
Pilatus PC-9: 226
Pilatus/Britten-Norman BN-2B Islander/Defender:
    227
Pilatus/Britten-Norman BN-2T Turbine
    Islander/Defender: 228
Piper PA-31 Navajo: 229
Piper PA-34 Seneca: 230
Prowler, see Grumman EA-6B
Pucará, see FMA 1A 58A
Puma, see Aerospatiale/Westland SA.330
PZL I-22 Iryda: 221
PZL Mielec TS-11 Iskra: 219
PZL Swidnik Mi-2 'Hoplite': 220
PZL Warszawa-Okecie PZL-130 Orlik: 222
PZL-130 Orlik, see PZL Warszawa-Okecie

**Q**

Q-5 'Fantan', see Nanchang

**R**

Rafale A/B/C/M, see Dassault-Breguet
Raven, see Grumman/General Dynamics
    EF-111A
RC-135, see Boeing
RF-5E Tigereye, see Northrop
RH-53, see Sikorsky

Rockwell B-1B Lancer: 231
Rockwell International Turbo Commander 690B: 235
Rockwell OV-10 Bronco: 232
Rockwell OV-10D Bronco: 233
Rockwell T-2 Buckeye: 234

## S

S-2 Tracker, see Grumman
S-3 Viking, see Lockheed
S-58, see Sikorsky
S-65, see Sikorsky
S-70, see Sikorsky
S-76/H-76, see Sikorsky
SA.316B/319B Alouette III, see Aerospatiale
SA.321 Super Frelon, see Aerospatiale
SA.330 Puma, see Aerospatiale/Westland
SA.341/342 Gazelle, see Aerospatiale
SA.360 Dauphin, see Aerospatiale
SA.365 Dauphin 2, see Aerospatiale
Saab 35 Draken: 236
Saab 105: 237
Saab AJ37 Viggen: 238
Saab JA37 Viggen: 239
Saab JAS39 Gripen: 241
Saab SF37/SH37 Viggen: 240
Saab Sk37 Viggen: 240
Sea Cobra, see Bell AH-1J/T
Sea Harrier, see British Aerospace
Sea King, see Westland
Sea Knight, see Boeing Vertol CH-46
Sea Ranger, see Bell Model TH57
Sea Stallion, see Sikorsky CH-53
Seabat, see Sikorsky SH-34
Seahorse, see Sikorsky SH-34
Seasprite, see Kaman H-2
Seneca, see Piper PA-34
SEPECAT Jaguar A/E: 242
SEPECAT Jaguar B/S: 243
SEPECAT Jaguar International: 244
SF.260, see SIAI-Marchetti
SF37/SH37 Viggen, see Saab :
SH-60B/F, see Sikorsky :
Shenyang J-6 'Farmer': 246:
Shenyang JJ-5: 245:
Sherpa, see Shorts 330/C-23 :
Shin Meiwa SS-2A (US-1): 247:
Shorts 330/C-23 Sherpa: 248:
SIAI-Marchetti SF.260: 249:
Sikorsky CH-34 Choctaw: 250:
Sikorsky CH-53 Sea Stallion: 251:
Sikorsky CH-53E/MH-53E: 252:
Sikorsky EH-60: 254:
Sikorsky HH60: 254:
Sikorsky RH-53: 253:
Sikorsky S-58: 250:
Sikorsky S-58 (H-34 Choctaw/Seabat and Seahorse): 250
Sikorsky S-65: 251
Sikorsky S-70: 254
Sikorsky S-70B: 255

Sikorsky S-76/H-76: 256
Sikorsky SH-60B: 255
Sikorsky SH-60F: 255
Sikorsky UH-60: 254
Sk37 Viggen, see Saab
Skyhawk, see McDonnell Douglas A-4
Skymaster, see Cessna Model 337
Skytrain, see Douglas C-47
SOKO G-2A Galeb: 257
SOKO G-4 Super Galeb: 258
SOKO J-1/RJ-1/JT-1 Jastreb: 259
SOKO P-2 Kraguj: 260
SOKO/IAv Craiova J-22 Orao/IAR-93: 261
SR-71, see Lockheed
SS-2A (US-1), see Shin Meiwa
Starfighter, see Aeritalia (Lockheed) F104S
StarLifter, see Lockheed C-141
Stratofortress, see Boeing B-52H
Strikemaster, see British Aerospace (BAC)
Su-15 'Flagon', see Sukhoi
Su-17 'Fitter', see Sukhoi
Su-20 'Fitter', see Sukhoi
Su-21 'Flagon', see Sukhoi
Su-22 'Fitter', see Sukhoi
Su-24 'Fencer', see Sukhoi
Su-25 'Frogfoot', see Sukhoi
Su-27 'Flanker', see Sukhoi
Sukhoi Su-15 'Flagon': 262
Sukhoi Su-17 'Fitter': 263
Sukhoi Su-20 'Fitter': 264
Sukhoi Su-21 'Flagon': 262
Sukhoi Su-22 'Fitter': 264
Sukhoi Su-24 'Fencer': 265
Sukhoi Su-25 'Frogfoot': 266
Sukhoi Su-25T, Su-25TK, Su-25UB, Su-25UT and Su-25UTG: 267
Sukhoi Su-27 'Flanker': 268
Super Etendard, see Dassault-Breguet
Super Frelon, see Aerospatiale SA.321
Super Galeb, see SOKO G-4
Super Puma, see Aerospatiale AS.332

## T

T-1, see Fuji
T-2, see Mitsubishi
T-2 Buckeye, see Rockwell
T-28 Trojan, see North American
T-33, see Lockheed
T-38 Talon, see Northrop
T-45 Goshawk, see British Aerospace/McDonnell Douglas
T.Mk 4, see British Aerospace (HS) Harrier
Talon, see Northrop T-38
TAV-8B Harrier II, see McDonnell Douglas/BAe
Texas Ranger, see Bell Model 206L
Thunderbolt II, see Fairchild Republic A-10A
Tigereye, see Northrop RF-5E
Tomcat, see Grumman F-14
Tornado, see Panavia
TR-1 and U-2R, see Lockheed
Tracker, see Grumman S-2

Transall C-160: 269
TriStar, see Lockheed L-1011
Trojan, see North American T-28
TS-11 Iskra, see PZL Mielec
Tu-16, see Tupolev
Tu-22 'Blinder', see Tupolev
Tu-22M 'Backfire', see Tupolev
Tu-95 'Bear', see Tupolev
Tu-95 MS, see Tupolev
Tu-142 'Bear', see Tupolev
Tu-160 'Blackjack', see Tupolev
Tucano, see EMBRAER EMB-312
Tupolev Tu-16 (bombers, missile carriers and tankers)": 270
Tupolev Tu-22 'Blinder': 271
Tupolev Tu-22M 'Backfire': 272
Tupolev Tu-95 'Bear': 273
Tupolev Tu-95 MS: 274
Tupolev Tu-142 'Bear': 275
Tupolev Tu-160 'Blackjack': 276
Turbine Islander/Defender, see Pilatus/Britten-Norman BN-2T
Turbo Commander 690B, see Rockwell International
Tutor, see Canadair CL-41
Twin Otter, see de Havilland Canada DHC-6
Twin Star, see Aerospatiale AS.355
Twin Two-Twelve, see Bell Model 212

## U

U-16 Albatross, see Grumman
UH-60, see Sikorsky

## V

V-22 Osprey, see Bell/Boeing Vertol
VC10, see British Aerospace (Vickers-Armstrongs/BAC)
Veltro 2, see Aermacchi M.B.339K
Viggen, see Saab AJ37, JA37 etc
Vought A-7 Corsair II: 277
Vought F-8E (FN) Crusader: 278

## W

Wasp, see Westland
Westland Lynx Army variants: 280
Westland Lynx Navy variants: 279
Westland Sea King HAR/HAS: 281
Westland Sea King HC/Commando: 282
Westland Wasp: 283
Wild Weasel V', see McDonnell Douglas F-4G

## Y

Y-8, see Harbin
Y-11, see Harbin
Y-12, see Harbin
Yak-38 'Forger', see Yakovlev
Yakovlev Yak-38 'Forger': 284
YS-11, see NAMC (Nihon)